THE EMERGENCE
OF MODERN TURKEY

STUDIES IN MIDDLE EASTERN HISTORY

General Editors
Bernard Lewis
Itamar Rabinovich
Roger Savory

THE EMERGENCE
OF MODERN TURKEY

BERNARD LEWIS

THIRD EDITION

NEW YORK   OXFORD
OXFORD UNIVERSITY PRESS
2002

956.1
L673e
2002

Oxford University Press

OXFORD   NEW YORK
ATHENS   AUCKLAND   BANGKOK   BOGOTÁ   BUENOS AIRES   CAPE TOWN
CHENNAI   DAR ES SALAAM   DELHI   FLORENCE   HONG KONG   ISTANBUL   KARACHI
KOLKATA   KUALA LUMPUR   MADRID   MELBOURNE   MEXICO CITY   MUMBAI   NAIROBI
PARIS   SÃO PAULO   SHANGHAI   SINGAPORE   TAIPEI   TOKYO   TORONTO   WARSAW

and associated companies in

BERLIN   IBADAN

Copyright © 2002 by Oxford University Press, Inc.

First issued, under the auspices of the Royal Institute of International Affairs,
by Oxford University Press, London, 1961.
Reprinted, 1962; and, with corrections, 1965 and 1966.
Second edition issued by Oxford University Press, London,
as an Oxford University Press paperback, 1968.
Third edition published in 2002 by Oxford University Press, Inc.
198 Madison Avenue, New York, New York 10016
http://www.oup-usa.org

Oxford is a registered trademark of Oxford University Press

Library of Congress Cataloging-in-Publication Data

Lewis, Bernard.
    The emergence of modern Turkey / Bernard Lewis.—3rd ed.
        p. cm.
    Includes bibliographical references and index.
    ISBN 0-19-513459-1 (alk. paper) – ISBN 0-19-513460-5 (pbk.)
    1. Turkey—History—20th century.   I. Title.

DR583.L48 2001
956.1—dc21

                                        2001031411

Printing (last digit): 9 8 7 6 5 4 3 2 1
Printed in the United States of America on acid-free paper

CONTENTS

To

Jill and Ercüment
in friendship and gratitude

PREFACE TO THE THIRD EDITION

THE beginnings of this book date back to the academic year 1949–1950, most of which I spent in Istanbul. My primary purpose in being there was to work in the Turkish State Archives, newly opened to Western researchers, for a project in sixteenth-century history. But living in Turkey at that time, I could not but be aware of the momentous events that were taking place around me, and be deeply impressed—even inspired—by their rapid development. An invitation from the Royal Institute of International Affairs in London, better known as Chatham House, to write a book on modern Turkey as part of a series they were planning on the interrelation between the Islamic world and the West, gave me an opportunity to pursue this new interest in modern and recent history. In the course of the 1950s I made a number of trips of varying duration to Turkey—partly to read books, periodicals, and newspapers in Turkish libraries not readily available elsewhere, and partly to observe at first hand the continuing process of change. My typescript was completed in 1960, and the book, entitled *The Emergence of Modern Turkey*, was published in 1961 by the Oxford University Press in conjunction with Chatham House. Neither the author nor the publisher had expected a very large sale for a book of almost 500 heavily footnoted pages, dealing with a single, no longer major, country. It was with surprise as well as pleasure that we saw it go through four printings in hardcover in five years. This unexpected success stirred the publisher's generosity to the point of allowing me to make fairly extensive though still minor revisions in the second, paperback edition published in 1968.

The preparation of the second edition confronted me with an important question. Writing in the middle and late 1950s, I had chosen, as the cutoff point for my book, the Turkish general election of 1950—the first that was conducted in complete freedom and fairness, and resulted in the transfer of power from the ruling to the opposition party. Since my book was one of history, reaching back to the Middle Ages, and not of current affairs, it seemed right to end it at that point, rather than to switch from one type of writing to another, radically different, and try to cope with the rapidly changing scene in present-day Turkey.

I remained of the same opinion while preparing the new edition. The events at the time of the revision, like those at the time of the original composition, must certainly have colored my perception of earlier periods, but I decided to keep to the 1950 cutoff point, and to use the opportunity of revision to take account of the considerable body of new evidence and new studies that had appeared in the meantime. Subsequent reprints of the English text, in Britain and the United States, have been based on the 1968 edition, with only minor corrections of a few obstinate misprints that had somehow escaped all previous revisions. The same text served as the basis of three translations that were published in the immediately following years—into Turkish, by the Turkish Historical Society in Ankara; into Polish, by the Academy of Sciences in Warsaw; and into Hebrew, by the Hebrew University Press in Jerusalem.

The publication of a French edition in 1988 provided the occasion for another look, both at the book and at the subject with which it deals. Reading my own work, more than thirty years after I started writing it, almost twenty years since I last revised it, was in some ways a chastening, in other ways a reassuring, experience. Inevitably, there were things that I would have arranged or presented differently had I been writing the book afresh, but these were mainly matters of emphasis and presentation rather than of structure. In a few places, here and there, I made small changes to take account of new evidence, of new thinking— both my own and other people's—and of the insights afforded by subsequent events. But the major presentation and interpretation remained as they were, and, despite the passage of time and the increase of knowledge and experience, I was content to leave them so.

Curiously, the French publishers reduced my title to a subtitle and gave the book a new title: *Islam et laïcité: la naissance de la Turquie moderne.* When I asked a representative of the publishing house the reason for this, he replied drily: "Islam sells; Turkey doesn't." The new French title, despite the change of emphasis, is not inaccurate, since one of the major themes of the book is indeed the emergence of a secular, democratic republic from an Islamic empire. This makes it all the more remarkable that in the year 1994 a complete Persian translation appeared in Tehran. Iran is not a signatory of the international copyright convention, and this edition was published without contract or consent. I heard of it and procured a copy thanks to the good offices of an Iranian friend. One can only speculate why the Persian publisher and translator thought it worthwhile to translate and publish a lengthy, detailed book on one country, originally published in 1961, and ending its story in 1950. Was it offered as a model to be followed, or as a terrible example to be avoided?

After so long an interval since its first publication, it may be appropriate to reexamine the genesis of the book and discuss the subsequent development of the events and processes with which it deals. Several factors, it seems in retrospect, determined the basic approach, the dominant conception, and the final conclusions of the book. The first—if I may be excused for putting it in that place—was my own intellectual formation. My academic training had been as a historian, specializing in classical Islamic civilization. I had studied Arabic and Persian before I approached Turkish. In my historical studies I began with medieval Islam, proceeded to the Ottoman Empire, and then, later, to modern Turkey.

The very first time that I, as a student, ever set foot in Turkey, I came from Syria, where I had been working on my dissertation, and not, like most Western visitors, from the west. The fact that I first came to Turkey, so to speak, from the past and from the south instead of from the present and the west, gave me a different—and I would claim better—understanding of the country, of its history and culture, and therefore of its problems. Certainly, in considering the sustained endeavor to create a secular, modern, and democratic nation state, I was more keenly aware of the immensity of the task that the Turks were undertaking, the difficulties that they confronted, and, in consequence, more able to appreciate the quality and magnitude of their achievements.

A second determining factor, of at least equal importance, was the world situation during my formative years and during the period when the book was begun and completed. For the men and women of that generation, their whole lives, their every thought, was dominated and indeed shaped by the titanic struggles in which they had participated, or which they had at the very least witnessed—the defeat and, so it seemed at the time, the destruction of fascism by an alliance of democrats and communists; the ensuing struggle, commonly known as the Cold War, between these former allies to decide which of them would shape the future of the world; the emergence of a third, neutralist bloc in some of the countries liberated by the withdrawal of the Western Empires. In the fifties, these issues loomed very large, and the choices before us still retained something of the clarity, even the starkness, which they had through the war years and which they have subsequently lost.

This clarity of choice gave a special significance to the already dra-

matic development of events in Turkey at the time when this book
was conceived and written. What could be more illuminating, more in
accord with the mood of optimism that victory had brought and
which the Cold War had not yet dissipated, than the spectacle of a
nation liberating itself from ancient bonds—a country of age-old
authoritarian habits and traditions turning to democracy; a regime
that had for decades enjoyed a virtual monopoly of power setting to
work, systematically, to prepare, organize, and preside over its own
electoral defeat. Even now, more than fifty years later, despite all the
ensuing setbacks and frustrations—and there have been many—no one
who was there at the time can ever forget the excitement, the exhila-
ration, of Turkey's first giant step towards a free and open society.

Perhaps the most remarkable aspect was the very choice which the
Turks made and to which they have ever since adhered. The three
defeated Axis powers had democracy thrust upon them by the victors,
and although it has since survived in all three, this was by no means
clear at the time. In Eastern Europe, democracy, never very strong,
was extinguished by native Fascists and German Nazis, and the
embers were stamped into the ground by the new Communist rulers.
In the new states created by the ending of the West European empires,
democratic institutions of a sort were bequeathed by the departing
imperial powers and, in all but a very few, were soon abandoned or
rendered meaningless. Almost alone, the Turks made a free and conscious choice of their own for democracy and fashioned their own representative institutions. The process of domestic Westernization
found its natural counterpart in a foreign policy of Western alignment.
Between 1947 and 1952, Turkey sent a brigade of the Turkish army
to fight in the Korean War, joined the Council of Europe, and was
included in the Truman Doctrine and the Marshall Plan. In February
1952, Turkey became a full member of NATO, and in 1964, an associate member of the European Economic Community. This policy
came at a price but, despite troubles and disappointments, the Turks
have not abandoned their alignment with the West or their commit-
ment to the building of a free polity and society.

There have been many such disappointments, some of them of internal, some of external origin. Most of the characteristic features of modern Turkey—the open, capitalist economy, the secular national identity, the parliamentary system of government—were seen as part of a
process of Westernization. This process, which in a sense had been
going on for more than a century, had brought many changes, both
domestic and international. Within the country, there has been a grad-

ual, perhaps painful, but nevertheless genuine development of a Western way of life, renewed and sustained despite successive upheavals. It was no easy matter to create a parliamentary democracy in a land of authoritarian traditions, and no less than four times in the post-war period, in 1960, 1971, 1980, and 1997, the Turkish army intervened, directly or indirectly, in politics. This in itself was by no means unusual, and was a common event in all but the old, and a small minority of new, democratic countries. What was surely unique is that in Turkey, on all four occasions, the army, having accomplished its declared purpose of restoring stability, preserved or restored the rule of the civilian politicians, even permitting and accepting the defeat of its own political nominees.

Westernization has posed grave problems of identity for a people who, after all, came from Asia, professed Islam, and belonged by old tradition to the Middle Eastern Islamic world where, for many centuries, they had been unchallenged leaders. In some Muslim and even non-Muslim Asian and African countries, Kemalist Turkey's secularizing and westernizing policies were regarded as a betrayal of both Islam and Asia, and the Turks were denounced as lackeys of the West—as slavish imitators who had renounced their heritage and forfeited their self-respect. Even today, Kemal Atatürk, the founder and father of the Turkish Republic, occupies a prominent place in the demonology of Islamic fundamentalists in Iran, the Arab world, and elsewhere.

More dangerous was the hostility of the Soviet Union, which saw in Turkey's membership of NATO a double danger: on the one hand, an incitement to the large Muslim, predominantly Turkic populations conquered by the Czars and retained by the Soviets; on the other, a direct strategic threat to Soviet positions on the Black Sea and in the Caucasian region. The Soviets therefore devoted great efforts to disrupting this alliance. One method was to try by whatever means possible to sow discord between Turkey and its NATO allies, notably the United States; another was to destabilize Turkey by encouraging and supporting opposition groups, both ethnic and ideological. Some of these efforts have had a lasting effect.

In the interwar period the Turks, busy with their own affairs, were not troubled by Asian and Islamic complaints. Indeed, for the most part, they were barely aware of these criticisms, which came from sources to which they attached no great importance. It was not until sometime later that they became aware of such new entities as the Third World and the non-aligned Bloc and began to take account of them in their political calculations. Nor, at first, were they too much disturbed by the manifest hostility of the Soviet Union. To most Turks at that time, Russia was the imperial power which in the course of centuries of expansion had wrested many territories from the Ottoman Empire and still ruled over the greater part of the Turkic peoples. In this perspective, Russia was still the implacable hereditary enemy against which, as in the past, they needed the friendship and support of the strongest powers in the West.

But even inside Turkey, there were significant groups that opposed these policies. Opposition to the pro-Western foreign policy alignment came initially from what one might call modish pan-leftism—fashionable ideologies and postures, imported from Paris, London, and New York. These ideologies were of course opposed to the United States, to NATO, to capitalist economics, and to military bases other than those maintained at the time by the Soviet Union in its satellite territories. Such views commanded considerable support in intellectual and, more particularly, academic circles, where they achieved an ascendancy not unlike that which they, for a while, enjoyed in France. They were helped by the spread of Marxism, in a variety of forms, among Turkish intellectuals, and by the development of Marxist-influenced political groups and, more effective, trade unions. Turkish Marxism had more in common with Western European, especially French, opposition groups than with the official and governmental ideologies of Eastern Europe.

As in other countries, fashionable leftism was often associated with another vogue, which one might call Third Worldism—the tendency to idealize the Third World, and the desire to identify with Third World resentments against the West. For many young Turkish intellectuals, this sympathy for the Third World had an added poignancy. But for the choices made by Atatürk and his associates, they too could have been sinless Afro-Asians instead of guilt-ridden Europeans. These attitudes were often linked with anti-Western and neutralist rather than pro-Soviet attitudes in foreign policy, and with a range of socialist programs for application at home.

Most of the leftist and socialist critics of post-war Turkish governments limited their criticism of Westernization to internal economic matters and to defense and foreign policy, and were content to retain the secular and modern, and for some also the democratic, aspects of Westernization.

More consistent and more comprehensive than the leftists and neutralists in their rejection of Westernization were the upholders of

Islam, both traditional and radical. In the authoritarian phases of Turkish Republican history, traditionalist Islamic views were without political effect. In the democratic republic they find free expression and command blocks of votes.

After the transfer of power in 1950, there were many signs of religious activity, notably the growing self-assertiveness of its proponents. Mosque attendance increased considerably; inscribed texts in Arabic script—previously unthinkable—appeared on the walls in public places. A spate of new publications included both scholarly works on Islamic history and doctrine and pamphlets of popular piety. Many Turks, after a long interruption, began to make the pilgrimage to Mecca. In 1950 there were almost 9,000 Turkish pilgrims, despite the refusal of the government at that time to give any allocation of foreign currency for this purpose. Perhaps most important was the emergence of a new and diverse religious press. Under successive governments, religious education was consolidated and expanded in schools and universities, and more especially, in the new network of so-called *imam-hatip* schools. Ostensibly for the training of imams and preachers, these provided both primary and secondary education under religious auspices and were favored by many in preference to the secular state schools.

All this has had some, though limited, effect in the realm of foreign policy. The change is most noticeable in Turkish relations with the rest of the Islamic world. Previously, the Turkish Republic, as a secular modern state, shunned all Islamic groupings, and was represented, if at all, by unofficial observers at inter-Islamic gatherings. In the 1970s, Turkey began to send high officials as representatives to such meetings. In May 1976, the Turkish government invited the Islamic foreign ministers' conference to convene in Istanbul and joined, albeit with some reservations, in supporting a series of strongly pan-Islamic resolutions which condemned virtually all non-Muslim powers ruling over Muslim populations, with the exception of India, China, and the Soviet Union. Since then Turkey has become and remains more actively involved in Islamic summit conferences and the various activities associated with them and even plays host to some of their agencies.

It is noteworthy that, while the resolutions of the inter-Islamic conferences are normally carried by consensus rather than by a vote, the Turks have made it clear that their participation in such consensus resolutions is always subject to two overall conditions—that they shall be committed to nothing contrary either to the Turkish Constitution and political system at home, or to the basic principles of Turkish foreign policy abroad. These two reservations, at once fundamental and comprehensive, have in general been maintained. At home, Islam is certainly a far more powerful force in Turkish public life than it has been at any previous time since the fall of the Ottoman Empire. Religious instruction is now an integral and accepted part of the educational system; religious literature is available everywhere; and graduates of the religious schools, in increasing numbers, are filling important public functions. While the more extreme elements, conservatives and radicals alike, appear to have made little headway, more moderate forms of Islam now affect a wide spectrum of political opinion and reach high in public life.

More important in domestic politics was the establishment, in 1970, of the first Islamic party, known as the National Order Party. Its founder was Necmettin Erbakan, a professor of engineering who was elected to the Assembly in the previous year as an independent. The party was closed down in 1971 and reappeared in its second avatar in 1973, under the name National Salvation Party. This time the party joined the governing coalition, and its leader became a vice premier and minister of state. The party was again suppressed after the intervention of 1980, and Erbakan, along with other politicians, banned from political activity. With the rest of them, he returned to political life in 1987, and reconstituted his party under the name of *Refah*, usually translated as Welfare Party (WP), though Prosperity Party would be more accurate. In the 1970s and 1980s religiously-defined parties won only a small and diminishing proportion of the votes. The 1990s brought a dramatic change. In the general election of 1991, religiously-defined parties significantly increased their representation. In the municipal elections of 1994, they won the mayoralties of both Istanbul and Ankara. The general election of December 1995 brought a further increase: The religious party, with approximately one-fifth of the total votes, was now, for the first time in the history of the Turkish Republic, the largest single party in the Assembly. Along with the municipal successes, this gain gave the party leader, Necmettin Erbakan, considerable influence and authority, and at the end of June 1996, with the agreement of his coalition partners, he formed a new coalition government with himself as prime minister.

Erbakan's government lasted less than a year and ended with his resignation on 16 June 1997, under pressure from his coalition partner on the one side and the military on the other. This was brought about by a number of factors. In the forefront of these was his program of Islamization, notably in the economic, social, and cultural fields, where, so it seemed, there was less danger of provoking a military intervention.

The role of the military in 1997 was a long way short of a coup d'état, or even a Turkish-style "intervention." The Turkish press styled it a "post-modern coup." Differing even from the situation in 1971, the military was only one of several factors involved. The general election of 1999 brought a change in the composition of the Assembly and therefore the emergence of a new government based on a new coalition, but no radical change in the general situation.

These developments were of course affected by changes in the international scene and notably by two major events—the Iranian Revolution of 1979 and the breakup of the Soviet Union, ending the Cold War, in 1991.

Foreign involvement in Islamic movements in Turkey was not new. Fairly soon after the creation in 1947 of the then militant Islamic Republic of Pakistan, its emissaries attempted for a while to provoke Islamic movements in Turkey. These attempts came to nothing and even provoked a secularist backlash. The Saudis and some other conservative Arab states are believed to have sponsored and funded Islamic activities, and these may have had some effect, particularly in the rapid development of an obviously well-financed Islamic press and literature. The Islamic revolution in Iran created a new and very different challenge to the Turkish principle of separation of religion and the state. This time the challenge came not from a cautious conservative monarchy but from a radical revolutionary republic which, like revolutionary republics elsewhere, believed it had a mission to bring its message to the whole world and particularly to that part of the world with which it shared a common universe of discourse. The neighboring Muslim state of Turkey, linked to Iran by so much shared history and culture, soon attracted Iranian attention. A notable example of Iranian involvement in Turkish politics occurred in February 1997, in a small town not far from Ankara. At a meeting convened by the local Municipality and the Welfare Party, the guest of honor was the Iranian ambassador to Turkey, who in a speech called on young people to take up arms and give their just punishment to those who had signed accords with the United States and with Israel. The regime responded promptly. The mayor was dismissed; the Iranian ambassador was declared persona non grata and sent home, with appropriate diplomatic protests. And there seems little doubt that this episode was one of the causes of the military intervention later in the same year.

The ending of the Cold War and the collapse of the Soviet Union removed some dangers and at the same time presented new challenges and opportunities. Six of the newly independent former Soviet republics were predominantly Muslim, five of them speaking languages related to Turkish and with a natural tendency to look to Turkey for help and guidance. Relations with the European Union were also affected; with the removal of the Soviet threat Europeans attached diminished importance to Turkish goodwill. Moreover, the Turks now had to compete with other—and in European eyes better qualified—candidates for admission. No longer preoccupied with the threat from the north, the Turks were able to devote more attention to the previously rather neglected countries beyond their southern and eastern frontiers.

One of the reasons for the continuing involvement of the Turkish military in the political process was the dangerous security situation, particularly the recurrent outbreaks of violence between rival extremists in the streets and on the campuses, and, far more serious, the growing Kurdish disaffection.

Minority problems were not new to the Turkish state, but in the past minorities had been conceived in religious, not ethnic, terms, and appropriate arrangements made for them. In the Ottoman Empire as in earlier Muslim states, the Greeks, Armenians, Jews, and some other smaller Christian denominations had enjoyed their own communal organizations, with special communal rights and privileges. These were revised and limited in the Turkish Republic, but by no means abolished, and the minorities were seen as having a definite place as such in the society. What had not occurred to anyone, either in the Empire or in the Republic, was that different ethnic groups within the majority Muslim community should constitute minorities—the very use of the word "minority" in this context was to most Turks odd and to many offensive. But the change in official nomenclature had made an important difference. The term "Ottoman," like the term "British," covered a number of different ethnic identities. Its replacement by the term "Turk" raised new issues.

The Kurdish problem was complicated by the fact that the Kurdish homelands were divided between Turkey, Iran, and Iraq, with smaller groups in Syria and the Transcaucasian republics. Of all these states, Turkey was by far the most open and the most free. It was therefore inevitable that the main thrust of the Kurdish movement should be directed against the Turkish regime. They were of course able to obtain help from other parties interested in destabilizing the Turkish State, notably Iran and Syria, and, in the past, the Soviet Union.

For some time Turkish governments tried to deal with the Kurdish problem by pretending that it did not exist. Turkish citizens of Kurdish origin were Turks like the rest, with the same duties, rights, and opportunities. That this was no false claim is demonstrated by the large number of men of Kurdish or partly Kurdish origin who rose to the highest offices in the state, including the presidency, the high command, and various government positions. But the tacit condition attached to such advancement was to avoid undue stress on their Kurdish origins.

For a long time, and for many of the Kurds of Turkey, this was acceptable. But for increasing numbers it was not, and their aspirations ranged from a minimum demand for the recognition and use of the Kurdish language, to a maximum demand for separation and independence. This last demand was often linked with radical ideologies of various inspirations, and found expression in a major armed insurrection in the southeast, accompanied by acts of terror in other parts of the country. This was launched in the mid-eighties and spearheaded by the Marxist Kurdistan Workers Party, usually known by the initials of its Kurdish name, the PKK.

For the military the Kurdish movement was primarily a security matter—the need to deal with a violent, seditious movement, the aim of which was no less than the breakup of the Turkish Republic. In political circles, particularly under Prime Minister, later President, Turgut Özal and some of his successors, there was a growing willingness to concede some merit to the cultural, though not the political, claims of the Kurds. Independence or even autonomy was out of the question, but the use of the Kurdish language was another matter. For some time, Kurdish books, grammars, and dictionaries have been freely available in Turkish bookshops, and there have been Kurdish broadcasts on private, though not as yet on government-controlled, radio and television. There are even avowedly Kurdish representatives in the Assembly in Ankara, as well as in provincial and local politics. Some have gone so far as to suggest an arrangement for the Kurdish areas similar to that of Wales or even of Scotland in the United Kingdom; others fear an Irish or even a Basque outcome as the more likely result of such a policy. Meanwhile the army, engaged in what its leaders see as a struggle against separatism and terrorism, continues to impose restrictions on Kurdish organizations.

Military spokesmen have repeatedly made it clear that in their view the two principal dangers to the Turkish state are the Kurdish problem and religious fundamentalism, the one threatening its national and territorial unity, the other its modern democratic institutions. A third danger is instability—the constant change and fragmentation in parliamentary coalitions, and even in the parties that compose them, opening the way for radicals and extremists of various kinds to disrupt the political and even the social order. As frequently stated by military spokesmen, it is the prime duty of the armed forces to protect the territorial integrity of the country and its constitution from internal as well as external enemies—and the army has made no secret of its view that it is the internal enemies that constitute the more immediate danger.

At first sight, it might seem there is little prospect for democracy in a polity where the army plays so powerful and so pervasive a role and has even institutionalized that role through the National Security Council. Yet such a view would be mistaken. In accordance with their statements, and in contrast with the general expectation, the army leaders repeatedly did exactly what they said they would do—restore order, restore democratic legality, and then return to the barracks.

The question inevitably arises as to why the Turkish Army, in contrast with the makers of military coups in so many other countries, chose to limit and end rather than consolidate their rule. Part of the answer is obvious. The army in politics means politics in the army, usually with damaging effects on military preparedness and efficiency. But this was also true in other countries, and it did not prevent the military from retaining its political power. Many in Turkey believe that the reason for this difference is Turkish membership of NATO and the regular and frequent cooperation between the Turkish forces and those of their NATO allies in joint exercises and even, occasionally, operations. The Turkish generals therefore have opportunities to measure their performance—both in political legality and military efficiency—against the forces of the most advanced and the most free societies in the world. The comparison proved salutary, and reminded the generals that their primary duty was to maintain their military efficiency and their ability to cope with any external dangers that might arise.

But there is more to the relative success of Turkish democracy than that. At the present day, democracy is the most widely respected form of government in the world, and democratic institutions have been introduced in many countries where they did not exist previously. Some form of election and some form of assembly are necessary parts of the dress of the modern state, just as trousers, jackets, and a peaked cap are a necessary part of the appearance of the modern officer. In many parts of the modern world democratic institutions are no more than an outward show to keep up with the prevailing fashions and, more practically, to qualify for various international benefits.

But there are countries, and Turkey is one of them, in which democratic institutions have really taken root and are showing promising signs of development. Each must be seen and studied in its own historical context, in the light of its own traditions and experience. In a very few countries, democracy is old and indigenous, the result of a long evolution. In most, it is recent and imported. Turkish democracy was neither bequeathed nor imposed, but represented the free choice of the Turks. True, they relied to a large extent on foreign models, but the choice—or mis-choice—of models was their own, and the pace and manner of democratic development were shaped by domestic much more than by foreign forces. This surely gave these institutions a much better chance of survival.

Democratic institutions are more likely to survive among people who are ready to accept and operate them, and this readiness in turn depends on the attainment of a certain level of economic, social, and political development. In this respect, the economic progress of the country and the emergence of an active and efficient entrepreneurial class are of key importance.

Democratic development can also be helped by the existence of older and more deeply rooted traditions which, though not perhaps in themselves democratic, may help to prepare people for democracy. The traditional Islamic background offers some such features: the notion of a law which is above the law, and to which the ruler himself is subject; and the notion of a contractual relationship between the ruler and the ruled, which may be dissolved if the ruler's actions and orders contravene the supreme law. True, these limitations on the sovereign power did not go very far. The law itself grants autocratic powers to the sovereign, and no procedure was ever set up, or even discussed, to determine which commands were and which were not lawful. The processes of modernization in the nineteenth and twentieth centuries did not improve this situation. On the contrary, they worsened it, on the one hand by placing new instruments in the hands of rulers to reinforce their power, on the other by abrogating or enfeebling the intermediate powers that had previously limited the effective exercise of sovereignty—notable among these, the provincial gentry, the urban patriciate and magistracy, and the religious and military establishments. This made it possible for the pioneers of Ottoman democracy to present their case not in terms of alien and unfamiliar ideas, but rather as a restoration of ancient liberties.

One of the factors most frequently adduced is the uninterrupted independence of the Turkish state. Turkey was one of the few Muslim states never colonized, never subjected to imperial rule or domination. The Turks were always masters in their own house and indeed, for a long period, in many other houses. When they lost their empire and were challenged even in their homeland, they won their war of independence, and were therefore able to achieve a degree of realism and, with it, a degree of self-criticism that had not been possible in countries where political life was dominated for generations by the struggle for independence and in which independence and freedom became virtually synonymous terms, to the detriment of the latter.

Despite, or perhaps because of, its independence, Turkey, of all non-Western countries, has had the longest and closest contact with the West. Recognizing Western superiority in both the battlefield and the marketplace, the Turks began to look at Western ideas and institutions, and made a deliberate choice for Westernizing reform. The Turkish experiment in parliamentary democracy has been going on for a century and a quarter, much longer than in any other part of the non-Western world, and its present progress therefore rests on a far stronger, wider, and deeper base of experience.

The Turkish struggle for democracy has confronted major problems, suffered heavy setbacks, and survived both. Despite these problems and setbacks—perhaps even because of them—Turkish democracy is by far the most successful among countries of comparable experience and tradition. In the Turkish story there are deviations and interruptions, normal in a situation of great strain and limited democratic experience. What is remarkable and distinctive is that after each derailment, the democratic process was put back on the rails, and the Turkish people continued their journey to freedom and democracy.

Twice before, in the course of their long history, the Turks have set an example and served as a model for others—under the Ottomans, of militant Islam; and under Kemal Atatürk, of secular patriotism. If they succeed in their present endeavor to create, without loss of character and identity, a liberal economy, an open society, and a democratic polity, they may once again serve as a model to many other peoples.

PREFACE TO THE SECOND EDITION

THE first edition of this book went to press in 1960. Since that date a good deal of new material has come to light. Important documents and memoirs have been published or examined, and numerous studies and monographs on modern Turkish history and thought have appeared, both in Turkey and in other countries. Minor changes were made in successive impressions of this book; the publication of a new edition provides an opportunity to make more extensive revisions. These are, inevitably, still somewhat limited, for both structural and practical reasons. Within these limits, I have tried to profit from the larger perspectives and deeper insights afforded by subsequent developments, both historic and historiographic; I have corrected some errors of fact and judgement, made good some omissions, and modified or amplified the presentation of a number of problems and events. The select bibliography has also been recast and brought up to date.

B. L.

London,
May 1967

PREFACE

THE theme of this book is the emergence of a new Turkey from the decay of the old. After an introductory examination of the sources and nature of Turkish civilization, the book falls into two parts. In the first the main events and processes are set forth in chronological sequence, not as a simple narrative history of Turkey, but rather as an attempt to trace and define the principal phases of change. The term of the study has been set in 1950, when the party of Atatürk was ousted from power in a free election which it had itself organized, and the country entered on a new phase in its history. In the second part of the book four aspects of change are examined in greater detail—the transformation of the corporate sense of identity and loyalty among the Turks, the transformation of the theory and practice of government, of religion and the cultural life which it dominated, and of the economic and social order. In a final chapter an attempt is made to draw some general conclusions on the nature of the Turkish Revolution and the measure of its accomplishment.

A separate note contains my thanks and acknowledgements to those who, in one way or another, have helped in the preparation of this book. Here I would like to express my gratitude to two scholars, neither of whom has been directly concerned with this book, yet both of whom have contributed largely to whatever merits it may possess. The first is my friend and colleague, Professor P. Wittek, whose conversation, over a period of many years, has enriched my understanding of Turkish history and civilization more deeply than any formal expression of thanks for help and guidance could indicate. The second is the late and deeply lamented Dr. A. Adnan Adıvar, to whose influence and teaching I owe my first acquaintance with Turkey and the Turks, my first knowledge of their language and literature, and an abiding concern that has shaped my life ever since.

London,   B. L.
January 1960

ACKNOWLEDGEMENTS

My grateful thanks are due to Miss Elizabeth Monroe, Professor Sir Hamilton Gibb, Professor A. T. Hatto, Professor P. M. Holt, Mr. A. H. Hourani, Professor J. C. Hurewitz, and Professsor D. A. Rustow for their careful reading of parts or all of my manuscript and for many helpful suggestions; to Dr. E. Atabay for taking photographs, and for aid and comfort throughout the preparation of this work; to Miss H. Oliver, for her painstaking and invaluable help in preparing the book for the press; to Professor D. A. Rustow for reading and correcting a set of proofs; to the late Mr. D. E. Pitcher for preparing the maps; to Miss M. Moyle for making the index; to Professor Franz Taeschner (editor of *Alt-Stambuler Hof- und Volksleben,* Hanover 1925), the Director of the Topkapı Sarayı Museum, and the Editor of *Hayat,* for their kind permission to reproduce illustrations. Parts of this book are based on matter previously published in the form of articles; I am greatly obliged to Professor G. E. von Grunebaum and the Chicago University Press (the editor and publishers of *Unity and Variety in Muslim Civilization,* Chicago 1955), and to the editors of the *Journal of World History, Middle Eastern Affairs, International Affairs,* the *Encyclopaedia of Islam,* and *Studia Islamica,* for their consent to this. Finally I should like to express my thanks to the Royal Institute of International Affairs for grants to cover the cost of my journeys to Turkey between 1954 and 1959, and for help and encouragement in the preparation of this study.

In preparing the revised edition, I have benefited from the comments of reviewers in a number of journals. To them I should like to express my appreciation. I am also deeply grateful, for privately communicated comments and suggestions, to the following: Dr. F. Ahmad; Professors Y. H. Bayur, R. H. Davison, U. Heyd, F. Iz, and E. Kuran; Dr. H. A. Reed; Professor D. A Rustow; Dr. M. E. Yapp.

ABBREVIATIONS

Ank. Univ. Dil ve Tar.- *Cog. Fak. Derg.*	*Ankara Üniversitesi Dil ve Tarih-Coğrafya Fakültesi Dergisi.*
BSOAS . . .	*Bulletin of the School of Oriental and African Studies.*
C. Or. contemp. . .	*Cahiers de l'Orient contemporain.*
EI¹, EI² . . .	*Encyclopaedia of Islam*, 1st and 2nd editions.
IA	*Islam Ansiklopedisi.*
Int. Aff. . . .	*International Affairs.*
Ist. Univ. Iktisat Fak. *Mec.* . . .	*Istanbul Üniversitesi Iktisat Fakültesi Mecmuası.*
J. As. . . .	*Journal Asiatique.*
JRAS . . .	*Journal of the Royal Asiatic Society.*
Jäschke, *Kalender* .	G. Jäschke and E. Pritsch, 'Die Türkei seit dem Weltkriege; Geschichtskalender 1919–28'. *Welt des Islam*, x (1927–9), &c. (see Bibliography).
MEA . . .	*Middle Eastern Affairs.*
MEJ . . .	*Middle East Journal.*
MER . . .	*Middle East Record.*
MES . . .	*Middle Eastern Studies.*
Mitt. Aus. Hoch. Univ. *Berlin*	*Mitteilungen der Ausland-Hochschule an der Universität Berlin.*
MSOS . . .	*Mitteilungen des Seminars für orientalische Sprachen*
OM . . .	*Oriente Moderno.*
R.C. As. J. . .	*Royal Central Asian Society Journal.*
R. Ét. islam. . .	*Revue d'Études islamiques.*
R. Fac. Sci. Éc. Univ. Ist.	*Revue de la Faculté des Sciences Économiques de l'Université d'Istanbul.*
RMM . . .	*Revue du monde musulman.*
R. hist. . . .	*Revue historique.*
RIIA, *Survey* . .	Royal Institute of International Affairs, *Survey of International Affairs.*
Tar. Derg. . .	*Tarih Dergisi.*
Tar. Ves. . .	*Tarih Vesikaları.*
TM . . .	*Türkiyat Mecmuası.*
TOEM . . .	*Tarih-i Osmani Encümeni Mecmuası.*
Türk Huk. ve Ikt. Tar. *Mec.* . . .	*Türk Hukuk ve Iktisat Tarihi Mecmuası.*
Vak. Derg. . .	*Vakıflar Dergisi.*
WI . . .	*Welt des Islam.*
ZDMG . . .	*Zeitschrift der deutschen morgenländischen Gesellschaft.*

NOTES ON TRANSCRIPTION

MANY different systems have been used for the transcription of Turkish in Latin letters. That used in the following pages is based on the official modern Turkish orthography. Some notes on pronunciation may be useful to readers unacquainted with Turkish. The descriptions given below are approximate and non-technical.

c —*j* as in *John*

ç —*ch* as in *church*

b, d —as in English, except that at the end of a syllable they are usually pronounced and sometimes written *p*, *t* (e.g. Recep, Ragıp, Ahmet, Mehmet for Receb, Rağıb, Ahmed, Mehmed). In transcribing Ottoman texts, I have retained the *b* and *d* as being nearer to the original.

ğ —after e, i—roughly as *y* in *saying*; after o, ö, u, ü—roughly as *w* in *sowing*; after a, ı—hardly sounded, but has the effect of lengthening the preceding vowel

ı —something between *i* as in *will* and *u* as in *radium*

ö —French *eu* as in *seul*, or German *ö* as in *öffnen*

ş —*sh* as in *shut*

ü —French *u* as in *lumière*, or German *ü* as in *schützen*

THE EMERGENCE
OF MODERN TURKEY

CHAPTER I

Introduction: The Sources of Turkish Civilization

Quis unquam tam sapiens aut doctus audebit describere prudenciam, miliciam et fortitudinem Turcorum? Qui putabant terrere gentem Francorum minis suarum sagittarum, sicut terruerunt Arabes, Saracenos et Hermenios, Suranos et Grecos.

GESTA FRANCORUM, *c.* 1100.

It is one of the strange things of Constantinople that for one copper coin one can be rowed from Rumelia to Frangistan or from Frangistan to Rumelia.

TURSUN BEG, '*Tarih-i Ebu'l-Fetih*', *c.* 1500.

'THE Turks are a people who speak Turkish and live in Turkey.' At first glance, this does not seem to be a proposition of any striking originality, nor of any very revolutionary content. Yet the introduction and propagation of this idea in Turkey, and its eventual acceptance by the Turkish people as expressing the nature of their corporate identity and statehood, has been one of the major revolutions of modern times, involving a radical and violent break with the social, cultural, and political traditions of the past.

The name Turkey has been given to Turkish-speaking Anatolia almost since its first conquest by the Turks in the eleventh century—given, that is, by Europeans.[1] But the Turks themselves did not adopt it as the official name of their country until 1923. When they did so, they used a form—*Türkiye*—that clearly revealed its European origin. The people had once called themselves Turks, and the language they spoke was still called Turkish, but in the Imperial society of the Ottomans the ethnic term Turk was little used, and then chiefly in a rather derogatory sense, to designate the Turcoman nomads or, later, the ignorant and uncouth Turkish-speaking peasants of the Anatolian villages. To

---

[1] The first occurrence of the name Turkey for the Anatolian lands conquered by the Turks is in a chronicle of the Crusade of Barbarossa, of 1190. By the thirteenth century the term is already in common use among western authors. See Claude Cahen, 'Le Problème ethnique en Anatolie', *J. Wld. Hist.*. ii (1954), 360.

apply it to an Ottoman gentleman of Constantinople would have been an insult.[2]

Even the term Ottoman was understood not in a national but in a dynastic sense, like Umayyad, Abbasid, and Seljuk, and the Ottoman state was felt to be the heir and successor, in the direct line, of the great Islamic Empires of the past. The concepts of an Ottoman nation and an Ottoman fatherland, as foci of national and patriotic loyalty, were nineteenth-century innovations under European influence. They were of brief duration.

Until the nineteenth century the Turks thought of themselves primarily as Muslims; their loyalty belonged, on different levels, to Islam and to the Ottoman house and state. The language a man spoke, the territory he inhabited, the race from which he claimed descent, might be of personal, sentimental, or social significance. They had no political relevance. So completely had the Turks identified themselves with Islam that the very concept of a Turkish nationality was submerged—and this despite the survival of the Turkish language and the existence of what was in fact though not in theory a Turkish state. Among the common people, the rustics and the nomads, a sense of Turkishness survived, and found expression in a rich but neglected folk literature. The governing and educated groups, however, had not even retained to the same degree as the Arabs and Persians an awareness of their identity as a separate ethnic and cultural group within Islam.

The Turkish national idea, in the modern sense, first appears in the mid-nineteenth century. Many factors contributed to its development—European exiles in Turkey, and Turkish exiles in Europe; European Turcological research, and the new knowledge which it brought of the ancient history and civilization of the Turkish peoples; the Russian Turks and Tatars, who encountered Russian pan-Slavism and reacted against it with a growing national consciousness of their own, nourished—by an odd paradox—by Russian Turcological discoveries; the influence of the subject peoples of the Ottoman Empire, who as Christians were more open to national ideas coming from the West, and who

---

[2] A text studied by Cahen shows that already in the thirteenth century a bourgeois of Konya 'uses the designation "Turk" exclusively for the "barbarous" and "unbearable" Turkoman frontier population' (Cahen, in G. E. von Grunebaum, *Unity and Variety in Muslim Civilization* (1955), p. 330).

in time helped to transmit the infection to their Imperial masters.

At first these ideas were limited to a small circle of intellectuals, but gradually they spread far and wide, and their victory was finally symbolized by the official adoption, for the first time, of the names of Turkey and Turk for the country and people of the Republic. The growth of the sentiment of Turkish identity was connected with the movement away from Islamic practice and tradition, and towards Europe. This began with purely practical short-term measures of reform, intended to accomplish a limited purpose; it developed into a large-scale, deliberate attempt to take a whole nation across the frontier from one civilization to another.

After the nationalist and modernist movements had established themselves, an interesting new development appeared—the assertion of identity with earlier, pre-existing local civilizations. This movement has its parallels in some other Islamic countries, and is of course a consequence of the importation of the European idea of the secular and territorial fatherland and of a mystical and permanent relationship between the land and the people who inhabit it. In Turkey it gave rise to the so-called Anatolianist movement and, later, to the theories, fathered by Atatürk, of the Turkish origin of such ancient peoples as the Sumerians, the Trojans, and, above all, the Hittites.[3]

This movement was partly political, with the purpose of encouraging the Turks to identify themselves with the country they inhabit—and thus at the same time of discouraging dangerous pan-Turanian adventures. But despite its politically inspired excesses and absurdities, Atatürk's Anatolian theory contained, or rather brought to light, important elements of truth.

We may then distinguish three main streams of influence that have gone to make modern Turkey: the Islamic, the Turkish, and a third, composite one that for want of a better name we may call local.

1. *Local*

The Muslim Turks who came to Turkey were marked by a complex and diverse pattern of tradition and culture. One strain is the Anatolian, the importance of which was stressed in the Turkish

---

[3] It is interesting that while the Turks claimed to be kinsmen and descendants of the ancient Anatolians, they made no such claim concerning the Byzantines, who had the threefold disadvantage, for this purpose, of being Greek, Christian, and above all, extant.

official thesis. The Hittites have left the most striking remains
and have been the subject of the most publicized theorizing,
and the other ancient peoples of Anatolia have no doubt also
left their mark. The Anatolian is, however, not the only strain.
The Ottoman Empire from its first century was a Balkan as well
as an Anatolian power, and Rumelia was for long the main centre.
Only in our own day has it lost its central position, together with
that of Constantinople-Istanbul, the Imperial city with its
millennial traditions of state and civilization, the ancient link
between the European and Asian territories of the Empire.

Any visitor to Turkey, especially one entering from the south or
the east, must at once be struck by the vigorous survival of these
local traditions within Turkish Islam. Many things will bring
them to his attention—the Anatolian village house and mosque,
so different in style and structure from those of Syria and Iraq;
the Balkan, almost European tonalities of Turkish music of the
kind called popular, as against the 'classical' music in the Perso-
Arabic manner; the Byzantine-looking cupolas on the mosques
and the Greek and south-east European decorative motives in
both formal design and peasant handicrafts.

The survival of Anatolian elements in modern Turkey is now
beyond dispute. There is no need to assert that the Turks are
Hittites or that the Hittites were Turks—but it is clear that there
was a large measure of continuity. This becomes clearer with the
parallel progress of archaeological and anthropological work in
Anatolia today. It is true that there was large-scale Turkish
colonization in Antolia, but the indigenous population was
neither exterminated nor entirely expelled. The Greek upper class
and the Greek cultural layer were replaced—and in time the
inhabitants were reassimilated, this time to Islamic and Turkish
patterns. They carried over much of their own culture, especially
in what pertains to agriculture and village life—the alternation of
the seasons, sowing and reaping, birth, marriage, and death.
With these things the newly imported Islamic culture, here as
elsewhere essentially urban, had less concern.

The Rumelian influence, after the conquest, came from the top
rather than from the bottom. Unlike Anatolia, most of Rumelia
was never assimilated either to Islam or to the Turkish language.
The peasant masses remained Christian, alien in language and
culture as well as religion, outside the cultural horizon of the

Turks. But the Balkan peoples had an enormous influence on the Ottoman ruling class. One of the most important channels was the *devşirme*,[4] the levy of boys, by means of which countless Balkan Christians entered the political and military *élites* of the Empire. Nor was that all. Even the local Christian landed ruling class was not wholly destroyed, as was once thought, but survived to some extent on its lands, and was incorporated in the Ottoman system. In the fifteenth century there were still Christian Timariots—military fief-holders—in Albania.[5] Then and later, Rumelian Christian troops served with the Ottoman forces, both as feudal cavalry and as common soldiers, while converted Rumelians were to be found holding fiefs and commands all over the Asiatic provinces of the Empire. The great role of the Albanians and Bosniaks in the Ottoman Empire is well known. Together with other Rumelians, they continued to play an important part in the reforms and revolutions of the nineteenth and twentieth centuries.

The Byzantine heritage of Turkey was at one time much exaggerated. Some historians attributed almost everything in Ottoman state and society to one or other source in Byzantium, and spoke of massive borrowings of Byzantine institutions and practices after the capture of Constantinople in 1453. It is now generally agreed that much of this is erroneous, and that in fact the Byzantine elements in Ottoman civilization are very much smaller than had previously been supposed. Moreover, these elements date from before the conquest of Constantinople, in most cases indeed from before the establishment of the Ottoman state. Some borrowings can be traced back to the time of the Anatolian Seljuks—others even to the Abbasid Caliphate, from which they came to Turkey as part of classical Islamic civilization itself. It was natural for the Seljuks to borrow during their long cohabitation with Byzantium, at a time when that state had not yet dwindled into the pale shadow that the Ottomans encountered.[6]

[4] On this term, and the practice that it denotes, reference may be made to the article 'Dewshirme' in *EI*[2] (by V. L. Menage). The compulsory levy of boys, originating in early Ottoman times, died out in the seventeenth century.

[5] See Halil İnalcık, 'Timariotes chrétiens en Albanie, au XV siècle, d'après un registre de timars ottoman', *Mitt. des Österreichischen Staatsarchivs*, iv (1952), 118–38.

[6] Köprülüzade Mehmet Fuat (=M. F. Köprülü), 'Bizans Müesseselerinin Osmanlı Müesseselerine Te'siri hakkında bazı Mülâhazalar', *Türk Huk. ve İkt. Tar. Mec.*, i

Yet, if the Byzantine elements have been exaggerated and misdated, they are nevertheless there. Though perhaps fewer, they are at the same time older and more deeply rooted—older perhaps than the Byzantine Empire. The survival of Byzantine motives in architecture has already been mentioned. But something as central and as typical in a society as its religious architecture cannot be an isolated phenomenon. The Byzantine elements in the Turkish mosque—so universal and so persistent—must express some deeper social and cultural affinity, all the more so in a society like Islam, where all is under the sign of religion. To suggest but one possible line of thought: perhaps we may associate the domed basilica type of mosque with the appearance—for the first time in Islam, and under Turkish rule—of an ecclesiastical hierarchy, with muftis presiding over territorial jurisdictions, under the supreme authority of the *Şeyh-ül-Islâm*, the Chief Mufti of the capital, whom we may describe, perhaps a little fancifully, as the Archbishop-primate of the Ottoman Empire. And here we may recall that hierarch and cupola are both oriental invaders even in Byzantium.

One other aspect of local influence may perhaps be considered here. Rumelia and Constantinople are part of Europe, and the Ottomans have from an early stage in their history been in contact with Europe—longer and more closely than any other Islamic state, not excluding North Africa. The Empire included important European territories, in which it absorbed European peoples and institutions. It also maintained contact with the West through trade, diplomacy, war, and—not least—immigration.

Mehmed the Conqueror had a knowledge of Greek and a library of Greek books. His entourage included the Italian humanist Ciriaco Pizzocolli of Ancona; his biographer was the Greek Critoboulos, his portraitist the Venetian Bellini.[7] Though unusual, this was not an isolated phenomenon. Not a little knowledge of the West was brought by the many renegades and refugees who sought a career in the Ottoman service, as well as by European diplomats and merchants. In the fifteenth century the Ottoman Sultans were quick to adopt the European device of artillery—often with European gunners and gun-founders. By the sixteenth

(1931), 165–313; Italian translation, *Alcune osservazioni intorno all'influenza delle istituzioni bizantine sulle istituzioni ottomane* (1953).

[7] E. Jacobs, 'Mehemmed II, der Eroberer, seine Beziehungen zur Renaissance, und seine Büchersammlung', *Oriens*, ii (1949), 6–30.

and seventeenth centuries Ottoman soldiers and sailors were trying, with varying success, to adopt European techniques of
warfare, while Ottoman scholars were making their first tentative
inquiries into European geography, history, and medical science.[8]
Before the nineteenth century Ottoman borrowings from Europe
were mainly of a material order, and were restricted in both scope
and effect. But today it is almost a truism that there can be no
limited and insulated borrowing by one civilization of the
practices of another, but that each element introduced from outside brings a train of consequences. We should perhaps reconsider
the significance and effects of such early Ottoman importations
from Europe as cartography, navigation, shipbuilding, and
artillery, followed in the eighteenth century by printing, military
engineering, and an Italianate style in Turkish architecture,
exemplified in the Nuruosmaniye mosque in Istanbul.[9]

2. *Turkish*

A visitor to Turkey will encounter at once the first and unmistakable sign of Turkishness—the Turkish language, which,
despite long subjection to alien influences, survives triumphantly.
Scholars have noted the remarkable capacity of Turkish to resist,
displace, and even supplant other languages with which it has
come in contact. With the Turkish language, as a sign of Turkish
tradition, the visitor may perhaps associate the habit of authority
and decision, and therefore of self-reliance, which the Turks have
retained from their historic role in the Islamic world.

Language was indeed the main—or at any rate the most readily
identifiable—contribution of the Turks to the diversified culture
of the Ottoman Empire. As once the Arabic language and the
Islamic faith, so now the Turkish language and the Sunni Islamic
faith were necessary qualifications of membership of the dominant
social class. In Ottoman Turkish was created a rich and subtle
means of expression, a worthy instrument of an Imperial civilization. The Ottomans had no racial arrogance or exclusiveness,
no insistence on 'pure' Turkish descent—nothing equivalent to
the segregation on a lower level of the *Mawālī*—the non-Arab

---

[8] A. Adnan, *La Science chez les Turcs ottomans* (1939). A more extensive treatment of
the subject by the same author in Turkish will be found in A. Adnan-Adıvar, *Osmanlı
Türklerinde İlim* (1943). See further below, ch. iii.

[9] See below, p. 440.

converts to Islam—by the Arab masters of the early Caliphate.[10] Islam and the Turkish language were the entry requirements which opened the door both to real power and to social status, to Albanian, Greek, and Slav as well as to Kurd and Arab.

For a time the Turks showed little national consciousness—far less, for example, than the Arabs or Persians. The pre-Islamic Turks were after all no savages, but peoples of a certain level of civilization, with their own states, religions, and literatures. Yet, save for a few fragments, all was forgotten and obliterated in Islam, until its partial recovery by European scholarship in the eighteenth and nineteenth centuries. There is no Turkish equivalent to Arab memories of the heathen heroes of old Arabia, to Persian pride in the bygone glories of the ancient Emperors of Iran, even to the vague Egyptian legends woven around the broken but massive monuments of the Pharaohs. Save for a few fragments of folk poetry and of genealogical legend, all the pre-Islamic Turkish past was forgotten, and even a newly Islamized Turkish dynasty like the Karahanids in the tenth century forgot their Turkish antecedents and called themselves by a name from Persian legend—the House of Afrāsiyāb.[11] Even the very name Turk, and the entity it connotes, are in a sense Islamic. Though the word Turk occurs in pre-Islamic inscriptions, it refers only to one among the related steppe peoples. Its generalized use to cover the whole group, and perhaps even the very notion of such a group, dates from Islam and became identified with Islam; and the historic Turkish nation and culture, even in a certain sense the language, in the forms in which they have existed in the last millennium, were all born in Islam. To this day the term Turk is never applied to non-Muslims, though they be of Turkic origin and language like the heathen Chuvash and Christian Gagauz, or citizens of a Turkish state, like the Christians and Jews of Istanbul.[12]

But the real Turkish element in Ottoman society and culture, if unselfconscious and unarticulated, is nevertheless profoundly important. It was revived in the late fourteenth century, when the

[10] cf. B. Lewis, *The Arabs in History* (1966), pp. 70 ff.

[11] In Iranian legend, re-echoed in Persian heroic poetry, Afrāsiyāb was king of Turan, a term which was later arbitrarily applied to the Turks.

[12] cf. P. Wittek, 'Türkentum und Islam. I', *Archiv für Sozialwissenschaft und Sozialpolitik*, lix (1928), 489–525; Osman Turan, 'Türkler ve Islâmiyet', *Ank. Univ. Dil ve Tar.-Coğ. Fak. Derg.*, v (1945–6), 457–85.

Ottomans, expanding from western into eastern Anatolia, encountered large groups of Turkish nomads, with their tribal organization and traditions intact—not yet scattered, disintegrated, and affected by local influences as in the western part of the peninsula.

During the first half of the fifteenth century there are a number of signs of the rise of a kind of Turkish national consciousness. It was at this time that the Ottoman Sultan assumed the old Turkish title of Khan; the cattle-brand of the Oğuz Turkish tribe of Kayı, from whom the Ottomans claimed descent, appeared as an emblem on Ottoman coins, and Ottoman historians and poets elaborated the Oğuz legend, which linked the Ottoman ruling house with a quasi-mythical Turkish antiquity and became the official account of the origins of the dynasty.[13] At the court of Murad II (1421–51) and his successors, Turkish poetry flourished and the study of Turkish antiquities was greatly in vogue. Even the Central Asian Turkish language and literature were for a while cultivated, and towards the end of the fifteenth century a literary school tried to write in pure and simple Turkish, without excessive use of the Persian and Arabic words and expressions that were already a part of the Turkish literary language.[14] This movement was limited and in many respects transitory, but it had an important effect in reaffirming the position of the Turkish language and thus of all that accompanies and is contained in language in the life of a people. It is significant too as the first major appearance, in the Ottoman state, of the nomadic Turkish element, which was now an important part of the Turkish population.

It is primarily as an ethnic reservoir that the Turkish nomadic tribes are important in the Ottoman Empire.[15] They were not a ruling element as such, but were rather treated with alternating mistrust and contempt by the state and the ruling groups. They were, however, the reserve on which the ruling class drew. The movement of the tribesmen into Ottoman society took place in several ways. One was the process of sedentarization, by which the nomads were settled on an increasing scale in different parts of

[13] P. Wittek, 'Le Rôle des tribus turques dans l'empire ottoman', *Mélanges Georges Smets* (1952), 665–76.
[14] Köprülüzade Mehmed Fuad (=M. F. Köprülü), *Millî Edebiyatın ilk Mübeşşirleri* (Ist., 1928).
[15] Wittek, in *Mél. G. Smets.*

Anatolia, and became peasant cultivators. This was partly due to the operation of normal economic processes, partly to deliberate government policy. The Ottoman Sultans from early times made extensive use of the method known as *sürgün*—the transfer of populations from one place to another for settlement and colonization.[16] Sometimes these deportations were penal, sometimes they were intended to serve political, economic, and military ends, as, for example, transfers of populations to newly conquered provinces or to disaffected areas. In all these movements the nomadic element played an important part. Nomadic settlement was not limited to the countryside. Evidence in both documentary and literary sources shows that there were tribal quarters in many towns. Such a process was inevitable in view of the close economic connexion between the town on the one hand and the peasants and tribes on the other—the two latter increasingly Turkish.

This seepage, so to speak, of Turks into the town and country population, and thus eventually into the governing *élite*, preserved and reinforced the Turkish character of Ottoman society, so that even the revolution of our time has been described with some justice as the emergence of a by now Turkish Anatolia, asserting itself against the cosmopolitan civilization of Constantinople and Rumelia—in other words, as a victory of Turks over Ottomans, typified by the transfer of the capital and the change of name of the country.

The conscious effort in modern Turkey to return to Turkism is important politically, as it affects the basis of polity and direction of policy of the state, but it is limited in its effects in other fields. The old Turkish civilizations were too thoroughly obliterated by Islam for any real revival of ancient Turkish culture to be possible. There have of course been attempts to revive it, the most noteworthy and most discussed being the language reform, the aim of which was to rid the language of the Persian and Arabic borrowings acquired during a thousand years of Islamic influence, and to return to a pure and unadulterated Turkish. There have also been some rather self-conscious but sometimes quite effective

[16] These transfers have been studied in a series of important articles by Ömer Lûtfi Barkan. See for example his 'Les Déportations comme méthode de peuplement et de colonisation dans l'Empire ottoman', *R. Fac. Sci. Éc. Univ. Ist.*, xi (1949–50), 67–131; Turkish section, 524–69.

adaptations of folk material—as for example the use of syllabic metres in place of the quantitative Perso-Arabic prosody, and the employment of Turkish melodies in modern orchestral and operatic compositions.[17] But modern Turkish literature and art owe far more to Europe than to any such deliberate experiments with old or popular material. The real importance of the Turkish strain in Turkey must be sought in uninterrupted survivals in the deeper layers of society—and these layers are now coming to the surface, with results yet to be seen.

3. Islam

We come now to the third factor—to Islam, which despite a period of eclipse has recently shown renewed vigour in Turkey, and is still clearly a major, if not the major element in the collective consciousness of a large proportion of the Turkish nation.

The Turks first encountered Islam on the frontiers—and their faith has from then till now retained some of the peculiar quality of frontier Islam, of the militant and uncomplicated religion of the frontiersmen.[18] The Turks were not forced into Islam, as were so many other peoples, and their Islam bears no marks of constraint or subjection. On the frontiers of the Caliphate, in East and West, the march-warriors had still maintained the simplicity, militancy, and freedom of early Islam, which elsewhere had been lost in the transformation of the old Islamic theocracy into an Oriental Empire. From all over that Empire, those who could not adapt themselves to the new order, those who for spiritual or material reasons felt the call of the frontier, joined the bands of the borderers and waged war for God, glory, and booty against the infidel and the heathen. In Central Asia, one of the two most important frontiers, the Turks, converted for the most part by wandering missionaries and mystics, joined in the struggle against their cousins who were still heathen, and, as the military classes of the Caliphate came to be more and more exclusively Turkish, began to play a predominant part in it. In the early eleventh century the first great independent Turkish sovereign in Islam, Mahmud of Ghazna, used his power to lead an army of Turks

---

[17] See below, p. 441.

[18] The significance of the frontier and of the frontier warrior (*gazi*) in the evolution of Turkish Islam has been studied by Professor Wittek in a series of notes, articles, and monographs beginning in 1925 (*ZDMG*, lxxix, 288 ff.). For a general survey see his *The Rise of the Ottoman Empire* (1938), where references to earlier studies are given.

to a frontier war on the grand scale, for the conquest of Hindu India. Later in the same century the Seljuks released a new wave of Turkish invaders across South West Asia, who wrested new territories for Islam from the Byzantine Empire, and infused into the Islamic Orient the martial and religious vigour which enabled it to withstand and eventually throw back the great European offensive of the Crusades.

The Islam of the Turkish frontiersmen was thus of a different temper from that of the heartlands of Islam. Unlike their brothers who had gone to Iraq or Egypt as Mamluks, and been brought up in the cosmopolitan atmosphere of the old Islamic capitals, the free Turks were Islamized and educated in the borderlands, and their Islam was from the first impregnated with the special characteristics of the frontier. Their teachers were dervishes, wandering ascetics and mystics, usually Turkish, preaching a very different faith from that of the theologians and the seminaries of the cities. Not for them was the subtlety—or the laxness—of Abbasid Baghdad, the easy-going tolerance and diversity of a mixed urban civilization—or the meticulous and exclusive orthodoxy of the schools. Theirs was a militant faith, still full of the pristine fire and directness of the first Muslims; a religion of warriors, whose creed was a battle-cry, whose dogma was a call to arms.

This was the faith—and the preaching—which the first Turks brought to Anatolia. And then, as the gazi, the dervish, and the nomad conquered, converted, and colonized the peninsula, the old Islamic traditions of government and civilization established themselves in what became the cities of a new sultanate, and the frontiersmen and dervishes moved on to seek new adventures on western fringes, by the Aegean, and in Europe. Anatolia became a province of the Middle Eastern Empire of the Seljuks, and the traditional pattern of Islamic life was gradually impressed on the country. Muslim bureaucrats and literati, jurists and theologians, merchants and artisans moved into the newly acquired territory, bringing with them the old, high, urban civilizations of classical Islam. The border moved farther westwards, and in time the new territories won by the Ottoman borderers in western Anatolia and in the Balkans were also transformed into a new Muslim Empire. Like Sivas and Konya under the Seljuks, so now under the Ottomans, first Brusa, then Adrianople, finally Constantinople became Muslim cities, centres of Muslim life and culture, decked with all the panoply of orthodox Islam.

From its foundation until its fall the Ottoman Empire was a state dedicated to the advancement or defence of the power and faith of Islam. For six centuries the Ottomans were almost constantly at war with the Christian West, first in the attempt—mainly successful—to impose Islamic rule on a large part of Europe, then in the long-drawn-out rearguard action to halt or delay the relentless counter-attack of the West. This centuries-long struggle, with its origins in the very roots of Turkish Islam, could not fail to affect the whole structure of Turkish society and institutions. For the Ottoman Turk, his Empire, containing all the heartlands of early Islam, was Islam itself. In the Ottoman chronicles the territories of the Empire are referred to as 'the lands of Islam', its sovereign as 'the Padishah of Islam', its armies as 'the soldiers of Islam', its religious head as 'the *şeyh* of Islam'; its people thought of themselves first and foremost as Muslims. Both Ottoman and Turk are, as we have seen, terms of comparatively recent usage, and the Ottoman Turks had identified themselves with Islam—submerged their identity in Islam—to a greater extent than perhaps any other Islamic people. It is curious that while in Turkey the word Turk almost went out of use, in the West it came to be a synonym for Muslim, and a Western convert to Islam was said to have 'turned Turk', even when the conversion took place in Fez or Isfahan.

A counterpart of this identification may be seen in the high seriousness of Turkish Islam, the sense of devotion to duty and of mission, in the best days of the Empire, that is unparalleled in Islamic history, not excluding that of the Caliphate. Which of the Abbasid Caliphs, for example, can show anything to compare with the loyalty, the intensity of moral and religious purpose, that clearly impelled the early Ottoman Sultans—the inexorable devotion to duty that made the aged and dying Sultan Süleyman the Magnificent face the hardships of yet another Hungarian campaign, and go from the comforts of his capital to the rigours of the camp and a certain death?

It is perhaps in the realm of law that one can see most clearly the seriousness of the Ottoman endeavour to make Islam the true basis of private and public life. The Ottoman Sultans gave to the *Şeriat*, the holy law of Islam, a greater degree of real efficacy than

it had had in any Muslim state of high material civilization since
early times.[19]. In a sense it may even be said that the Ottomans
were the first who really tried to make the *Şeriat* the effective law
of the state, to apply it throughout the land, and to give full
recognition and authority to the courts and judiciary that
administered it. The medieval Muslim Kadi cuts a miserable
figure beside his Ottoman colleague. Appointed by and answer-
able to the central authorities, he was compelled to abandon to
them important fields of jurisdiction, and was wholly dependent
on their rather dubious co-operation for the execution and enforcement of his judgments. The Ottoman Kadi on the other hand *was*
the central authority in the area of his jurisdiction, which in the
Ottoman system of provincial administration was known, significantly, as a kaza—the area administered by a Kadi, as a vilayet was
governed by a Vali. Moreover, he was one of a proud and powerful
hierarchy of juridical and theological authorities, ready to support
him in any clash with the military and political institutions, and
presided over by the *Şeyh-ül-Islâm* (or Chief Mufti) and the two
Kazıaskers in the capital, so great and revered, that the Sultan
himself rose to his feet to receive them when they came to offer
him their greetings at the Bayram festival.[20] The old Caliphs were
theoretically subject to the Holy Law, and could be deposed for
violating it—but this rule was a dead letter in the absence of any
authority or machinery for enforcing it. The Ottomans, however
recognized a supreme religious authority—the highest instance of
the *Şeriat*—with power to authorize the deposition of the sultan.
The actual role of this authority, the *Şeyh-ül-Islâm*, was of course
determined in the main by the play of politics and personalities.
The significant thing from our point of view is that such an
authority, with such a jurisdiction, should have existed at all and
have been recognized.

Another characteristic of Turkish Islam, of a rather different
kind but of similar significance, is the social segregation of the
non-Muslim communities. The Ottoman Empire was tolerant of
other religions, in accordance with Islamic law and tradition, and
its Christian and Jewish subjects lived, on the whole, in peace and
security. But they were strictly segregated from the Muslims, in
their own separate communities. Never were they able to mix

[19] J. Schacht, *An Introduction to Islamic Law* (1964), pp. 89 ff.
[20] *Kanunname*, quoted in Köprülü, in *Türk Huk. ve Ikt. Tar. Mec.*, i, 196.

freely in Muslim society, as they had once done in Baghdad and Cairo—nor to make any contribution worth the mention to the intellectual life of the Ottomans. There are few Ottoman equivalents to the Christian poets and Jewish scientists of the Arabic Golden Age. If the convert was readily accepted and assimilated, the unconverted were extruded so thoroughly that 500 years after the conquest of Constantinople, the Greeks and, to a lesser extent, the Jews in the city had not yet mastered the Turkish language—though neither people is lacking in linguistic versatility. One may speak of Christian Arabs—but a Christian Turk is an absurdity and a contradiction in terms.[21] Even today, after thirty-five years of the secular Republic, a non-Muslim in Turkey may be called a Turkish citizen, but never a Turk.

The first characteristic of Turkish Islam that we have noted is then—paradoxically—the extent to which the Turks have effaced themselves in Islam. We may find others. It is natural to look first to the popular, mystical, and more or less heterodox forms of religion which in Turkey, as in most other Muslim countries, flourish at the side of the formal, dogmatic religion of the theologians, and correspond to a far greater degree to the real religious beliefs and practices of the people. The different orders—*tarikats*[22]—that between them have commanded and perhaps still command the allegiance of the great majority of Turkish Muslims, certainly preserved much that is pre-Islamic in their beliefs, and still more in their traditions and observances. Turkish scholars have drawn attention to the Central Asian survivals—the elements of Shamanism, even of Buddhism and Manichaeism retained by the Central Asian Turks after their conversion to Islam and brought by them in various disguises to the West.[23] No less important are the many examples of Muslim-Christian (or Turco-Greek) syncretism in popular religious life.[24]

This kind of survival on the popular level is almost universal in Islam, and has its parallels in the persistence of old Celtic, Germanic, and Slavonic customs in a Christianized form in

[21] The use of the expression 'Christian Turk' to describe Christian populations of Turkish speech such as the Gagauz of the Dobrudja is of course restricted to the professional jargon of scholarship, and to very recent Turkish adaptations of it.

[22] See below, p. 398.

[23] See for example Köprülüzade Mehmed Fuad, *Influence du Chamanisme Turco-Mongol sur les ordres mystiques musulmans* (Ist., 1929).

[24] cf. F. W. Hasluck, *Christianity and Islam under the Sultans* (1928).

Europe. Popular Islam has always been looked upon with suspicion by the theologians and the state, perhaps more so in Turkey than elsewhere, and it is significant that even today the government of the Turkish Republic, though according tolerance and even encouragement to a limited revival of orthodoxy, has so far severely repressed all manifestation of activity by the *tarikats*.

It is, however, not on the popular, but on the formal level that we encounter one of the most characteristic qualities of Islam in the Ottoman Empire—that almost architectonic quality to which allusion has already been made. Here for the first time in Islamic history is created an institutional structure—a graded hierarchy of professional men of religion, with recognized functions and powers, worthy of comparison with the Christian priesthoods or those of the ancient Empires. The dictum that there is no priesthood in Islam remains true in the theological sense, in that there is no ordination, no sacrament, no priestly mediation between the believer and God—but it ceases to be true in the sociological and political sense. The origins of the great Ottoman religious institution can no doubt be traced back to the Sultanate of the Great Seljuks, when schools and schoolmen were organized to counter the threat of revolutionary heresy. But only in the Ottoman state did the religious institution reach maturity and fulfil its function as the guardian of the faith and the law.

We have now passed in review the three main trends in Turkish life and culture. In modern times there has been a fourth— Western civilization, which in Turkey as everywhere else in the world has struck with devastating impact against the existing order.

There are two concepts in relation to which we may consider those features and characteristics which set modern Turkey apart from her Muslim neighbours, and bring her nearer to both the merits and the faults of the Western world. One is the notion of process—the tendency to view a sequence of events not as a simple series but as a process in time, or, in organic terms, as a development; the second, related to it, is the notion of organism, of organic structure—the ability to conceive a whole made up of interrelated and interacting parts, rather than a mere congeries of separate, disjunct entities. These qualities are central to the modern Western form of civilization. They are the prerequisites of our physical and natural sciences; they determine our vision of the individual and the group, of man and the universe, and thus shape our institutions and our thought, our government and our arts, our industry, our science, and—save the mark—our religion. They make, to name but a few examples, the difference between the Western novel and the Oriental tale, Western portraiture and Oriental miniature, Western history and Oriental annals, Western government and Oriental rule—and perhaps between Western restlessness and Oriental repose.

For better or worse, these qualities have, in the course of the last century and a half, become more and more effective in Turkish public life—in the structure of state and law, in the formulation and direction of aspiration and policy, in the re-organization of social and even private life. They are already discernible in certain manifestations of the arts and sciences, where these go beyond the purely imitative. In the present forms in which these qualities appear in Turkey, they are certainly of Western and indeed recent provenance, and seem at times to be of but precarious tenure. But we may try, however tentatively, to see if they can be brought into relation with qualities in Ottoman or Turkish civilization which created, shall we say, a predisposition to accept them. The capacity for analysis and synthesis of the modern historian and the feeling for the development of character and plot of the modern novelist may have their precedents in the Ottoman chroniclers and memoranda writers, with their discussion of causes and analysis of effects. Even the modern constitutional republic is not entirely an importation. The Ottoman state, based on law and hierarchy, is in some ways nearer to it than to the amorphous and shifting society of classical Islam. The problem of the possible deeper affinities between Turkey and the West is of more than passing interest. In recent years the achievements and hopes of the whole reform movement have once again been brought into dispute and even, so it seemed for a while, into jeopardy. In the long run it will be the deeper rhythm of Turkish life, rather than the rapid surface movement of our time, which will determine the future relationship of Turkey with Islam, with the West, and with herself.

PART I
The Stages of Emergence

CHAPTER II

The Decline of the Ottoman Empire

For it has been well observed, that the arts which flourish in times while virtue is in growth, are military; and while virtue is in state, are liberal; and while virtue is in declination, are voluptuary: so I doubt that this age of the World is somewhat upon the descent of the wheel.

FRANCIS BACON, 'The Advancement of Learning', 1605.

The social condition of man corresponds to his individual condition, and in most matters the one is parallel to the other. . . . First of all, the natural life of man is reckoned in three stages, the years of growth, the years of stasis, and the years of decline. Though the times of these three stages are ordained in individuals, nevertheless these times vary according to the strength or weakness of individual constitutions . . . and these stages also vary in different societies . . . when the reckoning from the migration of the Prophet (upon him the best of greetings) had reached the year 1063, and the lofty Empire of Osman had attained its 364th year, in accordance with God's custom and the natural laws of civilization and human societies, signs of indisposition appeared in the complexion of this lofty Empire, and traces of discord in its nature and its powers. . . .

HACI HALIFE, 'Düstur ül-Amel', 1653.

THE decline of great empires has always been a subject of fascinated interest, and in our own day has a new poignancy, both for those who rejoice and for those who weep at the passing of Imperial greatness. The decline of the Ottoman Empire has also received its share of attention. though not of serious study.[1] The half-millennium of Ottoman history is still one of the most neglected of fields of study. Whereas recent research, both in Turkey and in the West, has increased our knowledge of the beginnings and of the end of the Empire, it has shed but little light on the processes of its decline. The modern Turkish historians, naturally enough, have devoted most of their attention to the early greatness and recent revival of their people, while such Western scholars as have discussed the subject have been content, in the main, to

---

[1] An exception is the essay on the decay of the Ottoman 'Ruling Institution', incorporated in H. A. R. Gibb and Harold Bowen, *Islamic Society and the West*, I/i (1950), 173 ff.

follow the analysis of the Ottoman historians themselves. Often, too, they have been influenced by the national historiographical legends of the liberated former subject peoples of the Empire in Europe and Asia. These have tended to blame all the defects and shortcomings of their societies on the misrule of their fallen Imperial masters, and have generalized the admitted failings of Ottoman government in its last phases into an indictment of Ottoman civilization as a whole.

'The decline and fall of the Roman Empire', Professor Jones has recently remarked, 'was the result of a complex of interacting causes which the historian disentangles at his peril.'[2] The peril is all the greater when, as with the Ottoman Empire, the essential preliminary work of detailed historical research is so little advanced. The great mass of Ottoman records for the seventeenth and eighteenth centuries are unpublished, almost untouched; even the chronicles have received only slight attention. The internal economic and social history in that period has hardly been studied at all, while the study of political history has progressed very little beyond the point to which it was brought by Hammer and Zinkeisen in the nineteenth century.

In what follows no attempt is made to cut through the complex web of cause, symptom, and effect. What is offered is a broad classification and enumeration of some of the principal factors and processes which led to, or were part of, or were expressions of the decline of Ottoman government, society, and civilization. They will be considered in three main groups—those relating to government, to economic and social life, and to moral, cultural, and intellectual change.

In the first group we may include the familiar changes in the apparatus of government—the court, the bureaucracy, the judiciary, the armed forces, which form the main burden of the famous memorandum of Koçu Bey, presented to Murad IV in 1630.[3] If the first ten Sultans of the house of Osman astonish us

[2] A. H. M. Jones, 'The Decline and Fall of the Roman Empire', *History*, xl (1955), 226.

[3] Koçu Bey, an Ottoman official of Macedonian or Albanian birth, was recruited by the *devşirme* and joined the palace staff, where he became the intimate adviser of Sultan Murad IV (1623–40). The memorandum which he composed for the Sultan in 1630 on the state and prospects of the Ottoman Empire has been greatly admired both in Turkey and among Western scholars, and led Hammer to call Koçu Bey 'the Turkish Montesquieu'. On the editions and translations of his treatise see F. Babinger, *Die Geschichtsschreiber der Osmanen und ihre Werke* (1927), 184–5. A new edition was

with the spectacle of a series of able and intelligent men rare if not unique in the annals of dynastic succession, the remainder of the rulers of that line provides an even more astonishing series of incompetents, degenerates, and misfits. Such a series as the latter is beyond the range of coincidence, and can be explained by a system of upbringing and selection which virtually precluded the emergence of an effective ruler. Similarly, the Grand Vezirate and other high offices, both political and religious, were filled and administered in such a way that what must surprise us is that they produced as many able and conscientious men as they did.

The breakdown in the apparatus of government affected not only the supreme instruments of sovereignty but also the whole of the bureaucratic and religious institutions all over the Empire. These suffered a catastrophic fall in efficiency and integrity, which was accentuated by the growing change in methods of recruitment, training, and promotion. This deterioration is clearly discernible in the Ottoman archives, which reflect vividly and precisely the change from the meticulous, conscientious, and strikingly efficient bureaucratic government of the sixteenth century to the neglect of the seventeenth and the collapse of the eighteenth centuries.[4] The same fall in professional and moral standards can be seen, though perhaps in less striking form, in the different ranks of the religious and judicial hierarchy.

Most striking of all was the decline of the Ottoman armed forces. The Empire could still draw on great reserves of loyal and valiant subjects, said Koçu Bey, writing in 1630. The Turkish soldier had suffered no loss of courage or morale, said Ali Paşa writing after the disastrous treaty of Küçük Kaynarca of 1774.[5] Yet the Ottoman armies, once the terror of Europe, ceased to frighten

published in Istanbul in 1939. A German translation by W. F. Behrnauer appeared in *ZDMG*, xv (1861), 272 ff. See further B. Lewis, 'Ottoman Observers of Ottoman Decline', *Islamic Studies*, i (1962), 71–87.

[4] In the sixteenth century the records are careful, detailed, and up to date; in the seventeenth and eighteenth centuries they become irregular, inaccurate, and sketchy. Even the quality of the paper becomes poorer. In this general picture of falling standards, the carefully kept registers of the Köprülü interlude stand out the more significantly.

[5] Ali Paşa had served as governor of Trebizond, where he founded a *derebey* dynasty. Two questions, he tells us, had profoundly occupied his thoughts: why the Empire from being so strong, had become so weak, and what was to be done to recover her former strength. His memorandum, still unpublished, is preserved in manuscript in Uppsala. A Swedish paraphrase was included by M. Norberg in *Turkiska Rikets Annaler* (Hernösand) v (1822), 1425 ff. See *EI²*, Djānīkli 'Alī Pasha' (by B. Lewis).

anyone but their own sovereigns and their own civil population, and suffered a long series of humiliating defeats at the hands of once despised enemies.

In the sixteenth century the Empire reached the effective limits of its expansion, and came up against barriers which it could not pass. On the eastern border, despite the victories in the field of Selim I and Süleyman, the Ottoman armies could not advance into Persia. The new centralized monarchy of the Safavids, then at the peak of their power; the high plateau of Iran, posing new problems of logistics and calling for new and unfamiliar techniques; the difficulties of leading against a Muslim adversary an army whose traditions since its birth were of the holy war against the infidels—all these combined to halt the Ottoman forces at the frontiers of Iran, and cut them off from overland expansion into Central Asia or India.

In Eastern waters they encountered the stout ships of the Portuguese, whose shipbuilders and navigators, trained to meet the challenge of the Atlantic, were more than a match for the calm-water ships of the Ottomans. Stouter vessels, more guns, better seamanship were what defeated the successive attempts of the Ottomans to break out of the ring, and swept Muslim shipping from the waters of the Indian Ocean.

In the Crimea and the lands beyond it they were halted by Russia. In 1475 the Ottomans had conquered Kaffa. Part of the Crimean coast passed under direct Ottoman rule, the Giray Khans of the Tatars became Ottoman vassals, and in 1569 the Ottomans even launched a plan to open a canal between the Don and Volga and thus, by acquiring a shipping route to Central Asia, to break out of the Portuguese noose.[6] But here too the Ottomans found their way blocked. At the same time as Western Europe was expanding by sea round Africa and into Asia, Eastern Europe was expanding by land across the steppe, southward and eastward towards the lands of Islam. In 1502 the once mighty Khanate of the Golden Horde was finally extinguished, and much of its territory absorbed by Russia. The successor Khanates of Kazan, Astrakhan, and Crimea lingered on for a while, but before

---

[6] On this project see the article of Inalcık, 'Osmanlı-Rus rekabetinin menşei ve Don-Volga kanalı teşebbüsü (1569)', *Bell.* no. 46 (1948), 349–402. English version: 'The Origins of the Ottoman-Russian Rivalry and the Don-Volga Canal 1569', *A. Univ. Ank.*, i (1946–7), 47–107.

long the Russians were able to conquer the first two, and to exercise a growing pressure on the third. The way was open to the Black Sea and the North Caucasus, the Caspian and western Siberia, where the advance of Russia barred and enclosed the Ottomans as did the Portuguese and their successors in the Eastern seas.

In Africa, desert, mountain, and climate offered obstacles which there was no incentive to surmount, while in the Mediterranean, after a brief interval, naval supremacy was lost to the maritime countries of the West.[7]

But the classical area of Ottoman expansion had been in none of these. Since the first crossing of the Bosporus in the mid-fourteenth century, Europe had been the promised land of the Ottomans—the 'House of War' par excellence, in which the power and the glory of Islam were to be advanced by victorious battle against the infidel. On 27 September 1529, after conquering Hungary, the armies of Süleyman the Magnificent reached Vienna—and on 15 October they began to withdraw from the still unconquered city. The event was decisive. For another century and a half inconclusive warfare was waged for Hungary, and in 1683 yet another attempt, the last, was made against Vienna. But the cause was already lost. The Ottoman Empire had reached the line beyond which it could not advance, from which it could only withdraw. The valour of the Habsburg, as of the Safavid armies, no doubt played its part in stemming the Ottoman onslaught, but is insufficient as an explanation of why the defenders of Vienna were able to halt the victors of Kossovo, Varna, Nicopolis, and Mohacs. There too we may perhaps find an explanation in the problems of a new and different terrain, calling for new techniques of warfare and especially of supply and transport.

It was after the halting of the Ottoman advance that the lag began to appear between the standards of training and equipment of Ottoman and European armies. Initially, the backwardness of

---

[7] Lûtfi Paşa, writing after 1541, could already see the danger to Turkey of the growing naval power of Europe. He quoted with approval a remark by Kemalpaşazade (d. 1533–4) to Selim I: 'My Lord, you dwell in a city whose benefactor is the sea. If the sea is not safe no ships will come, and if no ship comes Istanbul perishes.' He himself had said to Sultan Süleyman: 'Under the previous Sultans there were many who ruled the land, but few who ruled the sea. In the conduct of naval warfare the infidels are ahead of us. We must overcome them' (Lûtfi Paşa, *Asafname*, ed. and tr. R. Tschudi (1910), text 32–33, trans. 26–27).

the Ottomans was relative rather than absolute. Once in the forefront of military science, they began to fall behind. The great technical and logistic developments in European armies in the seventeenth century were followed tardily and ineffectively by the Ottomans—in marked contrast with the speed and inventiveness with which they had accepted and adapted the European invention of artillery in the fifteenth century. One possible contributory factor to this change is the fall in the flow of European renegades and adventurers to Turkey—but to state this is to raise the further question of why Turkey had ceased to attract these men, and why the Turks made such little use of those who did come.

The decline in alertness, in readiness to accept new techniques, is an aspect—perhaps the most dangerous—of what became a general deterioration in professional and moral standards in the armed forces, parallel to that of the bureaucratic and religious classes, which we have already noted. It led directly to what must be accounted, in the Ottoman as in the Roman Empire, one of the principal causes of decline—the loss of territory to more powerful foreign enemies. Modern historians have rightly tended to put the loss of territory to invaders among the symptoms rather than the causes of weakness, but the effect of the steady draining away of manpower, revenue, and resources should not be underrated. For Koçu Bey and his successors, the causes of these changes for the worse lay in favouritism and corruption. The different presuppositions of our time may incline us to regard these less as causes than as symptoms, and to seek their motives and origin in vaster and deeper changes.

During the sixteenth century three major changes occurred, principally of external origin, which vitally affected the entire life of the Ottoman Empire. The first of these has already been mentioned—the halting of the Ottoman advance into Europe. This was an event comparable in some ways with the Closing of the Frontier in the United States—but with far more shattering impact. The Ottoman state had been born on the frontier between Islam and Byzantine Christendom; its leaders and armies had been march-warriors in the Holy War, carrying the sword and the faith of Islam into new lands. The Ottoman gazis and dervishes, like the pioneers and missionaries of the Americas, believed themselves to be bringing civilization and the true faith to peoples sunk in barbarism and unbelief—and like them reaped the familiar rewards of the frontier warrior and the colonist. For the Ottoman state, the frontier had provided work and recompense both for its men of the sword and its men of religion and, in a deeper sense, the very *raison d'être* of its statehood. True, by the sixteenth century that state had already evolved from a principality of march-warriors into an Empire, but the traditions of the frontier were still deeply rooted in the military, social, and religious life of the Ottomans, and the virtual closing of the frontier to further expansion and colonization could not fail profoundly to affect them. The Ottoman systems of military organization, civil administration, taxation, and land tenure were all geared to the needs of a society expanding by conquest and colonization into the lands of the infidel. They ceased to correspond to the different stresses of a frontier that was stationary or in retreat.[8]

While the great Ottoman war-machine, extended beyond its range, was grinding to a standstill in the plains of Hungary, the life and growth of the Ottoman Empire were being circumvented, on a far vaster scale, by the oceanic voyages of discovery of the Western maritime peoples, the ultimate effect of which was to turn the whole Eastern Mediterranean area, where the Empire was situated, into a backwater. In 1555 the Imperial ambassador in Constantinople, Ogier Ghiselin de Busbecq, one of the acutest European observers of Turkey, could still comment that the Western Europeans basely squandered their energies 'seeking the Indies and the Antipodes across vast fields of ocean, in search of gold', and abandoning the heart of Europe to imminent and almost certain conquest.[9] But in about 1580 an Ottoman geographer, in an account of the New World written for Murad III, gave warning of the dangers to the Islamic lands and the disturbance to Islamic trade resulting from the establishment of Europeans on the coasts of America, India, and the Persian Gulf; he advised the Sultan to open a canal through the isthmus of Suez and send a fleet 'to capture the ports of Hind and Sind and drive away the infidels'.[10]

---

[8] The significance of the frontier and of the frontiersman in Ottoman government and society has been demonstrated by Paul Wittek. The whole question of the frontier as a cultural entity, with some reference to F. J. Turner's famous thesis on the significance of the frontier in American history, has been re-examined by Owen Lattimore in his 'The Frontier in History' (published in *Relazioni*, i, 105–38, of the Tenth International Congress of Historical Sciences, Rome 1955).

[9] *The Turkish letters of Ogier Ghiselin de Busbecq*, tr. by C. T. Forster and F. H. B. Daniell (1881), i, 129–30.

[10] *Tarih al-Hind al-Garbi* (Constantinople, 1142/1729), fol. 6b ff.

By 1625 another Ottoman observer, a certain Ömer Talib, could see the danger in a more pressing form:

> Now the Europeans have learnt to know the whole world; they send their ships everywhere and seize important ports. Formerly, the goods of India, Sind, and China used to come to Suez, and were distributed by Muslims to all the world. But now these goods are carried on Portuguese, Dutch, and English ships to Frangistan, and are spread all over the world from there. What they do not need themselves they bring to Istanbul and other Islamic lands, and sell it for five times the price, thus earning much money. For this reason gold and silver are becoming scarce in the lands of Islam. The Ottoman Empire must seize the shores of Yemen and the trade passing that way; otherwise before very long, the Europeans will rule over the lands of Islam.[11]

The effects on Middle Eastern trade of the circumnavigation of Africa were by no means as immediate and as catastrophic as was at one time believed. Right through the sixteenth century Eastern merchandise continued to reach the Ottoman Empire, coming by ship to Red Sea ports and Basra and overland across Persia, and European merchants came to Turkey to buy. But the volume of international trade passing this way was steadily decreasing. From the seventeenth century, the establishment of Dutch and British power in Asia and the transference of the routes of world trade to the open ocean deprived Turkey of the greater part of her foreign commerce and left her, together with the countries over which she ruled, in a stagnant backwater through which the life-giving stream of world trade no longer flowed.[12]

The European voyages of discovery brought another more immediate blow, as violent as it was unexpected. The basic unit of currency of the Ottoman Empire had been the silver *akçe*, or asper, in which all the revenues and expenditures of the state had been calculated. Like other Mediterranean and European states, the Ottoman Empire suffered from a recurring shortage of precious metals, which at times threatened its silver-based monetary system. To meet these difficulties, the Ottoman Sultans resorted to such well-tried measures as controlling the silver mines,

---

[11] The observations of Ömer Talib, written on the margins of a manuscript of the *Tarih al-Hind al-Garbi* in Ankara (Maarif Library 10024), were published by A. Zeki Velidi Togan, *Bugünkü Türkili (Turkistan) ve Yakın Tarihi*, i (1947), p. 127.

[12] On these questions see the important studies of Köprülü (in his additional notes to the Turkish translation of Barthold's *Muslim Culture (Islam Medeniyeti Tarihi*, 1940), pp. 255 ff.) and Inalcık in *Bell.*, no. 60 (1951), pp. 661 ff.

discouraging the export and encouraging the import of coin and bullion, extending the non-monetary sector of the state economy, and alternately debasing and reissuing the currency.

This situation was suddenly transformed when the flow of precious metals from the New World reached the Eastern Mediterranean. American gold, and, to a far greater extent, American silver had already caused a price revolution and a financial crisis in Spain. From there it passed to Genoa and thence to Ragusa, where Spanish coins of American metal are first reported in the 1580's.[13] Thereafter the financial impact on Turkey of this sudden flow of cheap and plentiful silver from the West was immediate and catastrophic. The Ottoman rulers, accustomed to crises of shortage of silver, were unable to understand a crisis of excess, or adequately to tax the new commercial inflow; the traditional measures which they adopted only served to worsen the situation. In 1584 the asper was reduced from one-fifth to one-eighth of a dirham of silver—a measure of devaluation which unleashed a continuous financial crisis with far-reaching economic and social consequences. As the price of silver fell, that of gold rose. Turkish raw materials became very cheap for European traders, and were exported in great quantities—including, despite prohibitions, even corn. Local industries began to decline, and the import of European manufactures expanded. Fiscal pressure and economic dislocation, accentuated by large-scale speculation and usury, brought distress and then ruin to large sections of the population. Before long there was a vast increase in coining, coin-clipping, and the like; the rate of the asper fell from 60 to the ducat to over 200, and foreign coins, both gold and silver, drove the debased Ottoman issues even from the internal markets. Twice in the seventeenth century the Ottoman government tried to stem the inflationary tide by the issue of a new silver currency; first, the *para*, which appeared as a silver coin in the 1620's, then the piastre, or *kuruş*, which appeared in the 1680's, in imitation of the European dollar. Both followed the asper into debasement and devaluation.[14]

[13] I am informed by Professor R. B. Serjeant that cheap silver of Portuguese provenance is reported slightly earlier in Southern Arabia, where it caused a drop in the rate of silver to gold.

[14] The effects on wages, prices, and currencies of the flow of American bullion, first studied for Spain in the classic monograph of Earl J. Hamilton (*American Treasure and the Price Revolution in Spain, 1501–1650*, 1934), were examined on a larger scale for the whole Mediterranean area in the great work of F. Braudel, *La Méditerranée et le monde méditerranéen à l'époque de Philippe II* (1949). Braudel's pointers on events in Turkey

Precisely at this time of monetary and financial crisis, the government was compelled to embark on a great expansion in its salaried personnel and a great increase in expenditure in coin. When Mehmed the Conqueror had faced a monetary crisis, he had reduced the numbers of paid soldiers and increased the numbers of cavalry sipahis, whose services were rewarded with fiefs and not coin.[15] But in the changed conditions of warfare of the sixteenth and seventeenth centuries this had ceased to be possible. The greatly increased use of firearms and artillery necessitated the maintenance of ever larger paid professional armies, and reduced the relative importance of the feudal cavalry-man. Both Koçu Bey and Hacı Halife note and deplore the decline of the sipahis and the increase in the paid soldiery which, says Hacı Halife, had increased from 48,000 in 1567 to 100,000 in about 1620.[16] Both writers are aware of the harmful financial and agrarian effects of this change. Understandably, they miss the point that the obsolescence of the sipahi had become inevitable, and that only the long-term, professional soldier could serve the military needs of the time.

The price was appalling. Faced with a growing expenditure and a depreciating currency, the demands of the treasury became more and more insatiable. The underpaid and over-sized salaried personnel of the state—civil, military, and religious—had growing difficulties in making ends meet, with the inevitable effects on their prestige, their honesty, and their further recruitment. Though the feudal cavalryman was no longer the main strength of the army, his decline was sorely felt in the countryside, as the old Ottoman agrarian system, of which he had once been the foundation, tottered and collapsed. In place of the sipahi, who resided in or near the fief in which he had a hereditary interest, palace favourites, parasites, and speculators became the recipients of

(especially pp. 393–4, 419–20, 637–43) were taken up and developed by Inalcık in his illuminating study, 'Osmanlı Imparatorluğunun Kuruluş ve Inkişafi devrinde Türkiye' nin Iktisadi Vaziyeti üzerinde bir tetkik münasebetile', *Bell.*, no. 60 (1951), 656 ff. See further the review of Braudel's book by Barkan in *R. Fac. Sci. Éc. Univ. Ist.*, xi (1949–50), 196–216.

[15] Inalcık, in *Bell.*, no. 60, 656 ff.

[16] *Düstur al-'Amal li-Islah al-Halal* (Ist., 1280/1863, as an appendix to the *Kavanin-i Al-i Osman* of Ayn-i Ali), pp. 131–2; German trans. by Behrnauer in *ZDMG*, xi (1857), 125. In this little treatise, written in about 1653, Hacı Halife examines the causes of the financial and other troubles of the Ottoman Empire. On changes in the Ottoman armies, see *EI*[2], 'Bārūd iv' and 'Harb iv' (by V. J. Parry).

fiefs, sometimes accumulating great numbers of them, and thus becoming, in effect, absentee owners of great latifundia. Other fiefs reverted to the Imperial domain.[17] But the growing inefficiency and venality of the bureaucracy prevented the formation of any effective state system for the assessment and collection of taxes. Instead these tasks were given to tax-farmers, whose interposition and interception of revenues became in time a prescriptive and hereditary right, and added to the number of vast and neglected latifundia.

The shrinking economy of the Empire thus had to support an increasingly costly and cumbersome superstructure. The palace, the bureaucracy, and the religious hierarchy, an army that in expenditure at least was modern, and a parasitic class of tax-farmers and absentee landlords—all this was far more than the medieval states or even the Roman Empire had tried to support; yet it rested on an economy that was no more advanced than theirs. The technological level of agriculture remained primitive, and the social conditions of the Turkish countryside after the sixteenth century precluded the appearance of anything like the English gentleman-farmers of the seventeenth and eighteenth centuries whose experiments revolutionized English agriculture.

These developments are not peculiar to Turkey. The fall in the value of money, the growing cost of government and warfare, the sale of offices and farming of taxes—all these are known in other Mediterranean and adjoining states, where they contributed to the rise of a new class of capitalists and financiers, with a growing and constructive influence on governments.

In Turkey too there were rich merchants and bankers, such as the Greek Michael Cantacuzenos and the Portuguese Jew Joseph Nasi—the Fugger of the Orient, as Braudel called him.[18] But they were never able to play anything like the financial, economic, and political role of their European counterparts. Part of the cause of this must undoubtedly be found in the progressive stagnation of Ottoman trade, to which allusion has already been made. But that is not all. Many of these merchants—especially those trading in Europe—were Christians or Jews—tolerated but second-class subjects of the Muslim state. However great their economic power, they were politically

---

[17] From the late sixteenth century onwards the cadastral registers in the Ottoman archives show a steady decrease in the number of *timars*, and a corresponding increase in the extent of Imperial domain.

[18] Braudel, p. 567.

penalized and socially segregated; they could obtain political power only by stealth, and exercise it only by intrigue, with demoralizing effect on all concerned. Despite the scale and extent of their financial operations, they were unable to create political conditions more favourable to commerce, or to build up any solid structure of banking and credit, and thus help the Ottoman government in its perennial financial straits. In England too finance and credit were at first in the hands of alien specialists, who have left their name in Lombard Street. But these were ousted in time by vigorous and pushful native rivals. In Turkey no such rivals arose, and in any case, in the general decline of the seventeenth century, even the Greek and Jewish merchant princes of Constantinople dwindled into insignificance. Fortunes were still made in Turkey, but their origin was not economic. Mostly they were political or fiscal in origin, obtained through the holding of public office. Nor were they spent on investment or development, but consumed or hoarded, after the fashion of the time.

Reference has often been made to the technological backwardness of the Ottoman Empire—to its failure not only to invent, but even to respond to the inventions of others. While Europe swept forward in science and technology, the Ottomans were content to remain, in their agriculture, their industry, and their transport, at the level of their medieval ancestors. Even their armed forces followed tardily and incompetently after the technological advances of their European enemies.

The problem of agriculture in the Ottoman Empire was more than one of technical backwardness, however. It was one of definite decline. Already during the reign of Süleyman the Magnificent, Lûtfi Paşa gave warning of the dangers of rural depopulation, and urged that the peasantry be protected by moderation in taxation and by regular censuses of village population, as a control on the competence of provincial government.[19] Koçu Bey reinforces these arguments; but by 1653 Hacı Halife reports that people had begun to flock from the villages to the towns during the reign of Süleyman, and that in his own day there

---

[19] Lûtfi Paşa, *Asafname*, ch. 4. Lûtfi Paşa's treatise, written after his dismissal from the office of Grand Vezir in 1541, sets forth rules on what a good Grand Vezir should do and, more urgently, on what he should avoid. In this booklet, written at a time when the Ottoman Empire was still at the height of its power and glory, the writer shows deep concern about its fate and welfare, and is already able to point to what, in later years, became the characteristic signs of Ottoman decline.

were derelict and abandoned villages all over the Empire.[20]

Much of this decline in agriculture can be attributed to the causes named by the Ottoman memorialists: the squeezing out of the feudal sipahis, the mainstay of the early Ottoman agrarian system, and their replacement by tax-farmers and others with no long-term interest in peasant welfare or land conservation, but only an immediate and short-term interest in taxes. Harsh, exorbitant, and improvident taxation led to a decline in cultivation, which was sometimes permanent. The peasants, neglected and impoverished, were forced into the hands of money-lenders and speculators, and often driven off the land entirely. With the steady decline in bureaucratic efficiency during the seventeenth and eighteenth centuries, the former system of regular land surveys and population censuses was abandoned.[21] The central government ceased to exercise any check or control over agriculture and village affairs, which were left to the unchecked rapacity of the tax-farmers, the leaseholders, and the bailiffs of court nominees. During the seventeenth century some of the more permanently established lease-holders began to coalesce with the landowners into a new landed aristocracy—the *ayan-i memleket* or country notables, whose appearance and usurpation of some of the functions and authority of government were already noted at the time.[22]

While agriculture declined, industry fared little better. The corporative structure of the guilds fulfilled a useful social function in expressing and preserving the complex web of social loyalties and obligations of the old order, and also, though to a diminishing extent, in safeguarding the moral level and standards of craftsmanship of the artisan. Their economic effects, however, were restrictive and eventually destructive. A man's choice of profession was determined by habit and inheritance, the scope of his endeavour limited by primitive techniques and transport, his

[20] Hacı Halife, ch. 1.

[21] See for example the list of *tapu* registers for the Arab provinces, given in B. Lewis, 'The Ottoman Archives as a Source for the History of the Arab Lands', *JRAS* (1951), pp. 149 ff. The great majority of the registers listed there are of the sixteenth century. After 1600 the surveys become less and less frequent, and the resulting registers more and more slipshod.

[22] cf. the remarks of Hüseyin Hezarfen, writing in 1669 (R. Anhegger, 'Hezarfen Hüseyin Efendi'nin Osmanlı devlet teşkilâtına dâir mülâhazaları', *TM*, x (1951–3), 372, 387. The *ayan-i vilayet* already appear occasionally in *Kanuns* of the sixteenth century (Barkan, *XV ve XVI inci asırlarda . . . Kanunlar*, i (1943), index).

manner and speed of work fixed by guild rule and tradition; on the one hand a sufi religious habit of passivity and surrender of self, on the other the swift fiscal retribution for any sign of prosperity, combined to keep industrial production primitive, static, and inert, utterly unable to resist the competition of imported European manufactures.[23]

Some have sought the causes of this backwardness in Islam or in the Turkish race—explanations which do not satisfy, in view of the previous achievements of both. It may, however, be possible to find part of the explanation of Ottoman lack of receptivity— perhaps even of Ottoman decline—in certain evolving attitudes of mind, inherited by the Ottomans along with the classical Islamic civilization of which they had been the heirs and renovators.

Classical Islamic civilization, like others before and after it, including our own, was profoundly convinced of its superiority and self-sufficiency. In its earliest, primitive phase, Islam had been open to influences from the Hellenistic Orient, from Persia, even from India and China. Many works were translated into Arabic from Greek, Syriac, and Persian. But with the solitary exception of the late Latin chronicle of Orosius, not a single translation into a Muslim language is known of any Latin or Western work until the sixteenth century, when one or two historical and geographical works were translated into Turkish.[24] For the Muslim of classical times, Frankish Europe was an outer darkness of barbarism and unbelief, from which the sunlit world of Islam had nothing to learn and little to fear. This view, though becoming outdated towards the end of the Middle Ages, was transmitted by the medieval Muslims to their Ottoman heirs, and was reinforced by the crushing victories of Ottoman arms over their European opponents. On the warlike but open frontier one could still exchange lessons with one's counterpart on the other side; through renegades and refugees new skills could still reach the Islamic Empire. But the willingness to learn these lessons was not there, and in time the sources also dried up. Masked by the still

---

[23] Sabri F. Ülgener, *Iktisadî Inhitat Tarihimizin Ahlak ve Zihniyet Meseleleri* (1951). Much light is thrown on these questions by Professor Ülgener's attempt to apply the methods of Weber and Sombart to the study of Ottoman social and economic history.

[24] See further B. Lewis, 'The Muslim Discovery of Europe', *BSOAS*, xx (1957), 415; also B. Lewis and P. M. Holt, eds., *Historians of the Middle East* (1962), pp. 180–91, where some earlier references to Western sources are discussed.

imposing military might of the Ottoman Empire, the peoples of Islam continued to cherish the dangerous but comfortable illusion of the immeasurable and immutable superiority of their own civilization to all others—an illusion from which they were slowly shaken by a series of humiliating military defeats.

In the military empire, at once feudal and bureaucratic, which they had created, the Muslims knew only four professions—government, war, religion, and agriculture. Industry and trade were left in large measure to the non-Muslim subjects, who continued to practise their inherited crafts. Thus the stigma of the infidel became attached to the professions which the infidels followed, and remained so attached even after many of the craftsmen had become Muslim. Westerners and native Christians, bankers, merchants, and craftsmen, were all involved in the general contempt which made the Ottoman Empire impervious to ideas or inventions of Christian origin and unwillingly to bend his own thoughts to the problems of artisans and vile mechanics. Primitive techniques of production, primitive means of transportation, chronic insecurity and social penalization, combined to preclude any long-term or large-scale undertakings, and to keep the Ottoman economy at the lowest level of competence, initiative, and morality.[25]

This apathy of the Ottoman ruling class is the more striking when contrasted with the continuing vigour of their intellectual life. An example of this may be seen in the group of writers who memorialized on the decline of the Empire, which they saw so clearly but were powerless to stop. We may point also to the brilliant Ottoman school of historiography, which reaches its peak of achievement in the work of Naima (1655–1716); to the Ottoman traditions of courtly and religious poetry, two of the greatest exponents of which, Nedim and Şeyh Galib, lived in the eighteenth century; to the Ottoman schools of architecture, miniature, and music. It is not until the end of the eighteenth century and the beginning of the nineteenth that we can speak of a real breakdown in the cultural and intellectual life of Turkey, resulting from the utter exhaustion of the old traditions and the absence of new creative impulses. And even then, behind the battered screen of courtly convention, the simple folk arts and folk poetry of the Turks continued as before.

In the late Middle Ages, the Ottoman Empire was the only

[25] Ülgener, pp. 193 ff.

state in Europe which already possessed the territory, the cohesion, the organization, the manpower and the resources to carry the new apparatus of warfare, the crushing cost of which was out-moding the city states and feudal principalities of medieval Europe, as surely as modern weapons have outmoded the petty sovereignties of Europe in our own day. In part perhaps because of that very primacy, it failed to respond to the challenge which produced the nation-states of sixteenth-century Europe, and the great commercial and technological efflorescence of which they were the scene.

Fundamentally, the Ottoman Empire had remained or reverted to a medieval state, with a medieval mentality and a medieval economy—but with the added burden of a bureaucracy and a standing army which no medieval state had ever had to bear. In a world of rapidly modernizing states it had little chance of survival.

The stages in the decline of Ottoman power and grandeur are well marked by public, international treaties. The first was the treaty of Sitvatorok, signed with Austria in November 1606. For the first time, this was not a truce dictated in Istanbul to the 'King of Vienna', but a treaty negotiated on the frontier and agreed with the 'Roman Emperor'. The Ottoman Sultan had at last consented to concede the Imperial title to the Habsburg monarch, and to treat with him as an equal.

The seventeenth century began with a concession of equality; it ended with a clear admission of defeat. In 1682 the Ottoman Empire, temporarily restored to health and vigour by the reforms of the Köprülü Vezirs, had launched one more major offensive, in the grand style, against its European enemies. The second failure before the walls of Vienna, in 1683, was decisive and final. The Austrians and their allies advanced rapidly into Ottoman territory in Hungary, Greece, and the Black Sea coast, and the Austrian victories at the second battle of Mohacs in 1687 and at Zenta in 1697 sealed the defeat of the Turks. The peace treaty of Carlowitz, signed on 26 January 1699, marks the end of an epoch and the beginning of another. This was the first time that the Ottoman Empire signed a peace as the defeated power in a clearly decided war, and was compelled to cede extensive territories, long under Ottoman rule and regarded as part of the House of Islam, to the infidel enemy. It was a fateful opening to the eighteenth century.

By the treaty of Passarovitz of 1718, Turkey made further cessions of territory. Though the mutual suspicions of her enemies enabled her to recover some ground during the war of 1736–9, the recovery was of slight duration. A new humiliation came with the treaty of Küçük Kaynarca of 1774, after a war in which Russian troops had carried all before them and a Russian fleet had entered the Mediterranean and threatened the very coasts of Anatolia. By this treaty, the Sultan renounced not only conquered lands inhabited by Christian populations, but old Muslim territory in the Crimea;[26] he also conceded to the Russian Empress a right of intervention which grew into a virtual protectorate over his own Orthodox Christian subjects.

Thereafter there was a halt. Apart from the loss of Bukovina to Austria in 1775 and of Bessarabia to Russia in 1812, the Ottoman Empire made no important cessions to foreign powers until a century later, when the process was resumed with the loss of Bosnia and Herzegovina to Austria and of Batum and Kars to Russia in 1878. During this period the main threat to the unity and integrity of the Empire came from within.

The humiliations of Carlowitz, Passarowitz, and later treaties further weakened the already waning authority of the central government over the provinces. Significantly, it was in the old Islamic territories in Asia and Africa that provincial independence first appeared and went farthest. These movements were in no sense expressions of popular or national opposition to Ottoman rule. Except in a few remote desert and mountain areas, such as Arabia, the Lebanon, and Kurdistan, neither the leaders nor the followers were local, but were drawn from either the Ottoman or the Mamluk military classes. In neither case had they any roots in local soil—in neither could they count on any serious local support. Most of them were rebellious and adventurous pashas and officers, profiting from the remoteness and weakness of the Sultan's authority to intercept a larger share of the revenues of their provinces and to transform them into virtually independent principalities. Such were Ali Bey in Egypt, Ahmed Jezzar in Syria, and the Mamluk lords of Baghdad and Basra. They were no more concerned with the language and sentiments of their subjects than

26 By the terms of the treaty, the Sultan renounced his suzerainty over the Tatar Khanate of the Crimea, which became independent. The second stage was completed in 1783, when Russia annexed the Crimea, and the Khanate was extinguished. On the Turkish reactions see below, p. 49 and n. 24.

was a medieval European feudal magnate; far less with their welfare.

Rather different was the position in Anatolia, where the independent *derebeys*—valley-lords, as they were called—won virtual autonomy about the beginning of the eighteenth century. These too began as officers or agents and became vassals of the Sultan. Unlike the pashas in the Arab lands, however, they struck root among the peoples whom they ruled and from whom they had sprung, and formed genuine local dynasties, with strong local traditions and loyalties. Their financial and military obligations to the Porte came to be well defined and regulated, and evolved into a regular system of suzerainty and vassalage. Their close and intimate relationship with their territories and peoples seem to have had a beneficial effect on both.

In Rumelia, still the main centre and stronghold of the Empire and the home of its governing *élites*, the central government was able to maintain some measure of direct control. But there too the *ayan*, the new aristocracy of 'notables', were steadily taking over the functions of government, and by the end of the eighteenth century the notables of Rumelia, with their private armies, treasuries, and courts of law, had rivalled the independence of the Anatolian valley-lords.

After each of the great military defeats of the eighteenth century, Ottoman statesmen and historians discussed with brutal frankness the decrepit state of the Empire and the abject performance of its armies. The treaty of Küçük Kaynarca and the subsequent annexation of the Crimea in particular gave rise to much heart-searching and discussion. Then, in 1787, a new war broke out between Turkey and Russia, joined in the following year by Austria. This time, distracted by events in Poland, Prussia, and France, the Russians and Austrians did not press the campaign as vigorously as previously, and in 1791–2 Turkey was able to make peace with Austria, at Sistova, and with Russia, at Jassy, on comparatively lenient terms.

During the war a new Sultan, Selim III, had been invested with the sword of Osman. Thirty-eight years of age at his accession, he was a man of greater ability and wider knowledge and experience than any who had emerged from the cage of princes in the Saray for a long time. Already as a young man he had entered, through his personal emissary Ishak Bey, into direct correspondence with the king of France, and showed a growing interest in European affairs. He was well aware that the respite of 1792 was due to difficulties elsewhere in Europe, and that there would be little time before Austria and Russia returned to the assault.

Selim's first problem was the modernization of the armed forces, and he began, reasonably enough, by setting up new military and naval schools. For these, however, he had to rely on foreign instructors. Such attempts at Westernizing the armed forces as had been made during the eighteenth century had all relied on French instruction, and it was natural for Selim, when he had prepared the list of foreign instructors and technicians whom he needed to recruit, to send that list to Paris. The time was the autumn of 1793.

CHAPTER III

The Impact of the West

It is certainly a good Maxim for an Embassadour in this Country, not to be over-studious in procuring a familiar friendship with Turks; a fair comportment towards all in a moderate way, is cheap and secure; for a Turk is not capable of real friendship towards a Christian.

PAUL RYCAUT, 'The History of the Present
State of the Ottoman Empire', 1668.

Familiar association with heathens and infidels is forbidden to the people of Islam, and friendly and intimate intercourse between two parties that are to one another as darkness and light is far from desirable.

ASIM EFENDI, 'History', c. 1809.

. . . sans perdre de temps je m'appliquai à l'étude de la langue française, comme la plus universelle, et capable de me faire parvenir à la connoissance des auteurs qui ont écrit sur les belles sciences.

SEID MUSTAFA, 'Diatribe de l'Ingenieur', 1803.

THE French Revolution was the first great movement of ideas in Western Christendom that had any real effect on the world of Islam. Despite the long confrontation of Christendom and Islam across the Mediterranean, and their numberless contacts, in peace and in war, from Syria to Spain, such earlier European movements as the Renaissance and the Reformation woke no echo and found no response among the Muslim peoples. It may at first sight seem strange that Islamic civilization, which in its earlier stages was so receptive to influences from Hellenism and Iran, even from India and China, nevertheless decisively rejected the West. But an explanation is not hard to find. When Islam was still expanding and receptive, the Christian West had little or nothing to offer, but rather flattered Islamic pride with the spectacle of a culture that was visibly and palpably inferior. Furthermore, by the very fact that it was Christian, it was discredited in advance. The Muslim doctrine of successive revelations, culminating in the final mission of Muhammad, enabled the Muslim to reject Christianity as an earlier and imperfect form of something which he alone possessed in its entirety, and to discount Christian thought and Christian civilization. After the initial impact of eastern Christianity on Islam in its earliest years, Christian influence, even from the high civilization of Byzantium, was reduced to a minimum. Later, when the advance of Christendom and the decline of Islam created a new relationship, Islam was crystallized—not to say ossified—and had become impervious to external stimuli, especially from the millennial enemy in the West.

Earlier Western Influences

All this does not mean that there was no Western influence in Turkey before the eighteenth century. On the contrary, the Turks, while rejecting Christianity, Christian ideas, and Christian civilization, still found many things in Christian Europe that were useful enough and attractive enough to borrow, imitate, and adapt.

No nation in the world [wrote the Imperial ambassador Busbecq in 1560] has shown greater readiness than the Turks to avail themselves of the useful inventions of foreigners, as is proved by their employment of cannons and mortars, and many other things invented by Christians. They cannot, however, be induced as yet to use printing, or to establish public clocks, because they think that the Scriptures, that is, their sacred books—would no longer be *scriptures* if they were *printed*, and that, if public clocks were introduced, the authority of their muezzins and their ancient rites would be thereby impaired.[1]

Firearms could be accepted, since they would be of service in the Holy War for Islam against the infidels; printing and clocks could not be accepted, since they served no such purpose, and might flaw the social fabric of Islam. The attitude of mind described by Busbecq is attested by many examples. When a Sultan wished to imitate the construction and armament of a captured Venetian galley, and some voices were raised in objection to this aping of infidel ways, the ulema ruled that for the sake of the Holy War it was permissible to learn from the infidels new ways of waging war against them. But when Jewish refugees from Spain asked Bayezid II for permission to set up printing presses in Turkey, he consented on condition that they did not print any books in Turkish or Arabic, and confined themselves to Hebrew and European languages.[2]

[1] Busbecq, i. 255 (pp. 213–14 of the Latin text in the Elzevir edition, Leiden, 1633).

[2] cf. the interesting observations of Nicolas de Nicolay, who visited Turkey in 1551, on the role of the Spanish and Portuguese Marranos: 'Oultre ce ilz ont entre eulx des couriers en tous arts & manufactures tres-excellens, specialement des Marranes n'as pas longs temps bannis & deschassez d'Espagne & Portugal, lesquelz au grand detriment & dommage de la Chrestienté ont apprins au Turc plusieurs inuentions,

The Ottoman state was born on the frontier between Islam and Christendom. For centuries the Ottomans and other Turkish principalities of march-warriors in Anatolia cohabited with Byzantium in the tense intimacy of frontier warfare—imitating and influencing one another in tactics and weapons, in clothing and diet, drawing closer to one another through the subtler workings of conversion, of assimilation, and of marriage by capture. Not a few of the Turkish frontiersmen were suckled and weaned by Greek mothers—not a few of the noble families of the early Empire were descended from converted Greeks. In the popular religion of both Greek Christians and Turkish Muslims, there are countless common saints, common festivals, and common holy places, which each group reinterpreted in its own way. Jalal ad-Din Rumi (1207-73), the great mystical poet of Konya— no Anatolian but an immigrant from Central Asia—tried his hand at Greek verse;[3] even Sultan Mehmed the Conqueror had Greek books and a Greek biographer, and the Sultans more than once called on the services of Greek architects for their mosques and Greek shipwrights for their fleet.[4]

Byzantine influence on the Ottomans was limited in the main to material things, and to the popular level of religious belief and practice. It died out in the course of the fifteenth century, under the impact of two events: the incorporation of the former frontier lands into the sphere of the old, classical Islamic civilization, and the decay and disappearance of Byzantium itself. Thereafter the general adoption of traditional Islamic institutions, attitudes, and conceptions served to reduce and to neutralize any influences emanating from the conquered House of War.

It is often overlooked that Western influence on the Turks is in a sense almost as old as that of Byzantium. Constantinople, two

artifices & machines de guerre, comme à faire artillerie, hardquebuses, pouldres à canon, boulets & autres armes. Semblablement y ont dressé Imprimerie, non iamais au parauant veue en ces Regions: par laquelle en beaux caracteres ilz mettent en lumiere plusieurs liures en diuerses langues, Grecque, Latine, Italienne, Espagnolle, & mesmement Hebraique, qui est la leur naturelle. Mais en Turc, ny en Arabe, ne leur est permis d'imprimer' (*Les Navigations, peregrinations et voyages, faicts en la Turquie*, Antwerp, 1576, p. 246). On the early history of printing in the Middle East, see L. Cheikho, 'Ta'rīkh Fann al-Ṭibā'a,' in *Mashriq*, iii (1900), 78 ff., 174, &c.

[3] Abdülbâki Gölpınarlı, *Mevlânâ Celâleddin* (1952), pp. 254 ff.; cf. P. Burguière and R. Mantran, 'Quelques vers grecs du XIIIᵉ siècle en caractères arabes', *Byzantion*, xxii (1952), p. 75.

[4] See above, p. 6 and n. 7; also Babinger, *Mehmed der Eroberer* (1953), p. 502.

and a half centuries before its conquest by the Turks, had suffered a more shattering conquest by Western invaders, and both the city and many of the provinces had been subjected to Western European government and institutions. Late Byzantine feudalism, which helped to shape the Ottoman system of military fiefs, had itself been reshaped under the impact of the Frankish feudalism of the Latin Empire of Constantinople and its dependent and successor principalities. When the Ottomans conquered the Morea, most of it had been ruled for the previous two centuries by French barons, Catalan adventurers, or Florentine financiers; its law was the feudal *Assises de Romanie*, based on the *Assises de la Haute Cour de Jérusalem*, a purely Western system of feudal law elaborated by the Crusaders in Palestine and later imposed by them on other countries which they conquered.

Once established in their new Imperial role, the Ottoman Turks found many points of contact with the West. What the Byzantine Empire had once been to the medieval Caliphate, Western Europe now was to the Ottomans—a rival empire and a rival civilization, the seat of a rival religion which it was the sacred duty of the Islamic Empire to subjugate and convert. Just as the Ottomans had succeeded the Caliphs as the sovereigns of Islam, so the Kings of Frangistan had succeeded the Emperors of Constantinople as Lords of the House of War. And as Baghdad had borrowed Greek fire from Constantinople, Istanbul might borrow artillery from Europe.

But in the intervals of war there was peace, and commerce; European diplomats sat in Istanbul; European merchants and scholars travelled in the Ottoman realms. Many came to stay; renegades and adventurers seeking a career in the Ottoman service, refugees from political or religious persecution, seeking shelter under the Ottoman power. Such was the mass migration of Jews from Spain and Portugal in the late fifteenth and early sixteenth centuries, bringing with them printing, and some medical and technological knowledge.

It was chiefly in the arts of war that the Turks were ready to turn to Europe for instruction. There are some rather dubious references to the use of firearms by the Ottomans as early as the fourteenth century. Their use of siege artillery is well attested in the early fifteenth century, and by the middle of the century they were already using field-guns at the second battle of Kossovo

(1448). Hand-guns were introduced at about the same time, and before very long gunners, musketeers, bombardiers, and sappers begin to play a central role in the Ottoman armed forces.[5]

The Ottomans showed equal readiness in adopting European techniques of naval construction and warfare. In the fifteenth century Venice was their model in shipbuilding, and improvements made by Venetian shipyards in the design and construction of galleys were closely watched and imitated. In the same way, in the course of the seventeenth century the Barbary Corsairs were followed by their Turkish overlords in building and operating large, square-rigged sailing ships, mounting twenty guns and capable of making long voyages on the open seas.[6]

With European naval construction, they also acquired a working knowledge of European maps and navigation. During the sixteenth century many European charts and portulans fell into Turkish hands. Of the theory of cartography they knew little enough, but they were soon able to copy and to use European sailing charts, and to make coastal charts of their own. Piri Reis (d. *c.* 1550), the first noteworthy Ottoman cartographer, seems to have known Western languages and made use of Western maps and geographical books. Hacı Halife (1608-57) was acquainted with the *Atlas Minor* of Mercator, which he translated into Turkish with the help of a French renegade in 1653-5. He incorporated data from this and from other standard European geographical works of the time, by Ortelius, Cluverius, and others, in his *Cihannüma*, or World-Mirror, for long the standard Ottoman geographical work. Another indication of Ottoman interest in Western geographical science at that time was the invitation issued by Murad IV (1623-40) to the Dutch Orientalist Golius to make a map of the Ottoman dominions. The invitation was not accepted.[7]

---

[5] On the Ottoman adoption of firearms and artillery see V. J. Parry, 'Bārūd', in *EI*².

[6] On the Ottoman fleet see I. H. Uzunçarşılı, 'Bahriyya iii' in *EI*², and the excellent survey by J. W. Zinkeisen in his *Geschichte des osmanischen Reiches in Europa*, iii (1855), 279 ff.

[7] Fr. Taeschner, 'Die geographische Literatur der Osmanen', *ZDMG*, n.s. 2, lxxvii (1923), 31–80; J. H. Kramers, 'Djughrafiya', in *EI*¹, suppl. For further appreciations of these and subsequent changes from special points of view see Mümtaz Turhan, *Kültür Değişmeleri* (1951) (social psychology), Ahmet Hamdi Tanpınar, *XIX Asır Türk Edebiyatı Tarihi*, i (1956) (literature and ideas); and Enver Ziya Karal, 'Tanzimattan evvel garplılaşma hareketleri', in Turkey, Min. of Ed., *Tanzimat* (1940), pp. 13–30. In this article Professor Karal gives a general survey of movements of Westernization before the *Tanzimat*.

The First Attempts at Westernization [8]

The first deliberate attempt at a Westernizing policy—the first conscious step, that is, towards the imitation and adoption of certain selected elements from the civilization of Western Europe —came in the early eighteenth century. The treaties of Carlowitz (1699) and Passarowitz (1718) had given formal expression and recognition to two humiliating defeats of the Ottoman Empire by the Austrians and their allies. On the other hand the example of Russia under Peter the Great suggested that a vigorous programme of Westernization and modernization might enable the Empire to throw off its weakness and once again become the terror of its enemies.

A Turkish document, written about the time of the treaty of Passarowitz, contains an imaginary conversation between a Christian and an Ottoman officer, in which they discuss the military and political situation. The purpose of the document appears to have been to prepare Ottoman ruling circles to accept defeat, by depicting as darkly as possible the unfavourable situation of the Empire. The conversation also, however, makes a comparison between the two armies, to the great disadvantage of the Ottomans, and would appear to embody a plea for military reform. [9]

The statesman chiefly responsible for the first attempt at reform was Damad Ibrahim Paşa, who became deputy Grand Vezir in 1716 and was Grand Vezir from 1718 to 1730. As soon as peace was restored he sent an Embassy to Vienna, in 1719, and in 1721 sent Yirmisekiz Çelebi Mehmed Efendi as ambassador to Paris, with instructions to 'make a thorough study of the means of civilization and education, and report on those capable of

---

[8] Information on these projects, from Turkish sources, will be found in the standard history of the Ottoman Empire by J. von Hammer-Purgstall, *Geschichte des Osmanischen Reiches* (1st ed. 1827–35, 2nd ed. 1835–40; French trans., *Histoire de l'Empire ottoman*, 1835–43). This may be supplemented by the later histories, written from European sources only, of Zinkeisen, and N. Jorga, *Geschichte des osmanischen Reiches* (1908–13). A useful outline will be found in C. von Sax, *Geschichte des Machtverfalls der Türkei* (1913). On the penetration of Western scientific knowledge to Turkey, see the pioneer works of Adnan, *La Science chez les Turcs ottomans*, and the fuller treatment by the same author in Turkish, Adnan-Adıvar, *Osmanlı Türklerinde Ilim*.

[9] Faik Resit Unat, ed., 'Ahmet III devrine ait bir islâhat takriri', *Tar. Ves.*, i (1941), 107–21.

application' in Turkey.[10] One of these, as we shall see, was printing. As early as 1716 a French officer, de Rochefort, submitted a
project for the formation of a corps of foreign engineer officers in
the Ottoman army, which, however, came to nothing.[11] In 1720
another Frenchman, the convert David known as Gerçek,
organized a fire brigade in Istanbul—the first of the long series of
reforms in municipal services that were to follow in the nineteenth
and twentieth centuries.[12] In the admiralty and navy too the new
mood was felt. The admiralty offices were reorganized, and an
important change made in ship construction. The three-decker
galleon was first built in Turkish dockyards in 1682, but few were
made. Under Ahmed III the construction of these ships was
resumed and improved, and the galley began to disappear from
the Ottoman fleets.[13]

These exchanges with Europe began to produce, for the first
time, some slight impact on cultural and social life. The wave of
Turquerie started by the Turkish Embassy in Paris in 1721 had its
counterpart in a rather smaller wave of Frankish manners and
styles in Istanbul. French gardens, French decorations, French
furniture acquired a brief vogue in palace circles. The Sultan himself built a fountain outside the palace gates which shows a
distinctly rococo style.[14] The Flemish painter van Mour (1671–
1737) enjoyed some success in the Turkish capital, where he
painted the portraits of the Sultan, the Grand Vezir, and other
dignitaries.[15]

Towards the end of Ahmed III's reign the unwonted interval
of peace which the Empire had enjoyed after the treaty of
Passarowitz was disturbed by the outbreak of war on the eastern
frontier, against Persia. In 1730 an Ottoman defeat at the hands
of Nadir Khan, who had just risen to power in Persia, touched off
a popular revolt in Istanbul, where resentment had been growing

[10] Cited by Karal, in *Tanzimat*, p. 19; Mehmed Said Efendi's report on his embassy
(*Sefâretnâme*) was several times printed in Istanbul, and appeared in a French translation by J. C. Galland (*Relation de l'Ambassade de Mehêmet Effendi . . .*) in Constantinople
and Paris in 1757.

[11] Hammer, 2nd ed., iv. 397.

[12] Osman Nuri [Ergin], *Mecelle-i Umur-i Belediye*, i (1922), 1170 ff. cf. below, pp. 387 ff.

[13] I. H. Uzunçarşılı, *Osmanlı Devletinin Merkez ve Bahriye Teşkilâtı* (1948), pp. 465 ff.

[14] On Turkish taste and fashions in this period see Ahmet Refik, *Lâle Devri* (1932).
Passages from this book were published in French translation in E. Saussey, *Prosateurs
turcs contemporains* (1935).

[15] A. Boppe, *Les Peintres du Bosphore au dix-huitième siècle* (1911).

against the extravagance of the court and the 'Frankish manners' of the palace circles. The Sultan was forced to abdicate, and the Grand Vezir and other dignitaries were put to death.[16]

The setback was only temporary. The most important Western innovations of the preceding reign—printing and naval reforms— were maintained, and soon a new start was made on the larger and more pressing problem of military reform. Already before the revolt Ibrahim Müteferrika, the director of the printing press, had presented a memorandum to Ibrahim Paşa; at the beginning of 1732 he printed it, and presented it to the new Sultan Mahmud I (1730–54). The memorandum, forty-nine pages long, is divided into three parts. In the first the author points out the importance, to all states and peoples, of a well-ordered system of government, and describes and comments on the various kinds of régime existing in other countries. In the second, he urges on his reader the impor- tance of scientific geography, as a means of knowing one's own lands and those of one's neighbours, as a useful adjunct to the military art, and as an aid to provincial and military administration; in the third, he examines the different kinds of armed forces maintained by the kings of Christendom, their training, organization, and discipline, in camp and in the field, their methods of waging war, and their military laws. Ibrahim, himself a convert, was careful to speak with proper disgust and contempt of the Frankish infidels, but at the same time makes clear the superiority of the Frankish armies, and the importance for the Ottomans of imitating them.[17]

Another convert was conveniently at hand to help in taking the first steps. The Count de Bonneval, a French nobleman, had, after a somewhat chequered career, arrived in Turkey in 1729. Apparently to avoid being extradited, he adopted Islam, took the name Ahmed, and entered the Ottoman service. In September 1731 he was summoned by the Grand Vezir Topal Osman Paşa, who gave him the task of reforming the Bombardier Corps on European lines. In 1734 a new training centre, the *Hendesehane*, or school of geometry, was opened in Üsküdar, and in the following

[16] On these events see Münir Aktepe, *Patrona Isyanı* (Ist., 1958); M. L. Shay, *The Ottoman Empire from 1720 to 1734* (Urbana, 1944).

[17] *Usūl al-Hikam fī Nizam al-Umam* (1144 A.H.); French translation, *Traité de la tactique*, Vienna 1769. For discussions of this book see G. Toderini, *Letteratura turchesca* (1787), iii. 97–108; Babinger, *Stambuler Buchwesen im 18 Jahrhundert* (1919), p. 15; Niyazi Berkes, 'Historical Background of Turkish Secularism' in R. N. Frye, ed. *Islam and the West* (1957), p. 51; idem, *The Development of Secularism in Turkey* (1964), pp. 42–45.

year de Bonneval was made a pasha of two tails and given the rank and title of Chief Bombardier.[18]

This school, and the 'corps of mathematicians' established under the command of de Bonneval's adopted son Süleyman, were not of long duration. The Janissaries were of course bitterly opposed to any such new-fangled notions, and despite an apparent attempt to keep the project secret from them, they found out about the school and forced its closure.[19]

The effort was not, however, entirely wasted. One of the teachers of the school, a certain Mehmed Said, the son of a Mufti from Anatolia, invented a 'two-arc quadrant' for the use of artillerymen and wrote a treatise illustrated with geometrical diagrams. Other writings of the time include a treatise on trigonometry, apparently based in part on Western sources, an anonymous Turkish translation of a treatise on military science by Count Montecuccoli, some medical works, and a few writings on European history and affairs.[20] Some interest in Westernization was also shown by the Grand Vezir Rağıb Paşa, an admirer of European science who is credited with having desired the translation into Turkish of a treatise of Voltaire on the philosophy of Newton.[21] It is reported by some sources that in 1759 he reopened the school of geometry, which functioned secretly in a private house at Karaagaç, near Sütlüce.[22]

A more serious effort began in 1773, with the opening of a new school of mathematics for the navy. In this and related projects the Turks were helped by the Baron de Tott, an artillery officer of French nationality and Hungarian origin, who had come to Turkey some years previously to study Turkish. He helped to form and train new corps of engineers and artillery, reorganized the gun-foundry, and for the first year or two taught rectilinear

---

[18] Tayyarzade Ata, *Tarih-i Ata* (1291–3 A.H.), i. 158. On Bonneval see H. Bowen, 'Ahmed Pasha Bonneval', in *EI*[2]; Mehmed Arif, 'Humbaracı-başı Ahmed Paşa Bonneval', *TOEM*, pts. 18–20; Osman Ergin, *Türkiye Maarif Tarihi* (1939 ff.), i. 44 ff.

[19] On the role and position of the Janissaries at this time see Gibb and Bowen, I/1. 56 ff.

[20] Adnan, *Science*, pp. 142 ff.   [21] Toderini, i. 130.

[22] Ergin, *Maarif*, i. 50; Adnan, *Ilim*, pp. 182–3. Another Turk who showed an interest in the West at this time was the diplomat Ahmed Resmi Efendi (1700–83), who went on embassies to Vienna in 1757, and to Berlin in 1763. Beside accounts of his embassies, he wrote an analysis of the causes of Turkey's defeat in the war of 1769–74, in which he urged the need for reform and reorganization. On him see Babinger, *Geschichtsschreiber*, pp. 309–12.

trigonometry and other subjects at the school of mathematics In these tasks he was assisted by some other foreigners, notably a Scottish renegade called Campbell, who after his conversion to Islam was known by the doubly incongruous name of Ingiliz Mustafa. It was he who replaced de Tott as chief instructor after the latter's return to France in 1775.

The nucleus of the student body was provided by the surviving pupils of the earlier schools, who were transferred to the new centre, as well as of serving naval officers. De Tott in his memoirs speaks of his 'white-bearded captains' and of 'sixty-year-old pupils'. In the following years the naval school of mathematics was expanded and developed, and provided the model for the military engineering, medical, and other schools set up by Selim III and his successors. We have a description of it by the Venetian priest Toderini, who was in Istanbul between 1781 and 1786. He found it well equipped with European maps and appliances, and with a library of European books, some with Turkish translations. There were over fifty pupils, sons of captains and Turkish gentlemen.[23]

The Russian annexation of the Crimea in 1783 gave the impetus to a new programme of reform, in which the Ottoman government was encouraged by the French, who were apprehensive of a possible Russian threat to their interests in the Levant. In October 1784, at the initiative of the Grand Vezir Halil Hamid Paşa and with the assistance of the French Embassy, a new training course was instituted, with two French engineer officers as instructors, working with Armenian interpreters.[24] After the outbreak of war with Austria and Russia in 1787 the French instructors were recalled, as their continued presence was regarded as a breach of

[23] On the history of the navy school see Ergin, *Maarif*, ii. 264 ff.; Mehmed Esad, *Mirât-i Mühendishane* (1312 A.H.), and the contemporary accounts of Toderini (i. 177 ff.) and de Tott, *Mémoires* (1785), *passim*.

[24] On the Turkish reactions to the Russian annexation of the Crimea, see Mustafa Nuri Paşa, *Netaic ül-Vukuat*, iv (1327 A.H.), 97: 'There [in Hungary] the Muslims had lived only in the towns and had had the character of visitors, while the mass of the population was Christian; Crimea, on the other hand, had a Muslim population of close on two million. Its loss therefore naturally affected the people of Islam far more, and its liberation became a prime objective.'

On the military reforms of the 1780's see Ahmed Cevdet Paşa, *Tarih* (1301–9 A.H.), iii-iv, *passim*; Nuri, *Netaic*, iv. 4 ff.; Uzunçarşılı, 'Sadrazam Halil Hamit Paşa', *TM*, v (1936), 213–67; Boppe, 'La France et le "militaire turc" au XVIIIᵉ siècle', *Feuilles d'Hist.* (1912), pp. 386–402 and 490–501. See further Adnan, *Science*, p. 155 and *Ilim*, pp. 183–5.

neutrality. This, and the strains of the war itself, hampered the development of the new schools, which remained inactive until the restoration of peace in 1792 gave the new Sultan, Selim III, the opportunity to make a new start.

Non-Military Innovations

The most important technical innovation from Europe outside the military field was undoubtedly printing. In a sense this had been known to the Turks for centuries. In the fourteenth century the Mongol rulers of Persia had printed and issued paper money, in obvious imitation of Chinese models, and at an earlier date the Turkic peoples of the Chinese borderlands had made use of a form of block-printing, common in the Far East. But all this had long since been forgotten, and the Ottoman Turks, like other Middle Eastern Muslim peoples, had no knowledge of book printing until it was introduced from Europe. This happened at the end of the fifteenth century, when Jewish refugees from Spain set up printing presses on Ottoman soil. The first Jewish press was established in Constantinople about 1493 or 1494, and others followed in various cities, notably in Salonika, which became the main Jewish publishing centre.

The Jews were followed by the other religious minorities. In 1567 an Armenian press was established in Constantinople by Apkar of Sivas, a priest who had studied typography in Venice, and a Greek press in 1627 by Nicodemus Metaxas, with machinery and type imported from England.

The ban on printing in Turkish or Arabic[25] remained effective until the early eighteenth century, when its relaxation was due largely to the efforts of two men. One of them was Said Çelebi, son of the famous Yirmisekiz Çelebi Mehmed Efendi, who had gone to Paris as Turkish ambassador in 1721. Said Çelebi had accompanied his father on his journey, and during his stay in France seems to have acquired an interest in the art of printing and a conviction of its usefulness. On his return to Turkey he attempted to secure the support of the Grand Vezir for the setting up of a Turkish printing press in Constantinople. In this, despite the opposition of religious conservatives and the strong vested interest of the scribes and calligraphers, he was successful.

He found a kindred spirit in Ibrahim Müteferrika, the true

[25] See above, p. 41.

founder and director of the first Turkish printing press. Ibrahim was a Hungarian, probably a Unitarian, and had been a student in the seminary in Kolosvar. In about 1691 he either fled to or was captured by the Turks, and found his way to Istanbul. He became a convert to Islam, and made a career in the Ottoman service. In collaboration with Said Çelebi, he drafted a memorandum on the usefulness of printing, which was submitted to the Grand Vezir. Support came from an unexpected quarter when the *Şeyh-ül-Islâm* Abdullah Efendi was persuaded to issue a *fetva* authorizing the printing of books in Turkish on subjects other than religion. The printing of the Koran, of books on Koranic exegesis, traditions, theology, and holy law was excluded as unthinkable. Finally, on 5 July 1727, an Imperial ferman was issued giving permission for the establishment of a Turkish press and the printing of Turkish books 'in the high, God-guarded city of Constantinople'.

Presses and types were at first obtained from the local Jewish and Christian printers already working in the city, and recourse was also made to Jewish type-founders and compositors. Later, presses and types were imported from Europe, especially from Leiden and Paris. Some specialists in different aspects of typography were also brought from Germany and other European countries.

The first book appeared in February 1729. By the time the press was closed in 1742, seventeen books had been printed. Most of them were in Turkish, and dealt with history, geography, and language. They included, however, a Turkish grammar in French, an account by Mehmed Efendi of his Embassy in France in 1721, and a short treatise by Ibrahim Müteferrika himself on the science of tactics as practised by the European states. The press was reopened in 1784, since when the development of printing in Turkey proceeded rapidly.[26]

[26] On the early development of printing in Turkey see Babinger, *Stambuler Buchwesen*, and Selim Nüzhet Gerçek, *Türk Matbaacılığı*, I: *Müteferrika Matbaası* (1939); Osman Ersoy, *Türkiye'ye Matbaanın Girişi* (1959). On Ibrahim, see Niyazi Berkes in *Bell.* no. 104, (1962), 715 ff. and idem, *The Development of Secularism* (1964), pp. 36 ff.

The first book published from the Müteferrika press, the dictionary of Vankılı, appeared in Rejeb 1141, corresponding to February 1729. The first volume opens with an introduction by the editor, followed by the full texts of the fermans authorizing the establishment of the press, the *fetva* of the *Şeyh-ül-Islâm* declaring printing licit, and certificates of approval from the two chief judges and other dignitaries. These in turn are followed by a treatise on the usefulness of printing.

Turning from gunnery and typography to knowledge and ideas, we find far fewer traces of Western influence, for it is here that the Muslim rejection of Christianity and all that came from it was most effective. Though clever with their hands in making useful devices like guns, clocks, and printing presses, the Europeans were still benighted and barbarous infidels, whose history, philosophy, science, and literature, if indeed they existed at all, could hold nothing of value for the people of the universal Islamic Empire. During the reign of Mehmed II there was indeed the beginning of a scientific renaissance, but under his successors, in the words of a modern Turkish writer, 'the scientific current broke against the dikes of literature and jurisprudence'.[27]

In these dikes there were, however, a few small leaks, through which some knowledge of the West percolated into the circles of Muslim scholarship. Among the many thousands of historical manuscripts of the sixteenth and seventeenth centuries found in the libraries of Istanbul, none deal with Christian Europe, for the Muslim, like other civilizations before and after it, equated universal history with its own. But there are a few signs of interest. Ottoman chroniclers occasionally report events in darkest Frangistan, and one of them, Ibrahim Peçevi (1574–c.1650), even went so far as to use, through a translator, Hungarian Latin chronicles for his history of the Turkish campaigns in Hungary. Hacı Halife, whose interest in European maps has already been mentioned, is also credited with having prepared, probably in collaboration with a Frankish colleague, a history of the Franks, and Hüseyin Hezarfen, whose observations on the state of the Empire have already been cited, sought out the company of such European visitors to Istanbul as Galland, Marsigli, and Prince Kantemir, and made a study of European history. A little later Ahmed ibn Lûtfullah, known as Müneccimbaşı (d. 1702), wrote a universal history which includes a brief account of the principal monarchies of Europe—the second, it would seem, in Islamic historiography.[28] In the course of the eighteenth century, no doubt in connexion with the military training schools, a small number of books on European affairs were prepared or translated.

The occasional Ottoman interest in European geography has

[27] Adnan, *Science*, p. 57.

[28] On all these see B. Lewis, 'The Use by Muslim Historians of Non-Muslim Sources', in B. Lewis and P. M. Holt, eds. *Historians of the Middle East* (London, 1962).

already been mentioned. In addition there was some slight interest in European medicine. In the sixteenth century Jewish refugees from Europe wrote in Turkish on medicine and dentistry; in the seventeenth a Turkish translation appeared of a European treatise on syphilis, and one or two passages in other medical works suggest an acquaintance with European writings.[29] In general, however, Ottoman medicine remained faithful to Galen and Avicenna, as Ottoman science to Aristotle, Ptolemy, and their commentators. The discoveries of Paracelsus and Copernicus, Kepler and Galileo were as alien and irrelevant to most Ottomans as were the arguments of Luther and Calvin.

Of the aesthetic life of the West little or nothing was known in Turkey. Of Western art there was some slight influence; several of the Sultans called on the services of Western portrait painters, and Western influences undoubtedly affected Turkish architecture and decoration in the early eighteenth century. Of Western literature and music practically nothing was known. The great Western movements of ideas passed without even an echo in the lands of Islam.[30]

The Ideas of the French Revolution [31]

With the French Revolution, for the first time, we find a great movement of ideas penetrating the barrier that separated the House of War from the House of Islam, finding a ready welcome among Muslim leaders and thinkers, and affecting to a greater or lesser degree every layer of Muslim society.

The success of Western ideas in the Islamic world in the nineteenth century is often attributed to the advance of the material

[29] Adnan, *Science*, p. 98; U. Heyd, 'Moses Hamon, chief Jewish physician to Sultan Süleymān the Magnificent', *Oriens*, xvi (1963), 152–70; idem, 'An unknown Turkish treatise by a Jewish physician under Süleymān the Magnificent', *Eretz-Israel*, vii (1963), 48–53.

[30] One solitary exception to the general lack of interest in Western literature may be mentioned. Ali Aziz Efendi, an eighteenth-century diplomat and man of letters, was appointed ambassador to Berlin, where he died in 1798. He knew French and some German, and adapted some tales from French into Turkish. They were not entirely alien, being taken from Pétis de la Croix's Oriental collection, *Les Mille et un Jours* (Paris, 1710–12). See A. Tietze, 'Aziz Efendis Muhayyelat', *Oriens*, i (1948), 248–329 and 'Ali Aziz', in *EI²*.

[31] A more extensive treatment of this subject will be found in B. Lewis 'The Impact of the French Revolution on Turkey', in G. S. Métraux and F. Crouzet, eds., *The New Asia: readings in the history of mankind* (1965), pp. 31–59.

might of the West—to the establishment of European economic, political, and eventually, military supremacy in much of the Islamic world. The Muslim, no less than other men, is inclined to listen with greater sympathy and respect to the beliefs of those whom God has favoured with power and wealth in *this* world, and the visible success of the West was certainly a contributory factor, if not indeed a prerequisite, in making Western ideas acceptable to him. But this is not a sufficient explanation. The age of the Renaissance and the Discoveries saw great Christian advances in the western Mediterranean and in Asia, which, if to some extent offset by the still formidable power of the Ottomans, might nevertheless have produced some effect on the Muslims of the invaded areas, had might alone been sufficient to impel acceptance. Nor do European wealth and power explain why the ideas of the French Revolution, rather than any other of the competing Western modes of thought, should have won such wide acceptance. The initial attraction of these ideas—which were later modified to respond to the political needs of the time and place—is rather to be found in their secularism. The French Revolution is the first great social upheaval in Europe to find intellectual expression in purely non-religious terms. Secularism as such has no great attraction for Muslims, but in a Western movement that was non-Christian, even anti-Christian, and whose divorce from Christianity was stressed by its leading exponents, the Muslim world might hope to find the elusive secret of Western power without compromising its own religious beliefs and traditions.

During the century or so that followed the first percolation of these new ideas from Europe, the channels of transmission became broader and more numerous, the trickle grew to a river and then to a flood. While Western material culture transformed the structure and aspect of Islamic society, often for the worse, ideas from the West were affecting the very basis of group cohesion, creating new patterns of identity and loyalty, and providing both the objectives and the formulation of new aspirations. These new ideas may be summarized in three words: liberty, equality, and—not fraternity, but what is perhaps its converse, nationality.

Before 1800 the word liberty in the languages of Islam was primarily a legal term, denoting the opposite of slavery. In the course of the nineteenth century it acquired a new political connotation from Europe, and came to be the war-cry of the struggle against both domestic despotism and foreign imperialism. Organized liberty required constitutions, representative government, the rule of law—and these in turn involved secular authority and legislation, with a new class of lawyers and politicians, different from the Doctors of the Holy Law and the agents of autocratic rule of former times.

Equality tended to take on a different meaning. Social and economic inequality were not major grievances. Islamic society did not know the rigid social barriers and caste privileges of pre-revolutionary Europe; its undeveloped economy limited the opportunities both of acquiring and of spending wealth, and thus prevented the growth of glaring disparities between rich and poor. To some extent the gulf between the two was still bridged by the corporative structure of society and the moral and charitable traditions of Islam. But if appeals to the individual had little effect, appeals to the group struck a more responsive chord. Soon the demand was raised for equality between nations, in time linked with the new Western principle of national self-determination.

The Western concept of the nation as a linguistic, ethnic, and territorial entity was not unknown to the Islamic Orient, but was never the primary basis of group identity. This was the brotherhood of faith within the religious community, reinforced by common dynastic allegiance. To this day the Western notions of patriotism and nationality have never entirely superseded the older pattern—indeed, though dynastic loyalties have faded, religious loyalty is in our own day showing renascent vigour. The history of the reform movements in the nineteenth and early twentieth centuries is largely concerned with the attempt by Western-educated intellectuals to impose a Western pattern of secular political classification and organization on the religious community of Islam.

The immediate and contemporary impact of these ideas on Muslim Turks was, inevitably, limited and muffled. It was however the start of a process which, in time, was to transform the outlook, self-awareness, and expectations not only of Turkey but of all Islam. The first vital penetration of ideas took place during the years 1792–1807, beginning with the military reforms of Selim III and ending with his deposition. It is therefore necessary to give close attention first to the channels through which these ideas were transmitted from France to Turkey, second to the response to these ideas of the Turks of that time.

The Channels of Transmission

By far the most important of these was military instruction. From Renaissance times onwards Islam had been the pupil of Christendom in the arts of war, especially in the more technical branches such as engineering, navigation, and artillery. For some time the imposing military façade of the Ottoman Empire masked the growing internal decline in skill and inventiveness, which found expression in the prominence of Western renegades or employees among the gun-founders and gunners of the Ottoman armies and the shipwrights and navigators of the Ottoman fleets. By the eighteenth century the rulers of the Empire, stimulated by a series of defeats at the hands of their despised Christian adversaries, began to give intermittent attention to the need for modernizing the equipment and training of their armies.

The restoration of peace in 1792, and the preoccupation of Europe with the problems of the French Revolution, gave the new Sultan Selim III the opportunity to plan and in part execute a large-scale reform of the Ottoman armed forces, intended to bring them up to the level of contemporary Western armies in technical equipment, training, and skill.

Such attempts at reform as had been made during the eighteenth century had all been under the guidance of French instructors, usually working in the French language. The latest was that of 1784, while Selim was still heir-apparent.[32] In this project both the initial impulse and the main guidance came from the government of France, and Selim himself had entered into correspondence with Louis XVI, who had given him good if somewhat patronizing advice.[33] Such nuclei of trained officers as were available in Istanbul had been taught by French teachers and with French textbooks. The only treatises available in Turkish were translations from French, printed at the press of the French

[32] See above, p. 49.
[33] Uzunçarşılı, 'Selim III' ün Veliaht iken Fransa Kralı Lüi XVI ile muhabereleri', *Bell.*, no. 5–6 (1938), 191–246; Tahsin Öz, 'Fransa Kıralı Louis XVI ci'nin Selim III' e Namesi', *Tar. Ves.*, i/3 (1941), 198–202 (with the French text of a letter from Louis XVI to Selim III); cf. Karal, *Selim III' ün Hat-ti Hümayunları; Nizam-i Cedit* (1946), pp. 11 ff.

Embassy—the best equipped press in the city.[34] What little knowledge of European languages Turkish intellectuals possessed was of French.

It was therefore natural that the Sultan should turn once again to France for help in preparing his New Order—*Nizam-i Cedid*—in the armed forces. There was an additional reason for him to do so. In an exchange of notes written on the eve of the launching of the military reforms, the Grand Vezir reported to the Sultan the arrival of letters from the King of France on the New Order—*Nizam-i Cedid*—that had arisen in France as a result of the recent upheaval, and the Sultan expressed interest in this New Order.[35] It is not without significance that in these notes the same term is applied to the 'New Order' in France as was shortly afterwards applied to the whole programme of reform in Turkey.

At the same time Selim sent a special envoy, Ebu Bekir Ratib Efendi, to make direct inquiries in Europe. Ratib Efendi went to Vienna in 1791, with instructions to study Austrian conditions and also to gather information on other European countries. On his return in May 1792, he presented a detailed report on the military systems of the European states, and especially of Austria, as well as on government, society, and political thought. One of his informants in Vienna seems to have been the Austrian apprentice dragoman Joseph Hammer, later famous as the author of the *Geschichte des osmanischen Reiches* and other standard works on Turkey.[36]

In the autumn of 1791, while the returning Ottoman army was still at Silistria, the Sultan issued a command to twenty-two civil, military, and religious dignitaries requesting them to set forth their views on the causes of the weakness of the Empire, and their proposals for its reform. The twenty-two included two Christians, a French officer called Bertrand or Brentano, serving with the Ottoman army, and the famous Mouradgea d'Ohsson, the Armenian dragoman of the Swedish Embassy in Istanbul. They

[34] On the French Embassy press in Constantinople see Babinger, *Stambuler Buchwesen*, pp. 27–28, and Gerçek, *Türk Matbaacılığı*, pp. 99 ff. In the latter work reproductions will be found of the title-pages of these translations.

[35] Karal, *Selim III*, p. 30.

[36] Ratib Efendi's report, of some 500 pages, deals with military and administrative institutions in Austria and elsewhere, and quotes the views of European political philosophers on the need for a disciplined army, orderly finances, loyal and competent statesmen, and a prosperous population (ibid. pp. 31 ff.; cf. Cevdet, *Tarih*, v. 232 ff.; Von Hammer-Purgstall, *Erinnerungen aus meinem Leben* (Vienna, 1940), 25–27; idem, *Geschichte der osmanischen Dichtkunst* iv (Pest, 1838), 418 ff., and Babinger, *Geschichtsschreiber*, p. 330). Ratib was *Reis-ül-Küttab* from 1794 to 1796, and was executed in 1799.

presented their replies in the form of *Lâyiha*—memorials, a term reminiscent of the French *cahiers* of 1789. Though no doubt accidental, the resemblance was a portentous one.[37]

All agreed in laying the main stress on the need for military reform, but differed as to how best to accomplish it. On the one hand were the conservatives, who sought to recover the military glories of the Ottoman golden age by reverting to its military methods. Then there were the romantics and compromisers, who sought various ways of insinuating Frankish training and weapons into the existing military order by claiming that this was in fact a return to the pure Ottoman past. Finally there were the radicals, who believed that the old army was incapable of reform, and urged the Sultan to set up a new one, trained, equipped, and armed from the start along European lines. It was to this view that the Sultan himself inclined.

From the first these proposals for reform aroused the bitterest opposition, and the reformist memorials were attacked with spite and ridicule even in the palace. But the Sultan proceeded with resolution and energy. Setting up a small committee of reform supporters to assist him, he promulgated, in 1792 and 1793, a whole series of new instructions and regulations which came to be known collectively as the *Nizam-i Cedid*. They included new regulations on provincial governorships, on provincial taxation, on the control of the grain trade, and other administrative and fiscal matters. By far the most important, however, were those providing for a new corps of regular infantry, trained and equipped on European lines. To finance this experiment, a special new treasury was set up, with revenues from escheated and forfeited fiefs and from newly imposed taxes on spirits, tobacco, coffee, and other commodities. It is both interesting and significant that the term *Nizam-i Cedid*, originally applied to the regulations of the new system, came to be used almost exclusively of the new, regular troops established under it. Just as centuries earlier the Arabic abstract noun *sultān*, authority, had come to designate a man, so now did *Nizam-i Cedid*, new order, become the name of a body of men.[38]

[37] Cevdet, *Tarih*, vi. 3 ff.; Ahmed Asım, *Asım Tarihi* (n.d.), i. 34; Karal, *Selim III*, pp. 34 ff. and 'Nizam-i Cedide dair Lâyihalar', *Tar. Ves.*, i (1942), 414–25; ii (1942–3), 104–11, 342–51, 424–32; Berkes, in Frye, pp. 56–58.

[38] On the financial arrangements see Cevdet, *Tarih*, v. 289 ff. (on the reorganization

A central place in Selim's projects was assigned to his new military and naval schools, which provided training in gunnery, fortification, navigation, and ancillary sciences. In these schools Selim relied, very heavily, on French help. French officers were recruited as teachers and instructors, French was made a compulsory language for all students, and a library of some 400 European books acquired, most of them French, and including, significantly, a set of the *Grande Encyclopédie*.[39]

The change of régime in France in no way discouraged the Sultan from seeking French aid. In the autumn of 1793 the Ottoman government sent to Paris a list of officers and technicians whom it wished to recruit from France; as late as 1795 the *Reis-ül-Küttab*, Ratib Efendi, addressed a similar but longer list to the Committee of Public Safety.[40] In 1796 the French ambassador General Aubert Dubayet brought a whole body of French military experts to Constantinople with him.[41] French co-operation in the Ottoman military reform was interrupted by the Franco-Turkish war of 1798–1802, but was later resumed, and reached its peak with the mission to Turkey of General Sébastiani in 1806–7. Though the pure wine of revolution was by now diluted with Caesarism, this more familiar flavour, with the added spice of victory, can only have made it more palatable.

The result of all this was to create a new social element— a corps of young army and naval officers, familiar with some aspects of Western civilization through study, reading, and personal contact, acquainted with at least one Western language —usually French[42]—and accustomed to look up to Western

of the military fiefs), and vi. 61 ff.; Karal, *Selim III*, pp. 134 ff. On the military reforms see Cevdet, vi; Hammer, and Zinkeisen, v–viii *passim*, where further references are given; S. J. Shaw, 'The origins of O:toman military reform: the Nizam-i Cedid army of Sultan Selim III', *J. Modern Hist.*, xxxvii (1965), 291–306; idem, 'The established Ottoman Army Corps under Sultan Selim III', *Der Islam*, xl (1965), 142–84. Turkish documents are published and analysed in: Ergin, *Maarif*, ii, *passim*; Karal, *Selim III*, pp. 43–94; Uzunçarşılı, *Merkez ve Bahriye*, pp. 507 ff. (on the navy), as well as numerous other Turkish works.

[39] A. de Juchereau de Saint-Denys, *Révolutions de Constantinople en 1807 et 1808*, i (1819), 76.

[40] See H. von Sybel, 'La Propagande révolutionnaire en 1793 et 1794', *R. hist.*, xi (1879), 107–8; A. Debidour, *Recueil des Actes du Directoire*, ii (1911), 630 ff.; Karal, 'Osmanlı Tarihine dair Vesikalar', *Bell.*, no. 14–15 (1940), 175 ff.

[41] Juchereau, i. 68 ff.; ii. 12 ff.

[42] Italian too was fairly well known, however, especially in commerce and in the navy. Many of the earlier European loanwords in Turkish are Italian in form.

experts as their mentors and guides to new and better ways. These men could not, like most of their contemporaries, despise the infidel and barbarous West from an altitude of comfortable and unassailable ignorance—on the contrary, for reasons both of inclination and of interest they were aligned with the Westernizers against the reactionaries. But these neophytes of Western culture, filled with an often naïve enthusiasm for things Western,[43] soon found that the West had more to offer than mathematics and ballistics, and that their knowledge of French enabled them to read other things besides their textbooks. Some of these other things were available to them in their own college library. We may assume that others were brought to their notice by French instructors who, after 1792, were chosen and appointed by the government of the French Republic.[44]

During the same period, another of the reforms of Selim III opened a second window to the West—that of diplomacy. Until the end of the eighteenth century the Ottoman Empire maintained no permanent diplomatic representation in foreign countries. From time to time a special mission was sent to one or another foreign capital, for a specific purpose—but barely a score of these are recorded in the whole period up to 1792. For its normal dealings with foreign powers the Empire preferred to rely on the foreign ambassadors resident in Istanbul. Even with those, business was carried on chiefly through the intermediary of local Christian dragomans. Very few even of the highest officials of the state had any knowledge of a Western language or any direct experience of Europe.[45] In earlier times a very important role had been played by renegades, men of European birth and

[43] A good example is Mahmud Raif, who went to London in 1793 and whose book, in French, on the Ottoman reforms was printed at Scutari in 1797. He was killed by mutinous Janissaries in 1807. A more dubious figure is Seid Mustafa, author of the *Diatribe de l'ingénieur sur l'état actuel de l'art militaire, du génie et des sciences à Constantinople*, printed in Scutari in 1803, and reprinted by L. Langlès in Paris in 1810. According to Langlès Seid Mustafa was a graduate and later a teacher of engineering, and was also killed by the mutineers. Hammer-Purgstall, however (*Staatsverfassung*, i. 81 n) says that 'Seid Mustafa' was a fiction, and that the tract was written at the request of the Reis Efendi by the Greek dragoman Yakovaki Argyropoulo.

[44] cf. the chronicle of Asım Efendi, quoted below, p. 71.

[45] In 1770, when a Russian fleet under Admiral Spiridov sailed round western Europe into the Mediterranean and attacked the Turks in the Aegean, the Porte, apparently still using medieval maps, protested to Venice against their permitting the Russians to sail from the Baltic into the Adriatic. See Kramers, 'Djughrāfiya', in *EI*[1], suppl.

education, who often rose to the highest positions in the Ottoman service, and brought with them invaluable skills and knowledge. These were, however, rarely transmitted, and in any case by the eighteenth century ex-Christians had ceased to play any significant role in the councils of state, which were now more and more monopolized by the Muslim Turks. Civilian, lay-educated bureaucrats, of free Turkish parentage, began to play a growing role in the political and cultural life of the capital. They were becoming aware of the importance of Europe; some of them even saw the need for change.

It was no doubt with the intention of securing more direct and reliable information on European countries and affairs, as well as bringing Turkey into line with the normal practice of Western states, that in 1792 Selim III resolved to establish regular and permanent Ottoman Embassies in the major European capitals. The first was in London in 1793, followed after an interval by Vienna, Berlin, and Paris, where in 1796 Seyyid Ali Efendi arrived as the first Ottoman ambassador to the French Republic.[46] Among other duties, these ambassadors were instructed to study the institutions of the countries to which they were accredited, and to acquire 'languages, knowledge, and sciences useful to servants of the Empire'.[47] Most of these first diplomats were Ottoman palace or chancery officials of the old school, ignorant of Western languages and conservative in outlook. Most of them, to judge by their dispatches, learned little about the countries to which they were sent, and were not greatly impressed by what they did learn.[48] But they did not travel alone. Besides the inevitable Greek dragomans, they took with them young Turkish secretaries, whose duty it was to study the languages of Europe—and especially French—and to learn something of the ways of Western society.

[46] His general report on his mission was published by Ahmed Refik in *TOEM*, iv (1329/1911), 1246 ff., 1332 ff., 1378 ff., 1458 ff., 1548 ff. A selection of his dispatches was edited by Karal in *Fransa-Mısır ve Osmanlı Imparatorluğu, 1797–1802* (1940). The choice of London for the first resident Embassy is explained in Cevdet, *Tarih*, vi. 257–60. (cf. Uzunçarşılı, 'Ondokuzuncu Asır başlarına kadar Türk-İngiliz Münasebatına dair Vesikalar', *Bell.*, no. 51 (1949), 581 ff., and Karal, *Fransa-Mısır*, pp. 169 ff.

[47] Karal, *Selim III*, p. 79.

[48] On these embassies see T. Naff in *JAOS* (1963), 295–315; B. Lewis, 'Elči' in *EI²*; Zinkeisen, vii. 55; Cevdet, *Tarih*, vi. 88 ff.; 231 ff.; and 257 ff.; Karal, *Selim III*, pp. 163 ff.; Babinger, *Geschichtsschreiber*, pp. 331–2, where a bibliography of published documents is given. Many of the dispatches and reports of these ambassadors have since been published and examined by Karal, Uzunçarşılı, and other Turkish scholars.

These missions thus gave an opportunity to a number of young men to reside for a while in a European city, master a European language, and make the acquaintance of some of the revolutionary ideas current among their European contemporaries. Some of them, on their return, became officials at the Porte, where they formed a Westward-looking minority among the bureaucratic hierarchy similar to that created among the officers by the military and naval reforms.

So far we have spoken only of Muslims—but there were of course other elements in the Empire, Christian and also Jewish. The Jews seem to have been surprisingly little affected by Western influences in this period, and with one or two exceptions played no significant role. The Christians on the other hand—especially the Greek and Armenian *élite* of the capital—had for long been on terms of familiarity with the West, and thanks to their monopoly of the knowledge of Western languages had managed to gain an important position in the Ottoman state and economy. In the late seventeenth century the Phanariot Greeks gradually ousted the renegades and Levantines who had hitherto served as interpreters in dealings with foreign embassies. The Greeks, and to a lesser extent the Armenians, were familiar enough with Western culture—many of the wealthier families had for long been in the habit of sending their sons to be educated in Italian universities, especially in Padua. They were thus prepared, both linguistically and intellectually, to receive the new Western ideas of their time.

On the whole, however, the influence of the ideas of the Revolution on the Christians of Istanbul was not considerable. The churches of course used their authority against it; the wealthy and conservative Greek aristocracy too, recognizing the danger to the existing Ottoman order, preferred at first to preserve a régime in which they had so considerable an interest. Some converts to French ideas were found, however, among the Christians, more especially when the French began to address themselves directly to Greek and other national aspirations. Some Ottoman Christians—as for example Mouradgea d'Ohsson —may have played some small part in influencing Ottoman policy towards the French Republic; later they certainly played a vital role in bringing the ideas of the Revolution, with explosive effect, to the peoples of the Balkans. But their role in bringing Western ideas to the Muslim Turks is small and indirect, and is in the main limited to their functions as interpreters, language teachers, and translators. As Christians and as subject peoples they were doubly discredited, and unlikely to gain much of a hearing for any new ideas they might attempt to convey— the more so since their own secular and religious leaders were opposed to them. If anything, the minorities acted as a cushion— absorbing the impact of regular Western commercial and diplomatic activities in Turkey, and thus protecting the Turks from direct contact and contamination. What they did do, how- ever, was to provide a nucleus of people familiar, on the one hand, with Turkish, on the other, with French or Italian, and thus able, when required, to translate Western books, to act as interpreters for Western instructors, and to teach Western languages to aspiring Turks.

If the channels through which the ideas of the Revolution might flow into Turkey existed, their use was not left to chance, but was the subject of sustained efforts by the French. Partly out of general missionary enthusiasm, partly in order to secure the support of the still not negligible Ottoman power at a critical time, the French devoted much attention to winning sympathy in the Ottoman capital and provinces. From the first an important section of the French community in Istanbul adhered to the Revolution, and aroused the ire of the Austrian and Prussian embassies by the wearing of revolutionary emblems and the holding of revolutionary meetings.[49] In June 1793 citizen Des- corches (*ci-devant* Marquis de Sainte-Croix) arrived in Istanbul as emissary of the French Republic, with the double mission of winning Ottoman support for French policy and Ottoman sym- pathy for the Revolution. The inauguration of the republican flag was made the occasion of a public celebration, culminating in a salute from two French ships moored off Seraglio Point. They flew the colours of the Ottoman Empire, of the French and American republics, 'and those of a few other powers that had not sullied their arms in the impious league of tyrants'.[50] In a solemn ceremony a tree of liberty was planted in the soil of Turkey.

[49] E. de Marcère, *Une Ambassade à Constantinople*, i (1927), 45; Zinkeisen, vi. 861 ff.; Cevdet, *Tarih*, vi. 183 ff.

[50] Marcère, ii, 12–15. See further Sybel, in *R. hist.*, xi, 107 ff. on French propaganda in Turkey in this period. The published proceedings of the Committee of Public Safety contain several references to the expenditure of large sums of money in Turkey, for the purposes of the Republic. For further details, see B. Lewis, in *The New Asia*, pp. 40 ff.

The French government also took further steps to encourage its growth. In April 1795 the Foreign Ministry in Paris informed Descorches that the Committee of Public Safety had decided to re-establish the French printing press in Istanbul, and announced the dispatch of Louis Allier, director of the French *Imprimerie Nationale*, to take charge of it. Three other assistants were sent, together with two presses and a quantity of French type. The ambassador was instructed to use this press to the best advantage of the Republic.[51]

Far more important, however, than any pamphlets, bulletins, or newspapers was the effect of the unrecorded efforts of individual Frenchmen in Istanbul and elsewhere, who abandoned the mutually agreed exclusiveness that had kept Franks and Muslims from all but formal contacts in the past, and for the first time sought the intimacy and cultivated the friendship of Muslim Turks. Turkish-speaking Frenchmen, native Christians, and some Turks began to form a new society in the capital, in which the needs and ideas of the time were discussed, and the enthusiastic optimism of revolutionary France found a response among the few but highly placed Turks that looked to the West for guidance and inspiration.

The Turkish Reaction [52]

The Revolution seems to have made little immediate impression on the Turks, who, like other contemporary observers, at first

[51] Ibid. pp. 116 ff.; L. Lagarde, 'Note sur les journaux français de Constantinople à l'époque révolutionnaire', *J. As.*, ccxxxvi (1948), 271 ff.; Gerçek, *Türk Gazet.*, pp. 10 ff. In the latter work a reproduction is given of an entire issue of the *Gazette française de Constantinople*, dated 1 Floréal, year 5 (20 Apr. 1797). In July 1795 Descorches reported that he had distributed a bulletin in Turkish on the victories of the republican armies (J. Sorel, *L'Europe et la Révolution française*, iv (1909), 248).

[52] The contemporary Turkish historians are discussed in Babinger, *Geschichtsschreiber*, and in O. M. von Schlechta-Wssehrd, 'Die osmanischen Geschichtsschreiber der neueren Zeit', *Denkschriften der phil. hist. Classe der Kgl. Ak. der Wissenschaften*, viii (1856), 1 ff. The most important published chronicle is that of Ahmed Asım Efendi (? 1755–1819), who wrote the official annals of the Empire for the years 1791–1808 (*Asım Tarihi*. On Asım see Babinger, *Geschichtsschreiber*, pp. 339–40, Schlechta-Wssehrd, pp. 10–11, and the article on Asım in the *IA*, by Köprülü.) A far profounder treatment is that of Ahmed Cevdet Paşa (1822–95), whose 12-volume history of the Ottoman Empire from 1774 to 1826 must rank as one of the greatest achievements of Ottoman historiography. Cevdet's history is based to a very large extent on archive documents, many of which he quoted *in extenso*. Since the foundation of the Ottoman (later Turkish) Historical Society in 1910, Turkish historians have published an increasing number of studies and of editions of documents from the State Archives, which have

regarded it as a purely internal affair of no great consequence. Even when the Revolution spread by war to the neighbouring countries and convulsed Western Europe, the Turks still regarded it as an internal affair of Christendom, having no relevance to the Ottoman Empire, which as a Muslim state was immune to this contagion. Diplomatically, the preoccupation of the Christian powers with the revolutionary wars was even of benefit to the Porte. Ahmed Efendi, the Privy Secretary of Selim III, noted this in his journal in January 1792, and concluded: 'May God cause the upheaval in France to spread like syphilis to the enemies of the Empire, hurl them into prolonged conflict with one another, and thus accomplish results beneficial to the Empire, amen.'[53]

A new phase began with the partition of the territories of the Republic of Venice by the treaty of Campo Formio of 17 October 1797. By the fifth article of this treaty, the Ionian islands, together with the former Venetian possessions on the adjoining coasts of Albania and Greece, were annexed to the French Republic. France, the traditional ally of the Ottoman Empire, had become her neighbour—and ancient friendship could not stand the shock. Soon alarming reports began to come in from Morea—of liberty and equality on the borders of the Empire, of speeches and ceremonies recalling the ancient glories and liberties of Hellas and promising their restoration—of French intelligence with rebels and dissidents in Ottoman Greece and French plans to annex Morea and Crete.[54] French reassurances failed to comfort the Divan, and when General Tamara, the new Russian ambassador, repeated the warnings of his predecessor against the dangers of revolutionary France, he was listened to with greater attention.[55] Before long still more alarming reports began to arrive of French naval preparations in Toulon, and of a projected French attack on the Ottoman dominions. In the spring of 1798

meanwhile been rehoused and reorganized. (For brief accounts, see B. Lewis, 'Başvek-âlet Arşivi', in *EI*²; S. J. Shaw, 'Archival sources for Ottoman history: the Archives of Turkey', *JAOS* (1960), 1–12).

[53] Tahsin Öz, ed., 'Selim III ün Sırkatibi tarafından tutulan Ruzname', *Tar. Ves.*, iii (May 1949), 184. cf. Cevdet, *Tarih*, vi. 130. In Turkish syphilis is called Frengi.

[54] On the reports of Hasan Paşa, the Vali of Morea, see Karal, 'Yunan Adalarının Fransızlar tarafından işgalı ve Osmanlı-Rus münasebâtı 1797–8', *Tar. Semineri Derg.*, i (1937), 103 ff.; cf. Cevdet, vi. 280–1.

[55] Karal, *Tar. Sem. Derg.*, pp. 116 ff., where the official Ottoman record of the conversation with Tamara is given.

the *Reis-ül-Küttab*, Ahmed Atıf Efendi, was instructed to prepare a memorandum for the Divan on the political situation, and on the invitation extended by the Allies to the Porte to join an anti-French coalition. His report is worth quoting at some length. He begins with a general account of the French Revolution, presented, in accordance with Ottoman politeness, as something well known to his readers, but clearly intended to remove their illusions as to the real purport of the events in France.

It is one of the things known to all well-informed persons that the conflagration of sedition and wickedness that broke out a few years ago in France, scattering sparks and shooting flames of mischief and tumult in all directions, had been conceived many years previously in the minds of certain accursed heretics, and had been a quiescent evil which they sought an opportunity to waken. In this way: the known and famous atheists Voltaire and Rousseau, and other materialists like them, had printed and published various works, consisting, God preserve us, of insults and vilification against the pure prophets and great kings, of the removal and abolition of all religion, and of allusions to the sweetness of equality and republicanism, all expressed in easily intelligible words and phrases, in the form of mockery, in the language of the common people. Finding the pleasure of novelty in these writings, most of the people, even youths and women, inclined towards them and paid close attention to them, so that heresy and wickedness spread like syphilis to the arteries of their brains and corrupted their beliefs. When the revolution became more intense, none took offence at the closing of churches, the killing and expulsion of monks, and the abolition of religion and doctrine: they set their hearts on equality and freedom, through which they hoped to attain perfect bliss in this world, in accordance with the lying teachings increasingly disseminated among the common people by this pernicious crew, who stirred up sedition and evil because of selfishness or self-interest. It is well known that the ultimate basis of the order and cohesion of every state is a firm grasp of the roots and branches of holy law, religion, and doctrine; that the tranquillity of the land and the control of the subjects cannot be encompassed by political means alone; that the necessity for the fear of God and the regard for retribution in the hearts of God's slaves is one of the unshakeably established divine decrees; that in both ancient and modern times every state and people has had its own religion, whether true or false. Nevertheless, the leaders of the sedition and evil appearing in France, in a manner without precedent, in order to facilitate the accomplishment of their evil purposes, and in utter disregard of the fearsome consequences, have removed the fear of God and the regard for retribution from the common people, made lawful all kinds of abominable deeds, utterly obliterated all shame and-decency, and thus prepared the way for the reduction of the people of France to the state of cattle. Nor were they satisfied with this alone, but, finding supporters like themselves in every place, in order to keep other states busy with the protection of their own régimes and thus forestall an attack on themselves, they had their rebellious declaration which they call 'The Rights of Man' translated into all languages and published in all parts, and strove to incite the common people of the nations and religions to rebel against the kings to whom they were subject.[56]

In this document the French Revolution is clearly regarded as a danger which threatened the Ottoman Empire as well as the Christian states. The need to overcome it overrode both the traditional enmity between the Porte and her neighbours and the traditional friendship between the Porte and France.

The French landing at Alexandria on 1 July 1798, and the subsequent activities of the French in Egypt and Palestine confirmed Atif's reasoning. The long-term effects of the impact of revolutionary France on the Arab peoples are well known. But even the immediate effects were disturbing enough to induce the Ottoman government to embark on what in our time is called ideological warfare. In a proclamation distributed in Arabic in Syria, Egypt, and Arabia, a detailed refutation of revolutionary doctrines was offered:

In the Name of God, the Merciful and the Compassionate.

O you who believe in the unity of God, community of Muslims, know that the French nation (may God devastate their dwellings and abase their banners, for they are tyrannical infidels and dissident evildoers) do not believe in the unity of the Lord of Heaven and Earth, nor in the mission of the intercessor on the Day of Judgment, but have abandoned all religions, and denied the after-world and its penalties ... so that they have pillaged their churches and the adornments of their crucifixes and attacked their priests and monks. They assert that the books which the prophets brought are clear error, and that the Koran, the Torah and the Gospels are nothing but fakes and idle talk ... that all men are equal in humanity, and alike in being men, none has any superiority of merit over any other, and every one himself disposes of his soul and arranges his own livelihood in this life. ... With counterfeit books and meretricious falsehoods they

[56] Cevdet, *Tarih*, vi. 394 ff.

address themselves to every party and say: 'We belong to you, to your
religion and to your community', and they make them vain promises,
and utter fearful warnings. They are wholly given up to villainy and
debauchery, and ride the steed of perfidy and presumption, and dive
in the sea of delusion and oppression and are united under the banner
of Satan. . . .[57]

It is interesting to note which characteristics of the French
Revolution were most shocking to Atıf Efendi and to the author of
the proclamation, or were regarded by them as most likely to
shock their readers. Neither makes any reference to the execution
of Louis XVI, which had such an effect on Christian Europe.
Von Knobelsdorf, the Prussian chargé d'affaires in Istanbul,
reported in a dispatch of 11 March 1793 that 'le Grand Seigneur,
instruit jusqu'aux moindres détails de ce crime affreux, en fut si
affecté, qu'il en a été malade; tout le Divan, tout le peuple en
est saisi d'horreur'.[58] That the Sultan was sick with horror at
the execution of his royal brother is likely enough, but the violent
death of a sovereign was too familiar a feature of political life
in Istanbul to arouse much comment. Nor did even the abolition
of the monarchy attract much attention. The Ottomans had been
familiar for centuries with republican institutions in Venice and
Ragusa, and there was nothing in the mere establishment of a
republic to alarm them. What was by now disturbing ruling
circles in Istanbul was the secularism of the Revolution—the
separation of State and Church, the abandonment of all religious
doctrines, the cult of reason. At first the attempt of the French
to curry favour with the Muslims by stressing their rejection
of Christianity and affecting a sympathy for Islam awoke some
response, but soon—with Russian and Austrian assistance—the
rulers of the Empire realized the dangers that this proffered
friendship held for the traditional Islamic order and principles.
Their fears were well grounded—the whole subsequent history
of the Middle East has shown how great is the seductive power of a
Western revolutionary ideology divorced from Western religion.
Some indication of the degree of French success in this propaganda

[57] The Turkish text, from a document in the Istanbul archives, is given by Karal,
Fransa-Mısır, pp. 108 ff. The Arabic text, as brought to Acre by Sir Sidney Smith,
is given in an Arabic biography of Jazzar Paşa, attributed to Haydar Aḥmad Shihāb,
Ta'rikh Aḥmad Bāshā al-Jazzār (Beirut, 1955), pp. 125 ff.

[58] Zinkeisen, vi. 858-9 n. 2.

may be gathered from the frequent hostile allusions to it in Ottoman sources. At the same time they began to appreciate the explosive content of the ideas of equality and liberty, though it seems that the latter was at first regarded as a danger to the Christian subjects of the Porte rather than to the Turks themselves.

While France and Turkey were at war, the communication of French ideas to the Turks was at a disadvantage. Nevertheless, the swift and easy success of an army of less than 30,000 Frenchmen in conquering and ruling Egypt for over three years did not fail to impress, nor did the tolerance and sympathy shown by the French rulers of Egypt. By the terms of the peace, France withdrew from the Ionian islands as well as from Egypt, and thus terminated her brief tenure as a neighbour of the Porte. The voice of France, no longer shouting in Greek and in Arabic, became more audible in Istanbul.

While Brune, Ruffin, and Sébastiani worked to restore French influence at the Porte, a new Turkish ambassador, Mehmed Said Halet Efendi, served in Paris from 1803 to 1806. Halet was a convinced reactionary, and a hater of all things Western. But even his strictures on Frangistan, as he calls it, reveal how strong French influence was. Some extracts from his letters may illustrate the point:

I ask you to pray for my safe return from this land of infidels, for I have come as far as Paris, but I have not yet seen the Frangistan that people speak of and praise; in what Europe these wonderful things and these wise Franks are, I do not know . . .

Glory be to God, the minds and beliefs of these people! It is a strange thing that this Frangistan, with the praises of which our ears have for so long been filled, we found to be not only unlike what was said, but the reverse. . . .

If anyone, with the intention either of intimidating you or of leading you astray, praises Frangistan, then ask him this question: 'Have you been to Europe, or have you not?' If he says: 'Indeed I have been there, and I enjoyed myself awhile', then assuredly he is a partisan and a spy of the Franks. If he says, 'No, I have not been, I know it from history books', then he is one of two things—either he is an ass, who takes heed of what the Franks write, or else he praises the Franks out of religious fanaticism. . . .[59]

[59] Karal, *Halet Efendinin Paris Büyük Elçiliği, 1802–6* (1940), 32 ff.

Despite Halet's encouragement of the reactionary party in Istanbul, French influence continued to grow. The French victories of 1805 and the humiliation of Austria and Russia delighted the Sultan, and decided him to recognize Napoleon as Emperor. In August 1806 Sébastiani returned to Istanbul, and was soon able to involve the Porte in war with both Russia and England. The repulse of an English naval squadron from Istanbul, thanks in no small measure to the energetic intervention of Sébastiani and a number of French officers and volunteers, gave the French ambassador a position of unparelleled ascendancy at the Porte. But it was this very victory of French influence and the prominence of Frenchmen in the defence of Istanbul that outraged Muslim sentiment, and helped to provoke the reactionary rebellion that culminated in the deposition of Selim III in May 1807.[60]

The first trial of strength with the opponents of reform had already come in 1805, when the Sultan, hard pressed for troops, had ordered a general levy to provide men for the *Nizam-i Cedid* regiments, in place of the system of voluntary recruitment maintained until then. The levy was required from the Janissaries as well as from the general population. This bold measure brought to a head the smouldering resentment of the Janissaries and the ulema at the new order. Some brushes with Janissary regiments had already occurred in previous years. They now broke out in open revolt in Rumelia. A regiment of *Nizam-i Cedid* troops sent against them from Anatolia was crushingly defeated, and in the face of this crisis the reactionaries and the mob in the capital were able to enforce a suspension of the reforms. To avoid a general revolt, the Sultan was induced to dismiss his reformist advisers, send the *Nizam* troops back to Anatolia, and entrust the Grand Vezirate to the Aga of the Janissaries.

This capitulation postponed but did not avert the debacle. In May 1807 the *Yamaks*—auxiliary levies—mutinied against an order to put on European-style uniforms. The leader of the mutineers, Kabakçıoğlu Mustafa, was soon able to command powerful support in high quarters. He marched with his henchmen to Istanbul, where he set up headquarters in the Hippodrome and entered into close relations with the kaymakam of the Grand Vezir, Musa Paşa, and with the Chief Mufti. Armed with a list of the chief partisans of reform, he and his mutineers, with the

[60] Zinkeisen, vii. 455 ff.

help of a maddened mob, set to work to round them up and kill them. Some they killed in their own houses, others they dragged to the Hippodrome and slaughtered them there.

A decree by the Sultan abolishing the *Nizam-i Cedid* came too late to save his throne. On 29 May 1807, after a turbulent meeting at the Hippodrome, a deputation of Janissary officers called on the Chief Mufti to ask 'whether a Sultan, who by his actions and enactments had worked against the religious principles sanctified by the Koran, could continue to reign?' The Mufti, with a becoming show of surprise and reluctance, then authorized the Sultan's deposition, in the interests of the Muslim religion and the house of Osman. Selim was accordingly deposed, and his cousin Mustafa was proclaimed Sultan. The *Nizam* forces were at once dissolved, and the chief of the mutineers became command-ant of the fortresses of the Bosporus. In the capital the real rulers were the kaymakam and the Chief Mufti.[61]

It was a year or so after these events that Ahmed Asım Efendi, Imperial Historiographer, wrote his chronicle of the years 1791–1808. From his narrative we can draw a clear impression of the general effect of French influences in Turkey during these years. Asım approves of the reforms, which he hoped would restore the military strength of the Empire, and in an interesting passage he describes how Russia emerged from weakness and barbarism to the status of a great power by borrowing the sciences and techniques of the West.[62] But he is bitterly anti-Christian, con-sidering all Christian powers as inveterate enemies of Islam, and foreseeing nothing but evil consequences from agreements with them. In particular he detests the French, and reviles the pro-French party in Turkey as deluded fools.[63] His reference to the internal affairs of France are few and hostile. The republic was 'like the rumblings and crepitations of a queasy stomach',[64] its principles consisted of 'the abandonment of religion and the equality of rich and poor'.[65]

Of French activities in Turkey he has more to say. In a lengthy discussion of the successes and failures of the reforms of Selim III and the causes and circumstances of his fall, Asım Efendi devotes

[61] Zinkeisen, vii. 461 ff.; Juchereau, ii. 104 ff.; Cevdet, *Tarih*, viii. 139 ff.; Asım, ii. 178 ff.; Ata, iii. 44 ff.
[62] Asım, i. 265.   [63] Ibid. pp. 76, 175, &c.
[64] Asım, i. 78.   [65] Ibid. p. 62.

a great deal of attention to French influence. The French had presented themselves as friends and even as prospective converts to Islam, assuring the Turks of their hostility to Christianity and their intention of following the teachings of Muhammad. By intensive propaganda they had confused the minds 'not only of the great ones of the state but also of the common people'. To spread their pernicious ideas, they had sought the society of Turks, beguiling them with protestations of friendship and goodwill, and thus, through familiar and intimate social intercourse, had found many victims.

Certain sensualists, naked of the garment of loyalty, from time to time learned politics from them; some, desirous of learning their language, took French teachers, acquired their idiom and prided themselves . . . on their uncouth talk. In this way they were able to insinuate Frankish customs in the hearts and endear their modes of thought to the minds of some people of weak mind and shallow faith. The sober-minded and far-sighted and the ambassadors of the other states foresaw the danger of this situation; full of alarm and disapproval, they reviled and condemned these things both implicitly and explicitly, and gave forewarning of the evil consequences to which their activities would give rise. This malicious crew and abominable band were full of cunning—first sowing the seed of their politics in the soil of the hearts of the great ones of the state, then, by incitement and seduction to their ways of thought, undermining—God preserve us— the principles of the Holy Law.[66]

By the summer of 1807 the Emperor Napoleon was in alliance with his Imperial brother in Russia; the Sultan Selim III was dethroned and the party of reaction in power in Istanbul. The French Revolution seemed dead in the land of its birth, and its influence stifled in Turkey. But the cutting from the tree of liberty had struck root in the soil of Islam. It was to bear both sweet and bitter fruit.

The contemporary evidence of the influence of new ideas in Turkey is largely negative; it could hardly be otherwise. The cultural traditions and political conditions of the Ottoman Empire were conducive neither to the formulation nor to the

[66] Asım, i. 374–6; cf. Cevdet, *Tarih*, viii. 147–8, where an account is given of the influence of European instructors and experts, the exaggerated respect for European ideas and practices among young Turks, the aping of European manners and customs, and the appearance of 'heresy and materialism' in Istanbul.

expression of new political theories or programmes. As so often happens, the first appearance of heterodox ideas in an authoritarian society is known only from refutations and condemnations; when positive responses appear, they are sporadic and furtive, and, in Islamic societies especially, assume the traditional disguise of a return to the sanctified past. Evidence of the working of new ideas is elusive, but it exists—as for example in the unprecedented attempts, in 1807 and 1808, to define and demarcate political authority,[67] and in the gradual transformation of the old Ottoman practice of *Meşveret*, consultation, under the influence of European parliamentary ideas. In a very significant passage the historian Şanizade (d. 1826)[68] discusses the nature of consultative meetings. He is careful to base the holding of such meetings on Islamic precedent and ancient Ottoman practice, and to give warning against their misuse; at the same time he points out that such consultations are normally held, with beneficial effects, in 'certain well-organized states'—a striking euphemism for Europe—and attributes to those attending them a representative quality entirely new to Islamic political thought. The members of the councils consist of two groups, servants of the state and representatives of the subjects; they discuss and argue freely, and thus arrive at a decision.[69] It is in this seemingly casual, barely perceptible form that such radical and alien ideas as popular representation, free debate, and corporate decision make their first appearance in Ottoman writings. It would be arbitrary to assign a source for these ideas—the Revolution, the Enlightenment, or the ultimate example of the ordered liberties of England. This much, however, can be said—that the events of the French Revolution were the first to bring these ideas dramatically before the rest of the world, and the government of the French Republic the first to try and teach them.

---

[67] See below, pp. 75 and 447.
[68] On Şanizade see below, pp. 86–87.
[69] Sanizade, *Tarih*, iv, 2–3; cf. B. Lewis in *BSOAS*, xxix (1966), 385–6, and 'Hurriyya ii' in *EI*[2].

CHAPTER IV

The Ottoman Reform

*Moi-même, ivre de joie de voir ma patrie dans l'état que je desirois si ardemment,
éclairée tous les jours davantage du flambeau des sciences et des arts. . . .*

SEID MUSTAFA, 'Diatribe', 1803.

*In scanning over the riches of civilization, spread out before him for acceptance,
he contemptuously rejects those calculated to benefit his people, and chooses the
modern scientific governing machine, result of ages of experiments, with its patent
screws for extracting blood and treasure, conscription and taxation.*

ADOLPHUS SLADE, R.N., 'Record of Travels in Turkey, Greece, &c.', 1831.

IN the summer of 1807 the reform movement in Turkey seemed
to be extinguished. The reforming Sultan was deposed, his new-
style army disbanded, his reformist ministers dead or in hiding.
In their place the Chief Mufti and the Janissaries ruled the city—
the two forces most bitterly opposed to social and military change.

But the reform, though young, was a vigorous plant—vigorous
enough to survive both the violence of the Hippodrome mutineers
and the subtlety of the Chief Mufti. The latter began to have
difficulties with his governmental colleagues. In September 1807,
after mounting disagreements, he procured the dismissal of the
kaymakam Musa Paşa, who was replaced by another well-known
reactionary, Tayyar Paşa. In June 1808 he too was dismissed.
Swallowing his convictions, he took refuge with Bayrakdar
Mustafa, the Pasha of Silistria and military commander of the
Danube frontiers—the only important partisan of reform still
alive, at large, and in a position of power.

Bayrakdar Mustafa Paşa [1]

Mustafa the Standard-bearer (Bayrakdar) was born in Ruschuk, the son of a Janissary. After distinguished service in the war
against Russia in 1767–74, he lived on his estates near Ruschuk,
where he acquired the status of *ayan*. In 1805 he took part in the
revolt of the Janissaries at Edirne against the *Nizam-i Cedid*.

---

[1] On the Bayrakdar (also called Alemdar, with the same meaning) there are two
modern monographs based on original sources: Uzunçarşılı, *Alemdar Mustafa Paşa*
(1942); and A. F. Miller, *Mustafa Pasha Bayraktar* (1947). Detailed accounts will also
be found in Cevdet, Zinkeisen, &c.

Afterwards, however, he was won over, became an enthusiastic partisan of reform, and was given high military rank and his appointment in Rumelia.

His headquarters in Ruschuk now became the rallying-point of the surviving reformers, as well as of other opponents of the new régime in the capital. In the summer of 1808 he was ready to take the offensive. The Grand Vezir, Çelebi Mustafa Paşa, was still at Edirne with the army of Rumelia, and was virtually excluded from power by the ruling group in Istanbul. Bayrakdar Mustafa and his associates now moved from Ruschuk to Edirne, joined forces with the Grand Vezir, and together marched on Istanbul, where they obtained control of the city. The Sultan Mustafa IV, learning of their intention to restore Selim III, took the precaution of having him murdered. He himself was immediately after deposed, and his brother Mahmud became Sultan.

The Grand Vezirate of Bayrakdar Mustafa Paşa lasted only a few months, until November 1808, when he was overthrown and killed by a revolt of Janissaries. During that time, however, he began a most ambitious programme. He reconstituted the *Nizam* troops under a new name, revived and extended the reforming edicts, and convened a great Imperial assembly, to which he invited high officials, governors, pashas, and *ayan* from all over the Empire. Among those who came were the Beylerbeys of Rumelia and Anatolia, the governors of the provinces adjoining the capital, the heads of several of the powerful *derebey* families of Anatolia, and of course the high dignitaries of the capital. By the beginning of October some two-thirds of the invited guests had reached Istanbul, and the Bayrakdar, accompanied by the highest officers of state as well as by a number of the ulema, formally inaugurated the assembly in the Imperial palace. In a rousing address, he set before the assembled pashas· a programme of reform, including a thoroughgoing reorganization of the Janissary corps, which would have removed a whole series of long-cherished abuses, and, at the same time, confirmed the rights and privileges of the *derebeys* and *ayan*, the new provincial *élite* to which the Bayrakdar himself belonged.[2]

<hr/>

[2] Şanizade, i. 66–73. Cevdet, *Tarih*, ix. 3–7 and 278–83. On the significance of the 'deed of agreement' (*sened-i ittifak*) see Inalcık, 'Tanzimat Nedir' in *Tarih Araştırmaları* (1941), p. 249 (a brief restatement in English by the same author in 'Land Problems in Turkish History', *Muslim Wld.*, xlv (1955), 225; Dustūr (1966), pp. 6 ff.; also below, p. 447.

An agreement was soon reached between the *derebeys* and the central government, and reluctantly ratified by the Sultan. But attempts to put it into force soon alienated all but a few devoted friends, and in the following month all was ended by a rising of the infuriated Janissaries. Bayrakdar Mustafa died in the flaming ruins of his residence, and the Sultan himself, tarred with the brush of reform, owed his throne and perhaps his life only to the fact that he was the sole surviving prince of the house of Osman. Once again the reactionaries were in control. Only the Sultan watched and waited the opportunity to resume the reform, by first destroying the forces that opposed it.

Mahmud II [3]

Mahmud II, sometimes described as the Peter the Great of the Ottoman Empire, was born in the Saray in July 1785. There is a story, of dubious authenticity, that his mother was

[3] There is a vast literature on the Ottoman reforms inaugurated under Mahmud II and his successors, though as yet no comprehensive monographic treatment. The most recent general survey, by a Turkish historian using both Turkish and Western sources, is that given by Karal in his three volumes contributed to the large-scale Ottoman history published in Ankara by the Turkish Historical Society: *Osmanlı Tarihi* v (1789–1856), 1947; vi (1856–61), 1954; vii (1861–76), 1956. A collection of studies and surveys on various aspects of the reforms, by different authors, will be found in the volume *Tanzimat*, published in 1940 by the Turkish Ministry of Education on the occasion of the 100th anniversary of the first great reforming edict. Among Turkish historians of an earlier generation, Abdurrahman Şeref, the last Imperial Ottoman Historiographer and first president of the Ottoman Historical Society, is particularly illuminating. Of special value are his *Tarih Musahabeleri* (1340 A.H.) (a collection of essays on personalities and events in nineteenth-century Turkey) and his *Tarih-i Devlet-i Osmaniye* (1309 A.H.), a general history, including excellent surveys of administrative and institutional changes. General accounts of the period will also be found in the historical writings of Ahmed Rasim, *Osmanlı Tarihi* (1326–30 A.H.) and *Istibdaddan Hakimiyet-i Milliyeye* (1923–5). A brief outline of the reforms, using Turkish sources, was written by J. H. Kramers for *EI*[1] (*s.v.* 'Tanzimat') where numerous other articles will be found on Turkish personalities and institutions. Useful material will also be found in certain works by Western historians, although these are based exclusively or almost exclusively on Western sources. These include both contemporary and near contemporary works such as G. Rosen, *Geschichte der Türkei . . . 1826 . . . 1856* (1866–7), J. M. Bastelberger, *Die militärischen Reformen unter Mahmud II, dem Retter des osmanischen Reiches* (1874), F. Eichmann, *Die Reformen des osmanischen Reiches* (1858), and Ed. Engelhardt, *La Turquie et le Tanzimat* (1882–4) (this work was translated into Turkish and much used by Turkish historians); and also more modern works like von Sax, *Geschichte des Machtverfalls der Türkei*, Vienna 1913; Jorga, *Geschichte des osmanischen Reiches*; H. W. V. Temperley, *England and the Near East, I: The Crimea* (1936); F. E. Bailey, *British Policy and the Turkish Reform Movement* (1942). Among the many contemporary Western observers of the reforms, some are of special interest. The period of Mahmud II is well described by the Prussian soldier Helmut von Moltke,

French.[4] He himself certainly had no knowledge of French, nor of any other Western language.[5] His father was Abdülhamid I, during whose reign the first modern training schools were established in Turkey. His cousin, Selim III, seems to have exercised a profound influence on him, especially in the last year of joint seclusion, between Selim's deposition and his death. His education was that normal to an Ottoman prince—Turkish and the classical Islamic languages, religion and law, poetry and history. He had no direct knowledge of the West, nor any means of access to it save through intermediaries, since he knew no Western language, and little was available in Turkish translation.

After the violent end of Bayrakdar Mustafa Paşa, it was eighteen years before the Sultan could return to his projects of military reform. These years were not, however, spent in idleness. His first task was the war against Russia. After its conclusion in 1812, he set to work to restore or establish the authority of the central

Briefe über Zustände und Begebenheiten in der Türkei aus den Jahren 1835 bis 1839 (1891), and the English sailor Adolphus Slade, *Record of Travels in Turkey, Greece, &c.*, . . . *in the years 1829, 1830, and 1831* (1832). For Turkey in the 1840's and 1850's, there are excellent accounts in Charles White, *Three Years in Constantinople* (1846), and A. Ubicini, *Lettres sur la Turquie* (1853–4). The final phase of the *Tanzimat*, and the brief interlude of the first constitution, are described with knowledge and insight by the German consul and scholar A. D. Mordtmann, in his book published anonymously under the title *Stambul und das moderne Türkenthum* (1877). The major published Turkish chroniclers of the period are Şanizade, Cevdet, and Lûtfi. Şanizade (on whom see below, p. 84) was an Imperial Historiographer whose chronicle (n.d.) covers the years 1808–20. Cevdet Paşa's history (see above, p. 64 n. 52) goes only as far as 1826, but his observations and memoranda (*Tezakir, i-xxxix*, ed. Baysun (1953–1963); *Maruzat*, published in *TOEM*, nos. 78–93) tell us much about the events of his own time. Ahmed Lûtfi, who succeeded Cevdet as Imperial Historiographer in 1865, wrote a chronicle covering the period 1825–68, of which only the first eight volumes, as far as 1847, have been printed (*Tarih-i Lûtfi*, 1290–1328 A.H.). Among other Turkish historians of the time, mention may be made of Tayyarzade Ata, whose chronicle (*Tarih-i Ata*) is especially informative on court affairs and personalities; Mustafa Nuri Paşa, whose *Netaic ül-Vukuat* includes valuable surveys and analyses of development and reform in the government, armed forces, and finances; Mehmed Süreyya, to whom we owe an invaluable biographical dictionary of Ottoman worthies (*Sicill-i Osmani* (1308–15); and the Grand Vezir Kâmil Paşa, whose political history (*Tarih-i Siyasî-i Devlet-i Aliye-i Osmaniye*, 1327 A.H.) goes as far as about the mid-century. Besides these and other works of historiography, there are Turkish newspapers, periodicals, and pamphlets of the period, as well as a vast documentation in the state archives that has only to a very limited extent been examined or exploited by scholars.

[4] For a brief bibliographic note on the 'abundant literature' on this story, see J. Deny, 'Wālide Sultān', in *EI*[1], iv. 1118.

[5] Moltke, p. 408: 'so viel ist gewiss, dass der Grossherr nicht eine Silbe Englisch, Französisch oder Deutsch verstand'.

government in the provinces, most of which had a considerable measure of autonomy.[6]

All these powers and privileges Mahmud II was determined to suppress. In his view, with which many subsequent observers have agreed, no real progress towards reform would be possible until all power other than that emanating from him had been eliminated, and the Sultan's will made the sole source of authority in the provinces as well as in the capital. In two areas he failed—in Egypt, where he was forced to concede autonomous status to an Ottoman military adventurer who had made himself master of that country; and in the Morea, where he was compelled by the intervention of the powers to recognize the freedom of the Greeks. Elsewhere in the Empire, however, especially in Rumelia and Anatolia, he was largely successful in overcoming the rebellious pashas and local dynasts and notables, and in bringing the provinces under the effective control of the government in Istanbul.

The Suppression of the Janissaries [7]

In 1826, immediately after the surrender by the Greek insurgents of the fortress of Missolonghi, the Sultan was encouraged to resume the favourite project of his forerunners on the path of reform, and order the formation of a new-style army, with European training and equipment. A *Hatt-i Şerif* of 28 May 1826 established a new corps. The corps of Janissaries was to be maintained, but each battalion stationed in the capital was to provide 150 men for the new force. Though this new force was in effect a revival of the *Nizam-i Cedid* of Selim III, the Sultan was careful in his order establishing it to avoid any reference to the reforms or the reformers. On the contrary, he blandly presented the new force as a restoration of the military order of Süleyman the Magnificent, which since the days of Koçu Bey had been the panacea of all who sought to revive the strength of the Empire by reverting

---

[6] See above, pp. 37–38.

[7] The official Turkish account of the 'Auspicious Incident', is the *Üss-i Zafer* of Mehmed Esad (1243/1827); French translation by A. P. Caussin de Perceval, *Précis historique de la destruction du corps des janissaires* . . . (1833). cf. Nuri, *Netaic*, iv. 76 ff.; Kâmil Paşa, *Tarih-i Siyasî*, iii. 100 ff.; Rasim, *Osmanlı Tarihi*, iv. 1805 ff. There are also numerous descriptions and comments by Western writers, e.g. Rosen, i. 8 ff. For brief critical accounts of the episode see Temperley, pp. 15–21 and 402 n. 22; Bailey, pp. 34–35. The military reforms that followed are described in Lûtfi, i. 191–202 and 252–59; Ata, iii. 108 ff.; Nuri, *Netaic*, iv. 109 ff., and in Ubicini, letter 19.

to the practices of her golden prime. The Sultan even specified that the new force would not be instructed by Christians or foreigners, but only by Muslim officers familiar with modern military methods. The whole was approved by the Chief Mufti and the ulema, as being justified by the overriding needs of the Holy War against the infidels, and the document was signed and sealed by senior Janissary officers and civilian officials, including the Reis Efendi.

But the Janissaries, as Mahmud had no doubt anticipated, would not be persuaded. On 15 June, ten days after the formal inauguration of the new corps, they mutinied for the last time. Overturning their soup-kettles in the traditional gesture of revolt, the five Janissary battalions assembled in the Etmeydanı and soon gathered a furious mob, bent on repeating the massacre of 1807. But this time most of the populace was against them— and Mahmud was ready for them. A loyal senior officer, Ağa Hüseyin Paşa, had arrived with troops and guns, and against the heavy cannon the Janissaries were helpless. Not a whiff, but thirty minutes of grape-shot fired into the packed square and barracks sufficed to exterminate the Janissaries and to destroy a centuries' old institution, once the terror of Europe, lately the terror of the Sultans and their law-abiding subjects. A proclamation, issued on 17 June, abolished the corps of Janissaries, and set up in their place a new army, to be known as the *Asakir-i Mansure-i Muhammediye*, the victorious Muhammedan soldiers. Ağa Hüseyin Paşa—himself a former Aga of the Janissaries— commanded the new force. A month later, on the pretext that they had stirred up revolts of protest against the destruction of the Janissaries, the Sultan dissolved the dervish brotherhood of the Bektaşis, for centuries intimately associated with the corps of Janissaries. With the support of the Chief Mufti and the chief ulema, he outlawed the brotherhood, destroyed its convents, publicly executed three of its leaders, and exiled the rest.[8]

The massacre of the Janissaries, known to the reformers as the *Vak'a-i Hayriye*—the Auspicious Incident—completed the preparatory work which the Sultan had already begun with his campaigns to end provincial autonomy. The valley-lords and notables in the provinces, the Janissaries and dervishes in the capital, all those who restricted the arbitrary power of the Sultan, had been

[8] Rasim, iv. 1830 ff.

crushed and destroyed. Now no group remained that could challenge the Sultan's will from entrenched positions of ancient and accepted privilege; no armed force survived, other than the Sultan's own new-style soldiery—equipped with guns and gunners who no longer needed to fear the anger of the city populace. Even the ulema, the guardians of the Holy Law, with neither the Janissaries nor the crowd to appeal to, were gravely weakened in their task of moderating the despotism of the Sultan. The way was now clear to that radical reorganization for which Mahmud had been waiting for so many years.

Between the destruction of the Janissaries in 1826 and his death in 1839, Mahmud II embarked on a great programme of reforms; in them he laid down the main lines along which later Turkish reformers, in the nineteenth and to some extent even in the twentieth century, were to follow. In each field of reform, the creation of a new order was preceded by the destruction of an old one—and all these preliminary demolitions were made possible by the destruction of the Janissary corps, the central repository of military power of the traditional order.

Military Reforms

With the Janissaries safely out of the way, Mahmud was able to proceed more rapidly with his plans for a new-style army, the creation of which had been the prime objective of his less fortunate predecessors. In place of the Aga of the Janissaries he created a new office, that of Serasker. The title was an old one, given to army commanders in former times. As used by Mahmud, it came to connote an officer who combined the functions of commander-in-chief and Minister of War, with special responsibility for the new-style army. In addition, he inherited from the Aga of the Janissaries the responsibility for public security, police duties, fire-fighting, and the like, in the capital. In a period of growing centralization and enforced change, the police function came to be of increasing importance, and the maintenance and extension of the police system one of the chief duties of the Serasker. Husrev Paşa, who held office as Serasker at various times between 1827 and 1837, was particularly successful in this part of his work. The police were taken from the jurisdiction of the Serasker and placed under a separate *Zabtiye Müşiriyeti* in 1845.[9]

[9] B. Lewis, 'Bāb-i Ser'askerî' and 'Dabtiyya' in *EI²*.

In the summer of 1826 a code of regulations for the new-style army was prepared. It provided for a force of 12,000 men, to be stationed in Istanbul, and divided into eight sections. Orders were also to be issued for the recruitment of new-style troops in the provinces. The soldiers were to serve for twelve years.[10]

The restoration of peace, with the signing of the treaty of Adrianople in 1829, gave the Sultan leisure to take up more actively the training and equipment of his new troops, for whom there were still many tasks within the Empire. The most important of these was the impending reckoning with Muhammad Ali, the refractory Pasha of Egypt, whose strikingly successful efforts at Westernizing his army and navy had provided the spur that drove Mahmud and his ministers forward in the same direction. In the competition for the support and goodwill of the West, it was necessary to show that the Sultan could be as progressive and as liberal as his vassal. In the battle for Syria, it was necessary to put in the field forces capable of meeting the modern army of the Pasha of Egypt.

The Egyptian forces had acquitted themselves well in the campaign against the Greek insurgents, and provided a model of successful reform. It was to Cairo, therefore, that, in 1826, the Sultan sent his first appeal for help—a request to the Pasha of Egypt for twelve expert instructors.[11] It was, needless to say, refused with somewhat specious excuses, and the Sultan, like the Pasha before him, had to look to Europe for help. France, hitherto the source of military guidance and instructors, was compromised, first by her sympathy for the Greek insurgents, and later by her support for Muhammad Ali. The Sultan therefore looked elsewhere. Britain was tarred with the brush of philhellenism, and an offer from Palmerston in 1834 to send officers to train the Turkish army was turned down. In the following year some further attempts were made to arrange for British assistance to the Turkish forces. Some Turkish cadets were accepted at Woolwich, and three officers went to Istanbul to assist and advise in the reorganization of the army. They accomplished little, and a naval mission sent in 1838 fared no better. One of the reasons for their failure was no doubt the growth of Russian influence in Istanbul, which worked against any British connexion with the Turkish armed forces. Another was the resentment of the officers at the

---

[10] Ubicini, letter 19. [11] Lûtfi, i. 196.

slighting way in which they were received, and the quasi-menial status offered to them.[12]

The same attitude was noted by another European officer, who spent four years in Turkey. The Prussian Lieutenant, later Field-Marshal Helmuth von Moltke, reached Istanbul towards the end of 1835, on a private visit. While there he made a deep impression on the Sultan, who engaged his services as adviser in the training of his new army. The Sultan now turned to Prussia and Austria with requests that they send officers to Turkey and accept Turks in their military academies. Five Prussian officers were sent, and a few Turkish cadets accepted in Vienna. Though this was much less than had been asked for, it was an important beginning, and initiated a strong German influence and tradition in the Turkish army which later became very strong and lasted until the first World War.[13]

Moltke set to work on the inspection of the defences of the Empire and the preparation of plans for military reorganization. His letters show that he was far from satisfied with the results of his work. This lack of success he attributes in part to the failings of Mahmud II, whom he compares very unfavourably with Peter the Great of Russia; still more to the invincible contempt of the Turks for the European advisers:

. . . in Turkey even the least gift becomes suspect, as soon as it comes from the hand of a Christian . . . in Russia the foreigners may have been hated; in Turkey they are despised. A Turk will concede without hesitation that the Europeans are superior to his nation in science, skill, wealth, daring and strength, without its ever occurring to him that a Frank might therefore put himself on a par with a Muslim . . .

Few Europeans, he writes, had entered Turkey in as favourable circumstances as he and his colleagues. They had been received with the greatest solicitude by the first dignitaries of the Empire, who came to greet them, handed them pipes, and gave them seats of honour by their sides. But respect for them decreased lower in the social scale. 'The Colonels gave us precedence, the officers

---

[12] Bailey, pp. 146 ff. On British policies towards the Ottoman reform see further F. S. Rodkey, 'Palmerston and the Regeneration of Turkey 1830–41', *J. Mod. Hist.*, i (1929), 570–93, ii (1930), 193–225, and H. Temperley, 'British Policy towards Parliamentary Rule and Constitutionalism in Turkey (1830–1914)', *Camb. Hist. J.*, iv (1932–4), 156–191.

[13] Rosen, i. 234–5; Sax, p. 265. On the translation into Turkish of a Prussian military manual about this time see Ata, iii. 126 ff.

were still tolerably polite, but the ordinary man would not present arms to us, and the women and children from time to time followed us with curses. The soldier obeyed but did not salute.' Even the Turkish command did not dare to demand of the Turkish soldier that he show respect to a Gâvur.[14]

Education [15]

One of the most serious defects of the new army was its lack of officers. Soldiers could be found and drafted easily enough, and the teaching of new drill and new weapons did not offer insuperable difficulties. The production of a competent officer corps was, however, another matter. There were a few Western renegades and adventurers in the artillery and engineers, who provided a nucleus of technically trained officers. Otherwise all branches of the new army were desperately short of competent officers.

It was partly to fill this need, partly to meet the parallel need for competent civil servants, that Mahmud devoted increasing attention to education. Without adequate cadres of men able and willing first to receive and then to impart instruction, the whole edifice of reform was doomed to collapse.

Two schools were already in existence—the naval and military engineering schools established in 1773 and 1793 respectively. These had gone through some difficult days, but were now revived and functioning again. In 1827, in the teeth of strong opposition, the Sultan took the revolutionary step of sending four students to Paris; others followed later.[16] This step, like so many of Mahmud's other reforms, followed a precedent set by Muhammad Ali, who had sent a large batch of students to Paris in 1826, and individuals in previous years. Mahmud began with a batch of military and naval cadets, for whom places were found in various European capitals. They were the first outriders of a great procession of Turkish students to Europe, who on their return played a role of immense importance in the transformation of their country.

[14] Moltke, pp. 412–13.

[15] See Berkes, *The Development of Secularism* (1964), pp. 99 ff. Turkish histories of education in this period will be found in Mahmud Cevad, *Maarif-i Umumiye Nezareti Tarihçe-i Teşkilât ve Icraatı* (1339 A.H.) (an official history of the Ministry of Education with many documents); Ergin, *Maarif*, ii. For a contemporary Western impression see Ubicini, letter 9.

[16] Karal, *Tar. Os*, v. 166. A picture of the first group of students, taken in Paris in 1830, is reproduced in *Tanzimat*, facing p. 737.

In the same year, 1827, a medical school was opened in Istanbul —this time less than a month after the opening of Muhammad Ali's medical school at the Abu Zaʻbal hospital in Cairo. Its purpose was to train doctors for the new army. Physicians for the civil population were still trained at more traditional establishments, such as the medical division of the Süleymaniye *Medrese*, where the syllabus was still based substantially on the writings of Galen and Avicenna. The medical school included a preparatory section, giving an approximation to a secular primary and secondary education—the first in Turkey. The school was several times reorganized, the most notable reorganization being that of 1838, when it was transferred to Galatasaray, the seat of the old palace school of pages and a famous educational centre dating back to the reign of Bayezid II (1481–1512). The teaching was given partly in Turkish, partly in French, and the instructors included several brought from Europe.

In 1831–4 two further schools were opened, both directly military in purpose. One was the Imperial Music School (*Muzika-i Humayun Mektebi*), the function of which was to provide the new army with drummers and trumpeters to match its tunics and breeches. One of the instructors was Donizetti Paşa—a brother of the composer. More important was the School of Military Sciences (*Mekteb-i Ulum-i Harbiye*). This school, which was planned for some years before its inauguration in 1834, was intended to serve as the St. Cyr of the Ottoman army, and was modelled as closely as circumstances permitted on its French original. Here too foreigners played a dominant role in the teaching, and the mastery of a foreign language, usually French, was the first need and prerequisite of all studies. As in the medical school, there was a preparatory division for children.

So far Mahmud's educational measures had been mainly concerned with the army. In 1838, however, he took up the question of primary and secondary education for civilian purposes, and planned the creation of what he named *rüşdiye* schools— from *rüşd*, adolescence. Little progress was made during Mahmud's lifetime, but two new grammar schools were set up, at the Sultan Ahmed and Süleymaniye mosques, called *Mekteb-i Maarif-i Adliye*[17] and *Mekteb-i Ulum-i Edebiye*. Their syllabus was predominantly traditional, but included provision for teaching

17 Adliye refers to the Sultan's sobriquet Adlî, and has not yet acquired its later

French and modern subjects. Their purpose was to train government officials and translators, and, as with the military schools, their pupils were supported out of public or endowment funds. Their graduates include several leading figures of the next generation.

In an address to the students of the medical school at the inauguration of the new building in 1838, the Sultan remarked:

> You will study scientific medicine in French . . . my purpose in having you taught French is not to educate you in the French language; it is to teach you scientific medicine and little by little to take it into our language . . . work to acquire a knowledge of medicine from your teachers, and strive gradually to take it into Turkish and give it currency in our language. . . .[18]

With these words the Sultan had touched on a central problem of the educational and indeed of the entire reform project—the language barrier. The number of Muslim Turks with an adequate knowledge of a European language was still fantastically small. Some had been trained during the reign of Selim III, but most of them had perished during the Hippodrome massacre of 1807. Instructors, advisers, even technical officers in the army were Europeans, and their instruction, advice, and commands had to pass through the prism of translation and interpretation. For a while recourse was had to native Christian interpreters, but these had many drawbacks. The instruction of a Frankish teacher, repellent enough in itself, did not gain by the mediation of an Armenian or Greek interpreter, whose appearance and accent would, for Turkish hearers, add to its alien grotesqueness a ridiculous familiarity.

There was thus an urgent need for Muslims with a knowledge of languages—to learn and to teach the sciences of the West, to translate textbooks into Turkish, and, as part of this task, to create in the Turkish language the technical and scientific vocabulary needed to describe the many new objects and concepts imported from the West.

In these tasks two men made a contribution of outstanding importance. The first was Ataullah Mehmed, known as Şanizade

connotation of legal. Ihsan Sungu, 'Mekteb-i Maarif i Adliyenin Tesisi', *Tar. Ves.*, i (1941), 212–25; Cevad, pp. 25–26; Ergin, *Maarif*, pp. 324 ff.; Mardin, *Genesis*, pp. 207–8, 337–8. On the military school see D. A. Rustow, 'Harbiye', in *EI*[2].

[18] Quoted by Suheyl Ünver in *Tanzimat*, pp. 940–1.

(1769–1826).[19] By education one of the ulema, he was a man of encyclopaedic knowledge, and in 1819 was appointed Imperial Historiographer. He was dismissed and exiled in 1826, after the suppression of the Janissaries, because of his connexion with the Bektaşi fraternity. He was, however, no reactionary. He seems to have learnt several European languages, and made a study of European medicine and other sciences. His major work was a Turkish translation, probably made from an Italian version, of an Austrian medical textbook. It was accompanied by an explanatory treatise by Şanizade on physiology and anatomy, and by another translation of an Austrian work on vaccination. Şanizade's medical textbook marks the end of traditional and the beginning of modern medicine in Turkey; in it he created, for the first time, a modern medical vocabulary in the Turkish language, which remained in use until the linguistic reform of recent years.

The other major pioneer of modern science and terminology was Hoca Ishak Efendi (died 1834), a Balkan convert to Islam.[20] A native of Arta, near Yannina, and a Jew by birth, he is said to have known French, Latin, Greek, and Hebrew as well as Turkish, Persian, and Arabic. By 1815 he was a teacher at the school of mathematics, and during the following years became the chief instructor and guiding spirit of that institution. His most important work was a four-volume compendium of the mathematical and physical sciences, which brought to the Turkish student, for the first time, some knowledge of European mathematics, physics, and mechanics. Like Şanizade, he had to create new terms to express new concepts, and ranks with him as the creator of most of the scientific terminology in use in Turkey until recent times. Besides this work, Hoca Ishak produced a number of others, chiefly translations, on military science and engineering. He died in Suez in 1834, on his way back from a trip to Arabia where he had combined a pilgrimage to Mecca with the restoration of some installations in Medina.

[19] On Şanizade see Babinger, *Geschichtsschreiber*, pp. 346–7; Adnan, *Ilim*, pp. 192–5.

[20] On Ishak Efendi see Adnan, *Ilim*, pp. 196–7; Esad, *Mirât-i Mühendishane*, pp. 34–42; Lûtfi, iii. 167; M. Franco, *Essai sur l'histoire des Israélites de l'Empire ottoman* (1897), pp. 141–2; Faik Reşit Unat, 'Başhoca Ishak Efendi', *Bell.*, no. 109 (1964), 89–115. For a rather unfavourable contemporary impression of Ishak and his school see [J. E. de Kay], *Sketches of Turkey in 1831 and 1832, by an American* (1833), pp. 138 ff. (later referred to as *Sketches*). Many of Ishak Efendi's neologisms are still in use in the Arab countries at the present time.

Reforms in Government and Administration: the Language Question

A knowledge of Western languages was also needed in the conduct of public affairs, and especially in foreign relations. In the past, Ottoman sovereigns and ministers had felt no need to demean themselves by learning the barbarous idioms of Europe. Such contact as was indispensable was maintained through the European embassies in Istanbui, and conversations were held through the medium of dragomans, who were usually local Christians. Every Embassy employed one, and the Ottoman government itself maintained a functionary known as the Dragoman of the Sublime Porte or of the Imperial Council, who conducted both its conversations and its correspondence. This post, which lasted for over three centuries, was usually held by Christians, and in the course of the eighteenth century had become the preserve of a small group of patrician Greek families of the Phanar district of Istanbul.

It will be obvious that the holder of the post was in a position to exercise considerable influence on the foreign policy of the Empire. Nevertheless, the Greek monopoly was not challenged until 1821, when the Greek revolt raised obvious and serious difficulties. In that year the last Greek dragoman, Stavraki Aristarchi, was dismissed and executed, and the decision taken to entrust the post to a Muslim.[21]

It was not easy to find one. Selim's young men, few enough to start with, had for the most part perished or lost their proficiency and there were few others. As late as 1844, when Charles White was in Istanbul, he was able to name only a bare dozen of educated Turks with a competent knowledge of a Western language and some reading in Western books.[22]

After two or three weeks, says Şanizade, when papers in Greek or 'Frankish' were accumulating at the Sublime Porte, the Sultan transferred Yahya Efendi, a teacher at the school of mathematics, to the office of dragoman, first with a temporary and then with a permanent appointment. Şanizade rightly insists on the importance of this nomination, which placed this crucial post in safe, Muslim hands, and freed the professional use of foreign languages from the stigma of a gâvur trade.[23]

[21] Şanizade, iv. 20; Cevdet, *Tarih*, xi. 166.   [22] White, ii. 176.
[23] Şanizade, iv. 33–35; Cevdet, xii. 43. cf. *Sketches*, pp. 281 ff.

Yahya Efendi was himself a convert to Islam, and is variously reported as having been of Bulgarian, Greek, or Jewish origin. He was the founder of a dynasty in what became a new and vital official career. His son, Ruhuddin Mehmed Efendi, also educated at the school of mathematics, went to Paris in 1834 as dragoman to the Embassy of Mustafa Reşid Paşa; his grandson, Ahmed Vefik Paşa, entered the same service, which led him to a distinguished career as diplomat, statesman, and scholar.[24]

On Yahya's death in 1823 or 1824, he was succeeded by his colleague Hoca Ishak, from the school, who held the office until 1830, when he returned to his teaching.[25] In 1833 the Sultan took the problem more seriously in hand, and created a 'translation chamber' (*tercüme odası*) at the Sublime Porte, which was later followed by similar 'chambers' in the Seraskerate and other departments of state.[26] In 1834–6 he reconstituted the permanent Embassies in London, Paris, and Vienna, which had been allowed to lapse after the deposition of Selim III; resident missions in other European capitals followed. The young diplomats and dragomans who staffed these missions thus had an opportunity to undergo in person the direct impact of the West. The significance of that impact may be gauged from the fact that almost every one of the reforming leaders and statesmen of the next half-century had served in these embassies. Of the three chief architects of the *Tanzimat*, Mustafa Reşid Paşa went to Paris in 1834 and then to London; Âli Paşa went to Vienna in 1836; Fuad Paşa went to London in 1840. Among their outstanding collaborators Sadık Rifat Paşa was minister in Vienna in 1837, Mehmed Şekib was there in 1841, and Ibrahim Sarim Paşa served in London in

[24] See the biographies of Ahmed Vefik Paşa in Mahmud Kemal Inal, *Osmanlı Devrinde Son Sadrıazamlar* (1940–53), pp. 651–738, and Pakalin, *Son Sadrâzamlar*, iii. 45–359; also the articles by H. Bowen, 'Aḥmad Wafīk Pasha' in *EI²*, and by Tanpınar in *IA*. Some interesting personal impressions of Vefik Paşa will be found in Nassau W. Senior's *Journal Kept in Turkey and Greece in the Autumn of 1857 and the beginning of 1858* (1859); in Mordtmann's *Stambul*, and other Western authors. On Yahya Efendi see Esad, *Mirât-i Mühendishane*, pp. 33–34.

[25] Cevdet, *Tarih*, xii. 91.

[26] Lûtfi, iv. 99. On the dragomans of the Sublime Porte, in general, see Kramers, 'Tardjumān', in *EI¹*; Gibb and Bowen, I/i. 123; Ergin, *Maarif*, pp. 613–17 (n.i.); Uzunçarşılı, *Merkez ve Bahriye*, pp. 71–76. For a biographical survey of the Greek Chief Dragomans from 1661 to 1821, see Epaminondas I. Stamatiadis, Βιογραφίαι των Ἑλλήνων Μεγάλων Διερμηνέων τοῦ Ὀθωμανικοῦ Κράτους (1865).

1834.[27] Even the sons of these first diplomats, profiting from the opportunities of a stay in Europe in childhood or youth, filled a disproportionate number of high offices of state in the next generation. An outstanding example was Ahmed Vefik Paşa, the grandson and the son of interpreters, who went with his father to Paris in 1834 and spent the three years from 11 to 14 as a pupil at the Lycée St. Louis. Later he was ambassador in Paris, twice Grand Vezir, and President of the Chamber of Deputies in the Ottoman parliament of 1877. His literary and scholarly achievements were of at least equal significance. His Turkish dictionary, the first serious attempt at one by a Turk, had an importance analogous to that of Dr. Johnson's Dictionary in England; his translations of *Télémaque*, *Gil Blas*, and above all his brilliant adaptation of a group of plays by Molière, opened new paths and revealed new vistas in Turkish literature.

Centralization

Mahmud II lavished special care on his foreign service and on the training of young diplomats and civil servants in the use of foreign languages. This did not, however, help him very much in the larger, more difficult, and more complicated task of reorganizing and modernizing the internal administration of the Empire. The first essential of this task, as Mahmud saw it, was the centralization of all power in his own hands, and the elimination of all intermediate authorities, both in the capital and in the provinces. All power deriving from inheritance, from tradition, from usage, or from popular or local assent was to be suppressed, and the sovereign power alone was to remain as the sole source of authority in the Empire. Mahmud therefore continued his campaign in Rumelia and Anatolia, and succeeded in establishing direct central control over most areas. Only against the Pasha of Egypt was he ultimately unsuccessful.

At the same time as he extended the powers of the central government, he tried to improve the apparatus through which they were exercised. An ancient complaint of Ottoman officialdom had been its insecurity of tenure and exposure to confiscation which, according to Koçu Bey and his fellow memorialists, had led to a decline in competence and a weakening of moral fibre.

[27] On the beginnings of Ottoman diplomacy see J. C. Hurewitz in *MEJ* (1961), 141–52; on Sadık Rifat Paşa see below, p. 132.

Mahmud tried to improve the status of his civil officials, and to raise their standards both of proficiency and of honesty. In June 1826, two weeks after the destruction of the Janissaries, he issued a *Hatt-i Şerif* abolishing the office of Confiscation and Escheat and renouncing some of the previous reversionary rights of the treasury to heirless property and to the property of persons banished or condemned to death. This measure was no doubt costly to the treasury: it did, however, give to civil servants and indeed to others a measure of security of life and property such as they had not known before, and greatly facilitated the transaction of both public and private business.[28] The civil servants—products of the new schools, often of humble origin—grew in numbers, and became an important new element in Ottoman society.

Census and Survey

Two further measures of centralization came in 1831. One was the first Ottoman census and survey in modern times. The immediate objectives were conscription and taxation—men for the new army, and money to support it. Careful preparations were made, and a committee appointed, which conducted a census of the male population of Anatolia and Rumelia. Females, who were not subject to conscription, were omitted. To forestall popular resentment and fear at this unprecedented step, members of the ulema were included among the census-takers.

At the same time as the census, a land survey was made, to register landholdings and thus make possible a more efficient and accurate system of tax assessment and collection.[29]

'The Abolition of Feudalism'

This prepared the way for the second major change of the year —the abolition of the *timars*. The *timar*, or military fief, had been the basis of the distinctively Ottoman type of feudalism since the very beginnings of the Empire. The *timar* was a grant of land, in return for which the sipahi, a feudal cavalryman, was bound to render military service in person and with as many men-at-arms as were required by the size and income of his fief. From the end

---

[28] Lûtfi, i. 59; White, i. 109; Ubicini, letter 19.

[29] Lûtfi, iii. 142; Karal, *Tarih*, v. 159. Karal has also written a monograph on the census of 1831, entitled *Osmanlı Imparatorluğunda ilk nüfus sayımı* (1943).

of the sixteenth century the system had begun to decay. In the army the paid regular troops grew in importance at the expense of the feudal cavalry; in the countryside more and more *timars* were converted into crown lands and appanages and then leased out (*iltizam* or *mukataa*) to tax-farmers with purely financial and no military obligations. The decline of the sipahis as a class, and the gradual replacement of *timar* by *iltizam* in the country, are among the most frequently cited causes of Ottoman decline.

At the beginning of the nineteenth century, however, neither the sipahi nor the *timar* had yet disappeared. Extensive lands, especially in Anatolia, were still classed and held as *timar*, and in the armed forces there were still many who were paid by fief instead of, or as well as, from the treasury. The cavalry was still predominantly feudal, as were also many of the local levies raised in the provinces. The distinction between the different kinds of troops was not rigid, and it was not infrequent for Janissaries and other regulars to receive *timars*.

The policy of converting *timar* into domain and then leasing it as *iltizam* was adopted in a more rigorous form by Selim III, who needed ready money for his New Army and was not averse to weakening the basis of the old one. As Asım said:

Since the ancient revenues of the exalted Dynasty were not adequate to its present expenditure, and since it was a present necessity to organize an adequate income to cover the cost of the New Army, *timars* in the *eyalet* of Anatolia were to be taken over by the treasury. Though a group of ignorant people considered this to be manifest tyranny, it is obvious to people of sound judgement . . . that the martyred Sultan had acted in a way very far from tyranny.[30]

Indeed, Asım implies, considering the cowardly and miserable performance of the sipahis in the war against Russia, it was generous of the Sultan merely to divert the revenues of their *timars* to the use of the New Army, and to leave them to enjoy life and repose in their countries.

Mahmud's revocation of all remaining *timars* in 1831 was thus a logical continuation of the policies of his predecessors. The military aspect of the change was of secondary importance. The old-style cavalry had been dissolved at the same time as the Janissaries, the new army was growing, and the dissolution of the last

---

[30] Asım, i. 40–41; cf. Cevdet, *Tarih*, v. 289–90 and vi. 57 ff.

of the sipahis made no great difference in the military forces of the Empire. Those of the sipahis whose services were worth retaining were formed into four squadrons of cavalry, which provided the nucleus of a new regular cavalry arm. The remaining sipahis were given pensions.

What was more important was the liquidation of the last vestiges of feudalism. Even at this stage, the extent of *timar* land must have been fairly considerable, for the amount assigned for pensions came to 120,000 purses, or 60 million piastres (at that time about £750,000). The cost of maintaining the New Army, 12,000 men strong, was estimated in 1827 at 34,000 purses. There are reported to have been about 1,500 *timars* in Anatolia, and under 1,000 in Rumelia. These now became crown domains and were mostly leased out to tax-farmers. From the point of view of the revenue, the seizure of the *timars* seems to have been disappointing; by it, however, the Sultan tightened his hold on the provinces, and carried his policy of centralization an important step forward.[31]

Vakf[32]

The pensioning off of the sipahis and the seizure of the *timars* was a comparatively easy matter; it was an obvious corollary to the destruction of the Janissaries, and was, in a sense, the culmination of a process that had been going on for a long time. Far more dangerous and controversial was the subordination to the Sultan's control of another category of lands and estates— the *evkaf*, or pious foundations.

The *vakf* was an old Islamic institution,[33] well established in the Ottoman Empire. Originally it was a dedication of land or other revenue-producing property to pious purposes. In time the practice grew up of establishing family *evkaf*, for the benefit of

---

[31] On the *timar* system, see Deny, 'Tīmār', in *EI*[1]. On the abolition of the fiefs see Inalcık's study, 'Tanzimat Nedir', pp. 244 ff., and sources cited there; also Bailey, pp. 36–37.

[32] On the *vakf* reform, see Lûtfi, i. 205; Ubicini, letter 12; White, i. 236; Köprülü, 'Vakıf müessesesinin hukukî mâhiyeti ve tarihî tekâmülü', *Vak. Derg.*, ii. 23 ff. of Turkish text, pp. 31 ff. of translation; Temperley, pp. 31 and 405. Reference may also be made to the official history of the Ministry of Vakf, *Evkâf-i Humâyûn Nezaretinin Tarihçe-i Teşkilâtı* (1335). In this too Mahmud seems to have been following an example set by Muhammad Ali in Egypt, in 1812.

[33] Turkish *vakf* or *vakıf* (plural *evkâf* or, in the new Turkish, *vakıflar*), from Arabic *waqf* (plural *awqâf*). On the institution in general see *EI*[1] ('Wakf', by W. Heffening).

the founder's family and descendants, as a safeguard against the general insecurity of property rights. Except by a Sultan, *vakf* could only be made out of *mülk*, or freehold property, and not out of land held as fief, tax-farm, appanage, and the like. It was therefore comparatively rare in agricultural areas, and most frequent in and around the cities. In Istanbul and other cities most *mülk* had in the course of time become *vakf*, and almost all the building sites, fruit and vegetable gardens, orchards and vineyards in the city and its immediate environs had become, in fact or in name, inalienable and irrevocable pious endowments. The effective control and disposition of these *evkaf* and their revenues was usually in the hands of administrators and collectors (*mütevelli* and *cabi*), who belonged to, or were appointed by, members of the class of ulema. The Chief Mufti and other dignitaries, both religious and lay, had their own groups of *evkaf* under their control, each with his own arrangements for supervision. The most important were directly or indirectly under the control of the Muftis and Kadis, and thus constituted a major source of economic power for the religious institution.

In 1826, with the Janissaries out of the way, Mahmud was able to strike at this power. Ostensibly with the intention of ending the existing anarchy in *evkaf* administration and bringing them all under a single jurisdiction, he created a new Directorate (later Ministry) of *Evkaf*, into which the existing agencies of supervision were incorporated. But, in the words of the historian Mustafa Nuri Paşa, himself for a while a Minister of *Evkaf*, 'since some of the ministers were of tyrannical disposition and some of them were ignorant of important matters of law, the *vakf* administration brimmed over with abuses'.[34] Mahmud's aim was nothing less than to centralize the collection and expenditure of *Evkaf* revenues in his own hands, receiving them from the collectors and administrators and paying out what was necessary for the upkeep of religious buildings, the salaries of religious personnel, and other pious purposes. Mustafa Nuri's description of Mahmud II's *vakf* policy amounts to a charge of malversation, and concludes that the Ministry of *Evkaf*, 'which should have been the protector of the *evkof*, became their destroyer'.[35] Mahmud, it would seem, was not only the Peter the Great but also the Henry VIII of Turkey. From a different point of view, Charles

[34] Nuri, *Netaic*, iv. 100.   [35] Ibid. p. 101.

White was of the same opinion, at least as regards the Sultan's intentions:

Sultan Mahmoud II . . . seriously contemplated carrying this plan into effect, and would probably have done so had his life been spared. The government in this case would have paid the salaries of all sheikhs, priests, and persons attached to the sacred edifices, together with all repairs and expenses of their dependent institutions, and would have converted the surplus to state purposes. Various plans were suggested to Sultan Mahmoud's predecessors; but during the existence of the Janissaries, no one dared to interfere with the institutions, whence the oolema, intimately connected with the Janissaries, derived invariable benefit.[36]

Mahmud's attempt to divert *evkâf* revenues was not entirely successful. He did, however, initiate a process which gravely weakened the power of the ulema to oppose him. Under his successors, the diversion of *evkâf* revenues to state purposes was standard practice, so much so that many mosques and other genuinely religious endowments were starved of funds for their upkeep.

Communications

Another group of reforms that helped the Sultan in his policy of centralization was that concerned with the improvement of communications. In 1831 the first issue appeared of the *Takvim-i Vekayi*, the Ottoman official gazette.[37] This was not the first newspaper in Turkey. Between 1796 and 1798 the French Embassy in Constantinople had published a newspaper in French for distribution to the French colony and such others as knew the French language. In the 1820's some further French newspapers appeared, this time in Izmir. The most important of them was

---

[36] White, i. 236.

[37] On the development of the press see White, ii. 218 ff.; Ubicini, letter 11; Temperley, pp. 244–5; Slade, i. 273 ff.; Mahmud Kemal in *TOEM*, no. 96–97 (on the contributors to the *Ceride-i Havadis*), and the histories of the Turkish press by Ahmed Emin [Yalman], *The Development of Modern Turkey as Measured by its Press* (1914); Gerçek, *Türk Gazeteciliği, 1831–1931* (1931); Server R. Iskit, *Türkiyede Matbuat Rejimleri* (1939) 'Djarīda' in *EI²*; and Vedad Günyol in *IA*, vii. 367 ff. On the French papers: L. Lagarde, 'Note sur les journaux français de Constantinople', *J. As.* (1948), pp. 271–6 and 'Note sur les journaux français de Smyrne à l'époque de Mahmoud II', ibid. (1950), pp. 103–44.

Le Spectateur oriental. The real spur, however, was the publication in Egypt in 1828, by Muhammad Ali, of the *Waḳā'i'Miṣriyya*, the Egyptian gazette—the first indigenous newspaper published in the Middle East.

What the Pasha could do, the Sultan could do better, if later. In 1831 the first issue appeared of the *Moniteur ottoman*, in the French language, under the editorship of a Frenchman called **Alexandre Blacque**, the former editor of *Le Spectateur oriental*. A Turkish version, called *Takvim-i Vekayi*, followed a few months later. It was the first newspaper in the Turkish language, and is well described by Charles White: 'The contents of this journal were at first strictly limited to a reproduction of official appointments, extracts of judicial trials, and pompous descriptions of the Sultan's progress on state occasions.'[38] It remained the only newspaper in Turkish until 1840, when an Englishman called William Churchill published the first non-official Turkish newspaper, the *Ceride-i Havadis*. The second did not appear until 1860.

The *Takvim-i Vekayi* was required reading for public officials. Its efficacy as a means of making the Sultan's policies and purposes better known to his servants was greatly increased by the inauguration of a postal system in 1834. The first post road, from Üsküdar to Izmit, was formally opened by the Sultan, riding in a phaeton, followed by his suite in post-carts. They travelled as far as Kartal, where the Sultan received a petition in a local dispute arising out of the conversion of a Christian girl to Islam. A second postal route was opened from Istanbul to Edirne, and later others linked the main centres of the Empire. The purpose of the new postal system is indicated in the *Hatt-i Humayun* establishing it:

Since it is obligatory to secure the safety and procure the revenues of my Imperial realm, and since disorder has arisen and appeared in the matter of correspondence, on account of its not being known from whom and to whom the letters that are sent from my Gate of Felicity to the country and that come from the country to my Gate of Felicity come and go; therefore, in order to set this matter aright, it has occurred to my Imperial mind to deal with it in this way: as is the practice in other countries, so also in my lofty Empire, a responsible official being appointed to supervise the matter, and a suitable place assigned to it, men shall be established by him at appropriate places in

[38] White, ii. 218 ff.

Anatolia and Rumelia, so that henceforth no person shall despatch letters of his own accord, but both the people of Islam and the Raya and Frankish communities shall bring the letters and objects which they wish to send to the superintendent; these being registered in the book, shall be sent, &c., &c.[39]

There were other improvements in communications besides the post. New roads were built, and the introduction of a quarantine system facilitated movement between Turkey and Europe, which had previously been subject to vexatious delays. With the coming of the telegraph in 1855 and the first railways in 1866, the administrative centralization initiated by Mahmud was enormously strengthened.

Committees and Ministries

At the same time as he extended and strengthened the control of the central government over the provinces, the Sultan made a number of significant changes in the structure and organization of the central government staff. One purpose of these was to give to the apparatus and personnel of Ottoman government the nomenclature and outward appearance of their European equivalents, and thereby to impress European observers with the modernity and progressiveness of Turkey, and perhaps also to win for Turkey something of the elusive secret of Western power and efficiency. The change had very little success in either respect. European observers both contemporary and subsequent were contemptuous of a change that affected only externals and appearances, leaving the realities as they were before.

Clearly, to call the Grand Vezir and his colleagues ministers, dress them in frock-coats, provide them with offices, desks, and newly frock-coated staffs, did not change them overnight into the administration of a modern state. Mahmud's administrative reforms were, however, by no means ineffective—though their effects were understood by but few contemporaries, either Turkish or Western.

The most important was the breakdown of old traditions, of established rights and privileges, of institutions with powers and prestige deriving from the past instead of from the Sultan, and their replacement by a new set of institutions which, since they

[39] Karal, *Tarih*, v. 160–1; Lûtfi, iv. 162 ff. On ports and other communications see further Bailey, p. 136; Ubicini, letter 18.

had neither inherited dignity nor acquired esteem, depended entirely on the sovereign power.

The first changes came immediately after the destruction of the Janissaries, which here too cleared the way for the extension of the Sultan's control. Of the two chief limiting authorities in the capital, the old army was crushed and the ulema cowed. The Sultan hastened to make use of his opportunity. The Serasker and his staff at the Seraskerate became the nucleus of the civilian Ministry of War which, until the Young Turk Revolution, was able to maintain the control of the central government over the armed forces and prevent the recurrence of anything like the constant Janissary uprisings that had terrorized the Sultans of the preceding period.[40]

The former residence of the Aga of the Janissaries, near the Süleymaniye mosque, was turned over to the Chief Mufti, who thus for the first time acquired an office and department. Until 1826 the Chief Muftis had held courts and issued rulings from their own residences. Their revenues, their employees, their establishments had been entirely independent of the palace, subject only to the final power of dismissal. The creation of an office and department of the Chief Mufti (known as *Bab-i Meşihat* or *Fetvahane*) was the first step towards the bureaucratization of the ulema, which undermined their popular and effective power and gravely weakened their ability—and at times even their desire—to resist change. Another, of no less importance, was the subjection to government control of the *evkaf*.

Deprived of both their financial and their administrative autonomy, the ulema were weakened as against the central power, and were unable to resist successive diminutions of their competence, authority, and status. The appointment of teachers and control of schools and colleges was later transferred to a Ministry of Education; the appointment of judges and the administration of the law to a Ministry of Justice; and in time even the drafting of *fetvas* was entrusted to a committee of legal specialists in the Chief Mufti's office under the Fetva Emini, the commissioner of *fetvas*. The Chief Mufti himself became a government office-holder, with some consultative and advisory functions, and with only such effective influence as his own personal character could win for him.

[40] B. Lewis, 'Bāb-i Ser'askerī', in *EI²*. See also above, p. 80.

Many of the higher ulema, through conviction, interest or fear, had already acquiesced in the westernizing reforms. With the final loss of their independence, the gulf between them and the lower ulema—usually fanatical opponents of change—became very wide.[41]

The Sultan's first new department of state—war, *evkaf*, and the Mufti's office—were thus not so much measures of modernization as attempts to consolidate the gains won from the forces of the old order by the destruction of the Janissaries, and to render the army and the ulema incapable of reviving their ancient authority against the Sultan. A few years later Mahmud felt strong enough to tackle the Sublime Porte itself—the office of the Grand Vezir, which for nearly two centuries had been the real seat of Ottoman Government. In 1835 two departments, those of the Kâhya and of the Reis Efendi, were constituted as separate ministries—though remaining in the same building and performing the same duties—and named Ministries of Civil and Foreign Affairs respectively. Two years later the old office of the Defterdar was renamed Ministry of Finance, and the Defterdar himself joined the Grand Vezir and the Reis Efendi as a minister. The Ministry of Civil Affairs was renamed Ministry of the Interior in 1837, and in the following year the title of Grand Vezir was abolished and the incumbent was named Prime Minister. Later the title of Grand Vezir was restored.[42]

A Grand Vezir turned Prime Minister, with a couple of other new holders of ministerial titles, do not yet make cabinet government. Mahmud was, however, preparing the way for a system of government based on malleable and interchangeable groups instead of powerful and entrenched individuals. Some consultative committees had already existed in earlier times. Mahmud now created a Privy Council or Council of Ministers (*Meclis-i Hass* and *Meclis-i Vükelâ*) presided over by the Prime Minister. As the number of ministers increased under his successors, this body gained in importance. Of more immediate significance were two other bodies, created in 1836 and 1838: the Council for Military

[41] On the attitudes of the ulema to the reform, see U. Heyd, 'The Ottoman 'Ulemā and Westernization in the time of Selim III and Mahmud II', *Scripta Hierosolymitana*, ix (1961), 63–96. See also B. Lewis, 'Bāb-i Mashīkhat', in *EI²* and above, pp. 92–93.

[42] On the new ministries in general see Karal, *Tarih*, vi. 123 ff.; Şeref, *Tarih-i Devlet-i Osmaniye*, ii. 464 ff. and Lûtfi, iii. 145. See further B. Lewis, 'Başvekil' and 'Daftardār' in *EI²*.

Affairs (*Meclis-i Dar-i Şura-yi Askeri*) and the High Council for Judicial Ordinances (*Meclis-i Vâlâ-i Ahkâm-i Adliye*). These were small, executive groups, each consisting of a chairman, five members, and one or two secretaries. They were to play an important role in planning and executing the reforms of the immediately following period. In 1838 Mahmud also established committees for agriculture, trade, industry, and public works.[43]

While these changes in nomenclature brought little or no immediate change in the conduct of affairs, they did mark the first step towards the break-up of old, well-entrenched institutions and the renewal of the old conflict between the palace and the Porte. The changes became more of a reality when the old officials were replaced by a new generation of civil servants different in education, outlook, and social background from their predecessors. Their professional skill and solidarity on the one hand, and the growing complexity of government on the other, helped to curb the growth of palace rule, and to bring the centre of power back to the Pashas and functionaries at the Sublime Porte.

Social and Cultural Change

The medieval Egyptian chronicles tell us that after the great Mongol conquests of the thirteenth century, even the Muslim Sultans and Emirs of Egypt began to wear their hair long in the Mongol style. But in 1315 the Sultan decided to return to the Muslim practice of shaving his head. In the words of Maqrīzī (d. 1442): 'He went to the bath and shaved his whole head, and there did not remain one of the Emirs and Mamluks that failed to do likewise; and from that time the soldiers ceased to wear their hair long, and so it has continued until today.'[44]

From the rise of Islam until the coming of the European, the Mongol was the only infidel invader to establish an empire in the heartlands of Islam—and Mongol methods of warfare, Mongol laws and customs as well as Mongol styles of dress were for a while imitated and adopted even in such lands as Egypt, which remained beyond the reach of the Mongol sword.

[43] Ata, iii. 121 ff., 137 ff., 294 ff.; Lûtfi, v. 70, 106, 128, &c.; Karal, *Tarih*, vi. 116 ff.

[44] *Sulūk*, II/1 (Cairo, 1941), p. 148; L. A. Mayer, *Mamluk Costume* (1952), pp. 17–18; cf. Maqrīzī, *Khitat*, ii (Bulaq, 1270 A.H.), pp. 216–17 on the introduction of Mongol-style dress by Qalawun in the thirteenth century (D. S. Rice, *Le Baptistère de St. Louis* (1951), p. 13).

After the decline of the Mongol power, these influences de-creased and eventually disappeared, and the older Muslim customs were once again supreme. It is a measure of the impact of European power and prestige on Selim III and Mahmud II that they should once again have attempted to breach the defences of sartorial conservatism and clothe their troops in European-style uniforms—in a costume to which was attached the aura of success and victory.

In the code of regulations issued in 1826 for the new-style army, it was laid down that their uniforms were to consist of European-style tunics and trousers. Twenty years previously an attempt to put the auxiliary troops into Frankish dress had launched the mutiny of 1807 and led directly to the deposition of Selim III. This time the reform was accepted, though not without rumbles of opposition, and the troops were issued with 'a *şubara*, a drill-coat, a short tunic and vest of broadcloth, tight-fitting serge breeches, and frontier-boots'.[45]

The question of Frankish uniforms raised larger issues than could be settled in the quartermaster's stores. Since early times, dress and above all head-gear were the means by which a man indicated his religious allegiance and his social status. Apart from a ban on silk, the Muslim law does not actually prohibit any kind of garment, but there are countless traditions urging the Muslims to distinguish themselves, even in appearance, from the infidels and to avoid imitating their habits in dress as well as in all else. 'God and the angels give their blessing at the Friday prayer to those who wear the turban.' 'Two prostrations with the turban outweigh seventy without the turban.' 'The turban is the barrier separating belief and unbelief.' 'Distinguish yourselves from the idolators; let your beards grow and trim your moustaches.' 'He who imitates a people, becomes one of them.'[46]

[45] Lûtfi, i. 191–3.

[46] Cited in M. Canard, 'Coiffure européenne et Islam', *A. l'Inst. d'Ét. or.* (Algiers), viii. (1949–50), 200 ff. Slade's comments on some aspects of the reform in dress, written from quite another point of view, are worth citing: 'In no one thing did Sultan Mahmoud make a greater mistake, than in changing the mode of mounting the Turkish cavalry, which before had perfect seats, with perfect command over their horses, and only required a little order to transform the best irregular horse in the world into the best regular horse. But Mahmoud, in all his changes, took the mask for the man, the rind for the fruit.—European cavalry rode flat saddles with long stirrups; therefore he thought it necessary that his cavalry should be the same. European infantry wore tight jackets and close caps; therefore the same. Were this

These and many other similar sayings attributed to the Prophet helped to reinforce the general feeling that to abandon one's own form of dress and adopt another was an act of treason and of apostasy. Non-Muslims were forbidden to adopt Muslim dress; Muslims would not dream of adopting Christian or Jewish dress. Even within the Muslim camp, each order of society had its own distinctive head-gear; the different shaped head-gear of the ulema, the Janissaries, and the men of the pen distinguished them during their lifetimes, and were carved in stone on their tombs after their death.

It was thus·no easy matter to persuade ordinary Muslim Turkish soldiers to accept what for them were the distinguishing marks of the infidel, the stigmata of inferiority. Most difficult of all to accept was the hat, and even at the present time, in many Muslim countries, the head-covering is the last refuge of conservatism. The fez and the sidara remain as the final symbol of religious identification and allegiance, while the rest of the body has accepted the fitted garments of the West.

The *şubara* was a wadded cap, made of cloth, with a roughly cylindrical crown ending in a flap. It was worn in former times by the Bostancıs and then by the *Nizam-i Cedid* troops of Selim III. Its use by Mahmud's new-style army was of short duration. In 1828 a new head-gear, of North African origin, was shown to the Sultan, and won his approval. It was called the Fez. A meeting was convened at the office of the Chief Mufti, and presided over by the Grand Vezir, to discuss the problem of military head-gear. It was agreed that the *şubara* was in every way unsatisfactory, and a fez was examined and approved, despite hesitation on the part of some of those present as to whether it could properly be considered an Islamic head-covering. Strong measures were taken to forestall and, if necessary, to suppress popular opposition to this new head-gear, and orders were given for its issue to the army. A century later it had become so well acclimatized that it was attacked—and defended—as the emblem of Ottoman and Islamic traditionalism and orthodoxy.[47]

blind adoption of forms only useless, or productive only of physical inconvenience, patience; but it proved a moral evil, creating unbounded disgust' (ii. 210–11). For a contrasting comment see *Sketches*, p. 237.

[47] On the introduction of the fez see the study by Uzunçarşılı in *Bell.*, no. 70 (1954), 223–30. On the vestimentary reforms see further Lûtfi, i. 255–6; Rasim, *Osmanlı Tar.*, iv. 1826 n. 280; White, ii. 50 ff.; Slade, ii. 210 ff.; Temperley, p. 21; Bailey, p. 37; Karal, *Tarih*, v. 154, 161–2.

A modification to the fez, of the year 1845, may be related in the words of the Imperial Historiographer Lûtfi:

> Until this time, the tassels which the regular troops, as well as the generality of Imperial servants and subjects, attached to their fezzes were made of unspun silk. The damage that befell their threads from the wind, the rain, and other vile things made it an urgent necessity to have the tassels combed every day. To comb the tassels, there were people, mostly Jewish boys, who, like the bootblacks today, cried 'Let us comb your tassels' in the streets and market-places, and made a living by this. The women too, arranging things somehow, used to attach combed tassels to flat-topped fezzes; to make them rest more easily on their heads, they used to put wires inside the fez, and plates of silver instead of paper at the top. These silken tassels rightly came to be called by the people 'the tasselled curse'. This being so, and since it was a matter involving much trouble both for the military and for civilians, the principle was adopted that for the commanders, officers, and men of the army, plaited tassels of a designated and indicated weight were to be attached; that for military ceremonies badges of rank in the form of circular metal plates were to be attached to the crown of the fez, and that for other ranks plaited tassels were to be adopted instead of tassels of silk thread.[48]

In 1829 the clothing reform was extended to civilians.[49] A decree of that year sets forth in great detail the costume to be worn by different classes of officials on different occasions. In general, the robe and the turban were permitted only to the ulema. For other civilians the fez compulsorily replaced all other forms of head-gear, and robes and slippers gave way to frock-coats and capes, trousers, and black leather boots. Jewels, pelisses, and other adornments were to go, and even beards were trimmed. The Sultan himself set an example which spread from the court to the pashas and then through the various grades of officials. At the same time European chairs and tables began to appear beside the divans and cushions of the old order, and European social manners were adopted. The Sultan began to receive foreign diplomats according to European and not Ottoman protocol, gave receptions and chatted with his guests, and even went so far as to show deference to ladies. The Thursday day of rest—religiously neutral—was borrowed from France and introduced in

---

[48] Lûtfi, viii. 69–70; Karal, *Tarih*, vi. 279.   [49] Lûtfi, ii. 148, 269.

government offices, and, still more startling, the Sultan's portrait was hung on their walls.[50]

These changes were as yet still only on the surface. The Holy Law of Islam was still unchallenged, above all in social and family matters. Marriage and divorce, property and inheritance, the status of women and of slaves—all these were substantially unchanged, and at this stage the reformers do not seem to have thought of any kind of reform in religious institutions. 'In political matters', said Sadık Rifat Paşa to Stratford Canning in 1844, 'we shall defer entirely to the advice of Europe. In religious matters we need all our liberty. Religion is the basis of our laws. It is the principle of our government; His Majesty the Sultan can no more touch it than we can.'[51]

The Men of the Reform [52]

In the thirteen years between the destruction of the Janissaries in 1826 and his death in 1839, the Sultan attempted to carry out a programme of reform as extensive as that of Peter the Great in Russia and far more difficult. Peter was already an autocrat; Mahmud had to make himself one, overcoming the resistance of the old, deeply-rooted Ottoman Islamic tradition of society and government, the opposition of well-entrenched and popularly supported classes both in the capital and the provinces, and, most of all, the ancient and profound contempt of Islam for the infidel and its rejection of anything bearing the taint of infidel origin.

The example of Peter the Great was not unknown in Turkey; it was cited by the chronicler Asım as an illustration of how a weak and backward country could win power and greatness by borrowing Frankish devices.[53] It was not to Peter, however, that Mahmud looked for a model; it was to his admired predecessor Selim, whose work he was determined to complete, and to his hated rival the Pasha of Egypt, whose example he was resolved to better.

[50] Lûtfi, v. 50 (portrait); iv. 100 and v. 55 (Thursday day of rest).

[51] Cited by P. Graves, *Briton and Turk* (1941), p. 23; cf. the observations of Fuad Paşa, cited by Cevdet, *Tezakir*, i. 85.

[52] The most comprehensive biographical data will be found in Inal, *Sadrıazamlar*, a series of biographies of the Ottoman Grand Vezirs from Mehmed Emin Âli Paşa (appointed 1852) to the end. See also *EI¹*, *EI²*, and *IA*, where biographies of many personalities will be found, with further bibliographical indications. Appreciations of some of the literary figures of the time—including many politicians—will be found in E. J. W. Gibb, *A History of Ottoman Poetry*, iv (1905), and in Tanpınar, Berkes, and Mardin. [53] See above, pp. 71–72.

But the task was appallingly difficult. Even when the forces of reaction had been beaten into submission, there was still the problem of finding suitable men to devise and apply the reforms. The Sultan himself, strong-willed and violent, was profoundly ignorant of everything Western. There were still lamentably few of his countrymen who were any better placed. Peter had invited great numbers of West Europeans to help him in his reforms. Muslim fanaticism prevented Mahmud from inviting more than a small number of foreigners, and from making much use of those who did come. Even a knowledge of European languages was still a rarity; and this gap was only gradually filled by the missions abroad and the Translation Office in Istanbul.

The men at Mahmud's disposal were thus poorly equipped to carry out the tasks assigned to them. Still worse was the growth and spread of corruption in the new civil service. Complaints of corruption were often heard under the old régime. They became more frequent under the new one. The increased cost of a Westernized style of living; the continuing insecurity of tenure and property; the chronic financial disorders of the reformist ministries, and above all the breakdown, without replacement, of traditional moral standards, all helped to make the new civil servants cynical and venal. In the old order there had been an accepted set of social loyalties and obligations, to which most men had tried to conform. With the destruction of the old order this complex web of social relationships and loyalties was torn asunder, and in its place came a new set of imported and alien institutions, with little meaning for the new officialdom and none at all for the people whom they ruled. There had always been a gulf between the rulers and the ruled. It now became fantastically wide, as the progress of Westernization added to the differences of power and wealth those of education and outlook, home and furnishings, even food and dress.

Reşid Paşa, Mahmud's chief instrument in the establishment of direct Imperial control in Eastern Anatolia, Armenia, and Kurdistan, was by no means well-disposed to the reforms. Husrev Paşa (1756–1853), who was Serasker between 1827 and 1837 was, however, a fanatical supporter of the reforms, and was able both to train and present to the Sultan a body of new-style troops, and to maintain order by rigorous police methods. Though he later became Grand Vezir, he never learnt to read or write, and his contributions to reform, if vigorous, were often ignorant and violent. His successor as Serasker, Hafiz Paşa, was also favourable to modern military methods, and took Moltke with him on a campaign in Mesopotamia.

On the civilian side, the most powerful man in the early years of Mahmud's reign was Halet Efendi, a convinced reactionary who had been ambassador in Paris from 1803 to 1806 and had returned to Turkey with a reinforced hatred of Europe and everything European. He defended the Janissaries and opposed military reform until his fall and execution in 1822. Another ex-ambassador to Paris, Galib Paşa (1763–1828), who had served in France in 1801, was far more positive in his attitude to the West. He held various offices under Mahmud II and became Grand Vezir in 1823, holding the office for only nine months. He is credited with having had a fine understanding of Turkish and European political problems, and with having exercised a formative influence on the rising generation of reformist statesmen.

In the 1820's and 1830's the rival poets Akif Paşa (1787–1845) and Pertev Paşa (d. 1837) alternated in the high offices of state. Though both were thoroughly conservative and traditional in their upbringing and political outlook, Akif nevertheless made a contribution of some importance to the progress of the reforms by casting off the cumbersome and convoluted chancery style until then current in Ottoman official usage, and initiating the development of a simpler and more direct prose style better suited to the needs of a modern state.[54]

Mustafa Reşid Paşa [55]

Far more important than any of these, however, was Mustafa Reşid Paşa (1800–58), in many ways the real architect of the nineteenth-century Ottoman reforms. He was born in Istanbul, the son of a *vakf* official who died when he was only ten years old. He was taught to read by his father, and then attended the mosque school, but did not complete a formal higher education in the *medrese*, of the type customary at that time. He was protected by a

---

[54] On Halet, see Seref, *Tar. Mus.*, pp. 27–38, Karal, *Tarih*, vi. 279, and *EI²*, s.v. (by E. Kuran); on Husrev Paşa, *EI¹* and *IA*, *s.v.*; on Galib Paşa, Babinger, *Geschichtsschreiber*, p. 331, and Uzunçarşılı in *Bell.*, no. 2 (1937), 357 ff.; on Akif and Pertev, Gibb, *Ottoman Poetry*, iv. 323 ff. and Tanpınar, pp. 60 ff.

[55] On Mustafa Reşid Paşa: Reşat Kaynar, *Mustafa Reşit Paşa ve Tanzimat* (1954); Cavid Baysun, 'Mustafa Reşit Paşa' in *Tanzimat*, pp. 723–46; Şeref, *Tar. Mus.*, pp. 75–87; and the general works on the period, by Karal, Şeref, Temperley, Rasim, &c.

relative by marriage, Ispartalı Seyyid Ali Paşa, with whose help he entered government employment at an early age. His talents soon won him advancement, and in 1832 he was appointed *Amedi*, a post which made him in effect chief secretary to the Reis Efendi, the official in charge of foreign affairs.

In 1834 he was sent as ambassador to Paris—the first of a series of diplomatic appointments. Among those who accompanied him was Ruhuddin Efendi, the dragoman—the son of Yahya Efendi, who had been a teacher at the naval school and later dragoman of the Porte, and the father of the more famous Ahmed Vefik Paşa. On his way to Paris he passed through Vienna, where he had a conversation with Prince Metternich. Soon after his arrival in Paris, he set to work to master the French language, and by 1839, when on another visit to France he was received by Louis Philippe, he was able to converse with the king without an interpreter. While in Paris he became friendly with the venerable Orientalist Silvestre de Sacy, who helped him in learning French and in meeting important people.

After holding various other diplomatic and official appointments, he became Minister of Foreign Affairs, and was on a special mission to London when the news arrived, in 1839, of the death of Mahmud II and the accession of his son Abdülmecid.

Abdülmecid: the Rescript of the Rose Bower[56]

The new Sultan was determined to continue his father's work, and was supported in this by his mother, the Valide Sultan Bezm-i Alem, a remarkable woman who exercised considerable influence over her son and consequently over the government of the Empire. The moment was a critical one. Muhammad Ali, the rebellious Pasha of Egypt, had resumed hostilities against the Porte, and on 24 June his armies had inflicted a crushing defeat on the Ottoman forces at the battle of Nezib. It was no doubt in part to demonstrate to Europe that the Sultan's government, as well as that of the Pasha of Egypt, could produce a liberal and modern régime, that

[56] On Abdülmecid see *EI²* and *IA*, *s.v.* On the Rescript of 1839, see the important comments of Cevdet Paşa (*Tezakir*, i, 7 ff.) and of Prince Metternich (Engelhardt, i. 47–51; cf. Metternich's *Mémoires*, Paris, 1884, vi. 378–86). Further discussions and comments in Lûtfi, vi. 59 ff.; Nuri, *Netaic*, iv. 97 ff.; Ata, iii. 203 ff.; Kâmil Paşa, *Tarih-i Siyasî*, iii. 191 ff.; White, i. 110–20; Ubicini, letter 2; Rosen, ii. 16 ff.; Engelhardt, i. 35 ff.; Şeref, *Tar. Mus.*, pp. 48 ff.; Jorga, v. 390; Sax, pp. 278 ff.; Temperley, p. 157; Bailey, pp. 193 ff.; Kaynar, pp. 164 ff.; Karal, *Tarih*, v. 173 ff.

the new Ottoman ministers produced the famous Noble Rescript of the Rose Bower (*Hatti-i Şerif* of Gülhane), promulgated on 3 November 1839.[57]

Husrev Paşa had become Grand Vezir after the succession of the new Sultan, but Reşid Paşa, who had returned post-haste from London to direct foreign affairs in the new ministry, took the main initiative in drafting and promulgating the first of the great reforming edicts which are collectively known in Turkish history as the *Tanzimat*—the Reorganization.

The Noble Rescript proclaimed such principles as the security of life, honour, and property of the subject, the abolition of tax-farming and all the abuses associated with it, regular and orderly recruitment into the armed forces, fair and public trial of persons accused of crimes, and equality of persons of all religions in the application of these laws. It was this last that represented the most radical breach with ancient Islamic tradition, and was therefore most shocking to Muslim principles and good taste.

The laws and traditions of Islam, the policy and practice of the Ottoman Empire, agreed in prescribing tolerance and protection for the non-Muslim subjects of the state, and in granting them a large measure of autonomy in their internal communal affairs. This toleration, however, was predicated on the assumption that the tolerated communities were separate and inferior, and were moreover clearly marked as such. To give up this principle of inequality and segregation required of the Muslim no less great an effort of renunciation than is required of those Westerners who are now called upon to forego the satisfactions of racial superiority. Of the two prejudices, that of the Muslim against the infidel had stronger roots both in tradition and in morality. The Muslim could claim that he assigned to his inferiors a position of reasonable comfort and security; he could moreover claim that his discrimination related not to an accident of birth but to a conscious choice on the most fundamental questions of human existence. Infidel and true believer were different and separate; to equalize them and to mix them was an offence against both religion and common sense.

[57] The text of this, and of other Turkish laws of the nineteenth and early twentieth centuries, will be found in the *Düstur* (Ist., 1871–1928); translations of some of them in G. Aristarchi, *Législation ottomane* (1873–88) and G. Young, *Corps de droit ottoman* (1905–6).

Another striking feature of the Noble Rescript is its frank reference to 'new rules'. In traditional Muslim usage the word *Bid‘a*, innovation, was the converse of *Sunna*, the accepted practice of the orthodox, and it came to be in effect a synonym for heresy. This attitude is well summed up in a saying attributed to the Prophet that 'the worst things are those that are novelties, every novelty is an innovation, every innovation is an error, and every error leads to Hell-fire'.[58] It was in this spirit that earlier reforms were often presented not as something new, but as a reversion to ancient practice. The Noble Rescript also begins with a pious allusion to the mighty and honoured past, but goes on to speak frankly of the creation of 'new institutions' to secure for the Empire the benefits of good administration.

The most important of these was the Council of Judicial Ordinances (*Meclis-i Ahkâm-i Adliye*), more commonly known as the Council of Justice. This body had been set up two years previously by Sultan Mahmud II.[59] It was presided over by the Serasker Husrev Paşa, and consisted of the president, five members, and two secretaries. The Noble Rescript laid down that this body was to be enlarged by the addition of new members, and to exercise a supervisory and quasi-legislative function.

A few months later, in March 1840, a new Imperial Rescript (*Hatt-i Humayun*) gave details of the reorganization of the Council of Justice, which, in various forms, played a central role throughout the period of the *Tanzimat*.[60] At about the same time Reşid Pasa introduced a completely new system of centralized provincial administration, modelled on the French system of prefectures and *départements*, with salaried officials in charge of them, to replace the loose-knit, quasi-feudal association of pashas and tax-farmers of earlier times. It was, however, some time before this ambitious project could be put into effect.[61]

Other reforms, foreshadowed in the Noble Rescript, followed rapidly, relating principally to two matters—justice and finance. Both involved radical breaches with the past.

[58] cf. B. Lewis, 'Some Observations on the Significance of Heresy in the History of Islam', *Studia Islamica*, i (1953), pp. 52 ff.
[59] Lûtfi, v. 106 ff.   [60] Lûtfi, vi. 92 ff. cf. Bailey, p. 199.   [61] See below, pp. 384 ff.

Legal Reform [62]

In the strict theory of the Muslim jurists, there could be no legislative power in the state, since law came from God alone and was promulgated by revelation. Theoretically, therefore, there was no law other than the *Şeriat*, the unchangeable, God-given law of Islam, and no judiciary other than that which administered it. In earlier Islamic Empires legal practice had made some compromise with reality, recognizing custom and the will of the ruler as legally effective, and applying them in administrative or customary tribunals outside the system of the *Şeriat* courts. The Ottoman Sultans, down to Mahmud II, had issued *Kanuns*, which are sometimes described as laws. The description is not, however, accurate. The Ottoman *kanun* is in no sense a legislative enactment, but rather a codification of existing law— a tabulation of legal rules. In fact the Ottomans went further than any previous Muslim régime in establishing the sole authority of the *Şeriat* and its exponents, and in eliminating or reducing the operation of such other systems of law and judicature as were in existence. The administrative, commercial, military, and equity courts which had existed under the Caliphate disappeared, and the Muftis and Kadis, organized in a hierarchy under the supreme control of the *Şeyh-ül-Islâm* in Istanbul, achieved an exclusive competence in all matters of law and justice concerning Muslims.

The promulgation in May 1840 of a new penal code did not at first appear to be a revolutionary step. The name given to it— *Ceza Kanunnamesi*—indicated a desire to remain within the existing tradition of *Kanun*-making, and the provisions of the code, though influenced by French law, are mainly within the framework of the penal law of the *Şeriat* itself. There are, however, one or two significant changes, which prepared the way for the more radical legal reforms that were to follow. One of these is the affirmation of the equality of *all* Ottoman subjects before the law. Another is the preparation and promulgation of a legal code, consisting of a preamble and fourteen articles, by a corporate body entrusted with that task. Though the code was confused in thought and expression and ineffective in application, it marks the first

[62] On the penal and commercial codes see Engelhardt, i. 40; Ubicini, letter 7; Lûtfi, vi. 102–4; *Tanzimat*, pp. 176, 214, 226; Temperley, p. 163; Bailey, p. 200; Karal, *Tarih*, v. 177.

tentative appearance, in the Ottoman state, of the legislative principle and of a legislative body.

The significance of this innovation seems to have escaped the ulema, who offered no resistance. They were, however, more perturbed by the creation, in the same year, of a new *ad hoc* court of justice, in the newly created Ministry of Commerce, to hear commercial disputes, and still more by the preparation, under the inspiration of Reşid Paşa, of a new commercial code based on French models. This raised an ancient dispute of the Muslim jurists, who recognized the new code as a derogation from the *Şeriat*, and forced its suspension. Dealing with partnerships bankruptcies, bills of exchange, and similar matters, it was derived almost entirely from French commercial law. When Reşid had introduced it to the High Council in 1841, he was asked whether it was in conformity with the Holy Law. ' "The Holy Law has nothing to do with the matter", said Reşid. "Blasphemy", protested the *Ulemas* present. The young Sultan promptly dismissed his minister of enlightenment.'[63]

Finance [64]

One of the provisions of the Imperial Rescript had stated that: 'steps shall be taken for the formation of banks and other similar institutions, so as to effect a reform in the monetary and financial system, as well as to create funds to be employed in augmenting the sources of the material wealth of my Empire'.

The point was a crucial one. From first to last finance was the Slough of Despond of the Turkish reformers, in which their brightest hopes were bemired, their cleverest plans befouled and engulfed. Two basic objectives were never met—a solvent treasury and a stable currency; and in their absence the apparatus of government was clogged and neglected, its servants became cynical and corrupt.

The reforming Sultans inherited from their predecessors the unfortunate practice of meeting a deficit by debasing the currency. During the reign of Mahmud II the form and name of the Ottoman coinage was changed 35 times for gold and 37 for silver issues, and the rate of the Turkish piastre or its equivalent to the

---

[63] Temperley, p. 163.

[64] On the Ministry of Commerce, see Lûtfi, vi. 28 and 145; on the finance committee, ibid. p. 125; on the banknote issue, ibid. p. 127; White, ii. 71; Ubicini, letter 14.

pound sterling, fell from 23 in 1814 to 104 in 1839. The effects of these changes on the economy of the Empire and on the standard of living and integrity of salaried officials were disastrous.

In April 1840 an Imperial ferman authorized the establishment of an Ottoman bank, to be formed along European lines, with a guaranteed subvention from the government of 30 million piastres a year for fifteen years. In the following year the Turkish government made its first issue of paper money. These papers, though sometimes described as banknotes, should more properly be termed treasury bonds. They were to carry interest at the lavish rate of 12 per cent., payable twice yearly, and the total issue was not to exceed 60 million piastres. There were no guarantees, and no date of redemption was specified. In the following year the interest rate was halved, and a part of the issue redeemed, but new issues soon followed, and within ten years the original amount was trebled. For a while these bonds remained fairly steady, and in 1844 the government, together with the new bank, was able to introduce a set of new measures for the safeguarding of the currency. These involved the withdrawal of the old coinage and the issue of a new currency on European lines, consisting of a gold pound of 100 piastres. For the moment all was well, but in banking and finance the reformers had an explosive device which was beyond their capacity to handle. By the time of the Crimean War the circulating treasury bonds, unnumbered and easily counterfeited, heavily discounted in terms of gold, had become a menace. A foreign loan was therefore negotiated in 1858, for the purpose, only partially accomplished, of withdrawing them; it initiated a series which led directly to the bankruptcy and collapse of 1875.

The Fall of Reşid: Interruption of Reform

At the beginning of 1841 the reforms suffered a setback. Reşid Paşa was dismissed, and in the following year the new system of provincial administration and taxation was dropped and the old partnership of military governors and tax-farmers restored.[65] Even under the reactionaries, however, the process of reform did not entirely cease. In 1842 the Council was reconstituted and a more moderate régime emerged; in the following year an

---

[65] Engelhardt, i. 50; Temperley, p. 165.

important change was made in the organization of the army, which was now reorganized in five army corps, with a period of five years' service for regular soldiers, followed by seven in the reserves (*Redif*). Recruitment was by a form of conscription, with the drawing of lots, and all matters of training, equipment, weapons, and organization were on Western lines.[66]

Reşid Paşa: the Second Phase

In 1845 a new phase of reform began, and Reşid Paşa returned to the Ministry of Foreign Affairs. In the following year he was appointed to the Grand Vezirate, an office which he held six times.

The Sultan had meanwhile made his own preparation. In January 1845 he issued a *Hatt-i Humayun*, in which he said that apart from the military reform, with which he was fully satisfied, all his other proposals for the benefit of his subjects had been misunderstood and misapplied by his ministers; the main reason for this lamentable fact was the general ignorance of the population. This should be remedied by the establishment of good schools throughout the Empire, so as to disseminate useful knowledge and thus make possible the introduction into other branches of the government of the improvements already tried in the Ministry of War.[67]

The Assembly of Provincial Notables[68]

It was no doubt with the same idea of associating the population with the reforms that a little later in the same year the Sultan took the unprecedented and potentially dangerous step of consulting his people. From each province of the Empire two men were to be sent to Istanbul 'from among those who are respected and trusted, are people of intelligence and knowledge, who know the requisites of prosperity and the characteristics of the population', in order to consult with the High Council. They were to be sent at the expense of the local treasuries, and lodged in Istanbul as 'honoured guests in the *konaks* of the great'. When these instructions arrived in the provincial capitals, 'persons were elected from among the prominent and respected people' and travelled to Istanbul, where they were given a document

---

[66] Lûtfi, vii. 74; Engelhardt, i. 71; Ubicini, letter 19.   [67] Lûtfi, viii. 8.
[68] Ibid. pp. 15–17; cf. Engelhardt, i. 76.

explaining the purpose for which they had been convened, and were asked their views on the present state and further needs of the reform.

The delegates seem to have been confused by this new and unfamiliar procedure, and, not knowing what they were expected to say, preferred to say nothing. The Sultan then resorted to the method of sending roving commissions to the provinces in both Europe and Asia, to investigate and report on the state of the reforms. They travelled for about seven or eight months, and in accordance with their instructions reported their findings to the Sublime Porte by every post. These were considered by the High Council, which occasionally took action on them. Some officials were dismissed or transferred, some army officers and naval engineers set to work to prepare maps and inspect some roads and ports, but for the most part, in Lûtfi's words, 'the orders of most of them were pawned to neglect and incoming papers were locked in the box of abrogation'.

Education [69]

Of rather more effect were the educational measures that followed the *Hatt-i Humayun* of 1845. In March of the same year a circular of the Porte appointed a committee of seven, 'of men well-versed in the judicial, military, and civil sciences',[70] to investigate the existing schools and prepare places for new ones. Among its members were Âli Efendi, Under-Secretary of Foreign Affairs and director of the chancery of the Divan, and Fuad Efendi, Chief Dragoman of the Divan.

The committee reported in August 1846. Its report, as was normal, was elaborate and unrealistic, providing for an Ottoman state university, a system of primary and secondary schools, and a permanent Council of Public Instruction. The creation of a university and of a network of schools was a difficult task, the accomplishment of which stretched over many years and encountered many obstacles. The foundations of the University were laid, and a medal struck depicting the completed building, but work on the building was abandoned when the walls were only a few feet high. The secondary schools, called *rüşdiye*, came slowly,

[69] Ubicini, letter 9; Engelhardt, ii. 7; Rosen, ii. 86; Bailey, p. 214; Temperley, p. 234; Ergin, pp. 355 ff.; Cevad, *passim*.

[70] Translation of the circular in Ubicini, doc. XIII.

and by the mid-century there were six of them, with 870 pupils; a poor result if compared with the programme, but creditable in relation to reality. The Council of Public Instruction was created immediately, and in 1847 became a Ministry.

The change, though perhaps unimpressive in terms of the number of schools and pupils provided, was nevertheless significant. Both the Sultan and his committee had been careful to pay lip-service to the primacy of religion in education—'the first of the necessities of this life', said the circular of March 1845, 'is to know the duties and obligations which religion imposes on man'. The effect of the change, however, was to set up new schools, with teachers and curricula outside the scope of the ulema and the religious sciences which they cultivated, and thus prepare the way for a system of secular education. The creation of a separate Ministry of Education confirmed the removal of this important matter from the sole jurisdiction of the ulema.

Law and Justice

Even more delicate than the question of education was that of law and justice, which to an even greater extent had been a preserve of the ulema. So far the reformers had not dared to set up any formal legislative organs, any system of courts and judges outside those of the *Seriat*. There had, however, been a few tentative moves in that direction. The cautiously named Council of Judicial Ordinances had been given, by the edict of 1839, what were in effect legislative and quasi-judicial functions. In 1847 mixed civil and criminal courts were constituted, with European and Ottoman judges in equal numbers, and with rules of evidence and procedure drawn from European rather than Islamic practice.[71]

In 1850 a more radical step was taken—the promulgation of Resid Pasa's Commercial Code, prepared some years previously, and delayed by his fall from power in 1841. It was to be administered in the tribunals of commerce.[72] The promulgation of this Code was the first formal recognition in Turkey of a system of law and of judicature independent of the ulema, dealing with matters outside the scope of the *Şeriat*. Such a recognition was by

[71] Lûtfi, vi. 102; Engelhardt, i. 83

[72] *Düstur*, i. 375 ff.; Young, vii. 55 ff.; Aristarchi, i. 275 ff.; *Tanzimat*, p. 196; Temperley, pp. 163, 232.

no means new in Islam. It was, however, a radical departure from previous Ottoman practice, and the harbinger of a complete legal and social revolution. A revised penal code followed in 1851.

The Fall of Reşid Paşa: 1852

More than once Reşid Paşa was unseated by the reactionaries. The most serious setback was in 1852, when, after his dismissal from the Grand Vezirate, his new system of provincial administration was abrogated and the whole movement of reform came to a standstill. Already in the previous year the British ambassador Stratford de Redcliffe had written in a private letter: 'The *great game of improvement* is altogether up for the present.'[73]

There is no doubt that one of the compelling motives that had led Reşid Paşa to promulgate this high-sounding programme of reform had been the need to win the goodwill and support of the European powers against that other and, in his time, more successful Westernizer, Muhammad Ali of Egypt. In view of this, some Western observers, seeing the appalling discrepancy between the Noble Rescript of the Rose Bower and the ignoble realities of less fragrant purlieus, concluded that the whole reform was no more than window-dressing, intended only to deceive the Western powers, without making any real change in the state of affairs in Turkey. To adopt such a view, however, is to disregard the long course of events which, since the eighteenth century, had prepared the way for the reform; the long working out, in the century that followed, of the principles and beliefs contained in it, and, at the moment of its promulgation, the deeper convictions and aspirations of Mustafa Reşid Paşa and other men of his generation.

Âli and Fuad Paşas: the Imperial Rescript of 1856

A new phase began in 1854. The poor performance of the new-style army against the Russians had revealed the hollowness of the reforms, and it was once again urgently necessary to convince Europe of the sincerity and good, intentions of the Ottoman government. The Sultan's government therefore again offered Europe the only evidence she would accept of progress and improvement—that is, a movement towards a greater resemblance to herself.

The reformers returned to power, and the Grand Council of

[73] March 1851, cited in Temperley, p. 242.

Justice was reorganized, being divided into two bodies, one more
strictly concerned with legal matters, the other, known as the
High Council of Reform (*Meclis-i Âli-i Tanzimat*), with general
responsibility for the whole programme of reform.[74]

For most Europeans the touchstone of Turkish sincerity was the
treatment of non-Muslims. In May 1855 the government declared
its intention—embodied in the reform charter a few months
later—to abolish the two principal measures of discrimination
against them. The poll-tax, which had been demanded from the
protected non-Muslim subjects of the Muslim state since the
beginnings of Islamic government, was solemnly abolished, and
the privilege of bearing arms—i.e. of military service—which
had been restricted to Muslims for almost as long, was thrown
open to all. However, since after centuries of exemption the non-
Muslim subjects had developed a disinclination or were found
unsuitable to serve in the army, which in any case offered
them few attractions as a career, they were required, instead
of serving, to pay an exemption tax called the *bedel*. This was
levied in the same way as the abolished poll-tax.[75]

On 18 February 1856 a new reform charter, the Imperial
Rescript (*Hatt-i Humayun*), was promulgated by the Sultan, as
part of the preliminaries of the treaty of Paris and the acceptance
of Turkey as a participant in that concatenation of discords known
as the Concert of Europe. The Rescript—prepared under strong
pressure from the British ambassador and his French and Austrian
colleagues—reaffirmed the principles of the edict of 1839, again
abolished tax-farming and other abuses, and laid down, in terms
more specific and categorical than previously, the full equality of
all Ottoman subjects irrespective of religion. Turkey had once
again declared her good intentions. The West had concerned itself
more directly with their fulfilment.

In the preparation and promulgation of this new charter
Reşid Paşa, for long the leader of the reformers, had no part.[76]

[74] Young, i. 2.

[75] Engelhardt, i. 126–7; Eichmann, pp. 436–40; Davison, *Reform*, p. 53; *EI²*
('Badal' by H. Bowen); *IA* ('Bedel-i Askeri' by S. S. Onar). On this question generally
see Roderic H. Davison, 'Turkish Attitudes concerning Christian-Muslim Equality
in the Nineteenth Century', *Am. Hist. R.*, lix (1953–4), 844–64.

[76] Cevdet's comments on the edict of 1856 are contained in *Tezakir*, i. 67 ff., where
some sharply critical memoranda of Reşid Paşa are also given. See also Engelhardt, i.
139 ff.; Rosen, ii. 239 ff.; Jorga, v. 482; Sax, pp. 342 ff.; Rasim, iv. 2048 ff., and, on
the whole period, R. H. Davison, *Reform in the Ottoman Empire 1856–1876* (1963).

Though he was twice again Grand Vezir, for short periods, before his death in 1858, the leadership of the reform had passed into the hands of his former disciples and present rivals, Âli Paşa and Fuad Paşa. These two men led the reform for the next fifteen years.[77]

Âli Paşa (1815–71) was born in Istanbul, the son of a shopkeeper. Like Reşid Paşa, he entered the civil service as a boy, and rose through the ladder of official promotions. In 1833, having acquired some knowledge of French, he was attached to the Dragoman of the Porte, whose staff was increased in that year from two to four assistants to cope with the increasing volume of translation work. While in this employment he made good progress in French, under a French teacher, and in 1836 went to Vienna on the staff of the special envoy Ahmed Fethi Paşa. This was the first of a series of diplomatic appointments, which culminated in his nomination as ambassador in London in 1840. On his return to Turkey in 1844, he became a member of the Council of Justice, and thereafter held a number of high positions, mostly in association with Reşid Paşa. In 1852, when Reşid Paşa was dismissed, Âli Paşa succeeded him as Grand Vezir. Though on this occasion he held the post only for two months, he remained at the centre of events. In 1854 he became president of the newly formed High Council of Reform, and a little later returned to the Grand Vezirate, before the promulgation of the *Hatt-i Humayun*. Thereafter he held the Grand Vezirate and other offices at various periods, and played a dominating role in the reform movement until his death in 1871.

His closest associate and collaborator during this period was Fuad Paşa (1815–69). He too was born in Istanbul, but with a very different background and education. He was the son of Keçecizade Mehmed Izzet Efendi (d. 1830), a well-known Ottoman poet, scholar, and statesman, who had for a while enjoyed high rank and favour under Mahmud II, and who played a role of some importance in the movement for linguistic and literary reform. Fuad himself entered the medical school which Mahmud had established at Galatasaray in 1827, and after graduating entered the new army medical corps. His knowledge of French, however, was of more immediate use than his medical training. In 1837 he joined the Translation Office and in 1840 went to London as Embassy dragoman and then First Secretary.

[77] On Âli and Fuad Paşas see *EI*[1], *EI*[2], *IA*, and Inal, *s.vv.*

Thereafter he held many diplomatic appointments, and in 1852 became Minister of Foreign Affairs under Âli Paşa. He too was a member of the High Council of Reform, of which he later became president, and was actively concerned in the preparation of new projects and the drafting of new laws. Besides his work as statesman and diplomat, he was a scholar of some quality, and collaborated with the historian Ahmed Cevdet in composing the *Kavaid-i Osmaniye* (1851), the first Turkish work on Turkish grammar to be printed, and a landmark in the linguistic reform.

Together with Reşid Paşa, Âli and Fuad were the chief archi-tects and executants of the *Tanzimat*. Like him, they owed their first steps towards advancement to their knowledge of a foreign language. For the shopkeeper's son, as for the others, French was the talisman that made the clerk a translator, the translator an interpreter, the interpreter a diplomat, and the diplomat a states-man. At a time when the Ottoman Empire was obsessed with the sheer problem of survival in a world dominated by an aggressive and expanding Europe, the positions of trust and decision in-evitably went to those who knew something of Europe, its languages, and its affairs. The new *élite* of power came not from the army, not from the ulema, but from the Translation Office and the Embassy secretariats. What had once been a despised and quasi-menial task, contemptuously left to Greek dragomans whose services helped to preserve their Ottoman masters from the defilement of contact, now became the school of statecraft and the battlefield of power.

Legal Reforms

The reforms of Âli and Fuad continued along the lines laid down by their predecessors. The legal reform was carried a few steps further, with the introduction of a land code[78] and a new penal code[79] in 1858, a reorganization of the commercial tribunals, which were amalgamated with the mixed courts in 1860,[80]

---

[78] Text in *Düstur*, i. 165; trans. in Young, vi. 45 ff. and Aristarchi, i. 57 ff.; studied by [F.A.] Belin ('Étude sur la propriété foncière . . . en Turquie', *J. As.*, 1862) and Barkan ('Türk Toprak Hukuku Tarihinde Tanzimat ve 1274 (1858) Tarihli Arazi Kanunnamesi', in *Tanzimat*, pp. 321–421). See also Inalcık, 'Tanzimat Nedir'.

[79] *Düstur*, i. 527 ff.; Young, vii. 1 ff.; Aristarchi, ii. 212 ff.

[80] *Düstur*, i. 445; Young, i. 226.

and further commercial[81] and maritime[82] codes, all of French origin, in 1861 and 1863.

The commercial codes were a logical development from Reşid Paşa's first initiative. The penal code marked a more considerable advance. It was more elaborate and more carefully devised than its predecessors of 1840 and 1851. The main part of it derived from French law, but with several significant omissions, additions, and emendations.

In many ways more important than either the commercial or the criminal codes was the new land law of 1858. This, like the Egyptian land reform of the same year, was basically an attempt to apply to the problems of the countryside the panacea of formal Westernization. Western villages were populous, Western agriculture was prosperous—therefore the system of land tenure and occupancy must be amended so as to make it more European. The last *timars* had been abolished by Mahmud; the abolition of the system of tax-farming had for some time been one of the objectives of the reformers, and some progress had been made in accomplishing it. The general trend of the reforms was to abrogate the earlier agrarian relationships and progressively to extend and confirm the rights of use, of possession, and of ownership. Leaseholders and tax-farmers acquired freehold ownership, with full rights of disposal and succession, confirmed by the possession of documents issued by the Survey Department. The actual cultivators, their rights and status much diminished, became share-croppers or hired labourers, at the mercy of a reinforced landlord class which was the principal beneficiary of the reform. The harmful effects of the new law were modified only by the inefficiency of its application.

Âli and Fuad Paşas were men of the second generation of reform. Much that for their predecessors was strange and new was already part of their normal lives. More secure than Reşid Paşa both in their convictions and in their personal positions, they could afford to be more cautious and practical. To European observers, their rate of progress seemed lamentably slow, and in October 1859 the representatives of the European powers presented a joint memorandum complaining to the Grand Vezir of the lack of progress in applying the charter of 1856.[83]

[81] *Düstur*, i. 780; Young, vii. 155.

[82] *Düstur*, i. 466; Young, vii. 103; Aristarchi, i. 344.

[83] Engelhardt, i. 161 ff.; Rasim, iv. 2092 ff.

Financial Troubles [84]

The disagreements of the powers, however, prevented them from taking any effective action to follow up the protest, and before very long the Ottoman Empire was concerned with more pressing matters—with the growing financial crisis. Finance had always been the weak point of the reformers. Now the treasury was empty, the army unpaid, and the populace, feeling the pinch, increasingly hostile to both Europeans and reformers. The government had for some time been raising short-term loans, at high rates, from local bankers in Galata. During the Crimean War, Turkey had obtained loans, for war expenditure, from her British and French allies. Further loans in 1858 and 1860 brought only temporary relief, and in 1861 the crisis came to a head. British and French help enabled the Ottoman government to convert its local loans and create a new financial instrument—the Imperial Ottoman Bank. A new loan, negotiated by the bank, was used to retire the treasury bonds. These measures, together with minor fiscal and administrative reforms, brought some improvement, but did not long postpone Turkey's career towards bankruptcy and foreign financial control.

Abdülaziz: Reaction [85]

On 25 June 1861 the Sultan Abdülmecid died, and was succeeded by his brother Abdülaziz. Abdülmecid had been a mild well-intentioned ruler, and personally well disposed to the reform movement. He knew some French—the first of his line to use a Western language; he read the Paris newspapers, and introduced or accepted many European practices at his court.[86] His successor was a man of a different temper. Capricious and violent, obstinate and irascible, he soon fell foul of the reformers, whose work was impeded and often nullified by his interference.

[84] On Ottoman finances see A. du Velay, *Essai sur l'histoire financière de la Turquie* (1903); Belin, 'Essai sur l'histoire économique de la Turquie', *J. As.*, 1885; Davison, *Reform*, pp. 110 ff.; Cevdet, *Tezakir*, ii. 226 ff. and Rasim's note on the loans (iv. 2028 ff.).

[85] On Abdülaziz see Haluk Y. Şehsuvaroğlu, *Sultan Aziz* (1949); also the relevant articles in *EI*² and *IA*, and sources quoted there. Comments from British diplomatic sources are cited by Temperley in *Camb. Hist. J.*, 167 ff.

[86] On some of these, see Rasim, iv. 2009 ff., n. 289. Cf. Cevdet, *Tezakir*, ii. 87 f., and Lewis in *MES* (1965), 287.

There had been tyrants before in the house of Osman—though far fewer than is sometimes thought; but the abrogation of the traditional restraints on the one hand, and the introduction of a new, Westernized apparatus of surveillance and repression on the other, had given to the absolutism of the imperial government a scope and an impact unknown in earlier times.

Âli and Fuad Paşas were, however, able to use this power for reform, and in 1864 a new Law of Vilayets regulated the provincial administration along lines that were to remain effective to the end of the Empire and beyond.[87]

The French Note of 1867: New Reforms [88]

In February 1867 the French government, supported by England and Austria, presented a note to the Porte urging a more active policy of reform, and setting forth detailed suggestions. The Sultan was violently opposed to the idea, but gave way to the pressure of events. For the next three years Âli and Fuad Paşas ran the state and a stream of new laws and institutions followed.

Later in 1867 an invitation from Napoleon III to visit the Paris International Exhibition gave the Sultan the occasion to make a journey to Europe—the first made by an Ottoman Sultan for any purpose but war. He was received at the courts of Paris, London, and Vienna, and also met the King of Prussia.[89]

Justice and Education

The reforms of the next two years were once again concerned with the two major topics of law and education. In April 1868 the High Council was reorganized, and two new bodies created from it; a Divan of Judicial Ordinances (*Divan-i Ahkâm-i Adliye*) and a Council of State (*Şura-yi Devlet*). The former was a revised version of the earlier Council of Justice, with judicial functions. The latter, modelled on the French *Conseil d'État*, was in effect a high court of

---

[87] *Düstur*, i. 608–24; Young, i. 36–45. See further Engelhardt, i. 193–8; Karal, *Tarih*, vii. 153; Temperley, p. 237; Sax, pp. 372 ff.; Davison, pp. 114 ff.; cf. below, p. 381.

[88] Engelhardt, i. 237 ff.; ii. 1 ff.; Sax, pp. 380 ff.; Davison, pp. 234 ff.

[89] On this visit, see the account written by Halimi Efendi, chief court secretary, who accompanied the Sultan as interpreter: ed. Necib Asim in *TOEM*, no. 49–62 (1337 A.H.), pp. 90–102. Also Ali Kemali Aksüt, *Sultan Aziz'in Mısır ve Avrupa Seyahatı* (1944).

appeal in administrative cases, with some consultative and quasi-legislative responsibilities.[90]

The same year saw the opening of the Imperial Ottoman Lycée at Galatasaray.[91] In this school the language of instruction was French (except for purely Turkish subjects), and a serious attempt was made to give a modern and Western curriculum of secondary education. A few such schools had already been established by foreign missions, notably the American Protestant Robert College (1863); the Galatasaray school was, however, the first serious attempt by a Muslim government to provide modern education at secondary level in a Western language. Another new feature was the teaching of Muslim and Christian pupils side by side—a step towards religious de-segregation.

The influence of the Galatasaray school on the rise of modern Turkey has been enormous. As the need for administrators, diplomats, and others with a Western education and a capacity to handle Western administrative apparatus became more and more pressing, the graduates of Galatasaray came to play a preponderant role in the politics and administration of the Ottoman Empire and, after it, of the Turkish Republic. The Imperial Ottoman Lycée had no playing-fields, but not a few of the victories of modern Turkey were won in its classrooms.

Probably the most important legal reform of the nineteenth century was the promulgation of the new civil code, known as the *Mecelle*, the first section of which appeared in 1870.[92] It was completed in 1876. The code was very largely the work of Ahmed Cevdet Pasha (1822–95), a scholar, historian, and jurist of genius who was a leading figure in the intellectual life of his time. After holding various official posts, he was appointed president of the Divan of Judicial Ordinances in 1868. As such,

[90] *Düstur*, i. 703 ff.; Young, i. 3 ff., 159 ff.; Aristarchi, ii, 38 ff.; B. Lewis in *MES* (1965), 290–1. On the high hopes entertained of the Council of State by the Turkish liberals, see Tanpınar, p. 190.

[91] Engelhardt, ii. 10; Ergin, *Maarif*, ii. 400; Ihsan Sungu, 'Galatasaray Lisesi'nin Kuruluşu', *Bell.*, no. 28 (1943), pp. 315–47; Davison, pp. 246 ff.

[92] Many editions and translations of the *Mecelle* are available. For a brief general account by a Turkish lawyer see S. S. Onar, 'The Majalla', in Majid Khadduri and Herbert J. Liebesny, eds., *Law in the Middle East*, i (1955), 292–308. On the legal work of Ahmed Cevdet Paşa see Ebul'ulâ Mardin, *Medenî Hukuk Cephesinden Ahmet Cevdet Paşa* (1946), and, more briefly, H. Bowen, 'Ahmed Djawdat Pasha' in *EI*[2]. Cevdet's own views are given briefly in *Tezakir*, i, 62–64. On his conflict with Hasan Fehmi see *EI*[2], *s.v.* (by B. Lewis).

he was in effect Minister of Justice, and was later officially confirmed in this title when a separate Ministry of Justice was recognized. His achievements include the institution of courses in law, at the Ministry, for judges, the elaboration of a new set of secular courts, the *Nizami* courts, with their own judiciary and procedure and with Courts of Appeal at the 'Divan of Judicial Ordinances'.

Cevdet Paşa had, during an earlier tenure of office on the Committee of Justice, played some part in producing the penal and land codes. He was now called upon to deal with the vaster problem of a new civil code, to replace the existing confusion. Âli Paşa was anxious to follow the precedent of the commercial code, and to adopt parts of the French *Code Civil* as the civil law of the Empire. Cevdet, however, preferred to remain within the Islamic tradition, and to prepare a code which, while modern in form and presentation, would be firmly based on the *Şeriat*. He and his committee had their way; the result of their endeavours, a digest rather than a code of *Şeriat* law of the Hanafi school, must rank as one of the great achievements of Turkish jurisprudence. It remained in force in Turkey until abrogated by the Republic in 1926, and still forms the basis of the legal systems of several of the Ottoman successor states in Asia.

In 1869 the partnership of the two reform leaders was dissolved by the death of Fuad Paşa.[93] Âli Paşa, probably the abler of the two, but the less popular among his countrymen, was left to cope with a renewed financial crisis, and soon made himself still more disliked by raising the tithe rate. The Franco-Prussian war of 1871 reduced the prestige of France and therefore of the reform, and Âli Paşa was already weakened and isolated when he died, after a three-month illness, in September 1871.

The reformers were dead; France, their patron and guide, was defeated, and a mood of reaction set in against any foreign intervention. Even Ottoman Christians were dismissed from public office, and greater stress was laid on the Islamic character of the Empire and the need for Islamic unity, in a form foreshadowing the pan-Islamic doctrines current in the next decade.

[93] For a useful survey of the documents and problems relating to the so-called political testament of Fuad Paşa, see Davison, 'The Question of Fuad Paşa's "Political Testament" ', *Bell.*, no. 89 (1959), 119–36.

Under Abdülaziz the doctrine was more actively advanced
that the Ottoman Sultan was not only the head of the Ottoman
Empire but also the Caliph of all Muslims and the heir, in a sense
not previously accepted, of the Caliphs of early times. At a
time when most Muslim lands in Africa and Asia were falling
under European colonial rule, this new claim quickly won
considerable support, and the Ottoman Caliphate provided a
rallying point for the forces opposed to Westernization and to the
West.[94]

The death of Âli Paşa and the triumph of the reaction provide a
convenient halt at which to consider the efforts of the reformers,
and the effects and limitations of their achievement.

Conclusions

In European writings on the nineteenth-century Turkish reforms it has become a commonplace that the reforms were still-
born. 'The *Tanzimat* stopped at the doorstep of the Sublime
Porte.'[95] Yet a comparison of Turkey in 1800 with Turkey in 1871
will reveal many profound changes—soon enough to show that,
for better or worse, the *Tanzimat* were more than a sop to Europe
or a pious expression of good intentions by naïve would-be
reformers.

The general feeling of Europe was that the ancient institutions
and structure of the Empire were barbarous and irretrievably bad,
and that only the adoption, as rapidly as possible, of a European
form of government and way of life would admit Turkey to the
rank and privileges of a civilized state. This view was urged on
Turkish statesmen with considerable vigour by the governments
and embassies of the European powers, and eventually came to be
accepted, at least tacitly, by a larger and larger proportion of a
Turkish ruling class, which was deeply aware of the power,
wealth, and progress of Europe as compared with their own
backwardness, poverty, and weakness. Their attitude is well
expressed in a famous poem by Ziya Paşa (1825–80) one of the
outstanding intellectual figures of nineteenth-century Turkey:

> I passed through the lands of the infidels, I saw cities and mansions;
> I wandered in the realm of Islam, I saw nothing but ruins.[96]

[94] See below, pp. 323 ff. and 340–3.
[95] Cited in Geoffrey Lewis, *Turkey* (1955), p. 35.
[96] This poem, written in Geneva in 1870, will be found in many Turkish anthologies.

But in questioning the common assumption that the reforms were ineffectual, we may also question the related assumption that what effect they did have was beneficial, and represented an improvement on what had gone before.

Already in the first half of the nineteenth century some voices were raised in doubt. Perhaps the most penetrating comments are those of Adolphus Slade, a British naval officer who visited Turkey many times from 1829 onwards, and acquired an intimate knowledge of the language, the country, and the people. His basic criticism is that the reformers destroyed an old order which was not in itself evil, but on the contrary contained much that was enviable:

Hitherto the Osmanley has enjoyed by custom some of the dearest privileges of freemen, for which Christian nations have so long struggled. He paid nothing to the government beyond a moderate land-tax, although liable, it is true, to extortions, which might be classed with assessed taxes. He paid no tithes, the vacouf sufficing for the maintenance of the ministers of Islamism. He travelled where he pleased without passports; no custom-house officer intruded his eyes and dirty fingers among his baggage; no police watched his motions, or listened for his words. His house was sacred. His sons were never taken from his side to be soldiers, unless war called them. His views of ambition were not restricted by the barriers of birth and wealth: from the lowest origin he might aspire without presumption to the rank of pasha; if he could read, to that of grand vezir; and this consciousness, instilled and supported by numberless precedents, ennobled his mind, and enabled him to enter on the duties of high office without embarrassment. Is not this the advantage so prized by free nations? Did not the exclusion of the people from posts of honour tend to the French revolution? I might infinitely extend the parallel existing between nations removed by ages of knowledge. One more example, rather burlesque, however, than correct. The Janizzaries of Constantinople somewhat resembled a chamber of deputies, for they often compelled their sovereign to change his ministers, and any talented, factious member among them, with the art of inflaming men's passions, was sure to obtain a good employment in order to appease him.[97]

It appears on p. 29 of the very useful collection of 'Turkish poetry under Western influence' ed. by Kenan Akyüz, *Batı Tesirinde Türk Şiiri Antolojisi* (1953). For discussions of Ziya Paşa and his work see Gibb, *Ottoman Poetry*, v. 41–111, and below, pp. 138 ff.

[97] Slade, i. 275–6 (2nd ed. p. 145).

This order Mahmud destroyed, and in its place offered nothing but his own unbridled will:

> For this freedom, this capability of realizing the wildest wishes, what equivalent does the Sultan offer? It may be said none. I do not think that the Osmanleys would have objected to a uniform system of government, with the burthen of a standing army which would have defended their honour, provided their liberties had been respected. But instead of engrafting his plans on the old system, which—embracing a respected hierarchy, an hereditary noblesse, and a provincial magistracy—offered such facilities, with a studious care not to shock prejudices, idle, but sanctified; to make it appear that he aimed at rendering European subservient to Asiatic, rather than Asiatic to European, manners, he rejected all subterfuge, and prematurely disclosed his schemes of self-aggrandizement and appropriation which disgusted his subjects, and changed their respect for him into something less than honour.[98]

Moltke passes a similar judgement:

> For the accomplishment of his purpose it was indispensable for him to raze to the ground any other authority within the compass of the Empire and to unite the whole plenitude of power in his own hand; to clear the site before setting up his own building. The first part of his great task the Sultan carried through with perspicacity and resolution; in the second he failed.[99]

After Mahmud, the men of the *Tanzimat* tried to erect a new structure on the terrain which he had levelled with such violent and destructive haste. But they were working in a style and with materials that were unfamiliar to them, with unskilled and resentful workmen, and alien and therefore mistrusted foremen— or none at all.

Nevertheless they accomplished a great deal. In the world of the nineteenth and twentieth centuries, Turkey had to modernize herself or perish, and the men of the *Tanzimat*, with all their failings, laid the indispensable foundation for the more thorough modernization that was to follow. Their legal and administrative reforms were often ill judged and incompetently applied—but in a world of railways and telegraphs the old feudal structure of the Empire could not survive, and there was in reality little freedom of choice. Perhaps their greatest achievement was in

---

[98] Slade, i. 276–7 (2nd ed. p. 146).   [99] Moltke, pp. 409–10.

education. In the schools and colleges set up during the nineteenth century, slowly and painfully a new educated *élite* was
evolved, with a new spirit, and a new and clearer perception of
realities. The problems of moral and spiritual adjustment were
enormous, and there were many, far too many, who fell into
frustration, cynicism, and corruption. The new class of officials
emerging from the schools were often ignorant, superficial,
corrupt, and separated from those over whom they ruled by a
widening gulf; but even this was better than the ignorant self-
assurance of those whom they replaced. And among these new
officials there was a high proportion of men of loyalty, integrity,
and responsibility, with a real understanding of the problems and
difficulties of their country, and a determination to face and
overcome them. The infusion of this new spirit into the dominant
classes of the Empire was a slow, often a heart-breaking business,
but by the twentieth century it had produced a ruling *élite* with the
knowledge, the capacity, and above all the sense of responsibility
and decision to carry through the great social and political
revolution that made modern Turkey. The value of that *élite*
to Turkey is strikingly confirmed by the penalties of its absence
in other countries with a similar legacy and similar problems.

The difficulties facing the nineteenth-century reformers were
enormous. The forces opposing them, even though pursuing
objectives which were ultimately unrealizable, were none the less
truculent and menacing. There was much about the reforms to
arouse resentment and dislike. The political, social, and economic
changes they involved seemed to offer some kind of threat to the
interests of almost every group in Turkish society; to almost all
they appeared as a triumph over Islam of the millennial Christian
enemy in the West. For the reforms were basically the forcible
imposition, on a Muslim country, of practices and procedures
derived from Europe, with the encouragement, if not the insistence, of European powers, and with the help of European experts
and advisers. Military defeat and political humiliation had indeed
shaken the torpid and complacent trust of the Turks in their own
invincible and immutable superiority, but the ancient contempt
for the barbarian infidel, where it yielded, often gave place to
rancour rather than emulation. The reforms were not endeared to
the Muslim population by the obvious and active interest of the

Christian powers in furthering them; the granting of equal status to non-Muslims within the Empire was to many the final insult and outrage.

By 1871 the reform had already gone far enough to make a simple policy of reversion to the past impracticable. The destruction of the old order had been too thorough for any restoration to be possible; for better or for worse, only one path lay before Turkey, that of modernization and Westernization. She could move fast or slowly, straight or deviously; she could not go back.

CHAPTER V

The Seeds of Revolution

In front of the central gate one encounters a statue of freedom; she has a staff in her hand and is seated on a chair. Her appearance and manner convey this meaning to spectators: 'O worthy visitors! When you look upon this fascinating display of human progress, do not forget that all these perfections are the work of freedom. It is under the protection of freedom that peoples and nations attain happiness. Without freedom, there can be no security; without security, no endeavour; without endeavour, no prosperity; without prosperity, no happiness! . . .

SADULLAH PAŞA, 'The Paris Exhibition', 1878.

The substance of the ideas of 1789 is not the limitation of the sovereign power, but the abrogation of intermediate powers.

LORD ACTON, 'Nationality', 1862.

THE Turkish word *hürriyet*, freedom, derives from the Arabic *hurriyya*, an abstract noun formed from *hurr*, free. In classical Islamic usage it is employed commonly in a legal and social, exceptionally in a philosophic sense. In the former it denotes the converse of slavery, of the servile status, sometimes also exemption or privilege; in the latter freedom of will—the converse of pre-destination.[1] At no time does it seem to have had the meaning which Cicero, in imitation of Aristotle, gave to the Latin *libertas* —that of citizenship, of the right to share in the conduct of government.

It was in the course of the eighteenth century that the word first began to acquire a new significance in Turkish. Reports from France, translations of French manifestoes, helped to familiarize the new notion.[2] The first reception was not favourable. In 1798

[1] See the dictionaries of classical Arabic by Freytag, Lane, Dozy, &c. The social meaning is noted especially in Muslim Spain (cf. the Spanish *Vocabulista aravigo en letra castellana* of Pedro de Alcala, Granada 1505, *hurr* = 'franco previlegiado': Dozy, i. 262). The philosophic meaning is rare, freedom of will being denoted by other words.

[2] The term first used for political freedom was the now obsolete *serbestiyet*, a pseudo-Arabic abstract formation from *serbest*, an Ottoman term of Persian origin, connoting the absence of limitations or restrictions. It was normally used in a fiscal context. *Serbestiyet* was only gradually replaced by the now common *hürriyet*. In Ruphy's Arabic word list, prepared for the French expedition in Egypt at the beginning of the nineteenth century, *hurriyya* is given as equivalent to *liberté*, but with the restriction 'opposé à l'esclavage' (J. F. Ruphy, *Dictionnaire abrégé François-arabe* (Paris, An X [1802], p, 120). In the sense of 'pouvoir d'agir' Ruphy prefers the Arabic term *sarāh*). As

the Reis Efendi Atıf, reporting on the proceedings of the French in the areas they had occupied on the Adriatic coast, remarks that 'their action in recalling the form of government of the ancient Greeks and installing a régime of liberty in these places reveals beyond any need for comment or explanation the evil intentions in their minds'.[3]

Nationalism and liberalism—Atıf had correctly diagnosed the two forces that in the nineteenth century were to do so much to destroy the Empire. Later in the same year the Sultan tried to refute these dangerous new ideas, describing French liberty as mere libertinism and anarchy:

> In this vain belief and preposterous opinion they have erected new principles and set new laws, and established what Satan whispered to them, and destroyed the bases of religions, and made lawful to themselves forbidden things, and permitted themselves whatever their passions desire, and have enticed into their iniquity the common people, who are as raving madmen, and sown sedition among religions, and thrown mischief between kings and states. . . .[4]

But despite these and other efforts to destroy it, the slip from the tree of liberty planted in the soil of Turkey struck root. Before long another development heightened the interest of thoughtful Turks in liberty, equality, and the rule of law. During the first half of the nineteenth century growing numbers of Turks, especially among those who had had the opportunity to travel in the West, were becoming disagreeably aware of the backwardness and poverty of their own country, as contrasted with a Europe which was rich and powerful beyond belief, and which, in its limitless self-confidence and aggressiveness, seemed to be bringing the whole world within its grasp. The old question: 'Why is the Empire declining?' had now to be restated: 'Why is the Empire declining while Europe advances and progresses, and what is the secret of European success?'

For a while the secret was believed to lie in European manufactures and technical devices, which were the sole merits of an

late as 1841 Handjeri, in his *Dictionnaire français-arabe-persan et turc*, 3 vols. (Moscow, 1840–1) renders 'liberté civile' and 'liberté politique' by *ruhsat-i şeriye* and *ruhsat-i mülkiye* respectively, and it is only about the mid-century in the new newspapers and periodicals that we begin to find *hürriyet* in the sense of political freedom. See *EI*[2] ('Hurriyya ii', by B. Lewis).

[3] Cevdet, *Tarih*, vi. 400–1; cf. B. Lewis in *Slav. R.*, xxxiv (1955), 232–5.

[4] Ferman of 1798; cf. above, p. 67.

otherwise contemptible crew of barbarians. The redoubtable Halet Efendi, who was ambassador in Paris from 1803 to 1806, expresses this view in its crudest form:

> God knows, their minds and their comprehension are such, that the difference between them and the people of Islam is like the difference between boatmen and scribes among us. Their strategems and policies are crude; before they even formulate an intention one can understand what they are going to do; these successes they have won arise only from our own lack of zeal, for they have no soldiers as brave as ours, no ministers like our ministers, and our artillery officers are more competent than theirs. Their capital consists of nothing but talk. God knows, I am of the opinion that if, as an emergency measure once every three or four years, 25,000 purses of aspers were to be set aside, and five factories for snuff, paper, crystal, cloth and porcelain, as well as a school for languages and geography set up, then in the course of five years there will be as good as nothing left for them to hold on to, since the basis of all their current trade is in these five commodities. May God bestow some zeal on our masters, Amen.[5]

Industry and science—factories and schools; these were the talismans by which both Mahmud II in Turkey and Muhammad Ali in Egypt tried to conjure up the wealth and power of Europe, and thus maintain the European-style armies which were their prime concern. The same basic ideas have underlain the work of many subsequent reformers and innovators.

But once a door had been opened in the wall separating Islam from Christendom, it was no longer possible to control and select the traffic in ideas that passed through it. Young Turks were learning European languages, studying with European teachers travelling in Europe—it was inevitable that they should extend their reading and their interests somewhat beyond the acquisition of the technical skills assigned to them.

The talisman did not seem to be working too well; some further secrets concerning its correct application must be discovered. To the eager young Turkish visitor to Europe, in search of the elusive source of European strength, it seemed natural to seek it in those features of European life and government which were most different from his own. Liberalism, in the 1830's and 1840's, was the sacred cause of enlightenment and progress, combining the hopes both of the noblest of idealists and the most practical of

[5] Karal, *Halet*, pp. 32–33; cf. above, p. 69.

business men and technicians—and what, to the visiting Oriental, could be more peculiar, more distinctive of the West, than constitutional and parliamentary government?

One of the first to argue along these lines was Sadık Rifat Paşa (1807–56), who went to the Turkish Embassy in Vienna in 1837 and later held a number of senior appointments in Istanbul.[6] One of his writings is a twelve-page essay entitled 'Concerning the Condition of Europe' of which a first draft was prepared during his embassy in Vienna.

In this essay he sets forth some ideas on the essential differences between Europe and Turkey, and those respects in which the latter should seek to imitate the former. Like many of his generation, Sadık Rifat was deeply impressed by the wealth, industry, and science of Europe, and saw in these the chief means of regenerating his country. But he also links European progress and prosperity to certain political conditions. The basis of the prosperity of European states, he explains, is the steady increase in numbers of the population, the improvement in cultivation of the country, and the maintenance of tranquillity and security. But these in turn depend on

the attainment of complete security for the life, property, honour, and reputation of each nation and people, that is to say, on the proper application of the necessary rights of liberty. This being so, this kind of security and these rights of liberty are maintained with exceeding care and concern; since individual subjects and likewise countries are not made and created for states, but on the contrary, by the wisdom of the Almighty King, the sovereigns of the world were only vouchsafed the grace of God in order to protect and safeguard the welfare and prosperity of countries, therefore in the conduct of the affairs of government they act in accordance with the rights of the nation and the laws of the state, and no kind of arbitrary or violent action occurs. . . . Since these matters occupy, for the civilised states of Europe, the position of the alphabet of their basic policy, it is a matter of urgent necessity to strive with the utmost exertion of will and endeavour to secure the conditions by which they may also be attained for the Empire. . . .[7]

[6] On Sadık Rifat Paşa see Tanpınar, i. 88 ff.; Şeref, *Tar. Mus.*, pp. 115 ff.; Ali Fuat, 'Ricali Tanzimattan Rifat Paşa' in *TTEM*, n.s. i/2 (1930), 1–11; Mardin, *Genesis*, pp. 169 ff.; Berkes, *Development*, pp. 130 ff.

[7] A version of Sadık Rifat's memorandum was published by Şeref, pp. 125 ff. A somewhat variant text will be found in Sadık Rifat's collected writings, *Müntehabât-i Asar* (n.d.) which includes a brief biography of the pasha.

Rifat's basic ideas are well within the framework of traditional Islamic political thought. His concern is with justice rather than liberty—with the obligation of rulers to rule according to law and to treat their subjects justly and benevolently. But the idea that the subject has a *right* to such treatment is a new one, in marked contrast to the older conception summed up in an Arab dictum: 'If the Caliph is just, his the reward and yours to be thankful. If he is unjust, his the sin and yours to be patient.'[8]

When Rifat speaks of 'the rights of the people' and 'the rights of liberty', he is expressing new ideas, derived from France, and still imperfectly understood. We find them again in the Essay on Europe of Seyyid Mustafa Sami, a former chief secretary of the Turkish Embassy in Paris. In this essay, published in 1840, the author speaks with admiration of the European form of government, of freedom of religion, of equality and security before the law, of liberty and progress.[9]

Both writers stress the importance of science in creating prosperity, and are aware of a connexion between science and freedom. But freedom for them still means equality and security before the law—the security of the subject from arbitrary and illegal actions by the government, and not his right to share in it. The statesmen of the *Tanzimat* held the same opinion, and tried, by making new laws and establishing new courts, to protect the subject from arbitrary action by the government or its agents. The triumph of science, the rule of law, and the spread of education are jointly celebrated in the somewhat ponderous ecstasies of Sadullah Paşa's (1838–91) ode on 'The Nineteenth Century':[10]

The rights of person and possession are protected from attack,
A new order has been given to the world of civilization.

[8] Ibn 'Abd Rabbihi, *Kitāb al-'Iqd al-Farīd*, i (Cairo, 1940), 10; cf. B. Lewis, 'The Concept of an Islamic Republic', *WI*, i (1955), 7.

[9] Tanpınar, pp. 93 ff. Another work of the time, of great importance in the spread of liberal and constitutional ideas, is the account written by the Egyptian Azhari Shaykh Rifā'a Rāfi' al-Tahtāwī of his stay in Paris during the years 1826–31. Rifā'a's book, which appeared in Bulaq in Arabic in 1834 and in a Turkish version in 1839, includes a translation, with comments, of the French constitution, a discussion of the 1830 revolution, which the author witnessed, and a description of how constitutional and representative government functions as a safeguard against tyranny.

[10] Akyüz, *Antoloji*, pp. 66 ff. The poem will also be found in other anthologies. For other examples of his writings see Ebüzziya Tevfik, *Nümûne-i Edebiyat-ı Osmaniye* (1306 A.H.), pp. 280 ff.

Amr is not Zeyd's slave, nor is Zeyd Amr's master,[11]
A clear and indubitable rule establishes the basis of equality.
The spread of science has enlightened the minds of men,
The printing press has completed what was lacking.
Alas, the Western lands have become the daysprings of knowledge,
Nothing remains of the fame of Rūm and Arab, of Egypt and Herat.
The time is a time of progress, the world is a world of science,
Is the survival of societies compatible with ignorance?

Even the Sultans and their ministers gave some recognition to the new ideas on the relationship between sovereign and subject. The Noble Rescript of the Rose Bower of 1839 lays down that the new institutions, to be set up for the better government of the Empire, must cover three major points, the first of which is 'the guarantees ensuring to our subjects perfect security for life, honour and fortune'. The Imperial Rescript of 1856 goes still further, and reaffirms in its very first article that

the guarantees promised on our part by the Imperial Rescript of the Rose Bower and the laws of the *Tanzimat* to all the subjects of my Empire, without distinction of class or religion, for the security of their persons and their property and the preservation of their honour, are today being confirmed and consolidated, and efficacious measures shall be taken in order that they may have their full and entire effect.

These guarantees are impressive enough on paper, and led some observers to describe the reforming edicts as the Charters of the Ottoman Empire. The reformers themselves were no doubt sincere in their intentions, and Sultan Abdülmecid had, in 1845, gone so far as to convene an assembly of provincial notables for consultation. But in fact the autocratic authority of the central government was not decreasing but increasing throughout the nineteenth century. The old and well-tried checks on the Sultan's despotism had all gone: the corps of Janissaries, with its ancient privileges and its deep conviction of corporate identity and prerogative; the feudal sipahis; the local dynasties of the valley-lords and the provincial magistracy of the *ayan*; the separate power of the ulema, controllers of the law, religion, and education, buttressed by an independent hierarchy of dignitaries and underpinned by vast independent revenues. These, and all other intermediate powers, had been abrogated or enfeebled, leaving the

[11] Amr and Zeyd are Arab personal names, traditionally used in Islamic law books—the John Doe and Richard Roe of the Holy Law.

sovereign power with nothing but the paper shackles of its own edicts to restrain it. These edicts, alien in their conception and irrelevant in their application to the problems of an Islamic Empire, had little chance of success. Their purpose and purport were meaningless or suspect to the mass of the Sultan's subjects; the men entrusted with their enforcement were inept and half-hearted; nor was there any group, any force among the different classes of the population which might, in its own interest, have impelled their effective application.

But the growth of autocracy, if unchecked, did not pass un-noticed—and in the Europe of the mid-nineteenth century there was no lack of ideologies of revolt. Islam was no longer insulated. Young France, Young England, Young Germany, were an inspiration to Young Turkey also. Turkish students and diplomats witnessed—may even have shared in—the heart-lifting events of 1848. After the suppression of the Hungarian rising of that year, a number of Hungarian and also some Polish revolutionaries sought refuge in Turkey.[12] As rebels against Russia and Austria they could be sure of a sympathetic welcome, and this time they brought new ideas against which their hosts were no longer immune.

The mounting economic difficulties of the country, the replace-ment of the easy-going Sultan Abdülmecid by the more despotic Abdülaziz, and the growing power of the central government and bureaucracy, brought matters to a head, and during the 1860's a new phase began in which the argument was no longer whether to accept or reject the Westernizing reforms, but whether—and how —to limit the autocratic power of the state. An important new element in the situation was the upsurge of the new, school-trained intelligentsia, with some religious support, against the entrenched oligarchy of senior bureaucrats and ulema. The former were drawn from a wide range of social backgrounds; the latter often— though by no means always—belonged to a small group of established families.

The new phase of reform was opened not by government enact-ments but by literary manifestoes, and the first leaders of Young Turkey were not politicians but poets and writers.

[12] See below, p. 345.

The Literary Movement [13]

From about the middle of the century the spread of Western ideas and the acclimatization of Western social and political attitudes among the Turks was greatly accelerated by the rise of a new Turkish literature, differing both in form and in content from classical Ottoman writings. In it the literature of France had begun to replace the classics of Iran as the source of inspiration and the model for imitation.

Three men are usually credited with being the pioneers of this new literature; Ibrahim Şinasi (1826–71), Ziya Paşa (1825–80), and Namık Kemal (1840–88). Ibrahim Şinasi was a poet, dramatist, and journalist.[14] The son of an artillery officer, he received his first instruction in French from one of his father's colleagues, a French renegade in the Ottoman service, and himself obtained a post in the artillery office. Thanks to the protection of Reşid Paşa he was able to join one of the Turkish student missions to Paris, where he stayed for four or five years. According to Turkish literary tradition he took part in the revolution of 1848, and hung a republican flag on the Pantheon. Certainly he was a young student in Paris during or shortly after those heroic days, and cannot but have been marked by them. While he was there, he is said to have been befriended by Samuel de Sacy, the son of the famous Orientalist Silvestre de Sacy, and to have made the acquaintance of the poet Lamartine, by whose writings he was much influenced.

On his return to Turkey he re-entered the government service, and became a member of the newly created Council of Education. He was, however, viewed with disfavour because of his Westernized manners. A particular grievance was his shaving of his beard —a practice due, according to one source, to a skin infection,

---

[13] The pioneer account of Turkish literary and intellectual movements in the nineteenth century is that given by Tanpınar, in the work already cited. Works in Western languages include A. Bombaci, *Storia della letteratura turca* (1956); Ş. Mardin, *The Genesis of Young Ottoman Thought* (1962); N. Berkes, *The Development of Secularism in Turkey* (1964). A very useful series of selections will be found in the *Türk Klasikleri*, published by Varlık Yayınları, Ist., 1952 ff.

[14] On Şinasi see *EI*[1] ('Shināsī', by J. Deny); Gibb, *Ottoman Poetry*, v. 22–40; Tanpınar, pp. 155–88; Şinasi (*Türk Klas.*, xxv); Ebüzziya, *Nümûne*, pp. 220–48; Akyüz, *Antoloji*, pp. 1–15; Mardin, pp. 252 ff.; and the relevant passages in the general literary histories and anthologies.

according to another, to Frankish influence. A beardless official was as much an oddity at that date as a bearded one would be today, and before long Âli Paşa himself ordered Şinasi's dismissal from the Council of Education, in a document demanding 'the abrogation of his rank, the cancellation of his appointment, the cessation of his salary'.[15]

Âli Paşa's objection to Şinasi was not confined to his bare chin; there was the more serious matter of his being a protégé of Reşid Paşa. Other nominees of Reşid Paşa, impeccably bearded, were also removed by the great reformer's disciples and rivals. On Reşid Paşa's return to the Grand Vezirate, Şinasi was reinstated in his former appointment. The death of Reşid in 1858 deprived him of his protector, but also took the sting out of Âli and Fuad Paşas' antagonism, and for some time Şinasi was untroubled by official hostility.

From this time onwards he became increasingly occupied with literature and with journalism—a new profession and a new form of expression in Turkey. From 1862 he edited his own journal, the *Tasvir-i Efkâr*, which came to play a role of great importance in the intellectual life of the country. In 1865, for reasons that are not quite clear, he seems to have feared official anger, and left once again for Paris, from where he did not finally return until after the death of Fuad Paşa in 1869. He himself died in Istanbul in 1871.

Şinasi's political ideas were cautious and tentative, and contained no radical criticisms of the existing order. The general line of his thought is, however, indicated in an ode which he wrote to Mustafa Reşid Paşa at the time of the promulgation of the Imperial Rescript of 1856—that is, shortly after his own return from his studies in France:

> Life, property and honour are the candles of our hearts,
> Your justice is a lantern to guard us from the blast of oppression.
>
> You have made us free, who were slaves to tyranny,
> Bound as if in chains by our own ignorance.
>
> Your law is an act of manumission for men,
> Your law informs the Sultan of his limits.[16]

The radical implications of the last couplet will be obvious.

[15] Şinasi, *Türk Klas.*, p. 6.

[16] Ibid. pp. 42-43; Akyüz, *Antoloji*, p. 8; Bombaci, p. 426.

Also a protégé of Reşid Paşa was Ziya Paşa, the second of the three pioneers of the new literature.[17] The son of a clerk in the customs house at Galata, he was educated at the grammar school which Sultan Mahmud II had opened by the Süleymaniye mosque, and entered the civil service at the age of seventeen. In 1854, thanks tó the influence of Reşid Paşa, whose goodwill he had won, Ziya was appointed third secretary to the Sultan, and embarked on a new career in the Imperial household. It was at this stage that he began to study French, and soon acquired sufficient mastery of the language to translate French books into Turkish.

Like Şinasi and other protégés of Reşid Paşa, he was not viewed with favour by Âli and Fuad Paşas, the more so since he seems to have used his position in the palace to warn the Sultan against Âli Paşa. Eventually Âli Paşa secured his removal from the Imperial household. Ziya then held various minor posts, and at the same time joined with Namık Kemal and other young men in forming the Young Ottoman Movement. In 1867, faced with virtual banishment as titular governor of Cyprus, he fled to Europe together with a number of his Young Ottoman associates.

Between 1867 and 1872 Ziya remained an exile, first in Paris, then in London, and finally in Geneva. During these years he wrote some of his most vigorous criticisms of the régime of Âli and Fuad Paşas, and of the changes they were making in Turkey. After the death of Âli Paşa, he was authorized to return to Turkey, where in 1876 he was made governor of Syria, with the rank of vezir and pasha, by Sultan Abdülhamid. He died in Adana in May 1880.

Ziya Paşa was by no means a consistent Westernizer. While urging the importance of learning Western languages, he disapproved of the imitation of Western literary models, since each civilization had its own genius:

> Is there not a difference of climate?
> Is the situation of East and West the same?
> Could Racine or Lamartine adorn a Kasida like Nefi?
> Could Senai or Farazdak write plays like Molière?[18]

[17] On Ziya Paşa see Gibb, *Ottoman Poetry*, v. 41–111; Tanpınar, pp. 279–321; Ziya Paşa (*Türk Klas.*); Ebüzziya, *Nümûne*, pp. 249–79; Akyüz, *Antoloji*, pp. 16–41; Mardin, pp. 337 ff., &c.

[18] Ziya Paşa, *Türk Klas*, p. 68 (from *Harabât*, Introduction, sect. 15).

He is by no means enthusiastic about the granting of equal status to non-Muslims, and in his famous satire against Âli Paşa he criticizes the minister's moves in that direction:

> If but the help of God assist in his purpose clear,
> Full soon will these gypsies sit on the couch of the Grand Vezir;
> It is but the Jews alone that form the exception here,
> For of Greeks and Armenians both doth he make Bey and Mushir;
> The equality of rights to perfection brought hath he.[19]

In a bitter attack on the fashions of his time, he observes:

> To impute fanaticism to men of zeal
> To ascribe wisdom to men without religion is now the fashion.
>
> Islam, they say, is a stumbling-block to the progress of the state
> This story was not known before, and now it is the fashion.
>
> Forgetting our religious loyalty in all our affairs
> Following Frankish ideas is now the fashion.[20]

But Ziya, despite his cultural and religious conservatism, did not himself disdain to follow Frankish ideas, suitably disguised. The most potent of these was constitutional government. His views on this matter are contained in two works, both written during his exile. The first, entitled 'Dream',[21] describes a vision which Ziya saw while sleeping on a bench in Hampstead Heath, and is curiously reminiscent of the visionary dialogue of the seventeenth-century poet Veysi,[22] and similar works. In his dream Ziya has a conversation with Sultan Abdülaziz, and warns the Sultan of the parlous state of the country. The Sultan accuses Ziya of having tried to undermine his authority by recommending the formation of a national assembly, and Ziya replies that the creation of such an assembly would bring Turkey into line with the practice of civilized states without infringing the lawful rights of the sovereign.

Now condescend to look at the states of this continent of Europe. Apart from Russia, does arbitrary government remain anywhere? And is not even Russia gradually trying to imitate the systems of

[19] Tr. by E. J. W. Gibb, *Ottoman Poetry*, v. 105–6.

[20] Akyüz, *Antoloji*, p. 38 (*Terkib-i Bend*, no. x).

[21] An abridged text of *Rüya* (Dream) will be found in Ziya Paşa, *Türk Klas.*, pp. 111–19.

[22] On Veysi see Gibb, *Ottoman Poetry*, iii. 208 ff.

government of the other European states? Are the Emperors of France and Austria, the Kings of Italy and Prussia, the Queen of England less than the Russian in might and majesty? . . . Since the lofty Dynasty is also considered one of the family of Europe, it is not within the bounds of possibility for us to remain in this way at variance with all the world.[23]

The Sultan, in Ziya's dream, is still not satisfied, and points out that while these other states each rule over one nation, his subjects are of various religions, and since each group would pursue its own interests, a national assembly would only provide a platform for conflict and give rise to dissension and disunity. Ziya agrees, and says: 'Yes, Sire, if the national assembly to be created here were to begin with the privileges of the French or English parliaments, this observation would indeed be in place.'[24] But this is not what he has in mind. The Ottoman assembly, for the reasons noted, must begin with limited powers, which may, however, be extended when this can be done with safety. The dream ends when Ziya is awakened by a park-keeper.

In another essay written during his exile Ziya takes as his text the tradition attributed to the Prophet that 'difference of opinion within my community is an act of divine mercy'.[25] This saying, which was usually cited to legitimize the coexistence of different schools of Holy Law, was given a new meaning by Ziya, and used by him to justify the creation of an assembly where truth would emerge from the clash of different opinions, and in which responsible statesmen would have to submit their actions to the test of criticism and opposition.

The same tradition is cited in a famous ode to freedom by the third and by far the most gifted of the trio of literary innovators. Namık Kemal was born in Tekirdağ in 1840, to an aristocratic family.[26] His father was the court astronomer, and the somewhat

[23] Ziya Paşa, *Türk Klas.*, p. 115.   [24] Ibid. p. 116.
[25] Text in Ebüzziya, *Nümûne*, pp. 257–61; *Türk Klas.*, ed., pp. 138–41.
[26] On Namık Kemal see *EI*[1] ('Kemal', by Th. Menzel); Tanpınar, pp. 322–432; Namık Kemal (*Türk Klas.*); Ebüzziya, *Nümûne*, pp. 294–493; Akyüz, *Antoloji*, pp. 42–65; Berkes, in Frye, pp. 65 ff.; Mardin, pp. 283 ff., &c. Among many modern Turkish works on Namık Kemal, special mention may be made of Mithat Cemal Kuntay, *Namık Kemal* (1944–56); and Mehmed Kaplan, *Namık Kemal*; *Hayatı ve Eserleri* (1948). A useful selection of his journalistic writings will be found in Mustafa Nihat Özön, *Namık Kemal ve İbret Gazetesi* (1938).

impoverished descendant of a line of Ottoman officials. His mother, of Albanian birth, was the daughter of a governor. He was educated at home, and was taught French as well as Persian and Arabic. Following the normal course of young men of his class and time, he entered the civil service at the age of seventeen and found a niche in the Translation Office of the Customs, and then of the Sublime Porte.

He soon came under the influence of Şinasi, and collaborated with him on the journal *Tasvir-i Efkâr*, of which he took over the editorship when Şinasi fled to France in 1865. At first his contributions consisted exclusively of translations, but then the need to deal with such events as the second Polish revolution of 1863–4 and the American Civil War sharpened his perceptions and improved his skill as a political journalist and essayist. His essays on Ottoman affairs brought him into trouble with the authorities, and in 1867, together with Ziya and the other Young Ottomans, he fled to Europe.

The next three years were spent in exile, in London, Paris, and Vienna. There he occupied himself with the publication of opposition journals, with the study of law and economics, and with the translation of a number of French works into Turkish.

On his return to Turkey in 1871 he resumed his journalistic activities, and in 1873 produced the patriotic drama *Vatan*.[27] This aroused such dangerous enthusiasms that the author was imprisoned in Cyprus, where he remained for over three years. After the deposition of Sultan Abdülaziz in 1876, he was allowed to return to Istanbul, and took some part in the preparation of the constitution, though, like Ziya, he was debarred from offering himself as a candidate. Later he fell foul of Sultan Abdülhamid, and spent most of his remaining years in detention or exile. He died in Chios in 1888.

Namık Kemal is best known in Turkey as the apostle of two ideas: freedom and fatherland. In a long series of articles, essays, novels, plays, and poems he brought to the Turkish Muslim reader these two characteristic ideas of the French Revolution, but in a form adapted to Muslim traditions and attitudes.

Despite his fervent patriotism and liberalism, Namık Kemal was a sincere and devoted Muslim, and the Fatherland of which he

[27] See below, p. 158.

speaks, though he uses a term denoting territory and not community, is Islamic no less than Ottoman. Throughout his life he remained firmly attached to traditional Muslim values and beliefs, and was often sharply critical of the men of the *Tanzimat* for their failure to safeguard and preserve the best of the old Islamic traditions, and to let them inspire and direct the new institutions which had to be imported from Europe. He upheld Islamic values and defended Islamic achievements against European belittlers, and even advanced the idea of a pan-Islamic unity, under Ottoman leadership, to accept, adapt, and diffuse modern civilization through Asia and Africa, and thus create an Eastern balance of power to counter that of Europe.

He was profoundly impressed by the achievements of European civilization. The backwardness of Islam, however, was in his view relative rather than absolute; it was not due to any inherent defect in Islam itself, but to the domination of the West, which had deprived the East of the opportunity of self-advancement. The Islamic state had to modernize itself, but in doing so it should not slavishly imitate Europe and abandon its own laws, beliefs, and traditions. On the contrary, he argued, all that is best in European civilization derived from or could be paralleled in classical Islamic civilization, and the Muslim, in adopting these things, was returning to what was deepest and most authentic in his own tradition. Here Namık Kemal used a line of argument that was to become typical of a certain trend of romantic and apologetic writing among Muslims. Sometimes its purpose was to win the respect of Westerners or Westernizers for traditional Islamic values. More frequently, in this period, it was intended to make the ideas of the reformers more palatable to orthodox Muslims.

Namık Kemal's political theory derives largely from Montesquieu and Rousseau, his ideas on the practice of government from the parliaments of London and Paris. One of the deepest and most lasting influences on his political thinking was Montesquieu's *Esprit des Lois*, of which he began to publish a translation in 1863. In later essays he tried to make the ideas of Montesquieu compatible with the principles of the *Şeriat*—a task which, like the earlier Muslim attempt to marry Aristotelian philosophy and Koranic theology, involved some reinterpretation of both. For Kemal, the wise and just rules of the *Şeriat* are none other than the natural law of which Montesquieu speaks, and 'the nature of things', from which law arises, could therefore be identified with a somewhat sufistic conception of God Himself.

According to the law-makers, there is no greater task than striving, from the point of view of abstract good, to bring to light origins and consequences. With us the *Şeriat* determines good and evil. Among the people of our country the compatibility of these consequences with abstract good can be known by testing the case against this touchstone of justice.[28]

One of the basic rules of natural—i.e. of divine—law is freedom. Kemal was not the first to speak of human rights and parliamentary government in Turkey, but he was the first to correlate them, and to achieve a clear vision of freedom and self-government under law. Sadık Rifat Paşa had spoken of the natural human right to freedom, but had seen no way of safeguarding it except by exhorting the sovereign to rule justly. Ziya Paşa spoke of constitutions and assemblies—but saw in them only a device of government, a means of giving the Ottoman Empire the appearance, and perhaps also some of the perquisites, of a Western state. For Kemal too the primary duty of the state is still to act justly; but he also has a clear idea of the political rights of the citizen, which justice requires the state to respect, and also of the means by which they may be safeguarded. Typically, these ideas, of French and British origin, are equated with principles of Islamic law:

Every book treats the subject of political rights with different subdivisions. However, the points on which the greatest measure of agreement exists among authors are such general principles as the sovereignty of the nation, the separation of powers, the responsibility of officials, personal freedom, equality, freedom of thought, freedom of the press, freedom of association, enjoyment of property, sanctity of the home.

The sovereignty of the people, which means that the powers of the government derive from the people, and which in the technical language of the *Şeriat* is called *Baya*, is not an authority which has happened to become attached to the abstract meaning expressed by the word 'public' or 'people'; it is a right necessarily arising from the personal independence that each individual by nature possesses.

[28] 'Hukuk', from *Ibret*, no. 5 of 1872, reprinted in Özön, *Ibret*, p. 51.

'Everyone is Emperor in his own world'. . . .

To keep the government within the limits of justice, there are two basic devices. The first of them is that the fundamental rules by which it operates should no longer be implicit or tacit, but should be published to the world. . . . The second principle is consultation, whereby the legislative power is taken away from the government. . . .[29]

For these ideas Namık Kemal tried valiantly to find precedents in the Islamic past. The sovereignty of the people he identified with the *Bay'a* (Turkish *Biat*), the ceremonial acceptance of a new Caliph on his appointment, which constituted the contract between the new sovereign and his subjects. For the principle of government by consultation and representation he was able to find justification in the Koran itself, notably in the verse in the third *Sura* when the Prophet is commanded to be lenient with his followers and to take counsel with them.[30] This verse was frequently quoted by Namık Kemal, Zyia Paşa, and their friends and became one of the favourite texts of the nineteenth-century Turkish and other Muslim liberals. Kemal went further, and tried to show that the Ottoman Empire itself, before the beginning of the reforms, had practised a form of representative government. Even the Janissaries, until their abolition, served as a kind of 'armed consultative assembly of the nation'.[31]

These attempts to identify European parliamentary institutions with traditional Islam are no doubt open to damaging criticisms from the point of view of Muslim law, theology, and history. They did, however, succeed in winning acceptance far beyond the Ottoman frontiers, and in convincing a generation of Muslim intellectuals who were no longer wholly satisfied with traditional Islam, but were sufficiently attached to it to feel a need to restate and justify their Islamic faith and heritage in terms of their newly acquired Western values. The effects of their ideas can be seen after the Young Turk Revolution when, in the speech from the throne at the opening of the Ottoman parliament on 14 November

[29] 'Hukuku Umumiye', from *Ibret*, no. 18, of 1872; reprinted in Ebüzziya, *Nümûne*, pp. 357–8 and Özön, *Ibret*, pp. 96–97.

[30] Koran, iii. verse 153.

[31] Kaplan, p. 107. This idea, which Kemal expresses in a number of places, might possibly derive from Slade (*Travels*, i. 276; cf. above p. 123). That Slade was read in Turkey is attested by N. W. Senior (p. 36), who found Vefik Paşa 'reading Captain Slade's "Turkey", of which he praised the fidelity'.

1909, the Sultan began with a reference to 'the parliamentary form of government prescribed by *Şeriat*'.[32]

For the actual form of representative government to be adopted even Namık Kemal could find no model in Islamic law and history, but was compelled to look abroad. His choice fell on London. Although his Western knowledge and reading were fundamentally French, the Paris Chamber under Napoleon III was too authoritarian for his taste. In his view, the Ottomans

could very well be governed under a more liberal constitution than that of France. . . . Since the French are of a very fiery disposition, they are always inclined to change. The basis of their actions is reason, but, under the impulsion of one specious sophism they spoil the result of a thousand sound deductions. . . . Since the great republic, they have constituted thirty or forty different forms of government. . . . The Ottoman people, on the other hand, thanks to their innate gravity and calm, are in no danger of running to extremes. . . . In the course of six centuries we have made hundreds of revolts; in all of them the men who governed were changed, but the form of government remained. . . .[33]

Namık Kemal is thus very far from agreeing with Ziya Paşa's view that the Ottomans would be wise to begin with restricted parliamentary powers.

In an article entitled 'Progress', and published in the *Ibret* in November 1872, Kemal speaks in glowing terms of London. 'What need is there to wander through all the civilized countries? If a man will but stroll about London with an attentive eye, he will be bewildered by the wonders that he sees. If London be called the model of the world, it would be no exaggeration!' He goes on to speak in rapturous terms of the schools and colleges, libraries, theatres, hospitals, and factories of the English capital, above all of its parliament, 'the cradle of most of the political principles that we see in the world . . . and the embodiment in stone of the indomitable power of public opinion against authority'.[34]

[32] I. Goldziher, *Vorlesungen über den Islam* (1925), p. 380 n. 20, and Turkish press, 15 Nov. 1909.

[33] Kaplan, p. 108, quoting *Hürriyet*, no. 12.

[34] 'Terakki', from *Ibret*, no. 45 of 1872, reprinted in Ebüzziya, *Nümûne*, pp. 308 ff. and Özön, *Ibret*, pp. 176 ff.

This was the form of government, these the resources and methods, that were needed to save the Ottoman Empire from destruction. Could they be won? To this question Kemal answers with true Victorian optimism:

> It took Europe two centuries to reach this condition, and while they were the inventors in the paths of progress, we find all the means ready to hand . . . can there be any doubt that we too, even if it takes us two centuries, can reach a stage when we would be counted as one of the most civilized countries?[35]

New Media: the Press [36]

Namık Kemal and his friends had, however, no intention of waiting two centuries to catch up with a Europe which, it is implied, would meanwhile remain stationary. Their plans called for a more immediate programme of modernization and of social and political reform, the difficulties of which they grievously underestimated. Progress depended on free institutions, and free institutions were maintained by public opinion. The Ottoman liberals therefore set to work to create and instruct a Turkish public opinion which, they hoped, would play the same role in Turkey as its counterparts in Paris and London.

One of their chief media in this was the press, the importance of which, in the Western world, they were quick to realize. The first non-official periodical in Turkish, the weekly *Ceride-i Havadis* (Journal of News) had been started in 1840 by William Churchill, and was continued by his son after his death in 1864.[37] This journal, which in its form and style was moulded on the official gazette, devoted rather more space than the latter to international affairs. In its early years it encountered some difficulties, and in 1843 was forced to close down for a while, possibly as a result of Russian pressure. Later it resumed publication, and seems to have been given a government subsidy. This, and a growing revenue from advertisements, kept the journal going, though, like the official gazette, it did not achieve regularity of publication.

[35] Ibid.; Özön, p. 187.

[36] On the early history of the press in Turkey see Emin, *Press*; Gerçek, *Türk Gazet.*; Iskit, *Türkiyede Matbuat Rejimleri*; *IA* ('Matbuat II/I' by Vedad Günyol); Tanpınar, pp. 224 ff.; above, p. 93 n. 37.

[37] Gerçek, pp. 35 ff.

The outbreak of the Crimean War brought new opportunities. The journalist Churchill covered the fighting for English newspapers, and his reports, which were also published in special supplements by the *Ceride-i Havadis*, gave the news-hungry Turkish reader a new insight into the function and value of the newspaper in the modern state. To keep in touch with this growing circle of readers, the editors of the *Ceride-i Havadis* began to simplify the language in which the journal was written, gradually abandoning the cumbersome chancery style which they had previously shared with the official gazette, and adopting a simpler and more direct form of language. Turkish journalese was born in their columns. As well as news, they published articles and features, often in serial form, and thus gave a first apprenticeship in literary journalism to a number of Ottoman men of letters, perhaps including Şinasi.

Apart from the colourless official gazette, the *Ceride-i Havadis* enjoyed a virtual monopoly of journalism in the Turkish language for twenty years. During that time it played an important pioneer role, accustoming the Turkish reader to news and features, and training a generation of journalists, as well as of printers, distributors, and other necessary adjuncts of the newspaper trade. In 1860 it had to encounter another aspect of the world of Western journalism—competition. In that year Çapanzade Agah Efendi, a scion of an aristocratic *derebey* family and a senior member of the Translation Chamber of the Sublime Porte, took the initiative in founding a new weekly, the *Tercüman-i Ahval* (Interpreter of Conditions). Associated with him as editor and writer was Ibrahim Şinasi, the poet and modernist. The opening paragraphs of his first leader are a good example of the mixture of styles, ideas, and traditions of the first journalists and liberals:

Since people who live in a social body are thereby charged with legal obligations, the expression of one's ideas by word and by pen concerning the interests of one's country must assuredly be reckoned as one of the acquired rights. If written proof of this contention be sought, it may suffice to point to the political newspapers of the civilized nations whose minds have been opened by the power of knowledge.

This argument is also in a sense confirmed as regards the Exalted Dynasty, in that when the High Council of Reform was constituted, official permission was given to the public to submit, in writing, proposals concerning the laws and regulations. And moreover, the newspapers which, with the permission of the Exalted Government, the non-Muslim subjects in the Ottoman realms still publish in their own languages, have perhaps more freedom than is their right. But when we come to discuss truly Ottoman newspapers, for some reason no member of the dominant nation has up to now been willing to trouble himself with the regular publication of a non-official newspaper. Now at last, thank God, under just Imperial auspices, it has become possible to make good the deficiency of the past. So that in this way, upon a report given from the General Council of Education, which approved the purport of a recently submitted memorandum concerning a petition for the publication of a newspaper in Turkish, the Privy Council of Noble Ministers also approved the matter and, in this connexion, the Imperial consent was also vouchsafed.[38]

Churchill responded to this challenge by publishing a daily version of his paper five days a week, and for a while there was keen rivalry between the two publications. Before long, however, the new weekly ran into difficulties. In the increasingly authoritarian mood of the 1860's there were some who thought that Şinasi and his friends were exercising 'perhaps more freedom than is their right'. As a result of an article probably written by Ziya Paşa, the *Tercüman-i Ahval* was closed by government order for two weeks—an early precedent in Turkey for government suppression of a newspaper.

Şinasi himself, finding his freedom of expression restricted, left the *Tercüman-i Ahval* after only twenty-five issues, and in June 1862 began to publish his own paper, the *Tasvir-i Efkâr* (Illustration of Opinion). This paper adopted a slightly more advanced position, though its radicalism was cultural rather than political. Şinasi did, however, devote some attention to political matters, and spoke from time to time of the need for financial and legal reform. In this he was followed by his more famous disciple Namık Kemal. Kemal made his journalistic debut in the *Mirat* (Mirror), a journal which appeared in March 1863 and of which only three issues were published. Significantly, he began with an annotated translation of parts of Montesquieu's *Considérations sur les causes de la grandeur et de la décadence des Romains*. A little later he began to contribute to the *Tasvir-i Efkâr*, and when Şinasi went

[38] Reprinted in Şinasi (*Türk Klas.*), pp. 72 ff.

to Paris in 1865 took over the editing of the paper. By temperament far less circumspect than Şinasi, he began to give the paper a more outspokenly political character, and his trenchant editorials on foreign and internal questions soon began to attract the attention of authority.

Still more radical in tone and content was the *Muhbir* (Informer), the first issue of which appeared on 1 January 1867, the last on 8 March. This was edited by Ali Suavi Efendi (1838–78).[39] Unlike many of the liberals and intellectuals of the time, he had not emerged from the landowning and official classes, but was the son of a villager who had come to Istanbul and made a poor livelihood by polishing paper. Ali Suavi received a traditional education in the *Medrese*. A schoolmaster by profession, he taught in the new *ruşdiye* schools in Bursa and Filibe (Plovdiv), and was dismissed from the latter for his alleged demagogy. His vigorous and somewhat sensational articles in the *Muhbir* aroused the ire of the Grand Vezir, who exiled him to Anatolia. From there he escaped to Europe where for a short time he continued to publish the *Muhbir* in London. In the meantime several other papers had begun to appear in Istanbul, among which mention may be made of the *Ayine-i Vatan* (Mirror of the Fatherland). This publication, the first issue of which appeared on 14 January 1867, was—apart from the short-lived *Mirat*—the first illustrated Turkish paper, and also the first to bear the name of Fatherland.

This rapid increase in the numbers and vigour of the press began to cause concern to the government, which, after the accession in 1861 of Sultan Abdülaziz, was becoming more and more autocratic. On 1 January 1865 a press law entered into force—the first of its kind in Turkey.[40] This laid down strict rules for the conduct of the press, and provided for the establishment of a Press Commission, to sit at the Sublime Porte and supplement the police courts in the enforcement of the law. A 'notification' of 12 March 1867 made the intentions of the government clear:

A part of the local press, not recognising the spirit by which journalism should be inspired in the East, has made itself the passionate

---

[39] On Ali Suavi see Kuntay, *Sarıklı İhtilâlcı Ali Suavi* (1946); Tanpınar, pp. 204–23; Mardin, pp. 360 ff.; and a rather impressionistic account by Falih Rıfkı Atay, *Başveren İnkilâpçı* (n.d., preface dated 1951).

[40] *Düstur*, ii. 220; Young, ii. 321 ff.; Aristarchi, iii. 320 ff.

organ of all the extreme parties and of tendencies essentially hostile to
the general interests of the country . . . the Sublime Porte therefore
reserves the right, whenever the general interest of the country may
require it, to act through administrative channels and independently
of the law of the press, against those newspapers which do not recognise
the above-stated principles, whose observance is an essential condition
of a national press. . . .[41]

These measures introduced a period of severe pressure, culminating in the suppression of several newspapers and the departure for Europe of their more prominent contributors. For the
next few years the most significant Turkish newspapers were
published in exile in London, Paris, and Geneva. In the words
that introduce the first London issue of one of them: '*Muhbir*
has found a country where it is not forbidden to tell the truth,
and appears again.'[42]

Turkish officials, faced with a new problem, were learning the
techniques of influence and control of the press. But Turkish
journalists had also completed, in a remarkably short time, the
evolution from report to comment, from comment to criticism,
from criticism to opposition, and from opposition to defiance.

Organized Opposition: the Young Ottomans [43]

The reforms of Mahmud II and his successors had created
a new administrative and governing *élite* in the Empire, literate,

[41] Young, ii. 326; Aristarchi, iii. 325–6.

[42] *Muhbir*, no. 1, 31 Aug. 1867 (the front page is reproduced in Gerçek, *Türk Gazet.*)

[43] The only detailed history of the Young Ottoman movement was that written by
Ebüzziya Tevfik, and published serially in the *Yeni Tasvir-i Efkâr*, 1909. Most subse-
quent versions are based on this. Useful brief accounts will be found in Akçuraoğlu
Yusuf [=Yusuf Akçura], 'Türkçülük', in *Türk Yılı*, 1928, pp. 294 ff.; Tarık Tunaya,
Türkiyede Siyasî Partiler, 1859–1952 (1952), pp. 91 ff.; Kaplan, pp. 54 ff.; Ahmed
Bedevi Kuran, *Osmanlı İmparatorluğunda İnkılâp Hareketleri ve Millî Mücadele* (1956),
pp. 57 ff.; and Karal, *Tarih*, vii. 299 ff. The most detailed documentation on the movement with special reference to the role of Namık Kemal is contained in Kuntay's
biography, vol. i. On the connexion of Ottoman princes with the Young Ottomans see
the notes of Abdülhamid, published in *TTEM*, nos. 90–92 (1926). A survey of the
political ideas of the movement, with many illustrative quotations from their writings,
was contributed by Ihsan Sungu to the *Tanzimat* anniversary volume ('Tanzimat ve
Yeni Osmanlılar', in *Tanzimat*, pp. 777–857). Finally, among the Turkish sources,
mention must be made of two excellent interpretative essays, the first historical, the
second literary, by Şeref, *Tarih Musahabeleri*, pp. 172 ff., and Tanpınar, pp. 189 ff. The
earliest Western accounts were those of the Turcophiles Léon Cahun and Arminius
Vambéry (see below, p. 340), who met the Young Ottomans in Paris and London.
Cahun wrote a brief account of them in the *Histoire générale* of Lavisse and Rambaud

idealistic, and ambitious. The transformation of Ottoman government and society had given them new opportunities and appetites; the translation and imitation of European writings had filled their minds with new beliefs and ideas. When therefore, in the second half of the nineteenth century, the growing autocracy of the Sultan and his ministers began to irk them and entrenched seniors blocked their advancement, they did not lack instruction either in the ideology or in the technique of opposition and revolution.

It is customary to begin the history of the Turkish liberal protest against absolutism with what is known as the Kuleli Incident, of 1859. In that year a small group of conspirators plotted to depose and if need be assassinate Sultan Abdülmecid. The plot was discovered, and the leaders were deported to Asia as prisoners. Several European writers describe this unsuccessful plot as the first attempt to introduce constitutional and parliamentary government. More recent research, however, would seem to indicate that the conspirators had no such aim or programme in mind—on the contrary, they disapproved of the concessions already made to the Christians. They were acting *against* the Sultan and his ministers rather than *for* any particular principles, and were thus concerned with an *attentat* and coup d'état on orthodox lines.[44]

Liberal and constitutional ideas had of course been known in the Ottoman Empire for some years. They appear, if faintly, in

(xi. 543 ff.), while Vambéry described them in an article in the *Deutsche Rundschau* of October 1893 (cited by Paul Fesch, *Constantinople aux derniers jours d'Abdul-Hamid*, 1907, p. 323. For further Western notices see Gibb, *Ottoman Poetry*, v. 60 ff.; Engelhardt, ii. 3 f.; Sax, pp. 383 f.; G. L. Lewis, *Turkey*, p. 36; E. Rossi, 'Dall' Impero ottomano alla Repubblica di Turchia, Origine e Sviluppi del Nazionalismo Turco sotto l'Aspetto politico-culturale', *OM*, xxiii (1943), 361 ff.; Davison, in *Am. Hist. R.*, 1954, pp. 851 ff.; idem, *Reform*, pp. 172 ff. The only monographic treatments of the Young Ottomans are those of Yu. A. Petrosian, '*Novye Osmani' i Borba za Konstitutsiyu 1876 g. v. Turtsii* (1958) (I owe my knowledge of this work to Professor A. Tietze) and Ş. Mardin, *The Genesis of Young Ottoman Thought* (1962).

[44] The Kuleli Incident has been discussed by many authors, and variously interpreted. For Engelhardt (i. 158–9), followed by Jorga (v. 517), Vambéry, and some others, it was a liberal movement, the first attempt to establish constitutional government. V. I. Shpilkova, in a recent article in *Problemy Vostokovedeniya*, i (1959), 100–4 (summarized in *MEJ*, xiii (1959), 347), goes even further, and describes it as a 'progressive and anti-monarchist plot' that failed through lack of mass support. The Turkish historian Uluğ İğdemir, whose book *Kuleli Vakası hakkında bir Araştırma* (1937) is the only monograph on the subject based on Turkish documentary evidence, regards it as a petty *attentat* on traditional lines, devoid of any liberal ideological content but

the writings of Sadık Rifat Paşa, and had some influence on the reforms of Sultan Abdülmecid and Mustafa Reşid Paşa. As far back as 1808 the reformist Grand Vezir Bayrakdar Mustafa Paşa had convened an Imperial assembly in Istanbul to approve his programme of reform,[45] and in 1829 Muhammad Ali Pasha in Egypt had gone a step further in nominating a consultative council of 156 members, which met for a few days each year.[46] In 1845 Abdülmecid himself had experimented, without success, with an assembly of provincial notables.[47] More recently, in 1861, the Bey of Tunis had proclaimed the first constitution of European type in a Muslim country. While reserving executive power to the Bey, it shared the legislative power between him and a Grand Council of sixty members, who were, however, nominated.[48] Finally, in 1866 the Khedive Ismail in Egypt made the first experiment with an elected assembly, by setting up a consultative body with a restricted electorate and still more restricted functions.[49]

It is in the 1860's in Turkey that we find for the first time an unmistakable liberal critique of government action, and a programme of constitutional reform. These ideas first appear in the circle of Şinasi, Namık Kemal, and their friends, and find a somewhat guarded expression in the journals of that time.

The first attempt to organize a definite group seems to have come in 1865. In June of that year a small group of six, one of whom was Namık Kemal, held a meeting and established a secret society. Little is known of its original programme, though we are told that one of the founder members, Ayetullah Bey, came to the first meeting with 'two important books, concerning the Carbonari and a secret society in Poland'.[50] Later a programme based on that of the Carbonari seems to have been

expressing rather a reaction against the trend of Westernization and the neglect of the Holy Law. Iğdemir's findings, based on documents in the Turkish archives, are reinforced by Roderic Davison with evidence from Western diplomatic records ('European Archives as a Source for Later Ottoman History', in *Report on Current Research on the Middle East 1958*, pp. 38–41). See further Karal, *Tarih*, vi. 95–97; Tunaya, *Partiler*, pp. 89–90; Kuran, pp. 49 ff.; Cevdet, *Tezakir*, ii. 83 ff.

[45] See above, p. 75.

[46] J. Landau, *Parties and Parliaments in Egypt* (New York, 1954), p. 7.

[47] See above, p. 112.   [48] *EI*², s.v. 'Dustūr'.   [49] Landau, p. 7.

[50] Ebüzziya Tevfik, in *Yeni Tasvir-i Efkâr*, issue of 20 June 1909; cf. Akçuraoğlu p. 295; Kaplan, p. 58.

adopted. The society grew rapidly, and at a later date was able to claim 245 members. Two princes of the Ottoman house, Murad and Abdülhamid, showed interest in the society, though it later became clear that Abdülhamid's intentions were from the first hostile.

Another prince who played a role of far greater significance in the movement was Mustafa Fazıl, of the Egyptian ruling house.[51] A son of the redoubtable Ibrahim Paşa, he was the brother of the Khedive Ismail and had been his heir until June 1866, when he was ousted by a change in the law of succession, obtained from the Sultan by the Khedive. Prince Mustafa Fazıl therefore had some reason to oppose the Sultan and the Grand Vezir, and is believed to have cherished the ambition of becoming the first minister of a constitutional empire, instead of or as well as Khedive of Egypt. It would, however, probably be unjust to ascribe his interest in reform purely to pique or private ambition, though these no doubt had their effect. The prince took an active interest in the Ottoman liberals, and from Paris sent an open letter to the Sultan, in French, telling a few hard truths about the state of the Empire and proposing constitutional and other reforms. This document caused great excitement among the liberals; it was translated into Turkish by Namık Kemal, Ebüzziya Tevfik, and Sadullah, and printed and distributed in great numbers by the staff of the *Tasvir-i Efkâr.*[52]

The government, though informed by spies of the formation of the group, had hitherto taken no measures against it. This last act, however, provoked Âli Paşa, who in February 1867 had become Grand Vezir again, to swift if disguised action. Of the leaders of the group, Ali Suavi was exiled to Kastamonu, in Anatolia, while Kemal and Ziya were given official postings in the provinces which amounted to decrees of banishment.

It was at this time that the first revolutionary committee received its name. At the beginning of February 1867 the Belgian newspaper *Le Nord* had published a report that Prince Mustafa Fazil had founded a banking establishment in Turkey. In a letter correcting this mis-statement, the prince referred to his

[51] On Mustafa Fazıl see Ebüzziya Tevfik in *Yeni Tasvir-i Efkâr*, issues of 31 May, 1 June, &c., 1909; M. Colombe, 'Une Lettre d'un prince égyptien du XIXe siècle au Sultan Ottoman Abd al-Aziz', *Orient*, v (1958), 23–38; Kuntay, *Namık Kemal*, i. 311 ff.; Mardin, pp. 276 ff.

[52] Text in Colombe, pp. 29 ff.; Turkish in *Yeni Tas. Ef.* 1–5 June 1909. cf. Kuntay, pp. 277 ff.

supporters in Turkey as 'jeune Turquie', a phrase that was no doubt inspired by the Young Italy, Young France, Young Germany of earlier decades in Europe. This *démenti* was copied from the Belgian paper by the *Courrier d'Orient* of Pera, the editor of which was on friendly terms with the Ottoman liberals, and thence translated into Turkish in the *Muhbir* of 21 February 1867. The name appealed to Ali Suavi and Namık Kemal, who tried various Turkish equivalents for it, eventually deciding on *Yeni Osmanlılar*—New or Young Ottomans. This, together with the French *jeunes Turcs*, appeared as the heading of the publications of the group.[53]

When Âli Paşa's orders became known, Prince Mustafa Fazil, a man of considerable wealth, invited the leaders of the 'Young Turks' to Paris, and in the middle of May they left Istanbul on a French steamer. Ali Suavi, escaping from his Anatolian exile, joined them in Paris, and then went on to London, where on 31 August 1867 he published the newspaper *Muhbir*. Ali Suavi, however, soon fell foul of his colleagues. A man of strong religious convictions and a pilgrim to Mecca, he is described by a modern Turkish writer as a liberal theologian, by another, perhaps more accurately, as a turbanned revolutionary. Namık Kemal and Ziya were also sincere and devoted Muslims, but they were not prepared to support him in his insistence on a religious reform as the starting-point of a revived Islamic state and law, nor in his attacks on the Christians. Ali Suavi's ambition and obstinacy soon led to a break, and in 1868 the Young Ottomans produced their own paper, the first issue of which appeared on 29 June. Its name was *Hürriyet* (freedom).[54] From the first Namık Kemal and Ziya Paşa were closely associated with this journal, and seem to have been responsible for editorial policy. The first issue contained two leading articles, probably both by Kemal, which laid down the two main points in the Young Ottoman programme. One of them, entitled 'Love of One's Country is Part of the

---

[53] *Yeni Tas. Ef.* of 31 May 1909; Colombe, p. 25; Sungu, in *Tanzimat*, p. 777 n.1; Kuntay, *Namık Kemal*, i. 289–90; Mardin, pp. 32 ff.; Davison, pp. 201 ff. Among those concerned with the distribution of the letter in Istanbul, Kuntay mentions two Europeans—the French lithographer H. Cayol, a convert settled in Turkey, and the Hungarian bookseller Daniel Szilágyi, a political refugee.

[54] The front page of the first issue is reproduced in Gerçek, *Türk Gazet.* On Kemal's stay in London see Kuntay, i. 533 ff.

Faith',[55] speaks of patriotism, and puts forward the idea of an
Ottoman patriotism similar to that of the European countries.
The other, headed, 'And Consult with Them in the Matter',[56]
uses this Koranic quotation as a peg on which to hang a plea for
consultative and representative government. These two themes
were developed in most of the subsequent issues of the journal,
and are linked with more detailed and specific criticisms of the
domestic, foreign, and especially the financial policies of Âli Paşa.

Meanwhile, Ali Suavi's *Muhbir* had closed down in London,
and Ali Suavi himself moved to Paris, where he began to publish
a new journal called *Ulum* (Science). The breach between him
and the Young Ottomans grew wider, and when they returned
to Turkey after the death of Âli Paşa, he, with perhaps a more
accurate assessment of conditions in Turkey, elected to stay in
France. He continued to publish in Paris and then, during the
Franco-Prussian War, in Lyons. It was at this period that he
began to express, for the first time, the idea of a *Turkish* as distinct
from an Islamic or Ottoman loyalty. His publication, which
reached Turkey through various channels, aroused some interest.
Speaking of the *Muhbir*, the official historiographer Lûtfi says:

> The said journal, appearing every week in London, was in numerous
> ways, sometimes through the letters of merchants, sometimes by un-
> known means, distributed in many copies, so that few were
> unacquainted with its purport. The ultimate purpose of this was to
> deride the principles of the state, to enumerate and elaborate the
> errors of the ministers, and perhaps to frighten the minds of Europe.
> So great was the demand for it among the people that copies were
> heard to have been sold for up to one pound.[57]

Ali Suavi did not return from exile with the rest of the Young
Ottomans after the amnesty of 1871; he did, however, return to
Istanbul in time to perish in a dramatic but ineffective interven-
tion in the events of 1878.

Another seceder of some interest was Mehmed Bey (1843–
74).[58] Unlike Ali Suavi, he was not a man of the people, but a

[55] 'Ḥubb al-Waṭan min al-Īmān', an Arabic dictum dubiously attributed to the
Prophet.
[56] Namık Kemal, *Külliyat*, iii. 165–75; see also above, p. 144.
[57] Quoted in Kaplan, p. 65.
[58] On Mehmed Bey see Kuntay, *Namık Kemal*, i. 414 ff.; Şeref, *Tar. Mus.*, pp. 173 ff.;
Kaplan, p. 67; Mardin, p. 12 and *passim*; Davison, pp. 189, 210 ff. There is a brief
biography in Mahmut Kemal [Inal], *Son Asır Türk Şairleri*, pp. 942–51.

member of the palace and governing circle. His father was a Minister of Posts, his father-in-law the former Grand Vezir Mustafa Naili Paşa, and his uncle the notorious Mahmud Nedim Paşa, several times Grand Vezir under Sultan Abdülaziz. Mehmed Bey had studied in France, and worked in the Translation Office; he had been one of the founder members of the original secret committee in Istanbul, and, according to some, its moving spirit. More radical than the Young Ottomans, he parted from them and published a paper called *Ittihad* (Union) in Turkish, Greek, Arabic, and Armenian. Then, moving to Geneva, he joined with Hüseyin Vasfi Paşa in publishing a journal called *Inkılâb* (Revolution). A new and portentous word had entered the Turkish political vocabulary. Mehmed Bey is said to have had some connexion with the Carbonari, and contributed to French radical newspapers. In the Franco-Prussian War he fought as a volunteer with the French army and then with the Commune, returning to Turkey shortly before his death in 1874.

Not a great deal is known of the European connexions of the Young Ottomans. Their headquarters were the Paris residence of Prince Mustafa Fazıl, who put them in touch with French political circles and more especially with French Foreign Office officials. According to the historian Abdurrahman Şeref, one of those whom they met in Paris was Léon Cahun, whose ideas on Turkish nationality and history, expressed in his book *Introduction à l'histoire de l'Asie* (1896), were later to have so great an effect on Turkish political thought.[59]

In June 1867 Sultan Abdülaziz went on a state visit to France. Prince Mustafa Fazıl, who still cherished the hope of achieving high office in Istanbul, seized this opportunity of restoring himself in the Sultan's good graces. When the Sultan landed at Toulon, the liberal prince was there to greet him and 'at the moment of the august arrival of the august and imperial person, to pay homage as a faithful slave'.[60] He was now able to ingratiate himself with the Sultan, and accompanied him to Paris, London, Vienna, and Budapest. From there he returned to Paris on 10

[59] Şeref, *Tar. Mus.*, pp. 175–6. For a later letter from Cahun to Namık Kemal see Kuntay, i. 530–2.
[60] Ebüzziya Tevfik in *Yeni Tasvir-i Efkâr*, issue of 17 Sept. 1909; cf. Kaplan, p. 63. On the Sultan's European journey see Kuntay, i. 546 ff., and above, p. 119. A new supporter for the Young Ottomans appeared, in the person of the Khedive Ismail. See the documents published by Abdülkadir Karahan in *Yeni Sabah*, 14–23 May 1961.

August, by permission of the Sultan, to settle his affairs before following him to Istanbul.

These 'affairs' included the Young Ottomans. When the Sultan reached Paris, the Young Ottomans, as a result of pressure from the Ottoman Embassy, were asked to leave, and went to Britain —Reşad, Nuri, and Mehmed to Jersey, Ziya, Namık Kemal, Ali Suavi, and Agah, to London. The prince now made financial arrangements for the Young Ottomans, assigning them living allowances and also funds to cover their publications. He then left for Istanbul where he later became a minister.

The defection and departure of their princely patron threw the Young Ottomans into disarray. In protest against what they regarded as a betrayal, Ali Suavi and Mehmed Bey refused to accept the allowances assigned to them by the prince. The others accepted his money, and, though Ziya Paşa later included some unkind remarks about him in his satirical *Zafername*, they seem to have regarded his appointment as a success for their cause rather than as a betrayal of it. Deprived, however, of his guiding and authoritative hand, they began to break up as a group, and gave way to the internal squabbles that are so often the fate of *émigré* politics. Towards the end of 1870 Namık Kemal, through intermediaries, managed to make his peace with the Grand Vezir Âli Paşa, and returned to Istanbul.

In September 1871 Âli Paşa died, and the Young Ottomans, who had always tended to take a naïvely personal view of the causes they were defending and opposing, prepared to return home. The arch-enemy, the ruthless autocrat, was at last out of the way, and now all would be well.

Namık Kemal, after spending a few months in Vienna, had already arrived in Istanbul on 25 November 1870. The rest, encouraged by the death of Âli Paşa, followed in the course of 1871 and 1872. Only Mehmed and Suavi remained abroad, the former fighting for France, the latter still mistrustful of the régime that followed the death of Âli Paşa.

Events proved him wholly right. Âli Paşa may have been authoritarian; he may have despised such new-fangled notions as constitutional government and freedom of the press. He was however, an able and honest ruler, and a sincere partisan of reform, which he did something to advance. None of these things can be said of his immediate successors, under whose fumbling

rule the Empire slid into a downward slope of bankruptcy,
rebellion, repression, war, and defeat. More and more the
Sultan, headstrong and wilful, became the effective ruler of the
Empire; the Grand Vezir, Mahmud Nedim Paşa, did little but
pander to his costly and destructive whims.

Immediately after his return to Turkey Namık Kemal resumed
his journalistic activities, and in June 1872 took over the newspaper *Ibret*. By this time there was quite a number of Turkish
newspapers and magazines in Istanbul, but Kemal's articles and
essays in the *Ibret* gave it an importance unequalled in the annals
of the Turkish press.[61] His editorship, however, lasted less than a
year, for in April 1873 a new crisis resulted in a second exile, this
time to Cyprus. The crisis was touched off by the performance, at
the Gedik Paşa theatre, of Kemal's play *Vatan yahut Silistre*
(Fatherland or Silistria). The first original Turkish play, Şinasi's
Marriage of a Poet, had been a brief comedy of manners, comment-
ing on the status of women and the practice of marriage among
the Turks—and published in a magazine. This one dealt in a
more violent manner with a more explosive subject—and was
performed before an enthusiastic audience. Its theme was patriotism, the doctrine, new to a Muslim people, of the love and loyalty
men owe to their country. The four acts of the drama deal with an
episode in the defence of the Turkish fortress of Silistria against the
Russians in 1854. The play burns with fervent patriotic sentiment,
and is full of rousing appeals to the Ottomans—not the Turks—
to love their country and defend it against its enemies. In it the
ideas formulated in Kemal's leading articles in *Hürriyet* and *Ibret*
find dramatic and poetic expression.

The play was first performed on 1 April 1873, amid scenes of
wild enthusiasm; the next and following days letters of rapturous
praise and support were published in the *Ibret*.

All this was not viewed with favour by authority. Namık
Kemal, recently permitted to return from exile in Europe, was
still under a cloud. Any manifestation of popular enthusiasm was
suspect, all the more so when it was associated with the alien and
subversive idea that the people owed loyalty not to the Sultan
and his ministers, not to the Islamic community and its authorized exponents, but to an abstract and unfamiliar entity called the
Fatherland. A lively and pointed report in the *Ibret* on the scenes

[61] A selection of his editorials will be found in Özön, *Namık Kemal.*

at the performance of the play provided the occasion for government action. On 5 April an order was published closing the newspaper, on the grounds of irresponsibility, sedition, and impudence. A defiant farewell editorial was promptly followed by the arrest and deportation of Kemal and several of his associates. No doubt his other activities and associations had helped to bring this about.[62] When Ziya and Kemal had fled to Europe in 1867, they had been threatened with nothing worse than provincial governorships, in such remote places as Cyprus and Erzurum. But by 1873 conditions had become harder. Ziya, it is true, having no further grievance after the death of Âli Paşa, had provisionally made peace with authority, and held various government offices. Kemal, however, continued to think, write, and agitate. These activities, coupled with his probable contacts with the heir-apparent Prince Murad, made him too dangerous to leave at large. This time, therefore, he was deported under close arrest, and kept in Famagusta, in Cyprus, for thirty-eight months, during the first part of which he was in solitary confinement. This imprisonment ended only with the deposition of Sultan Abdülaziz in 1876.

In the seventies conditions deteriorated rapidly. The army and navy—with its new ironclads the third strongest in Europe—had cost vast sums. The Sultan's extravagance and the reckless borrowing of his ministers threw the state finances into chaos. Crop failures brought hardship and discontent; anti-European feeling became general and intense. In October 1875 the Grand Vezir Mahmud Nedim Paşa announced that interest payments on the Ottoman Debt would be halved, with catastrophic effects on the standing and credit of the Ottoman government in Europe. The provinces were in turmoil. In July 1875 an insurrection had broken out in Bosnia and Herzegovina. This had spread to Bulgaria, where its bloody repression by Ottoman irregular forces led to a cry of outrage all over Europe. The murder, on 6 May 1876, of the French and German consuls at Salonika by a mob further embroiled the Porte with the European powers, leaving it bankrupt, discredited, and alone to face the war that was looming on the northern horizon.

[62] Accounts of these events will be found in the biographies of Namık Kemal, notably in Kuntay, ii/1, chs. 1–16. A lucid summary, with quotations from the contemporary sources, will be found in the appendix to Özön's edition of the play *Vatan yahut Silistre* (1943).

Midhat Paşa and the Constitution[63]

On 10 May 1876 the Softas, or theological students, of the Fatih, Bayezid, and Süleymaniye *medreses* rioted outside the Sublime Porte, demanding the dismissal of the Grand Vezir Mahmud Nedim Paşa and the Chief Mufti Hasan Fehmi Efendi. Some of them, it is said, measured the railings outside the Porte, to see if they were high enough to hang the Grand Vezir on them.[64] The evidence indicates that these riots were not wholly spontaneous. Sultan Abdülhamid—admittedly not an impartial witness—says that the riots were arranged and paid for by Midhat, whose fellow plotters behind the scenes included Rüşdi Paşa, Damad Mahmud, Halim Paşa, Hayrullah Efendi, and Murad.[65] There is also other evidence that the riots were organized, if not by Midhat Paşa and Prince Murad, then at least by others favourable to their interests. Riots by theological students were nothing new in Turkey; since the sixteenth century at least they had played an important and sometimes dangerous role in

[63] The dramatic events of 1876–8 have formed the subject of an extensive literature, of which only a few items can be mentioned here. Turkish memoirists of the period include Ismail Kemal (*The Memoirs of Ismail Kemal Bey*, ed. by Sommerville Story, 1920), Ali Haydar Midhat (*The Life of Midhat Pasha*, 1903, and, in Turkish, *Hatıralarım 1872–1946*, 1946), and even the Sultan Abdülhamid, some of whose dictated notes were edited, after the Revolution, in the journal of the Turkish Historical Society (*TTEM*, nos. 90–92, 1926). Among contemporary Western observers, some are of special interest; A. D. Mordtmann, whose *Stambul* was published anonymously; Sir Henry Elliot, *Some Revolutions and other Diplomatic Experiences* (1922); and Sir Edwin Pears, *Forty Years in Constantinople* (1916) and *Life of Abdul Hamid* (1917); G. Washburn, *Fifty Years in Constantinople* (1909); Paul Fesch, *Constantinople aux derniers jours d'Abdul-Hamid*; E. de Kératry, *Mourad V* (1878). Among earlier Turkish historians, mention may be made of Ahmed Midhat, whose *Üss-i Inkilâb* (1294/1877) presents the official justification of Abdülhamid's accession; Osman Nuri, *Abdülhamid-i Sani ve Devr-i Saltanatı* (1327/1909, published after his deposition); Rasim, *Istibdaddan Hakimiyet-i Milliyeye*; Şeref, *Tar. Mus.*, pp. 187 ff. Among modern Turkish writers, the following deal with various aspects of the period: Kuran, pp. 82 ff.; Kuntay, *Namık Kemal*, ii. pts. 1 and 2; Kaplan, pp. 96 ff.; Karal, *Tarih*, vii. 352 ff.; Haluk Y. Şehsuvaroğlu, *Sultan Aziz*; *Hayatı Hal'ı Ölümü* (1949); for monographic treatments of the first constitutional period see Bekir Sıtkı Baykal, '93 Meşrutiyeti', *Bell.* nos. 21–22 (1942), 45–83 and no. 96 (1960), 601–36; Petrosian, *Novye Osmani*, pp. 71 ff.; Temperley, in *Camb. Hist. J.*, pp. 169 ff.; R. Devereux, *The First Ottoman Constitutional Period* (1963).

[64] Şeref, *Tar. Mus.*, pp. 192 ff.; Kuran, pp. 82 ff.; Ismail Kemal, p. 108; Midhat, *Life*, p. 81; Şehsuvaroğlu, 60 ff. pp.; 'Abdülhamid-i Sani'nin Notları', *TTEM*, pp. 92 ff.; Tunaya, *Partiler*, pp. 96–97; Ismail Hami Danişmend, *Izahlı Osmanlı Tarihi Kronolojisi*, iv (1955), 253–4.

[65] *Notlar, passim*, espec. pp. 93–94.

Ottoman affairs, and are a phenomenon of some significance in the social history of the country.[66] The prearranged and prepaid student demonstration for the purpose of procuring a change of ministry was, however, something new. It introduced into Turkey a tradition well established in parts of Europe, and set a precedent that was followed many times, especially in the successor states.

The Sultan gave way to their pressure, and two days later dismissed both Mahmud Nedim Paşa and Hasan Fehmi Efendi. Mütercim (Translator) Rüşdi Paşa now became Grand Vezir, with Hüseyin Avni Paşa as War Minister and Hasan Hayrullah Efendi as Chief Mufti; Midhat became President of the Council of State—a post he had already briefly held in 1868–9. Between the Sultan and his new ministers, however, there was a complete lack of confidence, and a showdown could not long be delayed. On 25 May the British ambassador, Sir Henry Elliot, reported in a dispatch that

the word 'Constitution' was in every mouth; that the Softas, representing the intelligent public opinion of the capital, knowing themselves to be supported by the nation—Christian as well as Mahometan— would not, I believed, relax their efforts till they obtained it, and that, should the Sultan refuse to grant it, an attempt to depose him appeared almost inevitable; that texts from the Koran were circulated proving to the faithful that the form of government sanctioned by it was properly democratic, and that the absolute authority now wielded by the Sultan was an usurpation of the rights of the people and not sanctioned by the Holy Law; and both texts and precedents were appealed to, to show that obedience was not due to a Sovereign who neglected the interests of the State. . . .[67]

Sir Henry was perhaps a trifle naïve with his talk of 'public opinion', 'the bulk of the Nation', and the like, but he was accurate enough in his assessment of the trend of events. The arguments he cites, and the purpose for which they were adduced, were the logical culmination of the teachings of the Young Ottomans, the influence of whose ideas will readily be recognized.

On 30 May 1876, armed with a ruling from the Chief Mufti authorizing the deposition of the Sultan, and fortified with suitable

[66] See for example Mustafa Akdağ, 'Türkiye Tarihinde . . . Medreseli Isyanları', *Ist. Üniv. Iktisat Fak. Mec.*, xi (1949–50), 361–87.

[67] Elliot, pp. 231–2; also cited, with slight variations, by Midhat, *Life*, p. 81; cf. Temperley, in *Camb. Hist. J.*, p. 172.

political and military preparations, the ministers formally declared that Abdülaziz had ceased to reign, and installed Murad as Sultan in his place. Those primarily responsible were Midhat Paşa, Hüseyin Avni Paşa, and the head of the war college, Süleyman Paşa.[67a] The old Sultan went quietly, writing a letter of abdication in favour of his successor; the new one at once issued a decree confirming all the ministers in their posts.

The accession of Murad V seemed like a victory for the liberals. He had for some years been both in contact and in sympathy with the Young Ottomans, several of whom now received palace appointments. Namik Kemal, recalled from Cyprus, became his private secretary; Sadullah was given the key position of chief of the palace secretariat.

The satisfaction of the liberals with their new sovereign was, however, of short duration. Murad had been a prince of high intelligence, widely read in both Western and Turkish writings, with a keen and informed interest in European literature, science, and affairs. In 1867 he had accompanied Abdülaziz on his European tour, and had made an excellent impression. This, and the knowledge of his secret contacts with the exiled liberals, had led the Sultan to treat him with increasing suspicion, and to force upon him a life of virtual seclusion under surveillance. The strains of this life, and the solace of alcohol, were too much for a nature already subject to nervous disorder, and by the time of his accession Murad was already well on the way to mental derangement.

Two unfortunate shocks, following immediately on that of accession to the throne, completed his mental collapse. The first was the violent death of Abdülaziz, who was found in the Çirağan palace with his wrists slashed a few days after his deposition. The second was the murder of Hüseyin Avni Paşa and other ministers by Çerkes Hasan, a Circassian infantry captain who had been *aide-de-camp* to Prince Izzeddin, the son of Abdülaziz, and who ran amok at a cabinet meeting. Shocked out of his wits by these events, the new Sultan became incapable of making any public appearance or attending to any public business. After consultations with

---

[67a] On the preparations for the deposition, and the roles of those who organized it, see Davison, *Reform*, pp. 327 ff.

Turkish and foreign doctors, it seemed clear that the Sultan's condition was incurable.[68]

In the midst of foreign war and domestic crisis such a situation soon became intolerable, and the ministers, however reluctantly, began to consider the possibility of a second deposition. The next heir was Murad's younger brother Abdülhamid. On 27 August 1876 Midhat went to see him at his mother's palace at Nişantaş, to obtain his prior promise of sympathy for the liberal cause. The prince was shown a draft of the constitution which the ministers proposed to introduce; he gave it his approval and the pledge of his support. This preliminary having been completed, the Grand Vezir obtained from the Chief Mufti a ruling authorizing the deposition of the Sultan on grounds of mental incapacity, and on 31 August the unhappy Murad was deposed and Abdülhamid proclaimed Sultan in his place. Namık Kemal is said to have begged Midhat, with tears in his eyes, to postpone the deposition of Murad, but without avail.[69] The deposed Sultan was taken to the Çırağan palace, where he died in 1904 after twenty-eight years of captivity.

Twice within four months the Sultan had been deposed and replaced by the decision of his ministers. These events were not without precedent in the annals of the house of Osman, and many of the ministers, as well as the public, would no doubt have been content with a simple exercise of armed force, initiated by the political and ratified by the religious authority, along traditional lines. Midhat, however, had other ideas.

Midhat Paşa was born in Istanbul in 1822, the son of a Kadi from Ruschuk.[70] While still in his teens he obtained a post in the office of the Grand Vezir, and thereafter rose rapidly in the service of the Porte. In 1858 he spent six months' study leave in Europe, visiting London, Paris, Vienna, and Brussels. After his return he held various governorships and won a reputation as an able and conscientious administrator. In 1864 he was summoned

---

[68] On the Çerkes Hasan incident, see Uzunçarşılı, 'Çerkes Hasan Vakası', *Bell.* no. 33 (1945); on Murad's medical condition, idem, 'Beşinci Sultan Murad . . .' ibid. no. 38 (1946), and B. Lewis, in *MES*, i (1965), 294.

[69] Ismail Kemal, p. 118. On Murad V see *IA* and *EI*[1], *s.v.*, where further references are given.

[70] There are biographies of Midhat Paşa by his son Ali Haydar (see above, p. 156 n. 63) by Inal, *Sadrıazamlar*, pp. 315–414, and by Pakalın, *Son Sadrâzamlar*, i. 189–445. See further *EI*[1] and *IA s.v.*

to the capital to advise on the new law of provincial administration, and later in the same year he was made governor of the newly constituted vilayet of the Danube, formed by combining the former vilayets of Silistria, Vidin, and Nish. In this office, and in the governorship of Baghdad to which he was transferred in 1869, Midhat showed outstanding ability, giving the provinces security and prosperity such as they had long not known. In August 1872, after the fall of Mahmud Nedim Paşa, he was appointed Grand Vezir by Sultan Abdülaziz. He was not, however, the man to serve as the instrument of Abdülaziz's capricious absolutism, and was dismissed after a tenure of only two and a half months. During the next few years the manœuvres of rival cliques at the Sublime Porte brought him in and out of various ministerial offices, none of which he held for very long and in none of which he made any great impression.

As early as the winter of 1875, Midhat Paşa explained to the British ambassador Sir Henry Elliot that the object of his group was to obtain a constitution:

The Empire [he said] was being rapidly brought to destruction. . . . The only remedy that he could perceive, lay, first, in securing a control over the Sovereign by making the Ministers, and especially as regarded the finances, responsible to a national popular Assembly; secondly in making this Assembly truly national by doing away with all distinctions of classes and religions . . . thirdly, by decentralisation and by the establishment of provincial control over the governors. . . .[71]

Plans for the new constitution seem to have been set on foot immediately after Midhat joined the government in May 1876. A committee of statesmen and ulema was given the task of drafting the text, which was completed towards the end of the year. Like so many other constitutions of the nineteenth century, it was greatly influenced by the Belgian constitution of 1831, both directly and through the more authoritarian Prussian constitutional edict of 1850. Like the latter, it did not derive from a constituent assembly, but was promulgated by the sovereign power. This happened on 23 December 1876, a few days after Midhat had been reappointed to the Grand Vezirate by Sultan Abdülhamid.[72]

[71] Elliot, p. 228; cf. the manifesto of the 'Muslim Patriots', of 9 March 1876 (Mordtmann, *Stambul*, ii. 90 ff.)

[72] On the constitution see Baykal; G. Jäschke, 'Die Entwicklung des osmanischen

The promulgation of the Ottoman constitution in 1876 has been the subject of much debate in Europe between Turcophiles and Turcophobes, whose arguments and judgements in Turkish matters are often determined by considerations quite independent of the merits or shortcomings of the Turks. The criticism has often been made that the constitution of 1876 did not represent any real desire to reform or change the government of the Empire, but was simply a piece of window-dressing, a manœuvre intended to throw dust in the eyes of the Western powers and to circumvent their plans of intervention in the interest of the subject peoples.

The circumstances in which the constitution was promulgated and the manner in which it was applied would seem, at first sight, to confirm the validity of this criticism. The ruthless suppression of the rebellions in the Balkan provinces, followed by the defeat of the Serbs in the war they had begun against the Empire in June, had precipitated an international crisis. By November Russia was already preparing for war, and Disraeli had made it clear that the British government would not acquiesce in a partition of the Ottoman Empire. In December, as a last attempt to avert war, a conference of the powers was convened in Istanbul, to discuss peace terms between Turkey and Serbia, and the reorganization of the Balkan provinces with reforms under the supervision and guarantee of the powers. The day before the conference was due to open, Midhat became Grand Vezir;

while the plenipotentiaries were engaged upon the initial formalities, the thunder of cannon announced to the capital the proclamation of a new Turkish constitution of the most elaborate kind, so framed as to provide an excuse for the argument that the Porte was now actively embarking upon far-reaching reforms and could dispense with the proffered assistance of the Powers.[73]

The inference is perhaps excusable. This was not the first time that a major reform had come at a moment when the goodwill of the Western powers was needed. The Noble Rescript of the

Verfassungsstaates', *WI*, v (1918), 5 ff.; *IA* ('Kanun-i Esasi' by Hüseyin Nail Kubali); *EI²* ('Dustūr' by B. Lewis). The Turkish text will be found in the various editions of the *Düstur* and is reprinted, in the new Turkish script, in A. S. Gözübüyük and S. Kili, *Türk Anayasa Metinleri* (1957), pp. 25 ff.; among the numerous translations the most useful is the scholarly German version of F. von Kraelitz-Greifenhorst, *Die Verfassungsgesetze des osmanischen Reiches* (1919).

[73] R. W. Seton-Watson, *Disraeli, Gladstone, and the Eastern Question* (1935), p. 122.

Rose Bower, of 1839, came soon after the disastrous defeat of the Ottoman army at Nezib, when European support was needed against the victorious Muhammad Ali of Egypt; the Imperial Rescript of 1856 had followed immediately on the Crimean War, when Western goodwill was required in securing a peace treaty favourable to Turkey; and now the appointment of a reformer as Grand Vezir and the proclamation of a liberal constitution were perfectly timed to circumvent plans for intervention and protection, and to rally Western support in the war with Russia that was looming ahead.

These considerations were no doubt well to the fore in Midhat's mind in 1876, as in the minds of the earlier reformers in 1839 and 1856. The timing of the reforms, and the dramatic manner of their presentation, were no doubt influenced by the desire to secure political advantage from them. But it would be a grave error to conclude from this that the constitution and the earlier reforms were nothing but diplomatic subterfuges, intended to deceive foreigners but to change nothing at home. Certainly both the reformers and the liberals, no less than their conservative opponents, were loyal Muslims and Osmanlis, concerned to defend the integrity and sovereignty of the Empire from whatever threat. But the best of them were hardly less serious in their devotion to reform and to liberalism, which they believed to be in the best interests of the Empire. By 1876 the cause of reform was a century old in Turkey, and already had a tradition, an impetus, and indeed an achievement of its own. The liberal cause was much younger, but already it had produced a not inconsiderable ideological literature, and had won firm and ramified support within the Ottoman governing *élite*. When Midhat spoke to Elliot in 1875 of the need in Turkey for responsible and popular government, he no doubt hoped to please the ambassador and incline his government in Turkey's favour; but he was also quoting arguments and ideas that had become commonplace in the publications of the Young Ottomans during the preceding decade, and were accepted by many hopeful young men in the service of the Sublime Porte. In the same way when he asserted, in an article in the *Nineteenth Century*, that 'in Islam the principle of government rests upon bases essentially democratic, inasmuch as the sovereignty of the people is therein recognized' he was not, as one historian has suggested, trying to pull the wool over the eyes of the gullible English reader,[74] but was reproducing an argument which was familiar from the writings of Namık Kemal and Ziya, and which has since become an article of faith with Muslim liberals, reformists, and romantics.

There was one, however, among the prime movers in 1876 who had no sympathy whatever for liberalism or democracy, and whose use of the constitution and the constitutionalists was purely cynical and opportunistic. That one was the Sultan, Abdülhamid II.

It was not long before the new Sultan began to show his hand. Midhat's appointment as Grand Vezir had been timed to coincide with the meeting of the ambassadors' conference in Istanbul. On 20 January 1877 the conference ended—and on 5 February Midhat was ignominiously dismissed and ordered to leave the country. In a statement to the powers, the Sultan justified this action by reference to article 113 of the new constitution, which authorized the Sultan 'to expel from the territory of the Empire those who, as a result of trustworthy information gathered by the police administration, are recognized as dangerous to the security of the state'.

The moment, as usual, was well chosen. At home, Midhat was being attacked on two sides, by the conservatives, who disliked the whole programme of reform, and by the liberals, led by Namık Kemal and Ziya, who found his measures entirely inadequate. During the ambassadors' conference the Sultan had already been at work undermining Midhat's position; when the conference ended there was no further obstacle to his dismissal.[75]

The constitution itself lasted a little longer. It had already been publicly proclaimed, with much pomp and circumstance. As well as diverting the European powers, the promises it contained had aroused such a response among sections of the population of Istanbul that it would have been inexpedient and perhaps dangerous to abrogate it at once. The Sultan therefore proceeded with arrangements for a general election—the first in Ottoman and indeed in Islamic history.[76]

[74] Seton-Watson, p. 123, citing the *Nineteenth Century* of June 1878.

[75] On the dismissal and banishment of Midhat see, *inter alia*, Seton-Watson pp. 146–7; Ismail Kemal, pp. 136 and 149; Midhat, *Life*, p. 145; Inal, *Sadrıazamlar* pp. 350 ff.; Baykal, pp. 67 ff.; Devereux, pp. 101 ff.

[76] For a record of the proceedings of the Ottoman parliament see Hakkı Tarık Us, *Meclis-i Meb'usân, 1293–1877* (1940–54). Western impressions of the Ottoman chamber will be found in the works, already cited, of Mordtmann, Pears, Fesch, &c.

The first Ottoman parliament met on 19 March 1877. It was not an impressive spectacle. A Senate of twenty-five nominated officials; a chamber of 120 deputies elected under official pressure and amid general indifference with a franchise and by a procedure that were already in conflict with the new constitution—these seemed to meet the Sultan's need for a puppet assembly which would give his régime a façade of liberal and democratic government, and provide a semblance of popular support and legal validity for whatever he found it expedient to do.

But even this assemblage of tame and inexperienced deputies began to develop a life of its own. It has been well described by Sir Edwin Pears, who was at that time correspondent in Istanbul of the *Daily News*:

It was the first time that representatives from such distant places as Baghdad, Albania, Armenia and Syria met together. Their discussions were singularly full of interest and even surprises. Though most of the members spoke of serious grievances which required redress in their own district, they were surprised to learn that their own constituencies were not alone as spheres of misgovernment. When the members for Jerusalem, Baghdad, Erzerum and Salonika met together, they found that the administration throughout all the country was corrupt, and they set themselves honestly to discuss their grievances and the changes in the system which were necessary to secure a remedy. Amongst the deputies were several able and thoughtful men. They had no traditions of parliamentary government, and some of the speeches were banal, speeches which would have been brought to an end by the Speaker had they been delivered in the Legislative Chamber either of England, America, or a British colony. They often had a tendency to personalities unconnected with public affairs, but more usually they attacked this pasha or that for abuses, for receiving bribes and refusing to do what was right unless he was paid for it. Had the Sultan been as wise as his sycophants represented him to be, he would have seen the value of such statements and would have allowed the deliberations of the Chamber to continue. There were at first absolutely no attacks whatever upon him, though many of his Ministers were personally charged with specific irregularities and misconduct. The discussions were a revelation to Turkish subjects. They showed that the government from one end of the country to the other required radical reform. The Chamber had at its head a President, Ahmed Vefyk, who had been Ambassador of Turkey at the Court of Napoleon III, was an excellent French scholar, and in education was no doubt the superior of nearly all the deputies. But in public and private life he had become despotic, and his superior, school-masterly manner as Chairman of the House was arrogant and sometimes amusing. He frequently stopped deputies in the midst of speeches, telling them that they knew nothing about the subject and were talking nonsense. Dr. Washburn, the President of Robert College, was present when a white-turbanned deputy, who was making a long and prosy statement, was suddenly pulled up by a stentorian shout from the President of 'Shut up, you donkey!' '(*Sus eshek*).[77] The orator sat down as if he were shot.

Meantime the accusations brought by members against the corruption of individual Ministers became more serious and definite in form. The claim that certain of the Ministers should be brought before the Chamber in order to answer charges against them was naturally opposed by the accused Ministers and was distasteful to Abdul Hamid. The hostility between the Chamber and the pashas became serious, and various correspondents predicted that within a short time the Chamber would upset the rule of the pashas, or the pashas would get rid of the Chamber.[78]

In the event it was the Sultan who got rid of the chamber. The first Ottoman parliament had ended on 28 June 1877 and a second, after new elections, had met on 13 December. The Sultan's task was made easier by the Russian war, which had begun in April 1877 and ended with the armistice of 31 January 1878. On 13 February 1878 the deputies went so far as to demand that three ministers, against whom specific charges had been brought, should appear in the chamber to defend themselves. The next day the Sultan dissolved the chamber, and ordered the deputies to return to their constituencies. Parliament had sat for two sessions, of about five months in all. It did not meet again for thirty years.

The End of the Young Ottomans

For the Young Ottomans, this was the end. They had been sharply critical of Midhat, suspecting him, not without some justification, of being another authoritarian reformer in the tradition of Mustafa Reşid, Fuad and Âli Paşas, willing to modernize and Westernize the administrative structure of the Empire, but without sympathy for their liberal and patriotic aspirations. Now, in the personal autocracy of the Sultan, the causes both of reform and of liberty seemed to be lost. The great age of the

---

[77] cf. Washburn, p. 119, for a slightly different version, in which Vefik Paşa deals not with a white-turbanned speaker but with a green-turbanned interruptor.

[78] Pears, *Abdul Hamid*, pp. 49–51.

Tanzimat had come to an end—and the liberals, who had been its keenest critics, were silenced.

At this point it may be opportune to review briefly the chief arguments used by the liberals against the Sultans, statesmen, and edicts of the *Tanzimat*. Their criticisms are far removed from those of the simple reactionaries, and, though they probably expressed the outlook of a far smaller body of opinion in Turkey, were far more significant for the understanding of what followed. These opinions are first adumbrated in the Istanbul press of the early 1860's, clearly and vigorously expressed in the newspapers published in exile, and developed, with greater circumspection, in those published after their return to Turkey.[79]

Some two years after his return to Istanbul from exile, Namık Kemal published an article in the *Ibret* under the heading 'Tanzimat'. In it he speaks eloquently of the high hopes that had been raised by the Rescript of the Rose Bower, and of the belief that at last the age of bloody and arbitrary rule was coming to an end.

Indeed [he says if] one looks at its external aspect, one would think it to have been made as a surety for the life, property, and honour of every individual. But the truth of the matter is that it was proclaimed for the purpose of securing the life of the state.[80]

The *Tanzimat*, in other words, was less a reform than a manœuvre, intended to accomplish a political, rather than a legal or social purpose. Thus far, the Young Ottomans seem to be in agreement with those European critics who saw in the *Tanzimat* no more than a piece of window-dressing designed to deceive the West—a paper reform which 'never passed the threshold of the Sublime Porte'. But the Young Ottomans saw farther than that. They knew that the successive reforms had indeed made many real changes in Turkey—and despite their own devotion to

[79] The best sources of information of the ideas of the Young Ottomans are the articles published by them in Turkey and especially abroad. Some of these articles were later reprinted in various collections and anthologies. A useful survey of their ideas, with lengthy quotations, will be found in Sungu's article in *Tanzimat*, already cited. Their political and social ideas are discussed in Tanpınar, pp. 189 ff.; Kaplan, pp. 105 ff.; Mardin, *passim*; Berkes, pp. 208 ff. For an examination of the influence of the political philosophy of Montesquieu, Rousseau, and Voltaire, see Kâmiran Birand, *Aydınlanma Devri Devlet Felsefesinin Tanzimatta Tesirleri* (1955).

[80] *Ibret*, no. 46 of 1872, cited by Sungu, p. 778.

progress and reform, there was much in these changes that they disliked.

The fundamental charge which they brought against the statesmen of the *Tanzimat* was that of arbitrary and absolutist government. The old safeguards, the old balances provided by law, custom, and established interests had been abrogated or eliminated. The limiting power of the Janissaries, in which Namık Kemal affected to see a kind of armed popular assembly, had been destroyed; the Holy Law itself had been disregarded or violated, and replaced by a caricature of Western laws which was in fact neither Western nor Islamic, and which, being unreal and ineffectual, left the sovereign power free from any check at all. The reforming edicts had brought some changes in administrative procedures, but had done nothing to protect the subject against arbitrary rule. The point is well made by Namık Kemal in an article in *Ibret*.

The Rescript of the Rose Bower is not, as some have supposed, a fundamental charter for the Lofty Empire. It consists of a declaration which, while reiterating some of the principles of the Holy Law which is our only true Charter, sanctions a number of administrative measures in the line of European thought.

Had the Rescript not confined the general precepts of law set forth in its preamble to personal freedom alone, which it interpreted as security of life, property, and honour, but also proclaimed such other basic principles as freedom of thought, sovereignty of the people, and the system of government by consultation, then only could it have taken the character of a fundamental Charter for the Islamic Caliphate.[81]

In fact, said the Young Ottomans, they had done none of these things. They had taken away the rights which the people enjoyed under the old, Islamic order, and had given them none of the rights which belonged to the European system of government that they were introducing. By their actions they were discrediting Islamic government in the West, and Western government among Muslims.

In introducing a foreign form of goverment, under foreign pressure or advice, the men of the *Tanzimat* had thrown the country wide open to foreign influence and interference of every kind. Foreigners had been given the right to own land in Turkey,

[81] *Ibret*, no. 46 of 1872, cited by Sungu, pp. 844–5.

and were acquiring positions of control in every branch of the economic and public life of the Empire. To domestic tyranny, the men of the *Tanzimat* had added foreign exploitation.

A direct result of these policies was the economic ruination of the Empire. In an article published in *Hürriyet* in 1868, Namık Kemal reviews the economic situation. 'In this world wealth is obtained from three sources, agriculture, industry, and trade.' Ottoman agriculture was potentially one of the richest in the world, but was being crushed by reckless conscription and taxation. 'The second is industry. Industry is a product of intelligence. This being so, is it not a pity that a nation endowed, like the Ottomans, with extraordinary quickness of mind should be obliged to import from abroad even the clothes that it wears? . . .' The reason was a suicidal fiscal policy which, under the specious name of free trade, had stifled Ottoman industry and thrown the country into the hands of European exporters. The same causes, aggravated by the lack of roads and of educational facilities, had led to the backwardness and poverty of Ottoman trade.[82]

A subject of frequent and violent attack by the Young Ottomans was the government policy of borrowing money from abroad. Until the time of the Crimean War Turkey had incurred no foreign debts. From 1854, however, the Sultan's government began to raise loans in Europe, on terms that were ruinous to the Empire and that led to complete financial collapse.

For these and other reasons, the men of the *Tanzimat*, far from lightening the burdens that weighed on the Empire in the days of its decay, had greatly added to them. In the words of Ziya Paşa, 'if from 1000 to 1255 [1592 to 1839] the Empire had advanced on the road to decline at the pace of a two-horse carriage, from 1255 to 1285 [1839 to 1869] it had rushed with the speed of a railway-train'.[83]

The remedy for all these ills was constitutional and parliamentary government. The Holy Law must be restored, for it alone corresponded both to the traditions and to the needs of a Muslim people. This would not, however, mean a simple rejection of Westernization and a return to the immediately preceding past; what was needed was a return to the true spirit of early Islam,

[82] Cited in Sungu, pp. 825–7.

[83] *Hürriyet*, no. 36 of 1869; cited in Sungu, p. 816.

which recognized the sovereignty of the people and the principle of government by consultation. These could best be ensured by a constitutional apparatus of an assembly and a supreme court which, though imitated from European models, would be adapted to the needs of a Muslim people living under the God-given law of Islam.

The ideas of the Young Ottomans are clearly derivative, and it is easy to recognize the sources from which they were drawn. The jurisprudence of Montesquieu, the politics of Rousseau, the economics of Smith and Ricardo provided their theoretical foundations, while many even of their specific criticisms of *Tanzimat* policies are influenced by the comments of European observers. The judgements of Slade, in particular, seem to have had a marked influence on them. Their ideas are often confused and naïve, as for example when they ascribe the economic backwardness of Turkey simply to the incompetence of Turkish ministers and the rapacity of European merchants, or when, on a different level, they discuss the problems of law, power, and democracy.

Nevertheless, despite these gaps and obliquities in their vision, they saw more and further than most other Turks of their time. Their understanding of the problems of change in Ottoman society was deeper than that of the mechanicians of the *Tanzimat* and their ideal, if vague, was not an ignoble one. Many new and significant ideas first found Turkish expression in their writings, and their influence on the thought and action of the generations that followed was very great indeed.

In 1876 their ideal of constitutional liberty under Holy Law seemed about to be realized. A new constitution promised all those rights and liberties of which they had learned from their European teachers, and did so in the name of the Sultan-Caliph, the guardian of the Holy Law.

The collapse of the constitution, and the squalid despotism that followed it, were bitter blows. Some of the Young Ottomans, abandoning their ideals, found employment in the Sultan's service. Others suffered banishment, imprisonment, and death. Namık Kemal, the most brilliant among them, was imprisoned for nearly six months as a common criminal in Istanbul, and then exiled to Chios, where he was detained for two years. Later he was given minor government posts in the Aegean islands, where he spent the rest of his days until his death on 2 December 1888. It occurred the night after he received an Imperial order for-bidding him to print or continue the history of the Ottomans on which he was then working.

In a poem written not long before his death, Namık Kemal gives expression to the mood of desperation that held Young Turkey in those days:

> Let us truly renounce all ambition and all desire
> Let us break the cage of flesh, if it trammels our resolve
> As long as every breath of our motherland moans with sorrow,
> 'Come to my help!' she says. See, this is the voice of God.
> Zeal becomes us; mercy is God's,
> The verdict of the future belongs neither to beggar nor Emperor,
> Listen to her anguish that is told in her sigh
> See, what says the breath of our motherland as she moans.
>
> .   .   .   .   .
>
> Our country is no more; yet still it is, while you and I are there,
> In this condition we can have no greater enemy than ourselves.
> We are in the hands of the foe; for the sake of God, O countrymen,
> Enough! Let us indeed renounce every personal wish and desire![84]

[84] 'Murabba'; Akyüz, *Antoloji*, pp. 58–59.

CHAPTER VI

Despotism and Enlightenment

In any scheme of reform, I believe your attention will be far more usefully directed to persons than to paper institutions. Good officers, well selected for a length of time, will create suitable traditions of administration which will gradually harden into institutions, and, made this way, reformed institutions will regenerate a people. But if they are merely written in a pretentious law, they will have no other effect but to disturb the few traditions that are left and to give perpetual subject-matter for diplomatic wrangling.

LORD SALISBURY TO SIR HENRY LAYARD, 25 June 1878.

Since present circumstances are unfavourable to the full discharge of the duties of parliament, and since, according to the constitution, the limitation or curtailment of the period of session of the said parliament in accordance with the needs of the time form part of the sacred Imperial prerogatives, therefore, in accordance with the said law, a high Imperial order has been issued . . . that the present sessions of the Senate and Chamber, due to end at the beginning of March . . . be closed as from today . . .

PROCLAMATION OF 14 FEB. 1878.

Government by a chief who is obeyed from custom, and who is himself restrained by custom from mere tyranny, may at certain stages of culture be better than anything else which can be substituted for it. And representation, even when it is possible, is not an unchanging entity, but an expedient capable of an infinite number of variations.

GRAHAM WALLAS, 'Human Nature in Politics', 1929.

THE last of the Young Ottomans to make his peace with the government and return from exile was Ali Suavi, the turbanned revolutionary and man of the people. He was also the first to try and overthrow Abdülhamid.

After the deposition of Abdülaziz, Ali Suavi at last returned to Turkey. By the time he reached Istanbul, Murad had been deposed, and Abdülhamid had taken his place. The Sultan and the revolutionary seem at first to have been on good terms, and Ali Suavi was given the important appointment of director of the Galatasaray school. In December 1876 he and his English wife acted as hosts to H. A. M. Butler-Johnstone, a British member of parliament who was visiting Turkey, and claimed to be a personal emissary of Disraeli.[1] Soon, however, he formed a political committee, the so-called Üsküdar committee, which met in his house.

Relations between Ali Suavi and the new Sultan deteriorated rapidly. On 19 May 1878, when the Russians were almost at the gates of Istanbul, an advertisement appeared in the daily *Basiret*, signed by Ali Suavi, announcing that in the next day's issue he would expound and explain the remedy for the country's difficulties. This seems to have been a prearranged signal, for on the next day, at about 11 in the morning, some 500 men assembled in front of the Çırağan Palace, most of them Muslim refugees from the lost provinces. Led by Ali Suavi, about 100 of them forced their way into the palace, where they tried to release Murad and proclaim him Sultan. A police contingent, summoned by the palace staff, soon arrived, and dealt rapidly with the movement. Hasan Paşa, the police commandant of Beşiktaş, boasted to the end of his days of how he had felled and killed Ali Suavi with a blow of his cudgel. Twenty others were killed, and thirty wounded. A court martial pronounced one sentence of death, later commuted to life imprisonment, and several of deportation. The first rising against Hamidian rule was at an end.[2]

The deposed Sultan was still not without friends, and now sought them in a new direction. When, after the ignominious failure of the Suavi attempt, Murad was confined in the Malta Pavilion in the Yıldız palace grounds, he smuggled a note to one of them, saying: 'If you do not save me from this place, the Malta Pavilion will be my grave.'

The recipient of this dramatic appeal for help was Cleanthi Scalieri, a Greek subject living in Istanbul. His importance lay in his position as master of the Prodos masonic lodge, and the exalted European connexions to which this admitted him. Scalieri at once wrote an open letter to Abdülhamid, and sent it to the English-language newspaper *Eastern Express* with a demand, backed by threats, that it be published. The editor of the paper, Whitaker, referred the letter to the Palace counsellor Said Paşa, 'who shrugged his shoulders and said "publish" '. The publica-

[1] Seton-Watson, p. 129. R. Blake (*Disraeli*, London, 1966, p. 616) sees no justification for this claim.

[2] A detailed study of this first rising, based on archive documents, was published by Uzunçarşılı, 'Ali Suâvi ve Çırağan Vak'ası', *Bell.*, no. 29 (1944), 71–118. See further Kuntay, *Ali Suavi*, pp. 160 ff.; Tunaya, *Partiler*, pp. 98–100; Kuran, pp. 119–21; Ismail Kemal, pp. 120–1, 145–6; Pears, *Abdul Hamid*, p. 48.

tion of the letter provoked the Sultan to immediate reprisals against the newspaper, its editor and even, it is said, against Said Paşa; but the publicity achieved its effect, and Murad was restored to relative security in the Çırağan palace.[3]

Scalieri and his masonic friends did not leave the matter at that. From a report submitted to Sultan Abdülhamid, it seems that an attempt was made to persuade the German and English lodges, the heads of which were the Emperor Wilhelm and the Prince of Wales, to use their influence and secure the intervention of the German and British ambassadors in Istanbul in favour of Murad.

Nothing came of this suggestion. Scalieri then became associated with a group of Turkish conspirators, led by Nakşibend Kalfa, a palace servant of Murad's mother, Aziz Bey, a high official of the Inspectorate of *Evkâf*, and Ali Şefkati, a former official of the Council of State and a friend of Namık Kemal. The aim of this group, like that of Suavi, was to depose Abdülhamid and restore Murad to the throne. Members swore an oath 'to strive to work to the best of my ability for the safety of the nation (*millet*)' and a plan was prepared for a coup d'état.[4]

A traitor denounced them to the Sultan, who ordered police action. The members of the committee were besieged in Aziz Bey's house, where they had their headquarters. Some of them, including Scalieri himself, Nakşibend Kalfa, and Ali Şefkati, managed to escape abroad. The rest were arrested, tried by court martial, and sentenced to varying terms of imprisonment, or confinement to a fortress.[5]

This attempt to restore Murad, like that of Ali Suavi, had little effect, except perhaps to reinforce the autocratic tendencies of the new Sultan. But the Scalieri–Aziz Bey committee, insignificant as it was, revealed several new and interesting features. However incompetently, they did organize a group of conspirators to plan and execute a coup d'état; their purpose was not merely to replace one prince by another, but to depose an autocrat and enthrone in his place one whom they believed to be more liberal and progressive in his views. This belief was based on Murad's

[3] Uzunçarşılı, 'V Murad tedâvîsine ve ölümüne dair', *Bell.*, no. 38 (1946), 320 n.6.

[4] Uzunçarşılı, 'V Murad'i tekrar padişah yapmak isteyen K. Skaliyeri-Aziz Bey Komitesi', *Bell.*, no. 30 (1944), 264.

[5] On the Scalieri plot see Uzunçarşılı's article cited in the preceding note. Further, Tunaya, *Partiler*, pp. 100–2; Kuran, pp. 121–4; Mardin in *MEJ* (1962), 171. In 1879, Ali Şefkati published the first anti-Hamidian journal in exile.

past connexion with freemasonry, and it was through masonic channels that the conspirators directed some of their efforts. Finally—and this is perhaps the most remarkable feature—the conspiracy united a Christian with Muslims in a common cause, the safety of the 'nation', which for some of them at least must have had a secular and no longer a purely religious meaning.

The revolt of the returned exile Ali Suavi and the conspiracy of the Greek freemason Cleanthi Scalieri deepened the suspicion with which the Sultan regarded new and liberal ideas, and made him still less willing in any way to relax or divide his authority. The constitution remained in abeyance, the constitutionalists were either exiled or, if willing, incorporated in the apparatus of despotism. In 1881 Midhat Paşa, who, under British pressure, had been allowed to return to Turkey, was arrested and brought to Istanbul, where he was tried and found guilty of having caused the assassination of Sultan Abdülaziz. Under foreign pressure, the death sentence imposed on this trumped up charge was commuted to life banishment, and in April 1883 he was murdered in his prison in Arabia.[6] The Sultan was again an autocratic ruler, unrestrained by any legal or social checks, unchallenged by any opposition movement—and with his rule vastly reinforced by a new and immensely improved apparatus of repression.

The new Sultan, though bitterly hostile to liberal or constitutional ideas, was by no means entirely opposed to reform and Westernization in which, judiciously selected and applied, he saw the means of reinforcing both the Ottoman Empire and his own position in it. Abdülhamid was far from being the blind, uncompromising, complete reactionary of the historical legend; on the contrary, he was a willing and active modernizer, the true heir of Sultan Abdülaziz and the statesmen of the *Tanzimat*, against whose autocratic reformism the Young Ottomans had levelled the first Turkish liberal critique of despotic government. Politics apart, the first decades of Abdülhamid's reign were as active a period of change and reform as any since the beginning of the century, and saw the accomplishment of much that had been only started or sketched under earlier rulers, more famous

---

[6] On the arrest and subsequent fate of Midhat Paşa, see Uzunçarşılı, *Midhat ve Rüştü Paşaların Tevkiflerine dair Vesikalar* (1946) and *Midhat Paşa ve Taif Mahkûmları* (1950).

for their reforming zeal. It would not be an exaggeration to say that it was in these early years of the reign of Abdülhamid that the whole movement of the *Tanzimat*—of legal, administrative, and educational reform—reached its fruition and its climax. And so, too, did the tendencies, already discernible under the *Tanzimat* régimes, towards a new, centralized, and unrestrained despotism.

A key figure in the Sultan's reforms was Mehmed Said Paşa (1838–1914), sometimes known as Küçük (little) Said.[7] He was born in Erzurum, the son of a diplomat and the descendant of a family of ulema.[8] After a successful career in the government service, he became Grand Vezir for the first time in October 1879, and held the office almost continuously until 1885. He was Grand Vezir again in 1895 and in 1901–3, as well as on three occasions after the revolution of 1908.

A good indication of Said Paşa's ideas and policies can be obtained from the lengthy memorandum on the reforms needed by the Empire which, in accordance with what had become an established Ottoman custom, he submitted to the Sultan in 1880.[9]

In a lengthy historical preamble, that clearly owed much to a study of earlier memorialists, Said Paşa demonstrates that 'the advancement of a state can only be secured through knowledge and uprightness',[10] and that it was through the decay or disappearance of these qualities that the Ottoman Empire fell into a decline. The remedy is to restore them, and the means are education and justice.

Educational reform is the first prerequisite to any further improvement.

In order to remedy this situation, first and foremost a serious and powerful effort must be made to improve public education. As long as public education is not disseminated, there will be no leaders capable

[7] On Said Paşa, see *EI*[1] *s.v.* (by Th. Menzel). *IA s.v.* (by E. Kuran), Inal and Pakalın. His memoirs were published in three volumes—*Said Paşanın Hâtırâtı*, 1328 A.H. (analysed by K. Süssheim, 'Die Memoiren Küçük Said Paša's . . .' in *Orientalische Studien Fritz Hommel*, ii (1916), 295–312). Said Paşa was one of the first modern Turkish statesmen to publish his memoirs. He was followed by many others.

[8] It is interesting that Said Paşa prided himself on his authentically Turkish descent—one of the earliest appearances of this theme in Turkish politics. See Süssheim, p. 301 n.4.

[9] The memorandum appears in *Hâtırât*, i. 418–36. A translation of this, with some other documents from the memoirs, was made by the late Mr. Harold Bowen and awaits publication.

[10] *Hâtırât*, i. 423.

of directing the internal and external affairs of the Empire soundly, no judges who can administer the public laws justly, no commanders who can run the Army efficiently, and no finance officers who can show how to manage and increase the sources of revenue in accordance with economic principles. None of the institutions and operations that serve public prosperity and wellbeing can be brought into existence as long as education is not disseminated. . . .[11]

In short, Said Paşa goes on to explain, education is necessary for the efficient conduct of public affairs, for the life of a civilized community, for defence against foreign enemies, 'and even, henceforth, in order to keep under control the Christian populations, whose minds are now being opened by education. . . .'

Education is not, however, sufficient in itself; there is also a need for uprightness, the absence of which produces hypocrisy, falsehood, and a lack of patriotism (*hubb-i vatan*). To prevent the ruination of the Empire by the spread of these vices, the state must stamp out corruption, and must itself set a better example than hitherto of honest and upright behaviour. 'Though the Islamic religion defends justice, the government's neglect, for some time past, of this stern duty has reached a point when it can no longer be denied.'[12] To remedy this, there must be a reorganization of the law courts and a revision of legal procedures; in addition, there must be law schools to train a new generation of lawyers and judges.

Said Paşa then goes on to discuss a number of civil, military, and administrative matters, and finally comes to what he calls 'the fundamental and vital problem of the Empire . . . that of finance'.[13] He has no objection to further loans, provided that the terms are equitable, that there is no infringement of Ottoman rights, and that the money is spent on capital improvements and not on covering a budgetary deficit. But the real answer is financial reorganization and reform, the main points being the rationalization of the currency, the publication of proper annual budgets and balances, the adoption of an equitable and efficient tax system, and the introduction of a proper system of accountancy for government financial transactions. This will also help to make possible the urgently needed public works for the improvement of agriculture, industry, and trade, and for the extension of communications.[14]

[11] *Hâtırât*, i. 423   [12] Ibid. p. 424.   [13] Ibid. p. 433.   [14] Ibid. p. 434.

Educational Reform [15]

Educational reform, in Said Paşa's view, was the essential prerequisite to all further improvements, and it was in this field that the Hamidian régime made its first and greatest effort.

Its most impressive achievement was in higher education, where the number of schools and the number of students were both considerably increased. The *mülkiye* school, established in 1859 as a training centre for civil servants, was in 1877 reorganized and expanded, especially in the senior classes, and the curriculum revised to include modern subjects. Boarding facilities were also added for students from the provinces.[16] From a first graduation, in 1861, of 33 students, the numbers rose by 1885 to 395 of whom 295 were boarders. This school, the first purely civilian institution among the new modern centres of higher education in Turkey, remained, even under the pressures of the later Hamidian régime, an important intellectual centre and a forcing-ground of new ideas. Its teachers included such men as Murad Bey (d. 1912), later a leader among the Young Turks, Recaizade Mahmud Ekrem (1846–1913), a poet and literary reformer and a disciple of Namık Kemal, Abdurrahman Şeref (1835–1925), a historian—all of them men of high calibre and profound influence.[17]

Like the *Mülkiye*, the *Harbiye* or War College at Pangalti was maintained and extended, as were also the military and civil medical schools and a few other foundations, such as the artillery, naval and military engineering schools, inherited from the earlier reformers. But that was not all. To the existing schools, Abdülhamid added no less than eighteen new higher and professional schools. Though some of them were of short duration, their influence as a whole was considerable. They included the schools of finance (1878), law (1878), fine arts (1879), commerce (1882), civil engineering (1884), veterinary science (1889), police (1891), customs (1892), and an improved new medical school (1898).

Most ambitious of all was the founding of a Turkish university.

[15] The most detailed account of educational developments in this period will be found in Ergin, *Maarif*. For a brief British account of Turkish education, extracted from the Embassy Annual Report for 1907, see C. P. Gooch and H. W. V. Temperley, *British Documents on the Origins of the War*, v (1928), 29–31.

[16] And abolished in 1902 (Ergin, *Maarif*, p. 516).

[17] Ibid. pp. 510 ff., and Ali Çankaya, *Mülkiye ve Mülkiyeliler* (1954).

This project, first mooted in 1845, had run into many difficulties, and suffered from several false starts. It was not until August 1900 that, after long preparation, the Darülfünun, later known as the University of Istanbul, opened its gates. Turkey had at last acquired a university—the first truly indigenous modern university in the Muslim world.[18]

To provide students for all these new colleges, a large-scale expansion of the primary and secondary schools became necessary, as well as of teachers' training colleges to provide their staffs. The earliest training college had been opened in 1848; the first statistical statement published after the 1908 revolution shows 31 in operation, in vilayet and sanjak centres as well as in the capital.

Modern elementary education was provided in the *rüşdiye* schools, the first of which had been opened in Istanbul in 1847. From 1875 separate military *rüşdiye* schools were established, to prepare for admission to military high schools and colleges. Under Abdülhamid *rüşdiye* schools were set up in the centres of all the 29 vilayets and 6 independent *mutasarrıflıks* of the Empire, as well as in many kaza centres in Turkey proper. These led to the *idadi* schools, which provided middle and early secondary education. The first *idadi* was opened in Istanbul in 1875. A special education tax imposed in 1884 made it possible to establish seven-class schools in vilayet centres and five-class schools in sanjak centres all over the Empire. At the same time the network of military schools was extended, and in 1904, military schools were opened in Damascus, Baghdad, Erzincan, Edirne, and Manastir.

The apex of the system of secondary education was provided by the two great public schools of Galatasaray and Darüşşafaka.[19] Both were inherited from the *Tanzimat* period, the former an Imperial, the latter a private foundation. In the Hamidian period the Galatasaray school, originally a Franco-Turkish enterprise, became more Turkish in character. Latin was dropped from the curriculum, the proportion of Turkish pupils increased, and the school became more and more the favourite place of education for the sons of the ruling classes—the landowning, military, and bureaucratic families of the capital. Its teachers included some of

18 Ergin, *Maarif*, pp. 997 ff.
19 Ibid. pp. 400 ff. and 743 ff.; Sungu, in *Bell.*, no. 28 (1943), 315–47.

the leaders of Turkish scholarship and letters—its pupils were the sons of the ruling *élite*, preparing to succeed them.

Judicial and Legal Reform[20]

A whole generation of schoolboys and students were toiling in the schools of Turkey to achieve the first of Said Paşa's remedies —knowledge. The second, justice, on which would largely depend the use they made of their knowledge, proved more difficult of access.

The most important legal reforms of the Hamidian era occurred during the first few years of the Sultan's reign, and were in reality the completion of a process begun under the *Tanzimat*. These were a group of four laws, promulgated in May and June 1879, of which two dealt with the organization of justice and the courts and two with legal procedure. A Ministry of Justice had been established by ferman and given authority over the commercial courts. It was now reorganized, and given control over all non-religious courts. Another law provided for the regulation of the *nizamiye* courts—the mixed courts established some years previously to try lawsuits between Muslim and non-Muslim litigants.[21] At the same time two further laws dealt with procedural matters—the first providing for the execution of judgements, the second embodying a code of civil procedure.

One of the main purposes of these changes was to meet foreign criticisms of Ottoman justice, and thus prepare the way for the abrogation or limitation of the foreign judicial privileges recognized by the capitulations. In this the Ottoman legislators were unsuccessful. The laws on execution of judgements and on civil procedure were not recognized by the foreign missions, and were in consequence never actually applied in mixed law suits.[22] The extraterritorial privileges of the foreign communities remained firmly established, and the Ottoman courts, limited in their competence to cases involving Ottoman subjects only, were untroubled by foreign observation or criticism.

The failure to meet foreign criticism seems to have put an end to legal reform; domestic criticism, at the time, seemed less

---

[20] On the legal and judicial reforms of this period, see Engelhardt, ii. 237–4; *EI* s.v. 'Tanzimat' (by J. H. Kramers); Nuri, *Abdülhamid-i Sani*, ii. 700 ff.; Mardin, *Ahmet Cevdet.*

[21] Karal, *Tarih*, vi. 167 ff.   [22] *EI*, iv. 658.

important. In 1888 the official drafting committee, which was set up in 1869 and which had produced the *Mecelle* code of civil law and the code of civil procedure, was dissolved by order of the Sultan. Work on the revision and codification of other branches of law was not resumed until after the revolution of 1908.[23]

The Ministry of Justice continued to function, and under the leadership of such able men as Ahmed Cevdet Paşa, made some progress in extending and rationalizing the system of non-religious courts for civil, commercial, and criminal cases. But in a time of increasing autocracy and repression, justice was an early casualty, and the high hopes of the reformers were bitterly disappointed.

Communications

The Sultan's repressions bred discontent and resentment, which the young men being educated in the Sultan's schools found ways of expressing. New communications provided the means for the rapid dissemination of new ideas and movements.

The best known development was in the railways.[24] At the accession of Abdülhamid there were only a few hundred miles of railway line in Turkey. The first line, a British concession, linked Izmir with Aydın, through the Menderes valley; 80 miles long, it was opened to traffic in 1866, and helped to develop south-western Anatolia. The others included a 58-mile line from Haydarpaşa to Izmit, completed in 1873, and a link between Istanbul and Edirne of 198 miles—the first stage of the Orient Express.

From about 1885 a burst of railway construction, most of it by foreign concession-holders, increased the railways of Turkey from several hundred to several thousand miles of track. The figures are not in themselves impressive; as late as 1913 the Ottoman Empire in Europe and Asia possessed a total of 3,882 miles of line—less than the kingdom of Belgium.[25] But the importance of these lines cannot be judged only by their mileage. When, on 12 August 1888, the first direct train left Vienna on its way to Istanbul, a new breach was opened in the crumbling wall that

[23] Mardin, pp. 151 ff.

[24] There is a vast literature on the Turkish railways. For brief accounts, from different points of view, see R. Hüber, *Die Bagdadbahn* (1943); E. M. Earle, *Turkey, the Great Powers, and the Bagdad Railway* (1923); Nuri, *Abdülhamid-i Sani*, ii. 715 ff.

[25] E. G. Mears, and others, *Modern Turkey* (1924), p. 222. According to Nuri, ii. 717, there were 1,145 km. (=711 miles) of track in 1878.

separated Turkey from the West. It grew steadily wider. Hitherto, communications between Istanbul and the European capitals had been by slow and indirect sea routes, via Marseilles or Odessa. Henceforth there was a regular and direct railway service. The traffic on the new line increased every year, still more so after the introduction of a special international train known as the Orient Express. The name reflects the viewpoint of the Europeans who planned, built and operated it—but for a whole new generation of Turks it was the express to Europe, and the Sirkeci railway terminus in Istanbul the ante-room to freedom and modernity.

A move in the opposite direction was symbolized by the Hejaz Railway, linking Damascus with Medina. Begun in 1900, this was paid for by donations from Muslims all over the world, and played an important part in the Sultan's pan-Islamic policies.

The building of roads lagged behind that of railways, and in some areas there was even a retrogression, when the old roads were supplanted by the new railway lines and allowed to fall into disrepair. The ports, too, suffered from neglect and inefficiency. One of the reforms suggested by Lord Salisbury in 1877 was an improved postal service, and an official from the British General Post Office, Mr. Scudamore, was sent to Turkey to help organize a modern, central, postal service. His efforts had only a very limited success, and most people still preferred to patronize the extraterritorial post offices maintained, under cover of the Capitulations, by the foreign diplomatic missions.[26]

More striking was the spread of the telegraph—a service of direct value to the government for defence and home security, and not merely an amenity for the public.[27] Like so many other innovations and inventions, the telegraph was first brought by the impetus of war. The first lines in Turkey were laid by the British and French during the Crimean War; the first message—sent in September 1855, from Shumna via Edirne to Istanbul and from Istanbul to Europe—stated that 'Allied forces have entered Sevastopol'.

[26] Pears, *Abdul Hamid*, pp. 189–91.

[27] The best history of the telegraph in Turkey is that given by Ergin in his account of the telegraph schools (*Maarif*, pp. 517 ff.). See further Karal, *Tarih*, vii. 273. For a medieval parallel, the use of the postal system by the Caliphs, see *EI²* ('Barīd', by D. Sourdel).

The Turks were quick to realize the value of this new medium of communication. When the war was over, the Frenchman Delarue, who had laid the Edirne-Istanbul line, was given a concession to extend the service to other parts of the Empire. By 1864 there were already 76 telegraph stations, with 267 leagues of line in use and 304 more under construction.[28] By the accession of Abdülhamid, the greater part of the Empire was linked to the capital by a network of telegraphic communications.[29]

Two men share the credit of founding Turkish telegraphy; Feyzi Bey, a member of the Translation Office of the Sublime Porte, who became the first Turkish communications officer, and Mustafa Bey, the inventor of the Turkish morse code and the trainer of the first group of Turkish telegraph operators. In 1861 Mustafa Bey, who had been appointed director of the Edirne telegraph office, sent the first telegram in Turkish, 128 words long, to Istanbul.

The government now took the question of telegraph personnel seriously in hand, and in the same year decided to set up a school for telegraph operators in Istanbul. The course was of two years duration, and included theoretical, technical, and practical instruction. The school seems to have been closed down in about 1880, but other provision for the training of telegraphists was made. In the 1870's and 1880's instruction in telegraphy was even included in the curricula of the Galatasaray and Daruşşafaka schools, and from 1883 specially selected students were sent to Paris for more advanced instruction. This ceased in 1892, when all the Turkish students in Paris were recalled after a number of them had taken part in a Young Turk political demonstration. Instruction continued in the Turkish schools, notably the Daruşşafaka, and in the early years of the twentieth century a centre for practical instruction appears to have been established. The telegraphic network was under the control of a separate ministry—the Ministry of Posts and Telegraphs.[30] The first minister, Agah Efendi, was the pioneer of modern postal services in Turkey.

It is not difficult to see the reasons for this wide expansion of telegraphy, in which the Ottoman authorities showed a speed and efficiency in striking contrast with most of their other activities.

The point was well made by Sir Charles Eliot, in a book published in 1900:

little as the Turks like railways, they are great patrons of the telegraph, because it is the most powerful instrument for a despot who wishes to control his own officials. It is no longer necessary to leave a province to the discretion of a governor, and trust that he will come home to be beheaded when that operation seems desirable. With the telegraph one can order him about, find out what he is doing, reprimand him, recall him, instruct his subordinates to report against him, and generally deprive him of all real power.[31]

In other words, the telegraph was a potent instrument of centralized and autocratic rule, and Abdülhamid, following the example of his predecessors, made the most of it. Already at the end of the century there was a vast network of telegraphic communications, covering the whole of the Empire, and centred on Istanbul. And in each station, however remote, there was an operator, usually young, with enough modern education to read his manual, and enough science to do his job,—a natural recruit for the Young Turk committees.

Press and Publications [32]

Yet another of the media of communication underwent a considerable development during the reign of Abdülhamid—the printed word. And here, too, the results were in many ways far removed from the Sultan's purposes and intentions.

The censorship, already well established in the time of Abdülaziz, was maintained and reinforced, and extended from newspapers to almost all printed matter. At first, newspapers and periodicals were allowed some measure of freedom of comment—but this was rapidly reduced, and a censorship of often farcical strictness imposed.[33] The name of the deposed Sultan Murad V might not be mentioned—so a newspaper report of the restoration, in 1904, of the fifteenth-century mosque of Murad II in Bursa, spoke of 'the mosque of the heaven-dwelling father of his majesty

[31] Odysseus [Sir Charles Eliot], *Turkey in Europe* (1900), pp. 158–9.

[32] The main works on the history of the Turkish press are cited above, p. 93 n. 37. On the press under Abdülhamid see especially Fesch. A useful survey of the movement of publication in Turkey will be found in Iskit, *Türkiyede Neşriyat Hareketleri Tarihine bir Bakış* (1939). For a survey of the Turkish press in 1906–7 by G. H. Fitzmaurice see Gooch and Temperley, v. 24–29.

[33] cf. Fesch, p. 36.

Sultan Mehmed the Conqueror'.[34] Regicide was an even more
dangerous subject—so the Turkish newspapers attributed the
sudden and simultaneous deaths of the king and queen of Serbia
in 1903 to indigestion.[35] In the same way the Empress Elizabeth
of Austria died of pneumonia, President Carnot of apoplexy,
President McKinley of anthrax.[36] The position of the press in
Turkey was well summed up by Paul Fesch in a work published
on the eve of the Young Turk Revolution:

> For thirty years, the press has ceased to exist in Turkey. There are
> indeed newspapers, many of them even, but the scissors of the censor-
> ship cut them in so emasculating a manner that they no longer have
> any potency. If I dared, I would call them gelded newspapers—or
> rather, to keep the local colour, eunuchs. Far be it from me to mock at
> an infirmity which they are the first to deplore and which they cannot
> in any way remedy. They are to be pitied. I can understand that they
> prefer this diminished life to total death—I would do the same—with
> a patience the more resigned in that their virility will sprout again
> of its own accord the day their persecutor disappears and that they are
> only waiting for that day to prove it.[37]

Even the emasculated and ineffectual newspapers of the Hamidian era, however, made some contribution to the modernization
of Turkey, if only by increasing their numbers and readership and
thus accustoming more Turks to the European habit of reading the
news every day. No less important than the newspapers were the
periodicals and books that were issuing in growing numbers from
the printing presses, to satisfy—and again arouse—the appetites
of the new literate classes. At the time of the accession of Abdülhamid, there were still only a few printing presses in Istanbul.
The official Ottoman yearbook of 1883 lists 54 presses in the city;
that of 1908, no less than 99.[38]

Book printing, like the newspaper press, was under strict
censorship. Nevertheless, the output increased steadily, and a bibliography, prepared in 1890 by the Young Turk leader Murad,[39]
lists some 4,000 books published in Turkish during the first
fifteen years of Abdülhamid's reign. Of these, some 200 dealt with
religion, nearly 500 were language primers, readers, grammars,
dictionaries, &c., 1,000 dealt with scientific and scholarly subjects,

[34] Gerçek, *Türk Gazet.*, p. 77.   [35] Ibid. p. 78.   [36] Fesch, p. 54.
[37] Ibid. p. 50.   [38] Iskit, *Neşriyat*, pp. 97 f. and 113 f.   [39] See below, p. 193.

over 1,000 consisted of fiction, poetry, drama, &c., and over 1,200 contained laws and rules and regulations of various kinds.[40]

Of these, the most important are the literary works, and works of popular science and scholarship. Turkish intellectuals, debarred from politics and from political thought, turned either to 'pure literature' or to scholarship. In both fields the Hamidian period, thanks to the energies and talents thus diverted, is one of rapid and significant development.

A characteristic figure of the period is Ahmed Midhat (1844–1912), journalist, novelist, historian, and popularizer.[41] The son of a poor Istanbul draper and a Circassian mother, he was educated at the *rüşdiye* school in Nish, where his elder brother held a government appointment. Ahmed himself entered the civil service by the usual method of recommendation and apprenticeship, and continued his studies privately, also studying French and 'Western knowledge' under the guidance of a Christian colleague. He enjoyed the patronage of Midhat Paşa, and served under him in both the Danube province and Iraq.

In 1871 he left the state service, and devoted himself entirely to writing and printing. In the course of his journalistic activities he seems to have become associated in some way with the Young Ottomans, and in 1872 was exiled to Rhodes. In 1876, after the deposition of Abdülaziz, he was permitted to return to Istanbul, where he resumed his work as writer, printer, and publisher. His circumspection during the critical months that followed enabled him to win and retain the goodwill of Abdülhamid; in 1877 the publication of a book justifying the Sultan's accession and title to the throne won him the directorship of the official gazette and state printing press. Thereafter, he held a number of official appointments.

All this led inevitably to a permanent breach with the Young Ottomans and with their liberal and revolutionary successors. After the revolution of 1908 he was retired from his various official positions, ostensibly under the age-limit, and was subjected to sharp criticism. An attempt to resume the literary work which he had long since sacrificed to his official career was abandoned in the

[40] Iskit, pp. 100 ff.

[41] See *EI*[2] ('Ahmed Midhat', by B. Lewis); *IA* ('Ahmed Midhat Efendi', by Sabri Esat Siyavuşgil); Tanpınar, pp. 433–66. A selection of his writings was published in the *Türk Klas.*

face of hostile opinion and altered tastes, and his last years were spent in teaching at the University and elsewhere.

Ahmed Midhat was a man of no great literary talent; his close association with the Hamidian régime brought him the dislike and contempt of the new generation of Turkish intellectuals. Yet this acquiescent mediocrity was able to make a contribution of no small importance to the intellectual and cultural development of Turkey.

The most important of his variegated journalistic activities was the publication of the daily newspaper *Tercüman-i Hakikat* (the Interpreter of Truth), which he edited with a small group of associates. This paper, founded by Ahmed Midhat in 1878, continued for many years, and was one of the most important of the Hamidian period.[42] For a while the newspaper included a literary supplement, which from 1882 to 1884 was edited by the well-known author Muallim Naci[43] (1850–93), and engaged in violent literary controversies. Another, perhaps more significant, supplement was a weekly for schoolboys, distributed among the pupils in the *rüşdiye* schools.[44] The greater part of the copy of the *Tercüman-i Hakikat* was provided by Ahmed Midhat himself, who poured out an unceasing flow of stories, articles, serials, and features, original, adapted, and translated. In addition, he published an enormous number of books, estimated at more than 150. These fall into two main groups, fiction and popular knowledge. The former were widely read, and played a great part in developing new tastes and interests among a public still almost entirely unacquainted with Western literary forms and themes. The latter include a vast number of works on history, philosophy, religion, ethics, science, and other subjects, through which Ahmed Midhat was able to bring some idea of modern European knowledge to the Turkish reader in a simple and attractive form. Of special interest among these are a universal history in three volumes (1880–2) and a series of separate histories of European countries, in fourteen volumes (1871–81), which were among the first works to give the Turkish reader some insight into the history of the world outside the Islamic œcumene.[45]

[42] Emin, *Press*, p. 63.

[43] On Muallim Naci see *EI*[1] ('Nādjī', by Th. Menzel) and Tanpınar, pp. 596 ff.

[44] Gerçek, pp. 75–76; *IA*, vii. 370.

[45] cf. B. Lewis, 'History-writing and National Revival in Turkey', *MEA*, iv (1953), 218–27.

A contemporary of Ahmed Midhat, whose career followed a slightly different line, was Ebüzziya Tevfik (1849–1913).[46] Acquainted at an early age with Şinasi and Namık Kemal, he became associated with the Young Ottomans, whose historian he later became, and in 1872 was exiled to Rhodes with the others. He too made his peace with Abdülhamid, in whose reign he became a member of the Council of State and Director of the School of Arts. He proved, however, less compliant than Ahmed Midhat, and was in due course exiled again, first to Rhodes and then to Konya. Thanks to this he was able, after his return to Istanbul in 1908, to play some role in the parliament and press of the Young Turk period.

Under Abdülhamid Ebüzziya's activities were, of necessity, literary. They consisted chiefly of the publication of a fortnightly magazine (1879 onwards) and the editing of a series of well over a hundred books, written or translated by various authors, and known as the Ebüzziya library. His own writings, besides Turkish literary and historical matters, deal also with such topics as Gutenberg, Buffon, and Napoleon. All these works were widely disseminated and read, and helped to form the opinions and outlook of the new generation.

More ambitious, intellectually, were the efforts of Ahmed Ihsan [Tokgöz] (1869–1942), a graduate of the *mülkiye* school who gave up a promising official career in order to become a journalist.[47] While employed as a translator on an Istanbul evening paper, the *Servet* (Treasure), he brought out an illustrated scientific supplement, called *Servet-i Fünun* (Treasure of Science) which a year later he was able to publish as an independent periodical, owned and edited by himself. The first issue, which appeared on 27 March 1891, described itself as an 'illustrated Ottoman journal', devoted to literature, science, art, biography, travel, and fiction. In its first phase, it was modelled on the French *L'Illustration*, and was a kind of pictorial news magazine relying chiefly on foreign sources for both pictures and text. From the first it had a certain literary interest, with a Westernizing tendency, and published translations from Daudet and other French writers.

This new journal rapidly attracted the interest and support of

[46] *IA s.v.* (by Fevziye Abdullah).
[47] *EI*[2] ('Aḥmad Iḥsān', by K. Süssheim—G. L. Lewis).

the young writers of the time. In January 1895 one of the most distinguished among them, the poet Tevfik Fikret[48] (1867–1915) took over the editorship, and from that time onwards the character of the journal changed radically. He remained in control until 1901, when he resigned after a disagreement with Ahmed Ihsan. About the same time the journal fell foul of the censors, who condemned as seditious an article translated from the French by the journalist Hüseyin Cahid [Yalçın][49] containing a passing reference to the 'régime of 1789'.[50] After a few weeks of suppression the journal was permitted to reappear, with Ahmed Ihsan again in charge, but the best contributors had gone, and the journal lost its interest and its influence. After the 1908 Revolution it appeared for a while as a daily newspaper.

It was during the six years of Tevfik Fikret's editorship that the *Servet-i Fünun*,[51] with the collaboration of the most gifted writers of the time, really made its impact on Turkish opinion. In a sense the *Servet-i Fünun* group and the 'New Literature'—*Edebiyat-i Cedide*—which they propounded were conservative, even reactionary. Rejecting the tendencies towards the simplification of the language that had appeared in the preceding period, they wrote in a style that was deliberately recondite and obscure, laden with learned Persian and Arabic words and expressions, and addressed only to a highly educated *élite*.

Even this, however, was in part an expression of the Western influence that appears so strongly in the Turkish literature of the time. The men of the 'New Literature' were rejecting simplicity, despising words 'worn out in the mouth of the common people'.[52] They were not rejecting the literature of the West; there, on the contrary, under the prevailing influence of the French symbolists, they were able to find an aesthetic justification for that retreat into the ivory tower which the Hamidian censorship had imposed upon them. Despite their linguistic conservatism, Tevfik Fikret and his associates went much farther than their predecessors in imitating and adapting French models. Though political criticism was barred, social comment could be and was made through the

---

[48] On Tevfik Fikret, see *EI*[1] ('Tewfīḳ Fikret', by Th. Menzel); Akyüz, *Tevfik Fikret* (1947); Bombaci, pp. 449–54. For a selection of his writings see *Türk Klas.*

[49] Hüseyin Cahit Yalçın, selected works (ibid. xlix).   [50] Ibid. p. 4.

[51] On the *Servet-i Fünun*, see 'Serveti Fünun Edebiyatı Antolojisi', in the *Türk Klas.*; Bombaci, pp. 447 ff.

[52] U. Heyd, *Language Reform in Modern Turkey* (1954), p. 15.

fictional analysis of the social life of the time. One of the main tasks of the *Servet-i Fünun* was to make known to the Turkish reader something of the intellectual and cultural life of Europe, especially of France. Such a message, even in a parnassian, symbolist literary form, still held a profoundly revolutionary content; there is a symbolic quality in the suppression of the journal for a passing allusion in a translated article to the French Revolution—and perhaps also in the subsequent career of the translator.[53]

The *Servet-i Fünun* avoided politics, even though many of its authors held strong political opinions and Tevfik Fikret himself was more than once in trouble with the authorities. A bolder line was taken by the weekly *Mizan* (Balance), founded in 1886.[54] It was suppressed in 1890, and later restarted in exile. In the first issue, the editor discussed the importance, form, and proper contents of the press in civilized countries, and promised his readers to supply them with news, to discuss political questions, and to correct European misapprehensions about Turkey.

The editor, Murad Bey (1853–1912), known as Mizancı, was a person of some interest.[55] A native of Daghistan, in the Caucasus, he completed his education, perhaps including a university course, in Russia before settling in Turkey in 1873. Like so many Muslim emigrants from the Russian Empire, Murad found a ready opening for his talents and qualifications, and was employed for some time in the Council of the Public Debt. Later he became a teacher of history at the *Mülkiye*, where, according to the testimony of some of his pupils, he exercised a profound influence on the rising generation. Through his books, and still more through the weekly *Mizan*, he was able to extend that influence far beyond his classroom. Ahmet Emin [Yalman], the historian of the Turkish press, describes him as 'the leading figure in the press of the time . . . the idol of the intellectual classes'.[56] Under Hamidian rule the next stages—the suppression of the *Mizan*, and, after an interval, the flight to Egypt and Europe of its editor—followed inevitably. Among the Young Turks abroad he won a position of authority and leadership which ended only when he yielded to the Sultan's

---

[53] See his selected works in *Türk Klas.*   [54] *IA*, vii. 371.

[55] On Murad Bey see E. E. Ramsaur, *The Young Turks* (1957), index; Fevziye Abdullah, 'Mizancı Mehmed Murad Bey', *Tar. Derg.*, iii–iv. 67–88.

[56] Emin, *Press*, p. 65.

blandishments and returned to Istanbul to take up an official appointment in 1887.

With the increasing severity of the censorship from about 1890–1 onwards, the most significant and interesting productions of Turkish journalism were the newspapers and periodicals published, in growing numbers, by the Young Turk exiles in France, Switzerland, England, Egypt, and elsewhere. Nevertheless, even the press in Istanbul, though debarred from any serious political comment or even news reporting, continued to form its readers in new ways of thought, to inculcate, no doubt unconsciously, European social ideas and attitudes, and to bring to them some notion, however garbled, of the larger, modern world of which Turkey was now a part.

In 1891, before the growth of Young Turk activities abroad led to a worsening of the position of the press at home, there were six Turkish daily newspapers. Within a few years the pressure from above had reduced their number to three, all in receipt of government subsidies and under strict palace control. The *Tercüman-i Hakikat* has already been mentioned. The other two—the *Ikdam* (Effort) and *Sabah* (Morning)—both had fairly substantial circulations, the former about 15,000 and the latter about 12,000.[57] These numbers may seem small in comparison with the present-day circulations of 100,000–200,000 of some of the Istanbul papers. At that time, however, they were sufficient to keep the papers going even when the subsidies ceased, to reach and influence the members of the numerically small educated *élite*, and to provide a training, an outlet, and a livelihood for the followers of a new profession—journalism. It is significant that both papers managed to survive the revolution of 1908, and to play a role of some importance under the régimes that followed it.

The First Revolutionaries [58]

In spite of these changes, the government of Turkey was still the accepted and recognized prerogative of an *élite* of professionals,

[57] Emin, *Press*, p. 78.

[58] A detailed monographic study of the opposition movements under Abdülhamid, based on both Turkish and Western sources, will be found in Ramsaur's *Young Turks*; additional material in Ş. Mardin, 'Libertarian movements in the Ottoman Empire 1878–1898', *MEJ* (1962), 169–82; idem, *Jön Türklerin siyasî fikirleri 1898–1908* (1964); Berkes, *Development*, pp. 289 ff., and in several Turkish works, notably those of Tunaya, A. B. Kuran, and Bayur.

who retained all the rights and duties of politics, including that of opposition. It was, therefore, among the servants of the state that the pioneers of revolutionary change emerged; it was in the schools —those nurseries of the civil and military *élite*, so carefully tended by the Sultan himself—that the seeds of revolution were sown.

Many Turkish writers have described the atmosphere of discontent and revolutionary ferment in the Hamidian schools, especially in the provincial centres, less subject to the immediate control of the palace. Even in the Imperial Lycée of Galatasaray in Istanbul, feeling against the Sultan was very strong. Hikmet Bayur, who graduated from the Lycée in 1909, has described how, two years before the Young Turk Revolution, the pupils were assembled on various festivals for the distribution of sweets and ordered to shout 'Padişahım çok yaşa'—long live the Emperor!

We, however, or at least the great majority of us, used to shout 'Padişahım başaşağıya'—down with the Emperor. Among those who shouted in this way were the sons of ministers and even of such close associates of the Emperor as the palace chamberlains . . . the youth even of the circles nearest to the Emperor neither loved nor respected him. . . .[59]

This universal disgust no doubt took some time to reach the level described by Hikmet Bayur. But already in the first decades of Abdülhamid's rule there was discontent and frustration in the schools, where teachers and students alike read the forbidden writings of Namık Kemal and Ziya Paşa, talking and dreaming of freedom and fatherland. Niyazi Bey, the hero of the revolution of July 1908, describes in his memoirs how, already as a young schoolboy in the 1880's, he imbibed from the teachers of French and history—the choice is significant—the ideas of

loyalty, progress, humanity, and love of country. . . . They used to tell us stories about the patriotism of the old Ottomans and the French. . . . When we used to talk about the affairs of the world, with schoolmates and other people . . . the name of [Namık] Kemal Bey, of that great and respected writer, . . . and his works were mentioned.

. . . Would it not be our duty to defend the fatherland and repel the attacks of the enemy? Why then is there no trace, in our courses and syllabuses, of fatherland or of training of the mind? Why do they force us to conceal a whole set of feelings that by religion, reason and logic

[59] Hikmet Bayur, 'İkinci Meşrutiyet devri üzerinde bazı düşünceler', *Bell.*, no. 90 (1959), p. 269. Bayur is a grandson of Kâmil Paşa.

are sacred to us? Why do they not give us books to read that would serve to develop and elevate these feelings? ...

In fact, however, Niyazi and his friends were introduced by a teacher to such writings, including the poems of Kemal, under whose influence 'an intoxicating patriotism prepared my heart, my innocent heart, for revolutions . . .'

When Niyazi went to the War College at Pangaltı in 1882, he found that Kemal, whose works placed him 'among the greatest men of the nation, the greatest leaders of politics, the zealots of the community' was proscribed, together with the rest of the liberals. 'Even to mention their names or their works was considered a mortal sin.'[60]

There were, however, many sinners. Ali Kemal, Rıza Tevfik, and others have described how the teachers of the *mülkiye* and other schools talked to them of freedom, and introduced them to the writings of the proscribed Young Ottoman authors. The authorities were aware of this, and tried to replace them with safer and more submissive teachers. Ali Kemal remarks: 'At that time teachers like Murad Bey and even Ekrem Bey were removed from the *mülkiye* school because of their intellectual freedom. In their place dull and stupid men were brought.'[61]

An order of the time forbids teachers to diverge from the syllabus and provides for the 'exemplary punishment of teachers acting in a way contrary to the principles of loyalty'.[62] These measures, however, had only limited effect, and failed to prevent the spread of subversive views among the cadets and schoolboys. These young men, the future soldiers and administrators of the Empire, were given the most advanced and most modern education that the state could offer; it was inevitable that they and their teachers should, sooner or later, reach some radical conclusions on the conduct of the state which they were to serve.

Organized Opposition

The first organized opposition group was formed in 1889—the centenary, as a Turkish historian has pointed out, of the

[60] *Hâtırât-i Niyazi* (1326 A.H.), pp. 14–15. The influence of Namık Kemal is attested by other Young Turk memoirists. See, for example, Kâzım Nami Duru's account of how he read Namık Kemal while still a cadet at the military *idadi* school at Manastir, and secretly made a copy of one of them which reached him in manuscript form (*Ittihat ve Terakki Hatıralarım* (1957), p. 6).

[61] Cited in Ergin, *Maarif*, pp. 504 ff.   [62] Ibid. p. 513.

French Revolution.[63] Its founders were four medical students, meeting in May in the garden of the military medical college, halfway between the old Imperial palace and the new railway terminus. The founders were Ibrahim Temo, an Albanian from Ohrid, Mehmed Reşid, a Circassian from the Caucasus, Abdullah Cevdet and Ishak Sükûti, two Kurds from Arabkir and Diyarbakır respectively. Some accounts add a fifth name—that of Hüseyin-zade Ali, from Baku, in the Russian Empire.[64]

The new society grew rapidly, winning adherents among the cadets in the civil, military, naval, medical, and other higher schools in Istanbul. Like their predecessors, the Young Ottomans of 1865, these new conspirators seem to have taken the Italian Carbonari as their model, and formed themselves into numbered cells, in which each member also had a number. Temo, the first member of the first cell, was 1/1.

By means of the French post office in Galata, the conspirators were able to maintain contact with Paris, where in the meantime the first organized group of exiles had constituted itself. A small group of Ottoman liberals had been living there since the closing of parliament by Abdülhamid, and one of them, a Lebanese Maronite and former member of the Ottoman parliament called Khalil Ghanim,[65] had started a journal, in France, called *La Jeune Turquie*. The name was no doubt a conscious evocation of the memory of the Young Ottoman exiles of the 1860's.

In 1889 the director of education of Bursa, Ahmed Rıza Bey, obtained permission to visit Paris to see the exhibition. Arriving there, he joined the group of exiles, and soon became a dominant figure among them.

Ahmed Rıza (1859-1930), one of the most consistent and fearless of the Young Turks, is in many ways a key figure among them.[66] He was born at Istanbul, the son of Ali Rıza Bey, nicknamed 'Ingiliz Ali' because of his knowledge of English and his

[63] Tunaya, *Partiler*, p. 104.
[64] Ramsaur, p. 14; Tunaya, *Partiler*, p. 104; Kuran (1956), pp. 134 ff. Biographical notes on these personalities will be found in Ibrahim Alâettin Gövsa's useful compendium, *Türk Meşhurları Ansiklopedisi* (n.d.). On Abdullah Cevdet see further *EI*[1] suppl. ('Djewdet', by K. Süssheim).
[65] The role of this Ottoman Syrian Christian seems to have been overlooked by the historians both of Turkish and Arab nationalism. See Ramsaur, p. 22.
[66] On Ahmed Rıza, see Ramsaur, Tunaya, Kuran (1956), Bayur, *passim*, and Mardin, *Jön T.* (1964), pp. 123 ff. Surprisingly, he is missing from both the Turkish and Leiden Encyclopaedias of Islam.

friendship with Englishmen during the Crimean War; his mother was an Austrian or Hungarian lady converted to Islam. Ingiliz Ali had been a member of the first parliament, and had been exiled to Ilgin, where he died. Ahmed Rıza went to school at Galatasaray, and was then sent to study agriculture in France. It was on his return to Turkey, from his studies, that he was appointed director of education in Bursa. This post he abandoned in order to undertake a vaster project of re-education from abroad.

In Paris Ahmed Rıza fell under the influence of Pierre La-fitte, a disciple of Auguste Comte who instructed him in the positivist philosophy that was to dominate his thinking. In 1895, in association with other exiles, he began to publish a fortnightly journal, the *Meşveret*. The name—a word of Arabic origin meaning consultation—is an echo of earlier arguments, drawn from the Koran, for consultative government.[67] The device under it—*Intizam ve Terakki*—Order and Progress, is that of the Positivists. It is probably through this positivist influence that the group in Istanbul now changed its name from *Ittihad-i Osmani*, Ottoman Union, to *Ittihad ve Terakki*, Union and Progress.[68]

The *Meşveret*, smuggled through the foreign post offices and other channels, began to circulate in Istanbul, helping both to increase the numbers of the society and, as an inevitable consequence, to bring it to the attention of the authorities. At about the same time Murad Bey presented a memorandum on necessary reforms to the Sultan and then, feeling no doubt that his point could be made more effectively from beyond the Sultan's reach, fled to British-occupied Egypt, where he began to publish his *Mizan*, this time in a form openly critical of the Sultan and his régime.

The Sultan retaliated by arresting some of Murad's friends in Istanbul, and arresting or exiling the known leaders of the opposition groups. Far from being crushed, the conspirators were now driven from theory to practice, and prepared a coup d'état which was to depose the Sultan in August 1896. The plot was, however, betrayed to the Sultan, and swift police action led to the arrest of almost all the conspirators. Although the charge was virtually one of rebellion or treason, the court martial that tried the plotters imposed no sentences of death. Instead, the unsuccessful conspirators were exiled, in accordance with the old

[67] See above, pp. 144 and 155.   [68] Ramsaur, pp. 23 ff.

Ottoman practice, to remote provinces of the Empire—to Anatolia, Mosul, and Syria, and, for the most dangerous, to Fezzan in Libya. Kâzım Paşa, the general commanding the first division in Istanbul, and leader designate of the coup d'état, was punished with nothing worse than the governorship of Scutari in Albania.[69]

In spite of the failure of this first attempt to overthrow the Sultan, the Young Turk agitation continued to grow in Istanbul, notably among the students. It was actively encouraged by the exiles in Egypt and Europe, whose publications circulated in Turkey, and who managed, chiefly through the foreign post offices, to keep in touch with their friends at home. Çürüksulu Ahmed, a former teacher at the War College who had fled to France, corresponded secretly with some of his former pupils, and had a hand in the formation of two cells or committees at the War College. They were known, significantly, as the Hüseyin Avni and Süleyman Paşa groups—after the Minister of War and the War College commandant who took part in the deposition of Sultan Abdülaziz.[70]

At the beginning of June 1897 a special court martial was set up, presided over by Major-General Reşid Paşa, 'the tormentor of the country's youth'.[71] Its purpose was to crush the freedom movements among the cadets, and a grim, slow procession of arrests, detentions, and deportations filled the bleak corridors of the Taşkışla barracks. Political prisoners previously held at the Arsenal (Tersane) and elsewhere were transferred to Taşkışla for examination and trial, and then sent on their road to exile. On 28 August a party of seventy-eight prisoners—army, navy, medical officers, cadets from the military academies—emerged after 102 days at Taşkışla, and proceeded to the Kabataş quay, where they were put on board a steamer appropriately named the *Şeref* (Honour). They arrived on Wednesday 3 September at Tripoli, and were dispatched to military prisons.[72]

In spite of these repressions, the Young Turk movement continued to grow alarmingly, and the Sultan, feeling that the main impulse came from the exiles abroad, tried a new approach—that of reconciliation.

The situation among the exiles was not entirely happy. They were split up among a number of centres—the most important

[69] Ibid. pp. 31–34. [70] Ramsaur, p. 45; Fesch, p. 341; Tunaya, *Partiler*, p. 104.
[71] Kuran, p. 143. [72] Tunaya, *Partiler*, p. 105; Kuran, pp. 144 ff.

in Paris, Geneva, and Cairo, with smaller groups in Folke-
stone, London, and elsewhere. Differences, both personal and
ideological, had begun to appear among them. These were
aggravated when, towards the end of 1896, Murad Bey moved
from Egypt to Europe, where he soon emerged as a successful rival
of Ahmed Rıza for the leadership of the Young Turks. Murad
became the leader of the Geneva branch of the Committee of
Union and Progress, and his *Mizan*, now appearing in Geneva,
rivalled and surpassed Ahmed Rıza's *Meşveret* as an organ of
Young Turk opinion.[73]

It was at this juncture that the Sultan began to make approaches
to the leaders in exile. A first mission, consisting of Yusuf Ziya Paşa
and Ebüzziya Tevfik, produced no results, but in August 1897
Major-General Ahmed Celâleddin Paşa, a Circassian confidant of
the Sultan, succeeded in persuading Murad, in Geneva, to accept
a truce and return to Istanbul.

This defection was a shattering blow to the Young Turks. For a
while the attempt was made to present this as a genuine negotiated, armed, truce. Murad, said a report of the time, 'without
accepting any personal favour, will go alone to Constantinople
as hostage. It is a new sacrifice on his part, for in the event of a
resumption of hostilities, he will undoubtedly pay for this movement with his life.'[74]

Murad did not, in fact, pay with his life; instead, he became a
member of the Council of State. That his intentions were honour-
able at the moment of his return to Istanbul is generally conceded;
but his defection, its exploitation by the Sultan, and the more
flagrant betrayals of some of his associates, spread a wave of
demoralization through the movement, especially inside Turkey.
What was worse, Murad, the hero and idol of the movement, had
set an example of compromise and submission that others were to
follow. Two of the original four members of the Committee at the
Medical School, Ishak Sükûti and Abdullah Cevdet, arrived in
Europe about this time. With Tunalı Hilmi, who had started the
'Ottoman Revolutionary Party' in Geneva in 1896, Mehmed
Reşid, one of the founder members of the Committee, and other

[73] Ramsaur, pp. 37–39; Fesch, p. 338; Mardin, *Jön T.*, pp. 46 ff.

[74] Ramsaur, pp. 49–50; Fesch, p. 343; Fevziye Abdullah, p. 84. For a very detailed
account of the mission of Ahmed Celâleddin Paşa and the defection of Murad, see
Kuran, pp. 151 ff.

Young Turk militants, they succeeded in reviving the Geneva centre and in December 1897 launched a new journal, the *Osmanlı*. They remained, however, in touch with the Sultan, and in 1899 struck a bargain—apparently a renewal of an earlier agreement with Murad—whereby the Sultan undertook to release political detainees in Libya, and they to refrain from attacking him. In addition, Sükûti, Cevdet, and Hilmi accepted salaried appointments, the first two as medical officers to the Ottoman Embassies in Rome and Vienna respectively, the third as Embassy secretary in Madrid. Abdullah Cevdet, despite his intellectual pre-eminence and his undoubted contributions to the ideology of Young Turkism, found it hard to live down this apparent betrayal. It was no more than apparent. The *Osmanlı* was restarted in England, where it survived precariously until 1904. The defectors were among its financial supporters, and later returned to active opposition. [75]

Meanwhile, Ahmed Rıza and his friends in Paris remained impervious to both the blandishments and the threats of the Sultan and his emissaries, and continued to publish and distribute the *Meşveret*, now almost the sole organ of the Young Turk cause. And then, in December 1899, when Young Turk prospects seemed to be at their lowest ebb, both in Turkey and in Europe, the movement was suddenly galvanized into life again by the dramatic flight, from Istanbul to France, of a small group of new recruits from an unexpected source—from the Imperial family itself.

Damad Mahmud Celâleddin Paşa (1853–1903) was the son of a Vezir and the grandson, by his mother, of Sultan Mahmud II. [76] His wife was a daughter of Abdülmecid and a sister of Abdülhamid, to whom he was thus doubly related. His departure, with his sons Sabaheddin and Lûtfullah, was a heavy blow to the Sultan.

The arrival of the royal rebels was of course a great addition of strength and prestige to the Young Turks. It also had the effect of accentuating the divisions among them. Murad and Abdullah Cevdet had both successfully challenged for a while the leadership of Ahmed Rıza—and had then surrendered themselves into insignificance. Now a new and more enduring rival appeared,

[75] Ramsaur, pp. 53–54; Fesch, p. 346. cf. Kuran, pp. 204 ff.; K. Süssheim, 'Djewdet', in *EI*[1] Supplement; 'Hilmi' in *EI*[2]; Mardin, *Jön T.*, pp. 93 ff.

[76] On the intervention of the Damad and his sons, see Ramsaur, pp. 54 ff.; Fesch, p. 356; Kuran, pp. 228 ff.

high in prestige and firm of principle, to confront the positivist prophet of the *Meşveret*. Between the two there followed a polarization of opinion, that split the Young Turks in exile until the Revolution, and in office until the end of the Empire.

This new leader was Prince Sabaheddin (1877–1948) who rapidly emerged as the chief personal and, later, ideological rival of Ahmed Rıza.[77] The cleavage between the two wings of the movement became apparent and was made permanent in 1902, at a Young Turk congress convened in Paris to restore and confirm the unity of the movement. The idea of such a congress was first mooted by the two princes, in an appeal put out by them during a visit to Egypt in 1900.[78] The congress finally assembled on 4 February 1902, at the private house of a French well-wisher, under the presidency of Prince Sabaheddin.[79]

According to reports that have been published, two important questions came up during and after the congress. One was the argument, put forward by Ismail Kemal, that 'by propaganda and publications alone a revolution cannot be made. It is therefore necessary to work to ensure the participation of the armed forces in the revolutionary movement.'[80] Ismail Kemal, in his memoirs, describes how with Prince Sabaheddin's approval, he set to work to organize a military coup, and actually succeeded in interesting the British government in his plans. They came, however, to nothing.[81]

It was on the other question, that of intervention, that a serious split developed. The Armenian participants, mindful of the massacres of 1894–6, were anxious to seek the intervention of the European powers as a guarantee of effective reform in the Ottoman Empire. Ahmed Rıza and most of the Turks in the Committee of Union and Progress were opposed to this; the problem was, in their view, a purely internal one, and any outside intervention would be unnecessary and even harmful. Prince Sabah-

---

[77] On Sabaheddin, see Ramsaur, pp. 81–89; Kuran, pp. 317 ff. and 400 ff. &c.; Fesch, *passim*; Mardin, *Jön T.*, pp. 215 ff.

[78] Ramsaur, p. 65; Kuran, pp. 267 ff.

[79] On the Paris congress of 1902 see Ramsaur, pp. 66 ff.; Fesch, pp. 364 ff.; Kuran, pp. 317 ff.; Tunaya, *Partiler*, pp. 106 ff.

[80] Kuran, p. 321.

[81] Ismail Kemal, *Memoirs*, pp. 308 ff.; cf. Ramsaur, p. 76 ff. For a somewhat different version see Kuran, pp. 326 ff.

eddin agreed on this occasion with the Armenians, and a resolution was passed including a reminder to the Europeans

that is is their duty in the general interest of humanity to ensure that the clauses in the treaties and international agreements concluded between themselves and the Sublime Porte are put into effect in such a way as to benefit all parts of the Ottoman Empire.[82]

Ahmed Rıza and his friends remained implacably opposed to this policy, and the difference between his party and that of Prince Sabaheddin begins to crystallize from now onwards as one between Turkish nationalism and Ottoman liberalism. The minority statement makes interesting reading.

. . . We, the minority, convinced that the Powers are guided by interest and that this interest is not always in accord with that of our country, therefore utterly reject an action which infringes the independence of the Ottoman Empire. Nevertheless we are not, as has been claimed, hostile to Europe; on the contrary, one of our chief desires is to see European civilization spread in our country, notably its scientific progress and its useful institutions. We follow the path traced by Europe and, even in our refusal to accept foreign intervention, we draw inspiration from the patriotic resolution of which all the European peoples, jealous of their independence, have shown themselves rightly proud.[83]

The Prince now proceeded to found a new society in Paris, with the princely name of 'the League for Private Initiative and Decentralization'. Like its rival the Committee of Union and Progress, the League set up branches among the Turkish diaspora, as well as in various parts of the Ottoman Empire. They seem to have concentrated on Asiatic Turkey, and branches are mentioned in Erzurum, Trabzon, Izmir, Alanya, as well as in Damascus and Latakia in Syria.[84] In Istanbul the League seems to have been represented by the 'Revolutionary Society' (*Cemiyet-i Inkılabiye*), founded in September 1904 by a group of students and schoolboys.[85]

The somewhat ponderous name of the League derives from the writings of Edmond Demolins, a French writer by whom Prince Sabaheddin was profoundly influenced.[86] Demolins's book *À Quoi*

[82] Fesch, p. 371; Ramsaur, p. 71
[83] Fesch, pp. 372 3; Ramsaur, p. 69.   [84] Tunaya, *Partiler*, pp. 142 ff.
[85] Ibid. pp. 149 ff.   [86] Ramsaur, pp. 82 ff.

tient la supériorité des Anglo-Saxons? was published in 1897, and
translated into English immediately after. It attracted a good deal
of attention at the time, and in particular aroused the interest of
Muslim reformers, liberals, and modernists looking for an explanation of the backwardness of their own societies. The book was
quickly published in an Arabic version in Egypt,[87] and seems to
have had no small impact on Arab and Turkish thinking.
Demolins's thesis, briefly, was that the superiority of the Anglo-
Saxons rested on their superior education, which developed
personality and individual initiative—confidence in oneself,
instead of the confidence in the collectivity usual in other human
societies. Within this framework of historical and educational
theories, Prince Sabaheddin developed his idea of a federalized,
decentralized Ottoman state. A constitutional monarchy, on
British lines, would provide a minimum of central government;
for the rest, the different peoples and communities of the Empire
could satisfy their aspirations and safeguard their rights in
regional and local government and in a public life eman-
cipated from collective or governmental control. The German
Orientalist C. H. Becker, writing in 1916, grimly commented on
this doctrine:

> one may imagine what would have resulted if such theorists had been
> able to put their ideas into practice, if English individualism had been
> introduced in a country, millions of whose inhabitants are still in a
> state of ethnic collectivism, not to mention the irredeemable dissolution
> of Turkey into various European spheres of influence.[88]

Prince Sabaheddin's ideas, despite some initial success, were in
fact foredoomed to failure. The Armenians and other Christian
nationalities, whom he tried so hard to conciliate, found little to
attract them in an Ottoman federation, and preferred to seek the
fulfilment of their political aspirations outside the Empire
altogether. For the Turks, already irritated by the clashes and
arguments with the Armenian committees, private initiative and
decentralization seemed a much less satisfying slogan than union
and progress. The growing menace, from dissident nationalism
and foreign imperialism, to the integrity of the Empire made
decentralization seem a dangerous if not suicidal formula. The

---

[87] Tr. by Aḥmad Zaghlūl Pasha; see C. C. Adams, *Islam and Modernism in Egypt*
(1933), p. 312.   [88] C. H. Becker, *Islamstudien*, ii (1932), p. 355.

growing pre-eminence of the army in the revolutionary movement gave the direction of the latter to an institution and a profession that were inevitably imbued with a spirit of authoritarian centralism. Neither private initiative nor decentralization held much appeal for the Prussian-trained officers of the Turkish army.

Between 1902 and 1906 the Young Turk movement continued to expand and to ramify. New groups appeared in Geneva and Cairo. Even in Istanbul, apparently for the first time since the defection of Murad, revolutionary groups began to appear once more among the cadets and students of the military and civil schools.[89]

Then, in 1906, came the really important development—the establishment of revolutionary cells among serving officers in field formations. The first of such organizations seems to have been the 'Fatherland and Freedom Society' established by a small group of officers in Damascus, among them Mustafa Kemal, in the autumn of 1906. Branches were formed in Jaffa and Jerusalem, among the officers of the Fifth Army Corps.

Of more permanent significance was the committee formed in Salonika, at about the same time, among the officers of the Third Army Corps. The early history of this group is obscure, but it seems that Mustafa Kemal and the Damascus group played some role in getting it started. The vital phase began in September 1906, with the foundation of the 'Ottoman Freedom Society' by Ismail Canbulat and Midhat Şükrü [Bleda]. Its first supreme committee, of ten men, included Bursalı Tahir, headmaster of the military *rüşdiye* school in Salonika and a well-known scholar, Talât, chief clerk in the correspondence division of the Salonika directorate of posts and telegraphs, and a number of army officers.[90]

Events now moved rapidly. The cadets had by now become captains and majors, with men and arms under their command; the parlous state of the armed forces, and the increasing dangers of secession and aggression, made a change of régime an urgent necessity obvious to any patriotic and aspiring young officer. These were not of the kind that was to be familiar in subsequent Middle

[89] Tunaya, *Partiler*, p. 107. This revival of activity in Istanbul is not mentioned by Ramsaur.

[90] Ramsaur, pp. 95 ff.; Tunaya, *Partiler*, pp. 113 ff. and 150–2; Kuran, pp. 377 ff. There is some conflict of evidence on the personal role of Mustafa Kemal in these events.

Eastern revolutions—ambitious young subalterns, drawn from new and rising social classes, using the discipline and cohesion of the army to destroy an old social order and initiate a revolutionary upheaval. They were members of a ruling *élite*, prepared by education to command and to govern; their complaint was that they were not permitted to do so effectively. The army, mistrusted by the Sultan, was starved of money and equipment, its pay in arrears and its weapons obsolete. Smart, young officers, with up-to-date training for an out-of-date army, could not but be painfully aware of the inadequacy of the defences of the Empire, in the face of the dangers that were looming. Their political ideas were simple and rudimentary—freedom and fatherland, the constitution and the nation.

In December 1907 the Armenian Tashnag society took the initiative for a second attempt at the unification of the anti-Hamidian forces. A congress was again held in Paris, at which both Ahmed Rıza and Prince Sabaheddin were present; the latter was elected chairman.[91] This time the congress was held partly *in camera*, and seems to have been concerned with immediate practical decisions. Theoretical and ideological questions were left aside, and a large measure of agreement reached on an immediate programme of action. Only on one ideological matter did the opposing wings come together; on a proposal of the positivist Ahmed Rıza Bey, the liberals and the nationalists agreed to confirm the rights of the Caliphate and Sultanate.[92]

The real centre of events, however, was no longer among the exiles, but among the officers in Turkey, where new groups were being formed in Macedonia and Anatolia. In September 1907 the Salonika group had merged with the old Union and Progress organization in Paris, which thus acquired new vigour and prestige.[93] The Salonika officers seem, however, to have remained very independent in their affairs, using the committee in Paris as they used the masonic lodges in Turkey—because it was convenient to do so—but without paying much attention to the ideologies in either place.

By 1908 there was much to encourage the conspirators in Turkey. In the Far East, an Oriental but constitutional Japan had

[91] On the second Paris congress see Ramsaur, pp. 124 ff.; Tunaya, *Partiler*, pp. 107–8; Kuran, pp. 408 ff.

[92] Tunaya, *Partiler*, p. 108.   [93] Ramsaur, pp. 121 ff.

a few years previously defeated a European but autocratic Russia —and both Russia and Persia had accepted this demonstration of the superiority of democratic institutions, and had introduced, the one by precaution, the other by revolution, constitutional and parliamentary régimes. In Europe, the meeting of the English and Russian sovereigns at Reval on 9–10 June 1908 seemed to portend the obsequies of the Sick Man of Europe, and suggested an urgent need for the constitutional nostrum.[93a] And in the Empire, a wave of mutinies or rather strikes spread from Anatolia to Rumelia as Abdülhamid's unpaid, underfed, and ragged soldiery rose in desperation to demand the satisfaction of a few basic, minimum human needs.

The Constitutional Revolution [94]

In the early months of 1908 these troubles seemed to be spreading to the Third Army Corps, stationed in Macedonia. Alarming reports began to reach the Sultan's government in Istanbul, and in the late spring a commission was sent to Salonika to investigate the situation. The Sultan had accumulated vast archives of alarming reports from his spies over a period of many years, and seems at first to have seen no reason for precipitancy. This time he was mistaken. The Young Turk officers, by now seriously concerned at the growing threat to the Empire from inside and outside, were ready to overthrow a régime so incompetent in its defence. By the time the Sultan was ready to take action, it was too late.

The appointment of two successive commissions, to investigate and to punish, brought matters to a head. One young officer, attached to the staff of Hilmi Paşa, seems to have aroused suspicion and, characteristically, was invited to visit Istanbul in order to 'explain the situation and receive a promotion'. The officer in question, wisely mistrusting the motives behind the

[93a] See Jaeschke in *WI*, vi (1961), 265.

[94] There are many political, personal, and journalistic accounts of the revolution of 1908. Much useful material is given in the relevant parts of Kuran (*Inkılâp*) and of Hikmet Bayur's comprehensive history of the Turkish revolution—*Türk Inkılâbı Tarihi* (1940 ff.). An excellent summary of political developments will be found in Tunaya, *Partiler*, pp. 161 ff. and a brief account in idem, *Hurriyetin Ilânı* (1959). For a recent documentary study see Uzunçarşılı, '1908 yılında ikinci Meşrutiyetin ne surette Ilân edildiğine dair vesikalar', *Bell.* no. 77 (1956), 103–74.

invitation, preferred to disappear into the Resne hills. His name was Enver Bey.[95]

On 4 July another officer, Major Ahmed Niyazi—at that time far more important in the councils of the Young Turks—followed him into the hills. Niyazi, however, did not go alone and in secret. He went with a substantial body of men, and with arms, munitions, and money seized from the company stores. At the same time, he addressed a declaration to the Palace Secretariat, the Inspectorate-General of Rumelia, the vilayet of Manastir, as well as letters of accusation to the commandant of the gendarmerie at Manastir and the gendarme officer at Resne.[96] His attitude is summed up in a note written, on the eve of his departure, to his brother-in-law, Ismail Hakkı Bey, kaymakam of the kaza of Manastir, to whose care he entrusted his family:

I shall set out, with the help of God, in about an hour, and will therefore write briefly. . . . I see no point in lengthy explanations. The cause is known. Rather than live basely, I have preferred to die. I am therefore going out now, with two hundred patriots armed with Mausers, to die for our country. As to my family, please send them to Istanbul, as I explained to you yesterday, with my nephew Şevki, tomorrow if possible, otherwise Sunday. For the rest, either death or the salvation of the fatherland![97]

In the event, it was not Niyazi who died. That fate was reserved for Şemsi Paşa, the general appointed by the Sultan to suppress the mutineers and rebels. On 7 July Şemsi Paşa was shot in broad daylight as he was coming out of the telegraph office in Manastir; his assassin, one of the officers of the force that he commanded, walked calmly and unmolested away.[98]

The mutiny now spread rapidly among the different units of the Third Army Corps in Macedonia, and began to affect the Second Army Corps in Edirne. The Committee of Union and Progress came out into the open, adopting the mutineers and rebels and formulating a clear political demand—for the restoration of the constitution.

The Sultan at first attempted to resist this demand, and to deal with the leaders of the movement by the time-dishonoured alter-

[95] Ramsaur, p. 134; Kuran, pp. 425 ff.   [96] Niyazi, pp. 83 ff.
[97] Ibid. p. 73; cf. Uzunçarşılı, in *Bell.*, no. 77, 107 ff.
[98] Pears, *Forty Years*, p. 229; Ramsaur, p. 135; Y. H. Bayur, *Türk. Ink. Tar.*, 2nd ed., i/1, 455 ff.; Kuran, p. 427. Uzunçarşılı, pp. 109 ff.

natives of espionage, bribery, and repression. But this time all of them failed.[99] The spies despatched by the Sultan to report on the loyalty of the officers in Macedonia were detected, and added to the resentment of the army at this kind of insult and humiliation. The shower of decorations, promotions, and warrants for arrears of pay evoked no response from the dissident officers; the generals entrusted with repressions were fired on by their own men.[100]

The armies of Salonika and Manastir were now openly opposed to the Sultan, and were assured of the support of the Second Army Corps at Edirne. Even the faithful Anatolians, dispatched from Izmir to Salonika, were infected by Young Turk propaganda.[101] On 20 July the Muslim population of Manastir rose in revolt and seized the military stores.[102] Other outbreaks followed, notably at Firzovik (Ferizovič), in Kosovo province, where an angry gathering swore on oath to restore the constitution. They sent an ultimatum demanding this of the Sultan, failing which they would march on the capital and depose him.[103] Similar demands, some supported by similar threats, were reaching the Yıldız Palace by telegraph from other Rumelian centres. One of the most menacing is said to have come from Serez, demanding the immediate restoration of the constitution. If the Sultan refused, the heir apparent would be proclaimed as Sultan in Rumelia, and an army of 100,000 men would march on Istanbul.[104] Others took matters into their own hands. On the 23rd, the constitution was proclaimed in Manastir, followed within hours by other towns. Finally, after two days of hesitation and discussion, the Sultan gave way, and on 23 July announced that the constitution was once again in force. The mutiny had become a revolution, and the revolution had achieved its goal. Only the details of the millennium remained to be arranged.

[99] Pears, *Forty Years*, p. 234.   [100] Ibid. pp. 231–2.

[101] Ibid. pp. 203–4; Niyazi, p. 220; Uzunçarşılı, p. 111; Bayur, i/1, 468–9.

[102] Cevat, *Ikinci Meşrutiyetin İlânı* (1960), p. 160; Knight, *The Awakening of Turkey* (1909), pp. 192–5.

[103] Uzunçarşılı, pp. 124–7; Bayur, i/1, 469–72.

[104] Uzunçarşılı, pp. 132–4. No such telegram was found in the Yıldız papers by Uzunçarşılı; that such threats were made or implied is, however, attested by Kâmil Paşa (*Kâmil Paşanın . . . Said Paşaya Cevabları*, (1327), p. 51), Tahsin Paşa (*Abdülhamit ve Yıldız Hatıraları* (1931), p. 263) and Memduh Paşa (*Esvat-i Sudur* (1328), p. 78). See Bayur, i/1, 477.

CHAPTER VII

Union and Progress

In order to warn our Muslim and Christian countrymen against the system of government of the present régime, which violates such human rights as justice, equality, and freedom, which withholds all Ottomans from progress and surrenders our country to foreign domination, an Ottoman Society of Union and Progress has been formed, composed of men and women all of whom are Ottomans.

PROGRAMME OF THE OTTOMAN SOCIETY OF UNION AND PROGRESS, *c.* 1890.

And although time has only partially fulfilled so many generous hopes, or has turned them to bitterness, I refuse to believe that they were totally insincere. I shall always count on it, on the contrary, among the most enlarging experiences of my life to have been in Constintinople in 1908, and to have seen a people at one of those rare moments when it really lives.

H. G. DWIGHT, 'CONSTANTINOPLE, SETTINGS AND TRAITS', 1926.

SOME ten years before the revolution, the poet Tevfik Fikret had written a famous ode—*Sis* (Mist)—describing the decay of Istanbul under the tyranny of Abdülhamid:

> Once more a stubborn mist has swathed your horizons . . .
> A dusty, fearsome darkness, which the eye
> Takes care not to pierce, for it is afraid.
> But for you this deep, dark veil is right and fitting,
> This veiling becomes you well, O scene of evil deeds . . .
> Yes, veil yourself, O tragedy, veil yourself, O city;
> Veil yourself and sleep forever, whore of the world![1]

In 1908 the triumphant optimism of the revolution was given words by the same poet:

> Now we are far from that accursed night,
> The night of calamity has joined the nights of oblivion,
> Our eyes have opened to a radiant morning.
> Between you, O world of renewal, and that ill-omened night
> There is no kinship; you are noble and great.
> There is no mist or shade about your face, only splendour and majesty,
> A bursting brightness like the dawning sun.[2]

The long night of Hamidian despotism was over; the dawn of freedom had come. The constitution had once again been proclaimed and elections ordered. Turks and Armenians embraced

---

[1] Akyüz, *Antoloji*, p. 236.

[2] Ibid. p. 239. The poem, entitled 'Rücu' (Return) is dated 24 July 1908. The same poet's disillusionment, a few years later, is expressed in the famous poem *Han-i Yağma*.

in the streets; the age of freedom and brotherhood had come. The writings of that time reflect an almost delirious joy, which found its echoes even in the sceptical European press.

The second Turkish constitutional régime lasted longer than the first, but it too ended in failure, bitterness, and disappointment. The dangers and difficulties, at home and abroad, were too great; the defenders of the constitution were too few, too weak, too inept. Though the constitution remained in force and elections were still held, the régime degenerated into a kind of military oligarchy of the Young Turk leaders, which ended only with the defeat of the Ottoman Empire in 1918.

A Turkish historian of the Turkish Revolution, in a book published in 1940, has remarked that 'there are very few movements in the world that have given rise to such great hopes as the Ottoman Constitutional Revolution; there are likewise very few movements whose hopes have been so swiftly and finally disappointed.[3]

Even at the time, and still more later, there were many foreign observers who, out of prejudice, misunderstanding, or disappointment were ready to write off the whole Young Turk movement and revolution as mere window-dressing, as yet another attempt to mislead the West with a show of change while leaving the basic realities of Turkish life unchanged, perhaps unchangeable. Others went even farther, and tried to explain the Young Turks as something alien and irrelevant, an interlude by foreign players, unconnected with either the preceding or the following acts. In this way various writers, mostly adherents of the conspiratorial conception of history, have attributed the revolution of 1908 to the Jews, the Freemasons, the Roman Catholic Church, the positivists, the house of Orléans, the German General Staff, and the British Foreign Office.[4]

[3] Y. H. Bayur, *Türk Ink. Tar.*, i. 225.

[4] On these various stories, see Ramsaur, pp. 88 ff., 103 ff., 107 ff., 140 ff. The story of a Jewish Masonic plot, because of special circumstances, received for a while a wide circulation outside the circles in which this approach to history usually flourishes, and therefore requires a brief notice. Originating in a line of clerical and nationalist thought familiar on the Continent, it was taken up in some British circles, and a few years later was seized upon by Allied propagandists as a means of discrediting their Turkish enemies. The Young Turks, since the revolution, had been remarkably successful in their propaganda among non-Ottoman Muslims, both with pan-Turkish and pan-Islamic appeals (see below, p. 337). It seemed therefore a good idea to demonstrate that they themselves were neither Turks nor Muslims. A characteristic

The Young Turk Revolution was in fact none of these things; it was a patriotic movement of Muslim Turks, mostly soldiers, whose prime objective was to remove a fumbling and incompetent ruler and replace him by a government better able to maintain and defend the Empire against the dangers that threatened it. Ottoman non-Muslims played a small and diminishing role in the movement and the régimes that grew out of it; foreigners hardly any at all. The young officers were little interested in ideologies and social panaceas as such. The fundamental question that concerned them was survival, the survival of the Ottoman state which they and their fathers had for generations served, and both their actions and their discussions revolved around this central problem. *Bu devlet nasıl kurtarılabilir?*—How can this state be saved?

It is, perhaps, through the different solutions that were sketched and attempted for this problem, that the Young Turk Revolution, despite its disappointments and its failures, was so profoundly

statement will be found in R. W. Seton-Watson's *Rise of Nationality in the Balkans* (1917, pp. 135–6): 'The main fact about the Committee of Union and Progress is its essentially un-Turkish and un-Moslem character. From the very first hardly one among its true leaders has been a pure-blooded Turk. Enver is the son of a renegade Pole. Djavid belongs to the Jewish sect of Dunmehs. Carasso is a Sephardim Jew from Salonika. Talaat is an Islamised Bulgarian gipsy. Achmet Riza, one of the group's temporary figureheads, is half Circassian and half Magyar, and a Positivist of the school of Comte.' An admittedly fictionalized picture of the Young Turks will be found in John Buchan's famous romance *Greenmantle*, where for good measure Enver Paşa is made a Polish Jew. This curious story of Enver Paşa's Polish origin is probably due to a confusion with Enver Celâleddin Paşa, a general staff officer who was the son of the Polish renegade Count Constantine Borzęcki (on whom see below, p. 339).

The Turks of the Young Turk period were very far from thinking in such terms as 'pure-blooded Turks', and no doubt Turkish-speaking Ottoman Muslims of Balkan, Caucasian, and other origin played a considerable part in the movement. There seems, however, to be no evidence at all, in the voluminous Turkish literature on the Young Turks, that Jews ever played a part of any significance in their councils, either before or after the Revolution, or that the Masonic lodges were ever more than an occasional cover for their secret meetings. The Salonika lawyer Carasso, whose name is frequently mentioned by European opponents of the Young Turks, was a minor figure. Cavid, who did play a role of great importance, was a *dönme* (a Judaeo-Islamic syncretist sect founded in the seventeenth century) and not a real Jew; he seems in any case to have been the only member of his community to reach front rank. (For some interesting observations on the role of the *dönme* and the Turkish reaction to it see Leskovikli Mehmed Rauf, *Ittihad ve Terakki Cemiyeti ne idi?* (1327 A.H.), pp. 79 ff. In November 1911 Ebüzziya Tevfik, who had several times expressed concern about Zionism, for the first time connects the masonic lodges with Jewish purposes. He is careful to exonerate the Unionists, whose use of the lodges for their own purposes was justifiable when the need for secrecy was paramount. See 'Italyan Farmason Locaları ve Siyonizm', *Mecmua-i Ebüzziya*, no. 121 (1329 A.H.), pp. 129–34.)

important in the development of modern Turkey. In the few years of freedom that followed the ending of Abdülhamid's autocracy, there was an opportunity for discussion and experiment such as the country had never known before. In a spate of periodicals and books, the basic problems of religion and nationality, of freedom and loyalty in the modern state, were discussed and examined; in the new parliamentary and administrative apparatus that followed the Revolution, new methods of government were devised and put to the test. And even though the discussions ended in silence and the experiments in dictatorship, new hopes and new appetites had been created which could not be indefinitely denied.

The Young Turks in Power [5]

From the first, the Young Turks in power were divided between the two tendencies that had already appeared during the phase of opposition and exile. On the one hand were the liberals, in favour of some measure of decentralization and of some autonomous rights for the religious and national minorities; on the other, the nationalists, coming out more and more clearly for central authority and Turkish domination. The instrument of the latter was the Committee of Union and Progress, at first as the silent and self-effacing power behind the throne, later as an unashamed contender for supreme authority. The liberals, divided into many different groups, formed a series of ephemeral parties, the most important being the *Ahrar*, or liberal party of 1908 and the so-called Liberal Union of 1911.[6] Neither was able to accomplish very much.

[5] The years 1908–18 are well documented, in both Turkish and foreign sources. From the time of the Revolution onwards, there was a flood of memoirs, reports, journalistic, diplomatic, and political accounts, &c., often containing important material. A few major and many minor Turkish figures of the time have left memoirs, which have so far hardly been touched by Western scholarship. The only extensive historical treatment is that given by Y. H. Bayur in his large-scale history of the Turkish Revolution. Among shorter treatments, mention may be made of the useful if somewhat wilful chronology of events prepared by Danişmend, *Kronoloji*, iv. 356–455; Sax, pp. 545–654 (the best informed, on Turkish internal developments, of those who treat Turkish history in terms of the 'Eastern Question'); Emin, *Turkey in the World War* (1930); Tunaya, *Partiler*, pp. 161–398 (for an invaluable account, with documents, of political parties and ideologies); Feroz Ahmad, 'Great Britain's Relations with the Young Turks 1908–1914', in *MES*, ii (1966), 302–29. Finally, mention should be made of the detailed and documented biographies of the Grand Vezirs given by Inal in his *Sadrıazamlar*.

[6] On these parties see below, pp. 378 ff.

At first it seemed that liberal and moderate ideas were indeed about to prevail. Said Paşa and Kâmil Paşa,[7] the first two Grand Vezirs of the constitutional era, were elder statesmen who enjoyed both the support of the Ottoman liberals and the respect of most others. But whatever the intentions of the Young Turks, they were almost at once subjected to a series of blows, from inside and outside the Empire, that threw them into a mood of anger, bitterness, and frustration. It is difficult to judge how sincere the Young Turks may have been in their promises and proclamations of freedom and. equality; it is, however, undeniable that the immediate response of Europe and of the Balkan Christians to the heart-lifting events of July 1908 was what, in Turkish eyes, could only be described as aggression and betrayal. Austria seized the opportunity to proclaim the annexation of Bosnia and Herzegovina; Bulgaria declared her independence; Crete announced her union with Greece. The precedents had been set which were to be followed by Italy, in her attack on Ottoman Tripolitania in September 1911, and by the Balkan States, in their combined attack on Turkey in October 1912.

While the Christian subjects and neighbours of the Turks were demonstrating the unworkability of a multi-national Ottoman state, the Turks themselves vividly illustrated some of the dangers of weakened central control. On 13 February 1909 the Committee, dissatisfied for various reasons with Kâmil Paşa's government, secured his fall and replacement, as Grand Vezir, by Hüseyin Hilmi Paşa,[8] another survivor of the old régime, but more acceptable for the moment to the nationalist Young Turks.

Both the Sultan and the liberals were now opposed to the régime, and both have been accused, not without some colour, of complicity in the events that followed. During the preceding months, the constitutional revolution had been sadly tarnished, in the public eye, by the immediate loss of territory and prestige, and by the failure of the millennium, in general, to make its appearance. Anger was mounting against the Committee, too, because of the cavalier way in which, while remaining in the

---

[7] On Said Paşa, see above, p. 175 n. 7. Kâmil Paşa is missing in both *EI*[1] and *IA*. There are, however, biographies by his grandson H. K. Bayur, *Sadrazam Kâmil Paşa Siyasî Hayatı* (1954), and Inal, *Sadrıazamlar*, pp. 1347–472. Kâmil's own memoirs published in 1911, refer to the period of Abdülhamid.

[8] On Hüseyin Hilmi Paşa, see Inal, *Sadrıazamlar*, pp. 1654–703, and *EI*[2] *s.v.* (by F. Ahmad).

background, they manipulated government appointments. They were also accused of using intimidation and murder against political opponents, and when, on 7 April, Hasan Fehmi, the liberal editor of the *Serbesti*, was mysteriously murdered on the Galata bridge in Istanbul, the Committee was widely believed to be responsible, and became the object of much criticism and abuse.[9]

On 12 April, after a week of mounting tension, the Committee of Union and Progress published a statement in the press reiterating that it was no longer a secret association, but had become an ordinary political party.[10] The same night,.only one month after the fall of Kâmil Paşa, an armed, reactionary rising broke out. Some part in this rising was played by the so-called Muhammadan Union, an extremist religious organization founded on 5 April at a meeting in the Santa Sophia mosque.[11] Its journal, the *Volkan*, edited by a Bektaşi dervish called Vahdetî, posed as a champion of Muslim orthodoxy and of a 'revolutionary Islamic internationalism'.[12] Another exponent of these ideas was none other than Murad Bey,[13] the erstwhile radical and renegade—now a purveyor of militant pan-Islamism, and a stalwart of the Muhammadan Union. The actual rising took the form of a mutiny by the soldiers, largely Albanian, of the First Army Corps stationed in Istanbul. It began on the night of the 12–13 April, when some *chasseur* and infantry units mutinied in their barracks, crossed the Galata bridge in the early morning, and assembled in the Santa Sophia Square outside the parliament building. They encountered little resistance, and were joined by mutineers from other units as well as by some mollahs and theological students. Other bands gathered in the main centres of the city. The demands of the mutineers were simple—'The *Şeriat* is in danger, we want the *Şeriat*!' Some of them added that they did not want college-trained officers.

The government floundered helplessly in the crisis; the Sultan obliged with the time-honoured response to violent dissatisfaction —a change of Grand Vezir. Further, he promised protection for

[9] For contemporary Western accounts of these events, see Francis McCullagh, *The Fall of Abd-ul-Hamid* (1910), pp. 23 f., 71 ff.; Pears, *Forty Years*, pp. 274–5.

[10] McCullagh, p. 74.   [11] Tunaya, *Partiler*, p. 261.

[12] Ibid. pp. 226–3; cf. Lowther's comments in Gooch and Temperley, v. 319.

[13] See above, p. 193 n. 55, and Fevzíye Abdullah, pp. 85 ff.

the Holy Law and an amnesty for the soldiers who had mutinied to defend it. On 15 April a circular went out to all provincial governors, instructing them to safeguard the *Şeriat*. In the Chamber, the positivist Ahmed Rıza was deposed from the speaker's chair, where he had reigned since the Revolution, and Ismail Kemal elected in his place.[14]

The counter-blow was not long delayed. News of the reactionary rising was soon telegraphed to Salonika, and an 'Army of Deliverance',[15] commanded by General Mahmud Şevket Paşa, advanced on Istanbul. With him were Niyazi and also Enver, who had returned post-haste from the Turkish Embassy in Berlin on hearing the news. His chief of staff was Mustafa Kemal. The deliverers reached the capital on 23 April, and occupied it, after some clashes with the mutineers, on the following day.[16]

The reactionary movement was by no means limited to Istanbul. With suspicious simultaneity a wave of outbreaks spread across Anatolia. Particularly bad were the events in the Adana district, which culminated in the massacre of thousands of Armenians. Responsibility for this was variously allocated. While Europe was appalled by Turkish brutality, Muslim opinion was shocked by what seemed to them the insolence of the Armenians and the hypocrisy of Christian Europe.

The Turks were, however, well aware of the painful effects produced by these massacres in Europe, which had not yet forgotten the horrors of Hamidian repression. They were at some

---

[14] Ismail Kemal, *Memoirs*, p. 335.

[15] This is the common European designation. In Turkish it is simply called *hareket ordusu*—Action Army.

[16] The mutiny is known in Turkish annals as the '31 March Incident', following the old-style Greek calendar then in use for various purposes. Contemporary accounts will be found in McCullagh; A. Sarrou, *La Jeune-Turquie et la Révolution* (1912), pp. 77 ff.; Pears, *Forty Years*, pp. 257 ff. H. G. Dwight, *Constantinople; Settings and Traits* (1926), pp. 425 ff.; Sir W. M. Ramsay, *The Revolution in Constantinople and Turkey* (1909), pp. 11 ff. as well as in the reports of foreign diplomats, e.g. Gooch and Temperley v. 313–19). Among Turkish accounts are those of Ismail Kemal (*Memoirs*, pp. 329 ff.); Ali Fuad Türkgeldi (1867–1935—a former palace Chief Secretary and Counsellor to the Grand Vezirate, whose memoirs cover events in the palace and cabinet from the Young Turk Revolution to the end of the Empire), *Görüp İşittiklerim* (1951), pp. 25 ff.; Ali Cevat, *Ikinci Meşrutiyetin İlânı ve otuzbir Mart Hadisesi*, ed. Faik Reşit Unat (1960); Hasan Amca (pseud.), *Doğmayan Hürriyet* (1958), pp. 67 ff.; and a very detailed one by Yunus Nadi, *Ihtilâl ve Inkılâb-i Osmanî* (1325 A.H.) (an abridged paraphrase of this was published in the newspaper *Cumhuriyet*, in twenty instalments, in Mar.–Apr.1959). The fullest accounts are those of McCullagh and Yunus Nadi. See further Kuran, pp. 460 ff.; Y. H. Bayur, *Türk Ink. Tar.* 2nd ed., i/2, 182–217; Danişmend, iv. 370.

pains to remove it. On the Sunday after the entry of the deliverers into Istanbul, some fifty men who had fallen in the fighting were solemnly buried, with a public ceremony, in a common grave. In a speech delivered over the grave, Enver Bey 'emphasized . . . that Moslems and Christians were lying side by side in token that they, living or dying, were henceforward fellow-patriots who would know no distinction of race or creed'.[17]

The liberals had supported the mutiny, and shared its defeat. The Unionists had been badly shaken, and now set to work to restore their position. Their first task was to depose Sultan Abdülhamid who, having managed to survive the 1908 revolution, was now sent into ignominious exile in Salonika.[18] The new Sultan, Mehmed Reşad, was at the mercy of the Committee, who made a clean sweep of the palace and put their own nominees into key positions there.[19] From now on, the Committee of Union and Progress became the real masters of Turkey. What they meant by 'no distinction of race or creed' became clearer a few months later, with the publication of the new 'Law of Associations' on 23 August and the 'Law for the Prevention of Brigandage and Sedition' on 27 September.[20] The first of these prohibited the formation of political associations based on or bearing the name of ethnic or national groups, and was followed immediately by the closure of the Greek, Bulgarian, and other minority clubs and societies in Rumelia. The second authorized the formation of special 'pursuit battalions' from the army, and prescribed strong

[17] Pears, *Forty Years*, p. 282.

[18] The deposition of Abdülhamid has been described by many writers, most of whom have concentrated on the final phase—the unanimous vote of parliament to depose him, and the sending of a delegation of four, two deputies and two senators, to convey the decision of parliament to the Sultan. Interesting information on an earlier phase is given in the memoirs of Ali Fuad Türkgeldi, who describes the pressures used by Talât Bey to extract a *fetva* authorizing the Sultan's deposition from the reluctant religious authority. When Talât demanded that the *Şeyh-ül-Islâm* accompany him to parliament, the latter objected that he was too ill. 'What is the matter with you?' asked Talât. 'I can't hold my water,' said the *Şeyh-ül-Islâm.* 'Then bring a bed-pan with you, and come', said Talât (Türkgeldi, p. 36). See further Cevat, pp. 79 ff.; Pears, *Forty Years*, pp. 284 ff. and *Abdul Hamid*, pp. 295 ff.; McCullagh, pp. 265 ff.; Danişmend, iv. 376 ff.

[19] Halid Ziya Uşaklığil, who was appointed palace Chief Secretary at this time as a nominee of the Committee of Union and Progress, gives a lively picture of the fear and apprehension with which he was awaited by the palace staff and even by the Sultan himself. (*Saray ve Ötesi*, i (1940), 12 ff.)

[20] Y. H. Bayur, *Türk. Ink. Tar.*, i. 306.

measures for the disarming and repression of armed bands and of the famous Balkan *komitadjis*. Severe penalties were imposed for failure to report *komitadji* activities to the authorities and for the unauthorized possession of weapons. To complete the pattern, steps were taken, for the first time, to conscript non-Muslims into the armed forces.

Whatever the measure of sincerity that lay behind the promises of the Ottoman constitution, the march of events soon made those promises unrealizable. The spread of nationalism among the subject peoples of the Empire, and the final contamination, by the nationalist virus, of even the Turkish masters of it, ended for ever the 'Ottomanist' dream of the free, equal, and peaceful association of peoples in a common loyalty to the dynastic sovereign of a multi-national, multi-denominational empire.[21] In August 1910 the British acting Consul in Manastir reported a speech allegedly made by Talât Bey to a 'secret conclave' of the Salonika Committee of Union and Progress, in these terms:

You are aware that by the terms of the Constitution equality of Mussulman and Ghiaur was affirmed but you one and all know and feel that this is an unrealizable ideal. The Sheriat, our whole past history and the sentiments of hundreds of thousands of Mussulmans and even the sentiments of the Ghiaurs themselves, who stubbornly resist every attempt to ottomanize them, present an impenetrable barrier to the establishment of real equality. We have made unsuccessful attempts to convert the Ghiaur into a loyal Osmanli and all such efforts must inevitably fail, as long as the small independent States in the Balkan Peninsula remain in a position to propagate ideas of Separatism among the inhabitants of Macedonia. There can therefore be no question of equality, until we have succeeded in our task of ottomanizing the Empire—a long and laborious task, in which I venture to predict that we shall at length succeed after we have at last put an end to the agitation and propaganda of the Balkan States.

In a comment written a few days later, the British ambassador, Sir Gerald Lowther, remarked to Sir Edward Grey:

That the Committee have given up any idea of Ottomanizing all the non-Turkish elements by sympathetic and Constitutional ways has long been manifest. To them 'Ottoman' evidently means 'Turk' and

[21] Yorgi Bosho, a Christian deputy from the Balkans in the Young Turk parliament, infuriated the Turks by his ironic remark 'I am as Ottoman as the Ottoman Bank' (Talât, *Hatıralar* (1946), p. 15; Duru, *Hatıralarım*, p. 3; Ergin, *Maarif*, iv. 1132 n. 1).

their present policy of 'Ottomanization' is one of pounding the non-Turkish elements in a Turkish mortar. . . .[22]

The repressive and centralist policies of the Young Turks were by no means limited to the Christian subjects of the Empire. In both Rumelia and the Asian provinces, they followed a policy of Turkification, and attempted to impose the Turkish language on Arabs, Albanians, and other non-Turkish Muslims. Even in the capital, a new ferocity and ruthlessness appear in the treatment of the opposition elements. Whatever brutalities he condoned in the treatment of humble unbelievers in remote provinces, Sultan Abdülhamid had always hesitated to impose the death penalty on Turks and Muslims; at times he had gone to the limit of leniency in dealing even with armed sedition against himself, rather than shed the blood of members of the governing *élite*. The Young Turks—young, patriotic, soldierly, and efficient—had no such scruples. The suppression of the reactionary mutiny in April 1909 was followed by a court martial, the public hanging of a number of mutineers and reactionaries, and the repression of the liberals. The first to be hanged was Nadir Ağa, the chief Eunuch of the Imperial household.[23] Mahmud Şevket Paşa, the commander of the Army of Deliverance, proclaimed a state of siege in the city, which was extended for two years. In his newly created post as Inspector-General of the first three Army Corps, he occupied a position of great strength, and was described by some contemporaries as a dictator and even as 'a sort of Oliver Cromwell'.[24]

Şevket Paşa's main concern however, was defence, not politics, and the political effect of his intervention was to facilitate the return to power of the Committee of Union and Progress. Between 1909 and 1911 the Committee, first through alliances with senior officers and elder statesmen, then through its own men in and behind the government, became the dominant political force in the Empire. Its supremacy was by no means unchallenged, and rival factions, dissenting for personal or policy reasons from the dominant group, appeared inside as well as outside the Committee organization. Opposition was of more than one kind, as was

[22] Gooch and Temperley, ix 1. 207–9 (cited by Z. N. Zeine, *Arab-Turkish Relations and the Emergence of Arab Nationalism* (1958), p. 75). The editors are cautious about the authenticity of this report (pp. vii-viii).

[23] Pears, *Forty Years*, pp. 302–3.

[24] Ryan, *The Last of the Dragomans* (1951), p. 43; cf. Ahmad, 316–17; Sax, p. 573.

shown by the discovery, in July 1910, of a reactionary conspiracy
headed by the gendarme officer, Ali Kemal.[25]

The predominance of the Committee was, however, not
seriously shaken until 1911, when for the first time they had to face
a serious internal threat. The first signs of a parliamentary opposition had begun to appear in the first parliament after the restoration of the constitution. The crises that followed, however, and the
imposition and maintenance of martial law after the failure of the
mutiny, had impeded the development of any very effective constitutional opposition. At the beginning of 1911 the growing dissatisfaction in many quarters with the trend of events found
expression in the first major split in the Unionist ranks. A group
called the 'New Party' (*Hizb-i Cedid*) was formed, under the
leadership of Colonel Sadık and Abdülaziz Mecdi Bey, which
offered serious criticisms of the political and social policies
followed by the Committee.[26] On 23 April the group, with
rapidly growing support in the party, secured the publication of a
ten-point memorandum, based on its demands.[27] Most of these
were concerned with the better observance of democratic and
constitutional procedures, and with similar improvements. Some,
however, indicate another line of thought. Thus no. 6 seeks,
'while preserving general religious and national ethics and morals,
to make use of the advances and products of Western civilization
for the development of the Ottoman Empire': no. 7 demands 'the
maintenance and safeguarding, within the framework of the
constitution, of historic Ottoman traditions'; while no. 9 goes even
farther, and demands the amendment of certain clauses in the
constitution so as to reinforce the 'sacred rights of the Caliphate
and Sultanate'. In a speech, Mecdi Bey made the point clearer.[28]
There were, he said, three tendencies in the country—reactionary
fanaticism, recklessly fast progress, and the movement for cultural
progress with the preservation of existing customs and traditions.
It was the third that he and his friends desired. The appearance of
this rather right-wing group was paralleled by the emergence of a
left-wing splinter group, the Progress Party (*Hizb-i Terakki*) which,
however, remained more closely attached to the Committee and
its programme.[29]

[25] Sax, pp. 574–5.

[26] Tunaya, *Partiler*, p. 186; Sax, p. 588.   [27] The text is given by Tunaya.

[28] Sax, p. 589.   [29] Tunaya, *Partiler*, p. 187.

These matters were all thrashed out at a party congress held in August–September 1911. This, incidentally, was the last party congress held secretly in Salonika, which was shortly afterwards lost to the Ottoman Empire. The remaining congresses of the Committee of Union and Progress, those of 1912, 1913, 1916, 1917, and the final congress of 1918, assembled in Istanbul.[30] The 1911 congress—the first, according to a Turkish author, 'with heat and argument'—met in an atmosphere of great tension, generated by the threatening international situation.[31] After thundering against the Italian aggression at Tripoli, which occurred while the congress was in session, the delegates managed to reach a compromise in the form of a patriotic declaration of national unity.

These resolutions did little more than paper over the cracks. Some of the seceders remained outside the party, and other resignations followed, weakening the authority and diminishing the prestige of the once all-powerful Committee. On 21 November 1911 a new party was formed, the so-called Liberal Union,[32] by the merging of almost all the groups, parties, and personalities opposed to the Committee of Union and Progress.

Most of the founders of the Liberal Union were already members of parliament, and they were thus able immediately to form a parliamentary opposition. Their first real contest with the Unionists came when the party was only twenty days old. The appointment of the Foreign Minister Rifat Paşa as ambassador to London left a vacant seat in Istanbul. In the resulting by-election, there were two candidates; the Minister of the Interior, Memduh Bey, for the Unionists, and the liberal journalist Tahir Hayreddin[33] for the Liberal Union. The liberal candidate was elected by a majority of a single vote of the electoral college.

This by-election, held on 11 December 1911, was the first genuine electoral contest between two candidates, each representing a different party and programme. The victory of the opposition candidate created a new and unprecedented situation, and to many at the time seemed almost as important a victory

---

[30] Ibid. p. 189.   [31] Ibid. p. 191.

[32] In Turkish *Hürriyet ve Itilaf* (Freedom and Association). The official name in French was *Entente libérale*.

[33] He was the son of the liberal Grand Vezir Tunuslu Hayreddin Paşa (d. 1889) on whom see Inal, *Sadrıazamlar*, pp. 894–960; Pakalın, *Son Sadrâzamlar*, iv. 313–77; and *EI*[1] *s.v.* 'Khair al-Din'.

as the 1908 revolution itself. After the constitutional millennium, the democratic redemption was coming, and the Liberal
Union leader, Damad Ferid Paşa, prepared with vigour for the
role.[34]

Public opinion in the capital had asserted itself in a striking
form against the Unionist régime. Another voice was now raised—
that of the venerable Kâmil Paşa, one of the two most eminent
elder statesmen of the country, and a keen supporter of the
liberals against the Unionists. On 20 December 1911 Kâmil Paşa,
then wintering in Egypt, sent a letter to the Sultan, in which he
blamed the Unionists for the misfortunes of the Empire, and
demanded the raising of the state of siege and the dissolution of
the Committee of Union and Progress. At the same time he
proposed an alliance with England as the best means of preventing further disasters.[35]

Faced with this dangerous combination, against them, of
freedom and authority, the Committee acted swiftly against both.
In January 1912 the Unionists procured the dissolution of
parliament. In February they published Kâmil Paşa's memorandum in the press, and used it to discredit him; the tone was set
by Hüseyin Cahid [Yalçın], who discussed it in a leader entitled
'A Voice from the Grave'.[36] In April there was a general election
so well prepared and conducted that, out of a total of 275, only
six opposition members managed to slip through into the chamber.
The first opposition victory in a by-election had been followed by
the first general election held under the pressure of the dominant
party. A second precedent had been established. This election is
known in Turkish history as 'the big-stick election'.[37]

The Unionists now finally transferred their headquarters from
Salonika to Istanbul, where, with an obedient parliament and a
submissive Sultan, they seemed to be in full and undisputed
control. But difficulties were growing; the war against Italy was
going badly, and there were troubles in many of the provinces,
notably in Salonika. The Committee had crushed the liberal
parliamentary opposition by dissolving the old chamber and

[34] On Damad Ferid Paşa, see Inal, *Sadrıazamlar*, pp. 2029–94 and *EI*², s.v. (by
D. A. Rustow).
[35] H. K. Bayur, *Kâmil Paşa*, pp. 307–12; Sax, pp. 589–90.
[36] H. K. Bayur, *Kâmil Paşa*, p. 308 and n.1.
[37] Tunaya, *Partiler*, p. 322. cf. Kuran, pp. 496–7.

packing the new one through a shamelessly dishonest election. By thus illegally removing the legal opposition, the Committee inevitably called into being a new opposition, not democratic or parliamentary, but military and conspiratorial—a ghost from its own past. The Committee of Union and Progress had gone to Istanbul and become the oppressors—so once again young officers in Rumelia took to the hills, where they could now count on a welcome from the Albanian rebels.

In May–June 1912 a group of 'Saviour Officers' (*Halâskâr Zabitân*) was formed in Istanbul, apparently in relation with the rebel officers in Rumelia.[38] Their objective was to remove an illegal government and parliament, to break the power of the Committee of Union and Progress, to hold new and free elections, and to return to constitutional legality. Like all the opposition parties of the Young Turk period, this group of military conspirators demanded the withdrawal of the army from politics. The army would of course have to mend what the army had marred; after that it could return to its proper task of defending the Empire, leaving its government to the politicians and officials. Faithful to this principle, the group accepted no civilian recruits, and allowed its numbers to accept no governmental appointments.[39]

By the end of June the situation in Albania was causing serious alarm, and criticism of the Unionist government headed by Said Paşa grew rapidly. On 9 July the Minister of War Mahmud Şevket Paşa resigned. This sacrifice failed to appease the critics, and on 15 July the government felt it necessary to seek a vote of confidence from the Chamber. After speeches by the Grand Vezir and the Foreign Minister making light of the troubles in Albania, they obtained their vote with only four dissentients.[40]

The 'Saviour Officers' now went into action. A manifesto in the press, a declaration sent through the Army Council to the Sultan and, above all, certain ominous military movements and preparations, brought swift results. On 17 July, barely twenty-four hours after receiving their overwhelming vote of confidence from the Chamber, Said Paşa and his cabinet resigned. When the Sultan asked him a few days later 'Why did you resign? They still have confidence in you', Said Paşa replied: 'They have confidence in

[38] Tunaya, *Partiler*, pp. 345 ff.; Sax, p. 590; Y. H. Bayur, *Türk Ink. Tar.*, ii/1, 253–8.
[39] Ibid.. p. 347.   [40] Ibid. pp. 348–9.

me, but I have no confidence in them.'[41] On the day of the resignation the Saviours held a meeting at Bostancı, to which came a delegation of three pashas from the resigning government, to discover the Saviours' terms. These were simple: Nazım Paşa to be Minister of War, Kâmil Paşa to be a member of the government. The choice of Grand Vezir was left to the Sultan.

After unsuccessful approaches to Tevfik Pasa, the new cabinet was constituted on 21 July 1912. The Grand Vezir was the scholar and soldier Gazi Ahmed Muhtar Paşa (1839–1918);[42] Nazım Paşa and Kâmil Paşa became Minister of War and President of the Council of State respectively. At the end of October Kâmil Paşa again took over the Grand Vezirate.

With the formation of Gazi Ahmed Muhtar Paşa's government, known among the Turks as 'the great cabinet', [43] the first and basic demand of the opposition was met—the ousting from power of the C.U.P. Other steps soon followed. The state of siege was lifted on 23 July (and restored on 6 August), the C.U.P.-dominated parliament was dissolved on 5 August, and an oath exacted from all serving officers not to interfere in politics, as well as a written undertaking to the same effect: '. . . I swear by God and guarantee by my honour that I will not enter any political society, secret or public, nor interfere in any way whatsoever in the internal or external affairs of the state'. [44]

The government was already fully occupied with the Italian war when, on 2 October 1912, a new blow fell: the ultimatum of the Balkan allies. Peace was hastily signed with Italy on 17 October; the Balkan war began next day. The 'Saviour Officers' were now fully occupied with the waging of war, and the C.U.P., ousted but by no means destroyed, prepared for its return to power. Kâmil's cabinet, struggling with a desperate situation, seemed to many to be weak and incompetent, and, as the Balkan armies approached the walls of Istanbul, the Committee completed its plans.

---

[41] Türkgeldi, p. 35 and Inal, *Sadrıazamlar*, p. 1089.

[42] See Inal, *Sadrıazamlar*, pp. 1803–68.

[43] Also as the 'Father-and-son cabinet (*Baba-oğul Kabinesi*)', because of the presence of the Grand Vezir's son, Mahmud Muhtar Paşa, as Minister of Marine (Y. H. Bayur, *Turk. Ink. Tar.* ii/4, 219 ff. ; Danişmend, iv. 388; Sax, p. 591).

[44] Tunaya, *Partiler*, p. 350 n. 30.

On 23 January 1913, when the cabinet was believed—wrongly, as it appears—to be considering a proposal to cede Edirne to the Bulgarians, the Unionists launched their surprise assault on the Sublime Porte. Led by Enver Bey, a small party of officers forced their way into the cabinet room, shooting the Minister of War Nazım Paşa dead as they did so. At the point of their guns, the aged Kâmil Paşa wrote out his resignation, which Enver triumphantly took to the palace and presented to the Sultan.[45]

The Committee had made their preparations in the army, the police, the government offices. They were now firmly in power again, and secured the appointment of Mahmud Şevket Paşa as Grand Vezir. His murder, on 11 June 1913, provided them with the pretext for removing the last shreds of freedom and democracy. From then until 1918 Turkey was governed by a virtual military dictatorship, dominated by three men—Enver, Talât, and Cemal Paşas. Mahmud Şevket's immediate successor as Grand Vezir was Mehmed Said Halim Paşa (1863–1921), a member of the Egyptian Khedivial house and the author of a number of works pleading for an Islamic revival. He was, however, a captive of the Unionist leaders; finally in February 1917 he retired to the Senate, leaving Talât as Grand Vezir and the triumvirs openly in control.[46]

Enver Paşa[47] was born in İstanbul in 1881, the son of a father variously described, by his friends or enemies, as a railway official or a porter. A graduate of the War College in Istanbul, he soon joined the Young Turks, and first achieved fame as a 'hero of freedom' by his role in the revolution of 1908. After serving as military attaché in Berlin and then as a highly popular field officer, he returned to Istanbul and led the raid on the Sublime Porte. In 1913 he became Minister of War, general, and pasha;

---

[45] On the coup d'état see Sax, p. 591; Kuran, pp. 519 ff.; Danişmend, iv. 398 (where different versions of events are discussed). Y. H. Bayur, *Türk. Ink. Tar.*, ii/4, pp. 271 ff.; Inal, pp. 1411 ff. and 1874 ff.; H. K. Bayur, *Kâmil Paşa*, pp. 386 ff. Contemporary accounts in Türkgeldi, pp. 77 ff.; Cemalüddin Efendi (*Şeyh-ül-Islâm*, 1891–1908, 1908–9, 1912–13; he was deposed after the coup d'état and left for Egypt where he wrote his memoirs), *Hâtırât-i Siyasiye* (1336/1917), pp. 52 ff.; Pears, *Forty Years*, p. 331; Cemal Paşa, *Memoirs*, pp. 1 ff.

[46] On Mehmed Said Halim Paşa see Inal, *Sadrıazamlar*, s.v. Some of Said Halim's works, written in French, were translated into Turkish by the poet Mehmed Akif. A group of his writings was reprinted under the title *Buhranlarımız* (1330 A.H.).

[47] Enver Paşa, alone among the Young Turk triumvirs, has left no published memoirs. He is missing from both *EI¹* and *IA*, but is the subject of an important article by D. A. Rustow in *EI²*, s.v. Enwer Pasha.

In 1914, by marrying an Ottoman princess, he even acquired the title of Damad.

Cemal Paşa,[48] born in Istanbul in 1872, to a military family, was a man of a very different stamp from the flamboyant, reckless, and self-indulgent Enver. He too was a product of the War College and an early recruit to the Young Turks. After the coup d'état of January 1913 he became military governor of Istanbul, and showed great skill in organizing the police forces and directing their work for the preservation of the régime. He later became Minister of Marine and army commander in Syria. He was known as a man of high professional competence in military matters, of personal authority and responsibility, and of a cold, fanatical ruthlessness when he judged it necessary for the cause he served.

The third, and by far the ablest of the triumvirate was Talât Paşa,[49] born in a poor home in Edirne in 1874. After attending the local schools, he joined the staff of the telegraph office in Edirne, and in due course was promoted chief secretary of the directorate of posts and telegraphs in Salonika, where his position enabled him to render great service to the Young Turk cause. After the Revolution he rose rapidly in the councils of the C.U.P., and held various appointments, including that of Minister of the Interior for a while. In 1917 he became Grand Vezir. He was a man of swift and penetrating intelligence, forceful when necessary, but never fanatical or vengeful—'The Danton of the Turkish Revolution', according to a contemporary European observer.[50]

Under these three men the mechanism of state power was wound tighter and tighter. The opposition parties were broken up, their leaders exiled or made innocuous, and a ruthless repression applied which for a time approached the proportions of a reign of terror.

---

[48] Cemal Paşa's memoirs were published in Turkish (*Hâtırât, 1913–22*, 1922), German, French, and English (Ahmed Djemal Pasha, *Memories of a Turkish Statesman 1913–1919*, 1912. (cf. the Turkish volume, Cemal Paşa, *Hatıralar ve Vesikalar*, 1933). A modernized and annotated version was edited by Behcet Cemal (*Hatıralar*, 1959). See 'Djemāl Pasha', by D. A. Rustow, in *EI²*.

[49] The memoirs of Talât Paşa were edited by Huseyin Cahit Yalçın, *Talât Paşa'nın Hatıraları* (1946). Having attained to the Grand Vezirate, he qualified for a biography by Inal, *Sadrıazamlar*, pp. 1933–72.

[50] J. Østrup, *Det Nye Tyrki* (1931), pp. 77–78.

Their rule ended only with the defeat of Turkey in 1918, when the Committee of Union and Progress disbanded itself, its leaders fled abroad, and the liberal spokesmen emerged from exile, concealment, or insignificance to quarrel for the privilege of presiding over the dissolution of the Ottoman Empire.

The Achievements of the Young Turks

From 1908 until the final defeat of the Ottoman Empire in 1918, the Unionists were, except for brief intervals, the dominant political group. Even though they preferred, for much of the time, to leave the nominal leadership of the government to ageing survivors of the past like Said Paşa, Hüseyin Hilmi Paşa, or Ibrahim Hakkı Paşa, or, later, to an intermediate figure like Said Halim Paşa, it was the Young and not the old Turks who were the real masters.[51]

They have been harshly judged by history, and not without some cause. They have been blamed for many things—the brutalizaton of public life by violence, repression and terror; the intrusion of the army into politics, leading to the twin evils of a militarized government and a political command; the pursuit of policies, at home and abroad, that led directly to the destruction of the Empire.

The record of the ten years from 1908 to 1918 is indeed, at first sight, a black one. The high hopes of the Revolution were swiftly disappointed, and the orderly progress of constitutional government was ended in the wretched cycle of plot and counterplot, repression and sedition, tyranny, humiliation, and defeat.

Yet there is another theme in the story, one that is often overlooked amid the alarums and excursions of the Young Turk drama. The ultimate and desperate concern of all the Young Turk factions and committees was the survival of the Empire, by now in manifest danger; like their predecessors, both reformers and revolutionaries, they believed that certain radical improvements in Ottoman state and society were needed to save them from inner decay and foreign attack. Behind all the hectic struggles of those years, the Committee and the government found time to give their attention to some of these problems, and to try and solve them by legislative and by administrative action. Though their work was often ill conceived, incomplete, and frustrated by events, they did

[51] Y. H. Bayur, in *Bell.*, no. 90 (1959), 272.

nevertheless help to prepare the way, in many important respects, for the new Turkey that was to emerge after their disappearance.

One matter needing urgent attention was provincial and local administration. New difficulties had been added to old in the provinces and had, if anything, been aggravated rather than improved by reformist legislation. A new system of provincial and municipal government was now worked out and put into effect which, with only minor changes, provided the legal and administrative framework of the local and provincial government of the Turkish republic.

In Istanbul too the Young Turks made important and lasting changes. A new municipal organization provided for the more effective government of the capital of the Empire; an energetic programme of public works immensely improved the amenities of the city. The Young Turks may have failed to give Turkey constitutional government. They did, however, give Istanbul drains. Other improvements included the reorganization of the police, fire brigades, public transport services, and utilities. The famous packs of dogs that for centuries had patrolled the streets of the city were, by a decision of the municipal council, collected and shipped to a waterless island, to perish. They were replaced by relays of dustmen and scavengers.[52]

It was not only in Istanbul that the police were reorganized. The new-style gendarmerie, initiated in Macedonia under Abdülhamid, was now extended to many parts of the Empire, and training schools set up in Izmir and Beirut as well as Salonika. By a law of February 1912, the control of the gendarmerie was transferred from the Ministry of War to the Ministry of the Interior, and provincial gendarme posts placed at the disposal of the governors. A number of foreign, chiefly British officers and inspectors served in the Ottoman gendarmerie.[53]

The Young Turks, like most governments of their time, gave less attention to economic than to political and administrative problems. They did, however, attempt to tackle, with mixed results, one major economic problem—that of land[54] and also took the first steps in the policy of economic nationalism that was to

---

[52] Nuri, *Mec. Um. Bel.*, i. 960 ff.   [53] Pears, *Forty Years*, pp. 318–19; Sax, p. 606.
[54] On the land laws see E. Nord, *Die Reform des türkischen Liegenschaftsrechts* (1914); cf. below, pp. 448 ff.

develop under the Republic; in neither respect did they achieve any great success.

In social life, the movement of Westernization begun in the previous century gathered momentum. The old method of reckoning time gave way to the European twenty-four hour day. The Westernization of costume and manners went far enough to bring an anxious rejoinder from the religious authorities; in April 1911 the *Şeyh-ül-Islâm* issued a warning to Muslim women not to wear European dress, and in September of the same year the cabinet actually voted an order authorizing the arrest and fining of Muslims who publicly violated the fast of Ramazan.[55]

These measures, however, did little to halt the increasing modernization of society. An important factor was education, in which the Young Turks achieved their greatest successes. Building on the work of their predecessors, they created a new system of secular primary and secondary schools, teachers' training colleges and specialized institutes, with the reorganized University of Istanbul at the apex. A major change was the extension of educational opportunities for girls. Women of the highest classes of society had always had access to a good, private education; the *Tanzimat* reformers had added a few girls' schools, women's training colleges, and arts schools. The Young Turk régimes opened the doors first of the middle and secondary schools, then of the university, to girl students, thus preparing the way for their entry into the professions and into public life. The drain of men to the army during the war years created an urgent need for their services, and Turkish women, whose only possible professions had been nurse, midwife, or teacher, now appeared as doctors, civil servants, lawyers, and business women.

To women thus trained and employed, the seclusion of earlier times and the garments that symbolized it were an irritating and humiliating anachronism. Educated women were still few in numbers, but they enjoyed the sympathy and support of most men among the Young Turks; as a result the cause of female education and emancipation made noteworthy progress. In 1917 a new Family Law was approved, which marked an important step forward in the achievement of women's rights. The religious courts, which dealt with matters of family and personal status, were put under the jurisdiction of the Ministry of Justice—that is,

[55] Sax, p. 589

of a modern, secular authority, above the religious hierarchy. Though, in an Islamic state, it was not possible to remove the two chief disabilities of women, polygamy and repudiation, the law did contain a number of revisions in favour of women, giving them the right to insert and enforce certain stipulations in marriage contracts, including the right of divorce and monogamy. This law, which could probably never have secured a parliamentary majority, was enacted by emergency order, and a small number of educated women actually took advantage of it.[56]

Intellectual and Cultural Movements [57]

It is perhaps in its intellectual and cultural life that the Young Turk period is most interesting and most significant. The proclamation of the constitution released a vast surge of ideas and self-expression that the seal of the Sultan's censorship had for so long contained. On 25 July 1908 the *Ikdam* published 60,000, the *Sabah* 40,000 copies; by the afternoon copies were changing

[56] On the Ottoman Family Law see Jäschke, 'Der Islam in der neuen Türkei', *WI*, n.s., i (1951), 13; Halide Edib, *Turkey Faces West* (1930), pp. 130–1. On social and cultural developments, valuable insights may be obtained from the writings of European Orientalists who visited or studied Turkey during the Young Turk period, notably M. Hartmann, *Der islamische Orient*, iii; *Unpolitische Briefe aus der Türkei* (1910); C. Snouck-Hurgronje, *Verspreide Geschriften*, iii (1923) (espec. no. 37); Becker, *Islamstudien*, ii (espec. nos. 37 and 38).

[57] By far the most comprehensive and illuminating studies of the ideological movements and conflicts in the Young Turk period are those of Tarık Tunaya on the Westernizing and pan-Islamic tendencies in the political thought of the second constitutional period: *Türkiyenin Siyasî hayatında Batılılaşma hareketleri* (1960), *Islamcılık Cereyanı* (1962), and, from the point of view of public law '. . . Garpçılık Cereyanı', *Ist. Univ. Hukuk Fak. Mec.*, xiv (1948), 585–630, and '. . . Islamcılık Cereyanı', ibid. xix (1954), 1–41, and those of Y. H. Bayur, *Türk. Ink. Tar* ii/4, pp. 1 ff. Briefer and broader surveys by Tunaya will be found in his 'Türkiyenin Siyasi Gelişme Seyri içinde Ikinci "Jön Türk" Hareketinin Fikrî Esasları', in the volume presented by the Istanbul Law Faculty to Professor Tahir Taner (*Prof. Tahir Taner'e Armağan*, 1956), and in his *Partiler*, pp. 167 ff. Among other Turkish works see also Peyami Safa, *Türk Inkılabına Bakışlar* (c. 1938), and among earlier works, Ziya Gökalp, *Türkleşmek, Islamlaşmak, Muasırlaşmak* (1918) and reprints. For brief accounts in Western languages see Emin, *Press*, pp. 86 ff.; Rossi, 'Dall'Impero ottomano . . .', *OM*, xxiii (1943), 371 ff.; K. H. Karpat, *Turkey's Politics* (1959), 19 ff.; and three anonymous articles in the *RMM*, xxii (1913): 'Doctrines et programmes des partis politiques ottomans', pp. 151–64; 'Les Rapports du mouvement politique et du mouvement social dans l'Empire ottoman', pp. 165–78; and 'Le Panislamisme et le Panturquisme', pp. 179–220. According to Mlle A. M. Goichon (Jamâl ad-Din al-Afghânî, *Réfutation des matérialistes* (1942), p. 9), the last-named were written by S. H. Taghizade. More recent works by Professors Tunaya, Berkes, Mardin, and Ülken are listed in the bibliography.

hands at forty times the marked price.[58] A whole series of new literary, political, and other periodicals began to appear, and some of the major Young Turk organs were transferred from their places of exile to Istanbul. Voices that had long been silenced or muted spoke loud and clear; ideas long pent up now swirled into print. Although, after the mutiny of April 1909, repression and press control returned again to Turkey, even the coercion and bullying of the Unionists and the harshening conditions of the war years could never really quench the flow of new thought, expression, and argument.

In the literature of this period, foreign teachings once again provide the theoretical foundations of political and social criticism. The main source of these foreign intellectual influences is still France, but in place of the Enlightenment of the eighteenth century, the social science of the nineteenth century has come to dominate the thinking of Turkish reformers and revolutionaries. The first influence to emerge was that of Auguste Comte, whose positivist sociology inspired Ahmed Rıza to the first expositions of Union and Progress, and profoundly influenced the subsequent development of secularist radicalism in Turkey. Prince Sabaheddin, seeking a philosophy for his own rival school, found it in the teachings of Le Play and more especially of Demolins, whose ideas formed the basis of Sabaheddin's doctrines of individual initiative and decentralization. Finally, it was in sociology, especially that of Émile Durkheim, that Ziya Gökalp found the conceptual framework within which he constructed the first elaborate theoretical formulation of Turkish nationalism.

A common feature of all these schools is their tendency to treat sociology as a kind of philosophy, even of religion, and as a source of quasi-revealed authority on moral, social, political, and even religious problems.

The Young Turks seem to have been less concerned with political theory than their nineteenth-century predecessors. In the period of opposition, their view of the power they were opposing was often naïvely personal. Abdülhamid was a tyrant; he must repent or retire. Various definitions were given of his tyranny. Sometimes it lay in his violation of the Holy Law and of the traditional standards of conduct of the good Muslim sovereign. More often—and perhaps more sincerely—the Young Turks

[58] Emin, *Press*, p. 87.

condemned him for suspending the constitution and arresting the development of parliamentary government. In either case, it was his personal autocracy that was corrupting the political life of the country, excluding the 'light of civilization', and keeping the people backward, ignorant, and impoverished.

Our sovereign and our government [wrote Abdullah Cevdet in Geneva in 1897] do not want the light to enter our country: they want all the people to remain in ignorance, on the dunghill of misery and wretchedness; no torch of awakening may blaze in the hearts of our compatriots. What the government want is for the people to remain like beasts, submissive as sheep, fawning and servile as dogs. Let them hear no word of any honest lofty new idea. Instead, let them languish under the whips of ignorant gendarmes, under the aggressions of shameless, boorish, oppressive officials. . . . [59]

Against such a régime, revolt was both legitimate and necessary. The new régime to be established was still that of the earlier liberals—constitutional monarchy and parliamentary government. This would win for Turkey the respect of the West—always an important point with the Young Turks—and open the way to the political, social, and economic reforms that the country needed.

After the revolution of 1908 political discussion, naturally enough, became more concerned with current problems than with general principles. Political comment and criticism, though often wrapped up in imperfectly understood political terms and phrases borrowed from the European press, were basically concerned with one question—for or against the Committee of Union and Progress; and as the Committee became increasingly intolerant of criticism, the discussion of current issues became superficial and evasive.[60]

The Committee had no general objection to criticism; only to criticism of itself, and of its current actions. The discussion of the larger social, philosophic, and even—for the first time—religious issues was unimpeded, and the great debate about Turkey's future, begun by the Young Turks in exile, was now engaged with renewed vigour and extended scope.

Fundamentally the questions were the same as had been occupying Turkish statesman and memorialists since the sixteenth

[59] *Iki Emel* (1906), p. 4; Tunaya, in *Prof. Taner'e Armağan*, p. 3.
[60] Emin, *Press*, p. 95.

century—what is wrong with the Empire, why is it falling behind in the race with its infidel rivals, what must be done to save it? Many answers were offered and argued, some of them on lines already well known in the nineteenth century or earlier, some of them strange and new.

The problem of how to save the Empire from collapse or overthrow was old and familiar, even when the formulations and the solutions propounded bore a sociological and unfamiliar aspect. In discussing it, however, the writers and thinkers of this time found themselves face to face with a new and radical question, barely considered in earlier times; what was the nature of this entity that was to be saved? Official spokesmen and others continued to speak piously of 'the union of elements'[61]—the common Ottoman citizenship that was to unite all the Sultan's subjects, irrespective of race, creed, or language, in a single nationality and loyalty. Already during the Hamidian period, there were some among the Young Turks with sufficient perception—and sufficient frankness—to reject Ottomanism as an impossible fantasy. Their judgement was amply confirmed by the conduct both of the Turks and of their subjects during the years following the revolution. What existed was not a nation but a domination, the hegemony of the conquerors of an empire over the peoples they had conquered. The task of loyal members of the dominant group was to defend that group—its supremacy, or, failing that, its very existence—against the dangers that threatened it.

One of the most pressing of these dangers was uncertainty as to the very nature of that group. Were they Muslims, or were they Turks? Most of them, clearly, were both, but the question of whether the Muslim community or the Turkish nation was to be the basis of identity and focus of loyalty was one of the most hotly debated of the time. Much would depend on the answer—the social and cultural policies of the state, its international friendships and alignments, even, it might be, its territorial limits.

Linked with this question of corporate political identity were the deeper and vaster problems of civilization. To what civilization did the Turks belong—and in what civilization did their future lie? For the past millennium the Turkish peoples had formed a part—for long the dominant part—of the community of Islam, and their whole culture—religion and politics, law and

[61] In Turkish *ittihad-i anasir*.

art, society and government—was shaped in Islamic moulds and stamped with the imprint of the common Islamic past. For the past century they had been imitating the West, in an attempt—mainly unsuccessful—to save the Empire from collapse and win the respect of Europe by conforming to European patterns of culture and organization. With all its failures and disappointments, however, the movement of Westernization was continuing, and the Turkish people had come to a crisis of civilization—a turning-point in their history comparable, in its way, with that remote and half-forgotten time when their Central Asian ancestors had hesitated between China and Islam, and, then, too, had chosen the Western alternative.

Among the many solutions propounded in the writings of the Young Turk period to this crisis of culture, two general trends may be discerned—the Islamists and the Westernizers, with a wide range of compromise and confusion between them. Among the Islamists there were the four-square fundamentalists, for whom the faith and the Holy Law were the beginning and end of all wisdom, and derogation from them the cause of all Turkey's troubles. This view, commoner among the silent masses and the lower religious functionaries than among the articulate intellectuals, also found expression in the writings of such figures as the *Şeyh-ül-Islâm* Musa Kâzım Efendi (1858–1919).[62]

More important were the moderate Islamists, most of them men with some Western education, who saw the need for some measures of reform in Islam, and sought desperately for ways of achieving it, without endangering the religious and cultural heritage of Islam or the unity of the Islamic world. In their insistence on pan-Islamic unity, their anxious insistence that Islam is not an obstacle to modern civilization, that it is indeed the source and origin of European culture, they are strongly reminiscent of the apologetic and romantic writers of nineteenth-century Muslim India, by whom, indeed, they were influenced to no small extent. For them, the decline of the Ottoman Empire was due to the abandonment of Islam—and by this they did not mean, as did the orthodox ulema, the historic Islam of the law and the traditions, but an ancient and authentic Islam, which they themselves had rediscovered and reinterpreted. There was no need to

[62] On Musa Kâzım's writings, see Y. H. Bayur, *Türk Ink. Tar.*, ii/4, pp. 377 ff.; Tunaya, 'Islamcılık Cereyanı', *passim*.

go to the West for guidance in political and social matters, for all
the elements of political and social progress could be found in the
Islamic past, from which the West itself had borrowed. Science
and technology could be taken from the West—Islam offered no
obstacle to their adoption or their progress—but in government,
in law, in social usage, in education, in basic loyalty, Islam must
remain dominant.[63]

The moderate wing of the Westernizers differed from the
moderate Islamist more in mood and emphasis than in real
content. Civilization, says one of their outstanding spokesmen,
Celâl Nuri [Ileri][64] (1877–1939) is of two kinds, technical and
real. The West had reached the highest peak of technical civilization, but had not achieved and never would achieve any 'real'
civilization. Technical civilization could be transferred and
borrowed from one country to another; real civilization could
not, and the Ottoman reformers had made a great mistake in
confusing the two. Instead of limiting their borrowings to technical matters, they had tried to copy the West in a field in which
Islam was, in fact, superior.[65]

The same charge of superficiality, of blind and senseless copying
of everything European, is brought against the *Tanzimat* reformers
by other writers of this period.

The fallacy that everything seen in Europe can be imitated here
[says Ismail Hami, apparently following Moltke] has become a political
tradition among us. For example—by simultaneously introducing
Russian uniforms, Belgian rifles, Turkish headgear, Hungarian saddles,
English swords, and French drill—we have created an army that is a
grotesque parody of Europe.[66]

For the extreme Westernizers, the remedy was not less, but more
Westernization. The trouble with the earlier reforms, they said,
was that they had not gone far enough. Westernization was not a
matter of choice but of survival. 'Either we Westernize, or we are

---

[63] The writings of Mehmed Said Halim Paşa (see above, p. 221) may serve as
examples of this trend.

[64] On this important author there is still no monographic treatment. Some account
of his ideas will be found in the works cited above (p. 225 n. 57).

[65] Tunaya, 'Garpçılık', pp. 594–5.

[66] In the periodical *İçtihad*, no. 69 (1329 A.H.), p. 1508; cited in Tunaya, 'Garpçılık',
p. 591. Cf. Moltke, *Briefe*, 418.

destroyed,' wrote Ahmed Muhtar, in 1912.[67] The most consistent exponent of this view was Abdullah Cevdet, whose opinions were summed up in the phrase 'There is no second civilization; civilization means European civilization, and it must be imported with both its roses and its thorns'.[68] To borrow was pointless, to copy superficial and dangerous. The only answer was the complete acceptance of European civilization—the incorporation of Turkey as part of civilized Europe.

There were not many, at that time, who were prepared to go as far as that. When they did, and drew the logical inferences as to the place of Islam in such a Westernized Turkey, they aroused the bitter hostility of both pietists and patriots, and sometimes even the rigour of the law.

In 1912 the periodical *İçtihad*, edited by Abdullah Cevdet, published two articles entitled 'A Very Wakeful Sleep', describing a vision, seen in a dream, of the future of Westernization in Turkey. It was a wild and fantastic vision indeed. The Sultan would have one wife and no concubines; the princes would be removed from the care of eunuch and harem servants, and given a thorough education, including service in the army; the fez would be abolished, and a new headgear adopted; existing cloth factories would be expanded, and new ones opened, and the Sultan, princes, senators, deputies, officers, officials, and soldiers made to wear their products; women would dress as they pleased, though not extravagantly, and would be free from dictation or interference in this matter by ulema, policemen, or street riff-raff; they would be at liberty to choose their husbands, and the practice of match-making would be abolished; convents and *tekkes* would be closed, and their revenues added to the education budget; all *medreses* would be closed, and new modern literary and technical institutes established; the turban, cloak, &c., would be limited to certificated professional men of religion, and forbidden to others; vows and offerings to the saints would be prohibited, and the money saved devoted to national defence; exorcists, witch-doctors, and the like would be suppressed, and medical treatment for malaria made compulsory; popular misconceptions of Islam would be corrected; practical adult education schools would be opened; a consolidated and purified Ottoman Turkish dictionary

[67] *Ikdam*, no. 5716 (1328 A.H.), pp. 3–4; cited in ibid. p. 590 n. 18.
[68] *İçtihad* no. 89 (1329 A.H.), pp. 1890–1984; cited in ibid. p. 590.

and grammar would be established by a committee of philo-
logists and men of letters; the Ottomans, without awaiting
anything from their government or from foreigners would, by their
own efforts and initiative, build roads, bridges, ports, railways,
canals, steamships, and factories; starting with the land and
Evkâf laws, the whole legal system would be reformed.[69]

To his contemporaries, the vision of the wakeful sleeper must
have seemed a more than usually exuberant piece of fantasy; yet
there is no document of the time that more accurately foreshadows
the subsequent course of events.

The disputes between conservatives and radicals, between
moderates and extremists, are well summed up in an exchange of
views on the subject of education. Should there be more schools,
or more *medreses*; should the latter be maintained, reformed, or
suppressed? An Islamist journal, after arguing that instead of
opening new schools and colleges it would have been better to
reform the *medreses* and modernize their curricula, goes on to
remark that 'the two greatest universities of the world today,
Oxford and the Sorbonne, were in their time nothing but a couple
of *medreses*. It was by developing according to the needs of the
time that they achieved their present state of perfection.'

In reply to this argument the radical *İçtihad* reminded its
readers that this transformation of the Western universities had
taken place by a slow and gradual evolution, extending over four
or five centuries, and asked in conclusion: 'Have we the time to
wait so long?'[70]

It was while they were still discussing this question that, in
October 1914, the Turks stumbled into a major European war, as
allies of one group of European great powers against another.
By 1918 it was clear that their time had run out.

Turkey had already been at war from 1911 to 1913, but her
involvement in the clash of great powers was a new and shattering
experience. As elsewhere, the pressures of modern war forced rapid
changes; in Turkey, an oriental, Islamic country suddenly caught
in the close intimacy of alliance and conflict with major European
powers, these changes were especially violent and disturbing.
General mobilization snatched millions of Turks from their homes,
took them to new places, tasks, and associations, and made them

---

[69] Cited by Safa, pp. 51–55; cf. Tunaya, 'Garpçılık', pp. 493, 601–3, 606, 622.
[70] Safa, p. 33.

part of a great, modern, military organization. To fill the gaps they left, tens of thousands of Turkish women emerged from seclusion, and were accorded the equivocal privileges of emancipation for work. The economic pressures of war created new needs and opportunities—for speculation and profiteering on a catastrophic scale, but also for new commercial and industrial enterprises. The close alliance with Germany and Austria brought, in addition to military and financial support, educational, technical, and administrative guidance in many fields.[71] Under the lash of war, the weary empire of the Ottomans was stirred and shaken as never before. As the realities changed, so too did men's awareness of them—and the changes were at once swift, vast, and profound.

For a while, things did not go too badly. There were military victories—at Kut and Gallipoli against the British, in Eastern Anatolia against the Russians, and with the collapse of Imperial Russia in 1917 there were high hopes of a great new Turkish destiny in the East.

They were vain hopes. On both sides, the ramshackle, polyglot dynastic Empires collapsed under the impact of modern war. In Turkey, military defeat, economic ruin, and political ineptitude finally sapped the morale and loyalty even of the Muslim Turks.

[71] Turkey was fortunate in emerging from the first world war without the crippling burden of debt that affected the vanquished and most of the victors. Her debts to her defeated allies were cancelled by the treaties of Versailles and Saint Germain; her reparations to the victors were renounced in the treaty of Lausanne.

CHAPTER VIII

The Kemalist Republic

The basis of liberty, equality, and justice is the sovereignty of the nation.

MUSTAFA KEMAL.

Sovereignty should not be built on fear. Sovereignty that rests on guns cannot endure. Such a sovereignty, or dictatorship, must only be a temporary expedient in a time of upheaval.

MUSTAFA KEMAL, 1930

Revolutions are inevitable in the lifetime of nations. They may result in despotism, but they also launch nations on paths previously blocked to them.

MILOVAN DJILAS, 'The New Class', 1957.

At the end of 1918 it seemed that the Sick Man of Europe was about to die at last. Resentment against the dictatorship of the Young Turk leaders had been mounting for some time; the advance of the Allied armies lent it a force that could no longer be resisted. In July a new Sultan, Mehmed Vahideddin, a younger brother of Abdülhamid, had succeeded to the throne of Osman. In October the Young Turk ministers resigned, and the Sultan appointed Ahmed Izzet Paşa as Grand Vezir, with the task of seeking an armistice.[1]

After three days of preliminary negotiation, on 29 October a Turkish delegation led by the Minister of the Navy Rauf Bey[2] went on board H.M.S. *Agamemnon*, at anchor off Mudros, in the island of Lemnos, and signed an armistice next day.[3] The Young Turk pashas, Talât, Enver, and Cemal, fled across the Black Sea on the *stationnaire* of the German Embassy. An allied fleet of sixty ships sailed past the

[1] On Izzet Paşa, see Inal, *Sadrıazamlar*, pp. 1973–2028.

[2] Hüseyin Rauf [Orbay], born in 1881, was a naval officer who had become a national hero through his exploits as commander of the cruiser *Hamidiye*. He later played a role of some importance in the national struggle.

[3] On the armistice see Jäschke, 'Die Vorgeschichte des Waffenstillstandes von Mudros', *Or.-Rund.*, xviii (1936), 49–51, and sources quoted there, and *WI*, n.s., ii (1952), 126-8. Türkgeldi, *Mondros ve Mudanya Mütarekelerinin Tarihi* (1948), pp. 23 ff. For the period from the armistice onward, Jäschke's historical calendar, based in the main on Turkish press and official sources, is invaluable (Jäschke and E. Pritsch, 'Die Türkei seit dem Weltkriege; Geschichtskalender 1918-28' *WI*, x (1929), with continuations in subsequent issues, in the *MSOS*, and in separate publications (cited as Jäschke, *Kalender*, with date reference). The Ottoman chronology of Danişmend (above, p. 209 n.5) will also be found useful for the last years of the Ottoman Empire.

silent guns of the Dardanelles, and on 13 November anchored in the port of Istanbul.

General Izzet Paşa's tenure of office lasted only twenty-five days. Having achieved the armistice for which he was appointed, he gave place to Ahmed Tevfik Paşa, a former Grand Vezir and ambassador in London who would, it was hoped, be able to win the goodwill of the British. In the meantime, on 8 December, an Allied military administration was set up in Istanbul. Allied troops occupied various quarters of the city, strict Allied control was established over the port, tramways, defences, gendarmerie, and police, and on 8 February 1919 the French General Franchet d'Espérey, like Mehmed the Conqueror centuries before, rode into the city on a white horse, the gift of the local Greeks. The Arab provinces of the Empire were already in Allied possession, and had been promised independence. Allied forces now began to threaten even the Turkish provinces themselves. French troops advanced from Syria into Cilicia and the Adana district. British forces occupied the Dardanelles, Samsun, Ayntab, and other strategic points, as well as the whole length of the Anatolian railway. On 29 April 1919 Italian troops landed at Antalya, to take possession of some of the areas assigned to them by the secret wartime agreements of the Allies.

In Istanbul the new Sultan showed a disposition to follow in the footsteps of his elder brother and take over personal control of affairs. The Committee of Union and Progress had collapsed; its leaders had fled abroad. On 21 December the Sultan dissolved the Chamber of Deputies, and on 4 March 1919 appointed his brother-in-law Damad Ferid Paşa as Grand Vezir. Except for an interval of six months, from October 1919 to March 1920, Damad Ferid Paşa remained in power until October 1920, when Ahmed Tevfik Paşa returned to the Sublime Porte to hold office for just over two years, as the last Grand Vezir of the Ottoman Empire.

One of the first tasks of the Sultan and his ministers was to crush the remnants of the Young Turks. On 26 November 1918 court martial proceedings were opened against Enver and Cemal Paşas, *in absentia*. On 1 January 1919 they were dismissed from the army, and at the end of the month a new series of arrests and prosecutions began against the former leaders and supporters of the

Committee of Union and Progress.[4] Among the new leaders in the capital even the will to independent survival seemed to have failed and political discussion centred on the form which Turkish subjection was to take, and on the relative merits of an American or a British mandate.

There was indeed little room for hope. Exhausted by eight years of almost continuous warfare, the once great Ottoman Empire lay supine in defeat, its capital occupied, its leaders in flight. The country was shattered, impoverished, depopulated, and demoralized. The Turkish people, beaten and dispirited, seemed ready to accept almost anything that the victors chose to impose on them.

Almost, but not quite—for when, under cover of Allied warships, a Greek army landed at Izmir in May 1919, the smouldering anger of the Turks was at last kindled into an inextinguishable blaze. The cession of remote provinces inhabited by alien peoples could be borne, even the occupation of the capital could be suffered, for the occupiers were the victorious great powers of the invincible West, and their soldiers would sooner or later return whence they came. But the thrust of a neighbouring and former subject people into the heart of Turkish Anatolia was a danger—and a humiliation—beyond endurance.

The city and district of Izmir contained an important Greek population, and already in February 1919 Venizelos, the Greek Prime Minister, had presented a formal claim to them at the Peace Conference in Paris. The Italians, too, had a claim to Izmir, based on the superseded agreement of St. Jean de Maurienne, and it was largely in order to forestall the Italians that the Allies agreed to a Greek landing. On 15 May 1919, protected by British, French, and American warships, a Greek army landed at Izmir; after systematically occupying the town and surrounding district, they began to advance eastwards into the interior.

The Greeks made it clear from the first that they had come, not for a temporary occupation, but for a permanent annexation—to incorporate western Anatolia in a greater Greece on both shores of the Aegean, and thus bring nearer the 'Great Idea'—the restor-

[4] Danişmend, iv. 455–6; Jäschke, *Kalender*, Nov. 1918–Feb. 1919. For a transcript report of the trial of the Young Turk leaders, which opened on 27 April 1919, see *Takvim-i Vekayi*, 1335 [1919]. Divan-i Harb-i Örfi Muhakematı Zabıt Ceridesi.

ation of the departed glories of the Greek Christian Empire of
Constantinople.

The ultimate menace of the Byzantine 'Great Idea' to the
Ottoman Turkish state was clear enough to those who could see;
the immediate blow of the Greek occupation to the Turkish people
was felt in all the areas that they occupied. The Turkish reaction
was violent and instantaneous. In Istanbul, under the guns of the
occupying armies, there were great protest meetings, and the first beginnings of a secret resistance movement. On 23 May a vast, mass
demonstration was held in the Sultan Ahmed Square. In Anatolia,
the first armed clash occurred on 28 May at Ödemiş, where a small
body of Turks fought unsuccessfully to halt the Greek forces, and guerrilla warfare flared up along the line of Greek advance. The Turks
were ready to rise against the invader—only the leader was awaited.

Mustafa Kemal [5]

On 19 May 1919, four days after the Greek landing at Izmir,
Mustafa Kemal Paşa landed at Samsun, on the Black Sea coast of

[5] Mustafa Kemal, later Kemal Atatürk, is the hero of many popular biographies,
but still awaits a serious scholarly monograph. A bibliography of Turkish and foreign
works on Kemal and the Kemalist revolutions was published by M. Muzaffer Gökman, *Atatürk ve Devrimleri Tarihi Bibliyografyası* (1963; 2,157 items). The best short
biography is that contributed by a group of authors to *IA, s.v.* 'Atatürk' (now available
in English, *Atatürk*, Ankara, 1963). Of special interest are a group of Kemal's remin-
iscences, of which a French adaptation was published by Jean Deny, 'Les "Souvenirs"
du Gazi Moustafa Kemal Pacha', *R. Ét. islam.*, i (1929), 117–36, 145–222, 459–63.
The received version of the War of Independence and the subsequent struggles is that
given by Kemal himself in his famous six-day speech, delivered in October 1927.
(The Turkish text, simply entitled *Nutuk*, has been printed several times. Here reference is made to the two-volume edition published by the Ministry of Education,
1950–2. An English version, called *A Speech Delivered by Ghazi Mustapha Kemal*, was
published in Leipzig in 1929; this version, though apparently authorized, is not
satisfactory.) The account of events given in this speech, supplemented by Kemal's
other speeches and by such Turkish official publications as the *Histoire de la République
turque* (1935), has inspired most subsequent accounts of the Turkish Revolution and
Republic. Kemal's speech, though a remarkable achievement, inevitably reflects the
powerful personality of its author and the struggles in which he was engaged. Some
other Turkish sources are available, which, presenting independent testimony, make it
possible to amplify and occasionally rectify the received version. Mehmed Arif's
account of the struggle in Anatolia, *Anadolu İnkılabı*, was published in Istanbul in 1923.
Later, General Ali Fuat Cebesoy published an important series of memoirs
on the War of Independence (*Millî Mücadele Hatıraları*, 1953), on his embassy to
Moscow in 1920–2 (*Moskova Hatıraları*, 1955), and on the political struggle after his
return (. . . *Siyasî Hatıraları*, 1957–1960). Many other memoirs and documents have
appeared in Turkey including those of Kâzim Karabekir (abridged version,
İstiklâl harbimizin Esasları, 1951; suppressed in 1933; in extenso, *İstiklâl harbimiz*,
1960). A work of great literary merit, markedly different from the mass of

Anatolia, with orders from Istanbul to supervise the disbanding of the remaining Turkish forces. Instead, he set to work at once on the double task of organizing a movement and raising an army. Mustafa, later known as Kemal Atatürk, was born in Salonika in 1881, in a modest home. His grandfather had been an elementary school-teacher in Salonika; his father was a minor official who later became a timber merchant. Orphaned at the age of seven, Mustafa was brought up by his mother Zübeyde Hanım. In 1893, against her wishes, he entered the military *rüşdiye* school in Salonika; it was there that, in accordance with a common Turkish custom, he was given a second name by his teacher, and thus became Mustafa Kemal. In 1895 he went on to the military academy (*idadi*) in Manastir, and on 13 March 1899 entered the War College (*Harbiye*) in Istanbul as an infantry cadet. In 1902 he was assigned to a staff course, and in January 1905 graduated with the rank of staff-captain.

Mustafa Kemal's years at the War College coincided with some of the harshest repressions of Abdülhamid—and the College was one of the main centres of secret opposition. Despite all disciplinary measures, the cadets read the works of Namık Kemal and the Young Turk exiles secretly in their dormitories, and exchanged opinions on the ills of their country and the means of remedying them. Speaking of his years as a cadet, Mustafa Kemal later remarked:

autobiographic sagas by political and military veterans of the struggle for independence, is Yakup Kadri Karaosmanoğlu's *Vatan Yolunda, Millî Mücadele Hatıraları* (1958). A full critical study of the mass of Turkish and foreign documentation now available on the national struggle and the early years of the Turkish Republic is a task still to be undertaken. Among general studies of the Turkish War of Independence, mention may be made of two early ones by Jäschke ('Der Freiheitskampf des türkischen Volkes', *WI*, xiv (1932), 6–21) and A. J. Toynbee in RIIA, *Survey, 1925*, and a recent work by Elaine D. Smith, *Origins of the Kemalist Movement 1919–23* (1959). Useful information on particular problems and periods will be found in Jäschke, 'Beiträge zur Geschichte des Kampfes der Türkei um ihre Unabhängigkeit', *WI*, n.s., v (1957), 1–64; Dankwart A. Rustow, 'The Army and the Founding of the Turkish Republic', *Wld. Polit.* xi (1959), 513–52; Tevfik Bıyıklıoğlu, *Atatürk Anadolu'-da, 1919–21*, i (1959); idem, *Trakya'da Millî Mücadele* (1955–6); M. Tayyib Gökbilgin, *Millî Mücadele Başlarken* (1959–65), and Sabahattin Selek, *Millî Mücadele: Anadolu İhtilâli* (1965). A work by a Turkish author, Irfan Orga, *Phoenix Ascendant* (1959), diverges from the received version in its presentation of the roles of Kazım Karabekir and Rauf. Finally, for the course of events in Turkey since the Revolution, reference may be made to the regular surveys in *OM, WI*, and the *RIIA* Survey. Other works on Atatürk by Aydemir, Bayur, and Lord Kinross are listed in the bibliography.

I worked well at the usual lessons. On top of this, new ideas emerged among some of my companions and myself. We began to discover that there were evils in the administration and politics of the country, and we felt the urge to communicate this discovery to the thousands of students of the College. We founded a handwritten newspaper for them to read. We had a small organization in the class. I was in the committee, and I used to write most of what appeared in the paper.[6]

Inevitably, the apprentice conspirators were denounced and arrested. After a few months' detention Mustafa Kemal was released and given orders—half-posting, half-exile—to join the staff of the Fifth Army in Damascus. It was then that he had his first taste of active service, against Druze rebels. In 1906, together with a few friends, he founded a secret opposition group, and may have had some part in the Young Turk movement in Salonika. In 1907 he was promoted Major and posted to the Third Army in Macedonia. Then he got in touch with the secret Committee of Union and Progress, and took part in their work. His relations with the Young Turk leaders do not, however, seem to have been very cordial, and the revolution of 1908 did not bring him greatly to the fore. After the revolution he abandoned politics for a while, and devoted himself to his military career, publishing translations of General Litzmann's manuals on platoon combat drill (1909) and company combat drill (1910).[7] In 1910 he went on his first visit to Europe, to attend the great French military manœuvres of that year in Picardy. In the Italian and Balkan wars he served with distinction on several fronts, and during the uneasy peace that followed was posted to Sofia as military attaché. At the beginning of 1915, at his own urgent request, he was recalled to Turkey to take part in the war, and was given the command of the 'almost imaginary' 19th Division, then in process of formation at Tekirdağ, on the European shore of the Sea of Marmara. From there he and his division went to the Gallipoli peninsula, where he played a vital role in the successful defence of the Straits against the great British assault in 1915. This victory, which saved the capital from invasion, was one of the few major successes won by Ottoman arms during the war. To Mustafa Kemal it brought promotion, fame—and a posting to the remote eastern battle-front, many hundreds of miles from Istanbul, where a victorious national hero might be disagreeably conspicuous.

[6] *IA*, i. 720.   [7] *Atatürk'ün Askerliğe dair Eserleri* (1959).

Nuruosmaniye Mosque, Istanbul, completed 1755.
Turkish baroque; Ottoman plan with Italianate details

b. Vakıf Han, Istanbul, 1918; Young Turk neo-classical

a. Dolmabahçe Mosque, Istanbul, 1853; Tanzimat eclectic

ATABAY

a. Şişli Mosque, Istanbul, completed 1949

b. Atatürk Mausoleum, Ankara

b. Sultan Mahmud II, after the destruction of the Janissaries. (Painting in the Topkapı Sarayı collection)

a. Sultan Mahmud II, before the destruction of the Janissaries. (Painting in the Topkapı Sarayı collection)

President Kemal Atatürk

Ladies in Sultan Ahmed Square, 1907 (from *L'Illustration*,
reprinted in *Hayat*, 4 January 1957)

b. Günseli Başar ('Miss Turkey'), elected Miss Europe, 1951

a. Lady going to the bath, with a servant; (from a seventeenth-century Turkish miniature album)

a. Dance of the Mevlevi Dervishes (from a seventeenth-century Turkish miniature album)

b. Turkish football team

On 27 February 1916 he assumed a command at Diyarbakır, with the rank of general. A swift campaign against the Russians enabled him to recover Bitlis and Muş for Turkey (7–8 August 1916), and to win new honours for himself.

After further service in Syria and the Caucasus, he was on 5 July 1917 appointed to the command of the newly constituted Turkish Seventh Army, forming part of the so-called 'Yıldırım Army Group' under the German General Falkenhayn, in Syria. Disagreements with Falkenhayn led to his resignation and return to Istanbul in October 1917. Two visits to Europe followed, the first to Germany with the heir-apparent Mehmed Vahideddin, the second to Austria for medical treatment. In July 1918, still weak from illness, he returned to Istanbul, and on 7 August resumed command of the Seventh Army in Palestine. Six weeks later, on 17 September, Allenby began his final offensive north of Jerusalem, and the Turkish and German forces were driven out of Palestine and Syria. It was while Mustafa Kemal was preparing a last desperate struggle north of Aleppo that he heard of the signature of the armistice at Mudros. The next day, on 31 October, he was appointed commander of the Yıldırım Army Group, in succession to Liman von Sanders. Two weeks later his Army Group was dissolved and he himself summoned to the capital. He reached Istanbul on 13 November—the day of the arrival of the Allied fleets.

Despite his prestige as the only remaining victorious general in Turkey, Mustafa Kemal was not able to do very much in Istanbul. The Sultan and his friends were strongly opposed to all nationalist ideologies, which they held responsible for the misfortunes that had befallen the Empire; they were therefore anxious to discourage any popular movement of revolt which might, they felt, threaten the existing order as much as it threatened the invader. And so they continued the disarming of the Turkish forces, accepted successive Allied violations of the Armistice terms, ordered the Turkish troops in Izmir to offer no resistance to the Greeks, and suppressed any tendency to oppose or resist in the city. In the opening phrases of his historic speech on the revolution, delivered in 1927, Mustafa Kemal described the situation with characteristic vigour:

Those who had dragged the nation and the country into the Great War had thought only of saving their own lives and had fled abroad.

Vahideddin, who occupied the position of Sultan and Caliph, was a degenerate who, by infamous means, sought only to guard his own person and throne. The cabinet, headed by Damad Ferid Paşa, was weak, cowardly, and without dignity, subservient to the will of the Sultan, and ready to agree to anything that might protect him as well as their own persons.[8]

Realizing the hopeless condition of the capital, Mustafa Kemal decided to go to Anatolia, where some signs of revival were already noticeable. In December 1918 the first resistance groups had been formed, the so-called 'Societies for the Defence of Rights' (*Mudafaai Hukuk*). The first to appear were in Thrace and Izmir; others followed in Manisa and elsewhere in Anatolia, and set the pattern for national resistance movements in areas menaced or occupied by the enemy.[9]

The problem of how to leave the occupied capital and reach Anatolia proved unexpectedly simple. The Sultan, unaware of his intentions, was induced to give him an appointment as Inspector-General of the Ninth Army (in June 1919 renumbered Third Army), based on Samsun, on the Black Sea coast of Anatolia. His instructions were to restore order, to settle Muslim-Christian disturbances, to disarm and disperse the semi-military bands that had been operating in the area, and in general to supervise the disarmament and demobilization of the remaining Ottoman forces. Instead he set to work to establish links between existing resistance groups, to form new ones, and to prepare for the armed defence of the Turkish heartlands against invasion.[10]

Meanwhile, in the West, the victorious Allies were at last completing their arrangements for the disposal of the Sick Man's worldly goods. After a series of conferences in London and San Remo, a treaty was drawn up, and was signed by the representatives of the Allies and of the Sultan at Sèvres on 10 August 1920.

---

[8] *Nutuk*, i. 1; cf. *Speech*, p. 9.

[9] On these societies, see Rustow, in *Wld. Polit.*, xi. 541–2; Tunaya, *Partiler*, pp. 481 ff.; Jäschke, in *WI*, n.s., v. 19 ff.

[10] On the semi-legendary pre-history of the Kemalist movement—the activities of Kemal in Istanbul from November 1918 to May 1919—see the remarks of Jäschke, ibid. pp. 27 ff. and Rustow, pp. 537–8. See further Jäschke, 'Mustafa Kemals Sendung nach Anatolien', in F. Taeschner and G. Jäschke, *Aus der Geschichte des islamischen Orients* (1949), pp. 17 ff. and Y. H. Bayur, *Atatürk: Hayatı ve Eseri*, i (1963), 224 ff. For Kemal's own recollections, as recorded by a leading Turkish journalist, see Falih Rıfkı Atay, *Atatürkün bana anlattıkları* (1955), pp. 83 ff.

The treaty of Sèvres was very harsh, and would have left Turkey helpless and mutilated, a shadow state living on the sufferance of the powers and peoples who were annexing her richest provinces. It was far more severe than that imposed on a defeated Germany, and was received in Turkey with a national day of mourning.

It was, however, never implemented. While the Allies were imposing their terms on the docile government of the Sultan, a new Turkish state was emerging in Anatolia, led by men who rejected outright the treaty and the principles that underlay it, and condemned as traitors those Turks who had accepted it.

From the moment of his landing at Samsun, Mustafa Kemal had been hard at work in Anatolia, organizing the cadres of a national army, and preparing the ground for a war of liberation. In June he had a secret meeting in Amasya with Ali Fuad Paşa [Cebesoy], Hüseyin Rauf [Orbay], and Colonel Refet [Bele], and communicated with General Kâzım Karabekir Paşa, commanding the 15th Army Corps at Erzurum.[11] Soon afterwards he sent a circular telegram, in cypher, to a number of civil and military authorities in the country, setting forth his views. The opening phrases strike the keynote of the nationalist programme during the next few years:

1. The integrity of the country, the independence of the nation are in danger.

2. The central government is unable to discharge the duties for which it is responsible. As a result the nation is regarded as non-existent.

3. Only the will and resolution of the nation can save the independence of the nation.

The telegram then goes on to demand the convening of a congress, free from any influence or interference, to assert the rights of the nation before the world, and calls on each district to send delegates, in secret, to Sivas 'which is the safest place in

[11] Karabekir (*Istik. Harb.*, pp. 17 ff.; *Esaslar*, pp. 35 ff.) describes in his memoirs how, before leaving Istanbul early in April 1919 to take up his command in Erzurum, he called on Mustafa Kemal at his house in Şişli, and declared his intention of using the Army Corps at Erzurum as an instrument of national resistance, and thus preparing the ground for Kemal's own arrival and activities in Anatolia (cf. Gökbilgin, i. 79; Orga, pp. 73–74). In general, Karabekir's memoirs indicate a larger role in the movement in Anatolia than is allowed to him in Mustafa Kemal's historic speech, written, it will be remembered, after the break between the two men.

Anatolia for that purpose'.[12] At the same time Kâzım Karabekir sent out invitations for a meeting of delegates from the eastern provinces in Erzurum in July.

News of Mustafa Kemal's activities reached Istanbul, bringing joy to some quarters and alarm to others. The Minister of War called on him to return to Istanbul, and, when he omitted to do so, obtained an *irade* from the Sultan terminating his appointment. Mustafa Kemal, anxious to avoid any open act of rebellion against the legitimate Ottoman government, resigned his commission and put on civilian clothes.[13] He now turned to the Association for the Defence of the Rights of Eastern Anatolia, founded in Erzurum on 3 March 1919; this society, later registered in proper legal form at the vilayet of Erzurum, provided both an element of legal continuity and an instrument of organization.

On 23 July 1919 a congress of delegates from the eastern provinces, convened by the Association, assembled in Erzurum. Mustafa Kemal was elected chairman on the first day. The most important achievement of the congress, which continued until 17 August, was the drafting of the first version of the declaration which later came to be known as the National Pact (*Millî Misak*). During the congress Kâzim Karabekir received orders from Istanbul to arrest Kemal and Rauf, and to take over Kemal's post as Inspector-General. He refused to obey.[14]

On 4 September the second and more important congress opened at Sivas, attended by delegates from all over the country. Once again Mustafa Kemal was elected chairman, and directed the discussions of the meeting. The main business of the congress was to extend to the whole country the decisions taken at Erzurum, and to modify the organization established there accordingly. The 'Association for the Defence of the Rights of

[12] *Nutuk*, i. 30–31; *Speech*, p. 31. *Documents* (*Die Dokumente zur Rede*, 1927), no. 12. For Cebesoy's rather fuller account of proceedings at Amasya, see his memoirs, i. 69 ff.; further Karabekir, *Istik. Harb.*, pp. 57 ff.; Orga, p. 77; Gökbilgin, i. 145; Smith, pp. 14 ff., and *WI*, n.s., ii (1952), 130.

[13] On his resignation see Unat, 'Atatürk'ün Askerlikten Istifası . . .', *Tar. Ves.*, n.s., i (1955), 3–8; further Rustow, p. 546; Smith, p. 16.

[14] On the Erzurum congress see Cevat Dursunoğlu, *Millî Mücadelede Erzurum* (1946), pp. 107 ff.; *Nutuk*, i. 64 ff.; *Speech*, pp. 57 ff.; Arif, *Anadolu Inkılabı*, pp. 30 ff.; Cebesoy, i. 110 ff.; Karabekir, *Istik. Harb.*, pp. 83 ff.; *Esaslar*, pp. 66 ff.; Gökbilgin, i. 167 ff.; Orga, pp. 78 ff.; Smith, pp. 17 ff. On the history of the National Pact see Jäschke, 'Zur Geschichte des türkischen Nationalpakts', *MSOS*, xxxvi/2 (1933), 101 16.

Eastern Anatolia' now became the 'Association for the Defence of the Rights of Anatolia and Rumelia', with a permanent Representative Committee headed by Mustafa Kemal, and this new organization became the instrument of the political struggle ahead.

The political aims expressed at the Sivas congress were neither clear nor united. The delegates began by taking an oath never to revive the Committee of Union and Progress, and sending an address to the Sultan; they then went on to consider whether they should concern themselves with politics or not, and were by no means unanimous in agreeing to do so.[15] Even there, the idea of an American mandate, popular in some circles in Istanbul, was raised by some delegates, only to be rejected by the great majority.[16] The congress instead reaffirmed the principles of the Erzurum manifesto, and indeed strengthened the wording at some points, demanding the preservation of territorial integrity and national independence, and envisaging armed action against the occupying powers if necessary.

The congress lost no opportunity of reaffirming its loyalty to the Sultan, laying the blame on the Grand Vezir and the cabinet. On 10 September Mustafa Kemal telegraphed to Adil Bey, the Minister of the Interior:

You are preventing the nation from submitting their case to their sovereign. Cowards, criminals! You are engaged in treasonable conspiracies with the enemy against the nation. I did not doubt that you would be incapable of appreciating the strength and will of the nation; but I did not want to believe that you would act in this traitorous and murderous way against the fatherland and the nation. Think what you are doing. . . .'[17]

The next day a telegram was sent to the Sultan from the army commanders, reaffirming their loyalty to the throne and the sovereign, and begging him to 'deign to order the formation of a new government, loyal and respectful of the privileges of Your Majesty and of the Caliphate'.[18] Another telegram, signed by the

[15] *Nutuk*, i. 88; cf. *Speech*, p. 76.

[16] The *Nutuk* glosses over the fact, revealed by Cebesoy, that a telegram was actually sent from Sivas to the President of the Senate in Washington, asking for a fact-finding mission. The text of the telegram was later published in Washington. See Rustow, in *MEJ*, x (1956), 325–6; Cebesoy, i. 175–6.

[17] *Nutuk*, i. 131; cf. *Speech*, p. 114.   [18] *Documents*, no. 82.

'General Assembly of the Congress', was sent to the Grand Vezir Damad Ferid Paşa, accusing him both of trampling on the rights of the nation and of outraging the dignity and honour of the Sultanate.

The nation has no confidence left in any of you other than the Sultan, to whose person alone therefore it must submit its reports and petitions. Your cabinet . . . is coming between the nation and the sovereign. If you persist in this obstinacy for one hour longer, the nation will consider itself free to take whatever action it thinks fit, and will break off all relations between your illegal cabinet and the whole country. This is our last warning. . . . [19]

The immediate cause of these outbursts was the attempt by the Istanbul government, with some British help, to stir up the Kurdish tribes in the east against Kemal. These efforts had little effect, and precipitated the rupture between the Kemalists and Istanbul.

At first, however, relations with the capital showed signs of improvement. On 1 October Damad Ferid Paşa resigned, and was replaced by Ali Rıza Paşa, who, if not in favour of the Kemalists, was not actively opposed to them. He did go so far as to open negotiations, and on 20–22 October conversations were held at Amasya between Mustafa Kemal and a group of representatives of the Istanbul government led by the Minister of the Navy, Salih Paşa. Some measure of agreement was reached, involving the virtual recognition of the Kemalists by the government, and the acceptance by Istanbul of the main political principles of the Kemalist programme. [20] In December 1919, as a result of nationalist persuasion and pressure, new elections were held for the Ottoman parliament, which assembled in Istanbul on 12 January 1920. The Kemalists and their sympathizers had won a majority, and among the new members were some from the nationalist camp in Anatolia, including Rauf Bey. A fortnight later Parliament voted the National Pact, based on the declarations of

[19] *Nutuk*, i. 137; cf. *Speech*, p. 121. On the Sivas congress see further Arif, *Anadolu Inkılabı*, pp. 31 ff.; Cebesoy, i. 156 ff.; Karabekir, *Istik. Harb.*, pp. 179 ff.; *Esaslar*, pp. 94 ff.; Gökbilgin, ii. 3 ff.; Smith, pp. 19 ff.

[20] On the Amasya meeting, see *Nutuk*, i. 242 ff. and docs. 157–9; cf. *Speech*, pp. 208 ff.; Cebesoy, i. 252–4; Karabekir, *Istik. Harb.*, pp. 355 ff.; Gökbilgin, ii. 103 ff.; *Hist. Rep. turque*, pp. 42 ff.

Erzurum and Sivas, and formulating the basic demands for territorial integrity and national independence.

Mustafa Kemal and the 'Representative Committee', now established in Ankara, seemed in a strong position, with a sympathetic parliament in Istanbul and some measure of recognition from the government. Nationalist sympathizers in the capital became more active, and helped the Kemalists not only with words, but also by raiding Allied arms depots and sending their booty to Anatolia. The Allies, alarmed at these developments, reacted sharply. On 3 March Ali Rıza Paşa was forced to resign, and was replaced on 8 March by his Minister of the Navy, Salih Paşa. The same day the Allied Supreme Council decided on a reinforced occupation of Istanbul. On 16 March British forces entered the Turkish quarters of the city of Istanbul, and General Wilson, the Allied Commander, ordered the arrest and deportation of Young Turk and other suspected nationalist sympathizers. Some 150 were arrested in all, and a number of deputies, among them Rauf, deported to Malta. They were released late in 1921, in exchange for British officers arrested in Anatolia and held as hostages by the nationalists.

On 18 March 1920 the last Ottoman parliament in Istanbul held its last session. After unanimously voting a resolution of protest against the arrest of some of its members, it prorogued itself indefinitely. It did not meet again, and was finally dissolved by the Sultan on 11 April.

Matters now came rapidly to a head. On 19 March, the day after the prorogation of parliament in Istanbul, Mustafa Kemal called for elections to a new emergency assembly. It was to meet in Ankara, where the 'Representative Committee' had established itself on 27 December 1919. This small Anatolian hill town now became the headquarters of the nationalist resistance—the virtual capital of Turkish independence.

On 23 April a body of delegates, known as the Grand National Assembly, met in Ankara. Even now, the delegates were very reluctant to take any steps that might be construed as rebellious, and tried desperately to maintain legal continuity. So long as it was possible to do so, the nationalists proclaimed their loyalty to Mehmed Vahideddin, Sultan of the Empire and Caliph of Islam, and reaffirmed their desire to rescue him from enemy hands.

It soon ceased to be possible. On 5 April 1920 the Sultan had

recalled Damad Ferid Paşa to the Grand Vezirate, and opened a
new and bitter attack on the nationalists. On 11 April the *Şeyh-
ül-Islâm* Dürrizade Abdullah Efendi issued a *fetva* declaring that
the killing of rebels, on the orders of the Caliph, was a religious
duty; the Grand Vezir published a proclamation denouncing 'the
false representatives of the nation'; the Circassian Anzavur, who
had been fighting against the nationalists since September, was
given the title of pasha. On 18 April 'Disciplinary Forces' (*Kuvva-i
Inzıbatiye*) were formed to fight the nationalists, and on 11 May
Mustafa Kemal and other nationalist leaders were solemnly
sentenced to death, *in absentia*, by a court martial in Istanbul.
The Sultan and his government were preparing to use all weapons
—religious, political, military—in their last desperate assault on
the new power rising in Anatolia.

The nationalists replied in kind. On 3–4 May the Grand National
Assembly appointed a council of ministers. On 5 May the Mufti of
Ankara, Börekçizade Mehmed Rifat Efendi, issued a *fetva*, endorsed
by 152 other Muftis in Anatolia, declaring that a *fetva* issued under
foreign duress was invalid, and calling on the Muslims to 'liberate
their Caliph from captivity'. On 19 May the Assembly declared
Damad Ferid Paşa a traitor.[21]

These measures had, however, only limited effect in counter-
acting the immense prestige of such ancient and venerated offices
as those of the Sultan, the Grand Vezir, and the *Şeyh-ül-Islâm*. Anti-
nationalist riots broke out in many places, and irregular forces of
various kinds, encouraged and sanctified by the authority of Istanbul, harried the nationalists even in the neighbourhood of Ankara.

The nationalists, already militarily engaged against the
Greeks, the Armenians, and the French, were hard put to it to
defend themselves against the 'Army of the Caliphate'. In late
1920 and in 1921, however, events took a turn in their favour. The
signing of the treaty of Sèvres caused an immense revulsion of
feeling in Turkey against the régime that had accepted it; the
growing dissensions of the former allies made it possible for Kemal
to strengthen his position by judicious separate negotiation. In
Istanbul, on 17 October 1920, Damad Ferid Paşa, under strong
Allied pressure, resigned for the last time and gave place to Tevfik

[21] On these religious exchanges see Jäschke, 'Nationalismus und Religion im türkischen Befreiungskriege', *WI*, xviii (1936), 54–69, espec. p. 63; Rustow, 'Politics and
Islam in Turkey 1920–1955', in Frye, pp. 69–107, espec. p. 76.

Paşa. In Ankara, in January 1921, the ministers elected as chairman Fevzi Pasha [Çakmak], who had resigned the Ottoman Ministry of War and joined the nationalists the previous April.[21a] The progress of the struggle against the Greeks identified the Ankara régime with the national cause, and made opposition to it, rather than support for it, seem like treason and impiety in Turkish eyes.

The Greco-Turkish war falls into three stages, corresponding roughly with the campaigns of 1920, 1921, and 1922. In the first, the Turks, hopelessly outmatched in numbers and material, were badly defeated, and Greek forces advanced in both Anatolia and Rumelia. The second Greek campaign, in 1921, also opened well for the invaders, who made several important gains. The Turks, however, rallied. On 10 January a Turkish force under Colonel Ismet halted the Greeks in a valley near Inönü. In a second, more important battle, fought at Inönü on 31 March–1 April, Ismet, now promoted Brigadier, again repelled the invaders. It was from this engagement that Ismet Inönü, the collaborator and successor of Mustafa Kemal, later took his surname.

A new Greek advance began in July, and continued until the Greeks met the Turks on the Sakarya river. Then, on 24 August, a great battle took place, and the Turkish forces, under the personal command of Mustafa Kemal, won a decisive victory. The Greeks withdrew to a new line farther west. The victorious general was greeted by the Grand National Assembly with the title of 'Gazi'—victor in the holy war.[22]

The effects of the victory by the Sakarya were considerable. The nationalists were now internationally recognized as a powerful factor; by some as the real government of Turkey. The Soviets had already signed an agreement with them in March 1921, fixing the frontier and establishing friendly relations.[23] The French now did the same. In October a new Franco-Turkish treaty was signed with the nationalists, drawing up a new Turco-Syrian frontier far more favourable to Turkey than that laid down

[21a] On his rather mixed welcome, see Cebesoy, i. 367 ff.; Karabekir, *Istik. Harb.*, pp. 675 ff.

[22] On the significance of this title in earlier Turkish history see above, pp. 11 ff.

[23] On the history of the Russian treaty, see Jäschke, in *WI*, n.s., v. (1957), 44 ff. Among others, Jäschke quotes the important testimony of Cebesoy on the supply of arms and money by the Soviets to the Kemalists.

in the treaty of Sèvres, and providing for the French evacuation of Cilicia. The Italians too withdrew from their zone in southern Anatolia, stipulating only the retention by them of the Dodecanese islands. These withdrawals and agreements greatly strengthened the military position of the nationalist forces, who now in addition began to acquire large quantities of arms.

While the Turks had been growing in strength, the Greeks were weakened by dissension and changes of régime and policy at home. In August 1922 the third and final phase of the war began. The Turks won a crushing victory at Dumlupınar and, driving the Greeks before them, reoccupied Izmir on 9 September, thus completing the reconquest of Anatolia.

Mustafa Kemal now prepared to continue the struggle in European Turkey, and to drive the Greeks out of eastern Thrace. To do so, he had to cross the Dardanelles, still occupied by an inter-Allied force. The French and Italian contingents withdrew, but the British remained, and for a while an Anglo-Turkish clash seemed imminent. Finally, the British gave way to Kemal's demands, and on 11 October, 1922 an armistice was signed at Mudanya. By its terms, the Allied governments agreed to a restoration of Turkish sovereignty in Istanbul, the Straits, and eastern Thrace, which was occupied at once by 8,000 Turkish gendarmes. Full Turkish reoccupation was delayed pending the signature of a peace treaty. The Greeks acceded to the armistice on 14 October; on the 19th Refet Paşa, with a special commission from the Grand National Assembly in Ankara, crossed by the S.S. *Gülnihal* from Mudanya and entered the city of Istanbul.

The Treaty of Lausanne

The peace conference opened at Lausanne on 20 November 1922. Many months of diplomatic wrangling followed, until the treaty was finally signed on 24 July 1923. Its chief significance for Turkey was the re-establishment of complete and undivided Turkish sovereignty in almost all the territory included in the present-day Turkish Republic. At the same time the Capitulations, long resented as a symbol of inferiority and subservience, were abolished. Thus Turkey, alone among the defeated powers of the First World War, succeeded in rising from her own ruins and, rejecting the dictated peace imposed on her by the victors, secured the acceptance of her own terms. For the treaty of

Lausanne was substantially an international recognition of the demands formulated in the Turkish National Pact.

The military battle was won; the political programme of the nationalists had been achieved, and had been recognized by the world in an international treaty. What was to be done next? It was in his answer to this question that Mustafa Kemal showed his true greatness.

The point was well made by the Turkish journalist Falıh Rıfkı Atay, in his comparison between Mustafa Kemal and the Young Turk leader, Enver Paşa:

> Enver's special quality was boldness, Mustafa Kemal's was insight. . . . Had Mustafa Kemal been Minister of War in 1914, he would not have pushed the country into the First World War; had Enver entered Izmir in 1922, with the same *élan* he would have turned back, marched on Syria and Iraq, and lost all that had been won.[24]

There were indeed many distractions, which at that time might have enticed a warrior-hero. There were the lost Ottoman provinces in Europe and Asia, where the growing difficulties of the successor régimes might have favoured a reassertion of Turkish claims.[25] Nearer to the heart of Turkish nationalists, there were the 20 odd million Turkish-speaking Muslims of the fallen Russian Empire, which, in the throes of revolution, intervention, and civil war, might have offered a tempting field for political adventure.

But Kemal did none of these things. Once the war was over, he made peace with the Greeks, settling the ancient disputes between them by the brutal but effective method of an exchange of populations. He accepted the demilitarization of the Straits, to be ended only many years later and then by negotiation and agreement. Renouncing all foreign ambitions and all pan-Turkish, pan-Ottoman, or pan-Islamic ideologies, he deliberately limited his actions and aspirations to the national territory of Turkey as defined by treaty, and devoted the rest of his life to the grim, laborious, and unglamorous task of reconstruction. In a speech in 1923 he warned the people of Turkey:

> The successes which our army has gained up to now cannot be regarded as having achieved the real salvation of our country. These victories have only prepared the ground for our future victories. Let

[24] Atay, *Niçin Kurtulmamak* (1953), p. 6.

[25] On Kemal's refusal even to attempt the recovery of his birthplace, Salonika, see Orga, pp. 131–2.

us not be puffed up with military victories. Let us rather prepare for new victories in science and economics.[26]

The Political Reform

The first problem to be settled was, however, political—the form and structure of the Turkish state. The nationalists had from the first insisted on their loyalty to the sovereign; his actions against them and against what they regarded as the national cause were attributed to evil advisers and foreign control, from both of which they proposed to rescue him. But at the same time they had also formulated and adopted certain political principles which, in the long run, would prove incompatible with the survival of the Sultanate. As early as July 1920 Mustafa Kemal declared to the National Assembly in Ankara, amid applause: 'I think that the fundamental reality of our present-day existence has demonstrated the general tendency of the nation, and that is people's rights and people's government. It means the passing of government into the hands of the people.'[27] In August of the same year he made the same point again: '. . . Our point of view, which is people's rights, means that power, authority, sovereignty, administration should be given directly to the people, and should be kept in the hands of the people'.[28] It was about this time that the Assembly, with obvious reluctance, began to discuss constitutional questions. On 20 January 1921 it passed a 'Law of Fundamental Organizations', which began with the uncompromising declaration that 'sovereignty belongs without reservation or condition to the nation; the system of administration rests on the principle that the people personally and effectively directs its own destinies'. The subsequent articles went on to establish the position of the Grand National Assembly in Ankara as 'the only real representative of the people, and as the holder of both legislative and executive power'.[29]

[26] . . . *Millî Eğitimle ilgili Söylev ve Demeçleri*, i (1946), 10.

[27] *Atatürk'ün Söylev ve Demeçleri* (collected speeches), i (1945), 87.

[28] Ibid. pp. 97–98.

[29] The text will be found in the useful collection of constitutional documents by Gözübüyük and Kili, pp. 85–87, and of the laws and debates relating to the War of Independence and the Revolution by Kemal Arıburnu, *Millî Mücadele ve Inkılaplara ilgili Kanunlar* . . . i (1957), 11 ff. It is of interest that in late April 1921, when the Ottoman prince Ömer Faruk attempted to join the nationalists in Anatolia, he was politely but firmly advised by Kemal to stay in Istanbul (Jäschke, 'Auf dem Wege zur Türkischen Republik', *WI*, n.s., v (1958), 215–16, from a private communication).

With the Greeks and Allies at last out of the way, two forces remained, face to face, in Turkey; on the one hand a popular, nationalist government and Assembly, flushed with military victory and mass support; on the other the ancient supreme offices of the Muslim state and faith, still able to confer on their holders, however discredited by defeat and collaboration, an immense prestige and authority in the eyes of Muslim Turks of all classes.

The final clash between the two was precipitated by the Allied powers, who still insisted on recognizing the Sultan's government in Istanbul, and invited them as well as the nationalists to the peace conference at Lausanne. This twofold invitation and the prospect which it opened of divided Turkish authority at a crucial time, decided Kemal to terminate, once and for all, the political power of the throne.

The task was not easy. Kemal himself tells how he sounded some of his closest associates, and found them still loyal to the Sultanate. Rauf Bey, who had succeeded Fevzi as chief minister in July 1922, said:

> I am bound by conscience and sentiment to the Sultanate and Caliphate. . . . It is my duty to remain loyal to the sovereign: my attachment to the Caliphate is imposed on me by my education. Besides this, I would make a general observation. It is hard for us to control the general situation. This can only be secured by an authority that everyone is accustomed to regard as unapproachably high. Such is the office of Sultanate and Caliphate. To abolish this office and to try and set up an entity of a different character in its place, would lead to failure and disaster. It is quite inadmissible.

Refet Paşa, who was sitting near-by, agreed, and added that 'in fact, there can be no question of any form of government other than the Sultanate and Caliphate'.[30]

Mustafa Kemal had, however, reached his decision. The Sultanate and Caliphate were to be separated, and the former abolished. There would henceforth be no Sultan, but an Ottoman prince would hold office as Caliph only, with religious but not political powers. By this compromise Mustafa Kemal hoped to disarm the opposition of the religious elements to political change, to retain the advantages of a legitimate and revered authority

---

[30] *Nutuk*, ii. 684; cf. *Speech*, p. 573.

above politics, and at the same time to end the personal autocracy of the Sultan.

On 31 October Kemal put his proposals to a meeting of the association for the Defence of Rights. The next day they were submitted to the Assembly, where they formed the subject of long and heated arguments. Strong opposition to the proposals at once appeared, and the members of the Assembly's committee on *Şeriat*, mostly men of religion, raised all kinds of legal and theological objections. Kemal, sitting in a corner of the crowded committee room, saw that nothing very satisfactory to him was likely to emerge from these debates. The rest of the story is best told in his own words:

Finally, I asked the Chairman of the joint committee for permission to speak, and, jumping on the bench in front of me, I made this statement, in a loud voice: 'Gentlemen,' I said, 'Sovereignty and Sultanate are not given to anyone by anyone because scholarship proves that they should be; or through discussion or debate. Sovereignty and Sultanate are taken by strength, by power and by force. It was by force that the sons of Osman seized the sovereignty and Sultanate of the Turkish nation; they have maintained this usurpation for six centuries. Now the Turkish nation has rebelled, has put a stop to these usurpers, and has effectively taken sovereignty and Sultanate into its own hands. This is an accomplished fact. The question under discussion is not whether or not we should leave Sultanate and sovereignty to the nation. That is already an accomplished fact—the question is merely how to give expression to it. This will happen in any case. If those gathered here, the Assembly, and everyone else could look at this question in a natural way, I think they would agree. Even if they do not, the truth will still find expression, but some heads may roll in the process.

'As regards the theological aspect of the matter, there is no need for alarm or anxiety on the part of the reverend gentlemen. Let me give you a scholarly explanation.'

Having said this, I went on to give a lengthy explanation. Thereupon one of the deputies for Ankara, Hoca Mustafa Efendi said: 'I beg your pardon, sir, we were looking at the matter from another point of view. We have been enlightened by your explanations.'

The question was settled in the mixed committee. The draft law was quickly drawn up, and read on the same day at the second sitting of the Assembly. On a proposal to take a nominal vote, I mounted the tribune and said: 'There is no need for this. I believe that the Assembly will unanimously adopt the principles which will for ever preserve the independence of the country and nation!' Cries of 'Vote!' were raised, and finally the chairman put it to the vote and announced that it had been unanimously accepted. Only one opposing voice was heard saying: 'I am against it', but was drowned by cries of 'Silence!'

In this way, gentlemen, the final obsequies of the decline and fall of the Ottoman Sultanate were completed.[31]

The resolution passed on 1 November 1922 contains two articles. The first declared that 'the Turkish people consider that the form of government in Istanbul resting on the sovereignty of an individual had ceased to exist on 16 March 1920 [i.e. two and a half years previously] and passed for ever into history'; the second recognized that the Caliphate belonged to the Ottoman house but laid down that the Caliphate rested on the Turkish state, and that the Assembly would choose as Caliph 'that member of the Ottoman house who was in learning and character most worthy and fitting'.[32]

Mehmed VI Vahideddin did not wait for the Assembly's judgement of his learning and his character. On 17 November news was received that he had slipped out of the palace and boarded a British warship, on which he fled to Malta. Next day the Grand National Assembly in Ankara declared him deposed, and elected his cousin Abdülmecid as Caliph.

Mustafa Kemal now prepared for the next stages of the political struggle. His first need was for a political instrument. The Association for the Defence of the Rights of Anatolia and Rumelia had served well enough during the struggle for national liberation. It was not, however, adequate to the needs of a country enjoying peace and independence. Mustafa Kemal now set to work to transform it into a real political party. As early as 6 December 1922 he made his first announcement to the press about the formation of a new party, to be called the People's Party, and invited the educated classes of the country to communicate their views to him directly. In the new year he went on extensive journeys in Anatolia, and on 8 April 1923 published a manifesto with nine articles.[33] These reiterate his views on popular sovereignty, representative government, and the abolition of the

---

[31] *Nutuk*, ii. 690 ff.; cf. *Speech*, pp. 577 ff. Cebesoy's version of the abolition of the Sultanate is given in his memoirs, iii/1, 110 ff. On the question in general see Jäschke, 'Das Ende des osmanischen Sultanats', *Studien zur Auslandskunde, Vorderasien*, I/i.

[32] Text in Gözübüyük and Kili, pp. 90–91; Arıburnu, pp. 311–12.

[33] Text in Tunaya, *Partiler*, pp. 580–2.

Sultanate, and then go on to sketch a number of necessary reforms, especially in fiscal and administrative matters. In his 1927 speech, Kemal remarked of this manifesto:

> This programme contained essentially all that we have accomplished and applied until today. There were, however, certain important and fundamental questions that were not included in the programme, such as the proclamation of the Republic, the abolition of the Caliphate, the suppression of the Ministry of *Şeriat*, the closing of the *medreses* and *tekkes*, the introduction of the hat. . . . I did not think it right, by prematurely introducing these questions into the programme, to give the ignorant and the reactionary the opportunity to poison the whole nation. For I was quite sure that at the proper time these questions would be solved and the people would in the end be satisfied. . . .[34]

In spite of some complaints that the programme was brief and inadequate, it served as the starting-point of a new political development. On 16 April the Grand National Assembly, which in three years had grown from a rebel band to a national parliament, dissolved itself in preparation for new elections—the first real general election in many years. The elections, held in June, returned a new chamber of 286 deputies, which opened its proceedings on 11 August 1923. Two days earlier, on 9 August, the inaugural congress of the People's Party began its deliberations, under the presidency of Mustafa Kemal.[35] The Assembly elected Kemal as Head of State; Fethi [Okyar] replaced Rauf as Prime Minister.

The first major political act of the new Assembly was the ratification, on 23 August 1923, of the treaty of Lausanne, securing the international status of the new Turkey. At home, too, important consequences followed. On 2 October the last Allied contingents left Istanbul; on 6 October Turkish troops under the command of Şükrü Naili Paşa marched into the Imperial city. By a strange coincidence Damad Ferid Paşa died on the same day in Nice.

The Ankara government now faced a decision of fundamental importance. Its answer was not long delayed. On 9 October Ismet Paşa, at a meeting of the People's Party, moved a constitutional amendment, in the form 'Ankara is the seat of government of the Turkish state'. Four days later the Assembly formally decided on its adoption.

The decision meant a new breach with the past—a logical

[34] *Nutuk*, ii. 718 ff.; cf. *Speech*, p. 598.   [35] See below, p. 381

sequel to the abolition of the Sultanate. The Emperor had gone; the Imperial city was ill adapted to house the government of revolutionaries that had overthrown him. For nearly five centuries Istanbul had been the capital of an Islamic Empire; the pallid ghosts of a splendid past still flitted unhappily through the halls of the Saray and the Sublime Porte. Turkish Istanbul, with its mosques and palaces, its divines and courtiers; Pera, the Levantine suburb, with its cosmopolitan merchant community of concessionaires and compradors—these were too intimately associated with the past, in fact and in the mind of the Turkish people, to provide a centre for the new Turkey that Kemal wanted to build. And so a new capital was chosen, symbolizing and accentuating the changes that were taking place. The new state was based not on a dynasty, an empire, or a faith, but on the Turkish nation —and its capital was in the heart of the Turkish homeland.[36]

In the meantime Kemal had been preparing a still more radical change—the proclamation of the Republic. The abolition of the Sultanate and retention of a separate Caliphate had created a dangerous ambiguity in the headship of the state. There were many, in the Assembly and elsewhere, who saw in the Caliph the legitimate sovereign and head of state—a kind of constitutional monarch and, more especially, defender of the faith. Kemal, however, had other ideas. At the beginning of October reports began to circulate that he was going to proclaim a Republic, and they gave rise to impassioned opposition and discussion. At the end of October, after a series of carefully planned political manœuvres, Kemal came to the Chamber and proposed certain constitutional amendments which, he said, would remove the ambiguities and confusions in their political system. The draft amendment, prepared the previous night, included the phrases

The form of government of the state of Turkey is a Republic . . . the President of Turkey is elected by the Grand National Assembly in plenary session from among its own members. . . . The President of Turkey is the head of the state . . . and appoints the Prime Minister. . . .

At 8.30 in the evening, after hours of debate, the resolution was carried by 158 votes, with many abstentions but no dissentients. Fifteen minutes later, at 8.45, the deputies elected Mustafa

[36] G. J[äschke], 'Ankara wird Hauptstadt der neuen Türkei', *WI*, n.s., iii (1954), 262–7; Cebesoy, iii/2, 26–27, cf. below, pp. 377–8.

Kemal as first President of the Republic. He appointed Ismet Paşa as his first Prime Minister. The news was published all over the country the same night, and greeted after midnight in all parts by a salute of 101 guns.[37]

The Attack on the Theocracy

Among those who took part in the debate on the constitutional amendment was the distinguished historian Abdurrahman Şeref, the last Imperial Ottoman Historiographer, the first president of the Turkish Historical Society, and, at that time, a deputy for Istanbul in the Grand National Assembly.

> There is no point [he said] in enumerating all the different forms of government. 'Sovereignty belongs unconditionally to the people!' Once you have said that, you can ask whoever you like, and they will tell you that it means a Republic. That is the name of the new-born child. It seems, however, that some people dislike this name. Let them —it will make no difference.[38]

Not all the Sultan's former subjects were able to view the march of events with the same historical realism. In many quarters the proclamation of the Republic was received with enthusiasm, as the beginning of a new era. In others, it brought shock and grief, and profound anxieties as to the future. What did it mean? Would it merely replace the autocracy of the Sultan by that of Mustafa Kemal? How would it affect the Caliphate, and, with it, Turkey's standing as the leader of the Islamic world?

> No great intelligence is necessary [said an editorial in *Tanin*, on 11 November 1923] to understand that if we lose the Caliphate, the state of Turkey, with its five or ten million inhabitants, would lose all importance in the world of Islam, and in the eyes of European politics we would sink to the rank of a petty and insignificant state. . . . The Caliphate was acquired by the Ottoman dynasty and its retention in Turkey thus assured for ever; deliberately to create a risk of losing it is an action totally incompatible with reason, loyalty, and national feeling.[39]

The question of the Caliphate aroused interest far beyond the borders of Turkey, and brought anxious inquiries, especially from

---

[37] *Nutuk*, ii. 815 ff.: cf. *Speech*, pp. 657 ff.; Cebesoy, iii/2, 38 ff.; cf. ibid. 59–60. Texts and discussions in Gözübüyük and Kili, pp. 95 ff. and Arıburnu, pp. 32 ff. See also Orga, pp. 140 ff.

[38] *Nutuk*, ii. 812; cf. *Speech*, p. 655.   [39] *Nutuk*, ii. 830; cf. *Speech*, p. 669.

India, about the intentions of the republican régime. These last provoked the sharp comment from Kemal that 'those who had attacked the Caliphate were not strangers . . . they were Muslim peoples, who fought against the Turks under the British flag at the Dardanelles, in Syria, and in Iraq'.[40]

The main objection to the Republic, on the part of its conservative opponents in Turkey, was that it endangered the links of the Turkish people both with their own Islamic and Imperial past, and with the larger Muslim world of which they had for so long been the leaders. It was inevitable that the forces of tradition should rally around the person of the Caliph, the living symbol of their attachment to both. The Caliph Abdülmecid, by all accounts a mild and scholarly man, nevertheless lent himself to this role, and in January 1924 was subjected to a stinging reproof from the President of the Republic:

In his domestic establishment and more especially in his public appearances the Caliph seems to be following the path of his ancestors the Sultans. . . . We cannot sacrifice the Republic of Turkey for the sake of courtesy or sophistry. The Caliph must know exactly who he is and what his office is, and must content himself with it. . . . [41]

It was, it seems, the interest of Indian Muslims in the Caliphate that touched off the crisis which ended with its abolition. On 24 November 1923 three of the major Istanbul daily papers published the text of a letter to Ismet Paşa, signed by two distinguished Indian Muslim leaders, the Aga Khan and Ameer Ali. The two signatories pointed out that the separation of the Caliphate from the Sultanate had increased its significance for the Muslims in general, and begged the Turkish government to place the Caliphate 'on a basis which would command the confidence and esteem of the Muslim nations, and thus impart to the Turkish state unique strength and dignity'.[42]

Mustafa Kemal agreed with his opponents in seeing in the Caliphate the link with the past and with Islam. It was precisely for that reason that he was determined to break it.

Once again, the preparation was carefully planned. At the beginning of 1924 Mustafa Kemal went to Izmir, to preside over

---

[40] *Nutuk*, ii. 829; cf. *Speech*, p. 668.
[41] *Nutuk*, ii. 847–8; cf. *Speech*, pp. 682–3.
[42] RIIA, *Survey*, 1925, p. 571; Cebesoy, iii/2, 77–78.

large-scale military manœuvres, and stayed there for two months. With him were Ismet Paşa, the Prime Minister, Kâzım Paşa, the Minister of War, and Fevzi Paşa, the Chief of the General Staff. 'We were agreed on the need to abolish the Caliphate. At the same time we decided to suppress the Ministry of *Şeriat* and *Evkaf* and to unify public education.'[43]

On 1 March 1924 Mustafa Kemal opened the new session of the Assembly. In his speech, he emphasized three main points: the safeguarding and stabilization of the Republic, the creation of a unified national system of education, and the need to 'cleanse and elevate the Islamic faith, by rescuing it from the position of a political instrument, to which it has been accustomed for centuries'.[44]

The meaning of this third point was clarified next day at a meeting of the People's Party group. The President's proposals were discussed, and agreement reached on a series of motions, which were read to the Grand National Assembly on 3 March. They provided for the deposition of the Caliph, the abolition of the Caliphate, and the banishment of all members of the Ottoman house from Turkish territory. The next morning at daybreak the unhappy Abdülmecid was packed into a car and driven to a railway station to board the Orient Express—not the main Sirkeci station, where his departure might have provoked demonstrations, but a small one outside the city. The last of the Caliphs had followed the last of the Sultans into exile.[45]

In abolishing the Caliphate, Kemal was making his first open assault on the entrenched forces of Islamic orthodoxy. The traditional Islamic state was in theory and in the popular conception a theocracy, in which God was the sole legitimate source of both power and law, and the sovereign His vice-gerent on earth. The faith was the official credo of the established political and social order. The same Holy Law, coming from the same source and administered through the same judicature, embraced

[43] *Nutuk*, ii. 848; cf. *Speech*, p. 683; Cebesoy, iii/2, 64–65. See also *WI*, x (1924), 81.

[44] *Nutuk*, ii. 849; cf. *Speech*, p. 684.

[45] On the final phase of the Ottoman Caliphate, and its abolition, see Jäschke, 'Das osmanische Scheinkalifat von 1922', *WI*, n.s., i (1951), 195–217, 218–28; C. A. Nallino, 'La fine del così detto califfato ottomano', *OM*, iv (1924), 137–53 (reprinted in *Raccolta di Scritti*, iii (1941), pp. 260–83). Texts in Gözübüyük and Kili, pp. 98 ff., and Arıburnu, p. 329. Ismet Paşa's speech on this occasion is included in his collected speeches, *Inönü'nün Söylev ve Demeçleri*, i (1946), 87–93.

civil, criminal, and constitutional as well as ritual and doctrinal rules. The sovereign was the supreme embodiment of the Holy Law, maintained by it, and maintaining it. The ulema were its authorized defenders and exponents.

Since the beginning of the Ottoman reforms, great inroads had been made into the power of the ulema, who had been forced by successive reformers to surrender large areas of jurisdiction in legal, social, and educational matters. They still retained, however, great power and greater influence. A large part of the educational facilities of the country were under their control; the laws relating to family and personal matters were still dominated by the code which they administered; since the disappearance of the Sultanate and all the other institutions of the old régime, they remained the only power in Turkish society with the cohesion, the organization, and the authority to be able to challenge the leadership of the new régime.

More than once in the past, the ulema had delayed or frustrated the work of the reformers; Mustafa Kemal was determined that they should not hinder his revolution. The abolition of the Caliphate was a crushing blow to their whole hierarchic organization. It was accompanied by à series of others, abolishing the ancient office of *Şeyh-ül-Islâm* and the Ministry of *Şeriat*, closing the separate religious schools and colleges, and, a month later, abolishing the special *Şeriat* courts in which theologian-judges had administered the Holy Law. The new order was confirmed in the republican constitution, adopted by the Grand National Assembly on 20 April 1924, which affirmed the legislative authority of the Assembly and reserved the judicial function to independent courts acting 'in the name of the nation'.[46]

Radical changes of this kind inevitably aroused active and widespread resentment. In addition, opposition to Kemal's personal ascendancy was growing among those who had been most closely associated with him in the early phases of the national struggle. In the capital, a number of Kemal's former supporters broke away and began to form an opposition group, called the 'Progressive Republican Party'. Its leaders included Rauf and Generals Ali Fuad and Refet, who had been with him at the secret meeting in Amasya in June 1919, as well as General Kâzım

[46] On the constitution see below, pp. 362 ff.

Karabekir and other prominent civilian and military members of the nationalist old guard. On 21 November 1924 Mustafa Kemal appointed his old friend Fethi [Okyar], regarded as a liberal, as Prime Minister in place of Ismet.[47]

Political insurrection in the party was one thing; armed insurrection was another, and when, in February 1925, a Kurdish revolt broke out in the eastern provinces, Kemal acted swiftly and vigorously. The leader of the rebels was Şeyh Said of Palu, the hereditary chief of the Nakşbendi order. By the beginning of March the rebellion had spread to much of the south-east, and seemed to offer a serious threat to the republican régime. In Ankara the experiment in government by the President's loyal opposition was abandoned. On 3 March Fethi was dismissed and Ismet Paşa resumed the premiership, and on the following day a drastic 'Law for the Maintenance of Order' was rushed through the Assembly, giving extraordinary and, in effect, dictatorial powers to the government for two years.[48] They were renewed again in 1927 and did not finally expire until March 1929. At the same time special 'independence tribunals' were set up, in the east and in Ankara, the former with summary powers of execution. On the report of the tribunal in Ankara, the Progressive Republican Party was outlawed on 3 June. Fethi had meanwhile been appointed, on 11 March, as ambassador to France.

In the east swift military action crushed the rebellion; the 'independence tribunals' administered swift justice to the rebel leaders. Şeyh Said was captured in April and sentenced to death, together with forty-six of his followers, by an 'independence tribunal' in Diyarbakır, on 29 June. The sentences were carried out next day.

The Kurdish rebellion had been led by dervish *şeyhs*, who had urged their followers to overthrow the godless Republic and restore the Caliph. Kemal now reacted against the dervishes, closing their convents, disbanding their associations, and banning their meetings, ceremonies, and special garb.

[47] See Rustow, pp. 547–8; Orga, pp. 153 ff., and below, p. 375. The second part of General Ali Fuad Cebesoy's third volume of memoirs (*Siyasî Hatıralar*, 2, Istanbul 1960, especially 108 ff.) includes an account of the rise and fall of the Progressive Republican Party. See further F. W. Frey, *The Turkish Political Elite* (1965), pp. 323–35.

[48] Text and discussion in Arıburnu, pp. 174 ff.

It was at this time, and in this context, that Kemal made the first of his great symbolic revolutions—those dramatic changes of outward forms which expressed, in a manner at once vivid and profound, the forcible transference of a whole nation from one civilization to another. To the Westerner, the enforced replacement of one form of headgear by another may seem comic or irritating, and in either case trivial; to the Muslim it was a matter of fundamental significance, expressing—and affecting—his relations with his neighbours and his ancestors, and his place in society and in history. Islam was a faith and a civilization, distinct from other faiths and civilizations, uniting the Muslim to other Muslims, and separating him both from his heathen forefathers and his infidel neighbours. Dress, and especially headgear, was the visible and outward token by which a Muslim indicated his allegiance to the community of Islam and his rejection of others. During the past century modernization and reform had made great inroads into Muslim exclusiveness in matters of dress, and had created a new social gulf between the Westernized and the un-Westernized—the former comprising the male and secular elements of the ruling *élite*, the latter the rest of the population. But even among the immaculately trousered and jacketed dandies of the capital, one badge of distinctness had remained—the fez. This headgear, introduced a bare century earlier and fiercely resisted as an infidel innovation,[49] had been adopted and accepted by Muslims in Turkey and in many other countries, and had become the last symbol of Muslim identification. The rest of the Muslim's body might be Westernized, but his head remained Islamic—with the tall, red, challenging fez proclaiming at once his refusal to conform to the West and his readiness to abase his unimpeded brow before God.

Already in the Young Turk period there were some more consistent Westernizers who dismissed the possibility of a separate Islamic civilization, modern yet distinct. 'Civilization means European civilization', Abdullah Cevdet had written in 1911.[50] Mustafa Kemal was entirely of the same opinion. Speaking to the Assembly in November 1924, after the laws against the theocracy had gone into force, he remarked: 'The Turkish nation has perceived with great joy that the obstacles which constantly, for centuries, had kept Turkey from joining the civilized nations

[49] See above, p. 101.   [50] See above, p. 236.

marching forward on the path of progress, have been removed.'[51] 'Uncivilized people', he said on another occasion, 'are doomed to remain under the feet of those who are civilized.'[52] And civilization meant the West, the modern world, of which Turkey must become a part in order to survive. 'The nation has finally decided to achieve, in essence and in form, exactly and completely, the life and means that contemporary civilization assures to all nations.'[53]

The events of 1925 had shown that the forces of reaction were still powerfully entrenched, and able to offer serious resistance to the progress of Westernization. The removal of the Caliphate had not sufficed; a further shock was necessary—a traumatic impact that would shake every man in the country into the realization that the old order had gone, and a new one come in its place. The fez was the last bastion of Muslim identification and separateness. The fez must go.

In his speech of October 1927 Kemal explained his action in these terms:

> Gentlemen, it was necessary to abolish the fez, which sat on the heads of our nation as an emblem of ignorance, negligence, fanaticism, and hatred of progress and civilization, to accept in its place the hat, the headgear used by the whole civilized world, and in this way to demonstrate that the Turkish nation, in its mentality as in other respects, in no way diverges from civilized social life.[54]

The operation was carried through with characteristic speed and efficiency. In the last week of August 1925, on a visit to Kastamonou and Inebolu, Mustafa Kemal launched the first attack on the fez and the traditional garments still worn in provincial Anatolia. In a series of speeches he ridiculed them as wasteful, uncomfortable, and, above all, barbarous—unworthy of a civilized people. Addressing a crowd in Inebolu on 28 August he said:

> Gentlemen, the Turkish people who founded the Turkish republic are civilized; they are civilized in history and in reality. But I tell you as your own brother, as your friend, as your father, that the people of the Turkish Republic, who claim to be civilized, must show and prove that they are civilized, by their ideas and their mentality, by their

---

[51] *Söylev*, i. 320.   [52] Mustafa Baydar, *Atatürk diyorki* (1957), p. 46.

[53] *Söylev*, i. 325.   [54] *Nutuk*, i. 895; cf. *Speech*, pp. 721–2.

family life and their way of living. In a word, the truly civilized people of Turkey . . . must prove in fact that they are civilized and advanced persons also in their outward aspect. I must make these last words clear to you, so that the whole country and the world may easily understand what I mean. I shall put my explanations to you in the form of a question.

Is our dress national? (Cries of no!)

Is it civilized and international? (Cries of no, no!)

I agree with you. This grotesque mixture of styles is neither national nor international. . . . My friends, there is no need to seek and revive the costume of Turan. A civilized, international dress is worthy and appropriate for our nation, and we will wear it. Boots or shoes on our feet, trousers on our legs, shirt and tie, jacket and waistcoat—and, of course, to complete these, a cover with a brim on our heads. I want to make this clear. This head-covering is called 'hat'.[55]

The secret was out. Mustafa Kemal drove his point home two days later, in Kastamonu:

I see a man in the crowd in front of me [he said, pointing to a citizen]; he has a fez on his head, a green turban on the fez, a smock on his back, and on top of that a jacket like the one I am wearing. I can't see the lower half. Now what kind of outfit is that? Would a civilized man put on this preposterous garb and go out to hold himself up to universal ridicule?[56]

On 2 September a group of new decrees directed against the theocracy included a ban on the wearing of religious vestments or insignia by persons not holding a recognized religious office,[57] and an order to all civil servants to wear the costume 'common to the civilized nations of the world'—that is, the Western suit and hat. At first ordinary citizens were free to dress as they pleased, but on 25 November 1925 a new law required all men to wear hats, and made the wearing of the fez a criminal offence.[58]

The reaction of Muslim conservatives to this revolution can best be seen in a declaration issued in March 1926, on behalf of the

[55] *Söylev*, ii. 212–13; *Hist. Rép. turque*, p. 230.

[56] *Söylev*, ii. 219 ff.; *Hist.*, pp. 231–2.

[57] In December 1934 a further law prohibited the wearing of religious dress of any kind by clergy (*ruhaniler*) of all faiths, except in places of worship and during religious ceremonies. Exemptions from this law were granted to eight recognized religious chiefs.

[58] Jäschke, in *WI*, n.s., i (1951), 45–46. For Kemal's speeches on his trip to Kastamonu and Inebolu see also Mustafa Selim Imece, *Atatürk'ün Şapka Devriminde Kastamonu ve Inebolu Seyahatları 1925*, (1959).

'Islamic Religious Presidency of the Kingdom of Egypt', and signed by the Rector of the al-Azhar university and the Chief Mufti of Egypt.

It is clear [they said] that a Muslim who seeks to resemble a non-Muslim by adopting the latter's distinctive form of dress, will also come to take the same way as he in his beliefs and actions. That is why he who wears the hat because of an inclination to the religion of another and a contempt for his own is an infidel, according to the unanimous opinion of the Muslims. He who wears the hat in order to resemble non-Muslims, if he also adopts some of the practices of their religion, such as entering a church, is an infidel; if he does not do this, he is still a sinner. . . . Is it not folly to abandon one's own national way of dressing in order to adopt that of other people, when this desire for imitation can lead to the disappearance of our nationality, the annihilation of our own identity in theirs, which is the fate of the weak. . . .[59]

Statements of this kind, for obvious reasons, are not found in Turkey, but there can be little doubt that the pronouncement of the Egyptian divines substantially expressed the views of the Turkish opponents of the reform. The Caliph had, after all, been a remote and semi-mythical figure; the hat law affected every Turk in his own person, and the response was correspondingly greater. There were new disturbances in the east, and ominous stirrings elsewhere. The emergency 'Law for the Maintenance of Order', passed in March 1925 to deal with the Kurdish rebellion, was still in force, and the government was able to impose and enforce its will through the armed forces and the 'independence tribunals'. As Kemal grimly remarked:

We did it [i.e. the abolition of the fez] while the Law for the Maintenance of Order was still in force. Had it not been, we would have done it all the same, but it certainly is true that the existence of the law made it much easier for us. Indeed, the existence of the Law for the Maintenance of Order prevented the large-scale poisoning of the nation by certain reactionaries.[60]

Together with the fez, Mustafa Kemal changed some other symbols. The Turkish finance (*maliye*) calendar, based on a combination of the Greek months with the *hijri* year, had been in increasing use in Ottoman administration since the late eighteenth

[59] Quoted by Canard, in *A. l'Inst. d'Et. or.*, viii. 219–23.
[60] *Nutuk*, ii. 895; cf. *Speech*, p. 722.

century, and in 1917 had been adjusted to the Gregorian months, though still with a modified *hijri* year. On 26 December 1925 it was abolished, and the Gregorian calendar and era officially adopted. At the same time the twenty-four-hour 'international' clock was confirmed as the only legally valid method of measuring time.

Another, and more delicate matter, was that of female clothing. In his speech at Kastamonu on 30 August 1925, Mustafa Kemal had attacked the veil as well as the fez.

In some places I have seen women who put a piece of cloth or a towel or something like it over their heads to hide their faces, and who turn their backs or huddle themselves on the ground when a man passes by. What are the meaning and sense of this behaviour? Gentlemen, can the mothers and daughters of a civilized nation adopt this strange manner, this barbarous posture? It is a spectacle that makes the nation an object of ridicule. It must be remedied at once.[61]

Even the great reformer, buttressed as he was by the Law for the Maintenance of Order and the 'independence tribunals', did not venture to legislate against the veil. The unveiling of women, already accepted among the educated classes in the big towns, made only slow progress elsewhere. It was not until 1935 that a ban on the veil was proposed at a congress of the People's Party, and even then no action was taken.[62]

The Law Reform[63]

The 'outward aspect' of the Turkish people, or at least of its accessible male members, had been changed. There remained the more difficult task of transforming its 'family life and way of living' to accord with the 'common practice of civilized nations'. For this a radical reorganization of the entire legal system of the country was necessary.

[61] *Söylev*, ii. 220; *Hist.*, p. 234.

[62] Jäschke, in *WI*, n.s., i. 47. There were, however, municipal orders against the veil in some places.

[63] The best account and interpretation of the transformation of the legal system will be found in Count Léon Ostrorog, *The Angora Reform* (1927). See further Ali Fuad Başgil and others, *La Turquie* (1939), (no. vii in *La Vie juridique des peuples*, ed. H. Levy-Ullmann and B. Mirkine-Guetzevitch); Jäschke, in *WI*, n.s., i and Bülent Daver, *Türkiye Cumhuriyetinde Lâyiklik* (1955; on laicism), and a collection of papers by various authors in the Unesco *International Social Science Bulletin*, ix/1 (1957), 7–81.

The nineteenth-century reforms had already removed large areas of law from the domination of the *Şeriat* and the jurisdiction of its exponents. On 8 April 1924 Mustafa Kemal had gone still further, and had abolished the separate *Şeriat* courts. But even after all these changes, the *Şeriat* still remained in force in most fields of family and personal law, and was still administered by judges who, though they sat in secular courts, were still to a large extent, by training and outlook, doctors of the Holy Law.

Throughout the periods of the reforms, the exclusive competence of the *Şeriat* lawyers in matters of family and personal status had been left intact. Kemal was determined to end it. At the beginning of 1924 the Minister of Justice, Seyyid, proposed the restoration, in an improved form, of the liberal Family Law of 1917. Kemal, however, was not interested in a law based on the *Şeriat*, however much it had been liberalized and modernized by interpretative ingenuity.

> I wish to declare categorically [he said, in a speech at Dumlupinar on 30 August 1924][64] that the basis of civilization, the foundation of progress and power, are in family life. A bad family life leads inevitably to social, economic and political enfeeblement. The male and female elements constituting the family must be in full possession of their natural rights, and must be in a position to discharge their family obligations.[65]

A few days later, on 11 September 1924, a commission of twenty-six lawyers set to work on the task of adapting the Swiss civil code to Turkish needs. The completed code was voted by the Assembly on 17 February 1926, and entered into force on 4 October.

It is difficult to exaggerate the significance of this change in the development of Turkey. There had been many previous legal reforms, under the *Tanzimat* and Young Turk régimes, and not a few of the prescriptions of the *Şeriat* had been tacitly dropped, chiefly in the fields of administrative, commercial, and criminal law. But this was the first time that a reformer had dared to invade the intimacies of family and religious life, the inviolate preserve of the doctors of the Holy Law—and to do so, not by stealth, but by head-on attack. The God-given *Şeriat* was repealed by the Assembly, and its rules declared null and void, superseded by the

[64] Or on 26 Aug. according to the *Hist.*   [65] *Söylev*, ii. 183; *Hist.*, p. 223.

new Turkish civil code.[66] Polygamy, repudiation—all the ancient
bars to the freedom and dignity of women—were abolished. In
their place came civil marriage and divorce, with equal rights for
both parties. Most shocking of all, to Muslim opinion, the marriage
of a Muslim woman to a non-Muslim man became legally possible,
and all adults were given the legal right to change their religion
at will.

The voting of the Swiss civil code by the Turkish Assembly did
not, of course, transform Turkey overnight into a Middle Eastern
Switzerland. In the towns and in the villages near to the main
roads and railway lines, the new laws of marriage, divorce, and
inheritance were, in the main, enforced. In the countless villages
that made up the rest of the country, the old ways survived. A
marriage was usually registered with the civil authorities, to
ensure legitimacy and legal inheritance. The 'legal' wife was then
credited with the offspring of other wives, bound to their husbands
by the bonds of religion and custom, though without the con-
secration of the secular state. Even though the law gave them new
and extensive rights, there were few village women who dared—
or cared—to assert them against their husbands, fathers, and
brothers. Even in the provincial towns, though polygamy disappeared, the women of the un-Westernized classes for a long time
enjoyed very little real improvement in their status.

The citadel had, however, been breached. The authority of the
state, always so important in a Muslim country, was now unmistakably on the side of reform, and the defenders of tradition
were forced into the difficult and unfamiliar role of clandestine
resistance. Following on a series of other defeats, the ulema had
been driven from their last stronghold of power and influence; the
apparatus of the law and the coercive agencies of its enforcement were being used in a determined effort to break their power
for ever. Mustafa Kemal's purposes were made clear in his speech
at the opening of the new law school in Ankara, on 5 November
1925:

Gentlemen, when I speak to you of legal foundations, of the laws
required by our new needs, I am not merely referring to the dictum
that 'every revolution must have its own special sanctions'. While
restraining myself from useless recriminations, I must at the same time

[66] Jäschke, in *WI*, n.s., i. 36–37.

observe, with the deepest regret, how the efforts made by the Turkish nation for at least three centuries to profit from the means and benefits of modern civilization have been frustrated by such painful and grievous obstacles.

The negative and overwhelming force that has condemned our nation to decay, that has ultimately broken and defeated the men of initiative and drive whom our fecund nation has in no period failed to produce, is the law that has hitherto been in your hands, the law and its faithful followers. . . .

Think of the Turkish victory of 1453, the capture of Istanbul, and its place in the course of world history. That same might and power, which in defiance of a whole world made Istanbul for ever the property of the Turkish community, was too weak to overcome the ill-omened resistance of the men of law and to receive in Turkey the printing press, which had been invented at about the same time. Three centuries of observation and hesitation were needed, of effort and energy expended for and against, before the old laws and their exponents would permit the entry of printing into our country. Do not think that I have chosen a remote and ancient period, incapable of resuscitation, to illustrate the old law and the old lawyers. If I were to start giving you examples of the difficulties caused during our new revolutionary era, to me personally, by the old law and its exponents, I would run the risk of overburdening you. . . . All these events show that the greatest and at the same time the most insidious enemies of the revolutionaries are decayed laws and their decrepit upholders. . . .

It is our purpose to create completely new laws and thus to tear up the very foundations of the old legal system. . . .[67]

The most important of these new laws was undoubtedly the civil code. At the same time committees of jurists worked on others too, borrowing and adapting various Western systems of law to Turkish needs. Within a few years Turkey had new codes of obligations, commerce, maritime law, criminal law, and civil and criminal procedure, and a new system of judicature to administer them.

Conspiracy and Repression [68]

These reforms brought a renewal of activity by the opponents of

[67] *Millî Eğ. Söylev*, i. 29–30; cf. *Hist.*, pp. 207–8.

[68] On these events, details will be found in Jäschke's *Kalender*, the RIIA, *Survey*, *OM*, *WI*, &c.; the official version in the *Hist.*; Cebesoy's version in his memoirs, iii/2, 195 ff., including letters written by Rauf [Orbay] in London and Paris defending his record (pp. 226–42). Among other participants, Kılıç Ali has had his memoirs published (*İstiklâl Mahkemesi Hatıraları* and *Kılıç Ali Hatıralarını Anlatıyor*, 1955). For recent discussions see Karpat, pp. 46 ff., and Orga, pp. 165 ff.

the régime, who had been quiescent since the crushing of the Kurdish rebellion. On 15 June 1926, thanks to an informer, the police discovered a conspiracy in Izmir. Its leader was Ziya Hurşid, a former deputy who had opposed the abolition of the Caliphate in 1924; its purpose was to assassinate Mustafa Kemal by throwing a bomb into his car when he came to Izmir.

The conspirators were arrested, and on 16 June the Gazi entered Izmir unharmed. Two days later the 'independence tribunal', hastily transferred from Ankara, assembled in Izmir, and the Gazi issued a message to the nation, saying: 'One day I shall die, but the Republic will live on!'

The trial began on 20 June, in the Alhambra cinema in Izmir; the presiding judge was Ali [Çetinkaya], better known as Kel Ali, Bald Ali—an old soldier, a deputy, and a veteran of the Kemalist cause from the beginning. On 13 July sentences of death were pronounced against the accused, and carried out next day. The 'independence tribunal' now returned to Ankara, and began a new trial on 1 August, of a new batch of prisoners. On 26 August sentence of death was pronounced against a number of the accused, and carried out the same day.

The 'Law for the Maintenance of Order' had given Kemal the legal authority to deal not only with the insurgents in the east but also with political opponents in Ankara, Istanbul, and elsewhere. After the Kurdish rebellion, the Progressive Republican Party was outlawed, and a strict control clamped down on the opposition press. The Izmir conspiracy provided the opportunity to deal with its leaders as well as other opposition figures.[69] The 'independence tribunals' at Izmir and Ankara soon extended their inquiries far beyond the original conspiracy and conspirators, and, with scant concern for legal rules and procedure, embarked on what was, in effect, a prosecution of all the major political opponents of Mustafa Kemal. Some were acquitted—the four generals, Kâzım Karabekir, Refet, Ali Fuad, and Cafer Tayyar Paşas, all concerned in the proscribed Progressive Party, were too respected to be condemned, and were released, to the great and ominous satisfaction of the army and a good many civilians. Other prisoners were less fortunate. Among those executed were prominent survivors of the

[69] Whether the Progressive Republican leaders were in any way implicated in the Kurdish rising or in the Izmir conspiracy is still a matter of argument in Turkey. See, for example, Karpat, p. 47 n. 47.

Young Turk movement, such as the former Finance Minister, Cavid Bey, and even intimate associates of the Gazi during the war of independence, such as Colonel Arif. Rauf Bey, described as the arch plotter, had left for Europe before the plot was discovered, and was condemned *in absentia* to ten years' banishment.

By 1927 all opposition to the régime—military, religious, or political—had been silenced, and when elections were held in August and September 1927 for a third Assembly of the Turkish Republic, only one party, the Republican People's Party of Mustafa Kemal, was there to take part in them. It was after this election, from 15 to 20 October, that Mustafa Kemal delivered his famous speech to the Congress of the People's Party. Taking thirty-six hours to deliver, the speech contains the Gazi's description and justification of his proceedings from the moment when he landed at Samsun on 19 May 1919. It is still the classic account of the Kemalist Revolution.

Secularization: the Romanization of the Script [70]

The new session of the Assembly began unremarkably, with the re-election of Mustafa Kemal as President and the reappointment of Ismet as Prime Minister. Further projects were, however, in preparation, with the purpose of giving the Turkish state and people a more secular, more national, more modern—and less Islamic character.

The first step was little more than a formal ratification of the changes already accomplished. The second article of the 1924 constitution had begun with the words 'The religion of the Turkish state is Islam'—a formula retained, with appropriate modifications, since the first Ottoman constitution of 1876. On 5 April 1928 the People's Party resolved to delete this clause from the constitution, and five days later, on 10 April, the Assembly voted a law to that effect. At the same time three other clauses were amended to remove religious expressions and allusions.

The disestablishment of Islam was completed, and Turkey was now, legally and constitutionally, a lay state, secular and modern in her constitution, her laws, and her aspirations. But there remained one symbol, potent and universal, that bound her to the Orient and set her apart from the Western community of nations —the Arabic script. It was this final badge of Muslim identity

[70] See further, pp. 419 ff., below.

that was now to follow the Caliphate and the Holy Law into oblivion.

Reform of the alphabet was not a new topic. There had been proposals for an improvement of the Arabic script since the time of the *Tanzimat*, though nothing very much had come of them. The more radical idea of abandoning the Arabic script entirely and replacing it by the Latin alphabet was put forward and discussed in Turkey in 1923 and 1924, but was decisively rejected.

By 1927, however, the situation had changed. The Kemalist régime was now firmly in the saddle, and in possession of virtually dictatorial powers; the religious opposition was cowed and disheartened by a series of crushing blows. A new factor of some importance was the decision of the Soviet authorities to adopt the Latin alphabet in place of the Arabic for the Turkic languages of the USSR, thus providing both an example and an incentive to the government of the Turkish Republic.

Already in March 1926, immediately after the Soviet decision, the Minister of Education Necati had spoken of the political significance of romanization. Preparations went on during 1927, but nothing was heard in public until January 1928, when the first ranging shots of the preliminary barrage were fired. On 8 January the Minister of Justice, Mahmud Esad, a radical reformer who had played a major role in the repeal of the Holy Law, made a speech in which he praised the merits of the Latin script. A fortnight later the former Education Minister Hamdullah Subhi went further; 'The adoption of the Latin letters', he said, 'is for us a necessity. The old literature is doomed to moulder away.'[71] On 24 May the first legislative step was taken—the adoption, by law, of the 'international' numerals in place of the Arabic figures which Turkey had previously shared with other Muslim countries. On 26 June a special commission met at the Dolmabahçe palace in Istanbul, with the task of 'examining the possibility and the manner of adopting the Latin letters'. Kemal, in Istanbul for the summer, personally led and directed the discussions, and was no doubt responsible for the quick and expeditious way in which the commission conducted its business.

In six weeks the new alphabet was completed, and Kemal was ready to present it to the nation. On 9 August 1928 the

[71] Jäschke, *Kalender*, 21 Jan. 1928.

sometime Gazi Paşa, now President of the Republic, appeared in a new role—that of schoolmaster. The Republican People's Party was holding a fête that night, in the park at Seraglio Point, and many of its leading figures were present. Towards eleven o'clock the President himself appeared, and after a while he rose to address them.

My friends [he said], our rich and harmonious language will now be able to display itself with new Turkish letters. We must free ourselves from these incomprehensible signs, that for centuries have held our minds in an iron vice. You must learn the new Turkish letters quickly. Teach them to your compatriots, to women and to men, to porters and to boatmen. Regard it as a patriotic and national duty . . . and when you perform that duty, bear in mind that for a nation to consist of 10 or 20 per cent. of literates and 80 or 90 per cent. of illiterates is shameful. . . . The fault is not ours; it is of those who failed to understand the character of the Turk and bound his mind in chains. Now is the time to eradicate the errors of the past. We shall repair these errors, and in doing so I want the participation of all our compatriots. . . . Our nation will show, with its script and with its mind, that its place is with the civilized world.[72]

After this call to mobilization, the Gazi set out on a tour of the country, teaching and examining the populace in village squares, schoolrooms, town halls, and cafés. The Prime Minister and other dignitaries followed his example, and soon all Turkey was a schoolroom, with the nation's intellectuals, armed with blackboard and easel, teaching the people to read and write the new script. On 1 November 1928 the Assembly, on the first day of its new session, resolved to present the new alphabet to Mustafa Kemal on a golden tablet; on 3 November they passed a law establishing the new Turkish script and prohibiting the public use of the Arabic alphabet for the Turkish language after the end of the year. A few days later examinations were held to test the literacy of civil servants in the new script, and on 11 November a cabinet decision laid down the regulations of the 'School of the Nation'. Articles 3 and 4 read: 'Every male and female Turkish citizen is a member of this organization'; 'The chief instructor of the School of the Nation is His Excellency the President of the Republic, Gazi Mustafa Kemal.'[73]

[72] *Millî Eğ. Söylev*, i. 32–33; variant versions in *Söylev*, ii. 254–5; *Hist.*, pp. 248–9.
[73] Jäschke, *Kalender*, 11 Nov. 1928.

Various arguments have been put forward to explain and justify the revolution in the alphabet. The Arabic letters were ill suited to express the sounds of the Turkish language; they were difficult to teach and troublesome to print, and thus constituted a barrier to education and cultural expansion. These charges are not without foundation, and it is certain that the new script, clear, simple, and phonetic, showed the way to a great increase in literacy and a vast expansion of publications. But the basic purpose of the change was not so much practical and pedagogical, as social and cultural—and Mustafa Kemal, in forcing his people to accept it, was slamming a door on the past as well as opening a door to the future. The way was now clear to the final break with the past and with the East—to the final incorporation of Turkey into the civilization of the. modern West. This desire, with the danger inherent in it, is well expressed by the distinguished Turkish writer Mme Halide Edib Adıvar:

> We can conceive of modern civilization as an entirety. That is to say, we cannot put on Western civilization as a whole the label English, or French, or Italian. Therefore, even a nation that is a late-comer to this civilization is not simply their follower, but is also part of Western civilization. Total and slavish imitation of a model is the very opposite of the spirit of Western civilization. This point needs special attention from late-comers to this civilization.[74]

Experiment with Democracy

The law authorizing emergency powers was renewed in 1927 for a further period of two years. On 4 March 1929 it was allowed to run out, and the government announced that it would not be extended. At first there was no response to this relaxation of administrative control. Then, in December 1929, a new newspaper, *Yarın* (Tomorrow), began to appear and attracted attention by its criticisms of the government. As in 1924, the attack was not levelled against Kemal but against the Prime Minister Ismet and especially against his economic policies. In April the paper was suppressed for one day, and on 17 May its editor, Arif Oruç, was sentenced to a month's imprisonment on a charge of writing provocative articles. Before long he was back at work, and continued his criticisms of the government and of individual government officials.[75]

[74] Halide Edib Adıvar, *Türkiye'de Şark* . . . (1946), p. 11.
[75] Jäschke, *Kalender*, and *OM*, under the relevant dates.

This mild reaction presaged a second experiment with a tolerated opposition. The first hint came from Mustafa Kemal himself, who mentioned at a ball in Yalova that a new party was about to be formed. On 9 August 1930 Fethi, back in Turkey from his embassy in Paris, wrote a letter to Mustafa Kemal complaining of the failure of the government's fiscal and economic policies, of the lack of free criticism in the Assembly, and of the resulting irresponsibility of the cabinet. What was needed, he said, was an opposition, and he therefore requested the President's views on his proposal to found a new party. Kemal replied reaffirming his belief in freedom of discussion, and expressing his gratification at Fethi's acceptance of the basic principles of the secular Republic. The letter and reply were duly published, and on 12 August Fethi submitted the constitution of the Free Republican Party to the acting Vali of Istanbul with the request that it be registered in accordance with the law of associations. The programme included greater freedom, lower taxes, better and less government.[76]

The short and unhappy life of the Free Republican Party remains an obscure episode in the history of the Turkish Republic, and has given rise to many different explanations. Some believe that Mustafa Kemal really wished to create a multi-party democracy in Turkey, and abandoned the attempt only when reactionary violence proved that it was premature. Others have said that he aimed only at a tame, manageable opposition to release tension during a time of economic crisis, and crushed it when it seemed to be getting out of hand. Others again have interpreted the episode as a disagreement between Kemal and Ismet, the former seeking a counterweight to Ismet and the People's Party, the latter finally convincing him that the experiment was too dangerous. Certainly the Free Republican Party, founded by the authority of Mustafa Kemal and operating under his close supervision, was far less independent than the Progressive Party of 1924, and looked even less like a serious alternative to the party in power.[77]

Whatever the truth of the matter, it soon became clear that the experiment was both premature and dangerous. Fethi and Ismet were careful to maintain the fullest courtesy and friendliness

[76] Tunaya, *Partiler*, pp. 622 ff. Ahmet Ağaoğlu, *Serbest Fırka hatiraları* (Istanbul, n.d.); Süreyya Ilmen, *Zavallı Serbest Fırka* (1951); Frey, *Elite* (1965), pp. 335–43.
[77] Ibid.

towards one another, but the appearance of a licensed opposition provoked an explosion of accumulated hatreds and resentments from many different quarters. Fethi's speeches were followed by riots and disturbances, and there were ominous stirrings in the eastern provinces. Finally, in November, the Gazi's loyal opposition was disbanded. On 15 November Fethi accused the government, in the Assembly, of electoral malpractices, and shortly afterwards announced his decision to dissolve the Free Republican Party 'because struggle against the Gazi was impossible'.[78] This decision was made known to the Ministry of the Interior in a letter of 17 November 1930. Two other minor parties that had appeared at about the same time, the Popular Republican Party and the minute Workers' and Peasants' Party, were dissolved by direct government order.[79]

Economic Development [80]

In October 1929 the crash on the New York Stock Exchange ushered in the great depression, which swiftly spread across the world, bringing trade stagnation and falling prices, unemployment and ruin. Turkey, though still very imperfectly assimilated into the Western world of capitalist free enterprise, was badly hit by the fall in the prices of agricultural produce, on which she depended very largely for her export trade. Substantially self-sufficient in foodstuffs, she was able to feed her own people and shield them from the most terrible consequences of the depression. But her economic position in other respects was very vulnerable. The economic clauses in the treaty of Lausanne had restricted her power to impose certain tariffs, and had left her with a backward and undeveloped industry and a dangerously unfavourable balance of trade. For many vital supplies she was dependent on imports from the more advanced industrial countries, for which she paid with exports of raw materials. With the fall in prices, the Turkish leaders were soon faced with a grave economic crisis, caused by events beyond their reach or control, but demanding from them immediate remedial action.

---

[78] Jäschke, *Kalender*, 17 Nov. 1930.   [79] Tunaya, *Partiler*, p. 635.

[80] For a critical assessment of Kemalist economic policies see Z.Y. Hershlag, 'Turkey: Achievements and Failures in the policy of economic development during the inter-war period 1919–1939', *Kyklos* (1954), pp. 323–50, and the same author's book, *Turkey; an Economy in Transition* (n.d., preface dated 1958).

The first measures taken by the Turkish government—as by most other governments affected by the crisis—were orthodox and restrictive, palliative rather than remedial in their effects, and intended to reduce the volume of foreign trade and to cut down government expenditure. Already in June 1929, following the expiration of the restrictions imposed by the Lausanne treaty, the Assembly had approved a new tariff law; it was intended to give necessary protection to the nascent Turkish industries which the Kemalist régime had been trying almost since its inception, but without much success, to foster. The new tariff came into force on 1 October 1929, just before the beginning of the depression, and the emphasis of Turkish fiscal policy was inevitably shifted from the original objective of fostering industry to the immediate need for restriction and protection. On 4 December restrictions were imposed on currency dealings and purchases abroad, and the rate of the Turkish pound dropped to TL11.10 to the pound sterling.

These, and other measures that followed, transformed the balance of trade in Turkey's favour, and gave some measure of protection to local products; in time they placed the whole foreign trade of the country under government control. The Turkish leaders were, however, well aware that these restrictions, though helpful in their immediate effects. did nothing to bring about what the country most needed—an economic expansion that would develop her resources, endow her with industry, raise the standard of living of the people, and make her less vulnerable to the vagaries of international trade. But how was such an expansion to be accomplished?

The depression of 1929, and the hardships that resulted from it, brought a revival of anti-Western and anti-capitalist feeling. Once again, as in the early days of the struggle for independence, it seemed to many Turks that capitalism and imperialism—the two were more or less identified—were the real enemies, that it was the West, at once greedy and inefficient, that was enslaving the backward nations, by preserving and exploiting their backwardness. The Ottoman Debt, the Lausanne restrictions, the trade deficit—and now a terrible crisis which the fumbling and stricken West seemed utterly unable to control or remedy and in which the Turks, innocent bystanders, had become painfully involved.

Capital and initiative were urgently needed for development;

who could provide them? After the struggle to end foreign control and interference, the new republican régime did not look kindly on foreign capital, nor for that matter did foreign investors show any great desire to put money into Turkey.[81] Local capitalist enterprise was lacking in both capital and enterprise, and such people as still possessed wealth after the long years of war, occupation, and revolution were reluctant to venture it in undertakings of a new and unfamiliar kind. The government for their part did little to encourage local private enterprise. A régime of soldiers and officials, they had retained much of the traditional contempt for trade and traders, all the more so since the commercial class in the large towns still consisted very largely of Christians and Jews.

The West had failed; it was inevitable that many eyes should turn to another part of the world, where a rival, totally different system of economic organization was being tried. Soviet Russia, with all her difficulties, had been little affected by the crisis of capitalism. Her state-directed, state-operated economy seemed immune to the depression, and even the governments of the capitalist West, in apparent defiance of their own principles, were trying to solve the crisis by increasing state intervention in economic matters. Turkey was soon to follow—and surpass—their example.

Russian Influences

The suggestion has often been made that the introduction of the Turkish policy of etatism was inspired by the example and precept of the Soviet Union. Certainly, there were points of resemblance, and even of direct contact. Since the early days of the Kemalist movement, when the two outlaw, revolutionary régimes were drawn together by 'the common struggle which both peoples have undertaken against the intervention of imperialism',[82] relations between the Turkish and Soviet Republics had been friendly.

---

[81] Apart from short-term business credits, only one foreign loan was accepted by the Turkish Republic before 1933. That was a loan of $10 million negotiated by Ivar Kreuger in 1930, in return for a monopoly of match production in Turkey. This one experiment was not encouraging (Hershlag, *Turkey*, pp. 121–2. Orhan Conker and Émile Witmeur, *Redressement économique et industrialisation de la nouvelle Turquie*, 1937, pp. 198–200).

[82] Turco-Russian treaty of friendship, 16 Mar. 1921. Text in J. C. Hurewitz, *Diplomacy in the Near and Middle East*, ii (1956), 95. cf. Jäschke, 'Der Weg zur russisch-türkischen Freundschaft', *WI*, xvi (1934), 23–28; Hershlag, *Turkey*, pp. 77 ff., and above, p. 253.

After a temporary chill during the Lausanne period, they grew warmer in 1924–5, when a clash with Britain over the Mosul question again inclined Turkish sentiments away from the West and towards the Soviets, and led to the signature of a Russo-Turkish treaty of friendship on 17 December 1925.

This diplomatic friendship brought no ideological influences. Kemal had made it clear from the start that, whatever might be the arguments for Communism in Russia, he had no use for it in Turkey. On more than one occasion he specifically disavowed any affinity between Kemalist and Communist ideologies, and as early as January 1921 took steps to counter Communist activities in Turkey. In 1922 Rauf's government banned Communist propaganda; in 1925 the last semi-legal vestiges of the Turkish Communist Party were finally outlawed.[83] In Russia, these affronts to the Communist cause were swallowed for political reasons, and the ideologists of the Comintern were busy explaining that Kemal, though anti-Communist, could be regarded as progressive, and even revolutionary, since he was destroying the remnants of feudalism, pursuing liberal agrarian policies, initiating industrial development, and resisting the encroachments of the capitalist West.[84]

In 1928–9, in the course of a general ideological reorientation in Moscow, a new line of interpretation was adopted, and Kemal was abruptly transformed from a revolutionary hero to a reactionary tyrant.

Kemalism had ceased to be a mass movement, and was on the way to total capitulation. It had destroyed some, but by no means all, of the feudal vestiges in the Turkish villages, and its social basis was an alliance between the top layers of the bourgeoisie and the big landowners, plus the 'kulaks'. Kemal was said to rule by means of a unique mixture of terror and social demagogy, a special Turkish brand of 'national fascism' or 'agrarian Bonapartism'.

Kemal, according to this view, was a fascist; under his rule Turkey was falling back into Imperialist domination and social reaction.[85]

These changes inevitably affected relations between the two governments. The Russian reassessment of the Kemalist régime led to a renewal of Turkish Communist activity against it, which in turn led to new and more forceful repressive measures by the

[83] Tunaya, *Partiler*, p. 552; W. Z. Laqueur, *Communism and Nationalism* (1956), pp. 210–11 and *The Soviet Union and the Middle East* (1959), pp. 25–29.

[84] Laqueur, *Soviet Union*, pp. 87–88.   [85] Ibid. p. 105.

Turkish authorities. In the summer of 1929 these were reported in the Soviet press, which condemned, in strong language, the actions of the Turkish government and its economic policies. The Turkish press replied defending them, and drawing the attention of the Russians to some of their own shortcomings. When the newspapers on both sides are government organs, press polemics easily become international disputes.[86]

In these circumstances, it is the more remarkable that there should have been such a dramatic improvement in Turco-Russian relations a few months later. The first sign came in November 1929, when a commercial agreement with the USSR was initialed. On 11 December a company for trade with the USSR, founded by the Agricultural Bank and the Bank of Industry and Mines, began work. On 13 December the Soviet Deputy Commissar for Foreign Affairs, Karakhan, arrived in Ankara, where he was received by Mustafa Kemal, and on 17 December a 'Russo-Turkish Protocol' was signed, renewing the agreement of 1925. Relations became still closer in September 1930, when the Turkish Foreign Minister Tevfik Rüştü [Aras] went on a visit to Moscow. This was followed by other visits— Litvinov in Ankara in October 1931, Ismet Paşa in Moscow in April–May 1932, Voroshilov in Ankara in October 1933, Celâl Bayar in Moscow in July 1935. The most important of these visits was that of the Turkish Prime Minister and Foreign Minister to Moscow in 1932, where on 8 May they signed an agreement with the USSR for a loan of $8 million. Most of it was used for the development of the textile industry, through the Soviet-guided *kombinat* at Kayseri.

At a time when the West was still in the grip of the depression, the Soviets were thus able to offer a method of economic expansion, capital to initiate it, and experts to assist in its application. The Kemalist adoption of etatism was not due to any political or ideological leanings to the Soviet Union or to Communism, but to the sheer practical necessities of the moment. The country, still not fully recovered from the ruin and impoverishment brought by earlier struggles and upheavals, was now again stricken by the consequences of a world-wide crisis in which the Turkish leaders had neither responsibility nor control. Help was urgently needed; it must be taken where it could be found.

[86] Ahmet Şükrü Esmer, *Siyasî Tarih, 1919–39* (1953), pp. 204–5.

Etatism

The first hint of the new economic policy came in a speech of Ismet Paşa at Sivas in 1930, when he stressed the need for greater economic activity by the state. Then, on 20 April 1931, Mustafa Kemal published his famous manifesto, in which he set forth, for the first time, the six 'fundamental and unchanging principles' which were adopted the following month by a general conference of the Republican People's Party, and later incorporated in the constitution. They are still represented by the six arrows of the party crest. 'The Republican's People's Party', says the first article of the manifesto, 'is republican, nationalist, populist, etatist, secularist, and revolutionary.'

Of these principles, only one was new—that of *devletçilik*, usually translated etatism. It was defined in the third article of the manifesto in these words:

Although considering private work and activity a basic idea, it is one of our main principles to interest the State actively in matters where the general and vital interests of the nation are in question, especially in the economic field, in order to lead the nation and the country to prosperity in as short a time as possible.[87]

Further definitions of etatism were given, in the following years, by the party, the government, and Kemal himself. The spokesmen of etatism were at some pains to point out that they were not socialists. They had no intention of collectivizing the economy or establishing state monopolies; they would not touch agriculture at all, and had no desire to eliminate private enterprise from industry and commerce. Their purpose was to initiate and develop projects in fields which were of vital concern to the strength and well-being of the nation, and in which private capital was incapable, inactive, or dilatory.

In 1933 the first Turkish five-year plan was prepared, for the expansion of Turkish industry; it was approved on 9 January 1934, and completed in 1939. This plan was no doubt inspired by the Soviet precedent, and was certainly helped by the Soviet loan and Soviet advice. Its aim was the simultaneous development of consumer industries, chiefly textiles, and also paper, glass,

---

[87] *OM*, May 1931, pp. 225–6; official English version, from the 1935 programme, in J. Parker and C. Smith, *Modern Turkey* (1940), p. 238. Cf. Hershlag, *Turkey*, p. 86.

and ceramics, and of the basic industrial potential, especially iron, steel, and chemicals. The most important achievements were the Soviet-planned textile factory (the *kombinat*) at Kayseri, with 33,000 spindles, and the British-constructed iron and steel works at Karabük.[88]

As the five-year plan developed, the Turkish economic planners, though still reaffirming their respect for private enterprise, showed little interest in its expansion or even survival. Once again, the reasons were not doctrinal.

> The system of etatism applied in Turkey [said Mustafa Kemal at the Izmir Fair in August 1935], is not a system copied and translated from the ideas that socialist theoreticians have been putting forward since the 19th century; our etatism takes as its basis the private initiative and personal aptitudes of individuals, but at the same time, taking account of all the needs of a great nation and a broad land, and of the fact that so much still remains to be done, it rests on the principle that the state must take charge of the national economy.[89]

Economists have on the whole been severe in their judgement of the economic achievements of Turkish etatism. Undoubtedly, it endowed the country with many new industrial enterprises. There were factories for textiles at Kayseri, Eregli, Nazilli, Malatya, and Bursa; paper and cellulose at Izmir, artificial silk at Gemlik, glass and bottles at Paşabahçe, china-ware at Kütahya, sulphur at Keçiborlu, cement at Sivas. In heavy industry there were the great anthracite works at Zonguldak, and the iron and steel works at Karabük. But the efforts of the Turkish planners—and of their foreign advisers—were all too often inept, confused, and misdirected, and there are many tales of wasteful and inefficient factories, producing shoddy products at high prices.

> What we see in Turkey [says the Thornburg report] looks, not like a planned economy, but like a poorly managed capitalist economy in which most of the capital happens to be supplied by the government. . . . The result [of Soviet influence] is a hybrid which does not embody the best potentialties of either of its parents.[90]

The Thornburg report accuses the etatist planners not only of botching their own work, but also of preventing the expansion of

[88] See the comments in M. W. Thornburg and others, *Turkey, an Economic Appraisal* (1949), pp. 109 ff.
[89] Baydar, p. 87; cf. Hershlag, *Turkey*, p. 89, and below, pp. 469 ff.
[90] Thornburg, p. 39.

private enterprise which might otherwise have taken place. 'Private enterprise did not fail; it was deliberately discouraged.'[91] The report of the International Bank for Reconstruction and Development, on the other hand, concedes that 'under etatism Turkey has made substantial progress. It is doubtful whether comparable accomplishment would have taken place in this period under domestic private enterprise with the handicap of the Ottoman heritage.'[92]

Perhaps the most serious defect of the whole operation was the almost complete neglect of agriculture. 'Consequently', says Hershlag, 'the greatest natural asset of the country remained unexploited, agricultural production did not increase and only a limited labour force was released for urban industries.'[93]

The Last Years

During the 1930's the government of the Republic was mainly concerned with economic matters and, later, with the looming menace of Axis aggression. Mustafa Kemal did, however, find time for a few further measures of Westernization and reform. A second experiment, in 1930, with Western-style democratic government had been abandoned after a short time, and the attempt was not renewed until 1945.[94] But other forms of Westernization continued. In December 1934 women were given the right to vote in parliamentary elections and to be elected as deputies, and in the election of 1935 seventeen women were elected.

The same year 1935 brought two other notable innovations. The first was the compulsory adoption, by all Turks, of surnames; the second was the introduction, in all government and public offices, of a weekly holiday from 1 p.m. Saturday until Monday morning.

Both these measures involved radical departures from Islamic custom, albeit minor in comparison with those already accomplished. The weekly day of rest is a Jewish and Christian, but, though not unknown in Ottoman times, not a Muslim custom; the Muslim Friday is a day of public worship, but not a Sabbath, and traditionally it was the day of greatest activity in the markets centred round the mosque. There was some move-

[91] Ibid. p. 34.
[92] *The Economy of Turkey* (1951), p. 9.
[93] *Kyklos*, p. 324; cf. his *Turkey*, pp. 143 ff.
[94] See above, p. 279, and below, pp. 381–2.

ment towards a weekly day of rest in Ottoman times, but it remained informal. The weekly day of rest, on Friday, was first introduced by the Assembly for railway workers in 1920, and in 1924 was made general for all towns with more than 10,000 inhabitants. The transfer of the weekly day of rest from the Muslim Friday to the Christian Sunday had obvious economic and administrative advantages, and followed logically on the adoption of the Western clock and the Western calendar.[95]

The Turks, like most other Muslim peoples, were not in the habit of using family names. A man would be known by his personal name, given at birth, supplemented by a second name given in childhood, or by his father's name. Surnames existed, but were rare, and not in common usage. The more complex and extensive relationships of a modern society made a system of family names desirable; the adoption of the new civil code made it immediately necessary. A law of 28 June 1934 imposed on every Turkish citizen the obligation to adopt a surname with effect from 1 January 1935.[96] At the same time all non-military ranks and titles surviving from the old régime were abolished, and replaced by the new words *Bay* and *Bayan*—Mr. and Mrs. The Prime Minister was given, by the President, the name of the place where he had won a victory, and became Ismet Inönü. The President renounced his titles and received from the Assembly the name Atatürk—father-Turk. At the same time he dropped the excessively Arabic 'Mustafa' thus becoming Kemal Atatürk, the name by which he was known for the rest of his life, and after.[97]

In the early months of 1938, during a journey in Anatolia, Kemal Atatürk was taken ill.

After a brief recovery his condition worsened rapidly, and on 5 September he thought it advisable to make his will. On 1 November, when the new session of the Assembly opened its proceedings, the President's message was, for the first time, read for him by the Prime Minister, and on 10 November a stunned and anguished nation learned that the great leader who had guided it for nearly twenty years was dead. 'The Turkish fatherland', said the government communiqué, 'has lost its great builder, the Turkish nation its mighty leader, mankind a great son.'[98] On

[95] Jäschke, in *WI*, n.s., i. 50 ff. [96] Ibid. p. 53.

[97] The replacement of Kemal by the allegedly more Turkish-sounding Kamal was of brief duration, and did not pass into common usage.

[98] *IA*, i. 798.

16 November his coffin, on a catafalque draped with the Turkish flag, was placed in the great reception hall of the Dolmabahçe Palace in Istanbul, where for three days and nights an endless stream of mourners passed to pay their last respects. On the 19th Professor Şerefeddin Yaltkaya, a distinguished Islamic scholar and theologian, recited the Muslim funeral prayers over his body, and twelve generals carried the catafalque to a gun-carriage waiting outside the Palace. A mighty funeral cortége followed it to the Gülhane park, where the coffin was placed on board a torpedo boat and then transferred to the battleship *Yavuz*, the former *Göben*. From there it was landed at Izmit and taken by a special train to Ankara, where it was consigned, with full military honours, to a temporary tomb in the Ethnographical Museum. In 1953 it was transferred to its final resting place in the newly completed mausoleum at Rasat Tepe, on the outskirts of the capital.

Kemal Atatürk was a man of swift and decisive action, of sudden and often violent decision. A tough and brilliant soldier, a hard drinker and wencher, he was in all things a man of immense will and abounding vitality. By his contemporaries he was often called a dictator, and in a sense he certainly was. But in saying this one must remember that his rule was very different from that of other men, in Europe and the Middle East yesterday and today, to whom the same term is applied. An autocrat by personal and professional bias, dominating and imperious by temperament, he yet showed a respect for decency and legality, for human and political standards, that is in astonishing contrast with the behaviour of lesser and more pretentious men. His was a dictatorship without the uneasy over-the-shoulder glance, the terror of the door-bell, the dark menace of the concentration camp. Force and repression were certainly used to establish and maintain the Republic during the period of revolutionary changes, but no longer; and after the executions of 1926 there was little danger to life and to personal liberty. Political activity against the régime was banned and newspapers were under strict control. But apart from this, talk, and even books and periodicals, were comparatively free. Critics of the régime from the humbler classes were left alone; critics among the ruling *élite* were, in accordance with earlier Ottoman practice, punished with governorships or embassies in remote places. Violence was rare, and was usually in response to violent opposition.

The subsequent rise of military régimes in other Muslim countries in the Middle East has led some observers to see in Atatürk and his Revolution the prototype of these later movements. There is, however, very little resemblance between them. Atatürk was not a revolutionary junior officer seizing power by coup d'état, but a general and a pasha, taking control by gradual, almost reluctant steps in a moment of profound national crisis. He and his associates, though imbued with new ideas, were by status and habit men of the old Ottoman ruling *élite*, with centuries of military and Imperial experience. Even after the destruction of the Empire and the banishment of the dynasty, they still had the assurance and authority to demand—and receive—obedience, not needing either to court popularity or enforce submission. And so they were able to carry through their Revolution by a kind of paternalistic guidance, without resort to the whole monstrous apparatus of demagogy and repression familiar in the European dictatorships and their imitations elsewhere.

It was as a soldier that Atatürk first rose to lead his people—as the brilliant and inspired leader who snatched the Sick Man of Europe from his death-bed and infused him with a new life and vitality. His first great achievements were in the heroic mode—in fashioning an army, a movement, and a nation from the débris of the shattered Empire and driving the invaders from the national soil.

Yet it is not in these achievements, great as they were, that the true greatness of Atatürk lies. Rather does it lie in his realization that all this was enough—and yet not enough; that the military task was completed, and another, very different one remained. In 1923, at the moment of his triumph, there were many opportunities which might have tempted a military commander to seek more glory, or a nationalist leader to arouse new passions. He renounced them all, and with a realism, restraint, and moderation unusual among heroes, warned his people against all such heady adventures. The next task was at home—for when all the invaders, military, financial, political, had gone, there still remained the problem of rebuilding the country, already backward, now further weakened by long years of war and internal struggle. It is the supreme merit of Kemal Atatürk that he—the Ottoman soldier, the victorious hero, was able to see this, and to make the immense effort of imagination and courage that it required of him.

In a society that despised labour and trade, where ingenuity was an infidel trick and the military virtues the only universally accepted standard, the Gazi Pasha became a civilian President, and setting aside his uniform, appeared to his people in a top hat and evening dress. With this new image of himself Kemal Atatürk, the master of social symbolism, made it clear to his people that, for the time being, the age of martial valour in holy war had ended; the time had come for the solid, bourgeois virtues of industry, skill, and thrift, needed in the hard, unglamorous, but urgent task of developing the country and raising the standard of living of her people.

In his political ideas Kemal Atatürk was an heir to the Young Turks—more especially of the nationalist, positivist, and Westernizing wing among them. The two dominant beliefs of his life were in the Turkish nation and in progress; the future of both lay in civilization, which for him meant the modern civilization of the West, and no other. His nationalism was healthy and reasonable; there was no arrogant trampling on the rights or aspirations of other nations, no neurotic rejection of responsibility for the national past. The Turks were a great people of great achievement, who had gone astray through the evil effects of certain elements and forces among them; they must be restored to the path of progress, to find their place in the community of civilized nations. 'The Turks', he said in 1924, 'are the friends of all civilized nations. Countries vary, but civilization is one, and for a nation to progress it must take part in this single civilization.'[99]

Unlike so many reformers, Kemal Atatürk was well aware that a mere façade of modernization was worthless, and that if Turkey was to hold her own in the world of our time, fundamental changes were necessary in the whole structure of society and culture. Opinions are divided on the success and on the wisdom of some of his policies. If on the one hand there were complaints that the reforms were limited in their application to the towns and urban classes, and brought little change to the peasant mass of the population, on the other hand there were many who felt that the reforms were too violent and abrupt, and caused a rupture with the religious and cultural traditions of the nation that was harmful in its effects on the younger generation.

[99] Baydar, p. 49.

Whatever views one may hold on these points, this much is indisputable—that, at the darkest moment in their history, the Kemalist Revolution brought new life and hope to the Turkish people, restored their energies and self-respect, and set them firmly on the road not only to independence, but to that rarer and more precious thing that is freedom.

CHAPTER IX

The Republic after Kemal

Any human being who believes that the destinies of other human beings depend wholly upon him personally is a petty man, failing to grasp the most elementary facts. Every man is doomed to perish physically. The only way to stay happy while we live is to work, not for ourselves, but for those to come.

KEMAL ATATÜRK, March 1938.

The ultimate results of a social struggle can never be of the kind envisaged by those who carry it out. Some such struggles depend on an infinite and complex series of circumstances beyond the controllable range of human intellect and action. This is most true of revolutions that demand superhuman efforts and that effect hasty and radical changes in society.

MILOVAN DJILAS, 'The New Class', 1957.

On 11 November 1938, the day after Atatürk's death, the Grand National Assembly of Turkey unanimously voted to appoint Ismet Inönü, his lifelong friend and closest collaborator, as his successor. The vital decision seems to have rested with three men: Ismet Inönü himself, Marshal Fevzi Çakmak, the Chief of Staff, and Celâl Bayar, a banker and economist who had replaced Ismet Inönü as Prime Minister in September 1937. They agreed on Ismet as President, and co-operated in ensuring a smooth transition and a stable and continuous régime. The first President of the Turkish Republic was dead, but the Republic lived, and the second President was chosen and took office, without break or interruption. On 25 January 1939 Celâl Bayar was replaced as Prime Minister by Dr. Refik Saydam, who remained in office until his death in June 1942.

The spontaneous and moving demonstrations of grief by the great mass of the people at the death of Atatürk showed clearly that, whatever conflicts and repressions there might have been in the past, he had by then succeeded in winning the respect and indeed the love of the Turkish people. The old, reactionary opposition was crushed; no new opposition, offering not a mere return to the past but a different way forward, had yet appeared— and in the meantime a new generation was growing up in the schools that had never known any régime but the Republic.

It was as well that Inönü could count on a tranquil and loyal country, for difficult and dangerous times lay ahead. When Atatürk died, the war clouds were already gathering over Europe, and there is an oral tradition that his last political testament to his people had been 'to be as ready as possible and then, come what might, to stay on England's side, because that side was certain to win in the long run'.[1]

Authentic or not, this dictum seems to have expressed the views at least of Ismet Inönü, who on 19 October 1939 signed a treaty of alliance with Great Britain and France. But by the summer of 1940 there were few in Turkish government circles who shared them. Yakup Kadri Karaosmanoğlu, then Turkish ambassador at The Hague, has described how, when he returned to Ankara, after a shattering ordeal, in May 1940, and was 'bold enough' to state his belief that England would not be defeated, 'among all our statesmen only Ismet Inönü and Refik Saydam took me seriously'. The Secretary-General of the Ministry, far from attaching any importance to his views, accused him of misleading the President with false information.[2]

The fall of France, the hostile attitude of Russia, and the extension of German power or influence over most of Europe led the Turkish government to the conclusion that nothing would be gained by provoking a German invasion and an almost certain German conquest. They therefore decided, in June 1940, not to fulfil their obligations under the treaty of alliance. Instead, they embarked on a policy of uneasy and ambiguous neutrality, in which the one firm and guiding principle was the determination not to repeat the tragic error of October 1914. Turkish opinion was, to a large extent, sympathetic to the Allies, but from 1940 that sympathy was vitiated by a widespread conviction that the Axis would win; in June 1941, when German expansion in the Balkans had brought the German armies within 100 miles of Istanbul, the Turks tried to insure themselves by signing a friendship and trade agreement with Germany, in which, however, they stipulated that Turkey would maintain her treaty obligations to Britain.

After the German attack on Russia in 1941, Turkish feelings towards the Axis began to assume a more positive form. Russia

[1] Lewis V. Thomas and R. N. Frye, *The United States and Turkey and Iran* (1951), p. 89.
[2] Karaosmanoğlu, *Zoraki Diplomat* (1955), pp. 34–35.

was after all their ancient hereditary enemy, against whose relentless southward advance they had been fighting a desperate
rearguard defence for centuries; and the scanty reserve of goodwill built up during the period of revolutionary fraternity had
been dissipated by Soviet hectoring in 1939. In attacking Russia,
the Germans won the support of an important body of Turkish
opinion, and added genuine sympathy to the previous calculation.

The Allies, of course, increased their pressure on Turkey to join
what was now becoming the Grand Alliance. On 3 December 1941
President Roosevelt extended lease-lend aid to Turkey; in February
1943 Mr. Churchill visited Turkey and met Turkish statesmen at
Adana; in December 1943 President Inönü went to Cairo to meet
the British and American leaders. But Inönü still hung back, and
Turkish opinion in general supported him in his policy of
neutrality. One of the main considerations was mistrust of Russia,
and the widespread feeling that Nazi conquest and Soviet liberation were equally to be feared. 'What we would really like',
remarked a Turk during the war, 'would be for the Germans to
destroy Russia and for the Allies to destroy Germany. Then we
would feel safe.' This proved impossible to arrange, and by 1943
the ruling circles in Ankara began to realize that the Axis cause
was in any case doomed to defeat. From this time on the Turks
began to enter into ever closer economic and military relations
with the West, and aided the Allied cause in a variety of ways.
In August 1944 they broke off diplomatic relations with Germany,
and on 23 February 1945 declared war on Germany in order to
comply with the formalities of entry to the United Nations Conference in San Francisco.

The war years subjected Turkey to severe economic strains, and
increased the scale and severity of government intervention in
economic life. The etatist laws already provided the framework
for a system of wartime controls, and a 'National Defence Law',
approved on 18 January 1940, gave the government extensive
emergency economic powers. The second five-year plan, launched
in 1939, was nullified by the high rate of military expenditure and
the shortage of raw materials, and even agricultural production
was adversely affected by the maintenance of partial mobilization.[3]

Foreign trade, on the other hand, flourished. Turkish products

[3] Hershlag, *Turkey*, pp. 177 ff.

were in high demand, and were sold at strategic rather than commercial prices. This development, coupled with the high rate of government expenditure and the shortage of essential commodities, led to a considerable inflationary pressure.[4] Great fortunes were being made by the merchants, brokers, and agents in Istanbul. Partly because of tax evasion, but mostly because of the absence of any effective modern system of tax assessment and collection, these fortunes were substantially exempt from taxation or control by the government.

In these circumstances, the government decided on an emergency fiscal measure—a capital levy. Such a levy, in a country going through an economic and financial crisis, could be considered normal and justifiable, as a means of collecting revenue and as an instrument of control over the national economy. In fact, the levy was conceived and applied in a manner neither normal nor justifiable.[5]

The *Varlık Vergisi* (capital tax), as it was called, was approved by the Assembly on 11 November 1942, and came into force next day.[6]

Two groups had made the largest profits from the war; the large farmers, who had gained enormously from the rise in agricultural prices, and the merchants and middlemen of Istanbul, who had been in a position to exploit both the high value of Turkish exports and the desperate shortage of necessary imports. The farmers consisted almost entirely of Muslim Turks; the merchants were still largely, though not entirely, members of the three minority communities, the Greeks, Jews, and Armenians.

[4] Ibid. pp. 179–80.

[5] There are many accounts of the capital levy, the most accessible being those of L. V. Thomas and G. L. Lewis in the books already cited. For a detailed and documented account by a senior tax official see the work of Faik Ökte, cited below.

[6] Faik Ökte, the Defterdar (Director of Finance) of Istanbul, has recorded that when the details of the law were published in the press, his former Professor at the Faculty of Economics telephoned him early in the morning to ask for explanations. The conversation, as he relates it, ran as follows:
'—Faik, my boy, the text of the capital tax appeared in this morning's paper.
—Yes, Professor.
—Naturally the journalists got it wrong, they gave an incomplete text. . . .
—No, in all the newspapers I saw the text was complete. . . .
—How so, complete? No provision for objections or appeal! No indication of the rate of taxation. . . .
—That is the kind of tax it is, Professor.
—My boy, have you all gone mad!' (*Varlık Vergisi Faciası* (1951), p. 64.)

The tax law provided for a levy on property owners, owners of large farms, business men, and certain categories of taxpayers, who were paying tax on salaries or earnings. Owners of large farms could not be taxed at more than 5 per cent. of their capital; limited companies would be required to pay between 50 and 75 per cent. of their net profits for 1941. For other taxpayers, assessments would be made by special commissions, 'in accordance with their opinions'.

In this last category no rate of taxation was ever announced, no declaration of income or capital was ever required. The local tax boards made their estimates, and posted the lists of payments to be made. Their decisions were final, and not subject to appeal. Payment was required within fifteen days, failing which fines would be imposed. If payment was not made within a month the defaulters would be deported for forced labour.

It soon became apparent that the really important data determining a taxpayer's assessment were his religion and nationality. From subsequent revelations, it is known that the taxpayers were classified in two separate lists, the M list, for Muslims, and the G list, for non-Muslims (*Gayrimüslim*). Later, two other categories were added, E for foreigners (*Ecnebi*) and D for *Dönme*, members of the Sabbatayan sect of Jewish converts to Islam. *Dönmes* paid about twice as much as Muslims, non-Muslims up to ten times as much. Foreigners, on instructions from Ankara, were to be assessed at the same rate as Muslims,[7] but poor registration and inefficient administration led to the taxing of many foreigners as if they had been non-Muslim Turkish citizens, thus provoking the intervention of the foreign embassies and consulates on behalf of their nationals.

Early in January 1943 the press began to publish lists of names of defaulters, together with the amounts of their assessments, and it was announced that they would be sent to break stones for the new road at Aşkale. On 12 January the press announced relaxations for salaried persons, minors, women, the aged, and the sick. The remaining defaulters would be deported, and would have to pay the cost of their transport, food, and medical treatment if required. Tax defaulters serving with the colours would be transferred to the forced labour camps on completing their military service.

[7] Except for Jewish subjects of the Axis states, who were excluded from this privilege (Ökte, p. 81).

Although appeals were not allowed, taxpayers had a constitutional right of petition, and by January more than 10,000 petitions were received by the Revenue Department, almost all of which were rejected. Only a number of assessments, on persons already dead or businesses already bankrupt, were cancelled. Arrests and seizures of property went on daily, and the auction rooms were choked with confiscated property. The first party of deportees, numbering thirty-two, left Istanbul for Aşkale on 27 January.

The lists of names appearing in the press of defaulters and of persons arrested or deported, consisted almost entirely of non-Muslims—Greeks, Jews, and Armenians. The press, led by the pro-Axis *Cümhuriyet* and *Tasvir-i Efkâr*, expressed cordial approval, and spoke of people of 'alien blood', 'Turks only in name', who must be punished for their disloyalty and ingratitude.

In fact, it was the loyal, rather than the disloyal, who were punished. Those members of the minorities who had retained or obtained foreign protection at the time of the armistice and Allied occupation were able to get their assessments reduced to the Muslim level or something near it; those who had trusted in the new Republic and thrown their lot in with it, were subjected to victimization and punishment.[8]

Through the spring and summer the arrests, seizures, and deportations continued, almost all of non-Muslims. Many business men were ruined by assessments greater than their total possessions; others, though wealthy enough to pay, were bankrupted because no time was allowed them to find enough liquid money.[9] Most tragic was the position of the numerous poor—the artisans, wage-earners, and even the beggars, ragmen and boot-blacks, licensed occupations with lists of licence-holders in official possession. These, if non-Muslims, were in most cases taxed at figures wildly beyond their ability to pay, and then sold up for their failure to do so. Later, some remissions were granted in this category.

In June 1943 it was announced that the capital levy would be wound up by 31 July, and that persons who had not paid by that date would be deported to labour camps. The Prime Minister, in a speech to the People's Party congress on 15 June, denied indignantly that the capital levy had been used as an instrument to crush the minorities. It was true, he said, that 105 million out of the 270 millions collected so far had been paid by members of the

[8] cf. Ökte, pp. 123–4.   [9] Ibid. p. 149.

minorities and foreigners, but this was reasonable since they had all the real estate and sources of wealth in their hands.

By this time, the star of Germany was setting, and Western interest in the tax was becoming a source of discomfort.[10] On 21 September it was announced that the Finance Department was preparing lists of remissions and on 1 October Ahmet Emin Yalman, the editor of *Vatan*, published the first criticism of the tax to appear in the Turkish press.[11] At the end of October the Prime Minister gave an interview to the editor of a Greek-language newspaper in Istanbul, and denied that the minorities had suffered any injustice. In December 1943, just before Inönü's visit to Cairo to met Roosevelt and Churchill, the last deportees were brought back to Istanbul. On 15 March 1944—the day the Allies began their final assault on Monte Cassino—a law was passed by the Assembly releasing all defaulters still detained and cancelling all amounts still unpaid. The capital levy, in expiring, thus achieved its final ineptitude, by penalizing those who had made payment and rewarding those who had somehow managed to avoid it.

In a book written in 1947 and published in 1951, Faik Ökte, the Defterdar of Istanbul, tells with complete frankness the story of the origins, application, and end of the capital levy, in which, albeit with distaste and reluctance, he played the leading part required of him by his office. Turkey, he says, needed an extraordinary tax on capital, in the situation in which she found herself at that time. She did not need this misbegotten offspring of German racialism on Ottoman fanaticism.[12]

The receipts from the tax amounted to 314,920,940 Turkish liras—at the rate of exchange of that time, roughly £28 million. This was 74·11 per cent. of the total amount demanded.[13] In his final chapters the former Defterdar of Istanbul examines the results of the 'lawlessness and disorder'[14] involved in the enrich-

[10] Apart from occasional expressions of fatherly approval in Germany, the Turkish capital levy had hitherto passed without comment or criticism in the world press. The Allied conspiracy of silence seems to have been first broken in an Armenian weekly, *Hairenik*, in Boston, which on 30 June, under the title 'The Beast Breaks Loose Again', denounced the tax as a new piece of Turkish barbarism. A more balanced discussion appeared in a series of five articles in the *New York Times* from 9 to 13 Sept., which described the tax and its application in some detail, and considered the political implications of what had happened.

[11] Ökte, pp. 195–6.   [12] Ibid. pp. 38–39.   [13] Ibid. p. 197.
[14] Ibid. p. 209.

ment of the treasury by this amount. The business world of
Istanbul had been shaken and dislocated.[15] The tax had actually
worked to the advantage of the black market, enriching the large
operators by the opportunities it afforded them and increasing the
number of small operators by the ruination of legitimate businesses
and the destitution of those who had lived by them.[16] The tax
had failed to achieve its economic objectives, and had ended with
the complete collapse of the price policy that had inspired it.

The most precious currency that we lost by this tax in the realm of
finance was the confidence of the citizen in the state. . . . Industry,
commerce, all economic life can only live by breathing an atmosphere
of confidence; with the capital levy this atmosphere was poisoned. . . .[17]

The effect on Turkey's reputation abroad was even worse. The
good reputation which the Turkish Republic had won since its
establishment for financial probity and for religious tolerance was
shattered. It was not easy to build up again.

For the Turkish patriot, the most unforgivable aspect of the
capital levy was the degradation which it brought to the sovereignty and dignity of Turkey. By imposing unjust and discriminatory taxes on foreign citizens, Turkey invited the intervention
of the powers in her internal affairs; by then rectifying those
assessments under foreign pressure, the government of Atatürk's
Republic had themselves brought back the most shameful and
degrading features of the long-abolished Capitulations.

It is with this final comment that Faik Ökte ends his book: 'For
my part, I am still astonished that for this blow struck against the
honour and dignity of the state, we were not all of us, with the
Prime Minister at our head, indicted before the High Council.'[18]

The capital levy was a sad affair. It has been since described
and discussed by foreign observers and was probably, in the long
run, more harmful to the 'honour and dignity' of the Turkish
state than to its immediate victims. Its effects should not, however, be exaggerated. In a Europe dominated by Hitler's Germany, Republican Turkey's one essay in persecution was a mild
and gentle affair. For the Turks, it should be remembered,
Germany was an essential and central part of that Europe which
they so much admired and had for more than a century been
trying to emulate. They had seen how the Nazis behaved in
Germany and had also seen the statesmen of Europe accept them

[15] Ibid. p. 202.   [16] Ibid. p. 203.   [17] Ibid. p. 210.   [18] Ibid. p. 213.

and fraternize with them; subsequent denunciations of Nazi tyranny lost much of their cogency in following after the outbreak of war, and seemed to be no more than acts of political warfare. To the outside observer, Europe could no more disclaim the Germans than Germany could disclaim the Nazis.

The liquidation of the capital levy was accompanied by other evidences of diminishing German influence. In May 1944 demonstrations by students in Ankara led to the investigation by the police of pan-Turanian groups, accused of holding fascist, racialist, doctrines and—what was more to the point—of plotting to overthrow the régime and the constitution and establish a government that would bring Turkey into the war on the side of Germany.[19]

The trial and condemnation of the pan-Turanians in September 1944 was an obvious attempt to placate the Soviet Union; it failed in its purpose. In spite of this and other advances by the Turkish government, the Soviets would not be placated, and on 19 March denounced the Turco-Soviet treaty of friendship and neutrality which had been signed in 1925 and was due for another renewal. This opened the way to the presentation of a series of demands for territorial concessions, bases, and a revision of the 1936 Montreux Convention, governing the Straits; all these Turkey steadfastly rejected.

The eclipse of Nazi Germany by defeat, the estrangement of Soviet Russia by political conflict, removed the two influences which, during the 1930's and early 1940's, had seemed for a while to be supplanting the liberal and democratic West and setting Turkey an example of totalitarian autocracy in her path of modernization. Once again, as in 1918, the democracies had triumphed over their autocratic enemies, and were setting the tone of progress and development. And, although, in the hard years that followed, many nations and governments revised their estimates of the balance of power and prospects, and adjusted their allegiances accordingly, the Turks have seen no reason to abandon the Western alignment of their foreign policy, or the Westernizing trend of their internal development.

[19] On these movements see Jäschke, 'Der Turanismus und die kemalistische Türkei', in R. Hartmann and H. Scheel, eds., *Beiträge zur Arabistik, Semitistik und Islamwissenschaft* (1944), pp. 468–83; R. Oğuz Türkkan, 'The Turkish Press', *MEA*, i (1950), 142–9; C. W. Hostler, 'Trends in Pan-Turanism', ibid. iii (1952), 3–13 and *Turkism and the Soviets* (1957); Karpat, pp. 264 ff.

The Coming of Democracy [20]

Perhaps the most important single fact in the democratic development of post-Kemalist Turkey is that in May 1950 a really free and fair election was held which resulted in an overwhelming victory for the opposition over the government. After twenty-seven years of almost uninterrupted rule by the Republican People's Party, most of the time without any opposition party to challenge it, a government of that party presided over a free and peaceful election which resulted in its own defeat and replacement. This momentous event, without any precedent in the history of the country and region, bears remarkable testimony to the constructive work of the Kemalist régime, and to the political maturing of the Turkish people under its aegis. In a sense, the electoral defeat of the People's Party was its greatest achievement—a second revolution, complementing and completing that earlier revolution out of which the Party itself had sprung.

Democracy did not come easily to Turkey. The idea and the desire were not new. Unlike so many Eastern countries, where liberty is a synonym for independence, Turkey had had a genuine democratic movement, concerned not only with the rights of the nation against other nations, but also with the rights of the individual within the nation. But this movement, despite its widespread intellectual influence, had had little political success. Two constitutional régimes, in 1876 and 1908, begun with high hopes, had ended in frustration and failure, and even the populist régime of Kemal Atatürk, failing in its two experiments with tolerated opposition, had ended as the personal autocracy of the head of state.

After the death of Atatürk there was some deterioration. In the hands of lesser men than himself, his authoritarian and paternalist mode of government degenerated into something

[20] Accounts of post-war political developments in Turkey will be found in a number of general books, notably those of L. V. Thomas and G. L. Lewis. The most recent and comprehensive survey is that of Karpat. For details of events, Jäschke's *Kalender* (*Die Türkei in den Jahren 1942–51*, 1955), OM, WI, and the RIIA, *Survey* continue to provide useful information. To them may be added a number of new periodicals, notably *MEJ* (from 1947), *MEA* (1950–1963), *MER* (from 1960), *MES* (from 1964), *Orient* (from 1957), and *C. Or. contemp.* (from 1944). It is in the last-named that the most comprehensive coverage will be found. Among Turkish publications, one of unique value is Tunaya's *Partiler*, essentially a collection of documents relating to party politics in Turkey, but also including much valuable interpretation and presentation. See further Frey, *Elite* (1965), pp. 348 ff.

nearer to dictatorship as the word is commonly understood. The disappearance of Atatürk's own dominating personality and the rise of a new generation influenced by the constitutional ideas of the victorious West undermined the popular acceptance of authoritarian government inherited from the past, and forced the régime to rely more and more on simple repression. The strains and stresses of the war years, the burden of mobilization, the universal threat of foreign espionage and infiltration, all reinforced the need for a strong government, and lent some colour of justification to the repressive measures adopted. These included martial law, a strict control of the press and publications, and an extension of police powers and activities.

Then, after the war, came the swift and sudden change which ended one-party rule in Turkey and set the country, so it seemed at the time, on the high road to liberal, parliamentary democracy.

The process began in 1945 when Turkey joined the United Nations, and the Charter, which had recently been approved in San Francisco, came up for ratification in the Turkish Assembly.

The time and the atmosphere seemed favourable to democracy, and on 19 May the President himself, at a sports festival in Ankara, had spoken of land distribution and democratic development: 'In our political life democratic principles will prevail on a still greater scale.'[21] A group of members of the People's Party took the opportunity to propose a number of legal reforms which would guarantee, inside Turkey, those rights and liberties to which the Turkish government was giving its theoretical approval at the United Nations. The leaders of the group were Celâl Bayar, deputy for Izmir, a banker and economist who had played a part in the War of Independence and had been Prime Minister in 1937-9; Professor Fuad Köprülü, deputy for Kars, a distinguished scholar and historian and an outstanding figure in the intellectual life of Turkey, Adnan Menderes, deputy for Aydın, a lawyer and cotton-planter, and Refik Koraltan, deputy for Içel, a lawyer with extensive experience as judge and provincial governor. All but Köprülü were prominent and experienced members of the parliamentary group of the People's Party.

The party had always allowed some measure of internal discussion and criticism, and a free vote was often taken at a closed

[21] *C. Or. contemp.*, ii (1946), p. 294.

party meeting before an issue was made public in the Assembly. On this occasion too the issue was first raised inside the party. On 17 June 1945 six by-elections were due to be held, and the government decided not to appoint official candidates. A week earlier, on 12 June, a party group meeting was held to discuss the elections, and it was on this occasion that the four rebels presented a joint memorandum proposing certain changes in the party programme and in the law. The proposal was rejected by a vote that was unanimous except for the four signatories of the memorandum.[22] But this time the minority broke with precedent and persisted in bringing their proposal before the Assembly. On 15 August, when the United Nations Charter came before the Assembly for ratification, Menderes argued that 'Turkey, by signing the Charter, had definitely engaged to practice genuine democracy'.[23]

These arguments failed to shake the government or its tame majority, and the rebels now adopted the radical innovation of turning to the public. Ahmet Emin Yalman, editor of the newspaper *Vatan*, had more than once shown himself ready to defy both authority and public prejudice; he now opened the columns of his newspaper to the rebels, who in the third week of September 1945 published signed articles criticizing the 'totalitarian' line that the government and party were following and proclaiming their own belief in democracy.[24]

A period of acute political tension followed. On 21 September a secret meeting of the party decided to expel Menderes and Köprülü, for breach of party discipline; Koraltan now wrote an article in *Vatan*, defending Menderes and Köprülü, and declaring: 'I and my three colleagues have done nothing but work for the strengthening of the foundations of national sovereignty and the principles of the party. It is not we who have forsaken these principles; it is those who decided to expel our two colleagues.'[25] The party responded to this challenge, and on 27 November, by a vote of 280 to 1, the group decided to expel Koraltan himself. In the meantime Celâl Bayar had, on 26 September, resigned his membership of the Assembly. On 3 December, in solidarity

[22] Tunaya, *Partiler*, p. 648 n. 8.

[23] Yalman, 'The Struggle for Multi-Party Government in Turkey', *MEJ*, i (1947), 53.

[24] Yalman, *Turkey in my Time* (1956), p. 223.   [25] Tunaya, *Partiler*, p. 649 n. 11.

with his three colleagues, he resigned from the Republican People's Party.[26]

Violent attacks on the seceders appeared in the press, and for a while it seemed as though the Government were contemplating strong repressive action. Then, suddenly, there was a complete change of policy. On 1 November 1945, in his speech at the opening of the new session of the Assembly, President Inönü recommended a number of important changes: in place of the two-stage elections by colleges, there was to be a single, direct election, by secret ballot; laws restricting the constitutional liberties of the citizen, especially the laws relating to the press, associations, and the power of the police, should be repealed. Turkey, he said, was not a dictatorship, but it did lack an opposition party; the laws should be amended so that those who differed from their colleagues, instead of working as a clique or faction, could declare their convictions and programmes and function openly as a party.

This is the right road for the development of our political life; and this is the more constructive way for the welfare and the political maturity of the nation. We shall strive with all our strength so that differences of political opinion do not lead to enmity between our compatriots.[27]

On 7 January 1946 the President's desire for an opposition was gratified, when the Democratic Party was registered in Ankara.[28] Its founders were the four People's Party rebels of the previous year. They were soon joined by others, and began to prepare for their constitutional role of opposing and attempting to replace the government.

Their task was not made easy for them. In his speech in November, President Inönü had said that the next general election would take place in 1947, on the completion of the current term of the Assembly. In April 1946, however, the congress of the People's Party, with the obvious purpose of catching the new party before it was ready for an electoral contest, decided to put the date of the elections forward. The general elections were to be held on 21 July 1946; municipal elections were to be held immediately.

The Democrat Party decided to boycott the municipal elec-

[26] Tunaya, *Partiler*, p. 649 n. 12.
[27] Inönu, *Söylev*, i. 400; cf. *C. Or. contemp.*, iii (1946), 669 ff.
[28] On the slightly earlier opposition party of Nuri Demirağ, see below, p. 383.

tions, but to contest the general elections, in which they put up candidates for 273 out of 465 seats. Sixty-one were elected as well as six independents. The Democrat Party had shown itself a lusty infant. Democrat candidates had won considerable successes in the big towns, and would certainly have won many more elsewhere, had party and government officials in various parts of the country been able to resist the temptation to intimidate the voters and adjust the votes.

On 7 August a new People's Party cabinet was formed, headed by Recep Peker, who was regarded as representing the authoritarian wing of the party. He wasted little time; on 20 September amendments to the press law and penal code gave the government renewed powers of control, and an attempt was made to stop the mounting wave of criticism against abuses in the election by invoking the martial law that was still in force.[29]

The attempt failed. Turkey now had a vigorous and determined parliamentary opposition, and a lively and active independent and opposition press. Both played an important part in the progress towards democracy of the next four years. The struggle was not easy, but the democratic forces were much helped by the rise of new and more liberal elements within the People's Party itself.

Relations between government and opposition were at first bad, and mutual accusations and recriminations, in the Assembly and in the press, kept political tension at a high pitch.[30] Finally, President Inönü himself intervened, as a kind of umpire, in June 1947. He convened a series of meetings, together and separately, with the Prime Minister and the Democrat leaders, for an exchange of opinions and, more particularly, grievances. Then, on 12 July 1947, he issued a declaration describing these discussions and his own reactions to them.[31] In the multi-party state, he said, the President should be above politics, a non-partisan head of state, with equal duties to both parties. In the conversations, the government had accused the Democrats of sedition, the Democrats had accused the government, or some of its agents, of oppression. He found the first charge baseless, the second exaggerated; in any case, he had obtained assurances from both sides of good, democratic behaviour.[32]

[29] Yalman, *Turkey*, p. 229.   [30] Ibid. pp. 239–40.
[31] Text in Tunaya, *Partiler*, p. 688.   [32] Yalman, *Turkey*, p. 240.

The President's action did much to help the smooth functioning of parliamentary government in Turkey. It also had the immediate effect of precipitating a crisis in the ruling party, which became manifest at the summer meeting of the party parliamentary group, held on 26 August 1947. After eight hours of heated discussion, the meeting gave Recep Peker the vote of confidence that he asked for—but it was no longer unanimous. Thirty-five deputies, most of them young, voted against Peker. The press at once acclaimed them as heroes, and did not fail to point out that their number would certainly have been much greater had Peker not insisted on an open vote.[33] On 3 September six ministers resigned, and on the next day, when the Prime Minister asked the party group for authority to reconstruct the cabinet, the number of dissenters rose to 47, of abstainers to nearly 100. Recep Peker's second cabinet, faced by determined opposition inside as well as outside the party, lasted only a few days. On 9 September he resigned from office, and was succeeded by Hasan Saka, who remained in power until 16 January 1949. In his four cabinets and still more in the government of Professor Şemseddin Günaltay, who followed him, the liberal group within the People's Party occupied an important position.

Meanwhile the Democrat Party was also torn between extremist and moderate wings. After one or two minor splits and disagreements, a more serious one occurred in the summer of 1948, when a group of dissident Democrats, mostly deputies, accused the party of insufficient vigour in opposing the government, and founded a new party of their own. The National Party (*Millet Partisi*), founded on 20 July 1948, also rallied the support of some disgruntled members of the People's Party, and were able to persuade Marshal Fevzi Çakmak,[34] the former Chief of the General Staff, to give them the prestige of his name and leadership. The new party rapidly became a focus of more conservative and sometimes even anti-secularist opinion.[35]

Through this and other defections, the strength of the Democrat Party in the Assembly sank from 61 in 1946 to only 31 in 1950.[36] Nevertheless its strength and influence in the country continued to grow, the more rapidly as the restrictions on political activity

[33] Tunaya, *Partiler*, pp. 563–4; Yalman, *Turkey*, p. 243.
[34] See *EI*[2] ('Çakmak, Fevzi').   [35] Tunaya, *Partiler*, pp. 712–3 and n. 8.
[36] Ibid. p. 657.

were one by one relaxed. The Law of Associations was modified to allow opposition groups, and on 20 February 1947 a law was passed permitting the establishment of 'workers' and employers' unions and regional federations'.[37]

In December 1947 martial law was at last ended, and the press began to enjoy a freedom of expression and criticism previously unknown. The new cabinet of Professor Şemseddin Günaltay announced in its statement of policy on 23 January 1949: 'We shall take the rules of the Western democracies as our model. . . . Freedom of conscience is sacred to us . . .'. The next day the Prime Minister declared to the Assembly: 'I shall work sincerely to establish democracy. . . . For the future of our country, this is the only method that I, as an historian, can be sure of. . . . Demagogy leads to dissolution or dictatorship.'[38]

Certain restrictions, however, remained in force. The foreign policy of the government could not in effect be criticized, but this restriction was the less resented as there was a substantial measure of agreement between all parties on this matter.

All forms of Communism were, after an interval of uncertainty, banned. In 1945, profiting from the relaxation of censorship, a number of leftist publications began to appear. The first was the daily newspaper *Tan*, which reappeared in May after an interval of suspension, and, under the editorship of Zekeriya Sertel, began to express mildly pink opinions. Towards the end of the year other, more openly pro-Soviet journals appeared, notably the weekly *Görüşler* (Views) and the daily *Yurt ve Dünya* (Country and World).

Pro-Russian sentiments had never had much appeal for Turks; they were particularly odious at a time when the Soviet Government was presenting territorial and other demands to Turkey. At the end of November the greater part of the Istanbul press, including, after a day of hesitation, the opposition *Vatan*, launched a campaign against the leftists. On 4 December mobs of students attacked and destroyed the offices of *Tan* and *Yurt ve Dünya* as well as a number of bookshops reputed to stock Communist literature.[39] There was very little sympathy in Turkey for the Communists and fellow-travellers, who were regarded as little better than Russian agents. On the other hand, there were many

---

[37] See below, pp. 475 ff.   [38] Jäschke, *Kalender*, 23 Jan. 1949.
[39] Yalman, *Turkey*, p. 226.

who regretted that, in order to deal with them, recourse should have been made to such perversions of democracy as press demagogy and mob violence.[40]

In 1946, with the ending of one-party rule, attempts were made to form left-wing parties, none of them very successful. At least one of them was Communist inspired—the Socialist Workers' and Peasants' Party of Turkey, founded 20 June 1946 and led by a veteran Communist, of early vintage. The party was suppressed under martial law on 1 December 1946, and its leaders arrested on charges of Communist agitation. At the same time some pro-Communist papers and unions were banned.[41]

From this time on, in the face of growing Soviet hostility to Turkey, severe repression of Communist activities and ideas enjoyed general support—though at times this restriction was so interpreted as to make any serious discussion of social problems a hazardous undertaking. Occasional attempts to restrict the freedom of the press in other respects failed in the face of the new and potent force of public opinion.

Social Change

While Turkish politics were moving in the direction of a more effective parliamentary democracy, Turkish society had entered on the transition from the rooted and enclosed conformity of the traditional order to the modern community of mobile, participant citizens.[42]

The population of Turkey had been increasing very rapidly under the Republic—$13\frac{1}{2}$ million in 1927, 16 in 1935, nearly 18 in 1940, nearly 19 in 1945, nearly 21 in 1950. At the same time, the proportion of Turks living in cities was rising significantly, as the figures in the table on page 305 show.

The increase in urbanization naturally brought with it an increase in literacy, which rose, according to official figures, from 10·6 per cent. in 1927 to 20·4 per cent. in 1935, 30·2 per cent in 1945, and 34·6 per cent. in 1950. The breakdown of the last figure shows 43·2 per cent. literacy among the under sixteens, 48·4 per cent. among men generally, and 13·4 per cent. even in

[40] Thomas and Frye, p. 111.

[41] Tunaya, *Partiler*, p. 704; Laqueur, *Communism*, p. 215.

[42] On the significance of this process in Turkey, see D. Lerner, *The Passing of Traditional Society* (1958); Frey, *Elite* (1965).

villages—i.e. places with fewer than 5,000 inhabitants. Among males in cities the figure is as high as 72 per cent.

	Proportion of the population in cities with:		
	over 20,000 inhabitants	*over 50,000 inhabitants (percentage)*	*over 100,000 inhabitants*
1927	12·5	7·7	6·2
1935	13·0	8·0	6·4
1940	13·7	8·6	6·4
1945	14·1	9·5	7·4
1950	14·7	10·2	8·3

A literate, urban population develops new interests and habits, and is anxious to be kept informed of what goes on about them. The number and circulation of newspapers rose steadily; the number of wireless sets increased from 46,230 in 1938 to 176,262 in 1945, 240,525 in 1948, and 412,270 in 1951, mostly privately owned. In the same period the number of private letters sent was more than doubled, the number of telephones almost quintupled.[43] The novel and still more the short story flourished, theatres began to attract small audiences and cinemas larger ones, and football drew vast and passionate crowds.

The modernization of communications had begun in the nineteenth century, with the introduction of European-style coaches for the gentry of Istanbul. They were followed by coupés, victorias, omnibuses, trams, and finally cars. The increased traffic in the streets of Istanbul and the other cities soon led to further demands and reforms—paved roadways, sweeping and drainage, lighting and policing, and a modern municipal authority to supply and maintain these services.[44]

As the Turkish city was rebuilt and reorganized to cope with the new and expanding traffic that filled its streets, so the whole country was transformed by the new network of railways and roads. The replacement of the caravan by the train, of horse, ass, and camel by car, bus, and lorry, has made possible the movement

[43] Details in the statistical year books (*Istatistik Yıllığı*) published by the Turkish government. The above data was assembled from the very useful tables given by Lerner, and in *Investment in Turkey*, published by the U.S. Dept. of Commerce (1956).

[44] See below, pp. 393 ff.

of persons, commodities, and ideas on a hitherto undreamt-of scale, and has given the Turkish people a new mobility, social and mental as well as physical, that has prepared them for integration in the modern world.[45]

The Election [46]

On 15 February 1950, after long debates, the Assembly approved a new electoral law, in a form agreed by both the People's and Democrat Parties. A little later the parties began their electoral campaigns, with equal broadcasting time, access to halls for public meetings, and full press facilities. The People's Party spoke of agrarian reform and opportunities for private enterprise, and promised more democracy; the Democrats attacked them for their slowness, and demanded greater freedom, both political and economic—the relaxation of etatism, more private enterprise, and, for the workers, the right to strike. The National Party was more concerned with a relaxation of secularism and a revival of Islam.

Both of the two main contenders, the Democrats and the now dominant liberal wing of the People's Party, promised freedom and democratic progress. But perhaps even more significant than the promises of the two parties was the fact that they were making them—that government as well as opposition were actually wooing the electorate, instead of bullying them. In this new exercise the opposition were naturally more adept.[47]

On 14 May Turkey went to the polls. Of close on 8·5 million voters, 88 per cent. cast their votes. They elected an Assembly of 408 Democrats, 69 People's Party, 1 National Party, and 9 Independents. After twenty-seven years the People's Party had allowed itself to be defeated in a genuinely free and honest election and, having been defeated, had peacefully handed over power to the victors. The question may well be asked why it did so—why the party, with its immense powers of control and repression and its long unchallenged supremacy, was ready in this way to prepare, organize, and accept its own downfall.

---

[45] On mobility in its various aspects see Lerner, *passim.*

[46] For contemporary appreciations of the 1950 election, see S. J. Weinberger, 'Political Upset in Turkey', *MEA*, i (1950), 135–42; B. Lewis, 'Recent Developments in Turkey', *Int. Aff.*, xxvii (1951), 320–31.

[47] Thomas and Frye, p. 108.

Many explanations have been offered. Turkish cynics—who are very cynical—say that the whole thing was due to a miscalculation. The People's Party leaders, they say, were confident of a victory in a free election and for that reason alone allowed it to be free. Had they realized what would happen, they would have taken suitable precautions.

Such an explanation seems superficial and unsatisfactory. Most observers in Turkey in the months preceding the election were convinced that in a really free poll the Democrats would sweep the country—only they could not believe, even after the new electoral law, that a free election could really take place. The People's Party leaders must have been aware of the trends of opinion in the country. Moreover, the election itself was not an isolated phenomenon, but the last of a series of steps towards democracy extending over several years.

Foreign cynics, and some Turks, attribute these changes to a desire to please the West, and especially the Americans. They point to the economic difficulties and to the isolated and exposed position of Turkey at the end of the war, and argue that most of the liberalizing reforms of earlier times had come when Turkey needed the support of the West against her northern neighbour. In 1945 Turkey, as a result of her over-prolonged neutrality, was regarded with some disfavour in the West, while Russia might still have hoped for the acquiescence if not the support of her former comrades-in-arms. Faced with the Russian demands in 1945 and 1946 for bases in the Bosporus, as well as threats to the eastern frontier, Turkish statesmen may well have felt that some dramatic gesture was necessary to rally Western opinion to their side.

Western support was in fact forthcoming. The Turkish government, with British and American encouragement, stood firm against the Russian demands. In March 1947 the announcement of the Truman doctrine brought a new assurance of American support. In August 1949 Turkey became a member of the Council of Europe.

In foreign policy at least Turkey had identified herself fully and unreservedly with the West. Did this mean that the advance towards democracy inside the country was no more than a reflection at home of a policy pursued abroad or, to put it more crudely, a piece of window-dressing designed to please and flatter Turkey's Western allies?

No doubt the desire to impress and win over the West had its place among the motives that impelled Ismet Inönü to relax the authoritarian régime in 1945—just as the great Ottoman reforms that came at the time of the Crimean War and the Congress of Berlin were not unrelated to the need of the Ottoman Empire for Western Europe's help against Russia. But it would be a grave error to conclude from this that these various stages of Turkish reform were no more than diplomatic subterfuges. The rulers of Turkey were not likely to change their form of government and surrender power to an opposition, merely to please a foreign state. And, if they did not know it from the start, they must soon have realized that the extension or restriction of democratic liberties in Turkey would have only a limited influence on a decision in Washington to help or abandon them.

The liberal and constitutional movement in Turkey has a long history, going back to the first impact of Western political ideas on Turkish intellectuals. In the period following 1945 there were many indications of a pro-Western and therefore pro-democratic trend running much deeper than the temporary alignments of international relations. At the lowest level, it expressed itself in the prevalence of chewing-gum and leopard-skin shirts on the beaches of the Bosporus and the streets of Istanbul; at the highest, in the study of the English language and of English and American literature and history, in the university, the school, and the home, and in a self-criticism that verged at times on the morbid.

Many different factors contributed to this growth of pro-Western, pro-democratic feeling. The movement no doubt owed much to the prestige that attaches to military victory, and therefore to the characteristic institutions of those that have won it. It was further helped when the United States inherited the place of Germany, in Turkish eyes, as their main bulwark, and therefore model, in resistance to the ancient Russian threat. But there was more than that. In the Kemalist Republic a new generation had grown to maturity, for whom the main objectives of the nationalist creed had already been accomplished, and nationalism alone was no longer enough. Brought up in an age of intensive Westernization, they were deeply attracted by the Western liberal tradition, and saw in democracy not just a matter of fashion or diplomacy, but the means of achieving the final integration of Turkey, on a footing of equality and mutual respect, in the free Western world.

A more extreme form of the theory of American influence is the attribution of the change to direct American intervention. There is no doubt that American pressure was exerted rather strongly in favour of private enterprise and against etatism, and the moves of the People's Party government in this direction were no doubt due in large measure to the terms of American loans and the advice of American advisers. There is, however, no evidence supporting the theory of direct American action in favour of political change. The most that can be said is that they helped to create a favourable atmosphere.

Apologists for the People's Party claim that they had always been devoted to democratic ideals, and that only the harsh conditions of the war years prevented them from achieving them earlier. As applied to the cabinets that ruled Turkey during the war years, it is difficult to take this claim seriously; but much is certainly due to what one might call the Kemalist wing of Kemal's party—the younger men who grew up under the Republic and took the ideals and promises of their founder seriously, and who began to predominate in the final phase of People's Party rule.

There were also practical reasons for the change. By 1945 the strains of the war years had given rise to really serious discontent, and President Inönü may have sought to follow the example set by Atatürk in 1924 and 1930, and open a safety-valve of licensed and limited opposition. In Democrat Party circles the argument was sometimes put forward that Inönü intended no more than this, but the opposition, once started, went far beyond the restricted role intended by the government and became strong enough to force radical changes. There is probably some truth in this explanation, though it should be remembered that this development would not have been possible without a general change in the climate of opinion in Turkey, not least in the ranks of the People's Party itself.

The Democrat victory in 1950 was more than a change of party; it was a plebiscite. All who had a grievance against the People's Party—and after twenty-seven years there were many—found and took the opportunity to register a complaint against it. After so long a period, even a party of angels would probably have been swept out of office.

It is, however, possible to distinguish, among the vast mass of supporters of the Democrat Party in 1950, certain important interests and groups that played a role in the formation of the party and its policies. One of these is the country magnates, the large and medium landowners, especially in Anatolia. Before the Republic, the landlords and rich peasants had held a dominant position in rural Anatolia, not unlike that held by their equivalents beyond the southern and eastern frontiers. In some areas, notably in the east, virtual dynasties of landowners had survived the Ottoman reforms, and still enjoyed semi-feudal privileges over vast estates. The Kemalist Revolution brought radical changes. Like Mahmud II and the statesmen of the *Tanzimat*, Atatürk was a determined centralizer, and he resumed and continued their policy of eliminating the privileges and autonomies of the great *derebey* feudal families. By his day, it was only in the east that these survived in any numbers, and even there, after the rebellions, he had made a determined effort to break up the big estates.

The resentments of these magnates were reinforced by active fear when, after lengthy debates and controversies, a land reform law[48] was passed by the Assembly and entered into effect on 11 June 1945, by an odd coincidence the day before the Four presented their proposals for reform to the People's Party group.

It was, not surprisingly, the landowners, feudal or otherwise, who most feared the new law. But, while the law added the last straw to the growing resentments of the magnates against the People's Party, it did nothing to win them the goodwill of the peasantry. The peasants, weary of years of chivvying by People's Party officials and seeing no obvious benefit in the new law, were ready to take their line from the landlords and rich peasants, and to follow them in revolting against the People's Party régime. The peasants had got to the point of voting against the government; they still did so, however, under the guidance of their own rural leadership.

The influence of the magnates was not the only power that mobilized the accumulated resentments of the peasants against the People's Party. The leaders of the Muslim religious revival that had been growing steadily in force and scope for some years also favoured a change. Between 1946 and 1950 the People's Party had adopted an increasingly tolerant attitude towards the

---

[48] See below, pp. 474 ff.

manifestations of religious revival that were appearing in Turkey, but the religious leaders had never really forgiven the party of Atatürk for the enforced secularization of the 1920's and 1930's, and when the opportunity came to turn against the People's Party they gratefully seized it. Religious leaders still commanded considerable support in the country, especially in the villages and small country towns, and among the artisans and small shop-keepers in the larger cities. By an odd paradox, the introduction of modern communications extended the influence of religious conservatism. The village woman used to wear a veil only when she visited the town. With the development of roads and bus services, many villages all over Turkey have been brought within closer range of urban influences; for most of them, however, the centres of radiation are not Istanbul, Ankara, or Izmir, but the smaller provincial towns, traditionally and still today the strong-holds of religious and social conservatism. There are many villages where the veil has appeared for the first time as a result of technical progress.

Another and quite different element in the pro-Democrat camp was the new commercial and industrial middle class that had grown up in Turkey during the previous decades. These were increasingly restive under the etatist policies of the People's Party, against which they now revolted in the name of democracy and free enterprise. In a sense, the revolt against etatism was the measure of its success, for it was the etatist impulse, supplemented by the opportunities afforded by six years of neutrality in a world war, that led to the emergence of this new Turkish middle class. For this class, the more or less benevolent paternalism of the People's Party had become an irksome anachronism. They rallied with enthusiasm to a party which promised freedom of enterprise, and an economic system more akin to the expanding capitalism of the West.

The magnates, the peasants, the new commercial class, and the old religious class were probably the most important elements among the supporters of the Democrat Party in 1950. There were others too. The non-Muslim minorities, though they too had benefited from a much more liberal policy in the post-war years, could feel little affection for the party responsible for the fiscal pogrom of 1942, and supported the Democrat Party the more readily for its sympathetic attitude to commercial interests.

Popular rumour included even the army and the bureaucracy among those who transferred their allegiance to the Democrats— the latter with a very real grievance in a scale of salaries that had become absurdly inadequate in the face of the increased cost of living. Finally, there was the undifferentiated mass of the population—all those who during the twenty-seven years of People's Party domination had inevitably developed grievances of one sort or another against the government or its various agencies, and who were the more attracted by Democrat promises since the Democrat Party was unembarrassed by any previous record of government.

In spite of the strength and variety of Democrat support, the actual victory, when it came, was a surprise to all—mainly because people, both Turks and foreigners, simply would not believe that a party which had for so long enjoyed a monopoly of power would allow itself to be defeated or, if defeated, would quietly give way to the victors.

In the event, the prophets of doom were all confounded. The election was fair, orderly, and peaceful, and the transfer of power took place with no more fuss or incident than is usual in the oldest and securest of democracies.

The atmosphere immediately after the elections was almost apocalyptic. In Ankara a preacher in the Tacüddin mosque gave thanks to God in the Friday prayer for having freed Turkey from the government of the godless People's Party. Near Bursa, some peasants began to divide up the big estates, and when asked what they were doing, replied: 'Now we have democracy.' In Istanbul, taxi-drivers cocked the Turkish equivalent of a snook at policemen and refused to obey their orders—and even the policemen themselves seemed a little uncertain as to what powers they still retained. Discoloured patches of wallpaper appeared on countless walls, where once the portrait of Inönü had rested; off-the-mark vendors sold 'Democrat Lemonade' in the streets, and an eminent Turkish historian wrote of the election as 'the greatest revolution in the history of Turkey, accomplished without bloodshed . . . and leaving no further obstacle to her progress'.

The transfer of power by a free election was certainly a bloodless revolution, comparable, in its way, with the revolutions of 1876, 1908, and 1923. But it soon became apparent that once again, it was something less than the millennium. Peasants, taxi men, and others who had shown an excess of zeal in their interpretation of democracy duly received a lesson in political science. Policemen breathed again, and swung their truncheons with something like the old verve. And the historian gradually discovered that after all a few obstacles still remained on Turkey's path of progress and freedom.

PART II

Aspects of Change

CHAPTER X

Community and Nation

The Fatherland of a Muslim is the place where the Şeriat prevails.

M. SAID HALIM PAŞA, 1917.

Nation is not a racial, ethnic, geographical, political, or voluntary group or association. Nation is a group composed of men and women who have gone through the same education, who have received the same acquisitions in language, religion, morality, and aesthetics.

ZIYA GÖKALP, 1923.

The Fatherland is the sacred country within our present political boundaries, where the Turkish nation lives with its ancient and illustrious history, and with its past glories still living in the depths of its soil.

REPUBLICAN PEOPLE'S PARTY PROGRAMME, 1935.

IN the treaty of Küçük Kaynarca, of July 1774, the Sultan was forced to make two humiliating concessions. The first was the renunciation of the ancient Ottoman suzerainty over the Khan of Crimea and the Muslim Tatars of the northern Black Sea shore, who now became independent as a preliminary to their absorption by Russia nine years later; the second was the acceptance of certain rights of intervention, which became a virtual right of protection by the court of Russia over the Orthodox Christian Church in the Ottoman Empire.[1]

To compensate for this loss of suzerainty abroad and diminution of sovereignty at home, the Sultan himself asserted a new claim.

As to the practices of religion [says the treaty], the Tatars being of the same religion as the Muslims, and his Sultanian Majesty being as Supreme Mohammedan Caliph, they are to conduct themselves towards him as is prescribed in the rules of their religion, without, however, compromising their political and civil independence as has been laid down.[2]

[1] See arts. 7 and 14 of the treaty, which provided the basis for claims to rights of intervention far in excess of what is specified in the text.

[2] Art. 3. The title 'Supremo Califfo Maomettano', which appears in the Italian original text of the treaty, is increased in the French translation to 'Souverain calife de la religion mahométane'; in the Turkish version it is reduced to 'Imām al-Mu'minīn wa Khalīfat al-Muwahhidīn' (Cevdet, *Tarih*, i. 359)—a title connoting no such general claim as is asserted in the versions for foreign consumption. On this question see Becker, 'Bartholds Studien über Kalif und Sultan', *Der Islam*, vi (1916), 408 ff.; Nallino, *Raccolta di Scritti*, iii (1941), 245–6; Jäschke, in *WI*, n.s., i. 196–7.

The claim by the Ottoman Sultan to a kind of religious pontifi-
cate extending over Muslims other than his own subjects was new
and unprecedented. Since the extinction of the classical Islamic
Caliphate in medieval times, there had been no single, universally
recognized titular head of the whole Islamic community, and each
monarch had become, in effect, a Caliph in his own realms, using
some of the titles and exercising some of the prerogatives of the
Caliphate, but only as an adjunct to his secular sovereignty. The
assertion of religious authority beyond the frontier was a radical
departure—an attempt, for the first time since the fall of the
Abbasids, to establish a universal Islamic leadership, and to claim
it for the house of Osman. It is about this time that the legend first
makes its appearance, of how the last of the Abbasid Caliphs in
Cairo had transferred the Caliphate to the Ottoman Sultan
Selim I in 1517.[3] In the hard times that lay ahead, the Ottoman
claim to Muslim leadership was to arouse growing enthusiasm at
home, and win increased acceptance abroad.

The early nineteenth century was, for the peoples of Islam, a
period of defeat and humiliation, when the European powers,
having already demonstrated their military and commercial
superiority, moved forward to establish their direct rule. Napoleon,
by his swift conquest of Egypt in 1798, had shown the way,
demonstrating, at the same time, how ludicrously easy it was to
conquer and administer even one of the heartlands of Islam, and
how necessary it might be to do so in order to forestall a conquest
by a European rival.

The lesson was quickly learnt, and the European powers
swiftly staked out their claims across the whole length of the
Islamic world in Asia, Europe, and Africa. In India British para-
mountcy was by 1818 established in most of the peninsula; by 1849
no Indian state remained that was fully independent. In South East
Asia the British and Dutch swept away the last vestiges of independence, and incorporated the Malay lands firmly in the
European colonial system. Nearer home, the Turks saw the
southward advance of Austria and Russia bring important Muslim
territories under European rule, and offer a direct threat to the
security of both Turkey and Persia. In South Eastern Europe

[3] This legend, which first appears in d'Ohsson's *Tableau général de l'Empire ottoman*,
i (1788), 269–70, was probably invented to support this new claim; cf. Becker,
'Bartholds Studien', and R. Tschudi, *Das Chalifat* (1926), p. 20.

Bessarabia was lost to Russia; Greece and Serbia to new independent Christian states. In the North, Russia, which had long since liquidated and absorbed the Tatar Khanates of the Volga and the Caspian shores, in 1783 annexed the Khanate of the Crimea, and prepared for a further advance into the Caucasus. In 1806 the Russians captured Baku, the cession of which, together with Derbend, Shirvan, and other places, was confirmed by a defeated Persia in the treaty of Gulistan of 1813. Still further Russian annexations of Persian territory were sanctioned by the treaty of Turkmanchay of 1828.

The transfer of these Turkish-speaking, Muslim lands from Persian to Russian control, together with the absorption by Russia of the Christian kingdom of Georgia, brought Russian power to the eastern as well as the western borders of the Ottoman Empire. In this new configuration, not only the possession of its remoter provinces, but the very existence of the Empire was threatened.

These dangers did not pass unperceived in Istanbul. In 1822 Akif Efendi, later *Reis-ül-Küttab*, wrote a memorandum setting forth the dangers that menaced the Empire and the three possible choices that lay before it. After examining the attitudes of the Christian nations towards Islam, and their dealings with Turkey, still the most powerful of Muslim states, Akif tried to show how the Ottoman Empire, and the Muslims generally, could preserve their independence against Europe, and more especially against the encroachments of Russia which he regarded as the major enemy. In conclusion,

the Muslims must choose between three resolutions: either, faithful to the command of God and the law of Muhammad, we must, regardless of our property and our lives, defend to the last what provinces we still retain; or we must leave them and withdraw to Anatolia; or finally— which God forbid—we shall follow the example of the peoples of Crimea, India, and Kazan and be reduced to slavery. In fine, what I have to say can be reduced to this: in the name of the faith of Muhammad and the law of Ahmed, let us proclaim the Holy War and let us not cede an inch of our territory.[4]

Akif thus saw three possible courses before the Turkey of his day—defence, as champions of Islam, of the whole Empire,

[4] Cited in V. D. Smirnow, *Manuscrits turcs de l'Institut des langues orientales* (1897), item 26. My thanks are due to Professor P. Wittek for this reference.

subjection to colonial rule, or retreat to the Anatolian heartland, from which the Turks had first crossed into Europe. During the century that followed, the Turks unsuccessfully attempted the first, successfully avoided the second, and finally, under the pressure of events more than of ideas, successfully adopted the third.

In interesting contrast with the alternative resolutions described in 1822 by Akif Efendi was the challenge to choose between three different principles of loyalty thrown down in 1904 by Akçuraoğlu Yusuf (later known as Yusuf Akçura), a young Tatar from the Russian Empire, whose family had settled in Turkey. After completing his education in France, he found the Turkey of Abdülhamid closed to him, and returned to his native village in Russia. From there he sent an article to *Türk*, a periodical published in Cairo by a group of Turkish political exiles who had found a refuge in British-occupied Egypt. Yusuf's essay, entitled *Üç tarz-ı Siyaset* (three kinds of policy) was published in the issues of May and June 1904, and then reprinted as a pamphlet. Among the many ideological discussions published by the Young Turks in exile, it struck a new and significant note—that of Turkish, as distinct from Muslim or Ottoman, nationalism.[5]

In this essay, which was later to have great influence in Turkey, Yusuf formulates and examines three possible bases of unity in the Ottoman state. The first is Ottomanism, the aspiration of the nineteenth-century liberal reformers for a common Ottoman citizenship and loyalty, irrespective of religion or origin. The second is Islam, the traditional basis of the Ottoman Empire and its Muslim predecessors, since refurbished in the pan-Islamic policies of Abdülhamid. Yusuf discusses both of these at some length and dismisses them as failures. Ottomanism is a political loyalty, which Ottoman subjects owe to the state, but there is no Ottoman nation and it is wasted effort to try and create one. A pan-Islamic policy, aiming at a union of Islamic peoples, would encounter fewer internal obstacles. It would, however, be bitterly, and in all probability successfully, resisted by the Christian powers, and the Turks would gain nothing and lose much by squandering their efforts on an irrelevant and probably unrealizable ideal. As a third possibility he suggests Turkism—'a Turkish

---

[5] Yusuf's own account of the pamphlet, its origins, and its influence will be found in his invaluable survey of the Turkist movement, 'Türkçülük', *Türk Yılı*, i (1928), 396 ff.

national policy based on the Turkish race'. For such a policy, he argued, there were fewer internal obstacles than for Ottomanism, fewer external obstacles than for pan-Islam. A Turkist policy would rally the loyalties of the dominant Turkish race within the Ottoman Empire, and reinforce it with that of the many millions of Turks, in Russia and elsewhere, beyond the Ottoman frontiers.

The differences between the choices of Akif Efendi and of Akçuraoğlu Yusuf illustrate the evolution of Turkish ideas and ideologies during the intervening years. For Akif, the question of the basis of identity and loyalty simply does not arise. The Empire is an Islamic Empire, the champion of Islam as a whole, and the struggle in which it is engaged is the ancient clash of Islam and Christendom. The choice he offers is a purely practical one—between defence, retreat, and surrender. For Yusuf, on the other hand, it is the very basis of Turkish corporate identity that has become a matter of doubt and discussion. Islam is now only one of three alternative possibilities—and even then it is no longer the simple, strong, spontaneous loyalty to the House of Islam of earlier times, but a new, subtler, and feebler thing, a political response and an emotional reaction to alien challenges and influences, known by the appropriately hybrid name of pan-Islamism. Yusuf's two other alternatives—Ottomanism and Turkism—would have been meaningless to Akif and his contemporaries. The conflict and interaction of these ideas, and of the loyalties which they evoke, have, however, dominated Turkish political thought during the past century, and exercised a profound influence on the evolution of the Turkish state and nation. It would be rash to state that the Turkish people have made their final choice among the different paths that lie before them. This much, however, can be said—that in the Turkish Republic Akif's second best, the retreat to Anatolia, has been successfully adopted, though with a theoretical justification which would have been incomprehensible to Akif, and which is derived, with some important modifications, from the Turkist ideologies of which Akçuraoğlu Yusuf's third choice is an example.

Identity and Loyalty in Islam

In a well-known passage in his *Prolegomena*, the great Arab historian Ibn Khaldūn tells us that the Caliph Umar I once said to the Arabs: 'Learn your genealogies, and be not like the

Nabataeans of Mesopotamia who, if asked as to their origin, reply: "I came from such and such a village." [6]

It may be doubted whether the attribution of this dictum to Umar is authentic, but Ibn Khaldūn's historical flair did not betray him when he cited it as an expression of the sentiments of the Arabs at the time of the great Islamic conquests. The Arab conquistadores were a tribal aristocracy identified by descent and kinship, full of contempt for the land-bound peasants who were classified by the places they inhabited.

This identity of blood was at first reinforced, and then replaced, by an identity of faith—by the bond of a common acceptance of Islam, and common membership of the Islamic community. The nucleus of the later Islamic polity was the religio-political community which the Prophet founded and led in Medina—the *Umma dūn al-nās*, the community distinguished from the rest of mankind. [7]

Such distinctions were not new; Greeks and Barbarians, Jews and Gentiles, are obvious examples from the ancient world. The ancient Arabs too had divided mankind into Arabs and non-Arabs, *'Arab* and *'Ajam*, and this sentiment lived on into Islamic times. The distinction was ethnic, not territorial; there is not even a word in Arabic for Arabia, which is called the land or peninsula of the Arabs. In time, as the Arabian Arabs merged into the cosmopolitan Islamic Empire which they had created, the distinction *'Arab–'Ajam* was overshadowed by the antithesis *Muslim–Kāfir*—the vital and permanent division between believer and unbeliever, between the Muslims and the rest. This became and remained the fundamental division of mankind among the Muslim peoples—more important than kinship, language, country, or political allegiance. The world was divided into the *Dār al-Islām*, the House of Islam, and the *Dār al-Ḥarb*, the House of War, or lands under infidel rule, and between the two there was a perpetual state of war, interrupted only by truces, and preordained to end with the incorporation of the whole world into the House of Islam. Besides the *Ḥarbî* or infidel beyond the frontier, there was also the *Ẕimmî* (from Arabic *Dhimmī*), the protected non-Muslim subject of the Muslim state, whose position was determined by the *dhimma*, or

[6] *Muqaddima*, ed. Quatremère, i. 237; cf. F. Rosenthal's English translation, New York, 1958, i. 266.

[7] For a recent examination of the *Umma* by a social scientist see C. A. O. van Nieuwenhuijze, 'The Ummah; an Analytic Approach', *Studia Islamica*, x (1959), 5–22.

pact, between his community, called *millet*, and the dominant community of Islam.

The fundamental aim of Islamic policy was to incorporate the *Dār al-Ḥarb* in the *Dār al-Islām*, and to turn the *Harbî* infidels into Muslims or, if that were not possible, into *Ẕimmîs*. The essential classification—political, social, even economic—was Muslim, *Ẕimmî, Harbî*. This tripartite distinction between the believer, the subjugated unbeliever, and the hostile unbeliever was far more important than such divisions as Turks, Greeks, and Slavs in the Balkans or Turks, Persians, and Arabs in Asia. Loyalty to a place was known, but it was to a village or quarter, at most to a province, not a country; loyalty to one's kin was ancient and potent, but it was to the family or tribe, not to the nation. The ultimate loyalty, the measure by which a man distinguished between brother and stranger, was religion. For the Muslim, his fellow believer, of whatever country, race, or language, was a brother; his Christian neighbour, his own infidel ancestors, were strangers.

Among the different peoples who embraced Islam none went farther in sinking their separate identity in the Islamic community than the Turks. Though, as we shall see, some traces of a Turkish group self-awareness remained, the Turks retained but few memories of their pre-Islamic past and raised no racial barrier between Turk and non-Turk. The traditional Ottoman Turkish conception of the nature of the state and community in which they lived can clearly be seen, on two different levels, in their historiography and in their customs tariffs.

Until the early nineteenth century the Ottoman Turk regarded the society in which he lived as the culmination of two lines of development—or rather, since it is questionable how far the notion of development is present in traditional Islamic patterns of thought, of two series of historical events. The first of these began with the mission of Muhammad, the rise of Islam, and the establishment of the Caliphate; the second with the rise of the House of Osman and the Ottoman Empire. The link between the two was provided by the invasions of the Seljuk Turks and the creation of the Seljuk Sultanates, first in Persia and then in Anatolia. These events form the main theme of Ottoman historiography. The histories of the subject *millets* are treated only in so far as they affect Ottoman history. The history of the Christian neighbours and enemies of Turkey receives some slight attention;

the pre-Islamic history of the Turks and of Turkey receive none at all.[8] The classical Ottoman historians were products of an advanced and sophisticated civilization, and their writings must rank among its greatest achievements. It is the more remarkable that they should have been so totally uninterested, either in the history of their nation, before it was converted, or of their country, before it was conquered, for Islam.

The same scale of values is reflected, in a more material form, in the old Ottoman customs tariffs. In this, as in most Islamic fiscal laws, there are discriminatory rates of assessment. The Ottoman codes recognized these rates—the lowest for Muslims, the highest for *Harbîs,* and a medium rate for *Zimmîs.*[9] The believer, the hostile infidel, the subject infidel—these were the three recognized categories, and nationality, even political allegiance had no bearing on them.

After the basic loyalty to the Islamic community, the next loyalty was political—to the lawful head of the Islamic state. In the period following the Turkish and Mongol invasions of the Middle East, the dynastic principle became firmly established, and in the Ottoman Empire in particular the House of Osman, through the long centuries of its rule, came to enjoy. the unquestioning and spontaneous loyalty of most of its Muslim subjects —even of many of its Christian subjects. The Sultan may not always have been loved by his subjects, but he was generally accepted as the legitimate Muslim head of a Muslim Empire, and as the heir of the great Emperors of the Muslim past.

Within the Ottoman Islamic Empire the dominant group was Turkish. Despite the early prevalence of Arabs and Persians in the higher ranks of the religious hierarchy, and the influence at times of Persian as a courtly and polite language, the ruling language of the Empire was Turkish, and the court, army, and bureacracy alike made use of it. The cosmopolitan governing *élite* of the Empire was recruited from men of many races, but the use of Turkish was a normal adjunct of membership, and Turkish was usually the language spoken by their descendants.

On the other hand there is only sporadic evidence of any sense

---

[8] See B. Lewis, 'History-writing and National Revival in Turkey', *MEA,* iv (1953), 218 ff.

[9] Numerous examples will be found in the Ottoman *Kanuns,* notably in the collection edited by Ö. L. Barkan and published in Istanbul in 1943 (index under *harbi*).

of Turkish national identity. The first Turkish converts to Islam, as has already been noted, identified themselves completely with their new faith, and seem to have forgotten their separate Turkish past with astonishing rapidity and completeness. The Mongol conquests, which established the supremacy of an unconverted steppe people, still following its old religion, in the heartlands of Islam, brought the prestige of domination to the traditions and customs of the steppe, and aroused in the Turks as well as in the Mongols a new pride and interest in their own distinctive heritage. This development is especially noticeable during the fifteenth century. Timur (d. 1405), who initiated the second great wave of Mongol conquest, belonged to a Turkicized, Islamized tribe of Mongol ancestry, and by his time the Turks had come to predominate in the empires of the steppe peoples. Timur had a Turkish as well as a Persian chancery, and had his victories celebrated in Turkish chronicles which have unfortunately not survived.[10] Under his Timurid successors, the courts of Shiraz, Samarkand, and especially Herat became the centres of a Turkish cultural revival. Pre-Mongol Turkish writings were collected and studied, and a series of new translations and original works produced, which mark the beginning of a new Turkish literature. By far the most important among the authors was the great poet Ali Shīr Nevā'ī (1441–1501), who may in a sense be called the Chaucer of the Turks. The first major poet to use the Turkish vernacular, he both argued and demonstrated its fitness to serve as a literary medium, and exercised a profound influence in all the lands of Turkish speech.

The language used by Ali Shīr Nevā'ī was eastern or Chatagay Turkish, and in his day the main centres of Turkish life and culture were still in the East, and not in the remote, quasi-colonial territory of Anatolia. The Chagatay language was, however, well enough understood among the Anatolian Turks, and the writings of Nevā'ī and other eastern authors were known and appreciated. There were contacts of various kinds between the Ottoman and Timurid courts, and the prestige of the ancient centres of civilization in the east stood high among the rude pioneers of the western frontier. The first signs of a Turkish national revival in Turkey date from the reign of Murad II. During his reign the passage in the first book of the History of Rashīd al-Dīn (d. 1318), dealing with the early history of the Turkish tribes, was translated from

10 Bombaci, p. 125.

Persian into Turkish, and other works adapted or composed on Turkish antiquities. These stories were incorporated in the historical traditions of the Ottoman ruling house, which was now linked for the first time with Central Asian Turkish legends and traditions, and given a line of descent from the legendary hero Oğuz Khan.[11]

The Oğuz legend remained part of the official historiographic myth right down to the end of the Empire, but apart from this, the phase of Turkish antiquarianism and Turkish identification soon came to an end. The deflection of the Ottoman Empire away from a Turkish and back to an Islamic identity may be ascribed at least in part to three successive events. The conquest of Constantinople in 1453, rounding off the Sultanate of Rum, made the Turks more conscious of an Imperial, as distinct from a merely tribal mission. The rise of the Turkish but Shi'ite power of the Safavids in Iran cut them off from the eastern Turkish world, and flung them into bitter religious conflict with their nearest Turkish neighbours. The conquest of Syria and Egypt in 1516–17 and of Iraq in 1534 brought the ancient centres of Islamic Empire under their rule and conferred upon them the burden of an Islamic Imperial heritage and mission.

Under the double weight of the Imperial and Islamic traditions, in the twofold struggle against Christendom and heresy, the nascent Turkish sense of national identity was overlaid and effaced. In Ottoman writings up to the middle of the nineteenth century, and in many of them much later, the word 'Turkey' is not used. It was a Western term, used by Westerners to describe a country which the Turks themselves usually called 'the lands of Islam', 'the Imperial realm', 'the divinely guarded realm', or, when more local definition was required, 'the land of Rum'. The Roman name remained as common Turkish usage for the Ottoman Empire until comparatively modern times, and only gradually gave way to 'the Ottoman Dominions'. All these expressions were of course understood to include the whole of the Empire and not simply the area inhabited by the Turkish nation, the very existence of which was concealed.[12] When, in the mid-

[11] P. Wittek, 'De la défaite d'Ankara à la prise de Constantinople', *R. Ét. isl.* (1938), pp. 27 f. and 'Yazıjıoghlu 'Alī . . .', *BSOAS*, xiv (1952), 644 ff.

[12] Sometimes the term Rum was used to distinguish the old Ottoman provinces, i.e. Anatolia and Rumelia, from the Arab lands acquired after 1516.

nineteenth century, the Young Ottomans, under European influence, wished to speak of their country as 'Turkey', they were hard to put to it to find a Turkish equivalent for the name. At first they made use of the word Turkistan, a Persian formation meaning Turk-land. Later, probably because this term was already pre-empted for Central Asia, they abandoned it in favour of *Türkiye*, an adaptation of the European name, which in 1923 became the official designation of the country.

The word 'Turk' was indeed used, but only to denote the nomads or peasants of Anatolia. When Koçu Bey, in 1630, complains that the corps of Janissaries has been overrun with outsiders and interlopers, he speaks of 'Turks, Gypsies, Tats, Lazes, muleteers and camel-drivers, porters, footpads, and cutpurses'.[13] Even Halet Efendi, who went to Paris in 1803, seems to have been shocked to find himself called the 'Turkish ambassador', and, when congratulating himself on having countered a hostile manœuvre, remarks that this time they had not found him the 'Turkish ambassador'—i.e. the ignorant boor—that they wanted.[14] As late as 1897 an experienced British traveller in Turkey could still remark

at the present day the name 'Turk' is rarely used, and I have heard it employed only in two ways, either as a distinguishing term of race (for example, you ask whether a village is 'Turk' or 'Turkmen'), and as a term of contempt (for example, you mutter 'Turk Kafa', where in English you would say 'Blockhead').[15]

Yet, within a century of Halet's death, the Ottoman dynasty was deposed, Islam disestablished, and a secular Republic proclaimed, on the basis of the Turkish nation and the Turkish homeland. These new conceptions and new loyalties—the nation and the fatherland—struck deep roots in Turkey, and have, by modification, became associated with some of the deepest instincts of the Muslim Turkish people. Their origin and early development must, however, be traced in the workings of European influence.

European Influence: Patriotism and Nationalism

The modern conception of patriotism originated in Western Europe, where, first in England, then in France and other countries, the state ceased to be the king, and instead became

---

[13] Koçu Bey, chs. 5 and 9.   [14] E. Z. Karal, *Halet*, p. 55.
[15] Sir W. M. Ramsay, *Impressions of Turkey* (1897), p. 99.

identified with the nation, the people, or the fatherland. Echoes of the Greek *polis* and the Roman *patria*, drowned at the time of the Renaissance and Reformation by the clash of Church and State and of Church and Church, were heard more clearly in the Age of Reason. The new sentiment of nation and country began among the independent Western nations, where sovereignty and nationhood were axiomatic, and where nation-states, with well-defined national territories, in fact existed before the idea of the nation-state emerged. In these countries, the patriotic lovers of liberty were concerned with asserting the rights of the individual against domination by authority, rather than of the group against domination by other groups—in other words, not so much with independence, which they already possessed, as with freedom, which they were struggling to win.

This early, Western European type of nationalism was utilitarian, practical, and liberal; it dealt with nations defined by visible and objective criteria, such as territory and sovereignty. To some extent language too was a criterion, though it cannot have been a rigid one, since in the eighteenth century both Britain and France were countries of a plurality of languages. More important was the occupation of a common territory, defined by the jurisdiction of a common sovereign authority. It may thus more appropriately be called patriotism, rather than nationalism.

It was this Western European type of patriotism that first affected the Islamic world, and gave rise to the attempt, finally unsuccessful, to focus loyalty on an Ottoman fatherland, and on a vaguely defined Ottoman nation.

The two words used in Turkish for fatherland and nation were *vatan* and *millet*, and it is instructive to examine their semantic development. *Vatan* is a Turcicized form of *waṭan*, a classical Arabic word meaning place of birth or residence. A man's *vatan* might be a country, a province, a town, or a village, according to context. In this sense a *vatan* could inspire sentiment and loyalty, and these find frequent expression in classical literature—but the word had no more political significance than the English word home.

In the course of the nineteenth century the overtones of the French word *patrie* began to affect the Islamic word *vatan*. As early as the 1790's, Ali Efendi, the Turkish ambassador to the *Directoire*, in describing French arrangements for the care of disabled soldiers, speaks of men who had suffered 'in the cause of the Republic and out of zeal for their *vatan*'.[16] This was a new notion for Ali Efendi's time, and it is likely—for he was not a perceptive man—that he or his interpreter was merely translating literally from an original he did not understand. But by 1841 Handjeri's Turkish-French dictionary includes the equation *vatan = patrie*, together with new derivatives for patriot and patriotism, and examples of their use, in Turkish and French, which are purely Western in inspiration. By the mid-century *vatan*, in the political sense of fatherland, was in common use in the Turkish press, and in 1866 there was even a newspaper called *Ayine-i Vatan* (the Mirror of the Fatherland).

The word *millet*, from the Arabic *milla* and perhaps ultimately of Aramaic origin, occurs in the Koran with the meaning of religion. It was later extended to mean religious community, especially the community of Islam. In the Ottoman Empire it came to be applied to the organized and legally recognized religious communities, such as the Greek Christians, the Armenian Christians, and the Jews, and by extension also to the different 'nations' of the Franks. Even as applied to the Frankish nations the term was at first understood as having a primarily religious sense. Thus, the English were recognized in the sixteenth century as the 'Lutheran nation', and non-English Protestants were regarded as being under their protection. In the Empire, there was a Muslim *millet*, but no Turkish or Arab or Kurdish *millets*; there were Greek and Armenian and Jewish *millets*, but as religious communities, not as ethnic nations. Until the late nineteenth century, Greeks and Slavs alike formed part of the Greek Orthodox *millet*, while on the other hand Gregorian and Catholic Armenians formed separate *millets*. It is not until a comparatively late date that one encounters the idea of national entities transcending religious distinctions. Even then the idea is still recognizably alien, with dubious rights of domicile.

Both words—*vatan* and *millet*—occur in the Rescript of the Rose Bower of 1839, in a way which significantly reveals the confusion of ideas between the old Islamic loyalty and the new, imperfectly assimiliated patriotism. The text speaks of 'zeal for dynasty and nation (*millet*) and love of country (*vatan*)', in a

[16] Ahmed Refik, ed., '. . . Ali Efendinin Sefaretnamesi', *TOEM*, (1329 A.H.), p. 1459.

context which is quite clearly intended to refer to all Ottoman subjects irrespective of religion. Yet a little farther on, the same document speaks of 'the people of Islam and other nations (*millet*)' within the Empire, as separate and distinct entities. 'Other nations' and 'foreign nations' are common expressions in Turkish administrative and journalistic usage at the time. Both clearly mean nations other than Islam; 'foreign nations' mean those not under Muslim rule, and therefore correspond to the 'House of War' of earlier days. At no time do they include non-Ottoman Muslims, who, although they may be strangers, are not foreigners in the Islamic Empire. It is not until the 1860's that we find frequent reference to an Ottoman *millet*—and here too it is far from clear whether all Ottomans are meant, or whether this is a new name for the Muslims. In the first leading article of the *Tercüman-i Ahval*, published in 1860, Şinasi discusses the interests of the fatherland (*vatan*) and remarks that while the non-Muslim subjects of the Empire had their own newspapers, there were no 'truly Ottoman' newspapers, since hitherto no member of the 'dominant *millet*' had been willing to publish one.[17] In the same spirit, an article in the *Tasvir-i Efkâr* in 1862 speaks of 'the Ottoman *millet*, the owner and master of the country'.[18]

Namık Kemal, the apostle of liberal patriotism, adopts a milder tone, but he too, in his patriotic writings, shows that he never really distinguished between what was Ottoman and what was Islamic. A good example of this is a famous leading article, on patriotism, which he published in 1868 in *Hürriyet*, one of the journals issued by the Young Ottomans in exile. In an eloquent appeal to the patriotic pride of his readers, he reminds them that their country had produced such great sovereigns as Sultan Süleyman the Magnificent and the Caliph Umar, such men of learning as Farabi, Avicenna, Ghazali, and Zamakhshari; and he saw nothing incongruous in including medieval Arab and Persian Muslims, and an ancient Arabian Caliph, in his appeal to 'Ottoman' pride. The fatherland of Namık Kemal's loyalties included the Caliphs of Medina as well as the Sultans of Constantinople among its former rulers.

[17] *Tercüman-ı Ahval*, no. 1, 21 Oct. 1860. Reprinted in Özön, *Son Asır Türk Edebiyatı Tarihi* (1941), pp. 419–20, and in the Şinasi volume of the *Türk Klas.*, pp. 72–74.

[18] *Tasvir-i Efkâr*, 27 June 1862, reprinted in Özön, *Son Asır*, pp. 420–1; Sinasi (*Türk Kl.*), p. 74.

The Fatherland [he says in a later article] does not consist of imaginary lines drawn on a map by the sword of a conqueror or the pen of a scribe: it is a sacred idea, sprung from the union of the many lofty sentiments, such as nation, freedom, welfare, brotherhood, property, sovereignty, respect for ancestors, love of family, memory of youth. . . .[19]

A practical problem of the time illustrated the obstacles in the way of Ottoman patriotism. In May 1855 the Ottoman government announced that the duty and privilege of military service, hitherto restricted to Muslims, would be extended to the Christian subjects of the Empire. This declaration, issued to the ambassadors of the European powers, was part of the diplomatic preparation for the peace conference at the end of the Crimean War. The promise of the Porte included the abolition of the poll-tax levied on non-Muslims, as well as the admission of the Christians to the army, where they would be allowed to rise to the rank of colonel, and to the civil service, where they could rise to the highest grade.[20]

In early times, the Ottoman Sultans had not scrupled to make use of Christian auxiliaries and even, for a short time, to include Christian fief-holders in their feudal cavalry.[21] But all this was long past and forgotten; for many centuries the Ottoman armies had been the Muslim armies of a Muslim state, and the inclusion in them of Christian soldiers would have been a self-evident absurdity. In fact, the Christian beneficiaries of this act of emancipation were even less anxious to accept the privilege of arms than were the Muslims to confer it, and the attempt to recruit Christian soldiers was soon abandoned amid general satisfaction. Instead of serving in the army, the non-Muslim subjects of the Empire were permitted to commute their duty of military service to an exemption fee, the *bedel*,[22] which happened to coincide exactly, in the method of assessment and collection, with the abolished poll-tax. In this way the liberal reformers were able to serve both their instincts and their ideals.

In Europe, the promise and its abandonment were dismissed as just another piece of Ottoman insincerity. But in fact the Ottoman government gave long and earnest consideration to the problem

---

[19] *Ibret*, 22 Mar. 1873. Reprinted in Özön, *Namık Kemal*, p. 265; cf. Rossi, in *OM*, xxiii (1943), 364–5.

[20] Engelhardt, i. 126.   [21] cf. above, p. 5.   [22] See above, p. 116.

of non-Muslim recruitment, which, besides appealing to Western and liberal opinion, offered the tempting bait of a new accession of manpower for the depleted Ottoman armies. During the Grand Vezirate of Fuad Paşa a special commission discussed the matter. Cevdet Paşa, in his deposition to the commission, laid his finger on the essential difficulty. In times of special stress and urgency, he asked, when a commander wishes to urge his men to supreme endurance and self-sacrifice, on what basis is he to appeal to them? For Muslims, the most effective appeals are those of religion—holy war, martyrdom in battle, the struggle for the true faith against the infidel. These are the appeals to which they have been accustomed since childhood, and it is to them that they respond most readily. The loyalty, courage, and endurance of Muslim soldiers are due largely to their religious sentiments and devotion.

But in time of need, how could the Colonel of a mixed battalion stir the zeal of his soldiers? In Europe, indeed, patriotism has taken the place of religious devotion, but this happened at the end of their feudal period; their children hear the word fatherland (*vatan*) while they are still small, and so years later the call of patriotism has become effective with their soldiers. But among us, if we say the word 'fatherland' all that will come to the minds of the soldiers is their village squares. If we were to adopt the word 'fatherland' now, and if, in the course of time, it were to establish itself in men's minds and acquire the power that it has in Europe, even then it would not be as potent as religious zeal, nor could it take its place. Even that would take a long time, and in the meantime our armies would be left without spirit.[23]

Namık Kemal was not unaware of the difficulties and contradictions involved in the Ottoman fatherland. Other nations, he said, loved their fatherlands, but none of them could feel wholly confident and secure about their future. Every country had its own dangers and difficulties. The English feared Irish separatism and the Russian approach to India (which apparently formed part of the English *vatan*), the French strove to reconcile order and liberty, the Germans and Italians were anxious for their newly won unity, the Russians for their vast conquests. 'As for us, we imagine that the differences of race and religion among our countrymen might bring total dissolution to our country.'[24]

[23] Cevdet, 'Maruzat', *TOEM*, (1341 A.H.), p. 273; cf. his *Tarih*, vi. 18.
[24] *Ibret*, 22 Mar. 1873, reprinted in Özön, *Namık Kemal*, pp. 267-8.

Against this foreboding Namık Kemal offered his readers what proved to be specious reassurances. Diversity was not necessarily a weakness; with a wise policy it might even be a factor of progress. In any case, the various races and religions were so thoroughly mixed that, with one exception, there was no province of the Empire which could form a separate government or transfer to another state—for where could these people hope to find such freedom and tolerance as in the Ottoman Empire? The exception was the Arab lands. In them there lived a population of many millions, speaking a separate language and feeling themselves to belong to a separate race. But the Arabs were bound to the Empire by Islamic brotherhood and allegiance to the Caliphate, and their separation was not to be feared.[25]

Once again the real bond is Islam. The Christians would not leave because it would not be practicable for them to do so; the Arabs would stay because of Islamic brotherhood and loyalty. In a poem celebrating the 'Ottoman Fatherland', Namık Kemal proudly reminds his readers that it was in their country that Christ was born and ascended to heaven, that the light of God came down to Moses, that Adam found a substitute for Paradise, that Noah's Ark came to rest, that 'from the song of David and the moan of Socrates, religion and reason became keepsakes for one another'—that is, the Biblical and Hellenistic heritages merged in Islam—and he concludes

> Go, fatherland, swathe yourself in black in the Ka'ba,
> Stretch out an arm to the garden of the Prophet.[26]

It is in the last couplet that the poet's real loyalty finds expression. There was no Ottoman nation, and, as Akçuraoğlu Yusuf later remarked, it was wasted effort to try and create one. The Ottoman fatherland held many nations, which had once been held together, even the non-Muslims among them, by a common allegiance to the dynastic sovereign. The Ottoman liberals, and after them the Ottoman constitutionalists, tried to replace that allegiance by a new Ottoman patriotism, which would group all the many peoples of the Empire in a single political loyalty and identity. 'There is a new Ottoman nation . . .', said Ahmed Midhat, 'and Ottomanism consists in recognizing, as a basic political allegiance, the quality of subject of the Imperial

[25] *Ibret*, 2 July 1872, reprinted in Özön, *Namık Kemal*, pp. 84–85.
[26] *Vatan-i Osmani*, cited by Kaplan, p. 113.

Sovereign.'[27] The same principle appears in the programme of the Committee of Union and Progress, and formed the basic policy of the Young Turk government in 1908. But the cause was hopeless. The old dynastic allegiance was indeed being undermined by the new ideas of nationality coming from Europe, and affecting, in the first instance, the Christian peoples of the Empire. But when the national idea conquered them, they began to think of themselves, not as Ottomans, but as Greeks, Serbs, Bulgars, and Armenians. Against these heady visions the pallid doctrine of Ottomanism, so dubiously supported even by the Turks themselves, had little chance of success. The struggle of the Christian peoples for national independence and the Turkish reaction against it—armed insurrection and armed repression—created a new bitterness between Muslims and Christians. The Bulgarian rising of 1876, the Armenian revolutionary movement of the 1890's, the Cretan insurrection of 1896–7, the activities of the revolutionary committees, the famous *komitadjis*, in the Balkans, all helped to create in the Turks a profound mistrust of their Christian compatriots and of the European great powers looming behind them; at the same time the repressions and massacres with which the Turks responded reinforced the determination of the Christian peoples in the Empire to seek their salvation, not in citizenship, but in separation. In the end, the nationalist ideas that were destroying the Empire would reach even its Imperial masters. But in the meantime an older claim on their loyalty was again asserted.

Pan-Islamism [28]

When Namık Kemal felt the dawn of doubt as to the loyalty of the Arabs to the Ottoman Empire, he reassured himself with thoughts of Islamic brotherhood and allegiance to the Caliphate— to that throne of which the Arabian Umar, as well as the Turkish Süleyman, had been occupants.

During the second half of the nineteenth century new humiliations made the Muslims of the world more ready to turn to the Turkish Sultan for protection and leadership. In India the

[27] Rossi, in *OM*, xxiii. 367.

[28] The literature on pan-Islamism is extensive, and of unequal value. For brief introductions to the Ottoman variety see Rossi, pp. 366 ff.; anon., 'Le panislamisme et le panturquisme', *RMM*, xxiii (1913), 179–220; B. Lewis, in *MES*, i. (1965), 291–4; and, at greater length, Tunaya, *Islamcılık Cereyanı* (1962).

suppression of the last vestiges of the Mughal Empire, after the Mutiny of 1857–8, left the Muslims of that country without a focus for their loyalty, a Muslim sovereign to name in their prayers. In Central Asia the Russians conquered Samarkand in 1868, and reduced the Amirate of Bokhara to the status of a 'native state' in the Russian Empire. In Africa in 1881–2 the British occupied Egypt and the French Tunisia; in 1891 the Germans declared a Protectorate over Dar es-Salaam.

Already in the early 1870's, Namık Kemal was aware of a Western threat, both intellectual and imperial, to the Islamic world, and urged that the Ottomans take the leadership in defending Islam against it. His pan-Islamism was, however, cultural rather than political—'the way of uniting the people of Islam must be sought, not in political aims or doctrinal disputes, but in the presence of preachers, in the pages of books'.[29] His pan-Islamism was linked with his desire for modernization. Since the Ottomans were the nearest of the Muslims to Europe, they were the most advanced on the path 'of modernization, and were thus the natural leaders of Islam on this path. The Muslims would certainly unite one day in progress. But at the same time

Since the Caliphate is here, and since . . . in the suitability of the place and the readiness of the people in nearness to Europe, the present home of civilization, in wealth and in knowledge, this country is the most advanced of all the Muslim lands, this union of which we speak will surely have its centre here. . . . When that happens, the light of knowledge will radiate from this centre to Asia and Africa. Facing the balance of Europe, a new balance of the East will come into being, and in that way the scales of justice will come into the world of men. . . .[30]

Namık Kemal speaks of the union of Islam as being a general objective in his day. The Crimean War, the Indian Mutiny, the conquests of Britain, France, and Russia in Muslim lands, all helped to foster these ideas. Towards 1870 the Turkish Khans in Central Asia, about to be engulfed in the great wave of Russian imperial expansion, appealed to their Muslim brothers for help. Agents were sent to the Middle East, and contact made with the Sultan. Nothing came of these efforts, which were forgotten during the wars of 1877–8 and the interlude of liberal constitutional

[29] *Ibret*, 13 June 1872; reprinted in Özön, *Namık Kemal*, pp. 77–78.
[30] Ibid. reprinted in Özön, *Namık Kemal*, p. 33.

government. But pan-Islamism was not dead, and the third article of the 1876 constitution formally claims the 'high Islamic Caliphate' for the house of Osman. Under Abdülhamid a form of pan-Islamism became official policy—though with a very different content from Kemal's preaching of freedom and progress.[31] There was a wide range of pan-Islamic ideologies, from the Ottoman official version to the more radical teachings of the redoubtable Jamāl al-Dīn al-Afghānī (1839–97), the apostle of the Islamic reaction against the West. For most of their followers, the causes of the decline of Islam were to be sought, not in any internal weaknesses or defects, but in the aggressive imperialism of Christian Europe, which sought to enslave the Muslims and destroy Islam. The danger was twofold; the establishment of foreign political, military, and economic supremacy in the Muslim lands, and the undermining, by foreign intellectual influences, of the basic beliefs and values of Islam. The task was to drive out the foreign invaders, abolish foreign concessions and immunities, restore the true Islamic faith—and, some added, to reunite all the Muslims in a single state, under its lawful sovereign, the Caliph.

Such a task was obviously beyond the capacities of the Ottoman Empire, but the espousal of such a programme offered many advantages to Abdülhamid. Inside the Empire, the appeal to Muslim loyalty could win support for his efforts to repress the liberals, nationalists, reformers, and other opponents of his autocratic power. Outside the Empire, he might hope to rally an important body of Muslim opinion to his support and, by creating difficulties for the Imperial powers in their Muslim territories, forestall possible action against Turkey.

His policy was for a while remarkably successful. The Sultan's emissaries were at work in Algeria and in Egypt, in India and even in Japan, stirring up Muslim opinion, gaining new support for the Ottoman Sultanate, and taking full advantage of the new media of communication at their disposal. The measure of their success may be seen in the widespread concern aroused all over the

[31] O. Depont and K. Coppolani, (*Les Confréries religieuses musulmanes* (1897), pp. 257 ff.) attribute a major role in pan-Islamic propaganda to the dervish orders, some of whose leaders, resident in Istanbul, they regard as the Sultan's principal agents in this field. This interpretation, which has been followed by several subsequent writers (e.g. Nallino, in his article 'Panislamismo' in the *Enciclopedia Italiana*) is decisively disproved by Snouck-Hurgronje, 'Les Confréries religieuses, la Mecque et le Panislamisme', *Verspreide Geschriften*, iii. 189 ff. On the role of Afghani, see Nikki R. Keddie, in *MES*, iii (1966), 46–67.

Islamic world by the Greco-Turkish war of 1897—a local affair
that would have passed unnoticed in earlier times. Ottoman
victories were celebrated in many lands, and were followed by
stirrings or outbreaks among the Muslims in India and the East
Indies, Turkestan, Madagascar, and Algeria. Even after the
deposition of Abdülhamid, the Young Turks continued to enjoy
the support of the Muslim world in their struggles against their
Balkan enemies, and pan-Islamic solidarity was a matter of grave
—indeed exaggerated—concern to the Allies in the First World
War.[32] The last flickers of pan-Islamic sentiment can be seen in
the pathetic intervention of the Indian Muslim leaders on the
question of the Caliphate in 1923.[33]

Turkism [34]

In 1897, in a mood of passionate loyalty engendered by the
brief Greco-Turkish war, a young poet called Mehmed Emin
published a volume of verse entitled *Türkçe Şiirler* (Poems in
Turkish). Abandoning the formal language and quantitative
prosody of the Ottoman court poets, Mehmed Emin wrote in
simple popular Turkish and in the syllabic metre used in folk
poetry. Still more remarkable, he adopted a word which, in
Turkish usage, had connoted a boorish, ignorant peasant or
nomad, and proudly proclaimed himself a Turk—

> I am a Turk, my faith and my race are mighty

and in another place—

> We are Turks, with this blood and with this name we live.[35]

Mehmed Emin still defined his loyalty first by faith, and was
indeed a deeply religious man; but with this new word a new
concept of identity had found its way into the collective self-
awareness of the Turkish-speaking Ottoman Muslims.

[32] On the pan-Islamic activities and propaganda of the Young Turks see Y. H.
Bayur, *Türk Ink. Tar.*, ii/4, pp. 88 ff., 314 ff., 374 ff. On the Hejaz Railway see above
p. 185, and 'Ḥidjāz Railway' in *EI²* (by Z. H. Zaidi).

[33] See above, p. 263.

[34] On the Turkist movement, the classic account is that of Akçuraoğlu Yusuf in
Türk Yılı, i (1928), 290–455. See also U. Heyd, *Foundations of Turkish Nationalism*
(1950); Gökalp, *Turkish Nationalism and Western Civilization* (tr. and ed. by Niyazi
Berkes, 1959); Karpat; Rossi, in *OM*, xxiii. 361 ff.

[35] Reprinted in the Mehmet Emin volume in *Türk Klas.*, p. 18; Akyüz, *Antoloji*,
p. 20, &c. See Rossi, p. 371.

Ottomanism had proved a failure. Islamic loyalty still dominated the sentiments of the great mass of Turks, as it had done for centuries past, but its modern political avatar, pan-Islamism, had won only limited successes, and held, moreover, a diminishing appeal for the Western-educated, westward-looking younger intellectuals.

The Western European concept of the territorial and political nation had proved difficult of application to the Ottoman Empire, and was basically irrelevant to its historic situation and present needs. There was, however, another kind of national sentiment in Europe, that was to have far greater impact on the people of the Ottoman Empire. In central Europe, where there were no well-defined and long-established territorial nation-states such as England and France, the visible and external criteria of nationhood—land and state—were insufficient. In the continental Empires, there were Germans, Czechs, Poles, and Hungarians, but no Germany, no Czech-land, no Poland, and only a shadow of Hungary. None of these nations could be defined in terms of sovereign states; none could even be defined, with any precision, by their territorial limits. In place of the patriotism of Western Europe, a different sentiment arose—nationalism, romantic and subjective in its criteria of identity, all too often illiberal and chauvinistic in its expression.

This kind of national sentiment corresponded much more closely to the ethnic confusion of the Ottoman Empire, with its intermingled populations grouped by such intangible criteria as faith and kinship. Nationalism—loyalty to the group—evoked a ready response; patriotism—loyalty to one's country—for long remained alien and unintelligible.[36]

Among the peoples of the Ottoman Empire the last to be affected by the national idea were, not unnaturally, the masters

[36] English 'nationality' and French 'nationalité' indicate the country and state of which one is a citizen or subject. German uses 'Staatsangehörigkeit'—state-belonging—in this sense, and employs 'Nationalität' in an ethnic and not a legal sense. The same appears to be true of the East European languages—e.g. in Stalin's writings on the 'nationality problem' and in the Soviet visa form. In this case Turkish follows German, and not, as is usual in loanwords and neologisms, French usage. Turkish official forms usually contain two spaces, one for *tabiiyet*, which corresponds in meaning with the German 'Staatsangehörigkeit', the other for *milliyet*, an abstract form from *millet*. All citizens of the Turkish Republic are of Turkish *tabiiyet*; their *milliyet*, however, may be Greek, Armenian, Jewish, or, for the majority, Muslim and Turkish interchangeably. To this day Muslim is the more usual way of answering this question.

of the Empire themselves. It was only slowly, and under foreign influence, that the Turks at last began to recover a sense of their separate national identity as Turks, as a Turkish nation distinct from—though included in—the Ottoman state and the Islamic religion.

One of the most important sources of these ideas was the new European science of Turcology. From the eighteenth century onwards a series of Orientalists, working from Chinese and Islamic sources, had studied the history and languages of the eastern and pre-Islamic Turks. As a result of their work, a new picture emerged of the role of the Turkish peoples in the history of Asia and Europe, and new light was thrown on the hitherto obscure history of the Turks before they entered Islam. In time this new knowledge of a forgotten and rejected chapter in their history reached the Turks themselves, and helped to accomplish a great change in the way they conceived their corporate identity, their relations with other groups past and present, and their place in the two fundamental visions of the human predicament, the historical and the philosophic.[37]

One channel by which these new ideas reached the Turks was the student missions; by the mid-century these were going to European universities and academies in increasing numbers, and were inevitably affected by the ideas current there. Another was the group of Hungarian and Polish exiles who settled in Turkey after the unsuccessful revolutions of 1848, bringing with them the romantic nationalism of central Europe. Several of these, converted to Islam and permanently established in Turkey, played a role of some importance in the introduction of new ideas in Turkey. Such for example was the Pole Hayreddin, who contributed many articles to the newspapers *Terakki* and *Basiret*, and played some part in the founding of the Galatasaray school.[38] Another was Mustafa Celâleddin Paşa, *né* Constantine Borzęcki, author of a book, in French, entitled *Les Turcs anciens et modernes* and published in Istanbul in 1869; in this he argued that the Turks were ethnically akin to the peoples of Europe, and belonged to what he called the 'Touro-Aryan' race—the Turanian subsection of the Aryan race. The purpose of these theories was to demonstrate that the Turks were Europeans, and to minimize the differences dividing them from their European subjects. The historical

[37] B. Lewis, in *MEA*, iv. 218 ff.   [38] Sungu, in *Bell*, no. 78 (1943), 328.

section of the book includes a survey of ancient Turkish history based on the writings of a number of European Turcologists, and emphasizes the great role of the Turkish peoples in human history.[39]

Of Western Turcological writings two books in particular— neither of them of any great scholarly value—seem to have had a considerable influence. One was the *Grammar of the Turkish Language*, with a long historical introduction on the Turkish peoples, published in London in 1832 by Arthur Lumley Davids. A French translation appeared in 1836 and attracted Turkish attention. Its grammatical portions helped to inspire the *Kavaid-i Osmaniye* of Fuad and Cevdet Paşas, published in 1851, the first modern Turkish grammar to appear in Turkey. More important in the present context, its introduction served as the basis of a defence of the Turks—not, as would have been normal at the time, of the Muslims or Ottomans—written by Ali Suavi for the first issue of his fortnightly *Ulum*, published in Paris in 1869.[40]

Another author who influenced the growth of Turkish consciousness among the Turks was Léon Cahun, a French teacher and writer who became friendly with the Young Ottomans during their stay in France in the 1860's, and wrote extensively on Turkish subjects. His best-known book was the *Introduction à l'histoire de l'Asie*, published in 1896, containing a semi-scientific, semi-romantic account of the history of Asia in which great stress is laid on the role of the Turkish nomads of the Central Asian steppe. Cahun's book was published in a Turkish translation in 1899, and many Turkish writers testified to its formative influence.

Of far greater importance as a scholar than either of these was the Hungarian Arminius Vambéry (1832–1913), who during his residence in Turkey came into contact with many Turkish intellectuals, and retained their friendship and attention for years

---

[39] Akçuraoğlu Yusuf, pp. 304 ff.; Rossi, in *OM*, xxiii. 362. His son, Maj.-Gen. Enver Paşa, was a member of the Ottoman General Staff. Ömer Naili Paşa, a Hungarian refugee who became a senior Ottoman officer, is named as an influential and effective supporter of the Young Ottomans (Ebüzziya Tevfik, in *Yeni Tasvir-i Efkâr*, issue of 21 June 1909; cf. Kuntay, *Namık Kemal*, i. 359); another Hungarian, Daniel Szilágyi, is mentioned among the distributors of Young Ottoman pamphlets in Istanbul (Kuntay, *Namık Kemal*, i. 281). It is interesting to note that the *émigré* Turkish Communist poet Nazım Hikmet has adopted Polish nationality and the surname Borzęcki. See further Davison, *Reform* (1963), pp. 76–77.

[40] Tanpınar, pp. 220 ff. On Davids' influence see further Köprülü, *Millî Edebiyat*, pp. 45–46, and Heyd, *Foundations*, p. 105.

after. Turcology was especially cultivated in Hungary, where it derived encouragement from the theory, formerly held, of a common origin of the Magyars and the Turks, and from the Hungarian desire for Turkish support against the common danger of pan-Slavism.[41]

As early as 1839 Hungarian scholars used the word Turan, an ancient Iranian name for the country to the north-east of Persia, to describe the Turkish lands of Central and South East Asia, and applied the term Turanian to a group of peoples and languages comprising Turkish and Mongol as well as Finnish, Hungarian, and others. As a linguistic and ethnological classification this has long since been abandoned. As a political idea Turanianism and pan-Turanianism have retained some vigour.

In political circles in Turkey the impact of Turkish nationalist ideas was for long negligible. True, we do find Fuad Paşa, in a conversation with Stratford Canning, remarking that the Empire rested on four foundations, not one of which could be dispensed with: 'The Islamic religion (*millet*), the Turkish state (*devlet*), the Ottoman Sultans, and the capital in Istanbul.'[42] In this, however, Fuad Paşa was probably expressing no more than the sense of cultural identity of the Turkish-speaking ruling group within the Empire, perhaps in a form influenced by European usage. He was certainly not putting forward any idea of Turkish racial or ethnic identity and dominance.

For the first signs of a Turkish national consciousness among the Ottoman Muslims we must turn to the intellectual life of the nineteenth century, and especially to the writers on history and language. Ahmed Vefik Paşa (1823–91), scholar and statesman, the translator of Molière and Speaker of the first Ottoman parliament, is credited with being the first to stress that the Turks and their language were not merely Ottoman, but were the westernmost branch of a great and ancient family stretching across Asia to the Pacific. Süleyman Paşa (d. 1892) was the author of a universal history, published in 1876, which included a section on the pre-Islamic Turks—the first in modern Turkish historiography—based chiefly on Davids and other European writers. Şemseddin Sami Fraşeri (1850–1904) was an Albanian whose career illustrates the way in which the Balkan peoples, now

[41] Lewis, in *MEA*, iv. 218 ff.; Heyd, *Foundations*, pp. 104 ff.
[42] Cevdet, *Tezakir*, i. 85.

accessible to Western influences, served as carriers for new ideas. Though a philologist rather than an historian, Sami Fraşeri, by his lexicographic and encyclopaedic work, did much to help the growth of the new feeling of Turkish self-awareness. Perhaps the most important was Necib Asım (1861–1935), the first real Turcologist in Turkey. He was much influenced by Cahun, whose works he translated into Turkish, and also by the Turcological discoveries and publications in Europe, especially in Hungary, with which he had close personal connexions.

Towards the end of the nineteenth and the beginning of the twentieth century, the movement towards Turkism received a political impetus from another source, the Russian Turks—Muslim Tatars and Turks from the Volga, Central Asia, Azerbayjan, and Crimea, numbers of whom were coming to live in the Ottoman Empire. These exiles from Russia were often of a high standard of education; some of them had been through Russian high schools and universities. They were acquainted with the very considerable achievements of Russian Turcology; they had encountered—and reacted against—the pan-Slav movement and *mystique*; they were affected by the populist and revolutionary tendencies current among the intelligentsia of the Russian Empire, to which they belonged. At the same time they were familiar with the new political and social ideas current among some circles in the Ottoman Empire.

The Ottoman reaction to Balkan separatism, the Tatar revolt against Russian pan-Slavism, the response of Turkish and Tatar intellectuals to the new ideas and examples set by European nationalisms, the nourishment of Turkish pride by Turcological discovery—all these, at a time of Ottoman defeat and Muslim abasement, combined to encourage the growth of Turkism, of the new political movement based, not on a dynasty, a faith, or a state, but on a people—the Turkish people, in its vast territories extending from Europe to the Pacific.[43]

Although the terms Turan and pan-Turanianism remained in occasional use, the movement was in effect pan-Turkish, for the Muslim Turkish peoples, in Turkey and Central Asia, showed little interest in their putative Christian or pagan brothers in Hungary or Mongolia. Tatar intellectuals in Russia, led by the Crimean Gaspiralı Ismail or Ismail Gasprinski (1841–1914), began a new

43 See V. Minorsky, 'Turan', in *EI¹*.

kind of pan-Turkish movement, at first mainly cultural, then more and more political. Pan-Turkist ideas were also disseminated among the Turks in Turkey by *émigrés* from the Russian Empire, such as Akçuraoğlu Yusuf (1876–1939), Ağaoğlu Ahmed (1869–1939), and Hüseyinzade Ali (1864–1941).

Pan-Turkist ideas found little support among the Young Turk groups in exile, and such occasional expressions of them as Akçuraoğlu Yusuf's article, cited above, were either disregarded or refuted. The Young Turks were dedicated to the idea of the union—or association—of the Ottoman Empire, and Ottomanism, rather than Turkism, remained their official credo after their victory in 1908. But the march of events was leading in another direction. The loss of one province after another in Europe was solving the problem of the Christian subjects by ending their subjection, and left an empire not only dominated by Muslims, but also predominantly inhabited by Muslims. The defection of the Muslim Albanians, and the stirrings of dissent among the Muslim Arabs, both encouraged and were encouraged by the growing insistence on the Turkishness of what remained. On the one hand, there was a sharpening impression, both at home and abroad, that Ottomanism, in administrative practice, meant enforced Turkification; on the other, there was a mounting wave of pan-Turkish cultural and to a lesser extent, political activities, with a lively periodical literature and a network of Turkist clubs.

The first of these was the *Türk Derneği*, the Turkish Society, founded in Istanbul on 24 December 1908. With this society, the declared purpose of which was to study 'the past and present achievements, activities, and circumstances of all the peoples called Turk', the name 'Turk' emerged from the obscurity in which it had lain hidden, and the Turkist movement acquired its first platform in Turkey.[44]

The objectives of the *Türk Derneği* were scholarly and cultural—'to study and make known the ancient remains, history, languages, literatures, ethnography and ethnology, social conditions and present civilizations of the Turks, and the ancient and modern geography of the Turkish lands'. As well as a number of well-known Turkists, its members included Ottoman non-Muslims and foreign Orientalists; its president was the heir-apparent, Prince Yusuf Izzeddin. In 1911 the *Türk Derneği* began to publish a

[44] Akçuraoğlu Yusuf, pp. 435 ff.

monthly journal of the same name, of which only seven issues appeared.

The disappearance of the monthly *Türk Derneği* was followed very shortly by the appearance of a new journal, the *Türk Yurdu* (Turkish Homeland), which rapidly became the organ of a more systematic and political form of Turkism. Its founders were the poet Mehmed Emin, the author Ahmed Hikmet, Dr. Akil Muhtar, Ağaoğlu Ahmed, Hüseyinzade Ali, and Akçuraoğlu Yusuf. The three last-named were all Russian Turks; Akçuraoğlu Yusuf was the editor of the journal. In September 1912, when Ahmed Hikmet was sent to take up a consular appointment in Vienna, his place on the *Türk Yurdu* was taken by Ziya Gökalp (1876–1924), who was rapidly becoming the outstanding theoretician of the Turkist movement.[45] Under this editorial board, the *Türk Yurdu* became an important and influential organ, and a platform on which the major theoretical issues of cultural and political Turkism were discussed and elaborated.

Closely associated with the *Türk Yurdu* was the *Türk Ocağı*, (Turkish Hearth), a kind of club founded in 1912. Its aims were 'to advance the national education and raise the scientific, social, and economic level of the Turks, who are the foremost of the peoples of Islam, and to strive for the betterment of the Turkish race and language'. This it would do by opening clubs called Turkish Hearths, organizing courses, lectures, and debates, publishing books and pamphlets, and opening schools. The society would confine itself to national and social ends, and would take no part in politics, nor associate itself with any political party. The *Türk Yurdu* became its principal organ.[46]

The Turkish Hearths increased rapidly in number, not only in Istanbul but also in many provincial centres. Many prominent literary figures joined the movement, and contributed both to its journal and to the activities of its branches. In these centres, incidentally, mixed audiences met for the first time, and women were able to make their first appearance on a public platform, both as speakers and as performers in amateur theatricals.[47]

[45] On Ziya Gökalp see Heyd, *Foundations*, where further literature is cited. A selection of his writings, in English translation, was published by Niyazi Berkes. On the whole, Gökalp's influence seems to have been exercised more through personal relations than through his published works.

[46] Akçuraoğlu Yusuf, pp 439 ff.; Rossi, pp. 377 ff. On *Türk Yurdu* see further Esmeralda Yu. Gasanova, *Ideologiya burzuaznogo natsionalizma v Turtsii* (1966).

[47] Edib, *Turkey Faces West*, pp. 116–17.

Even in Salonika, the Rumelian capital of the Union and Progress movement, a Turkist trend soon appeared, and found expression in the literary review *Genç Kalemler* (Young Pens), founded in 1911. One of its regular contributors was Ziya Gökalp, who in his poem 'Turan', published in 1911, produced this much-quoted verse formulation of pan-Turanianism.

> The country of the Turks is not Turkey, nor yet Turkistan,
> Their country is a vast and eternal land: Turan![48]

For the Turkish exiles and immigrants from the Russian Empire, pan-Turanianism or pan-Turkism was indeed a political programme, which in its maximalist form implied the political unification of all the Turkish-speaking peoples, in Turkey, Russia, Persia, Afghanistan, and China, in a single state. The main obstacle to this, the power of Russia, would be overcome with the help of the Western states.

Among the Turks of Turkey this programme won only limited support. Their interest in the movement was social, cultural, and literary—a greater awareness of their separate identity as Turks, a new feeling of kinship with their rediscovered ancestors and their remote cousins, a new interest in Turkish language, folklore, and tradition. On the question of a closer political association with these cousins, Ottoman Turkish opinion was at first more cautious. The outbreak of war in 1914, with Turkey fighting Russia as the ally of two mighty military empires, aroused wider and more extensive hopes, and in 1914 Ziya Gökalp opened his poem *Kızıl Destan* (Red epic) with the couplet:

> The land of the enemy shall be devastated,
> Turkey shall be enlarged and become Turan.[49]

After a rebuff caused by the defeats of the Ottoman armies, these hopes flared up again after 1917, when the Russian Revolution and the collapse of the Russian Empire seemed to offer a tempting opportunity to liberate and unite the Turkish peoples and thus achieve the pan-Turkish dream. It was partly under the inspiration of such ideas that Enver Paşa embarked on his ill-fated schemes, the invasion of Trans-Caucasia in 1918, and his subsequent adventures in Central Asia.

[48] *OM* (1924), p. 576; Heyd, *Foundations*, p. 126; Rossi, p. 378.
[49] Heyd, *Foundations*, p. 43. See also G. Jäschke, 'Der Turanismus der Jungtürken', *WI*, xxiii (1941), 1–54.

The distinctions between the three brands—Islamism, Otto-manism, Turkism—are not always easy to see. The Ottomanists revealed that, despite their professions, they were not prepared to concede real equality to non-Muslims; the Turkists made it clear that their greater Turkish family was limited to those professing Islam, and excluded the rest. To this extent, both groups were Islamists, and the Ottomanist leaders were indeed ready to make use both of pan-Islamism and pan-Turkism when they suited their ends.

Ottomanism was manifestly dying; the question was whether Islam or Turkism would inherit its place, as the basis of cohesion and loyalty of the Turkish people. Ottomanism had been a loyalty to an Empire and a dynasty—but the Empire was breaking up, and the dynasty going into exile. Islam and Turkism had this in common, that they were both non-territorial; there was no country and no government in existence defined by either of them. The Muslim Turks of Turkey might classify themselves as Muslims—by faith and law; or as Turks—by language and real or imagined descent; they had not yet thought of defining them-selves as the people of a country—of Turkey.

Patriotism

It was this new idea—of a territorial nation-state based on the Turkish nation *in Turkey*—that makes its first appearance in the early days of the Kemalist Revolution. The National Pact of 1919–20, containing the basic demands of the nationalists in Anatolia, speaks of areas 'inhabited by an Ottoman Muslim majority, united in religion, in race and in aim', in which full and undivided sovereignty is required.

The Pact still speaks of 'Ottoman Muslims' and not of Turks, and the word Turk appears nowhere in the document. But Mustafa Kemal soon made it clear that he was fighting for the people of Turkey, and not for any vaguer, larger entity beyond the national frontiers, whether defined by religion or by race. In a speech delivered on 1 December 1921, he explicitly rejected these movements as useless and dangerous:

Gentlemen! Every one of our compatriots and coreligionists may nourish a high ideal in his mind; he is free to do so, and no one will interfere. But the government of the Grand National Assembly of Turkey has a firm, positive, material policy, and that, gentlemen, is directed to the preservation of life and independence . . . within defined national frontiers. The Grand National Assembly and government of Turkey, in the name of the nation they represent, are very modest, very far from fantasies, and completely realistic. . . .

Gentlemen, we are not men who run after great fantasies and present a fraudulent appearance of doing things which in fact we cannot do. Gentlemen, by looking as though we were doing great and fantastic things, without actually doing them, we have brought the hatred, rancour, and malice of the whole world on this country and this people. We did not serve pan-Islamism. We said that we had and we would, but we didn't, and our enemies said: 'Let us kill them at once before they do!' We did not serve pan-Turanianism. We said that we could and we would, and again they said: 'Let us kill them!' There you have the whole problem. . . . Rather than run after ideas which we did not and could not realise and thus increase the number of our enemies and the pressure upon us, let us return to our natural, legitimate limits. And let us know our limits. Gentlemen, we are a nation desiring life and independence. For that and that alone may we give our lives.[50]

The Ottoman Empire was dead. For centuries the Turkish people had squandered their energies and their blood in the useless struggle to conquer and defend alien lands and peoples. Now that Empire was gone, and for the Turks too its passing was a liberation from an intolerable burden. For their Muslim and Turkish brothers elsewhere the people of Turkey had the greatest sympathy and the warmest of feelings—but no more. Their destiny and their responsibility lay in their native land, which it was their duty to free, to defend, and to rebuild. From this task they must not be distracted by vast and visionary schemes of Islamic or Turanian unity, which were either outdated or premature.

The growth of cultural nationalism since 1908 had accustomed the new generation of Turks to the idea of Turkishness—of identity and loyalty based on the Turkish nation. The Kemalist Republic brought a new idea—that of Turkey—the land of the Turks. So new was this idea, that the Turkish language had even lacked a name for it. The Young Ottomans had used the Persian form Turkistan; Mehmed Emin had spoken of *Türkeli*—Turkland, and only during the Young Turk period had the name *Türkiye* come into common usage. It was first adopted officially by the Kemalist state in Anatolia, to mean the remaining central core of

[50] *Söylev*, i. 193, 195–6.

354 The Emergence of Modern Turkey

the Ottoman Empire inhabited by Turks. It was used as the name
of the country in the law of 1921, and in the republican constitution of 1924. In the forceful phrase of Peyami Safa, 'Pan-Islamism
sailed away from Istanbul with the Allied fleets and fled with
Vahideddin; Ottomanism was lynched at Izmid with Ali Kemal.'[51]

This new idea of the territorial state of Turkey, the fatherland
of a nation called the Turks, was by no means easy to inculcate
in a people so long accustomed to religious and dynastic loyalties.
The frontiers of the new state were themselves new and unfamiliar, entirely devoid of the emotional impact made by the
beloved outlines of their country on generations of schoolboys in
the West; even the name of the country, *Türkiye*, was new in conception and alien in form, so much so that the Turkish authorities
hesitated for a while between variant spellings of it.[52]

The Religious Minorities

A good example of the confusion of concepts and loyalties prevailing at this time can be seen in the Greco-Turkish exchange of
populations, arranged after the treaty of Lausanne. Greece and
Turkey had ended their conflict, and a separate agreement
between them provided for the permanent settlement of minority
problems by a compulsory exchange of populations. Between 1923
and 1930 about a million and a quarter Greeks were sent from
Turkey to Greece, and a rather smaller number of Turks from
Greece to Turkey.

At first sight this exchange seems a clear indication of the
prevalence on both sides of nationalistic and patriotic ideas, and
of the desire to give greater unity and cohesion to the nation and
the fatherland. Yet on closer examination of what actually took
place, it begins to appear that other ideas and other loyalties were
still at work. The Greeks of Karaman who were 'repatriated' to
Greece were Greek Christians by religion—yet most of them knew
no Greek. Their language was Turkish—which they wrote in the
Greek script—and the inscriptions in their abandoned churches
and cemeteries in Karaman still testify to their linguistic Turkishness. In the same way, many of the repatriated Turks from Greece

[51] Safa, p. 87; cf. Rossi, in *OM*, xxiii. 381. Ali Kemal (1867–1922) was Minister of
the Interior in Damad Ferid Paşa's cabinet, and a relentless enemy of the nationalists.
In November 1922 he was arrested in Pera and sent to Ankara for trial, but was seized
and lynched by a mob in Izmid.
[52] *WI*, n.s., ii (1953), 279; iii (1954), 278–9; iv (1955), 61.

knew little or no Turkish, but spoke Greek—and wrote it in the Turco-Arabic script. What took place was not an exchange of Greeks and Turks, but rather an exchange of Greek Orthodox Christians and Ottoman Muslims. A Western observer, accustomed to a different system of social and national classification, might even conclude that this was no repatriation at all, but two deportations into exile—of Christian Turks to Greece, and of Muslim Greeks to Turkey.

In general, the status of the religious minorities in Turkey is a good indication of the progress—and setbacks—of these new ideas. Toleration is of course a relative matter. According to the principles professed by modern democracies, toleration means the absence of discrimination. In that sense, the old Ottoman Empire was not tolerant, since non-Muslims were not the civic and social equals of the followers of the dominant faith, but were subject to a number of legal disabilities. But complete toleration is new and insecure even in the most enlightened modern democracies, and there have been appalling lapses from it. It would hardly be reasonable to look for it in the old Ottoman Empire. If we define toleration as the absence, not of discrimination, but of persecution, then the Ottoman record until the late nineteenth century is excellent. The well-known preference of the fifteenth-century Greeks for Muslim rather than Frankish rule was not without its reasons. The confrontation of Islam and Christendom in the fifteenth and sixteenth centuries has sometimes been compared with the cold war of the mid-twentieth. In making the comparison, we should remember that the movement of refugees then was from West to East.

With the visible decline of Ottoman power and the rise of European influence in the nineteenth century, there was a catastrophic change for the worse in the position of the Ottoman non-Muslims. The material relationship between Muslim and Christian had changed beyond recognition. Even the theoretical basis of association was gone. The old, mutually accepted relationship between Muslims and *Zimmîs*, conferring a definite and agreed status and rights on the latter, had been undermined and destroyed by new ideas and new ambitions. Liberal principles required the Turks to give the subject peoples full equality of rights in the state; national principles entitled these peoples to rebel against it, and set up independent states of their own;

Christian and Imperial principles enabled the powers of Europe to intervene on their behalf, supporting their claims both to citizenship and to secession. In these circumstances, suspicion, fear, hatred—and sometimes, we may add, the high example of Western intolerance—transformed the Turkish attitude to the subject peoples. Turkish weakness and uncertainty, in the face of foreign invasion and internal rebellion, often led to terrible oppression and brutality.

Most tragic was the case of the Armenians, who at the beginning of the nineteenth century were still known as the *Millet-i Sadıka*, the loyal community, and were described by a well-informed French visitor as the minority group most loyal to the Ottoman Empire and most trusted by the Turks. The change began with the Russian conquest of the Caucasus in the first quarter of the nineteenth century, and the creation of a Russian Armenia on the eastern border of Turkey, where the Armenian Church was established and recognized and where Armenian governors and generals ruled provinces and commanded armies. The political and cultural impact of Russian Armenia on the one hand, and the new national and liberal ideas coming from Europe on the other, powerfully affected the Ottoman Armenians, especially the rising middle class, and stimulated the growth of an ardent and active Armenian nationalist movement.

For the Turks, the Armenian movement was the deadliest of all threats. From the conquered lands of the Serbs, Bulgars, Albanians, and Greeks, they could, however reluctantly, withdraw, abandoning distant provinces and bringing the Imperial frontier nearer home. But the Armenians, stretching across Turkey-in-Asia from the Caucasian frontier to the Mediterranean coast, lay in the very heart of the Turkish homeland—and to renounce these lands would have meant not the truncation, but the dissolution of the Turkish state. Turkish and Armenian villages, inextricably mixed, had for centuries lived in neighbourly association. Now a desperate struggle between them began—a struggle between two nations for the possession of a single homeland, that ended with the terrible slaughter of 1915, when, according to estimates, more than a million Armenians perished, as well as an unknown number of Turks.

In the Turkish Republic, the constitution and the law accorded complete equality to all citizens. Yet even on the official side, in the structure and policies of the state, there were signs that, despite secularism and nationalism, the older idea that Muslim equals Turk and non-Muslim equals non-Turk persisted. In some respects the participation of non-Muslims in the public life of Turkey actually decreased after the establishment of the Republic, although their legal status on paper was higher than ever before. Certain forms of discrimination continued—for example, non-Muslims were called up for military service but did not bear arms and were not commissioned, while the number of non-Muslims in the civil service dwindled rapidly. All this can be largely but not wholly explained by their ignorance of Turkish and their self-isolation from the social and cultural world of the Turks. The cosmopolitan Islamic Empire had assigned a definite place and function to the non-Muslim minorities; the nationalist Republic could offer little to those who either would not or could not join the dominant group. While on the one hand Turkish-speaking Orthodox Christians from Anatolia were classed as Greeks and sent to Greece, the children of Muslim Bosniaks or Albanians, Kurds or Arabs settled in Istanbul were accepted as Turks. Significantly, religion still appeared on identity cards and other official documents, and the designation Turk was in common usage restricted to Muslims; the rest were known as Turkish citizens, but never as Turks.

Feelings towards the non-Muslims varied. The exacerbated hatreds of the last years of the Empire reached their climax after the 1918 Armistice, when many Ottoman Christians made no secret of their delight in the Allied occupation. Thereafter, as the memories of the occupation and of the war receded into the past, relations between Muslims and non-Muslims improved. The latter, despite successive improvements in their status, remained separate and distinct, extruded from the body of the nation. The fundamental weakness of their position was once again revealed in the episode of the capital levy in 1942–3.[53]

The Anatolian Fatherland

However strange the idea, however great the difficulties, a Turkish national state was in fact coming into being. The Balkans, for long the centre of gravity of the Ottoman Empire, were lost. The Arab countries, the heartlands of Islam, had gone their several ways. Anatolia, after the final bloody struggle against the Armenians and the Greeks, had been held as a Turkish land, and

[53] See above, pp. 297 ff.

even the capital was now transferred from cosmopolitan, Levantine, Imperial Constantinople to an Anatolian hilltown with a Seljuk citadel.

The idea of a Turkish nation had made rapid headway among the Turkish educated classes. It had, however, brought with it a new danger. The loss of the Empire was recent, and still rankled with many, to whom the idea of a comparatively small nation-state seemed unsatisfying and unattractive. In pan-Turkist circles and especially among the Tatar exiles, the idea was current that a new Imperial destiny awaited the Turks, whose task it was, not to revive the polyglot and multi-national Ottoman Empire, but to create a new pan-Turkish Empire of the Turkish and Tatar peoples from the Aegean to the China Sea.

To all such projects and ambitions Mustafa Kemal was firmly opposed. The Turks had a long and hard task to perform in Turkey. Their Turkish brothers elsewhere might enjoy their sympathetic interest and friendship; they must, however, work out their own political fate, and not try to distract the Turkish Republic from the work in hand to remote and dangerous adventures.

What was needed was patriotism rather than nationalism— loyalty to the existing, legally defined, sovereign Republic of Turkey, rather than to an ill-defined and variously interpreted entity like the nation.

The term *vatan*, fatherland, had had a chequered history in modern Turkey. In the mid-nineteenth century, according to Cevdet Paşa, it would have meant, to a Turkish soldier, no more than the village square; by the late nineteenth century, to Namık Kemal, it suggested the whole Ottoman Empire, including— perhaps especially—the Holy Cities of Arabia. For the pan-Turkist Ziya Gökalp in 1911, it was neither Turkey nor Turkistan but the vast land of Turan. Yet as late as August 1917, the Grand Vezir Mehmed Said Halim Paşa could still firmly assert that 'the fatherland of a Muslim is the place where the *Şeriat* prevails'.[54]

It was against this variegated background of traditions and ideas that Kemal sought to adapt and inculcate the new idea of an Anatolian Turkish fatherland. His aim was to destroy what remained of the Islamic and Ottoman feelings of loyalty, to

[54] Quoted in Inal, *Sadrıazamlar*, p. 1892.

counter the distractions of pan-Islamic and pan-Turkist appeals, and to forge a new loyalty, of the Turkish nation to its home-land. His chosen instrument was history. The Ottoman Histori-cal Society had been wound up. A new Turkish Historical Society was founded in 1930, to serve as the medium of state policy for the imposition of certain historical theories. Its tasks included the drafting of new historical syllabuses and textbooks, on patriotic lines, for use in schools and universities.

In 1932 a Turkish historical congress was convened in Ankara, which was inspired by Mustafa Kemal and attended by pro-fessors and teachers of history from all over Turkey, as well as by scholars and delegates from abroad.

The theory propounded by Kemal and his disciples was, briefly, that the Turks were a white, Aryan people, originating in Central Asia, the cradle of all human civilization. Owing to the progressive desiccation of this area, the Turks had migrated in waves to various parts of Asia and Africa, carrying the arts of civilization with them. Chinese, Indian, and Middle Eastern civilizations had all been founded in this way, the pioneers in the last named being the Sumerians and Hittites, who were both Turkic peoples. Anatolia had thus been a Turkish land since antiquity. This mixture of truth, half-truth, and error was pro-claimed as official doctrine, and teams of researchers set to work to 'prove' its various propositions.[55]

It would be a grave error to deride all this as the whim of an autocrat. Kemal was too great a man to organize an elaborate campaign of this sort out of mere caprice, or out of a simple desire for national self-glorification. One of the reasons for the campaign was the need to provide some comfort for Turkish national self-respect, which had been sadly undermined during the last century or two. First, there was the demoralizing effect of a long period of almost uninterrupted defeat and withdrawal by the Imperial Ottoman forces. Then there was the inevitable reaction to Western prejudice. It is difficult not to sympathize with the frustration and discouragement of the young Turk, eager for enlightenment, who applied himself to the study of Western

[55] Lewis, in *MEA*, iv. 224 ff. The 'historical thesis' is extensively discussed in the earlier publications of the *Türk Tarih Kurumu* (Turkish Historical Society), and in most of the general books about Turkey. For a rather forlorn recent statement of the former official purpose, see Ahmet Cevat Emre, *Atatürk'ün Inkılab Hedefi ve Tarih Tezi* (1956).

languages, to find that in most of them his name was an insult. In the English dictionary the Turk shares with the Jew[56] and the Welshman the distinction of having given his name to a term of abuse. The mixture of prejudice, ignorance, and cynicism that disfigures most European writings about the Turks can have given him no very high opinion of the European ideal of disinterested historical inquiry and the search for truth. His opinion will not have been raised by the readiness with which some European institutions and scholars, for political reasons, lent their encouragement to the Turkish official thesis. Once upon a time the Turk had been accustomed to despise his neighbours and his enemies from the comfortable altitude of superior religion and Imperial authority. Empire was gone, and the growth of secularism was depriving him even of the consolations of religion.

Though the encouragement of Turkish pride and self-respect was no doubt an essential part of Kemal's purpose, it was probably not his primary objective. This was to teach the Turks that Anatolia—Turkey—was their true homeland, the centre of their nationhood from time immemorial, and thus to hasten the growth of that ancient, intimate relationship, at once mystical and practical, between nation and country that is the basis of patriotism in the sovereign nation-states of the West.

During the years that followed, the wilder historical theories were quietly abandoned and decently buried, but the patriotic loyalty which they had served to encourage grew steadily. In the schools and universities of the Republic a new generation grew up for whom the Empire was a burden now happily cast off, and the now familiar rectangle of the Turkish Republic the focus of their loyalties and aspirations.

The widening gulf between Turkey and the eastern Islamic world; the gathering momentum of Westernization and modernization; the rise of a new secular-educated generation brought up to accept the Turkish Republic as the final fruition of land and people—all these fostered a deepening consciousness of territorial identity; the embattled neutrality of Turkey amid the swirling currents and buffeting storms of a Second World War made it at once more vivid and more concrete.

---

[56] This companionship in obloquy, which has parallels elsewhere in Europe, may in part account for the prominence of Jews among European Turcologists and Turcophiles, such as Davids, Cahun, Vambéry, and, of a different kind, Disraeli.

While the larger loyalties of the Muslim Turks were being transferred and modified in the as yet unresolved equation of Islam, Turkism, and Turkey, their lesser loyalties were still given, much as before, to the smaller, more local groupings of kin and craft, tribe and brotherhood. These even found a new function with the coming of contested elections. The best hope for the future lay in the sometimes painful emergence, out of all the groups, of the individual—better informed and more self-reliant, with a growing awareness of his place, his rights, and his duties in a free modern society.

CHAPTER XI

State and Government

O you who believe, obey God, obey the Prophet, and obey those among you who hold authority.

KORAN, iv. 62.

He who applies and administers a decision is always more powerful than he who makes it.

MUSTAFA KEMAL, 1921.

CENTRAL GOVERNMENT

Constitution [1]

DURING the nineteenth century the Turkish reformers tried, by legislative enactment, to give Turkey the form and structure of a European state. European laws and judiciary, European ministries and administrative procedures were copied with more or less fidelity, usually from French originals, and promulgated by Imperial decree. The culmination of this process saw the Ottoman constitution of 1876, the supreme achievement of the liberal reformers, which was to turn the Ottoman Empire into a parliamentary democracy, and the Ottoman Sultan into a constitutional monarch. The original, this time, was not French but Belgian, the Belgian constitution of 1831 combining the advantages of being liberal, monarchical, and written in French.

But the Ottoman Empire was not Belgium. The Belgian constitution worked well enough in Belgium, where it was the result of centuries of Belgian history, and where the Belgian parliament was the apex of a pyramid of responsible elected assemblies with its base in the Belgian parish and borough councils. A similar constitution, adapted into Turkish, was inevitably irrelevant, unrelated to Turkish conditions, and ultimately unworkable.

This constitution was not formally abrogated, but with the

---

[1] On the development of the Ottoman and Turkish constitutions see *EI*[2] ('Dustūr' by B. Lewis; revised version in *Dustūr*, Leiden 1966, pp. 6–24), and *IA* ('Kanun-i Esasi' by Hüseyin Nail Kubalı). Discussions of constitutional developments will be found in Jäschke, in *WI*, v. 5–56; Pritsch, 'Die türkische Verfassung vom 20 April 1924', *MSOS*, xxvi–xxvii/2 (1924), 164–251 and Jäschke, 'Auf dem Wege zur türkischen Republik', *WI*, n.s., v (1958), 206–18. See further above, pp. 160 ff., 256 ff., and 265.

closing of parliament by Abdülhamid on 14 February 1878 it was in fact tacitly suspended for thirty years. It was restored by the Young Turk Revolution of 1908; soon after, on 1 August a *Hatt-i Humayun* from the Sultan to the Grand Vezir Said Paşa declared the constitution to be fully effective and in force again, and supplemented it with a number of further provisions, extending the personal liberty of the subject and guaranteeing its inviolability. The Rescript prohibited arrest and search except by lawful procedures, abolished all special and exceptional courts, introduced for the first time the principle of freedom of travel, and guaranteed the security of the mails and the freedom of the press. A striking omission from this festival of freedom was that the notorious article 113 of the 1876 constitution, reserving to the Sultan the exclusive right to deport persons dangerous to the state, was for the moment left unchanged. It was abolished in the following year.[2]

The Rescript of August 1908, restoring the constitution, thus in fact made important additions to it. After the opening of parliament on 17 December 1908 further proposals for constitutional changes were made and debated. The need for revision was generally agreed on, and a constitutional commission was formed, to prepare draft proposals. Amid the burst of legislative activity of the first Young Turk parliament, there was no time for a detailed and systematic revision of the whole text of the constitution. Instead, the drafting commission produced a series of *ad hoc* amendments, modifying some articles and remaking or replacing others. The Bill became law on 21 August 1909.

These amendments, though piecemeal, amounted to a major constitutional change, the purpose of which is clear. The Committee of Union and Progress dominated both houses of parliament; the palace, even after the deposition of Abdülhamid, was still feared as the possible source of a reactionary coup. The amendments therefore aimed at strengthening parliament and weakening the throne. Both the Sultan and the Grand Vezir, whom the Sultan nominated, were reduced in stature and authority. The sovereignty of parliament was triumphantly affirmed.

The resulting weakness of the executive was found inconvenient

[2] On these and the following constitutional changes, see Jäschke, in *WI*, v. 20 ff.; texts in Gözübüyük and Kili (trans. in Kraelitz-Greifenhorst).

to the Young Turks themselves, and the constitutional struggles of the next ten years were caused by their efforts, sometimes fiercely resisted, to restore the executive power. The new Sultan, Mehmed V, proved himself a harmless and loyal collaborator, and the Unionists soon began to feel safe enough in their control of the palace and the Grand Vezirate to want them strong rather than weak. Towards the end of 1911 they submitted proposals to parliament to this effect. These were bitterly opposed by the opposition, on the grounds, it was made clear, that they would strengthen, not the Sultan, but the Committee of Union and Progress. In the parliamentary and constitutional crisis that followed, parliament was dissolved. After the elections of April 1912, the Unionists were securely in power, and on 18 May tabled more than 100 draft laws, including a proposal to amend several articles of the constitution. These amendments, increasing the Sultan's authority over parliament, became law on 28 May 1914. Subsequent amendments, in January 1915 and March 1916, still further increased the powers of the Sultan, who was now able to convene, prorogue, prolong, and dismiss parliament almost at his discretion.

The final amendment to the old constitution came in April 1918. The parliament inaugurated in May 1914 had reached its legal term, and new elections were due. These were clearly not possible at the time, and an amendment to the constitution authorized the prolongation of parliament, by emergency enactment, in time of war.

On 21 December 1918 the new Sultan, Mehmed VI, dismissed parliament and ruled through the Grand Vezir. New elections began in December 1919—the sixth and last general election in the Ottoman Empire. The Chamber assembled on 12 January 1920, prorogued itself on 18 March and was dissolved by the Sultan on 11 April. The last Ottoman parliament had ended its final session. Twelve days later the Grand National Assembly of Turkey held its opening session in Ankara.

Mustafa Kemal and the nationalists in Anatolia were at first very careful to maintain legal continuity. They made war against the foreign invader and occupier; not against the lawful sovereign or his government, to whom they were careful to show due respect. Kemal first came to Anatolia with an appointment from the Sultan. When he was deprived of this, some new status was necessary; he found it through the Association for the Defence of the Rights of Eastern Anatolia, with its headquarters in Erzurum. On 24 August 1919 Mustafa Kemal, 'former inspector of the Third Army, officer, retired', together with a group of similarly 'retired' associates, addressed a formal message to the vilayet of Erzurum, asking for legal recognition of the 'Representative Committee' of this association, 'in accordance with the Law of Associations'.[3]

This legally recognized 'Representative Committee' provided the link from the old to a new legality. When it seemed clear that the last legal parliament in Istanbul were no longer free agents, Kemal and his associates proceeded to hold elections to an emergency assembly to meet in Ankara. Even in this revolutionary action, Kemal still sought for continuity; his order to all vilayets, independent sanjaks, and officers commanding army corps begins by referring to the dissolution of parliament under foreign pressure, and the consequent inability of the deputies to perform their duties. For this reason, the national interest required the immediate convening of an assembly in Ankara, 'which will be furnished with extraordinary powers and will permit members of the chamber that has been dissolved to come to Ankara to take part in it'. Only then does Kemal 'in the name of the Representative Committee', go on to order elections, to be conducted by colleges of electors.[4]

When the assembly met, Mustafa Kemal was elected as its President; significantly, the vice-president was Celâleddin Arif, the last President of the Chamber of Deputies. On the third day, 25 April, the Assembly resolved on the creation of its executive arm. After a lengthy discussion, two commissions, an executive commission and a drafting commission, were elected, the second to draft proposals for a permanent executive, the first to act in the meantime. On 1 May 1920 the draft was submitted. After a heated debate it was passed and at once became effective. In accordance with its terms, a first 'Committee of Executive Delegates', of

[3] *Nutuk*, i. 67; *Documents*, no. 41; cf. *Speech*, p. 59. See also Jäschke, 'Die ersten Verfassungsentwürfe der Ankara-Türkei', *Mitt. Aus.-Hoch. Univ. Berlin*, xlii/2 (1939), 58.

[4] *Nutuk*, i. 420 ff.; *Speech*, pp. 364 ff.; cf. Jäschke, p. 59. On the formation and development of the Grand National Assembly see further the two important studies of Tunaya, 'Osmanlı İmparatorluğundan Türkiye Büyük Millet Meclisi Hükumeti Rejimine Giriş', in *Prof. Muammer Raşit Sevig'e Armağan* (1956); and 'Türkiye Büyük Meclisi Hükumeti'nin Kuruluşu ve Siyasi Karakteri' (offprint, Ist., n.d.), and of Bıyıklıoğlu, in *Bell.*, no. 96 (1960), 637–63.

eleven men, was elected. The Assembly had acquired a government.[5]

On 22 April, the day before the Assembly opened, Mustafa Kemal sent out a circular to the army and provincial administration, informing them that from the following day 'the National Assembly will be the lawful authority to which all civil and military authorities and the entire nation must turn'.[6]

The Assembly itself was less certain of its status and functions. It was a mixed body, including some 125 civil servants, 13 municipal officials, 53 soldiers (10 of them pashas), 53 men of religion (including 14 muftis), and 5 tribal chiefs. The remaining 120 odd members were engaged in commerce, farming, in the professions—including 40 merchants, 32 farmers, 20 lawyers, 1 journalist, 2 engineers, and a single artisan—a master gunsmith. No less than 92 of its members had belonged to the last Chamber of Deputies.[7]

Many of the members remained firmly attached to the Sultan-Caliph, and insisted that all their actions had a provisional and emergency character. The Assembly argued from the start that it could not be made to recognize a provisional head of government or to form a regency, and voted, perhaps a little ambiguously, that the Sultan-Caliph, when he had been liberated from his present constraint, would resume his functions within the framework determined by the laws which the Assembly would adopt.[8] Meanwhile, the liberation of the Sultan-Caliph from enemy hands was a prime objective of the Assembly and the conservatives went so far as to say that 'we find ourselves in the necessity of creating a government without a head'.[9] In fact, avoiding the term government, they approved the creation of a 'committee of executive delegates' to fulfil the same purpose.

The Assembly, which thus shied away even from the idea of forming an interim government, was far from desiring to frame a constitution. But the strong hand of its leader, and the relentless pressure of events, drove it irresistibly in that direction.

Mustafa Kemal thought from the start in terms of a constituent assembly. The bitter struggle fought against the Assembly by the Sultan's Government and by its irregular forces

[5] Tunaya, 'Karakter', pp. 6–11.   [6] *Nutuk*, i. 432; *Speech*, p. 375.
[7] Tunaya, 'Karakter', p. 5. On the composition of this and subsequent Assemblies see Frey, *Elite* (1965), pp. 161 ff.

[8] Jäschke, in *Mitt. Aus.-Hoch. Univ. Berlin*, xlii/2, p. 60; *Hist.*, pp. 52–53.

[9] Tunaya, 'Karakter', p. 7.

in Anatolia, even more than the occupation of parts of Anatolia by foreign armies, drove more and more of the deputies to follow his lead.

There were several paths which the drafters of a new Turkish constitution might take. The arguments of the Westernizers and the Islamists, brought into the open after 1908, were familiar. The Western forms of parliamentary democracy, though for the moment tarnished by Western hostility to Turkey, were well known, and moreover, bore the laurels of victory over their authoritarian opponents. In the East, a new system of government was arising out of the chaos of the Russian Revolution. In September 1920 a 'Congress of Eastern Peoples' assembled in Baku, to proclaim the message of revolutionary Communism to the peoples of Asia. Enver Paşa appeared in Moscow and elsewhere, and a Communist movement, known as the Green Army, for a while played a certain role in Anatolian affairs.

Turkish material interests at that moment lay with the Soviets against the West, and a friendly agreement between Kemal and the Bolsheviks was indeed signed in March 1921. But Kemal had no intention of making Turkey a Communist state, and managed with remarkable skill to avoid the closer embraces of his new and redoubtable neighbour.[10]

As early as August 1920 the Assembly was debating constitutional proposals, and devoting its attention to such problems of Western political thought as the separation of powers—a matter of great concern also to the Young Turk parliaments. Then, on 20 January 1921, the Grand National Assembly passed the 'Law of Fundamental Organizations'—in fact the provisional constitution of the new Turkey. The law, after declaring the sovereignty of the nation, went on to state that

the executive power and the legislative authority are vested and expressed in the Grand National Asembly, which is the only and real representative of the people.

The state of Turkey is administered by the Grand National Assembly and its Government bears the name of the 'Government of the Grand National Assembly'. . . .

[10] On the early relations between the Kemalists and the Bolsheviks, see Laqueur, *Communism*, pp. 205 ff. This account can now be amplified in the light of the memoirs of Gen. Cebesoy, the first Kemalist envoy to Moscow (*Memoirs*, ii); cf. Jäschke, in *WI*, n.s., v. 44 ff.

The remaining articles dealt with the holding of elections and the conduct of government business.[11]

The sovereignty of the people . . . the state of Turkey . . . these were new and revolutionary ideas, and their appearance in a constitutional enactment marks the first decisive step in the legal processes that transformed Turkey from an Islamic universal empire into a secular national state.

The transitional phase, which began with the formation of the Grand National Assembly, was completed with the proclamation of the Republic and the promulgation of the new constitution.[12]

The idea of a Republic in Muslim territory was strange, but not wholly new.[13] In the welter of theorizing on government and the state in the last years of the Ottoman Empire republican ideas did not appear, and it is indeed doubtful whether it would have been possible to express them.[14] But since 1918 republics had sprung up in several places. In the summer of 1918, after the dissolution of the ill-starred Transcaucasian Federation, the Turkish-speaking Muslims of Russian Azerbayjan proclaimed a republic—the first Muslim republic in modern times. Their example was followed by the Bashkir, Kirghiz, and other Turkic peoples of the former Russian Empire, who preferred to give this form to their short-lived freedom. Though all these republics were conquered and reconstituted by the Communists, the name and form of republican autonomy remained, and to many at that time bore great promise.

The republican idea soon began to appear outside Russia. As early as November 1918, the North African leader Suleymān al-Bārūnī made an unsuccessful attempt to establish an Arab republic in Tripoli. In Syria too republican ideas were current in some circles, and the institutions set up by the French mandatory authorities in Syria and Lebanon clearly tended towards republics,

---

[11] Jäschke, in *Mitt. Aus.-Hoch. Univ. Berlin*, xlii/2, and idem. in *WI*, n.s., v. 206–18. Text in Gözübüyük and Kili, pp. 85 ff.

[12] Debates in Gözübüyük and Zekai Sezgin, *1924 Anayasası hakkındaki Meclis Görüşmeleri* (1957); cf. E. C. Smith in *Ank. Univ. Siyasal Bilgiler Fak. Derg.*, xiii (1958), 82–105.

[13] cf. *EI*[2] *s.vv.* 'Djumhūriyya' and 'Ḥurriyya ii' (by B. Lewis).

[14] cf. the remarks of Atatürk, quoted by Emre, p. 5. On the first manifestations of republicanism, see the comments of Karabekir, *Istik. Harb* (1960), pp. 978, 1136–7, etc. Karabekir makes the startling allegation that Mustafa Kemal himself did not finally decide on a republic until a very late stage, and that he thought of retaining the office of Sultan and Caliph, though not necessarily in the house of Osman.

even though these were not formally proclaimed until after the Turks had set the example.

The world situation obviously favoured the republican cause. The great autocratic monarchies on both sides in the World War—Germany, Austria, Russia—had collapsed in ruin. France and America gave the example of old republics with power, wealth, and victory; Germany and Russia of new republics struggling to rise from ruin and defeat to something better. Britain, which might have provided the example of a monarchy both democratic and successful, was temporarily obscured from Turkish view by a bitter political conflict. The Turkish Assembly had already agreed that sovereignty belonged to the people. They could also see that success belonged to the republicans.

The proclamation of a Republic in Turkey was by no means unresisted. It has, however, never been seriously challenged; and with one major and several minor amendments, the constitution remained in force until 1960.

The Head of State

At first sight, the most striking change that took place as a result of the Kemalist Revolution was in the headship of the state. In place of the dynastic, divinely sanctioned Sultan-Caliph, there was a secular, elected, chief executive; in place of a bearded, braided emperor, a clean-shaven, dress-suited President.

But the change was more gradual and less abrupt than might appear. The tendency in the Turkish state throughout the nineteenth century had been towards increased personal despotism. The old Ottoman Sultans had been, within the limits of the Islamic law and the social system of the Empire, autocratic rulers. The Sultans of the seventeenth and eighteenth centuries, however, had lost most of their effective power to the vezirs and courtiers in the capital and to the pashas and notables in the provinces, and had little more effective power than a feudal king in medieval Europe. Under Selim III and his successors, and especially under Mahmud II and Abdülaziz, the personal ascendancy of the sovereign was restored—and not only restored, but carried to new heights unknown in earlier times. This was no longer the old Islamic autocracy, but a vastly strengthened personal despotism, freed from the limiting intermediate powers that had been swept away by the reformers, and sustained by such modern devices as the telegraph, the railway, and the gendarmerie.

This growth of personal rule was observed, resisted, and from time to time interrupted—though not for long. The constitutional interlude of 1876–8 ended in the reinforced personal rule of Abdülhamid; the constitutional millennium of 1908 expired in the dictatorship of the Young Turk triumvirate, of Enver, Talât, and Cemal Paşas.

This time it was no longer the Sultan who ruled, but a small group of ministers acting in his name. From a shadow Sultan to no Sultan proved, in the event, not too difficult a transition. Cemal and Enver were both soldiers; so too were Mustafa Kemal and Ismet. The incantatory flourish of constitution, parliament, party, and election does not hide the basic fact that the Republic was established by a professional soldier leading a victorious army and maintaining himself, in the early stages at least, by a combination of personal and military power.[15]

During Kemal's last years there seems to have been an estrangement between him and his old comrade-in-arms Ismet Paşa, and Ismet had been replaced as Prime Minister by Celâl Bayar, a banker and a civilian. But when Kemal died in 1938, it was the soldier Ismet who succeeded him as President—and a persistent rumour has it that it was the army that determined the final choice.

Yet the régime, though military in its origin and for a long time authoritarian in character, was never a mere military dictatorship. Perhaps because his personal autocracy could be grafted on to a living tradition, Kemal could dispense with the trappings of militarism, and tried to create a new republican and civilian legality. Both he and Ismet renounced military titles and uniforms; the constitution clearly subordinated the military to the civilian power, and the army withdrew into a silent loyalty. With the victory of the Democrat Party in the general elections of 1950, a civilian President and a civilian Prime Minister took over the government of Turkey.

Between 1923 and 1950 the Turkish Republic had only two Presidents. Kemal's re-elections by the Assembly were no more than a matter of form. In fact he enjoyed life tenure, with powers as great as those of any Sultan, appointing and dismissing Prime

---

[15] See Rustow, in *Wld. Polit.*, xi (1959), 513–52, and espec. 545–6.

Ministers and other ministers at will. Ismet Inönü inherited the same powers and for a while, during the difficult and dangerous years of the Second World War, even reinforced them. But in the period after 1945 there was a significant shift in authority. Democracy had won new laurels of victory—and the Assembly of the post-war years was more active and more demanding than its predecessors. The appearance, for the first time in many years, of a group of opposition members radically altered the situation, transferring the centre of internal political activity from the ante-room of the presidential palace to the lobbies of the Assembly. Ismet himself, by encouraging or permitting the growth of real parliamentary democracy in these years, and by attempting to place the presidential office above the political mêléc, helped the process.

In May 1950 the people, having owned sovereignty since 1923, exercised it for the first time. They elected an Assembly—the Assembly elected a President—the President appointed a Prime Minister. Both were civilians, of civilian background. The President remained the head of the state; the play of politics and personality would determine whether he would also remain the effective head of the government, or whether he would leave this task to the Prime Minister and himself withdraw into a largely formal primacy.

Ministers and Ministries

In the old Ottoman Empire the Sultan had been the sole repository and source of power in the state. He had appointed the Grand Vezir and other vezirs, the chief Finance Officer (*Defterdar*), the army and navy commanders, and other high officers of state. From early times, a state council, known as the Imperial Divan (*Divan-i Humayun*), assembled four times a week in the Topkapı Palace, in the room known as the Dome Chamber (*Kubbe-altı*). It was presided over by the Grand Vezir. Those who attended were the 'Dome Vezirs'—so-called because of their participation in this assembly, the Kaziaskers of Rumelia and Anatolia, the *Nişancı* (chief officer of chancery), the Defterdars, the Aga of the Janissaries if he held the rank of vizier, and, when he was in the city, the Kapudan Paşa of the fleet. It thus included the heads of the Chancery, the exchequer, the judiciary, and the armed forces, each of whom had his own personal staff and establishment.

During the seventeenth century this system was abandoned. The withdrawal of the Sultan Mehmed IV from Istanbul to Edirne and the energetic Grand Vezirate of the Köprülüs initiated a change in practice. In 1654 the Grand Vezir acquired an official residence and office, which came to be known as *Paşa Kapısı*, the Pasha's Gate or, more commonly, as *Bab-i Ali*, the Sublime Porte. This henceforth became the effective centre of the Ottoman Government, and the Grand Vezir its effective head. The *Divan-i Humayun* still met occasionally in the palace, but for purely ceremonial matters, while the real business of government was conducted elsewhere. There seems to have been no regular system of ministerial meetings, but in case of necessity the civil, military, and religious chiefs met at the Sublime Porte under the presidency of the Grand Vezir. If he were on campaign, they might meet in the palace of the *Şeyh-ül-Islâm* or the acting Vezir.

A new order began with the reforms of Mahmud II, who first tried to introduce the European system of ministries.[16] His first ministries were not really experiments in Westernization, but moves in an internal struggle, to bring the religious hierarchy under closer state supervision. It was not until some years later, in 1836–8, that the Sultan took the first steps towards the creation of ministries in the Western style, by giving Western titles to some of the officers of the Sublime Porte, and then even to the Grand Vezir himself.[17]

The change of style from Grand Vezir to Prime Minister was of short duration, lasting only for fourteen and a half months, after which the old title was restored. A second attempt to introduce the European title was made during the first constitutional interlude, then dropped after less than four months, then restored in the following year by Abdülhamid, then dropped again, after about three and a half years, in 1882. Thereafter the title Grand Vezir remained in official use until the end of the Empire.

These changes in the style of the chief minister were of no great importance, and the Turkish historian Abdurrahman Şeref is probably right in dismissing them as mere make-believe. The process, however, of extending the activities of government to new areas suggested by European example, and of creating new

[16] See above, pp. 96 ff.

[17] Şeref, *Tarih-i Devlet-i Os.*, ii. 470–5 (Interior) and 507 (Foreign Affairs), and *Tar. Mus.*, pp. 264 ff. (on the title of Prime Minister).

departments of the central government to deal with them, continued. In 1839 a Ministry of Works was set up, with the task of improving trade, agriculture, and economic life generally. In 1870 police matters, already withdrawn from the department of the Serasker (Commander-in-Chief), were handed over to a separate Ministry of Police; while the Seraskerate itself was evolving into a closer likeness of a Ministry of War. In 1879–80 this name was in fact briefly introduced and then dropped; it was reintroduced after the revolution of 1908.

Two other innovations greatly reduced the authority of the ulema. In 1857 a Ministry of Education took over and extended the former personal interest of the sovereign in schools and colleges, and transferred this important field from religious to secular control. In 1879 a Ministry of Justice assumed the direction of the new courts and judiciary set up by the reformers, and thus again reduced the area of religious jurisdiction.[18]

With these the main departments of state of the Empire were established. Subsequent additions were the Ministry of the Navy, the Ministry of Trade and Agriculture, separated from the Ministry of Works; the Ministry of Post, Telegraphs, and Telephones; and, by a decree of 30 July 1918, a Ministry of Food.

The advent of the Republic brought important changes. The ministries were of course all moved to Ankara, the new capital, where they were in time housed in separate buildings. Some of them, as the Ministries of Foreign and of Internal Affairs, for the first time became physically separate entities. But for all of them the departure from the old Imperial city, and from the overshadowing pressure of such ancient centres as the palace and the Sublime Porte, opened the way to a new phase of development in republican, secular Ankara.

The new régime created several new ministries, once again reflecting the extension of the area of government activity, notably in social and economic matters. A Ministry of Health and Social Welfare dates back to the days of the first Ankara government. A Ministry of Labour was established in January 1946, and has developed rapidly since then.[19]

[18] For a useful general survey of the ministries in the first half of the nineteenth century, see Şeref, *Tarih-i Devlet-i Os.*, ii, 464 ff.

[19] A. Gorvine and L. L. Barber, *Organization and Functions of Turkish Ministries* 1957).

The Civil Service

During the nineteenth century the term *mülkiye*, roughly 'civilian', came into general use, to designate the civil service, both central and provincial, as distinct from the other two branches of the government, the military (*askeriye*) and the religious (*ilmiye*). The Department of Internal Affairs, established by Mahmud II in 1836, was originally called *mülkiye*, and although this name was changed to *dahiliye* (internal) in the following year, the term *mülkiye* remained in general use for the non-military, non-ecclesiastical servants of the state.

The recruitment and maintenance of a civilian bureaucracy for the new and reconstructed ministries and departments presented various problems. Between 1833 and 1846 a series of ordinances laid down the tables of rank, precedence, titles, and honours for the new service, and incidentally established a new precedent by according them to offices instead of to officers.[20] But there were more practical problems to settle in the creation of a modern civil service.

One of the central problems was that of recruitment. The new system of secular schools set up by Mahmud II and his successors provided more recruits, but they were still sadly inadequate. In about 1872, in a memorandum to the Grand Vezir, Cevdet Paşa remarked:

If we are still deficient as regards judicial officials, we are even more deficient as regards executive officials, and are growing daily more so. It is an urgent necessity to expand the *mülkiye* school in accordance with the time and situation, to rearrange the programme of studies correspondingly, to employ its graduates progressively in important posts, and thus to train competent administrative officials. Our immediate obligation is to take care to choose and employ those who are already fairly experienced and thus put the state administration on the right path. If we give up finding jobs for men, and instead make it our policy to find men for jobs, then it is certain that within a short time officials capable of administering the country will emerge. . . .[21]

This doctrine, and Cevdet's immediately following argument, that these officials should be paid regular and adequate salaries, proved too revolutionary and too difficult. Recruitment in fact

---

[20] *IA* ('Bala', by Cavid Baysun), and sources quoted there.

[21] 'Vakanüvis Cevdet Paşa'nın Evrakı', *TOEM*, no. 44 (1333 A.H.), p. 103.

continued to be by patronage and apprenticeship. A young man in his early or middle teens joined a department on the recommendation of some well-connected relative. He served for a while as a kind of apprentice, making himself generally useful, and receiving no salary. Eventually he might hope to be assigned a rank and rate of pay, and thus enter on the ladder of officialdom. His further promotions depended only partly on his merits; partly also on seniority, and above all on favour.

Pay was low and irregular, but employment in the government service was still eagerly sought after. No other civil career offered equal prestige, or even equal security of tenure. Successive reforms, concerned more with the safety of the official than with his efficiency, made him almost immune from dismissal.

Under the Republic the position of the civil servant was changed several times by new laws, the basic one being that of March 1926.[22] These laws laid down regular conditions of service, an establishment, and a scale of salaries which has been honoured. Recruitment was partly by competition, partly by nomination, the latter right being granted to various central and provincial public authorities, for certain kinds of post only. The number of candidates accepted was often determined by considerations other than the number of known vacancies to be filled. Pay, though now regular, remained low, and its purchasing power was diminished by successive inflations. The high degree of centralization, both in the country as a whole and in each individual ministry, left but little room for independent initiative.

If the civil servant was helpless under the authority of his official superiors, he remained a great power in his relations with the common people. The role of the civil servant in Anglo-Saxon democracy is perhaps best expressed by the term civil servant. The Turkish official, at least in departments exercising some authority over the public, was no civil servant. The Turkish term is *memur*—literally, one who is commanded, and the word, of course, expresses his relationship to the authority that employs him. For the mass of the people, however, he was not a servant

---

[22] Başgil, p. 64. On the value to the young Republic of the trained reserves of manpower inherited from a much larger Empire, see the penetrating observations of D. A. Rustow, 'Foreign Policy of the Turkish Republic', in R. C. Macridis, ed., *Foreign Policy in World Politics* (1958), p. 315. On the role of the bureaucracy in the modernization of Turkey see further R. L. Chambers in Ward and Rustow, *Political Modernization* (1964), pp. 301–27.

but a master, or at least a shepherd, and was still accepted by the masses as such. Social attitudes rarely keep pace with changes of régime, and it was no easy matter to eradicate the vestiges of the centuries-old tradition whereby the official and the policeman wielded and shared in the autocratic authority of the Sultan. The fact that this authority was often benevolent and paternal, and those who wielded it conscientious and well intentioned, mitigated but did not resolve the difficulty. Political conceptions and practices changed greatly in Turkey, and the constitution recognized the people as the source of sovereignty, but the lower ranks of the hierarchy were less easy to persuade to part with their little brief authority—the more dear to them since it had ceased to carry with it any important economic privilege. The miserably inadequate salaries that most Turkish officials received did not improve their tempers. The processes of Westernization during the last century had made things worse rather than better. The need to conform to a Western social and sartorial standard added further financial burdens to the hard-pressed Turkish official, and the models offered by Western officialdom in Turkey and abroad were not always of the best. In Anatolia official arrogance was still modified by the innate courtesy of the old Turkish tradition. In Istanbul Westernization all too often resulted only in superimposing the morose fussiness of the French *fonctionnaire* on the alternating indolence and insolence of the Ottoman bureaucrat. A real change clearly required a re-education of both the official and the citizen. Among the most encouraging development of recent years are the many signs that this process has already begun.

The Cabinet

One of the more significant governmental reforms of Mahmud II was the establishment of the Privy Council—*Meclis-i Hass*. This body was in part a revival of the former *Divan-i Humayun*, in part an imitation of the Western Council of Ministers. It met twice weekly at the Sublime Porte, under the presidency of the Grand Vezir, and discussed current problems. Unlike the former Divan, it made no appointments, and dispensed no judicial decisions. Unlike a cabinet, it had no corporate existence or responsibility, and its members were all appointed directly by the Sultan. Even though the various ministers and high officials were in theory responsible to the Grand Vezir, in fact they were the Sultan's servants, individually nominated and dismissed by him.

At first the Privy Council was merely one of a number of such bodies, often eclipsed by others, such as the Councils of Justice, of Reform, and of Military Affairs, that dealt with more definite and tangible tasks. The gradual modernization of the administration, however, gave increasing importance to the central committee of ministers, which, under a Grand Vezir strong enough to impose his will on both his colleagues and the Sultan, could be a useful instrument of government. The efforts of Fuad Paşa, for example, to hold the Council together against the interventions of Sultan Abdülaziz, recapitulate the Western evolution towards cabinet government.[23]

The constitution of 1876 recognizes the existence of a Council of Ministers, presided over by the Grand Vezir, and assigns to it 'all important state matters, both external and internal'. There is, however, no approach to collective responsibility. The Grand Vezir and the *Şeyh-ül-Islâm* are appointed by the Sultan at his discretion; the other ministers are nominated by Imperial *irade* and all are individually responsible for their activities.

The Rescript restoring the constitution in 1908 made an important change, giving the Grand Vezir the right to appoint all the ministers other than the Ministers of War and of the Navy who, like the *Şeyh-ül-Islâm*, were to be appointed by the Sultan. These two exceptions, seen by the C.U.P. as a dangerous strengthening of the Sultan's powers, led to the fall of the Grand Vezir Said Paşa, and a few days later his successor, Kâmil Paşa, secured a new Rescript reserving the nomination of all ministers, other than the *Şeyh-ül-Islâm*, to the Grand Vezir.

The change was taken a step farther with the constitutional reforms of 1909. These laid down clearly that the Grand Vezir was responsible for choosing and forming the cabinet. They also laid down, for the first time, the collective responsibility of the ministers for the general policy of the government. The relationship between the cabinet, the sovereign, and parliament, with such questions as dismissal, resignation, and prorogation, remained the subject of bitter constitutional struggles right through the Young Turk period.[24]

[23] Karal, *Osmanlı Tarihi*, vii. 142 ff.

[24] Şeref, *Tar. Mus.*, pp. 348 ff.; cf. Cemalüddin, *Hatırat* (1917), pp. 11–12; Kraelitz-Greifenhorst, pp. 3 ff.; Jäschke, in *WI*, v. 20 ff.

As early as November 1921 Mustafa Kemal asked the Grand
National Assembly in Ankara to pass a law on ministerial responsibility, but without result. In July 1922 the Assembly reserved to
itself the right directly to elect the ministers and the Prime
Minister, and in April 1923 finally passed the Law of Ministerial
Responsibility.[25] This was confirmed in article 46 of the republican constitution, which reproduces the revised text of 1909.

Parliaments and Parties[26]

Turkey has had three periods of parliamentary government, the
first constitutional period, from 1876 to 1878, the second constitutional period from 1908 to 1920, and the third period, which
may be dated from the convening of the Grand National Assembly
in Ankara in 1920.

The constitution of 1876 provided for a two-chamber legislature;
an elected Chamber of Deputies, and a Senate nominated by the
Sultan, its members not to exceed one-third of the number of
deputies. The procedure was laid down in an *irade* of 28 October
1876, on a basis of restricted franchise and indirect elections.[27]
The elections of 1876 and 1877 were both held under this system.
An electoral law, the preparation of which was required by the
constitution, was actually drafted and discussed in 1877, but it
did not become law until after the revolution of 1908. The
remaining elections of the Ottoman Empire were held in accordance with its provisions.[28] These improved and extended the
framework of the *irade* of 1876, but retained the restricted franchise
and the system of electoral colleges.

The Grand National Assembly of Ankara consisted of a single
chamber, and the Kemalist governments never attempted to re-
introduce a second, whether nominated or elected. In other
respects the republican régime showed itself to be conservative in
electoral matters. The old electoral law remained in force, with

[25] Jäschke, *Kalender*; Gözübüyük and Kili, pp. 88, 92; *Nutuk*, ii. 663.

[26] The best available discussion of electoral systems and procedures in Turkey are
those of Tunaya in his *Partiler* and his article in English, 'Elections in Turkish History',
MEA (1954), 116–20. (cf. Tunaya and Reşit Ülker, *Mufassal Fihristli Özetli
Milletvekilleri Seçimi Kanunu ve İlgili Mevzuat*, 1954, for the texts of the electoral laws).
On parties, see *EI*[2] *s.vv.* 'Djam'iyya', 'Ḥizb ii', and the names of the individual parties;
Frey, *Elite* (1965), pp. 301 ff.; Payaslıoğlu in Ward and Rustow, pp. 411–33; Rustow
in La Palombara and Weiner, *Political Parties* (1966), pp. 107–33.

[27] Aristarchi, v. 306.   [28] Trans. in Kraelitz-Greifenhorst, pp. 65 ff.

its system of indirect or two-stage elections. It was not until 1946 that the system of direct election was accepted; it was fully applied in the general election of May 1950. Progress was more rapid in the extension of the franchise. As early as April 1924 the limitation of the franchise to tax-payers was abolished, together with some other restrictions. In 1934 the more radical step was taken of extending the vote to women, and henceforth all Turkish citizens, men and women, aged 22 and over, were entitled to vote.

A reform of far-reaching importance, going beyond the mere form and procedure of the elections, was brought by the new electoral law of 15 February 1950. This law, passed with the approval of both the government and opposition parties, made a number of changes, including the secret ballot and public counting of votes; by far the most significant was the transfer of the supervision and control of the elections, both centrally and locally, from the executive to the judiciary. This measure, by making the judge instead of the Vali the supreme electoral authority in each constituency, was one of the main guarantees of the free and fair general election of May 1950.[29]

In the Turkish electoral system the constituency was the vilayet, or province, which returned a certain number of members according to its population. The first constitution specified one member for 50,000 inhabitants; in 1923 the number was reduced to 20,000, then in 1934 raised again to 40,000. This last figure remained in force. The vilayets are of unequal size; thus Istanbul has a million and a half inhabitants, while Hakkâri has only some 50,000. In each vilayet the parties nominated candidates, to the number of seats assigned to that vilayet, and the voter had to indicate his choice. This in effect has meant, in most of the vilayets, voting by lists.

Between 1876 and 1950 fourteen general elections were held, two in the first period, four in the second, and the rest in the third. None were held between 1877 and 1908. Of these fourteen elections, only five—those of 1908, 1912, 1919, 1946, and 1950—were contested by more than one party. Of these five, only one —that of 1950—resulted in an opposition victory and a transfer of power.[30]

[29] Details in Tunaya and Ülker.

[30] Besides the People's Party, a number of independent candidates stood in the election of 1931.

The first beginnings of political parties in Turkey may be traced in the mid-nineteenth century, and already indicate the several different lines of development known to European party politics. The 'Society of Zealots', responsible for the Kuleli Incident of 1859, was a clique of conspirators, aiming at the violent overthrow of the régime by assassination.[31] The 'New Ottoman Society' of 1865 was a band of liberal patriots and idealists, aiming at education, persuasion, and influence.[32] At the same time Fuad Paşa, in his unsuccessful attempt to induce the pashas to act in concert against the Sultan's influence, was groping towards another and quite different kind of political party organization.

During the first constitutional period no parties emerged to contest the elections of 1876 and 1877, or to form groups in the parliaments of that time. It was not until the despotism of Abdülhamid was well established that a number of illegal, opposition groups were formed, with the common object of overthrowing it.

By far the most important of them was the Committee of Union and Progress, which dominated the parliaments of the second constitutional period. In the general election of 1908, only one other party, the Liberals (*Ahrar*), offered candidates. One, in Ankara, was elected; the others, in Istanbul, were all defeated. After the election, however, a number of deputies, chiefly Christians, began to form a parliamentary opposition group favourable to the liberals; several other new parties were formed, and also found supporters among disgruntled deputies.

None of these were, however, strong enough to offer any real threat to the monopoly of power of the Committee of Union and Progress. The only serious challenge came from the Liberal Union, which won a brief victory in the famous by-election of December 1911. It did not long enjoy it, and in 1913 the Committee, back in power,[33] established a virtual dictatorship. The opposition parties were suppressed, and some of their leaders exiled. The elections of May 1914 were held with one party only participating; the Committee remained the only party until the armistice in 1918.

The general elections of 1919 were contested by a large number of groups, new and old. Yet the only discernible victors were two groups that did not officially participate—the Committee of

Union and Progress, which no longer existed, having dissolved itself at its last party congress on 14–19 October 1918, and the nationalists who had already appeared in Anatolia.[34]

Of the many parties formed in Istanbul in the course of the year 1919, the most important was the Liberal Union, formally reconstituted, after a period of quiescence, in January of that year. Though it would be an exaggeration to describe it as the party in power, the Liberal Union and its leaders did play a role of some importance in the series of ministries that ruled in Istanbul between the end of the war and the end of the Empire. It failed however, to win any extensive following in the last Ottoman parliament.

The People's Party, created by Mustafa Kemal as the political instrument of his struggle for the reform of Turkey, was the direct successor of the Association for the Rights of Anatolia and Rumelia, which served during the phase of armed struggle for liberation. An inaugural general meeting was held in August 1923 and in November of the same year the new party took over the organization and assets of the now superseded Associations. A year later, in November 1924, the name of the party was changed to Republican People's Party.

Opposition groups were present in the Ankara régime almost from the beginning. In the summer of 1922 a splinter group was formed in the Association for the Defence of Rights, with the declared objective of resisting any personal despotism. The group approved the sovereignty of the Assembly, but opposed the autocracy of an individual—in other words, of Mustafa Kemal. It presented no candidates in the 1923 elections and thereafter played no further part in politics.[35]

On two occasions Mustafa Kemal experimented with a tolerated opposition—the Progressive Republican Party in 1924–5, and the Free Republican Party in 1930.[36] These experiments ended with the suppression of the opposition parties, and the reinforcement of the Gazi's control over the party in power, even to the point of personally nominating the candidates for parliament. After the party congress of 1935, the virtual coalescence of party and state was formalized; at the centre, the Minister of the Interior and the Secretary-General of the party were the same person; in the

[34] Tunaya, *Partiler*, p. 402.
[35] Ibid. pp. 537–8.   [36] See above, pp. 265–6 and 279–81.

provinces, the Vali was chairman of the provincial party organization.[37]

The party congress of 1939, after the Gazi's death, decided to separate the party somewhat from the state, and to experiment with another kind of opposition. Party and government appointments were dissociated, and an 'independent group' constituted among the People's Party deputies in the *Meclis*, with instructions to function as a parliamentary opposition. The group was abolished by the party congress of 1946.[38]

Apart from two brief episodes, the RPP was in undisputed control from 1923 to 1945, when other parties were again permitted. Since, during that period, the party in power was under no obligation to seize, to win, or even to defend its control of the state against political opposition, it had no need of those techniques, electoral or conspiratorial, which in varying circumstances are so important in party political life. The RPP was not so much a means of gaining and holding power, as an instrument for exercising it. Diverging from a pattern common in the Middle East and elsewhere, it was more than a clique of notables in the capital with allies in the provincial cities, grouped by personality rather than programme; it possessed a nation-wide constituency organization, and was dedicated to a consistent and realistic programme of work. Fulfilling many important functions, both educational and executive, it became in effect part of the apparatus of republican government. In every rural centre of Turkey there was a local RPP branch, whose officials were the agents of the Kemalist Revolution. It was they who guided the peasantry, by means varying from persuasion to compulsion according to circumstances, and in doing so took over many of the social and economic powers formerly wielded by the rural magnates. An outstanding example of the educational and social work of the party was the network of 'People's Houses' and 'People's Rooms' (*Halkevi* and *Halkodası*). These had their origins in the Turkish Hearths (*Türk Ocağı*), founded in 1912.[39] They were revived in 1924, and in 1927 held a congress in Ankara. By a resolution of the party conference of 1931, the RPP decided to take over and expand their activities, and to set up 'People's Houses' in towns all over Turkey. In 1940 these were supplemented by 'People's Rooms' in small towns and

---

[37] Tunaya, *Partiler*, pp. 570 ff.
[38] Tunaya, *Partiler*, pp. 573 ff.; Karpat, p. 396.   [39] See above, p. 350.

villages, and by 1950, when the RPP fell from power, there were over 4,000 such rooms, as well as nearly 500 houses. The purpose of these houses was avowedly to inculcate in the people of Turkey the principles of the Revolution, especially republicanism, nationalism, and laicism. This they did through lectures, classes, and meetings, libraries and publications, dramatic, sporting, and other activities, concerts and exhibitions, and social assistance and guidance of various kinds.

All these activities conform fairly closely, in form perhaps more than in content, to what became the pattern of the role of the party in the one-party state in Europe at that time—the Fascist Party in Italy, the Communist Party in Russia, the Nazi Party in Germany. In one respect, however, the Republican People's Party of Turkey differs most strikingly from its compeers elsewhere; for no other party of dictatorship prepared, organized and accepted its own peaceful supersession. Twice before—unsuccessfully—the RPP had experimented with a tolerated opposition. In 1945 it tried for a third time—and successfully procured its own defeat.

In 1945 and 1946 the Law of Associations and the penal code were amended to facilitate the formation and the operation of political parties besides the RPP. Political propaganda and activity became free, save only for two restrictions, on Communism and on clericalism—or, more precisely, anti-laicism. The advocacy of Communism or of the restoration of the Sultan-Caliph were contrary to the fundamental principles of the Republic, and could not be tolerated. Within these principles, the rights of opposition and criticism were conceded and recognized.

The first new party to appear and end the long monopoly of the RPP was the so-called National Recovery Party (*Millî Kalkınma Partisi*) founded on 18 July 1945, with an authorization from the Vali of Istanbul.[40] Its founders were Nuri Demirağ, a firm supporter of free enterprise and a sharp critic of the policy of etatism; Hüseyin Avni Ulaş, a member of the 'Second (opposition) Group' in the Association for the Defence of Rights in 1923; and Cevat Rifat Atılhan, who afterwards left and became associated with a number of extreme right-wing organizations.

This party, with its rather mixed leadership and programme, attracted little support; it did, however, establish precedents for organization and opposition, and was soon followed by many

[40] Tunaya, *Partiler*, pp. 639 ff.

others. Between 1945 and 1950 no less than twenty-seven parties came into existence, some with such resounding names as the Social Justice Party, the Workers' and Peasants' Party, the For the Fatherland Only Party, the Cleansing and Defending Party, the Defence of Islam Party, the Idealist Party, the Pure Democrats Party, the Free Democrats Party, the Land, Property, and Free Enterprise Party, as well as a variety of toilers and workers, socialists and liberals.

Of all these parties, however, only two were of any real political importance; the Democrat Party,[41] founded on 7 January 1946, and the National Party,[42] founded on 20 July 1948. In 1950, under the new electoral law, the Democrats won 407 out of 487 seats, and thus became the government of Turkey—the first in Turkish history to have won power by purely constitutional and parliamentary means. It remained to be seen whether they would exercise it by the same means.

Provincial Government

The Ottoman Empire in its classical form has been described, by a kind of loose analogy with medieval Europe, as a military feudalism. The basic unit of provincial government was the sanjak. Its governor, the Sanjak-Bey, was a military officer; he was paid by the grant of a fief; and his primary duty was to superintend and, in time of war, to mobilize the feudal cavalrymen holding fiefs in his province. A group of sanjaks formed an eyalet governed by a Beylerbey, or governor-general. The Beylerbey, whose term of office was usually brief, enjoyed a large measure of military and financial autonomy.

During the seventeenth and eighteenth centuries the decentralization of the Empire advanced rapidly. With the relative decline in importance of the feudal levies and the increase in the numbers and cost of the paid regulars, the concern of the central government in the provinces became more financial and less military. The surviving *timars* were sharply reduced by Selim III, and finally abolished by Mahmud II in 1831.

Meanwhile, however, the leasing of crown revenues to tax-farmers had led to the emergence of a new kind of feudalism, based on money rather than service. Coupled with the growth of

---

[41] Tunaya, *Partiler*, pp. 648 ff.; Karpat, pp. 408 ff.
[42] Ibid. pp. 712 ff.; Karpat, pp. 431 ff.

the autonomies of the *ayan* and the *derebeys* during the eighteenth century, it led to the almost complete loss of control over the provinces. The imposition on Mahmud II, by a conference of provincial notables, of a charter of provincial autonomy in 1808 marked the culmination of this process of feudal decentralization.

But Mahmud II, who gave formal recognition to the rights of the provincial notables, was determined to end them. After the conclusion of the war with Russia in 1812, he turned his attention to what he regarded as his first major task—the restoration or establishment of the authority of the central government in the provinces. By a series of military campaigns and police actions, he was able to overcome the rebellious pashas and the local notables, destroying the institutions as well as the autonomies of provincial government. The New Order created by Mahmud and continued by his successors was at once more centralized and more autocratic.[43]

In one respect Mahmud's campaigns left the old order unchanged. Although the provinces were brought under the direct control of the central government—which in the circumstances of the time meant the personal control of the Sultan—there was still no financial or fiscal centralization. Provincial revenues were still farmed out by *iltizam*, and the tax-farmer, though bereft of his political privileges, still interposed himself between the taxpayer and the treasury.

A fatal custom still exists [says the Rescript of the Rose Bower of 1839] although it can only have disastrous consequences; it is that of venal concessions, known under the name of 'Iltizam'. Under that name the civil and financial administration of a locality is delivered over to the passions of a single man; that is to say, sometimes to the iron grasp of the most violent and avaricious passions, for if that contractor is not a good man he will only look to his own advantage.

The Rescript goes on to abolish *iltizam*, and to decree that all Ottomans shall be subject only to fixed and direct taxation, 'according to their means'. A few months later, in December 1839, the government decreed that, with effect from 1 March 1840, governors of provinces, cities, &c., would be paid fixed salaries, that promotions to senior appointments would be made on merit alone, and that provincial governors would collect only the fixed legal taxes, through newly appointed civilian tax officials.[44]

[43] See above, pp. 77 and 89 ff.   [44] Bailey, pp. 198 ff.; Temperley, pp. 236 ff.

It was one thing to decree the millennium, quite another to apply it. The first effect of the abolition of the sale of offices was a shortage of money; the new financial administration, however well-intentioned, was inexperienced and inept; the new paper currency depreciated rapidly, and before long almost all classes of society felt their interests to be endangered by these alien and ineffective reforms.

In the wave of reaction following the dismissal of Reşid Paşa in 1841, the provincial reforms were abandoned, and the old fiscal system restored. In February 1842 the civilian tax collectors in the provinces were removed, and the collection of taxes returned to the military governors and their contractors, with the assistance of councils of local notables.[45]

These councils, established by Reşid Paşa, were modelled on the French *Conseils Départementaux*, with the difference that they were permanently in session, and interfered actively in the administrative and judicial affairs of the province. Inevitably, they became centres of bitter local partisan strife, and the executive power, caught between a remote and inactive central authority and a lively and obstructive local council, was reduced to complete ineffectiveness. Eventually some of the evils of premature centralization and democracy were removed. A ferman of 28 November 1852 restored the powers of the governor, making him once more the effective authority in his province. At the same time the legal powers of the police and army, weakened to the point when they could barely maintain order, were reaffirmed and extended.[46]

The compromise between the old and new orders was less than satisfactory, and it was natural that in the new phase of reform that followed the Crimean War attention should once again be given to the problems of provincial administration. The interest of the European godfathers of the reform was directed particularly to the Balkan provinces of the Empire, and in 1859–60 a proposal for an international commission of inspection in the European provinces was averted only by the Grand Vezir, Kıbrıslı Mehmed Paşa, going on one himself.[47]

Discontent and rebellion among the Balkan Christians had become an accepted feature of life in the Empire, but the spread

[45] Engelhardt, ii. 50.   [46] Ibid. i. 105–110; Karal, *Tarih*, vi. 31–32.
[47] Rasim, *Osmanlı Tarihi*, iv. 2095, ff.; Karal, *Tarih*, vii. 152.

of the disorder to the staunchly Muslim province of Syria in
1860–1—and the resulting foreign intervention—were a danger
signal that could not be ignored. Fuad Paşa himself, then Minister
of Foreign Affairs, went to Syria to investigate, and severely
punished the culprits.[48] In his notes on the troubles, Fuad Paşa
lays great stress on the maladministration from which the provinces of the Empire were suffering. In a country as large as the
Ottoman Empire, it was difficult to find an adequate number of
officials with the desired qualities. Many officials had in fact
misused governmental powers, and for this reason the tendency
had been to reduce their competence and strengthen the control
of the central government. This had brought some benefits,
but at the same time it had reduced the status and authority
of provincial officials and, in the eyes of a populace accustomed to being governed by quite other means, made them
appear as contemptible nonentities. In a country made up of
many races and religions, this feebleness and disrepute into
which the provincial administration had fallen led to grave
dangers.[49]

The problem of provincial government continued to exercise
Fuad Paşa and his circle. Inspectors were sent to the provinces,
including such well-known figures as the historian and jurist
Cevdet and the scholar and statesman Ahmed Vefik. A special
commission, presided over by Cevdet, was formed to examine the
inspection reports, and make recommendations.

In 1864 Fuad Paşa, who had meanwhile again become Grand
Vezir, had his solution ready—the new Law of Vilayets. His idea,
according to the evidence of Cevdet, was to group the provinces
into larger units, and place them under the control of carefully
chosen able and experienced men. These would be given greatly
extended discretion, and would need to refer to Istanbul only in
the most important matters. This would have the further advantage of freeing the ministers from ordinary routine, and
allowing them to concentrate on high affairs of state.[50]

On this basis a provincial code was drafted and promulgated in

[48] Rasim, iv. 2083 ff.; cf. W. Miller, *The Ottoman Empire and its Successors, 1801–1922* (1923), p. 302.

[49] Rasim, loc. cit; Karal, *Tarih*, vi. 31.

[50] 'Maruzat', in *TOEM*, no. 87 (1341 A.H.), 269–70; cf. Karal, *Tarih*, vi. 153 and Mardin, *Ahmet Cevdet Paşa*, pp. 53 ff.

1864. The old eyalets were replaced by substantially larger vilayets, twenty-seven in number, and each governed by a Vali with extensive powers. Within the vilayet a chain of authority was established. The vilayet was divided into sanjaks—the old, feudal name, but with quite a new meaning; the sanjak into kazas, the kaza into *nahiyes* and villages. Under the authority of the Vali, the sanjak was administered by a *mutasarrıf*, the kaza by a Kaymakam, the *nahiye* by a *müdür*, the village or quarter by an elected *muhtar* (headman). At vilayet, sanjak, and kaza levels there was to be an administrative council, formed by the Governor, the chief judge, the chief finance officer, and the chief secretary, together with four representatives of the population, two Muslim and two non-Muslim, and the religious heads of the Muslim and non-Muslim communities. The representative members were to be chosen by a complicated and restricted franchise. The council was to meet under the presidency of the governor. To avoid a return to the anarchy of the Rose-Bower experiment, the council was forbidden to interfere in judicial matters.

The Vali's administration was divided into civil, financial, police, political, and legal affairs. For each of these he had subordinate officials placed under his orders, though the finance officer, continuing a traditional Ottoman and Islamic practice, was responsible for his accounts directly to the Ministry of Finance. The Vali was also responsible for recruiting and appointing his staff. Apart from the councils, an annual general provincial assembly was to be convened, with four delegates elected by each sanjak, again two Muslim and two non-Muslim. These assemblies met for a few years, before they were abolished, together with the rest of the apparatus of representative government, by Abdül-hamid.[51]

This law, with its hierarchy of Valis, *mutasarrıfs*, kaymakams and *müdürs*, administering vilayets, sanjaks, kazas, and *nahiyes*, is clearly based on the French system of provincial administration, through the *départements*, *arrondissements*, cantons, and communes. Though Fuad Paşa's law gave the Ottoman Vali considerably more discretion than was enjoyed by the French *Préfet* on whom he was modelled, the general tendency of the law was towards

[51] Engelhardt, i. 193–8; Temperley, p. 237; Karal, *Tarih*, vii. 153; Sax, pp. 372 ff.; Ismail Hakkı Göreli, *Il Idaresi* (1952), p. 6; and Davison, *Reform* (1963), pp. 136–71. Text in *Düstur*, i. 4 ff.; trans. in Young, i. 29 ff. and Aristarchi, iii. 1 ff.

centralization and uniformity. It was more especially on the latter ground that it was criticized by Cevdet Paşa, an advocate, in general, of conservative gradualism. The provinces of the Empire, he said, differed greatly from one another, both in their geographical and their ethnographical circumstances, and could not all be treated in the same way. In each region an administrative reform should be undertaken, taking account of local conditions and of the historical background. Cevdet saw this as a process requiring much knowledge, skill, and time.[52]

Cevdet did offer general principles and observations. The classical Ottoman Empire had not been a centralized state. The *Tanzimat* reformers had attempted to introduce a centralized administration, but grave difficulties had arisen. Since then they had chopped and changed between centralized and decentralized government, with the result that all was confusion and anarchy. The first necessity was to decide on the general principle of government, and then to determine the duties and responsibilities of officials of all three groups, administrative, judicial, and military. Finally, officials should be regularly and adequately paid.

The servants of the state should be superior to the mass of the people in ability and competence. But if there is no recompense, outstanding persons among the population will have no inclination to the service of the state, and will choose other professions, leaving only mediocrities to carry on the business of the state. These, lacking all prestige in the eyes of the people, will be quite unable to administer men who are in fact their superiors.[53]

Order and consistency, recruitment and pay, the competence, integrity, and prestige of the service—Cevdet had put his finger on some of the main difficulties of applying a uniform, centralized administration in regions as diverse and as mixed as the Ottoman provinces. On the other hand, however, there were new factors favouring centralization, two of particular importance. One was the improvement in communications—the introduction of the telegraph at the time of the Crimean War, and the rapid extension of roads and railways from about 1862 onwards.[54] The other was the loss of several of the predominantly Christian Balkan provinces; this, by leaving the Empire more homo-

---

[52] Karal, *Tarih*, vii. 153.   [53] Cevdet in *TOEM*, no. 44 (1333 A.H.), 103.

[54] Karal, *Tarih*, vii. 267–73; cf. above, pp. 184 ff.

geneous, made it easier to devise and apply a national provincial system.

The law of 1864 was of course not immediately and universally applied. Nor was there any intention of doing so. In accordance with a common practice of the Ottoman reformers, Fuad Paşa began with a pilot project—the model and experimental vilayet of the Danube. This new vilayet, chosen for obvious political reasons, was entrusted to one of the ablest administrators in the Ottoman service—Midhat Paşa, himself one of the architects of the new system.

Midhat's term of office as Vali of the Danube province showed that, given the necessary goodwill and ability, the new system could work very well. Within two years he had restored order, introduced the new hierarchy, provided agricultural credits, extended roads, bridges, and waterways, started industries, opened schools and orphanages, founded a newspaper, and increased the revenues of the province from 26,000 to 300,000 purses.[55]

Midhat's success in reviving the Sick Man of Europe was not to the taste of the expectant heirs; in 1868, apparently as a result of various foreign pressures at the Porte, he was recalled, and in 1869 posted as Vali of Baghdad. There, in a remote and backward Asian province of the Empire, he was able to repeat his achievements, and bring order and progress to the people of Iraq.

With these successes to guide them, the Ottomans gradually extended the new system to the whole Empire, at the same time introducing such legislative modifications to the provincial code as seemed desirable. In 1871 a revised general provincial code delimited the functions and authority of provincial officials from the Vali down to the village *muhtar*.[56]

The constitution of 1876 contained a whole section relating to the provinces. This affirmed the principle of decentralization and the separation of powers in provincial administration, and declared that a special law would regulate the election of members of provincial administrative councils and general assemblies and the powers and duties of the Vali, these last to include public works, and the improvement of agriculture, industry, commerce, communications, and education.

[55] Midhat, *Life*, pp. 38 ff.; Karal, *Tarih*, vii. 154–5.
[56] *Düstur*, i. 625; Young, i. 47; Göreli, p. 7.

The question of provincial administration received earnest attention from the short-lived Ottoman parliament of March 1877, and a new vilayet law, of 101 articles, was actually debated and passed by the lower house. It had, however, not yet reached the Senate when parliament was closed, and the debate, the law, and the constitution itself were shelved indefinitely. Instead, a new law was published, in 1880, by a mixed commission of Ottoman and foreign officials. Its purpose appears to have been to answer the clauses in the treaty of Berlin relating to Ottoman administration, and to satisfy the powers that their requirements had been met. Significantly, this law is not included in the Ottoman corpus of laws. The basic Ottoman provincial law remained that of 1864, with minor subsequent amendments.[57]

The revolution of 1908 and the restoration of the constitution raised once again the question of the application of article 108, prescribing decentralization and the separation of functions in provincial government. After long investigations and deliberations by two successive special commissions, a draft law was submitted to parliament in 1910. The parliamentary consideration of this bill was protracted and difficult; inevitably, it was affected by the strains of the Tripolitanian and Balkan wars, and by the growing tendency towards a more centralized, more authoritarian régime. The law finally accepted, on 26 March 1913, has remained the basis of Turkish provincial administration ever since. To meet the requirements of clause 108 of the constitution, the jurists of that time evolved the theory of the dual character of vilayet government. The vilayet administration was conceived as having two aspects; one general, as components of the national apparatus of government, the other special or local, as decentralized administrative entities, with a recognized legal personality. By thus admitting the Western conception of corporate legal persons into the legal and administrative structure of the country, the legislators of 1913 were taking an important step away from Islamic and towards European legal principles. The aim of the law was to give the Vali the necessary powers and discretion to maintain order, carry out public works, and conduct local affairs effectively, while at the same time preserving the national authority of the Ministry of the Interior.[58]

[57] Engelhardt, ii. 250–5.   [58] Göreli, p. 17.

An important change in nomenclature was made by the 'Fundamental Law' of 20 January 1921, passed by the Grand National Assembly in Ankara. This divided the country into vilayets, the vilayets into kazas, and the kazas into *nahiyes*. The old title of sanjak was dropped, but in fact it was the older, large-scale vilayet that ceased to exist, since the old sanjaks now become vilayets, directly dependent on the central government.

The situation created by the law of 1913 was not changed by the proclamation of the Republic, nor by the republican constitution of 20 April 1924, which reaffirmed the principle of decentralization and separation of functions in provincial government. It was confirmed by the vilayet law of 18 April 1929, which remains in force.[59] This law confirms the dual character of the vilayet, as a territorial and administrative subdivision of the national government, with a Vali appointed from the capital, and at the same time as a unit of local government, with a recognized legal personality. In the latter capacity it has its own budget, its own legislative and executive branches, and can own property.

In the theory of Turkish law the vilayet and its subdivisions thus provide the local government of the country. In fact the control of the Ministry of the Interior in provincial affairs is very strict. The Vali, Kaymakam, and others are all ministry-appointed permanent officials. The vilayet budget is provided from the centre; it may be supplemented by loans, but not by local taxation, which the vilayet council has no power to impose. The council, an elected body, meets normally for forty days in the year, under the presidency of the Vali. If he disapproves its decisions, he may refer them to the Council of State in Ankara for a final verdict. The council's duties are to audit the expenditure of the previous year, and to pass the current budget, which has been prepared by the Vali and submitted to the vilayet permanent commission. The budgets must be finally ratified by the cabinet in Ankara and the President of the Republic. The vilayet council may also discuss and lay down policy on public works, agriculture, education, and social services. When it is not in session its functions are discharged by a four-man permanent commission.

The kaza is not a legal person, and has no elected assembly. Its administrator, the Kaymakam, is a subordinate of the Vali, but

---

[59] Ibid.; Başgil, p. 49; Jäschke, *Kalender*, under date; idem, 'Die grösseren Verwaltungsbezirke der Türkei seit 1918', *MSOS*, xxxviii (1935), 81–104.

is a central government official appointed from Ankara. The *nahiye*, the smallest sub-unit of the vilayet, is administered by the *müdür*, also a central government officer, but on a different ladder of promotion from the Kaymakam and Vali. He presides over a *nahiye* council, consisting of the local officials and technicians, together with one elected representative from each village or municipality. Finally, there is the village, established as a legal entity for the first time by the village law of 18 March 1924. The villagers elect a *muhtar* and council of elders, in which the school-teacher and the imam are *ex officio* members. Although the *muhtar* is an elected official who represents the villagers, he is also in effect, and usually in the first instance, an administrative officer, representing the central government in the village and carrying out whatever instructions reach him through the chain of command. Much the same is true of the *muhtar* in the *mahalle*, or quarter of a town. He too is subject to the authority of the vilayet for many purposes. For others, however, the *mahalle* is part of the municipality, a quite separate organization with a very different background and history.[60]

Municipal Government [61]

Although classical Islam was in many respects an essentially urban civilization, the classical Islamic system of law and government takes very little account of the city. Islamic law does not recognize corporate persons, and Islamic history shows no recognized, privileged cities, with corporate status and rights. Just as there was no state but only a ruler and his agents, no court but only a judge and his helpers, so there was no city but only a conglomeration of families, quarters, and guilds, each with their own chiefs and leaders.

The *Şeriat* contains no municipal code, and the town never became a legal or political entity—neither as a fief, nor as a commune. Those charged with its government were not municipal officers, nor yet feudatories; still less were they civil servants in the modern sense. For the most part they were royal officers, with revocable, delegated powers from the sovereign; or else members

[60] On Turkish provincial government see further *Kaza ve Vilayet Idaresi üzerinde bir Araştırma* (Ank., 1957); A. Gorvine, *An Outline of Turkish Provincial and Local Government* (1956).

[61] For a survey of Turkish municipal institutions see *EI²* ('Baladiyya', by B. Lewis). Details and documents in Nuri, *Mec. Um. Bel.*

of the religious class, charged with certain duties of prevention and enforcement, where the provisions of the Holy Law were concerned.

In Ottoman Istanbul police duties, fire-fighting, and public order generally were entrusted to certain military officers with regiments designated for these tasks. The supervision of the markets was the duty of the *muhtesib*, a member of the ulema class whose task it was to enforce the rules relating to prices and quality of merchandise offered for sale, and in general to act as a censor of morals and to maintain public decency and morality. The function of the *muhtesib*, a post going back to medieval Islamic times, is called *ihtisab*. A third official was the *Şehr-emini*, or City Commissioner. This office, which appears in Istanbul soon after the Ottoman conquest, was probably modelled on a Byzantine original, since there seems to be no trace of it in earlier Ottoman towns. The City Commissioner was not merely a royal officer but, more specifically, a palace functionary. His chief tasks were the financial supervision of the palace, the provision of food, clothing, and other palace needs, the maintenance and repair of the palace and of other royal and governmental buildings in the city, and similar duties. The office ranked high on the ladder of promotion of the finance branch of the bureaucracy. It was abolished in 1831.

The first approaches towards modern municipal government was made by Sultan Mahmud II, in the period after the destruction of the Janissaries. As with so many of his reforms, the purpose seems to have been to centralize and thus better to control certain functions previously performed by quasi-independent bodies—in this case the ulema. In 1827 an inspectorate of *ihtisab* was set up, which centralized certain duties, connected with market controls, inspection of weights and measures, &c., hitherto performed by the *muhtesib*. In 1829, with the same general aim of centralizing control and reducing the powers of the ulema, the system of *muhtars* was introduced in the quarters of Istanbul. Until that time there had been headmen in villages, whose duties, as far as the government was concerned, were chiefly fiscal. In towns, where no agricultural taxes were to be assessed and collected, there were no headmen, and the duties of keeping registers of the male population, recording movements, transfers, &c., were the responsibility of the Kadis and their deputies; in the quarters of the town they fell to the local imams. Under the new law these duties were transferred to the *muhtars*, of whom two, a first and a second, were to be appointed in every town quarter. The Imperial Historiographer Lûtfi says that the purpose of this measure was to end the laxness and incompetence of the imams.[62] A little later, the *muhtar* was reinforced by a committee of elders of from three to five persons. In time, this system was extended to other cities.

A new phase began in 1854, when two important changes were initiated. The first of these was the revival of the title of *Şehremini*, City Commissioner, in abeyance since 1831. Though the name was the same, the new office had nothing to do with the old; it was rather an adaptation of the French *préfecture de la ville*, and was chiefly concerned with the supervision of markets, the control of prices, &c.—the chief functions of the former *ihtisab*. The Inspectorate, established in 1827, was abolished, and its duties transferred to the Prefect, who was to be assisted by a city council drawn from the guilds and merchants.

This change in nomenclature seems to have had little practical effect, and complaints began to be made about official neglect of municipal problems. A few months later a decision was taken by the High Council of Reform to establish a municipal commission. The leading spirit in the commission was Antoine Aléon, a member of a rich French banking family that had settled in Turkey at the time of the French Revolution. The other members were drawn chiefly from the local Greek, Armenian, and Jewish communities. There were, however, some Muslim Turks, including the Chief Physician Mehmed Salih Efendi, one of the first graduates of Sultan Mahmud's medical school. The commission was instructed to report on European municipal organization, rules, and procedures, and to make recommendations to the Sublime Porte.

A number of factors had combined to induce the Ottoman government to take these steps. European financial and commercial interests in the capital had been growing steadily, and a new quarter was developing in Galata and Pera, with buildings, blocks of flats, shops, and hotels in European style. An important change was the vast increase in the number of horse-drawn carriages of various kinds. At the beginning of the nineteenth century there were few such carriages in Istanbul, since their use in the city was limited to a small number of privileged persons,

[62] Lûtfi, ii. 173.

such as the *Şeyh-ül-Islâm* and the Grand Vezir. A somewhat larger
number were allowed to ride on horseback in the city, and the
rest, even including many officers and officials, had to walk.
During the early nineteenth century these old rules were disregarded, and, says Cevdet Paşa, 'even some of the non-Muslim
subjects, without authorization, could be seen in public places on
caparisoned horses'.[63] Such unauthorized horse-riding by infidels,
'being unseemly in the eyes of the people', was banned, but the
numbers of carts and carriages, both the local varieties and
imported coaches from Europe, increased rapidly.[64]

All this created a demand, which was put forward by the
European residents, with the support of the Europeanized elements among the local population, for proper roads and pave-
ments, street-cleaning and street-lighting, sewers and water-pipes.
The presence in Istanbul of large allied contingents from the
West during the Crimean War gave a new impetus and a new
urgency to these demands, and, in the new phase of reform that
began in 1854, some attention was given to the problems of
municipal organization and services in the capital. Even the
liberal reformers took notice of these questions, and the poet
and publicist Ibrahim Şinasi contributed an article to the
Tasvir-i Efkâr on the lighting and cleaning of the streets of
Istanbul.[65]

The records of the proceedings of the High Council of Reform
on these matters reflect clearly the various preoccupations of the
Ottoman government. The creation of a city prefecture, under
the recently created Ministry of Commerce, was in part an
attempt to meet a new need by installing the relevant European
apparatus. There was also the usual desire to impress Western
observers. Ill-wishers, says a document in the Council's records,
had accused the Imperial government of doing nothing and caring
nothing for the adornment and improvement of the capital, and
were saying that nothing would come of the proposed system of
municipal districts. It was therefore necessary to show practical
zeal.[66]

---

[63] Cevdet, ix. 185–6.
[64] See M. Rodinson, 'Araba', *J. As.*, ccxlv (1957), 273–80.
[65] Reprinted in Ebüzziya, *Nümûne*, pp. 227–35.
[66] Quoted in Ergin, *Türkiyede Şehirciliğin Tarihî İnkişafı* (1936), p. 125.

The Commission sat for four years, and then presented a report to the High Council of Reform, recommending a number of municipal services and improvements. The Commission also recommended the imposition of a special tax for municipal purposes, the organization of separate municipal finances, and the appointment of itself to apply municipal laws and regulations.

The High Council of Reform decided to accept these recommendations, but to limit their application, for the time being, to an experimental municipality, to be established in the European quarter of Galata and Pera. This district, though the first to be organized, was officially named the sixth district, possibly, as a Turkish historian has suggested, because the sixth *arrondissement* of Paris was believed to be the most advanced of that city. The reasons for this decision are set forth in a protocol of 9 October 1857. Municipal services and improvements were badly needed, and should be provided; the cost should not fall on the state treasury, but should be met by a special levy from the townspeople who would benefit. It would be impracticable to apply the new system to the whole of Istanbul at once, and it was therefore decided to make a start with the sixth district, consisting of Pera and Galata, where there were numerous fine buildings. The district contained a large number of foreign establishments and a preponderance of foreign residents who were acquainted with the practice of other countries and would be willing to accept the expense of municipal institutions. When the merits of these institutions had been demonstrated by this example, a suitable occasion would be found to apply them generally.

The constitution and functions of the municipality of the sixth district, also known as the model district, were laid down in an Imperial *irade* of 7 July 1858. The municipal council was to consist of a chairman and twelve members, all appointed by Imperial *irade*, the chairman indefinitely, the others for three years. All were to be unpaid. The council would appoint a number of permanent officials, including a civil engineer and an architect, who would receive salaries. The municipality would have the right to assess, impose, and collect rates and taxes, to raise loans within limits laid down, and in certain circumstances to expropriate property. The chairman was to submit his budget to the council for discussion and inspection, and then to the Sublime Porte for ratification, without which it would not be valid.

These measures, while accepting and providing for the discharge of certain new responsibilities as to the town, hardly represent an approach to the European conception of municipal institutions. For one thing the reform was limited to a single urban district with a predominantly European population; more fundamental, there was still no recognition of the city as a corporate person, for such an idea remained alien to Islamic conceptions of law and government; nor was there any suggestion of election or representation. What was created was a new kind of administrative agency, appointed by and responsible to the sovereign power, with specified and limited tasks and with a measure of budgetary autonomy. Such special commissions were by no means new in Ottoman administration. The novelty lay in the kind of function entrusted to it.

The 'model commission' worked well, and in 1868 a code of municipal regulations was issued, which was to extend the system to the rest of Istanbul. Each of the districts of the city was to have a municipal committee, and to send its chairman and three delegates to a general municipal assembly for all Istanbul. This assembly, together with a Council of Prefecture, of six persons, appointed and paid by the Imperial government, was to function under the Prefect of the city, who was to remain a government official.

The provisions of this code seem to have remained a dead letter until 1876–7 when, under the impetus of the constitutional movement, new municipal codes were issued for the capital and for provincial towns. The Istanbul code of 1876 was a rearrangement of that of 1868, and proved as ineffectual. Finally, in 1878, a new and more realistic version was published, which in time was put into operation. This divided the city into ten municipal districts. The elaborate apparatus of councils and committees provided by the earlier codes was abolished. What was left was an appointed Council of Prefecture, to assist the Prefect, and a government-appointed director for each of the ten districts. This system, ensuring the full and effective control of the sovereign power, remained in force until the revolution of 1908.

In the provinces the policies of the reformers followed much the same line. Such earlier authorities as the *ayan* had been abolished. The *muhtar* system, inaugurated by Mahmud II, was introduced into the quarters of most of the larger towns, and the vilayet law of 1864 laid down regulations for their election. In the vilayet law of 1870, provision was made for the establishment of municipal councils in provincial cities, along the same general lines as in the code for Istanbul. There is no evidence that anything was done about this. Some attempt, however, seems to have been made to implement parts of the provincial municipal code of 1877, according to which each town was to have an elected municipal council, consisting of six to twelve members, according to population, with the district doctor, engineer, and veterinary surgeon as *ex-officio* advisory members. One of the councillors was to be mayor, not by election but by government appointment; the budget and estimates were to be approved by a municipal assembly, meeting twice yearly for this purpose, and in turn responsible to the General Council of the province.

After the revolution of 1908 a new attempt was made to introduce democratic municipal institutions. The law of 1876, with some amendments, was restored, and a serious attempt made to put it into effect. The experiment was not very successful. The personnel of the district committees, though enthusiastic, were inexperienced, and there was little co-operation between districts for common purposes. In 1912 a new law finally abolished the system. In its place a single Istanbul prefecture was established with nine district branch offices each directed by a government official. The Prefect was assisted by a general assembly of 54 members, to which 6 delegates were elected from each of the 9 districts. As in earlier electoral systems, the franchise was restricted by property and income.

In this as in so many other respects, the new régime was returning to a more centralized system of government, though without abandoning all the forms of democracy. In spite of many difficulties the Young Turk régimes did in fact make some progress in improving the amenities of Istanbul, notably in drainage, garbage disposal, and fire prevention.

This system remained in force in the early years of the Republic. The first municipal measure of the republican government was a law of 16 February 1924 setting up a prefecture in Ankara, with a 'General Assembly' of twenty-four members. The constitution followed broadly that established in Istanbul in 1912, but with some changes, the general effect of which was to restrict the autonomy of the municipality in financial and security matters and place it more strictly under the control of the Ministry of the Interior.

On 3 April 1930 a new law of municipalities was passed. The names *Şehr-emini* and *Şehr-emanet*—prefect and prefecture—were abolished, and replaced by *belediye* and *belediye reisi*, usually translated municipality and mayor. Under Sultan Abdülhamid, the offices of prefect and governor (Vali) of Istanbul had in fact been exercised by the same person. This arrangement, which secured complete governmental control over the municipal business of the capital, was criticized by the Sultan's liberal opponents, and in 1909 the new régime formally separated the prefecture from the governorship. The law of 1930 provided a compromise; in Istanbul, though not elsewhere, the office of mayor would be combined with that of Vali, and the incumbent nominated by the Ministry of the Interior. The vilayet and municipality administrations, however, would be separate, and the municipal councillors elected as elsewhere. This arrangement continued in force; it is interesting that whereas in Turkish documents the incumbent was usually called Vali, in foreign languages he was normally described as mayor. This Janus-like posture of the head of Turkey's largest city remained a subject of controversy. In the general election of 1950 the separation of the two offices and the creation of an elective mayoralty formed part of the Democrat Party programme.

The law recognizes municipalities, like villages, as having corporate legal identity and legally defined boundaries, and thus takes municipal government in Turkey across one of the most important barriers separating Islamic from Western legal concepts. It provides a set of rules governing the election and functioning of municipal bodies, and with some modifications has remained in force to the present day.

CHAPTER XII

Religion and Culture

Just as physical bodies have length, width, and depth, so the social consciousness also has three dimensions—nationality, religion, and modernity. I propose to test the validity of this observation first with regard to language, which is the best mirror of social consciousness.

ZIYA GÖKALP, 1913.

The Turkish nation is ready and resolved to advance, unhalting and undaunted, on the path of civilization.

MUSTAFA KEMAL, 1924.

IN April 1921, in occupied Istanbul, a religious service was held in honour of the fallen in the war of independence in Anatolia. Yakup Kadri Karaosmanoğlu, the distinguished Turkish author, was present, and has described in striking terms the thoughts and feelings that moved him. As he listened to the recitation of the *Mevlûd*, the ode in honour of the Prophet's birthday that serves in Turkey as a requiem, the realization came to him that his life during the past ten years, in pursuit of modernism and secular nationalism, had been a nightmare from which he was now awakening. The ideals which he and his contemporaries had followed were false and harmful; here was the truth. The true home of his people was not 'the national club, the cultural lecture, the political meeting', but the mosque and congregation, 'the house, home, and fatherland' of this nation. Only the simple, ignorant people had understood this and had preserved the true values which the intellectuals, with their apeing of the West, had forgotten.

Yesterday for the first time the common people, whom we had always despised as ignorant and idle, taught the intellectuals of this country some divine truths. One of these is that the heart is superior to the mind. Another is that apart from sincerity and devotion and simple faith there is no way of salvation. The third is that there must be no separation between the nation and the religious community.[1]

---

[1] Printed in Ergin, *Muallim Cevdet'in Hayatı, Eserleri ve Kütüphanesi* (1937), pp. 324–7; cf. Rossi, 'La cultura araba presso i Turchi', in *Caratteri e Modi della cultura araba* (1943), p. 236.

These words, written in April 1921, make strange reading in the light of the secularist policies adopted by the victors after the completion of those victories that had so deeply stirred Yakup Kadri's religious loyalty. That a man of his generation and of his education should, in the moment of profound national crisis, have rallied instinctively to Islam is striking enough; but it was more than a momentary or individual reaction. The independence movement itself, in its earlier phases, was strongly religious in character. Its aims were to rescue 'Islamic lands' and 'Islamic populations' from foreign—i.e. Christian—rule and its declarations were addressed to 'Muslim compatriots'.[2] One-fifth of the numbers of the first Grand National Assembly belonged to the class of professional men of religion, and some of them, both from the ulema and the brotherhoods, played an important part in the Kemalist movement.

Secularism and Laicism

On 5 April 1920 Damad Ferid Paşa formed his fourth cabinet, determined to destroy the nationalists in Anatolia, and on 11 April the *Şeyh-ül-Islâm* Dürrizade Abdullah issued his famous *fetva* against them.[3] The Caliph and the *Şeyh-ül-Islâm* both seemed to have gone over to the side of the invaders and occupiers, and in the bitter civil struggle that followed between the nationalists and the so-called 'army of the Caliphate', Turkish secularism for the first time became a serious political force.[4]

Though militant laicism was new, traces of what might be called anti-clericalism can be found in earlier periods of Ottoman history. The ancient chronicles, for example, reflect the resentments of the frontiersmen at being subjected to the hierarchy and restraints of Islamic orthodoxy; popular poetry, legend, and anecdote reflect the occasional doubts of the faithful as to the complete integrity and disinterestedness of their spiritual guides.

During the Young Turk period, secularist and positivist ideas enjoyed a certain vogue. Comte and Haeckel as well as Voltaire and Rousseau found their translators and admirers, with effects that sometimes went beyond the intellectual circle—as for example the Young Turk officers who made a point of honour of

[2] D. A. Rustow, 'Politics and Islam in Turkey . . .' in Frye, p. 71 n. 1; cf. Karabekir's insistence, in his memoirs, on the late adoption of secularism and republicanism.
[3] *EI*[2], *s.v.* Dürrizāde (by Unat and Rustow). See also above, p. 252.
[4] cf. Rustow, loc. cit; Jäschke, in *WI*, xviii. 54–69; Berkes, *Development*, (1964), pp. 431 ff.

drinking cognac and eating ham. More important than the out-and-out positivists were those who preached the separation of religion and the state—the forerunners of the laicism of the Republic. The most notable was the ideologist of Turkism, Ziya Gökalp. It was perhaps unfortunate that, to render the unfamiliar French term *laïque*, he should have used the word *lā-dīnī*, which could mean irreligious. In the opinion of a well-qualified Turkish observer, the resulting confusion between laicism and irreligion 'did much to lead the Muslim clergy, with the Shaykh al-Islam at their head, into a hostile attitude'.[5]

Besides these modernist tendencies, there was also something of a religious revival in the Young Turk period, which found expression in a number of influential magazines and books; both the intellectual and the political life of the second constitutional era were profoundly affected by the debates and conflicts between the different groups of modernists and religious conservatives.[6] The strength and aims of some of the latter can be seen in their repeated attempts, from the Volkan group onwards, to stir up Muslim fanaticism against the modest reforms of the Young Turk governments.

Through all these changes, the religious hierarchy in Turkey remained immensely strong. Despite the efforts of liberals, Ottomanists, and nationalists, the religious basis of the state had been reaffirmed by the assertion, in the late nineteenth and early twentieth centuries, of an Ottoman Caliphate; the religious loyalty of the people had been sharpened and intensified by the long series of foreign and civil wars, all of them against Christian adversaries. The First World War, with its German-made *jihad* and its British-made revolt in Arabia, blurred the simple lines of religious identity and conflict, but the Kemalist struggle to defend Anatolia against the ancient and familiar Greek Christian enemy brought a new intensity of religious identification and loyalty.

The defection of the Caliph and the *Şeyh-ül-Islâm* in the midst of the struggle were bitter blows, only partially atoned for by the counter-*fetva* of the Mufti of Ankara. Even after this the nationalists still tried to avoid a break; only twelve days after the *fetva* of

[5] Abdulhak Adnan-Adıvar, 'Interaction of Islamic and Western Thought in Turkey', in T. Cuyler Young, ed., *Near Eastern Culture and Society* (1951), pp. 125-6.

[6] For a survey of these ideological movements see Tunaya, '"Islamcılık" Cereyanı.' cf. above, pp. 229 ff.

The Emergence of Modern Turkey

Dürrizade the Grand National Assembly began its proceedings with public prayers and reaffirmed its loyalty to the Sultan. As late as February 1921 a pan-Islamic conference met in Sivas, for the obvious purpose of rallying world Muslim opinion to the nationalist cause.[7]

The bitter hostility of the supreme religious authorities in Istanbul, and the military and terrorist action of 'the army of the Caliphate' whom they launched against the nationalists, made the reconciliation impossible. Even so, Kemal attempted a compromise by retaining the Caliphate, under the Republic, after the Sultanate had been abolished.[8] But this compromise, utterly alien to the spirit of Islam, accorded neither with the traditions of the past nor with the needs of the moment, and was abandoned after a few months.

Within four years, in a series of swift and sweeping changes, Kemal repealed the Holy Law and disestablished Islam. The stages are well known—the restriction and then prohibition of religious education, the adoption of European civil and penal codes, the nationalization of pious foundations, the reduction and eventual elimination of the power of the ulema, the transformation of social and cultural symbols and practices, such as dress and headgear, the calendar and the alphabet. The coping-stone of the edifice of legal secularism was laid in April 1928, when Islam was removed from the constitution.[9]

But the frontal assault on the *Şeriat* and the hierarchy of its exponents was only one aspect of the religious conflict. There was another, less publicized by Western writers, but vitally important—the struggle with the dervish brotherhoods, known as *tarikat*, from an Arabic word meaning way or path.

The Tarikats [10]

Turkish Islam had always functioned on two levels; the formal, legal, dogmatic religion of the state, the schools and the hierarchy;

[7] Rustow 'Politics and Islam', pp. 75 ff.; Jäschke, in *WI*, xviii. 63 ff. (where translations of the two *fetvas* are given).

[8] See above, pp. 257 ff.

[9] For a detailed account of these changes, see Toynbee, in RIIA, *Survey, 1925*, i. 25–81; cf. the monthly surveys in *OM*, and above, pp. 262 ff.

[10] The Muslim *tarikats* have still received very little attention from Western scholarship. The only comprehensive study is still that of Depont and Coppolani, mainly concerned with North Africa and of course rather out of date. For Turkey it may be

and the popular, mystical, intuitive faith of the masses, which found its chief expression in the great dervish orders.

The interior of an Islamic mosque is simple and austere. There is no altar and no sanctuary, for Islam has no sacraments and no ordained priesthood. The imam—the authorized representative of orthodoxy—has neither priestly nor pastoral function; he is a leader in prayer, and a guide in religious law. Public prayer is a disciplined, communal act of submission to the One, remote, and immaterial God. It admits of no saints and no mediators, no drama and no mystery. Like Judaism and, with a few exceptions, Christianity, orthodox Islam has rejected dancing from among the devotional arts; unlike them, it has rejected music and poetry too, and confines its liturgy to the recitation of a few simple formulas of piety.

From early times the orthodox faith—austere in its worship, abstract in its teachings, remote and conformist in its politics— failed to satisfy the religious and social cravings of important sections of the population. In medieval times they had often found satisfaction in various Shi'ite sects, stigmatized by the ulema as deviant; since the Mongol invasions they had turned rather to the brotherhoods which, though frequently accused of heterodox leanings and regarded with suspicion by the hierarchy, had remained within the broad framework of Sunni orthodoxy.

To these brotherhoods, and their dervish leaders, the common people turned for help and guidance where orthodox Islam was lacking or deficient. To supplement the austere ritual of the mosque, there was the ecstatic prayer meeting in the dervish convent, aided by music, song, and dance. To compensate for the academic aloofness of the ulema, there was the warm, personal influence of the dervish, the friend, pastor, and guide; to bridge the orthodox gulf between man and God, there were saints and intercessors and holy men, and the hope of a mystical union with the Godhead.

supplemented by J. P. Brown, *The Dervishes* (1868; re-edited by H. A. Rose, 1927); Ubicini, letter 5; Hasluck, and, among more recent scholarly studies, H. J. Kissling, 'The Sociological and Educational Role of the Dervish Orders in the Ottoman Empire', in Von Grunebaum, ed., *Studies in Islamic Cultural History* (1954), pp. 23–35; Snouck-Hurgronje, iii. 149–206 (important corrections to Depont and Coppolani on the role of the *tarikats* under Abdülhamid); Marie Luise Bremer, *Die Memoiren . . .* (on the memoirs of a nineteenth-century dervish); on the role of the *tarikats* in the Young Turk period, Hartmann, iii. 14 ff. 69, 92 ff., 191 ff., 221 ff., &c., and *RMM*, xxii (1913), 171–2. In general, Jäschke, in *WI*, n.s., i. 58 ff.

All the dervish orders were to some extent unorthodox and their teachings and practices were the subject of repeated criticisms and denunciations by the custodians of the law. This did not prevent the brotherhoods from retaining and extending their influence over the Muslim masses, who found in the dervishes their real religious guides. While the ulema were becoming a wealthy, hereditary caste, the dervishes remained part of the people, with immense influence and prestige among them. Often, in earlier times, we find the dervishes as instigators of religio-social revolts— for piety against legalism, for sanctity against learning, for the masses against the ruling political and religious order. At other times we find them penetrating into the apparatus of government, and wielding a powerful though hidden influence on the actions of ministers and Sultans.

The different orders were by no means always in accord. Often there were bitter rivalries between them, aggravated by the personal antagonisms of their leaders, and the state did not, at times, disdain to pit them against one another.[11] These differences were sometimes doctrinal as well as personal and sectarian. Some orders stood comparatively close to orthodoxy, such as the Kadiris, the Halvetis, and the Nakşbendis—though the quietism and docility of the first contrasted strongly with the driving political ambitions of the second and the aggressive fanaticism of the third. Others, like the widespread Bektaşi and Mevlevi orders, were lax and latitudinarian, suspected of Shi'ite tendencies, and of pandering to the Christian and pagan beliefs and practices that had lingered on among the common people. Both had extensive followings in Turkey; both came to play a great role in the Ottoman Sultanate. The Bektaşis had their main support among village populations, especially in European Turkey. The origins of the order have been sought in Central Asia and even in Turco-Mongol Shamanism; later, in Anatolia and Europe, the Bektaşis absorbed a good deal of popular Christianity, and played an important role as a link between the Turks and their Christian subjects, for whom they offered a gentler transition to Islam. They were closely associated with the corps of Janissaries, serving as chaplains for its newly Islamized recruits. The Mevlevis were a more urban order, flourishing especially in the provincial towns of Anatolia, but with important branches in Rumelia also, notably in Salonika. They too obtained a position of influence in the state, thus counter-balancing the Bektaşis and their Janissary acolytes. The head of the Mevlevi order was a well-known and highly respected figure, and sometimes officiated at the ceremony of girding the sword of Osman, on the accession of a new Sultan.[12]

By the eighteenth century the brotherhoods had established themselves in almost every town and village in Turkey. Through their close links with the guilds and corporations, they were able to dominate the professional and social, as well as the religious life of the artisan and much of the merchant classes. Though primarily popular movements, they had their adherents and lay brothers in all walks of society, reaching even into the higher ranks of the governing *élite*. During the seventeenth and eighteenth centuries they even managed to penetrate the orthodox institution itself, and, by impressing a more personal and more ethical stamp on orthodox thought and education, helped to bring the two levels of Islam closer to one another.

In the revulsion against European conquest in the nineteenth century, the brotherhoods played an active role. Most of these actions were outside Turkey—the Nakşbendis in the Russian Caucasus, the Senusis in North Africa, the Khatmiyya in the Sudan, for example; their struggle against modernism and Western rule was bound to have repercussions in Turkey, however, and in the late nineteenth and early twentieth centuries several of the more activist orders seem to have created or revived branches in Turkey. Notable among these was the Ticani order, a Berber offshoot of the Halvetiyya, which spread to Turkey at a comparatively recent date.[13]

Little is heard of the brotherhoods during the period of *Tanzimat*, when, after some initial resistance,[14] they seem to have remained indifferent to the political arguments and changes of the time.

---

[12] For a brief general account of the Bektaşi order see *EI*[2], ('Bektāshiyya', by R. Tschudi); for a more detailed study, J. K. Birge, *The Bektashi Order of Dervishes* (1937); on their political role, E. E. Ramsaur, 'The Bektashi Dervishes and the Young Turks', *Moslem Wld.* (1942), pp. 7–14. On the Mevlevis, see *EI*[1] ('Mawlawiyya', by D. S. Margoliouth), and Gölpınarlı, *Mevlânâ'dan sonra Mevlevîlik* (1953).

[13] For their earlier history see *EI*[1] ('Tidjaniyya', by D. S. Margoliouth); for comments on their more recent activities in Turkey, see E. Marmorstein, 'Religious Opposition to Nationalism in the Middle East', *Int. Aff.*, xxviii (1952), 344–59.

[14] The Bektaşi were for a time banned, after the destruction of the Janissaries; see above, p. 79.

They return to prominence during the reign of Abdülhamid II, when several of their leaders, profiting from the religiosity of the Sultan, obtained positions of influence and dignity in his entourage. It is interesting, however, that the dervish leaders closest to the Sultan were Arabs, such as the Syrian Abu'l-Huda and the Hejazi Sayyid Ahmad As'ad, leaders of the Rifa'i order, or the Medinese Muhammad Zafir, leader of the Shadhiliyya, to which the Sultan himself is said to have belonged.[15]

The role of the brotherhoods in Sultan Abdülhamid's pan-Islamic policy has been greatly exaggerated. The more purely Turkish orders, the Bektaşis and Mevlevis, remained coldly indifferent, while even the Shadhili and Rifa'i orders seem to have used their twin vantage points, in Istanbul and in Arabia, more for mutual rivalries and recriminations than for a common pan-Islamic endeavour.[16]

Several of the orders, with their religious and political opposition to authority, seem to have sympathized with the Young Turk conspirators against Abdülhamid; the widespread and quasi-Masonic organization of the orders made them useful allies. The Bektaşis, in particular, seem to have had close links with the Young Turks, several of whose leaders, including Talât Paşa and Riza Tevfik, were members of the brotherhood. The *Seyh-ül-Islâm* Musa Kâzim Efendi was a Nakşbendi. Other orders, too, notably the antinomian Melamis, claim to have played an active role in the revolutionary movement.[17]

After the revolution of 1908 the brotherhoods attracted the attention of several of the rival political parties and factions. Their usefulness was obvious. They had wide distribution and profound influence; the high regard and affection in which they were held by the mass of the people contrasted both with the tarnished glories of the old political order and the untried innovations of the new. Young Turks and Old Turks tried to make the brotherhoods and convents the vehicles of their propaganda. In thus confusing popular religion and party politics, they established a practice which was followed to the end of the Empire, and which has not yet been extirpated in the Republic.

The political role of the brotherhoods during the second

[15] Snouck-Hurgronje, pp. 191–7.   [16] Ibid. pp. 149 ff.

[17] See Hartmann for the best information on the brotherhoods in this period. The various *tarikats* are listed in the index.

constitutional period is not easy to determine with any accuracy. Some, like the Nakşbendi order, seem to have been systematically opposed to any derogation from the rule of the Caliphate and the Holy Law; others, like the Bektaşis, seem to have rejoiced in the overthrow of the personal tyranny of Abdülhamid, and to have offered sympathy and even help to the Young Turks. In the main, however, the dervishes seem to have allowed themselves to be used as tools in a political game which they did not understand. Even the headship of some of the orders was affected. In 1908 Abdülhalim Çelebi, the hereditary chief of the Mevlevi dervishes, was deposed by the Young Turks and replaced by Veled Çelebi, a man of letters and a patriot, who contributed many articles in the press, and who formed and led a Mevlevi volunteer brigade during the First World War. In 1918 he was deposed by the Sultan's government, and replaced by his predecessor Abdülhalim, who, however, represented Konya in the first National Assembly. Veled Çelebi [Izbudak] served in the Assembly from 1923 to 1943, and played a role of some importance.[18]

In general the brotherhoods seem to have rallied to the support of the nationalists in Anatolia. The first Grand National Assembly included ten of their leading *şeyhs*, drawn from the Mevlevi, Bektaşi, and even the Nakşbendi order.[19] Their role there was an active one, and Kemal himself seems, at one time, to have sought an alliance with the Bektaşis. But relations with the dervishes, as with the ulema, were affected by the breach with Istanbul, and some of the brotherhoods gave active and effective support to the army of the Caliphate.

The great secularizing reforms of 1924 were directed against the ulema, not the dervishes; but it soon became apparent that it was from the dervishes, not the ulema, that the most dangerous resistance to laicism would come. The ulema, long accustomed to wielding the authority of the state, were unpractised in opposing it. The dervishes were used to independence and opposition; they still enjoyed the confidence and loyalty of the common people and, unlike the ulema, were untarnished by collaboration with the invader. In some areas, notably in the Kurdish provinces, veritable dervish dynasties had emerged, replacing the vanished *derebeys* and autonomous princes as the exponents of local particularism. The rebellion of 1925 has been described as a Kurdish nationalist or

[18] Gölpınarlı, *Mevlevîlik*, pp. 273 ff.   [19] Tunaya, 'Karakter', p. 5.

secessionist movement, but in view of its dervish leadership and
its declared objectives, it seems not unreasonable to accept the
government's description of it as a religious reaction against the
secularizing reforms. The two characters are in any case difficult
to distinguish. On 29 June 1925 the 'independence tribunal' in
Diyarbakır passed sentence of death on the leaders of the rebellion.
The same judgement ordered the closing of all the dervish convents
in Kurdistan.[20]

After this warning, Kemal prepared for a more comprehensive
attack on the brotherhoods and on the way of life that they
represented. In August 1925 he went on a visit to Kastamonu and
Inebolu. It was on this occasion that he and the officials accom-
panying him first wore Panama hats, and that, in a series of
speeches, he launched the great attack on the fez, the gown, the
shalvar, and the rest of the traditional garments of Turkish
Muslims. His attack, however, was not limited to the symbols of
the old way of life. In a speech delivered in Kastamonu on
30 August he spoke of the dervish convents, retreats, and brotherhoods, of their so-called saints and holy men, of the tombs to
which the ignorant and superstitious went to seek for help and
guidance.

... the aim of the revolutions which we have been and are now
accomplishing is to bring the people of the Turkish Republic into a
state of society entirely modern and completely civilized in spirit and
form. This is the central pillar of our Revolution, and it is necessary
utterly to defeat those mentalities incapable of accepting this truth.
Hitherto there have been many of this mentality, rusting and deaden-
ing the mind of the nation. In any case, the superstitions dwelling in
people's minds will be completely driven out, for as long as they are
not expelled, it will not be possible to bring the light of truth into men's
minds.

Kemal then gave some examples of these superstitions, and went
on to speak of the saints and their tombs, and more generally, of
the brotherhoods and their convents:

To seek help from the dead is a disgrace to a civilized community. ...
What can be the objects of the existing brotherhoods (*tarikat*) other than
to secure the well-being, in worldly and moral life, of those who follow
them? I flatly refuse to believe that today, in the luminous presence of
science, knowledge, and civilization in all its aspects, there exist, in

[20] cf. Cebesoy, iii/2, 153, and above, pp. 266 ff.

the civilized community of Turkey, men so primitive as to seek their material and moral well-being from the guidance of one or another *şeyh*. Gentlemen, you and the whole nation must know, and know well, that the Republic of Turkey cannot be the land of *şeyhs*, dervishes, disciples, and lay brothers. The straightest, truest Way (*tarikat*) is the way of civilization. To be a man, it is enough to do what civilization requires. The heads of the brotherhoods will understand this truth that I have uttered in all its clarity, and will of their own accord at once close their convents, and accept the fact that their disciples have at last come of age.[21]

The blow against the brotherhoods was not long delayed. On 1 September Kemal returned to Ankara, and on the following day, after a meeting of the cabinet, he announced a series of new decrees. By these decrees, confirmed by laws passed in November in the Assembly, the brotherhoods were dissolved and banned, their assets impounded, their convents and sanctuaries closed, their prayer meetings and ceremonies prohibited. Henceforth, Turkey was to be free from

şeyhs, dervishes, disciples, *dede, seyyid, çelebi, baba, emir, nakib, halife*, fortune-tellers, magicians, witch-doctors, writers of amulets for the recovery of lost property or the fulfilment of wishes, as well as the services, dues and costumes pertaining to these titles and qualities....[22]

These measures, accompanied by the ban on the fez and turban, aroused widespread resistance—far more than had the deposition of the Caliph and the repeal of the *Şeriat*. In the words of the official history:

The closing of the convents and monasteries, the abolition of the religious orders had naturally displeased the many fanatical *şeyhs* and dervishes, who, living in idleness in these homes of laziness, exploited the religious sentiments of the credulous people and put all their interests in the reaction. In several regions they tried to raise the people against the achievements of the Revolution and against the republican régime. But they were swiftly punished, and the nation adopted and rapidly assimilated these reforms.[23]

Significantly, the powers of the independence tribunals were renewed by the Assembly in February and again in May 1926; their work, supported by the military and even the naval forces of the Republic, was swift and efficient.

[21] *Söylev*, ii. 217 ff.; cf. *Hist.*, pp. 233–4, and Imece, pp. 59 ff.
[22] Jäschke, in *WI*, n.s., i. 61–62.   [23] *Hist.*, pp. 235–6.

By a curious oversight, article 75 of the constitution, guarantee-ing freedom of 'religion, doctrine, *tarikat*, or philosophic belief', had remained in force, even while the *tarikats* were dissolved and suppressed. This inconsistency was remedied by an amendment of 5 February 1937, rewording the article and omitting the reference to *tarikat*. The Minister of the Interior of the time made the purpose clear. The dervish brotherhoods were an evil legacy from the past, distracting the Turks from the true 'way', that of nation-alism, resting on the true knowledge, that of the positive sciences. This was the way of the greatest benefit for the material and moral life of the Turks.[24]

Religious Reform

The basis of Kemalist religious policy was laicism, not irreligion; its purpose was not to destroy Islam, but to disestablish it—to end the power of religion and its exponents in political, social, and cultural affairs, and limit it to matters of belief and worship. In thus reducing Islam to the role of religion in a modern, Western, nation-state, the Kemalists also made some attempt to give their religion a more modern and more national form.

The principle of the separation of religion from politics appears already in the Law against High Treason, passed by the Grand National Assembly on 29 April 1920 in response to the anti-nationalist *fetva* of Dürrizade, and containing provisions against the misuse of religion for political purpose. The principle was reaffirmed in the Criminal Code of 1926, which lays down penal-ties for those

who, by misuse of religion, religious sentiments, or things that are religiously considered as holy, in any way incite the people to action prejudicial to the security of the state, or form associations for this purpose. . . . Political associations on the basis of religion or religious sentiments may not be formed (Art. 163).

The same code prescribes punishments for religious leaders and preachers who, in the course of their functions, bring the admin-istration, laws, or executive actions of the government into dis-repute, or incite to disobedience (art. 241 and 242) or who conduct religious celebrations and processions outside recognized places of worship (art. 529).[25]

It was one thing to exclude the professional exponents of Islam

[24] Jäschke, in *WI*, n.s., i. 63.   [25] Ibid. pp. 54–55.

from the workings of a modern, national state. It was quite another to modernize and nationalize Islam itself. But the attempt was made. For the *tarikats* there could be no mercy. Their popular support, their radical traditions, their Masonic organization, all made them too little amenable to state control, too dangerous for experiment. The ulema, on the other hand, with their hierarchy, their schools, and their habits of intellectual and administrative discipline, seemed to offer a more favourable field for an experiment in Erastian Islam.

The reorganization of the hierarchy was initiated with the law of 1924, abolishing the office of *Şeyh-ül-Islâm* and the Ministry of Religious Affairs and pious foundations which, in the Ankara government, had taken over most of the functions of the *Şeyh-ül-Islâm's* department. In their place two separate offices were established, a Presidency for Religious Affairs (*Diyanet Işleri Reisliği*) and a Directorate-General of Pious Foundations (*Evkâf Umum Müdürlüğü*). The head of Religious Affairs was nominated by the Prime Minister, to whose department he and his office were attached. These duties were the administration of mosques, convents, &c., the appointment and dismissal of imams, preachers, muezzins, and other mosque functionaries, and the supervision of the muftis generally. The Directorate of Pious Foundations, not directly subordinated to any ministry, was responsible for the administration of the *evkaf* that had been taken over by the state, and for the maintenance of religious buildings and installations. From 1931 it also took over the payment of religious functionaries, leaving the Presidency of Religious Affairs with little more than the appointment of preachers, the censoring of their sermons, and the giving of an occasional ruling on a point of Holy Law.[26]

The bureaucratization of the ulema, begun by Mahmud II, had reached its logical conclusion. Islam had been made a department of state; the ulema had become minor civil servants. General education had already been taken out of the hands of the ulema. There remained the question of religious education, which the state now prepared to take over.

By the laws of 1924 the *medreses*—the old theological seminaries —were closed. The state did, however, make some attempt to provide for the further training of religious personnel. At the lower level, the Ministry of Education established some training

[26] Jäschke, in *WI*, n.s., i. 96 ff.; Rustow, 'Politics and Islam', pp. 82–83.

schools for imams and preachers; at the higher level, the old Süleymaniye *Medrese* was reconstituted as a faculty of divinity in the University of Istanbul—also, therefore, under the ultimate control of the Minister of Education of the Republic in Ankara.

This new faculty of divinity was intended to serve as the centre of a new, modernized, and scientific form of religious instruction, more appropriate to a secular, Westernized republic. In 1928 the faculty appointed a committee to examine the problem of reform and modernization in the Islamic religion, and to make proposals through the University to the Ministry of Education. The chairman of the committee was Professor Mehmed Fuad Köprülü; its members included the professors of psychology and logic as well as a number of theologians.

Its report, published in June 1928, begins with a clear assertion that religion is a social institution; like other social institutions it must meet the needs of social life and keep pace with change and development. 'Therefore, in the Turkish democracy, religion should also manifest the vitality and progress which it needs.'

It is almost impossible [the report goes on] with the modern views of society, to expect such a reform, however much the ground may be ready for it, from the working of mystic and irrational elements. Religious life, like moral and economic life, must be reformed on scientific lines, that it may be in harmony with other institutions. . . .

The recommendations of the committee, for the achievement of this purpose, was grouped under four headings. The first, 'the form of worship', speaks of the need for clean and orderly mosques, with pews and cloakrooms. 'People must be urged to enter into them with clean shoes.' The second, on 'the language of worship', insists that this must be Turkish, and that all prayers and sermons should not be in Arabic but in the national language. The third, on 'the character of worship', seeks to make worship beautiful, inspiring, and spiritual. For this the mosque needs trained musicians and also musical instruments. 'The need is urgent for modern and sacred instrumental music.' The fourth, and last, deals with 'the thought side of worship'. Printed, set sermons must be replaced by real religious guidance, which only preachers with the necessary philosophic training would be competent to give.[27]

[27] Cited in Lutfy Levonian, *The Turkish Press* (1932), pp. 174 ff.

It was possible to turn the Ottoman Sultanate into a national republic, with a president, ministries, and parliament. It was not possible to turn the mosque into a Muslim church, with pews, organ, and an imam-precentor. In all but one respect, the recommendations of the committee were a dead letter, and even the faculty of divinity itself proved to be premature. The teachers, themselves of the *medrese* tradition, did not take kindly to the task assigned to them, and the atmosphere of the time was not conducive to its realization. The abolition, in 1929, of Arabic and Persian as subjects of instruction in the secondary schools reduced both the numbers and the competence of the students. After some abortive attempts at reform, the faculty was finally suppressed in 1933, and replaced in due course by an Institute of Oriental Studies attached to the faculty of arts. During the nine years that the faculty of divinity existed, the number of its students dropped from 284 to 20. In the same period there was a parallel decline in the schools for imams and preachers, and the last two such schools were closed in 1932. Except for the comparatively unimportant schools for Koran-readers, formal religious education disappeared in Turkey, and the attempt to form a new class of modern religious guides was completely abandoned.

Only one of the recommendations of the 1928 committee had any practical consequences—that of the Turkicization of worship. Attempts were made to translate the Koran and the Traditions of the Prophet into Turkish, and in 1932 the Assembly voted a sum of TL4,000 for the preparation and publication of such a translation. It was not completed. An attempt to translate the mosque service into Turkish was abandoned in the face of opposition. In one respect, however, the government held firm. Even if Arabic were still to be used inside the mosque, it could not be tolerated in public places. Years before, Ziya Gökalp, the theoretician of Turkish nationalism, had demanded that the call to prayer, from the minarets of Turkish mosques, should be uttered in the Turkish language.[28]

> A land where the call to prayer from the mosque is recited in Turkish
> Where the peasant understands the meaning of the prayer in his worship,
> A land where in the schools the Koran is read in Turkish,
> Where, big and little, everyone knows the command of God—
> This, O son of the Turks, is your fatherland.[29]

[28] Heyd, *Foundations*, pp. 102–3.   [29] *Yeni Hayat*, 1918.

On 30 January 1932 the cry 'God is great' resounded from the minarets of Santa Sophia, for the first time, in Turkish, and shortly afterwards a version of the call, in 'pure' Turkish, was prepared by the Linguistic Society and published by the Presidency of Religious Affairs. A Turkish melody was ordered from the Conservatory in Ankara.[30] Muezzins all over Turkey were instructed in the new version, and an order issued early in 1933 superseded, though without actually banning, the call to prayer in Arabic. 'It seems that this one act of government interference in the ritual caused more widespread popular resentment than any of the other secularist measures.'[31]

Survival and Rebirth[32]

During the 1930's the pressure of secularization in Turkey became very strong indeed. Although the régime never adopted an avowedly anti-Islamic policy, its desire to end the power of organized Islam and break its hold on the minds and hearts of the Turkish people was clear. The prohibition of religious education, the transfer of mosques to secular purposes, reinforced the lesson of the legal and social reforms. In the rapidly growing new capital, no new mosques were built. Most striking, and most symbolic, was the fate of the great basilica of Santa Sophia in Istanbul. Sultan Mehmed the Conqueror, in the moment of triumph over Byzantium, had made it a mosque; the Republic made it a museum.[33]

In spite of all this, there is much evidence that the secularization of Turkey was never quite as complete as was sometimes believed. In the first place, there were many indications of the persistence, beneath the surface, of popular religion in the form of the cult of dervish *şeyhs*, especially in Anatolia. As late as 1930

---

[30] Jäschke, in *WI*, n.s., i. 74–75.   [31] Rustow, 'Politics and Islam', p. 84.

[32] Religious revival in Turkey in recent years has attracted the attention of many writers. Besides the writings of Jäschke and Rustow already cited, mention may be made of the following: Heyd, 'Islam in Modern Turkey', *R.C.As.J.*, xxxiv (1947), 299–308; B. Lewis, 'Islamic Revival in Turkey', *Int. Aff.*, xxviii (1952), 38–48; Thomas, 'Recent Developments in Turkish Islam', *MEJ*, vi (1952), 22–40; H. A. Reed, 'Revival of Islam in Secular Turkey', ibid. viii (1954), 267–82; A. L. Tibawi, 'Islam and Secularism in Turkey Today', *Quart. R.* (1956), pp. 325–37; Paul Stirling, 'Religious Change in Republican Turkey', *MEJ*, xii (1958), 395–408; W. Cantwell Smith, *Islam in Modern History* (1957), pp. 161–205. For a discussion of religion and politics by a Turkish scholar, see Karpat, pp. 271 ff.

[33] Rustow 'Politics and Islam', p. 84.

a striking incident occurred in Menemen, near Izmir. A young Kemalist officer called Kubilay heard a local dervish leader addressing the populace and attacking the régime. When he remonstrated, he was seized by the mob, held down, and slowly beheaded, amid the acclamation of the *şeyh* and his supporters. The guilty were punished, and a monument was erected to the memory of Kubilay, at which a ceremony of commemoration was held every year until 1951.

After the death of Atatürk there were rumours of a religious restoration, but apart from the return of Muslim chaplains to the army in May 1940 nothing very much happened. The first open sign of religious opposition to the secularist policy of the state appeared in 1940. In the previous year the Turkish Ministry of Education decided to publish a Turkish edition of the *Encyclopaedia of Islam*, the great co-operative work published in Leiden by an international team of European Orientalists. The Turkish edition was not to be a mere translation. Many articles which were out of date were to be revised or rewritten by Turkish scholars, and many new articles added, but the whole was intended to be in the same spirit of scientific scholarship as had informed the Leiden publication. A group of religious-minded Turks, led by Eşref Edib, who had been editor of the Muslim periodical *Sebil-ür-Reşad* in the Young Turk era, protested energetically against this project. They said that the so-called *Encyclopaedia of Islam* was not really an encyclopaedia of Islam but against Islam, and that it was the work of Christian missionaries, aimed partly at assisting missionaries in their endeavours and partly at undermining the basis of the Muslim faith. They criticized the Ministry of Education for sponsoring this allegedly anti-Islamic project, first in letters and articles in the press and then in a periodical which they published themselves. In 1941 they began the publication of a rival encyclopaedia of their own, entitled *Türk İslâm Ansiklopedisi* (Turkish Encyclopaedia of Islam), on the same pattern as the official one, but with all the contributions written from what they believed to be a strictly Muslim point of view. Each fascicule of their encyclopaedia was accompanied by a magazine supplement containing violent and often scurrilous criticisms of the current fascicules of the other encyclopaedia which were meanwhile issuing from the Ministry.

The new post-war democracy of Turkey gave a very much

greater degree of freedom of expression to almost all trends of opinion, including of course the religious leaders, who now proclaimed more and more openly their hostility to secularism and their demands for an Islamic restoration.

The first issue that was publicly debated was that of religious education. The debate began with private discussions and moderately phrased articles in the press, and then, on 24 December 1946, a full-dress debate was held on the subject in the Assembly in Ankara. Several members of the Government Party spoke in favour of restoring religious education, and although the Prime Minister firmly refused to accede to their request, the mere fact that the debate was held at all was widely regarded, in the rather authoritarian Turkey of that time, as portending a coming change of policy. A long controversy followed in the press, parliament, and elsewhere. Should religious education be tolerated? Should it be compulsory or optional in schools? Should it be controlled by the Ministry of Education or by the Presidency of Religious Affairs, which, after years of quiescence, was now burgeoning into new life? These questions were eventually settled by a compromise. At the beginning of 1949 religious education was reintroduced to Turkish schools. It consisted of two hours' instruction on Saturday afternoons, and was only to be taken by children whose parents specifically asked for it. The overwhelming majority did. The textbook was prepared by a joint committee of representatives of the Ministry of Education and the Presidency of Religious Affairs, and presents a modernized version of Islam which Muslims in, say, Mecca or even Damascus would probably have some difficulty in recognizing.

The next step came in October 1950, when it was decided to make religious education compulsory—or rather, when parents were required to opt out instead of in, as previously. This applied only to the fourth and fifth classes of the primary schools. For the rest of the school years religious instruction remained optional.

These changes, together with the growing interest in religious matters and the increase in public worship, raised the question of religious higher education. For many years there had been no higher religious instruction, and the religious revival therefore revealed an acute shortage of people competent to teach religion, even in schools, and to undertake the various religious functions in mosques. This lack of men with a serious religious education gave scope to fanatics and illiterates in the religious revival, often with unfortunate results. It was no doubt for this reason, at least in part, that the government decided to restore the faculty of divinity, which opened its gates to students in October 1949. Several features of the new faculty strike the outside observer. Unlike its predecessor, it was not in Istanbul, the old religious centre, with its great mosques, libraries, and traditions, but in Ankara, the new city, the heart of republican Turkey and the seat of the government. Unlike the old *medreses*, it was a part of the University, and therefore ultimately under the control of the Ministry of Education. The first chairs to be established included Islamic Art and History of Religions.[34]

After the war there were a number of signs of increasing religious activity, and one of the most striking was the growing self-assertiveness of religious functionaries. For a long time they had been very quiet and did not dare to raise their voices, certainly not in the towns, and hardly even in country places. Now they began to be much more in evidence. The wearing of religious garb outside mosques was still forbidden, but the beret, which presents obvious advantages for Muslim worship, became the social equivalent of the former turban of the religious hierarchy. For a time even the beret was banned in Turkey, precisely because it had assumed that character, but soon old gentlemen with beards and berets were to be seen in many places, voicing their views and demands with growing vigour. The survivors of the ulema had become more ambitious. Some of them openly demanded control of religious education, and they began, in a tentative way, to intervene in politics. In about 1950 they started a demand for the return of the *evkaf* to the Presidency of Religious Affairs, and if that is granted—it has not been yet—it will of course give them a great increase in power and influence.

Mosque attendance rose considerably. Many of the mosques were now equipped with amplifiers; inscribed Arabic texts appeared on the walls in cafés, shops, taxis, and in the markets, and were offered for sale in the streets. Religious books and pamphlets were written and published on an ever-increasing scale. Besides a great number of pamphlets of popular piety, there were

[34] Reed, 'The Faculty of Divinity in Ankara', *Muslim Wld.*, xlvi (1956), 295–312, and xlvii (1957), 22–35.

books on Islam, biographies of the Prophet and other figures, works on Islamic history, theology, and mysticism, translations of and commentaries on the Koran.

Quite a considerable number of Turks began to make the pilgrimage to Mecca. In 1950 there were nearly 9,000, in spite of the fact that the government gave no allocation of foreign currency for the purpose. Three of the major Istanbul dailies sent special correspondents to cover the pilgimage, and the popular press in general gave increased attention to religious matters.

Far more significant were the many signs of a revival of the *tarikats*, which had continued to exist secretly right through the republican era. It was natural enough that the dervish brotherhoods should be encouraged by the growing official tolerance of Islam to reassert themselves, but apparently the government was not prepared to extend the same indulgence to popular, mystical Islam as to orthodoxy. This government mistrust of the *tarikats* was not new. Even the sultans, in earlier times, had looked askance at some of the orders because of the suspicion of heterodoxy and dissidence attached to them, and of the dangerous, pent-up energies which they could release. During the war years there were occasional arrests of dervish *şeyhs*. A major episode began in April 1950 when a *şeyh* of the Ticani order, called Kemal Pilâvoğlu, was arrested and brought to trial in Ankara. The trial awoke very great interest; thousands of the *şeyh's* followers thronged the streets outside the court house, came into the court-room and interrupted the trial by shouting and demonstrating. Eventually, for the remainder of the proceedings, the court house had to be guarded by a cordon of 200 policemen. The *şeyh* claimed to have 40,000 followers. Later there were a number of similar proceedings against other orders—Nakşbendis in May 1950, Mevlevis in June, Kadiris in March 1951.[35]

A considerable religious press grew up in Turkey during and after the war, and by 1950 there were many periodicals devoted wholly or mainly to religious matters and to the propagation of religious ideas. These may be divided into three main categories. The most widely read were the popular journals, mainly weekly magazines, addressed primarily to artisans and peasants, to be read aloud where necessary. They presented a form of simple piety

[35] Rustow, 'Politics and Islam', pp. 97 ff.; Jäschke, *Kalender*, 1942–51, index 'Derwischorden'.

which probably very well reflected the mind of the people to whom they were addressed. A second group has been well described as 'Boulevard Fascism with religious colouring matter'. The outstanding example was *Büyük Doğu* (Great Orient), a rather scurrilous periodical, appearing at irregular intervals and edited by the poet Necib Fazıl Kısakürek. *Büyük Doğu* was clericalist, nationalist, and monarchist, and appeared to be a Turkish *calque* on the *Action Française*, with the House of Osman in place of the 'forty kings who in a thousand years made France'. The third and most interesting group consists of those journals with some intellectual pretensions. The most important were the *Türk İslâm Ansiklopedisi*, *Selâmet*, and *Sebil-ür-Reşad*. The last purported to be a revival of the journal of the same name published under the Young Turks. Most of the contributors were survivors from that period, and were incidentally also responsible for many of the religious books which were appearing. These journals appeared to enjoy the support of the Presidency of Religious Affairs.

The content of these journals was somewhat disappointing. The religious journals of the Young Turk period maintained a very high standard, and were written by men thoroughly conversant with Islam, its literature, its doctrines, its traditions. But most of these men were dead, and the few survivors showed all too plainly the scars of thirty years of frustration and isolation. In the absence of any religious higher education, no successors could appear to replace them. The journals were for the most part clericalist rather than religious in any real sense. They were xenophobe, usually anti-Western, often anti-Christian, treating most of what they discussed in a rather crude and violent political manner. Articles on India, for example, which occasionally appeared, consisted of communal pamphleteering, and showed no awareness of the very important religious problems and trends in modern Indian and Pakistani Islam. Much of their content consisted of apologetics, with the familiar distortion of true Islamic values by restating them in terms of the dominant Western concepts: the historical romanticism in the presentation of the recent and remoter Islamic past; the inferiority complex that induces learned Muslims to seize on chance remarks by one or other Westerner in praise of Islam and inflate their importance beyond all reason. This romantic approach to history is found in other Muslim countries, where Muslim thinkers strive unnecessarily to justify

their own civilization in Western terms. It has some novel variants
in Turkey, as, for example, in the parallel attempts to show that
the Ottoman ulema were really good Kemalists and Republicans
and that Kemal himself was a good and faithful Muslim.

Only occasionally does one find a serious attempt to face the
problems of Islam in the modern world and the role of Islam in a
modern state. Here the ideas derive mainly from two sources—
the Indian and Egyptian reformers of the nineteenth century.
Ahmed Hamdi Akseki, the late chief of the Presidency of Religious
Affairs, and Ömer Rıza Doğrul, one of the most active religious
journalists, were both good Arabic and English scholars, and
translated books from both sources.

It is still not easy to assess the political role of this religious
revival in modern Turkey. With the restoration of freedom of
opinion Islam necessarily became a political issue again, and the
fear of giving the advantage of religious support to the other side
led both of the major parties to give at least toleration, often
encouragement, to this movement. At the same time both the
Republican and Democrat Parties seemed anxious to keep it
within bounds. No interference was tolerated in matters which the
government regarded as vital. The *tarikats* were still held in check,
the *evkaf* were not restored. Despite the demands of some extremists, such changes as the return to the Arabic alphabet or the
repeal of the social legislation of the Republic were not under
serious consideration. At the same time it was clear that the
strength of the religious revival was such, that in a democratic
Turkey no party could dare to ignore it, or even perhaps to oppose
it. If the revival continued to grow in strength and momentum,
it was not impossible that even these reforms might be endangered.

What elements supported the religious revival? From 1924
religion was not an open political factor in Turkey, and its real
strength and basis of support are not very well known. The
younger intellectuals—those educated in the schools and universities of the Republic—seemed, with some exceptions, to be
very little affected and to regard it with feelings ranging from
irritation to contempt. The main opposition to it was in the
universities. But their dislike of the current form and leadership
of clerical reaction should not mislead us into thinking that they
had done with Islam itself. Islam is too deeply rooted an element

in the Turkish national identity to be lightly cast aside, and a form of faith more suited to nationalist intellectuals may yet awake a wide response.

Officials, as a class, are extremely sensitive to changes in the direction of the wind. In the civil service, in the army, and even in parliament piety became fashionable, and while by no means all favoured the full programme of the reactionaries, many felt that both for moral and for political reasons some restoration of Islamic belief and practice was necessary for the health of the Turkish people. The peasantry were still as religious as they had always been. For them there was no question of a revival—the only difference was that they could now express their religious sentiments more openly.

Perhaps one of the strongest elements supporting the revival was the class known in Turkey as the *esnaf*—the artisans and small shopkeepers in the towns. These were generally very fanatical, and, like the peasants, many of them were connected with one or another of the *tarikats*. Finally, the merchant class was interested in any additional form of insurance against Communism, and had a tradition of pious observance, at least in the provinces.

How far the religious revival was in fact an insurance against Communism was a subject of some discussion. The accusation is often made, in secularist quarters, that the revival, at least on the level of popular, dervish religion, was inspired by Communist agitators. The Anatolian brotherhoods have in the past been no strangers to a form of primitive religious communism which clever propagandists might exploit for political ends. Developments in other Muslim countries show that Communism is not averse to collaborating with movements of mass fanaticism where these appear to offer the best chance of undermining the existing order. How far this was happening in Turkey is anyone's guess—though on the whole the ancient and deep-rooted Turkish mistrust of Russian expansionism makes Turkey a singularly barren soil for Communist seeds.

The leaders of the religious revival were mainly men of the older generation, survivors from the Young Turk period. They seem to have recruited very few young men to their number, and many secularist intellectuals claimed that there was no real religious revival at all, but simply a reassertion by certain people of sentiments which for a long time they had to keep hidden and could now proclaim openly. The movement, they said, would die with the generation which sponsored it, and was only of transitory significance.

This point of view is difficult to accept. Islam has profound roots among the Turkish people. From its foundation until its fall the Ottoman Empire was a state dedicated to the advancement or defence of the power and faith of Islam. Turkish thought, life, and letters were permeated through and through by the inherited traditions of the classical Muslim cultures, which, though transmuted into something new and distinctive, remained basically and unshakeably Islamic.[36]

After a century of Westernization, Turkey has undergone immense changes—greater than any outside observer had thought possible. But the deepest Islamic roots of Turkish life and culture are still alive, and the ultimate identity of Turk and Muslim in Turkey is still unchallenged. The resurgence of Islam after a long interval responds to a profound national need. The occasional outbursts of the *tarikats*, far more than the limited restoration of official Islam, show how powerful are the forces stirring beneath the surface.

The path that the revival will take is still not clear. If simple reaction has its way, much of the work of the last century will be undone, and Turkey will slip back into the darkness from which she so painfully emerged. But that is not the only way, nor the most probable. In Turkey, as in other Muslim countries, there are those who talk hopefully of achieving 'a synthesis of the best elements of West and East'. This is a vain hope—the clash of civilizations in history does not usually culminate in a marriage of selected best elements, but rather in a promiscuous cohabitation of good, bad, and indifferent alike. But a true revival of a religious faith on the level of modern thought and life is within the bounds of possibility. The Turkish people, by the exercise of their practical common sense and powers of improvisation, may yet find a workable compromise between Islam and modernism that will enable them, without conflict, to follow both their fathers' path to freedom and progress and their grandfathers' path to God.

[36] See the thoughtful observations of H. A. Reed, 'The Religious Life of Modern Turkish Muslims', in Frye, pp. 108–48.

Script and Language [37]

According to a doctrine introduced to Turkey from Persia at the end of the fourteenth century, and adopted by the Bektaşi order of dervishes, the image of God is the face of man, the mark of man is language, and language is expressed in the twenty-eight letters of the Arabic script, which thus contain all the mysteries of God, man, and eternity.

Orthodox Muslims would not go as far as the *hurufiya*, as the followers of these teachings are called, in their reverence for the Arabic script. They would, however, attach special sanctity to the language and writing in which the Koran was revealed. For the believer, the text of the Koran—including the script in which it is written—is uncreated, eternal, and divine. In the mosque, where representational painting or sculpture would be regarded as blasphemy verging on idolatry, their place is taken by calligraphy. The interior decoration of the mosque is based on the extensive use of Arabic writing—the names of God, the Prophet, and the early Caliphs, the Muslim creed, and verses or even whole chapters from the Koran. Many different styles of writing are used, and in the hands of the great masters the art of calligraphy achieved an intricate and recondite beauty, the mainsprings of which are not easy of access for one brought up in the Western tradition. For Muslims, the Koranic text is literally divine; to write or read it is in itself an act of worship. These decorative texts are the hymns and fugues and icons of Muslim devotion—a key to the understanding both of Muslim piety and of Muslim aesthetics.

In many societies there is a close link between religion and writing—nowhere more clearly than in the Ottoman world. The language of the South Slavs is written in Latin letters by the Catholic Croats, in Cyrillic by the orthodox Serbs. In Syria the

[37] The best comprehensive study of this subject is Uriel Heyd's monograph, *Language Reform in Modern Turkey*. Among the numerous writings on the reforms in the Turkish language and script, the following may be mentioned: J. Deny, 'La Réforme actuelle de la langue turque', *En Terre d'Islam*, x, n.s. (1935), 223–47; Rossi, 'La Questione dell' alfabeto per le lingue turche', *OM*, vii (1927), 295–310; id., 'La Riforma linguistica in Turchia', *OM*, xv (1935), 45–57; id., 'Un Decennio di Riforma linguistica in Turchia, 1932–42', *OM*, xxii (1942), 466–77; id., 'Venticinque anni di rivoluzione dell' alfabeto e venti di riforma linguistica in Turchia', *OM*, xxxiii (1953), 378–84; H. W. Duda, 'Die Gesundung der türkischen Sprachreform', *Der Islam*, xxvi (1942), 77–100. For a history of the phases of linguistic reform and simplification see Agâh Sırrı Levend, *Türk Dilinde Gelişme ve Sadeleşme Safhaları* (1949).

common Arabic language has been written in Arabic script by Muslims, in Syriac script by Christians, in Hebrew script by Jews. Greek-speaking Muslims in Crete wrote Greek in Arabic letters, while Turkish-speaking Christians in Anatolia wrote Turkish in Greek or Armenian letters, according to their Church. Not language, but script was the visible and outward sign distinguishing Muslim from unbeliever.

Turkish had not always been written in the Arabic script. The oldest known Turkish writings—the eighth-century Orkhon inscriptions—are in a runic script, and during the eighth and ninth centuries the Uygur alphabet, of north Semitic origin, came to be extensively used in Central Asia. With their conversion to Islam, however, the Turks, like all other Muslim peoples from West Africa to Indonesia, adopted the Arabic writing. By the beginning of the present century they had been using it for close on a millennium, and all other kinds of writing had been long since forgotten.

The Arabic alphabet, though admirably suited to Arabic, is peculiarly inappropriate to the Turkish language. Although Turkish contains many loanwords borrowed from Arabic and Persian, its basic structure remains very different from both, with a range of forms and sounds that the Arabic script is unable to convey. Arabic writing is in itself by no means easy to learn; in Ottoman Turkish its difficulties were augmented by a gap between spelling and pronunciation wider even than in English.

The difficulty of Ottoman Turkish was not limited to the script in which it was written. The language itself had become heavy and artificial, borrowing not only words but also expressions and even grammatical rules from Persian and Arabic. In its best days Ottoman Turkish had been a magnificent instrument of expression, a worthy medium of an Imperial civilization; but in later times, and in the hands of inferior manipulators, it had become heavy, inelastic, and incredibly tortuous. For official use, a complex and intricate chancery style was evolved, full of allusion and artifice, and by the eighteenth and early nineteenth centuries Ottoman prose in general had degenerated into mere bombast—vast expanses of contorted syntax and swollen verbiage where the thin rivulet of meaning was lost in the trackless wilderness of words.

As long as writing was a privileged mystery, the perquisite

of the governing and religious *élites*, these difficulties did not greatly matter—on the contrary, they helped to restrict access and increase prestige. But the impact of Westernization and modernization in the nineteenth century raised new problems, to which liberal and national ideologies offered new answers. The Ottoman script and language were found inadequate as a medium of modern education and as a vehicle of modern knowledge and ideas; the new, secular literate class of officials, officers, lawyers, journalists, publicists, and politicians became increasingly impatient of the delays and restraints which their language imposed on them.

The first to raise the question of a reform in the script seems to have been Mehmed Münif Paşa (1828–1910), a Turkish publicist and public servant who was especially active in the translation and dissemination of Western scientific and scholarly literature. In May 1862, in a speech to the recently-founded 'Ottoman Scientific Society', he raised the question of a reform in the alphabet, as a necessary preliminary to the advancement and dissemination of science. Ottoman orthography was hard to teach, hard to learn; worse still, it was inaccurate and ambiguous, and could easily mislead instead of informing a reader. It was unsuited to the printing press, 'the most powerful instrument for the spreading of knowledge'; compared with the Western alphabet it was expensive and inefficient, needing two or three times as many characters. To meet these difficulties Münif Paşa proposed a reformed Arabic typography.[38]

Fourteen months later another proposal for typographical reform was made by Ahundzade Feth Ali, an Azerbayjani Turk who was Oriental Dragoman to the Russian governor of the Caucasus. Feth Ali came to Istanbul and presented to the Sultan a scheme for a revised alphabet to replace the ordinary Arabic letters used by Muslim peoples. His proposal was referred by the Grand Vezirate to the Ottoman Scientific Society for consideration. The Society, in its report, conceded the reality of the problem, but could not recommend the acceptance of Feth Ali's proposals as a solution.[39]

[38] Levend, pp. 167 ff.; Fevziye Abdullah Tansel, 'Arap Harflerinin Islâhı ve Değiştirilmesi hakkında ilk Teşebbüsler ve Neticeleri, 1862–84', *Bell.*, no. 66 (1953), 224 ff. On Münif Paşa see further Tanpinar, pp. 150 ff.; Mordtmann, i. 173 ff., Mardin, *Genesis* (1962), index, *s.v.*; and below, p. 437.

[39] Levend, pp. 169 ff.; Tansel, p. 226.

In 1869 the question became a matter of public controversy. An article in the newspaper *Hürriyet*, published by the Young Ottoman exiles in London, bitterly criticized the teaching of children in Turkish schools. While Armenian, Greek, or Jewish children at their parish schools learnt to read newspapers and letters within six months and to write letters within a year, Muslim children studied for many years without being able to read a newspaper, and even their teachers were usually unable to write a decent letter. The fault, said the author of the article, was not in the children, who were not lacking in natural intelligence, but in the whole system of education.

This article provoked an interesting reaction from Malkom Khan, then attached to the Persian Embassy in Istanbul. In a letter written in Persian to the editors of *Hürriyet*, he agrees that the system of Muslim education is bad, but lays the main blame on the Arabic script, the continued use of which makes adequate education impossible, and prevents the Muslims from attaining the level of European civilization. In the inadequacy of the Arabic alphabet, Malkom Khan saw the root cause of all the weakness, the poverty, insecurity, despotism, and inequity of the lands of Islam.

In a reply to Malkom Khan, published in *Hürriyet*, Namık Kemal concedes that the cause of Turkey's ills is lack of knowledge, but cannot agree that all can be blamed on the inadequacy of the alphabet. After all, he points out, English writing is as erratic and ambiguous as Turkish, yet in England and America illiteracy is very rare. The Spaniards, on the other hand, who enjoy a phonetic script, are far below the English or American level of education. In any case, Kemal says, the practical difficulties of changing the script would be insuperable.

In a letter written in 1878, Namık Kemal even gives some consideration to the possibility of writing Turkish in Latin letters. Among his objections to the adoption of the Latin alphabet are the difficulty of rendering Arabic letters in them, the awkwardness of writing from left to right ('for us, it would be like wearing trousers too narrow to bend at the knee'), and the irrelevance of alphabetic reform to the major educational problems. Some reform was indeed needed, as a practical measure, but it should take the form of modification of the Arabic letters, not of their abandonment.[40]

---

[40] Levend, pp. 170 ff.; Tansel, pp. 227–49.

The question of a reform of the Arabic script continued to be raised from time to time, especially in relation to typography. During the First World War another aspect of the problem appeared—the difficulties of military communication, in a medium so subject to ambiguity and error. Enver Paşa, the Minister of War, even went so far as to devise a modified Arabic script, to be used by Turkish officers in sending handwritten messages. Like other attempts at reform, it had little effect, and the end of the Ottoman Empire found the Arabic script still in a position of unchallenged supremacy.[41]

While the movement of alphabetical reform thus got off to a series of false starts, attempts at linguistic and stylistic simplification achieved more positive results. Already in the sixteenth century there had been a literary movement in favour of 'simple Turkish' (*Türkî-i basît*), to stem the flow of Persian and Arabic words and phrases into Turkish usage.[42] The movement had little effect, and the flow swelled into a flood tide.

A new phase began in the nineteenth century. One of the first reformers was the *Reis-ül-Küttab*, Akif Paşa.[43] A conservative in politics, totally ignorant of European languages and literatures, he nevertheless took part in a literary revolution. Abandoning the involved and ponderous 'bureaucratic style' (*usûl-i kalem*) that had become usual in Ottoman government offices, he attempted to return to a simpler style, more natural and more direct. This example was followed and bettered by others, and in the writings of a mid-nineteenth-century author like Cevdet Paşa we find a model of clear and elegant Ottoman prose.

Even in this form, however, the written language remained remote from the speech of the people, and largely unintelligible to the man in the street. Many officials, moreover, were unaffected by the new style, and continued to write their orders and memoranda in the obscure and verbose chancery style of the past. A more militant attack on the old style was initiated in 1868 by Ziya Paşa, this time with a political slant, both nationalist and democratic. In a famous article called 'Poetry and Prose' (*Şiir ve inşa*), written during his exile in London, Ziya attacks the classical Ottoman court literature as artificial and alien, a medley of imitations of Arabic and Persian originals. In its place, Turkish

[41] Levend, pp. 355 ff.   [42] See above, p. 9.

[43] On Akif, see Gibb, *Ottoman Poetry*, iv. 327 ff.; Tanpınar, pp. 60 ff.; above, p. 325.

writers should turn for inspiration to the neglected but authentic Turkish folk literature, where they would find the true genius and the real language of their people. The same obscure and artificial language was still used in government offices. This made for oppression and tyranny. An essential safeguard of the rights of the subject is that he should be able to understand the language of laws and administrative orders. Thus he would be able at once to recognize and denounce any violation of his rights.

At the present day, if the officially proclaimed orders and regulations are read aloud in the presence of the populace, is any useful purpose served? Are these documents produced only for those who are proficient in the art of writing, or are they to enable the common people to understand the orders of the government? The government has issued commercial regulations for everybody; there are orders and regulations concerning tithes and taxes and the like—but let the common people in Anatolia or Rumelia be askèd about them, and it will be seen that the wretches have no idea. That is why even now, in our country, the people do not know what the *Tanzimat* are or what reforms the new order has accomplished, and in most places therefore remain in the power of self-appointed local notables and tyrannical governors and officials, and are maltreated in the old, bad ways of before the *Tanzimat*, without being able to tell anyone their trouble. In France and England, on the other hand, if an official even partially violates an existing law the common people at once bring a claim against him, because the laws are written in a language which the people understand and are duly conveyed to everybody.[44]

Ziya Paşa's arguments found many supporters, more especially in his appeal for a more national language. Grammars and dictionaries began to appear, one of which, published in 1874, significantly referred to the language as Turkish instead of, as previously, Ottoman. A number of Persian and Arabic words which had never gone into common use were dropped from the dictionaries, while common Turkish words and expressions, previously debarred, were now admitted to dictionaries and works of literature. Persian and Arabic words in Turkish were now used according to Turkish grammar and not, as previously, according to the grammatical rules of their languages of origin. Correct Ottoman usage thus no longer rested on three sets of rules of

[44] Text in Ebüzziya, *Nümune*, pp. 271 ff. (reprinted in the new script in Levend, pp. 134 ff.).

accidence and syntax. Most striking of all, some of the exponents of the new nationalism began to point to the affinities between Ottoman Turkish and the Turkic languages in the East, and to suggest that it was from them, rather than from Arabic or Persian, that new terms should be borrowed.[45]

In general, the linguistic and stylistic reformers of the nineteenth century found it easier to formulate theories than to apply them. Ziya Paşa's essay, cited above, is a good example of the artificial and Persianized style which he condemns, and there were but few authors who managed to write the simple, popular Turkish which they held up as an ideal. Still more words of alien origin came into the language when nineteenth-century writers turned to Arabic and Persian, in much the same way as Europe turned to Latin and Greek, as a reserve store of roots from which new terms could be formed.

Already during the nineteenth century the first Turkish newspapers played an important role in the creation of a new, simpler Turkish prose style. After the revolution of 1908 the role of the press was vastly increased. The rulers of the revolutionary state were anxious to be understood—by Turks and non-Turks, at home and abroad. Above all, they were anxious to convey their message to the simple Turkish soldiery, on whom their power rested, and for whose allegiance there were dangerous competing interests.

The decade of Young Turk rule gave a great impetus to the development of simpler Turkish. The repeated struggles for power—whether electoral, demagogic, or military—needed swift and effective use of the new mass media of information. The series of wars in which the new régime was involved made a different but no less cogent demand for simple and accurate communication. The printing press and the telegraph both played a great part in the simplification of Turkish. The writers who, from 1911, produced the Salonika literary journal *Genç Kalemler* (Young Pens), drew up rules for a purified but not purist style. Even the bureaucracy played its part, using the new, simplified style in its orders and regulations. By the end of the Ottoman Empire, the high Ottoman mandarin style was already dead. Its place had been taken by a flexible, living idiom, based on the spoken language of the educated classes of

[45] Heyd, *Lang. Ref.*, p. 13.

the capital. It still contained, however, an immense vocabulary of Persian and Arabic words; though greatly simplified, it was still far from the vernacular of the common people.

The idea of romanization appeared very early in the history of the Kemalist state. It was discussed at the economic congress in Izmir in 1923, when a proposal for the adoption of the Latin alphabet was put forward and discussed. It was defeated, on 2 March 1923. An attempt to raise the matter in the Grand National Assembly the following year met with a similar lack of success.

Meanwhile definite action had been taken among the Turkish-speaking peoples east of the Turkish border. Already in 1921-2 experiments were made with a Latin alphabet in Azerbayjan and the North Caucasus, and in July 1922 it was reported that a memorandum on romanization from the Government of Azerbayjan had been received in Ankara. On 1 May 1925 a decree of the supreme Soviet of Azerbayjan established the Latin alphabet as the official script of the Azeri Turkish language. In the spring of 1926 a congress of Turcologists assembled in Baku, under Soviet auspices. One of its decisions was to introduce the Latin in place of the Arabic script in the Turkic languages of the Soviet Union, and in the following years a number of varying Latin scripts were introduced in Central Asia.[46]

One aim of this Soviet policy of romanization was to reduce the influence of Islam; another was no doubt to cut off contact between the Turks of the Soviet Union and those of Turkey, who were still using the Arabic script. The contrary consideration —that of maintaining contact between the different Turkic peoples—induced some Turkish nationalists to favour the adoption of the Latin script in Turkey. When, eventually, this was done, the Russians countered again by abolishing the Latin script and introducing the Cyrillic, thus reopening the gap between the Soviet Turks and Turkey.

This, however, was still in the future. In 1925-8 Azerbayjani exiles in Turkey were particularly active in urging the romanization of Turkish, by which they hoped to save their homeland from complete isolation. The idea of romanization fitted well with the policies of Kemal, though for different reasons. The Latin alphabet appealed to him less as a link with the Azerbayjan Republic than

---

[46] J. Castagné, 'La Latinisation de l'alphabet turk dans les républiques turko-tatares de l'U.R.S.S.', *R. Ét. islam.*, i (1927), 321-53.

as a barrier against the Ottoman Empire. By learning a new script and forgetting the old, so it seemed, the past could be buried and forgotten, and a new generation be brought up, open only to such ideas as were expressed in the new, romanized Turkish.

The new script was officially adopted in November 1928, and the old Arabic script outlawed from the New Year. The erection of this great barrier against the past obviously created a new and unprecedented opportunity for linguistic reform, and from the first there seems to have been a clear intention of exploiting it.[47]

It was not, however, until 1932 that the first practical steps were taken. On 12 July of that year, on a directive from Mustafa Kemal, the Turkish Linguistic Society was founded;[48] its task was 'to bring out the genuine beauty and richness of the Turkish language and to elevate it to the high rank it deserves among world languages'.[49] The work was planned like a military operation, and a series of committees appointed to organize and direct the assault on the various sectors—linguistics, etymology, grammar, terminology, lexicography, and the like.

Within two months the Society was ready to launch a general offensive. In September 1932 the first Turkish Language Congress assembled in the Dolmabahçe palace, in the presence of Mustafa Kemal himself. The proceedings of the Congress were widely publicized, and in the months that followed a number of decrees and directives gave governmental aid and sanction to its decisions. Apart from its scholarly work of collection, research, and publication, the Society's main task was the simplification and purification of the Turkish language. The idea was not new, but the scope, scale, and manner of the reform were very new indeed; for none of the earlier pioneers had ever conceived a reform as radical as that which the Society, with government support, undertook.[50]

The first task was the completion of a process already begun by earlier literary reformers—the reduction and eventual elimination of the Arabic and Persian grammatical and syntactical forms, many of which still remained embedded in Turkish literary usage. This was followed by a far more radical step—the assault

[47] Heyd, *Lang. Ref.*, pp. 24–25.
[48] cf. above, p. 353, on the parallel Historical Society.
[49] Statutes of the Society, art. 2; cited by Heyd, pp. 25–26.
[50] Heyd, *Lang. Ref.*, pp. 26 ff.

on the Arabic and Persian vocabulary itself. For more than 1,000 years the Turks had been a Muslim people, sharing in the common Islamic civilization of the Middle East. Arabic and Persian had been their classical languages, and had made a contribution to their vocabulary comparable in scale and content with the Greek, Latin, and Romance elements in English. The earlier language reformers had been content to remove foreign constructions, and foreign words that were rare, learned, or archaic. The radicals of the Linguistic Society were opposed to Arabic and Persian words as such, even those that formed an essential part of the basic vocabulary of everyday spoken Turkish. On the one hand, the Society prepared and published an index of alien words, condemned to deportation; on the other search parties collected and examined purely Turkish words, from dialects, from other Turkic languages, and from ancient texts, to serve as replacements. When no suitable words could be discovered, resuscitated, or imported, new ones were invented.

This planned exchange of lexical populations reached its height during the years 1933–4, when it coincided with a general movement of secularization and Westernization. It is significant that the hue and cry after alien words affected only Arabic and Persian—the Islamic, Oriental languages. Words of European origin, equally alien, were exempt, and a number of new ones were even imported, to fill the gaps left by the departed.

Some pruning of the exuberant verbiage of late Ottoman style was certainly necessary; the use of whole phrases and idioms from Arabic and Persian could obviously not continue in a language which was to be no longer the plaything of chancery scribes and palace littérateurs, but the medium of communication of a literate, modern, and advancing nation. Reform was needed—but not all would agree on the wisdom and success of the reforms accomplished. The attempt of the reformers to strip away the accretions of 1,000 years of cultural growth seemed at times to bring impoverishment rather than purity, while the arbitrary reassignments of words and meanings often led to confusion and chaos.[51]

In 1935, therefore, a new directive was issued. The invention

[51] A parallel movement in English might have imposed folkwain for omnibus, revived ayenbite and inwit for remorse and conscience, and renamed Parliament the Witenagemot.

and imposition of new words was halted, and a number of familiar and indispensable Arabic and Persian words were granted reprieve and naturalization. To provide a theoretical justification for this retreat, the doctrine was promulgated that 'a number of words which are used in our language and which until now were thought to have been taken from foreign languages had originally passed from Turkish into those languages'.[52] In other words, where it proved impracticable to provide a Turkish substitute for a foreign word, a Turkish etymology would serve instead.

This kind of theorizing, and some other dubious doctrines that were launched in aid of it,[53] never won much support outside the inner circle of the Linguistic Society, and were allowed after a time to fade into decent oblivion. The reform, however, despite occasional setbacks, continued, and achieved a final symbolic triumph when the Turkish constitution itself was translated into 'pure' Turkish and promulgated in January 1945.[54]

It was the last victory of the purists. No longer sustained by the firm hand of Mustafa Kemal, they faced a rising tide of criticism from teachers, writers, journalists, and scholars, who protested against what they regarded as an impoverishment and debasement of the language. Even the objective of simplicity, they said, had been forgotten, and a new, artificial official language created that was as remote and obscure to the ordinary Turk as the high Ottoman chancery style had been to his forefathers.[55]

In December 1949 the Linguistic Society, at its sixth congress, adopted a markedly more moderate position, and tried to give itself a less political and more scholarly character. In its subsequent work, though it has not entirely abandoned the idea of purity, it has been much more concerned with simplicity.[56] Finally, in December 1952, by an overwhelming majority, the National Assembly decided to withdraw the 'pure Turkish' constitution and repromulgate the text of 1924.

[52] Translated and quoted in Heyd, *Lang. Ref.*, p. 33.

[53] On the Sun-language theory (*Güneş-Dil teorisi*), proving that all civilization came from the Turks and all languages from Turkish, see Heyd, *Lang. Ref.*, pp. 33–34. Authorized expositions, in French and Turkish, will be found in the journal of the society, *Türk Dili, Belleten*, for 1937 and 1938.

[54] For a lexical analysis of the new text, see M. Colombe, 'Le Nouveau texte de la constitution turque', *C. Or. contemp.*, iv (1946), 771–808.

[55] Heyd, *Lang. Ref.*, pp. 44 ff.   [56] Ibid. pp. 84 ff.

The idea was mooted at the time of preparing yet a third version of the constitution which, avoiding both the archaism of the 1924 text and the artificiality of the 1945 version, would really be written in the living language of the country. Perhaps wisely, it was decided that parliament was not the place for linguistic discussions, nor the constitution the appropriate text for stylistic experiments.[57]

A comparison between the text of the 1924 constitution and the current language of Turkish literary, journalistic, and official usage will reveal how much the reform really accomplished. To the Turk of the present day, this thirty-five-year-old document, with its numerous Arabic and Persian words and constructions, bears an archaic, almost a medieval aspect. Though certainly more intelligible than the 'pure Turkish' version of 1945, it contains many expressions that are now obsolete, and must be explained to the Turkish schoolboy or student of the new generation. Even the famous speech of Mustafa Kemal, delivered in October 1927, has become a difficult and archaic text, requiring notes and explanations for the children of the new Turkey. The written language of today is unmistakably different from that which was used before the reform, and books a bare half-century old, even when transcribed into the new script, are as difficult for a Turkish schoolboy as Chaucer or even Langland for his English contemporary.

The main and really significant change has been to bring the written language closer to the spoken. In all countries there is a gap between the languages of speech and of writing, which differ from one another in texture, in style, and to some extent in grammar and vocabulary. In Ottoman Turkey they were two different languages, and an illiterate man could not hope to understand a normal written text even if it were read aloud to him.

In the new Turkey this gap has been closed. The language of books, newspapers, and government documents is the same as the spoken language—or at least, no more different from it than is normal in the countries of the West. Of the linguistic and cultural effect of this change in their language, only the Turks themselves can judge. The educational and social effects of the transformation will be obvious to all.

[57] Heyd, *Lang. Ref.*, p. 51.

Scholarship and Science

All these changes in the manner and form of expression were, in the last analysis, secondary to the greater and infinitely more difficult process of changing the ideas expressed. Modern civilization rested very largely on its scientific achievement. How were European science and the European scientific method to be adapted and adopted in Turkey?

The main instrument was of course to be education, and from the start the Turkish reformers, modernizers, and Westernizers have given a central place to education in their projects of reform. As far back as the mid-nineteenth century the first attempts were made to create an academy and a scientific society, for the encouragement of scholarship and science in the Ottoman Empire.

The *Encümen-i Daniş* (Society of Knowledge) was first suggested at the Council of Education in 1845, and was formally authorized by an Imperial *irade* in 1851. Obviously modelled on the Académie Française, it consisted of forty Turkish members and a number of corresponding members including such European Orientalists as Hammer, Bianchi, and Redhouse. Its programme included the encouragement of letters and sciences, and the advancement of the Turkish language. It was publicly inaugurated with a speech by Mustafa Reşid Paşa, indicating the part the Academy was to play in the renovation of the country. Its work was, however, impeded by the political instability of the time, and it petered out in 1862 without having accomplished more than the sponsorship of a few books.[58]

The *Cemiyet-i Ilmiye-i Osmaniye* (Ottoman Scientific Society), modelled on the Royal Society of England, was founded in 1861 by Münif Paşa, a graduate of the Translation Chamber, and was very much his personal creation and medium. Its most important achievement was the publication of the *Mecmua-i Fünûn*, journal of sciences, which was the first scientific periodical in Turkish. Including articles on history, geology, geography, and philosophy, as well as the natural sciences, it gave to its readers a clear and vivid picture of Western achievements in these fields, introduced them to the language and manner of modern science, and played a role in nineteenth-century Turkey analogous to that of the

[58] B. Lewis, 'Andjuman' in *EI²*.

Grande Encyclopédie in eighteenth-century France. It ceased publication during the cholera epidemic of 1865, and after a brief resumption some years later was closed down by Sultan Abdülhamid in 1882.[59]

The further development of scholarship in Turkey was considerable. With encouragement and support from successive governments, Turkish universities and learned societies have sponsored a truly impressive output of research and publication, notably in history, archaeology, language and literature, the general aim of which is to recover and illuminate the Turkish past. Great progress has also been made in the social sciences. Not all the work is of equal value, and some, notably in the 1930's, was directed to political rather than scholarly ends. Turkish scholars have, however, shown a growing regard for the standards and an increasing familiarity with the methods of critical scholarship, and in so doing have acquired a significance that is more than purely local.[60]

The adoption of European science, requiring entirely new attitudes as well as techniques, proved far more difficult. The first steps in the introduction of Western science into Turkish education were taken in the eighteenth century; by the beginning of the twentieth century scientific subjects were a normal part of the school curriculum, and have since found an important place in the universities. Yet the output of trained scientists was still inadequate to the needs of a modern state, and the volume of research below the Western level. It was easy enough to teach the new knowledge, with a scientific instead of a religious authority behind it. It was quite another matter to inculcate and develop the scientific mentality, without which no real scientific progress is possible. A Turkish psychologist, in an appraisal of the progress of Westernization published in 1959, saw in this the cardinal failure of the whole movement, and warned his countrymen, especially the intellectuals, of the consequences of their inability to master this fundamental element of the modern civilization of the West. Some

[59] 'Djem'iyyet-i 'Ilmiyye-i 'Othmāniyye' in *EI*[2]; Tanpınar, pp. 151–4; Cevad, *Maarif*, pp. 69 ff.; Berkes, *Development*, p. 178; Adnan-Adıvar, in Young, p. 124. Adnan notes that 'since the principal collaborators of the *Majmū'-i-Funūn*' had studied in England, most of their essays were inspired by Anglo-Saxon works'. On Münif Paşa see above, p. 427.

[60] On the historians, cf. B. Lewis, in *MEA*, iv. 218–27; Kerim K. Key, *An Outline of Modern Turkish Historiography* (1954).

have held that Western civilization derives from Greek, Latin, and Christian sources, and that therefore the Turks, who do not share its classical and Christian heritage, cannot hope to become full participants in it. To them he replied that modern Western civilization is, in essence, not so much classical and Christian, as scientific. Therein lies the cause of past failures, and the hope of future success, in the Westernization of Turkey.[61]

Literature and the Arts[62]

The starting-point of the new Turkish literature under European influence is, by convention, the year 1859, when Ibrahim Şinasi published a lithographed booklet containing 100 or so verse translations from Racine, La Fontaine, Lamartine, Gilbert, and Fénélon.[63] In the same year Münif Paşa, founder of the Scientific Society, published a group of dialogues translated from Fontenelle, Fénélon, and Voltaire,[64] introducing to his readers some strange and exotic notions on 'patriotism, social ethics, and female education', as well as other topics.[65]

Thereafter the translation movement developed rapidly. One result, of far-reaching effect, was the introduction of two entirely new genres—the drama and the novel. These translations and adaptations helped to familiarize Turkish readers and spectators with some aspects of European manners and customs otherwise entirely alien to them, and thus remotely to anticipate the acceptance of these customs by themselves. The number of readers and playgoers was no doubt very small—but so too was the number of those who made Turkey's successive revolutions.

The Westernization of Turkish literature—the genres, the forms, the themes, the prosody, and the style—proceeded rapidly. At first the new literature was largely derivative and imitative, chiefly of French models. But by the time of the Young Turk

---

[61] Turhan, *Garblılaşmanın Neresindeyiz* (1959); English translation, *Where are we in Westernization?* (1965). See also the same author's study of cultural change, *Kültür Değişmeleri*.

[62] On Turkish literature in the nineteenth and twentieth centuries, see the standard works already cited by Bombaci and Tanpınar, and the very useful Turkish manual by Özön, *Son Asır Türk Edebiyatı Tarihi*. Useful shorter accounts will be found in *EI*¹ ('Turks, literature' by M. F. Köprülü), and Key, 'Trends in Modern Turkish Literature', *Muslim Wld.*, xlvii (1957), 318–28.

[63] *Tercüme-i Manzume* (Ist., 1276 A.H.). On Şinasi see above, p. 136.

[64] *Muhaverat-i Hikemiye* (Ist., 1276–7 A.H.).   [65] Tanpınar, p. 152.

régime a new and original literature was emerging, in which the Western models are familiar and, so to speak, naturalized. Nor is that all. With the cultural radiation of the Turkist movement, Turkish writers achieved a new revival from within, drawing sustenance from old cultural roots deep in Turkish life. The cult of the medieval bard Yunus Emre, the revival of the Turkish syllabic verse of folk-poetry in place of the now almost abandoned Perso-Arabic prosody, the influence of folklore and folk literature on modern writing, are all reflections of the same tendency to look beyond the formal heritage of Ottoman court civilization to the long-neglected riches of Turkish popular life and art that lay beneath it. Nor has even the Ottoman past been wholly abandoned. The passing of years and the mellowing of memories have permitted a more impartial assessment of the values of the old culture, and in the work of some modern writers we find the interesting phenomenon of a consciously evocative neo-classicism, playing on the glories and legends of a past that has become remote and exotic to the Turks themselves. There could be no better proof of the magnitude of the change that had taken place.

The phases of Westernization in literature are closely paralleled in Turkish architecture, where we can observe the first Italianate influence in the so-called Turkish baroque of the eighteenth century, the mixture of styles in the nineteenth, to the point of introducing Corinthian columns and capitals into the design of the minaret, and the neo-classical and modernistic styles of the twentieth.[66]

The revival of Turkish folk tradition, though of considerable cultural influence, is of course of far less significance in modern Turkish literature than the massive and dominating influence of the West. This is still more so in Turkish art and music, where modern painters and composers, trained in the West, have broken away from the classical Islamic art and music of the Ottoman Empire, and have also sought inspiration in the folk arts of Anatolia.

The beginnings of modern Turkish art were formal and official. A museum was opened in 1868, a museum school in 1874, a School of Fine Arts in 1881. In the words of a modern observer,

---

[66] See further, Behcet Unsal, *Turkish Islamic Architecture* (1959), espec. pp. 28, 48, 56 and 68. A school of architecture was opened in 1894 (Ergin, *Maarif*, iii. 839).

the school based itself firmly, and unfortunately, on the usual western academic canons common to all Écoles des Beaux Arts; it ignored Turkish traditions of decorative art, of colour, pattern, line and arabesque, and turned to representational and academic art, which was European and foreign.[67]

Within this tradition some quite competent work was done, and the way opened to a fuller development in the twentieth century. Most of this was still Parisian painting in Turkey rather than Turkish painting, and it is only very recently that Turkish painters have begun to feel their way to an authentic idiom of their own. In this they are certainly helped by the growth of a non-representational art in Europe, that is more intelligible in terms of their own ancient traditions of calligraphy and design.

In 1926 a statue of Kemal by a Viennese sculptor was unveiled at Seraglio Point in Istanbul. It was followed by two others in Ankara, and then by many more all over Turkey. The significance of this public defiance of one of the most deep-rooted of Islamic prejudices was social and political rather than artistic; it did, however, prepare the way for the acceptance of this new art, where the complete absence of any inherited tradition—except perhaps for the newly discovered Hittite remains—posed problems quite different from the problems of synthesis confronting the writer, architect, painter, or musician.

As with so much else, the beginnings of Western music in Turkey were military. After the destruction of the Janissaries in 1826, the Sultan wished to find a substitute for the famous Janissary *Mehter* of reed-pipes, trumpets, cymbals, and kettle-drums. In 1831 Giuseppe Donizetti, brother of the more famous Gaetano, was invited to Istanbul to organize a band, and taught in the Imperial School of Music established by the Sultan.[68]

The first Turkish musical student in Europe was Saffet, a flautist, who went to France in 1886. A small number of others followed, and in 1923 a municipal Conservatory of Music was founded in Istanbul. The Republic went still further, founding and endowing a state conservatory in Ankara, a National Opera,

---

[67] J. Steegman, 'Turkish Painting', *The Studio*, May 1946, p. 130; cf. the comments of Georges Duhamel in *La Turquie nouvelle* (Paris, 1954), pp. 90 ff. On the history of the school see Ergin, *Maarif*, iii. 919 ff.

[68] Ergin, *Maarif*, ii. 311–15; Lûtfi, vii. 61 (on Donizetti's promotion to the rank of Miralay). According to a source quoted by Ergin, he later became a pasha. On a performance of Rossini by a 'military band' of 'royal pages', see Slade, i. 135.

two symphony orchestras, and a number of smaller schools and groups.

In spite of all this, and of a series of distinguished visitors and advisers from Liszt to Hindemith and Bartok, the acclimatization of Western music in Turkey hàs made but slow progress. A few talented Turkish composers and performers have won high reputations abroad, but the response to Western music, even among the Westernized intelligentsia, is still somewhat limited. As science after scholarship, so also does music limp after literature in the Turkish movement of Westernization—for music, like science, is part of the inner citadel of Western culture, one of the final secrets to which the aspiring newcomer must penetrate.

CHAPTER XIII

Élite and Class

First, let it be known to his Imperial Majesty that the origin of the good order of kingship and community and the cause of the stability of the foundations of the faith and the dynasty are a firm grasp of the strong cord of the Muhammadan law. For the rest, let the Imperial attention and favour be given to the men of religion, who with care and knowledge attend to the affairs of the subjects entrusted to the Emperor by God, and to the soldiers who give up their lives in the Holy War. Let him show favour to the worthy men of every class, and contempt for the unworthy.

> MEMORANDUM OF KOÇU BEY.

All Turks are equal before the law and are without exception obliged to observe it. Every kind of group, class, family and individual privilege is abolished and prohibited.

> TURKISH CONSTITUTION, 1924; Article 69.

In 1786, when the French ambassador Choiseul-Gouffier was urging military reform on the Turkish government of the time, he remarked in a letter home: 'Things here are not as in France, where the king is sole master; here it is necessary to persuade the *Ulema*, the men of law, the holders of high offices, and those who no longer hold them.'[1]

Choiseul-Gouffier was not alone in this judgement. In 1803 a Muslim visitor from India, Mirza Abu Talib Khan, remarked of the Turks:

> I learned that their Emperors have not the power of shedding blood unjustly, nor can they follow the bend of their inclinations or passions with impunity. On all affairs of consequence they are obliged to consult their nobles, who are kept in proper subjection by the hope of promotion or the fear of punishment. . . .[2]

Adolphus Slade, discussing the reforms of Mahmud II, accuses him of 'the entire subversion of the liberties of his subjects', and, realizing that 'liberties of the subject' might seem to his readers

---

[1] Léonce Pingaud, *Choiseul-Gouffier* (Paris, 1887), p. 82 (cited by Karal in *Tanzimat*, p. 23); cf. Heyd, 'The Ottoman 'Ulemā . . .', *Scripta Hier.*, ix (1961), 77.

[2] *The Travels of Mirza Abu ̄Taleb Khan . . . written by himself in the Persian language*, trans. by C. Stewart (London, 1814), iii. 60.

an odd expression to apply to Turkey, he goes on to explain how the Sultan, though despotic in name, had in fact been limited by many checks and restraints, which served to protect the people against tyranny.[3]

All this is in marked contrast with the familiar picture of the Turkish state, drawn by the majority of European travellers and political theorists from the Renaissance onwards, as the very model and prototype of autocratic and arbitary power. Thus, for example, Choiseul-Gouffier's comparison between the freedom of the French king and the restraints imposed on the Turkish Sultan is in specific contradiction with an earlier comparison between the two monarchies, made by no less a connoisseur of political power than Niccolò Machiavelli:

> The examples of these two different Governments now in our dayes, are, the Turk and the King of France. The Turks whole Monarchy is govern'd by one Lord, and the rest are all his Vassalls; and deviding his whole kingdom into divers Sangiacques or Governments, he sends severall thither: and those hee chops and changes, as hee pleases. But the King of France is seated in the midst of a multitude of Lords, who of old have been acknowledg'd for such by their subjects, and being belov'd by them, injoy their preheminencies; nor can the King take their States from them without danger.[4]

In the two and a half centuries between Machiavelli and Choiseul-Gouffier, many great and important changes had taken place. The evolution of the French monarchy is familiar enough— the ending of feudal independence, the reduction of the vassals to courtiers, the centralization of authority, the growth of royal despotism. The transformation of the Ottoman monarchy in the same period is far less known. Yet the history of the Ottoman Empire in this period was no cycle of Cathay; it was a time of great changes, in society and state—changes very different from the familiar pattern of European development, but equally relevant to the understanding of what followed.

The Breakdown of the Old Order

In the first half of the sixteenth century the classical Ottoman system was at the height of its power and efficiency, and it is small wonder that contemporary European observers saw in it the

---

[3] Slade, i. 214 ff.   [4] *The Prince*, trs. by E. Dacres (1640), ch. 4.

pattern and exemplar of a ruthless, centralized absolutism. If some, loyal to the entrenched privileges of the European estates, saw in the Sultanate the terrible example of arbitrary and capricious power, there were others who looked forward to the new European age of enlightened royal despotism in the nation-state, and saw in Turkey the model of the disciplined, efficiently governed centralized monarchy.

By an irony of history, at the very time when Machiavelli and other European political thinkers were contrasting the weakness of the French king with the might of the Turkish Sultan, processes were beginning in both countries which in time would reverse the roles of the two monarchs. In France the magnates would become courtiers, the autonomous regions administrative districts, and the king grow in power and authority over all his subjects and all his realm until he could truly say 'L'État c'est moi'. In the Islamic Empires the same Arabic word Sultān had denoted both the state and the sovereign; but there the courtiers became magnates, the provinces principalities, the slaves of the Imperial household its masters, and 'the lord of the world' the puppet of his wives, his eunuchs, and his slaves.

When Süleyman the Magnificent was invested with the sword of Osman in 1520, he became master of a perfect machine of absolutist government, over an empire stretching from Hungary to the borders of Persia, from the Black Sea to the Indian Ocean. True, he was subject to the unalterable provisions of the Holy Law, but the Holy Law itself conceded him almost absolute power, and the hierarchy of its exponents were the firm prop of his authority among the people. The government and the army—the men who ruled and the men who fought—were his personal slaves; privileged and immune as against the mass of the people, but totally without rights as against the will of their sovereign. The regular replacement of the old cadres by new intakes of slaves of humble origin forestalled the growth of a hereditary aristocracy at the centres of power, while at the same time the feudal gentry, bound to the Sultan by their revocable, functional fiefs, were nevertheless secure enough in their holdings to have an interest in the prosperity of agriculture and the well-being of the countryside.

The religious institution, as it has been called, enjoyed un-disturbed control of law, justice, religion, and education. Its head was the *Şeyh-ül-Islâm*, the Chief Mufti of the capital, presiding over a great hierarchy of kadis and muftis, with territorial jurisdictions like Christian justices and bishops. Its members, the ulema, were exempt from taxation, and unlike their colleagues of the slave establishment could transmit their possessions, and in effect their status, from generation to generation, thus forming perhaps the only secure hereditary possessing class in the Ottoman Empire.

The Ottoman historians date the decline of the Empire from the death of Süleyman the Magnificent, and it is indeed in the second half of the sixteenth century that the first signs of breakdown in the Ottoman institutional structure begin to appear.

One of these, to which the memorialists frequently allude, was the decay of the sipahi class.[5] As the feudal cavalry decayed, the standing army increased rapidly, and so too did the cost of maintaining it. This was no doubt one of the main reasons for the seizure of vacant fiefs. To secure a quick and easy cash return, the Sultan did not administer the revenues of these lands directly, but farmed them out on various kinds of leases and concessions. These were all of a monetary and not a military nature. Some were tax-farms, others were usufructuary assignments. At first they were for a brief term; later the practice spread of granting the tax-farmer a life interest which, by abuse, became heritable and alienable. The system spread rapidly all over the Empire. Not only crown lands were affected. Many fiefs were granted, as appanages, to dignitaries or favourites at court, who exploited them in the same way, and eventually many even of the sipahis farmed out the revenues of their *timars*.

The economic and social power derived from the permanent local control of tax-farms and leases produced a new propertied, influential class in the provinces, which soon began to play a prominent part in local affairs. This class interposed itself between the government and the peasantry, and intercepted much of the revenue. In theory they only held possession as lessees or tax-farmers, but as the government, through growing weakness, lost control of the provinces, these new landowners were able to increase both the extent of their holdings and the security of their tenure. In the seventeenth and eighteenth centuries they even began to usurp some of the functions of government.

[5] On the sipahi and the *timar*, see above, pp. 30 ff. and 90.

The Ayan *and* Derebeys[6]

The term *ayan* had been in use since early times in the general sense of provincial or local notables, usually merchants. It now came to denote a definite social group or class of old and new landlords, exercising important political functions. At first these were resisted as a usurpation, but amid the financial and administrative strains of the eighteenth century the central government found it expedient to delegate more and more of the conduct of provincial affairs, notably the running of the provincial towns, to the *ayan*, who began to resemble a freeholding landed gentry. They elected their own leaders and representatives, who were recognized rather than appointed by the government. In 1786 the government, fearing their growing power, tried to oust them from town government and to appoint its own city provosts, but after five years it was compelled to abolish the provosts and restore the rule of the *ayan* and their system of election.

By this time the *ayan* had become more than a provincial gentry and magistracy. In some areas, especially in Rumelia, some of the *ayan* maintained their own private armies, levied taxes, and dispensed justice, and at times there is no clear distinction between them and the *derebeys*, some of whom at least seem to have emerged from their ranks.

In Anatolia the *derebeys* had become a kind of feudal vassal-princes ruling over autonomous, hereditary principalities. In time of war they served, with their own contingents, in the Ottoman armies, which to a large extent came to consist of such quasi-feudal levies. Though given formal titles as collectors and intendants by the Sultan, they were in effect independent within their own territories. By the beginning of the nineteenth century almost the whole of Anatolia was in the hands of the various *derebey* families—only two eyalets, Karaman and Anadolu, remaining under the direct administration of the Porte.[7]

During the reign of Selim III the *derebeys* reached the summit of their power, and even began to play an important role in the affairs of the court and the capital, some supporting and others opposing the Sultan's programme of reform. In 1808 the Grand

[6] Uzunçarşılı, *Alemdar Mustafa Paşa*, pp. 2 ff., and 'Ayan', in *IA*; Miller, *Mustafa Pasha*, pp. 363–5; *EI²* ('Ayan', by H. Bowen); Gibb and Bowen, index. cf. above, p. 38.

[7] 'Derebey' in *EI²*, and above, p. 385.

Vezir Bayrakdar Mustafa Pasha convened a conference of *ayan* and *derebeys* in Istanbul, where they and the dignitaries of the central government signed an agreement of mutual support, recognizing and confirming their status. The 'Deed of Agreement' was ratified, much against his will, by Sultan Mahmud. Thus at the dawn of the nineteenth century the Sultan was brought to Runnymede, to sign a charter that gave formal recognition to feudal rights and autonomies in the Ottoman Empire. They were to be of short duration. Sultan Mahmud, like King John, had the will to suppress his baronage and gentry. The nineteenth century also supplied him with the means.[8]

Agrarian Change [9]

Selim had already made the first, unsuccessful attempts to curb the feudal autonomies of the magnates and restore the long-forgotten authority of the sovereign power. Mahmud, by a series of effective military and police actions in Europe and Asia, completed the process.

The suppression of these quasi-feudal autonomies did not, however, halt the important agrarian changes that had been taking place. Sultan Mahmud deprived the *ayan* of their armies and their courts; he left them in full, indeed in increased control of their lands.

It was not the *ayan*, but the sipahis who were deprived of their lands. In 1831 the *timars*, still comprising a considerable part of the agricultural land of Turkey, were taken over by the state.[10] They were not, however, administered directly by state agents, but were farmed out, in ways not unlike the leases on crown lands in earlier times, to tax-farmers and lessees of various kinds, who, coalescing with the survivors of earlier groups, begin to form a new landlord class in the Turkish countryside.

In the classical Ottoman land system *mülk*—freehold—was

[8] See 'Dustūr ii' in *EI²*, and above, pp. 75 ff.

[9] The economic history of Turkey in the nineteenth century is still to be written. In the meantime, the best guides on agrarian matters will be found in Barkan's study of the *Tanzimat* land laws, in *Tanzimat*, pp. 321–421, and Inalcik's 'Tanzimat Nedir?' in *Tarih Araştırmaları 1940–1941*, pp. 237–62. For briefer accounts in English see Inalcık, in *Muslim Wld.*, xlv (1955), 221–8, and Karpat, pp. 77 ff. Various aspects of Ottoman economic history are dealt with in the volume edited by Charles Issawi, *The Economic History of the Middle East 1800–1914* (1966), and in Z. Y. Hershlag, *Introduction to the Modern Economic History of the Middle East* (1964).

[10] See above, pp. 90 ff.

comparatively rare, and was to be found chiefly in towns or their immediate neighbourhood. It consisted normally of building land, together with some orchards, vineyards, and vegetable gardens in or near the town. Most farm land was *miri*—domain land—and was either granted as a *timar* to a sipahi or leased to a tax-farmer. During the period of Ottoman decline the latter became increasingly common, and the holders of such leases began to acquire, in fact though not in law, the rights and powers of freeholders.

This happened in several ways. The Sultans had always had the right to grant *miri* land as *mülk*, and occasionally did so to favoured or meritorious persons. Such estates became full legal freehold, alienable and heritable according to the *Şeriat* laws governing freehold property. Such grants, which involved the formal renunciation of the taxes due from *miri* but not *mülk* lands, were, not unnaturally, few and exceptional.

Another method was by forceful usurpation. In times and places where the authority of the Sultan was weak and remote, powerful individuals sometimes succeeded in seizing *miri* lands by force, exercising *mülk* rights over them, and obtaining subsequent recognition.

During the early nineteenth century the growth of freehold estates was maintained from two main sources. One was the sale of *miri* lands, as freehold, by the government, in order to meet deficits in the treasury. The other was the sale, by auction, of a special kind of lease conferring very extensive rights and powers on the purchaser.

It was by this kind of sale that many of the impounded *timar* estates passed into the hands of a new possessing class. Under Mahmud and his successors, such sales seem to have been very frequent. The purchaser, who was given a deed called *tapu temessükü*, had, in theory, no legal right to freehold ownership, but only a lease of revenues. In fact, however, his rights were steadily extended and confirmed, and the trend of most of the agrarian laws of the *Tanzimat* period was to transform these leases into something barely distinguishable from freehold. Changes in the rules concerning transfers and registration increased the value of the *tapu temessükü*, which became a veritable title-deed, while the laws were successively modified to allow inheritance by sons, daughters, and other relatives.

These leases were often of some size. The Land Law of 1858 prohibits the acquisition of a whole populated village as an estate by an individual. This would seem to indicate an awareness, by the statesmen of the *Tanzimat*, of the growth of large estates, and a desire to restrict it. This ruling seems, however, to have had little practical effect. The commercial and financial developments of the time, including the expansion of Turkish agricultural exports, brought a flow of ready money, and created a class of persons with sufficient cash to bid for leases, buy estates, and lend money on land. The new laws gave them legal powers to enforce contracts of debt and sale; the new police protected them from the hazards which formerly attended such enforcements.[11]

In this way, in the course of the nineteenth century, a new freehold landlord class came into existence, controlling much of the countryside of the Empire. In the Balkan provinces this gave rise to bitter social struggles, which continued after those countries had won their independence. In western and central Anatolia it produced the familiar figures of the Ağa, the rich peasant or landlord, dominating and often owning the village, and of his still more powerful protector, the merchant landowner residing in the town.

The position of the peasant was much worsened by these changes. As the *tapu*-holder became a freeholder, the peasant became a hired labourer or share-cropping tenant with no rights at all—so that his emancipation from feudalism left him rather worse off than before. As well as government taxes, he had to pay part of his crop as rent, and sometimes render personal service in addition. Turkish folk-literature in the nineteenth and fiction in the twentieth century reveal a bitter struggle between the impoverished and unhappy peasant and the landlords who dominate and exploit him. His only champion is the bandit—*eşkıya*—the runaway peasant who takes to the hills and fights against the oppressors and the government forces that maintain them.[12] There are many tales of such Anatolian Robin Hoods;

[11] See especially Inalcık, 'Tanzimat Nedir', pp. 244 ff. The whole course of development shows remarkable resemblances to what was happening in Khedivial Egypt, British India, and elsewhere in Asia and Africa.

[12] Information on the *eşkıya* will be found chiefly in the numerous locally produced works on local history. A notable example is the series of books by M. Çağatay Uluçay on the history of Manisa, including two volumes on brigandage and popular movements in Saruhan (*Saruhan'da Eşkıyalık ve Halk Hareketleri*, Manisa-Istanbul, i. 1944, ii. 1955).

their prototype is the famous Köroğlu, whose Sheriff of Nottingham was the *derebey* of Bolu.[13]

In some of the eastern versions, Köroğlu is not a countryman but a nomad. It is no accident, for the nomadic tribesmen had found their lives dislocated and disrupted by the social and economic changes of the time. The outstanding example is Çukurova, the plain of Cilicia, now a rich agricultural area with important industrial developments. In the nineteenth century it was a thinly populated and pestilential marshland, vaguely claimed by the chiefs of the nomadic Turkoman tribes of the surrounding mountains. In 1840, after a period of Egyptian occupation, it was returned to Turkey, and became part of the vilayet of Aleppo. The Egyptian administration had made some attempt to foster the cultivation of cotton, but with little effect, and the land remained empty.

A new phase began in 1866, when the Sultan's government embarked on a new programme of pacification and settlement. A military force, known as the 'Improvement Division'—*Fırka-i Islâhiye*—landed at Iskenderun, and advanced into the inner Taurus and Amanus mountains. These mountains, and the plain north and east of Adana which they dominated, were partly ruled by *derebey* families such as the Kozanoğlu of Kozan, the Menemencioğlu and the Kökülüoğlu, partly controlled by Turkoman tribes and bands of brigands. The aim of the expedition was to subjugate the independent *derebeys* and tribal chiefs, destroy the power of the bands and nomads, and thus prepare the way for agricultural settlement.

The pacification once completed, colonists were needed—and the displaced tribesmen were most unwilling to settle on the land. Three thousand families of Nogay Tatars, who had migrated from Russia after the Crimean War, were settled on both banks of the Ceyhan river above Misis, and Egyptian fellahin were imported to work on the new cotton plantations; they were later followed by Muslim repatriates from Crete, from Salonika, from the Balkans, and from North Africa, as these lands were successively lost to the Empire. Tribal rebellions were put down, and a period of social and often violent unrest culminated in the acquisition by private owners of almost the whole of what had become a flourishing area of intense cultivation.[14]

[13] On Köroğlu, see *EI*[1] and *IA s.v.*

[14] The chief source for these events is Cevdet Paşa, 'Maruzat', *TTEM*, 10/87, 12/89,

European Activities [15]

One of the factors leading to the settlement of the Cilician plain was the increased Western demand for cotton. In general, Turkey was becoming more involved in the economic patterns of development of the West. Until the Crimean War, the Ottoman government, despite the increasing burden of public expenditure needed for the new armies and administrative services, had managed to avoid incurring foreign debts. In 1854, the costs of waging modern war and the opportunities offered by a Western alliance combined to induce the Ottoman government to seek a loan on the money markets of London and Paris. On 4 August 1854 the Sultan issued a ferman authorizing the borrowing of £3 million. The interest rate was 6 per cent., the amortization 1 per cent., the issue price £80. Underwriters' commissions reduced the amount actually received still further, to about half the nominal amount, and the Ottoman government was obliged, within less than a year, to seek a further loan, this time of £5 million.[16] This new loan, for war purposes, was guaranteed by the British and French governments, with the result that the Ottomans were able to obtain more favourable terms. Rothschilds of London floated the loan at $2\frac{5}{8}$ premium and 4 per cent. interest.

The Anglo-French guarantee, while ensuring better terms, also brought the first infringements of Turkish financial independence. The guarantors had specified that the loan was to be used for war purposes; they also claimed the right to appoint a commissioner each, to supervise the employment of the funds and verify the treasury accounts. The work of the commissioners seems to have been effectively frustrated by the Ottoman officials with whom they dealt, but an important principle had been established.[17]

The war ended, but the demand for money grew and became

14/91 (1924–6) and *Tezakir*, iii, *passim*. See further Marie Luise Bremer *Memoiren*, p. 18; Hamit Sadi Selen, 'Türkiyede bir iç iskân örneği', in *Iskân ve Şehircilik Haftası Konferanslari* (Ank., 1955), pp. 91–97, and, for later developments and recollections, W. Eberhard, 'Nomads and Farmers in South-eastern Turkey; Problems of Settlement', *Oriens*, vi (1953), 32–49.

[15] On the loans and their effects there is a vast literature: see especially du Velay; D. C. Blaisdell, *European Financial Control of the Ottoman Empire* (1929). For a Turkish viewpoint see Refii Şükrü Suvla's article 'Tanzimat Devrinde Istikrazlar', in *Tanzimat*, pp. 263–88; English translation in Issawi, *Econ. Hist.*, pp. 95–106; for a brief summary, 'Duyûn-i 'Umûmiyye' in *EI²*.

[16] Blaisdell, pp. 28 ff.   [17] du Velay, p. 143; Blaisdell, p. 28.

more imperious. A first peacetime loan in 1858 to cover the with-drawal of the depreciated *Kaime*[18] brought only temporary relief, and soon the need to service earlier loans, coupled with the reckless extravagance of Sultan Abdülaziz, led to a mounting series of new loans, following one another at almost annual intervals. The inevitable end came on 6 October 1875, when the Sublime Porte announced its intention of paying in cash only half of the interest and amortization on the loans; the other half would be covered by the issue, during the following five years, of 5 per cent. bonds, which would be delivered to the bondholders.

In a time of mounting troubles, even this was impossible to maintain. In 1876 further payments were missed or deferred, and finally, on 20 December 1881, corresponding to 28 Muharrem 1299, the Ottoman Government issued the document known as the Muharrem Decree.[19] This decree, based on an agreement negotiated with representatives of the European bondholders, set up a 'Council of the Public Debt', which was henceforth to ensure the service of the Ottoman Public Debt. The Debt, by now amounting to nearly £200 million, was to be met from certain state revenues reserved for the purpose. The Council, directly controlled by and responsible to the foreign creditors, was to take full charge of them. The effect was to give Turkey a second and independent exchequer, controlling a large part of the national revenue. By 1911 the Council had a staff of 8,931 persons, as against 5,472 in the Imperial Ministry of Finance. Meanwhile, in 1910, the Ottoman government, after unsuccessful attempts in Paris and London, had raised a new loan of £11 million in Germany.[20]

The penetration of European finance was inevitably accompanied by extensive economic penetration in other fields also. Foreign capital began to play an important part in the development of the country, notably in communications and services, but also in agriculture and in the nascent Ottoman industries. Tobacco, for example, which provided employment for important numbers, was constituted a monopoly in 1884 and granted to a Franco-Austrian company. By 1914 the Company had made a profit of 30 million Turkish gold pounds, of which 23 million were paid in tax to the Council of the Public Debt. Railways,

---

[18] See above, p. 110. [19] du Velay, pp. 463 ff.; Blaisdell, pp. 90 ff.
[20] Conker and Witmeur, p. 46; Ahmad, 318.

---

tramways, and ports, gas, electricity, and water, were all operated by foreign concessionaire companies, as were also most of the few mines and factories.[21] By a law of 1867 foreigners obtained the right to own land.

These economic developments produced two important social consequences. One was the decline and ruination of native hand industries, which were quite unable to compete with the cheap, imported European goods. This process had begun as far back as the sixteenth century. In the nineteenth century it reached critical proportions, and caused severe unemployment and growing distress, notably in Anatolia.[22]

At the same time a new native middle class was coming into being, as buyers, agents, importers, distributors, and generally as the financial and commercial representatives of the foreign interests—in a word, as what are known in the Far East as compradors. The dangerous feature was that this new class consisted predominantly of non-Muslims. The Turk still preferred the three professions of religion, government, and war, and left commerce, with its degrading infidel associations, to the Christians and Jews. They accepted it, and some, notably among the Greeks and Armenians, grew rich and powerful.

The Christian Middle Class

There had been such Christian merchant classes in Turkey before, as for example in the sixteenth century, when the Greek Michael Cantacuzenos held court as a merchant prince in Ottoman Istanbul. In the sixteenth century the Turks had relied very heavily, in commerce, diplomacy, and many fiscal matters, on the Jews—the only community possessing the necessary aptitudes yet free from suspicion of treasonable sympathies with the Christian powers. The Jewish community declined together with the Ottoman Empire, and lost ground to the Greeks, Armenians, and Syro-Lebanese Christians. The Ottoman Jews did not experience any educational or intellectual revival comparable with those of the Christians, nor could they count in the same way on the favour of European merchants and the protection of European governments. Their economic and political position, already much weakened during the eighteenth century, suffered further blows after the destruction of the corps of Janissaries, with

[21] Ibid. pp. 47 ff.   [22] Karpat, pp. 81 ff.

which several prominent Jews had had close relations. The Greek and Armenian communities, as a consequence of the decline of Ottoman power, had become stronger and more cohesive, and profited both commercially and culturally from their contacts with the greater Christian world.[23] Many of them obtained *berats*—certificates—from the European embassies and consulates, which assured them important commercial and fiscal privileges. Originally intended to protect locally recruited interpreters and consular agents, these *berats* were granted or sold to growing numbers of local merchants, who were thus able to acquire a privileged and protected status. During the period of Western strength and Ottoman decline, the Capitulations, originally granted with almost contemptuous condescension for small groups of visiting foreign merchants, had been transformed into a system of extra-territorial privilege and immunity. By the sale of *berats* it was extended by abuse to many local merchants, who thus acquired a considerable advantage over their Ottoman fellow subjects.

The Turkish authorities attempted to curb the traffic in *berats*, and at the end of the eighteenth century Selim III tried to compete with the European consuls by himself selling *berats* to Christian and Jewish merchants. In return for a fee of 1,500 piastres, these *berats* conferred the right to trade with Europe, together with important legal, fiscal, and commercial privileges and exemptions. These grants, enabling Ottoman non-Muslims to compete on more or less equal terms with foreign or foreign-protected merchants, created a new privileged class, known as the *Avrupa Tüccarı*, the Europe merchants. In this class, the Greeks, thanks to their maritime skills and opportunities, were able to win a position of pre-eminence. It was reinforced by the advantages which they derived from the use of the neutral Ottoman flag during most of the years of the revolutionary and Napoleonic wars. The influence of the Ottoman Greeks inevitably declined after the creation of the Greek kingdom. The chief beneficiaries were the Armenians, already well established as money-changers and bankers; better trusted than the Greeks, better educated than the Jews, they moved into many positions previously held by both, and played a

---

[23] Gibb and Bowen, i/2, pp. 233 ff.; cf. A. H. Hourani, 'The Changing Face of the Fertile Crescent in the XVIIIth Century', *Studia Islamica*, viii (1957), 103 ff.

large part in the commercial and industrial developments of the nineteenth century.

In the early nineteenth century the *berat* system was extended to Muslim merchants, who for a slightly smaller fee, of 1,200 piastres, could obtain a *berat* of membership of the Muslim guild of the *Hayriye Tüccarı*, the 'merchants of benefaction'. The response was, however, meagre, and the merchant class remained predominantly non-Muslim.[24]

By the mid-century these terms and institutions had fallen into desuetude. The Christian merchants remained, however, and began to play a new and important role in the penetration of European commerce and investment. What distinguished them from such classes in earlier times was that, in addition to enjoying the patronage and protection of the European great powers, many of them now cherished national aspirations of their own that were ultimately incompatible with Ottoman loyalty. At the same time they—or rather their European patrons on their behalf—were putting forth comprehensive demands for civic and fiscal rights which effectively undermined the previously accepted principle of Muslim political primacy in the Empire.

The Muslim Reaction

The rise of a new Christian middle class, prosperous, self-assertive, and potentially disloyal, coincided ominously with the ruination of the Muslim Turkish craftsmen and small merchants. The contrast between the two led to a sharpening of religious and national tensions, and to a rising wave of hostility directed both against the foreigner and the Ottoman Christian. As early as the 1860's, Namık Kemal and his Young Ottoman companions had complained of the growing subservience of the Ottoman Empire to European economic interests, and had commented on both the laxness of Turkish statesmen and the thrust of the comprador class. In the main, however, the Muslim Turkish intelligentsia continued to find its outlet and careers in the service of the state, and its theoretical interests in the problems of the state, religion, and nation. Fundamentally unconcerned with the affairs of merchants, craftsmen, and peasants, it was content to leave both economic activity and economic criticism to others.

[24] Ubicini, *Lettres*, ii. 212 ff.; 310 ff.; 376 ff.; B. Lewis, in *MES*, i (1965), 288-9; idem, 'Berātlı' in *EI²*.

Industry[25]

One problem, however, did retain some attention—that of industrialization. The general decay of Ottoman industry dates from the early nineteenth century, when Turkey, along with many other countries, underwent the shattering impact of the expanding industrial capitalism of Europe, and a flood of cheap manufactured goods flowed into the Turkish market. The most important imports were textiles, and the old-established Turkish cotton and silk manufactures suffered accordingly. Other imports included ironware, knives, clocks, paper, and manufactured sugar, and once again the Turkish local industries failed to compete.[26]

The process begun in the first half of the nineteenth century was completed in the second half. Apart from a few necessary local craftsmen such as cobblers, tailors, and the like, the manufacturing arts disappeared almost completely, and Turkey became an exporter of raw materials and importer of manufactured goods. The altered demand for clothing and household accessories resulting from social Westernization on the one hand, and the restriction imposed on Turkish fiscal policies by the Capitulations on the other, no doubt helped to bring this about, but the main cause must be sought in the basic inability of a weak, pre-modern economy like that of Turkey to resist the competitive impact of modern capitalist industry.[27]

The value of industry as a source of wealth and power was soon realized in the Middle East. Such early observers as Halet Efendi and Sadık Rifat Paşa[28] comment on it, and such rulers as Abdül-mecid in Turkey and Muhammad Ali Paşa in Egypt tried to build factories and establish industries by decree. But industrialization was not a magic talisman that could be used, in a single flourish, to conjure up the gorgeous and fabulous treasures of the West. Perhaps the best example is Sultan Abdülmecid, a ruler of goodwill and progressive intentions, who during his reign encouraged or directly initiated the establishment of more than 150 factories. Only three of them have survived to the present day.[29]

[25] On Ottoman industries in the *Tanzimat* period, see Ömer Celâl Sarç, 'Tanzimat ve Sanayiimiz', *Tanzimat*, pp. 423–40; English translation in Issawi, *Econ. hist.* (1966), pp. 48–59; on the later period see Conker and Witmeur.

[26] Sarç, pp. 425–6.   [27] Ibid. pp. 427–34.   [28] See above, pp. 131 ff.

[29] Turhan, *Garblılaşmanın Neresindeyiz?*, p. 41; cf. Sarç, p. 435. In the same way Slade, in 1832, discussing Selim III, speaks of 'the manufactories (now in ruins) he established' (i. 211).

The state factories were ill conceived, inefficient, often irrelevant to the country's needs, and were only able to sustain a parasitic life on constant government subsidies. Most of them were closed or abandoned, sometimes after only a few months work. Such private industry as came into being was for the most part foreign controlled and foreign operated. It was inevitably limited, since industrial development, with all the immense difficulties arising from the lack of suitable personnel, could not compete in attractiveness with the quick, cheap, and easy export of the raw materials in which the country abounded.

The rather crude mercantilism of the statesmen of the *Tanzimat* was in any case hopelessly irrelevant, both to the bustling nineteenth century and to the fatalistic Turkish population. In the hands of a government too weak to enforce its policies, too poor to apply them, it could end only where it did, in failure, breakdown, and impoverishment.[30]

The Young Turks: Land Laws

Even by the early twentieth century the Young Turk revolutionaries, in their discussions and arguments both before and after the Revolution, devote comparatively little attention to economic matters. Their most important enterprise in this field was the reform of the land law, which had undergone no serious change since the law of 1858 and amendment of 1867.[31] A group of 'temporary' laws, passed in February 1910, brought important changes in the land law, especially on the questions of corporate ownership, mortgage, and inheritance. Further modifications were enacted in March 1911 and February 1913, the last providing for a regular system of delimitation and registration of real property, and estimation of values and revenues. As late as the war years, a further reform removed the last traces of the notorious *iltizam* system. These laws did indeed simplify the complex and often anomalous situation left by the *Tanzimat* reforms. They were, however, also responsible for some hardship among the small peasants. The basis of the new law of inheritance was the German civil code, but certain rules which in the German code applied only to real estate in towns were in the Turkish law extended— probably by inadvertence—to farmlands and forests. This led to

---

[30] See the penetrating observations of Sarç, pp. 439–40.
[31] See above, pp. 118 and 228.

excessive subdivision, to frequent dispossessions, and to grave dislocation and distress.[32]

Economic Nationalism

During the last years of the Empire, the growing nationalism of the Young Turks led them to initiate some economic and social changes which were to reach a fuller development under the Republic. During the reign of Abdülhamid, the economic penetration of the Empire by Europe, especially by Germany, had proceeded rapidly. It continued after the Revolution of 1908, but the Young Turks were becoming conscious of it, if only as a political problem—the infringement of Turkish sovereignty. The 'Turkish Hearths'[33] were particularly active in calling for greater national economic activity, as a prior condition for economic emancipation. A few rather desultory steps were taken to stimulate local enterprise. An attempt in 1913–14 to abolish the economic Capitulations[34] came to nothing, but a 'society for national consumption' was founded in July 1913, and launched a campaign to encourage the consumption of home-produced in place of imported goods.[35] The same year a law was passed to encourage industry, and a first industrial census, for the years 1913–15, was completed in 1915.[36]

Another instrument of this policy was a consumers' co-operative movement, started in Istanbul. As far back as 1860 Midhat Paşa, while governor of the Danube province, had established the first agricultural credit co-operatives. These, however, had no successors, and a genuine co-operative movement did not appear in Turkey until after the 1908 revolution. The producers' co-operatives never really got past the stage of making laws and preparing plans, but from 1909 onwards consumers' co-operatives appear in several districts in the capital, where their growth was encouraged by the shortages and difficulties of the war years. They disappeared when the war ended, perhaps because of the political

[32] Mardin, 'Development of the Shari'a under the Ottoman Empire', in Khadduri and Liebesny, pp. 287 ff. See also Nord; Louis Steeg, 'Land Tenure', in Mears, pp. 238–64.

[33] See above, p. 350.   [34] Karpat, p. 83.

[35] Y. H. Bayur, *Türk Ink. Tar.*, ii/4, pp. 494–6.

[36] Hallûk Cillov, 'Les Recensements industriels en Turquie', *R. Fac. Sci. Éc. Univ. Ist.*, xiii (1951–2), 163 ff. Conker and Witmeur, pp. 55 ff.

direction and exploitation to which they had been subjected.[37]

A first prerequisite to any national economic development was a genuinely national bank, for all the existing banks, including the Imperial Ottoman Bank, were more or less under foreign control. After some discussion, a party congress of the Committee of Union and Progress in 1916 decided on the establishment of a National Credit Bank. The bank was opened in January 1917; its capital was 4 million Ottoman pounds, half paid-up, and an issue of 400,000 £10 shares was expressly limited to Ottoman subjects. The guiding spirit seems to have been Cavid Bey, the Finance Minister; with him on the provisional board of directors were Hüseyin Cahid [Yalçın] and a number of prominent merchants.[38]

Under the auspices of the bank, other enterprises were begun, notably two insurance companies. The founding of companies by private enterprise with local capital was given wide publicity, and factories were opened with impressive ceremonies.[39] At the same time foreign companies were required by law to have a certain number of Ottoman subjects on their boards of directors. A law of 1916 had already required concessionary companies to keep their books and run their affairs in Turkish. A boycott of Greek-owned shops, ostensibly in reprisal for Greek ill-treatment of Turks in Macedonia, was also no doubt intended to increase the Turkish, as distinct from merely Ottoman participation in the advantages of commerce.[40]

These efforts to foster Turkish commerce and industry, made in the final phase of Ottoman decline, could achieve little, and in any case came to an end with the defeat of the Empire and the flight of the Young Turk leaders. They did, however, indicate some of the lines of economic policy and development which, at a later and more favourable time, the Turkish Republic was to follow.

[37] Orhan Tuna, 'Küçük San'atlar ve kooperatifçilik Meseleleri', *Istanbul Üniversitesi Çanakkale Haftası 1952* (1953), pp. 100–2. There is also a more detailed study on Turkish co-operatives by Z. Fahri Fındıkoğlu.

[38] Tunaya, *Partiler*, pp. 204–5; Karpat, p. 83. The National Credit Bank (*Itibar-i Millî*) was merged in 1927 with the Bank of Affairs (*İş Bankası*) which had been established in 1924.

[39] Tunaya, pp. 204–5.

[40] Bayur, *Türk Ink. Tar.*, ii/4, pp. 493–4; Emin, *Turkey in the World War*, pp. 114 ff.; Karpat, p. 84.

Social Change: the New Élite

It is not possible to identify, with certainty, any important changes in the economic basis of social prestige and political power in Hamidian Turkey. It is, however, possible—and for an Islamic society like the Ottoman Empire this is far more important —to distinguish certain new social and professional elements, and to observe their emergence among the governing and cultivated *élites* of the country. These new elements came from a wider variety of social backgrounds than their predecessors. This social diversification of the educated *élite*, and perhaps even more the sheer increase in its numbers, gradually ended the cosy intimacy of earlier struggles. The Young Ottomans and the first constitutionalists had, with few exceptions, all been members of the inner circle of prestige and power, on the same social level and often personally acquainted with the men of the régimes they were opposing, and therefore always able to reach some sort of personal accommodation with them before things became really serious. Even in the first decades of the Hamidian period this remained true, when the Sultan found it worth while to send a pasha to Europe to tempt the exiles home with promises of pardon and promotion.[41] But as the literate *élite* became larger and more diverse, the personal bond was weakened, the struggle for power became sharper and fiercer, and the penalties for failure more terrible and more final. Ironically, it was the Young Turks themselves, and not the old-fashioned Sultan, who inaugurated the large-scale execution of political opponents. By that time, the governing *élite* of the Empire had expanded beyond the dimensions of a family circle, and the change was reflected in the sharper conflicts and harsher tone of political life.

Among these new elements in the educated *élite* four are of special importance—officers and civil servants, lawyers and journalists. Men of these four professions played a role out of all proportion to their numbers in the preparation and establishment of the new Turkey.

Journalism and the law were entirely new professions in Turkey. Under the traditional order the only publicly recognized system of law and judicature was the *Şeriat*, the Holy Law of Islam. Its authorized exponents—muftis and kadis, jurisconsults and judges,

[41] See above, p. 200.

were men of religion, identified by education, status, and function with the theologians and preachers, and forming, with them, the great Islamic hierarchic institution under the supreme authority of the *Şeyh-ül-Islâm* in Istanbul. But the establishment of new, secular codes, and of new, secular tribunals to administer them, also created a demand for new secular lawyers—judges, to perform a task for which the old kadis showed themselves ill equipped, and also advocates, to exercise a profession and develop a skill not previously known in the Islamic world. Secular lawyers were at first few in numbers and importance; the training schools of Abdülhamid increased them in both respects, and helped to prepare them for the new role they were to play in the structure of a modern state.

Like advocacy, journalism too was a new profession, without precedents and therefore without social traditions or connexions. The first journalists, in the *Tanzimat* period, had been part-time amateurs, men of letters, officials, or politicians, dabbling with a new medium the full potentialities of which they failed to appreciate. To some extent this is still true of the Hamidian period, when many journalists combined their activities with government appointments, teaching, or other professions. There was, however, a clear and rapid development of professional journalism—of a class of men skilled in the collection, presentation, and discussion of news and earning their principal livelihood through the press. The growth of literacy—according to Ahmed Emin the rate was tripled in the last quarter of the nineteenth century—and the increased desire for news and other information made newspaper publishing a profitable enterprise, and gave the journalist a new standing and influence.

In some of the Arab successor states of the Ottoman Empire the radical advocates and journalists were able, for a while, to play a decisive role in political life. In the Turkish Revolution the role of the lawyers and journalists, though important, was subordinate to that of two other elements in the new *élite*—the officers and the civil servants.

The army and the bureaucracy were of course no new professions in Turkey; on the contrary, they had, together with the men of religion, formed the three pillars on which the traditional political and social order had rested. But unlike the men of religion, they had undergone a tremendous transformation. For more than a century the Ottoman state had lavished its best efforts on military and administrative reform—to create the modern army which alone could resist the European enemy, and the modern state on which, as time had shown, that army must depend. New methods and equipment, new schools and curricula, had produced a new kind of officer and official—open to Western influences and ideas, aware of the diminished status of their country, and adding to their ancient loyalty a new, radical patriotism inspired by European example. After all the changes and reforms, the military and bureaucratic classes, broadly recruited but self-perpetuating, retained a deep conviction of their privileges and responsibilities in the defence and government of the Empire—of a status and authority to which the rest of the population still gave automatic and spontaneous recognition. As late as 1920 the first Grand National Assembly of the Kemalist revolution, meeting in Ankara, included among its members 138 officials, 53 soldiers, and 53 men of religion—nearly two-thirds of the total.[42]

The Revolutionaries: Kemalist Populism

It is thus very difficult to isolate and identify any clear economic factors or forces in the earlier phases of the Turkish revolutionary struggle. The contenders for power were different groups or factions within the governing *élite*—all of them dependent on the state for a livelihood, and regarding the public service as a natural and proper career for men of their kind.

The Young Turks had, however, brought one important change —the broadening of the popular basis of political interest and participation. The army had always drawn its recruits from a wider circle than the religious hierarchy, with its entrenched dynasties of rank and wealth, or the bureaucracy, with its inevitable bias in favour of the capital and its insistence on traditional, formal education. The poor and the provincial, the low-born and the uneducated, all had their chance in the armed forces, and in the course of the nineteenth century the expanding, modernized army offered the most promising career open to talent.[43]

The Young Turk Revolution, and the emergence of the officer

[42] See above, p. 246; cf. the comments of D. A. Rustow in Macridis, pp. 315–16. See further Frey, *Elite* (1965), and Ward and Rustow, *Political Modernization* (1964).

[43] Rustow, in *Wld. Polit.*, xi. 515.

corps as the dominating factor in political affairs, thus broadened the range of political activity and concern far beyond the small circle of the palace and the Sublime Porte, within which they had previously remained. The events of the following years encouraged and accelerated this change. The series of elections, both general and local; the increase in literacy and the swift expansion of the press; above all, the growing practice of contenders for political power to appeal for public support by meetings and rallies and even local party branches, helped to create a new attitude to politics among many Turks who had previously regarded such matters as outside their competence and irrelevant to their lives.[44]

As well as political participation, the Young Turks also provided the first schooling in direct action. In 1913 they launched a simultaneous campaign of irredentist agitation and guerrilla activity in the vain hope of recovering the lost province of Western Thrace. It would seem that in the autumn of 1918, foreseeing the military defeat of the Empire, they began to make preparation for a resistance movement in Anatolia.[45]

In these circumstances, it is not surprising that some observers at the time, both Western and Turkish, should have regarded the new nationalist movement in Anatolia as a disguised reappearance of the discredited Committee of Union and Progress. In a sense, they were not entirely wrong. It soon became apparent, however, that something new and different was afoot—and there was some anxiety as to what it might be.

Ahmed Izzet Paşa, the Grand Vezir of the Armistice, tells in a letter how in the winter of 1920-1, when the return to the Greek throne of King Constantine had cooled the philhellene ardour of the Allied governments, they began to consider the possibility of an accommodation with the nationalists, and to make anxious inquiries about them. A number of British officers came to see him and, believing him to be in secret communication with the men in Anatolia, made searching inquiries into his political opinions and, especially, wanted to know whether the Anatolians were completely tied up with the Bolsheviks. Izzet Paşa replied that

this group consists in the main of military commanders and their staffs, of country notables and landowners, and of intellectuals; it is therefore inconceivable that they should have any inclination to Communist

[44] Ibid. p. 541.   [45] Ibid. p. 541-2.

theories. However, if the Western powers insist on applying unjustified pressure, it is not unlikely that they will throw themselves into the arms of Russia.[46]

Izzet Paşa, on his own statement, was choosing his words carefully; in doing so, he was giving a first formulation of what was, elsewhere, to become a classical political ploy. At the same time, his characterization of the nationalist movement was remarkably accurate, and his description of their attitude to Communism amply borne out by subsequent events.

There was, however, a time, in the early days of the movement, when Kemal himself gave voice to radical social and economic views. Speaking in Ankara on 1 December 1921, he had said:

If we must define our government sociologically, we would call it 'people's government'. . . . We are toiling people, poor people, who work to save their lives and independence. Let us know what we are! We are people who work and who must work to be saved and to live. For this every one of us has the right and the authority, but only by working do we acquire that right. There is no room, and no right, in our society for men who want to lie on their backs and live without working. Populism is a social principle that seeks to rest the social order on its work and its law. Gentlemen! We are men who follow a principle that entitles us, in order to preserve this right and to safeguard our independence, to struggle as a whole nation against the imperialism that seeks to crush and the capitalism that seeks to swallow our very nationhood . . . that is the basis on which our government rests, a clear sociological basis. . . . But what can we do if we don't resemble democracy, we don't resemble socialism, we don't resemble anything? Gentlemen, we should be proud of defying comparison! Because, gentlemen, we resemble ourselves![47]

Kemal's populism, which later found its way into the programme of the Republican People's Party and even into the Turkish constitution, was far from being an empty word. Besides its well-known political and cultural implications, it also connoted certain economic and, still more, social ideas, which found expression in several measures of the republican government. With the signing of the peace treaty with the West and the progress of Westernization, it had, however, lost its outspoken anti-capitalist quality, and had been more concerned with such

[46] Quoted by Inal, p. 1996; cf. Rustow, in *Wld. Polit.*, xi. 542.
[47] *Söylev*, i. 190–1. The last phrase has become a favourite text for quotation.

matters as the ending of surviving feudal privileges in the remoter areas of rural Anatolia.

On 17 February 1923 Mustafa Kemal inaugurated an economic congress in Izmir. In a speech of welcome to the assembled delegates, he spoke to them of the urgent need to seek and find the means of rapid economic development, and thus heal the economy of the nation from the wounds left by the neglect and incompetence of centuries:

Comrades, you come directly from the classes of the masses who really constitute our nation, and are chosen by them. You thus know at first hand the condition and the needs of our country and nation, the hopes and sorrows of our people. The words that you will utter, the measures that you will prescribe, may be considered as directly spoken by the people . . . the voice of the people is the voice of God.

Kemal then went on to discuss at length the futility of purely military power, the squandered blood and effort of the great Turkish Empires of the past:

My friends, those who conquer by the sword are doomed to be overcome by those who conquer with the plough, and finally to give place to them. That is what happened to the Ottoman Empire. . . . The arm that wields the sword grows weary and in the end puts it back in the scabbard, where perhaps it is doomed to rust and moulder; but the arm that holds the plough grows daily stronger, and in growing stronger becomes yet more the master and owner of the soil. . . .

In a word, national sovereignty must rest on economic sovereignty, without which political and military victories, however great, are empty and transitory. Likewise, without economic effort, the greatest and most sacred national objectives would be no more than paper enactments and empty fancies. The economic servitude of the public debts, the Capitulations, the concessions, must give way to a free and expanding national economy.

To achieve all this, great changes would be needed—the mechanization of agriculture, the development of industry, the improvement of communications: 'We must turn our country into a network of railways and motor roads . . . for while the West and the world use cars and trains, we cannot compete against them with donkeys and ox-carts on natural tracks.'

In this task, the whole nation would have to work together. The Turkish people were not divided into classes with conflicting interests. On the contrary, their existence and efforts were mutually necessary.

At this moment, my listeners are farmers, artisans, merchants and workers. Any of these can become the antagonist of another. But who can deny that the farmer needs the artisan, the artisan the farmer, the farmer the merchant, and all of them need one another and the worker.[48]

The congress continued its deliberations until 4 March. Although some of its discussions were devoted to such matters as the introduction of the Latin script, the congress did consider a number of economic problems, and at its final session passed an economic pact (*misak-i iktisadî*), which was to be the economic counterpart of the National Pact passed in both Ankara and Istanbul.[49]

The four groups mentioned in Kemal's speech—traders, farmers, artisans, and workers—were all represented at the congress, and met in separate groups. But the explicit rejection of class-war ideologies by Kemal in his opening speech set the keynote for the congress, and indeed for the social and economic ideologies of the Kemalist state, for a number of years.

This by no means meant the abandonment of the social radicalism—or populism—of the early days of the movement. On the contrary, during the 1920's two further measures of great importance were adopted, both in the field of agrarian reform.

The first of these was the abolition, by a law of 17 February 1925, of the tithes (*Âşar*). This tax, with its roots going back to the medieval Islamic fiscal system, had become a serious abuse, irregular in its incidence and often greatly exceeding the legal tenth. A law of 1840[50] had standardized the tithes at the rate of one-tenth, which was later reduced to one-twelfth. The tax was calculated on the gross product, and was not subject to any allowances. Providing a large part of the revenues of the state, it had constituted a heavy burden on the peasantry.

With the abolition of the tax, the state monopolies—tobacco, matches, alcohol, &c.—now came to be a major source of state

[48] Text of Kemal's speech in *Söylev*, ii. 99 ff.; cf. *Hist.*, pp. 270 ff. and 312.
[49] On the economic pact see *OM*, ii (1923), 593, 671, and the published proceedings, *Zabıtlar*; on the National Pact cf. above, p. 243.
[50] Barkan, in *Tanzimat*, pp. 354 ff.; Inalcık, in *Muslim Wld.*, xlv. 226.

revenue, and the main burden of supporting the state was thus transferred from the small peasants to the landlords and towns-people who were the monopoly's principal customers. The republican government, by this measure, thus brought a major change in the material situation of the village population, and no doubt helped to assure their loyalty, or at least their quiescence, during the upheavals that followed.

The other major reform undertaken by the Republic was in landownership. The introduction of the Swiss code in 1926 had unified and modernized the system of land tenure, thus legally terminating such traces of feudalism as remained in the country. Legal termination was, however, insufficient, and a number of great landowners, notably in the south and the east, still enjoyed the status almost of *derebeys* in the provinces. Even in the more advanced parts of the country, the large landowner in the town, with his ally or dependant the rich peasant in the village, still wielded enormous powers over the peasantry.

These powers the Kemalist régime sought—with only limited success—to reduce or eliminate. One method was land distribution —the granting of lands by the state to landless peasants and new immigrants. Land distribution laws were passed in 1927 and 1929, but progress was very slow, and between 1923 and 1934 only 711,000 hectares were distributed.[51] The most important dis-tributions were in the eastern provinces, where, in addition to its social policies, the government was anxious to break the power of the feudal and tribal chiefs that had led the rebellion of 1925.

In some parts, especially in the Aegean provinces and in Karaman, a new class of landowners, with medium-size estates, was formed when the lands formerly held by Greeks were given, after the exchange of populations, to Muslim immigrants and to veterans of the war of independence. These last, with their close connexions with the new régime, often took over the prestige and authority formerly exercised by the local agas and landlords.[52]

There was another change, even more damaging to the privi-leges of these landowners. All over the country local branches

---

[51] Barkan, 'La Loi sur la distribution des terres', *R. Fac. Sci. Éc. Univ. Ist.* (1944–5), pp. 44 ff.

[52] A vivid fictionalized picture of these changes in an Aegean village will be found in Kemal Bilbaşar's story *Pembe Kurt* (Pink Worm; Ist., 1953). See also above, p. 450.

of the People's Party were set up, with an active and well-defined role. In Kemal's Turkey the local party officials were the agents of the Kemalist revolution, giving 'advice' to the peasantry on a wide variety of subjects; in so doing they took over many of the powers formerly held by the magnates.[53]

The radicalism of the Kemalist régime in agrarian matters was not matched in its dealings with the urban working class. The Turkish working-class movement reached an important landmark in its development when it was able to participate, as a separate group, in the Izmir economic congress. During the period of the war of independence several attempts were made to form socialist and trade union groups, and, since their activities were directed chiefly against foreign enterprises, they were able to win a certain place in the national movement. Communist influences, however, appeared in several of these groups, and in the period after 1923, when Turkish policy was moving away from Russia and towards the West, the attitude of the state towards these movements became less tolerant. A labour code on liberal principles, which had been drawn up, was rejected, and a number of restrictions imposed. The emergency Law for the Maintenance of Order of March 1925 put an end to socialist and trade unionist activities.[54]

Etatism [55]

The world crisis of 1929 opened a new phase in the economic and social development of the Turkish Republic. The pressure of economic necessity impelled the Turkish state to undertake more and more extensive economic activities, and led it, in 1931, to adopt etatism as a central plank in its programme; at the same time, the rise of dictatorship and of dictatorial movements in several of the European states discredited political as well as economic liberalism, and made it easier for the Turkish state to

[53] See above, p. 382.

[54] On the Turkish labour and trade union movements see Lütfü Erişçi, *Türkiyede Işçi Sınıfının Tarihi* (1951); Kemal Sülker, *Türkiyede Sendikacılık* (1955); Tunaya, *Partiler*, pp. 463 ff.; Laqueur, *Communism*, pp. 205 ff. (on Communist movements); G. Haupt, 'Le début du mouvement socialiste en Turquie', *Le Mouvement Social*, no. 45 (1963), 121–37; Mete Tunçay, *Türkiye'de Sol Akımlar* (1967). Some Russian and other publications are listed by R. P. Kornienko in his review of Erişçi's book in *Sovietskoye Vostokovedenie*, iii (1957), 198–203. On the emergency law see above, pp. 269 ff.

[55] See above, pp. 286 ff.

acquire and exercise the new political powers that went with its new economic responsibilities.

The new policy does not seem to have been inspired by any new ideological trends, or to have been directly due to any external theoretical influences. The crisis had, however, brought a certain revival of anti-Western and anti-capitalist feeling in Turkey; the new economic co-operation with Russia brought some renewal of the comradeship of the early years of the Republic. It was in these circumstances that a new ideological trend appeared in Turkey, known by the name of *Kadro*, the periodical that was its organ. *Kadro* was published between 1932 and 1934; its leading figures were Yakup Kadri Karaosmanoğlu, a distinguished Turkish novelist and, later, diplomat,[56] and a number of other writers and intellectuals. The policy of the *Kadro* group, which at first enjoyed some measure of official support, has been described as 'a superficial combination of Marxism, nationalism, and corporatism'.[57] Turkey, according to their analysis, had no accumulated capital and therefore no class struggle; it was the duty of the state to accumulate and utilize capital, and thus forestall the emergence of a class struggle. In this new economic state, a cadre—*kadro*—of qualified and competent leaders would direct the state economy in the interests of the masses who would follow and accept their leadership. The Turkish Revolution was part of a world-wide struggle for liberation from capitalism and imperialism; the Turkish state was concerned primarily with the creation of an advanced technology and developed economy, with itself as both supreme arbiter and active director of all economic and social matters.

This blend of ideas from Rome, Constantinople, and Moscow was not of long duration. The frank discussion of economic and social problems, and the markedly radical character of some of the analyses and solutions propounded, led to the polite suppression of the journal and the exile of its editor as ambassador to Albania. The *Kadro* group was, however, the only one to undertake such analyses in Turkey in many years, and its influence on Turkish intellectuals has remained considerable.[58]

[56] On Yakup Kadri, see above, pp. 295 and 401.

[57] Karpat, p. 70. Dr. Karpat's examination of the *Kadro* group has formed the main basis of what is said here.

[58] Karpat, pp. 70–73. Yakup Kadri's account of the end of *Kadro* appears in his autobiographical work *Zoraki Diplomat* (The Unwilling Diplomat), pp. 22 ff. The

The acceptance of Russian models and the presence of Russian experts no doubt had their effect, irrespective of the wishes of the Turkish leaders, in extending state control and discouraging private industry. But apart from all this, the doctrine that 'the state must take charge' was, in a country like Turkey, an easy and familiar one, well in accord with the inherited traditions and habits of both the rulers and the ruled. To the Kemalist régime, authoritarian, bureaucratic, and paternalistic, the idea of state direction and control in economic life came as a natural and obvious extension of the powers, prerogatives, and functions of the governing *élite*. If economic development were really necessary, it would be undertaken by those who were responsible, in this as in all else, for the safety and well-being of the nation. It was far too important to be left to infidel business men and ignorant peasants.

Etatism thus meant, in effect, the intervention of the state as a pioneer and director of industrial activity, in the interests of national development and security, in a country where private enterprise was either suspect or ineffective. Some development had already been undertaken in the first ten years of the Republic, notably in the extension of the railways and the organization of the tobacco, match, and alcohol monopolies. The first Turkish five-year plan, applied from 1934 to 1939, attempted a massive advance.

'The main lines of the programme', says the Turkish official report, 'and the extent of the projected industries, were determined solely by the desire to enable the country to meet its requirements . . .'[59] Certainly they were not determined by normal economic considerations, and economists have found it easy to list the errors and failures of the etatist industrialization, responsibility for which must be shared between the Turkish planners and their foreign expert advisers.[60]

Nevertheless, with all their defects, the plans did bring an important increase in Turkey's industrial output, which between

journal, he says, was published with the consent of the People's Party, and its sole purpose was to clarify and explain the Party's principles. A rag-tag and bobtail of opportunists and bureaucrats could not run a revolutionary movement; a revolutionary party could not be constructed without cadres. They also wanted to demonstrate that the economic system called etatism was not the same as monopolism, and should not serve as a means of loading private and sectional interests on the back of the people. On *Kadro* see further the group of articles in *Forum* (Ankara), Oct.–Dec. 1958.

[59] *Turkey on the Way of Industrialization* (Ank., 1937), p. 38.

[60] See above, pp. 286–7.

1927 and 1939 rose from 0·14 per cent. to 0·23 per cent. of the world total. Only Russia and Japan reported more rapid industrial development.[61] Though productivity remained poor and urbanization slow, capital accumulation and investment advanced, bringing progress also in private industry, and there is some evidence of a rise in the standard of living, albeit a slow and limited one.[62] Perhaps more important than the economic achievements were the social changes which, unintended and probably undesired, followed in their wake. The economic activities of the Turkish government may have been incompetent and misdirected; they did, however, create new openings and new careers, and initiate the process which in time gave Turkey something she had never had before—a Turkish middle class of business men, managers, and technicians. The social and political consequences of the emergence of this new element were to transform Turkey in the next generation.

The War Years

During the gradual economic recovery of the 1930's, there was a slow but significant accumulation of capital in private possession. The many opportunities offered by Turkish neutrality during the war years gave a new impetus to this movement. The Turkish tax system, despite an overhaul in 1934, was still based on gross earnings, and was not supported by any modern apparatus of assessment, control, and collection. Bearing heavily on earners of fixed wages and salaries, it allowed both the merchants and the farmers to retain and accumulate their wartime riches, almost unscathed by direct taxation.[63]

Two emergency fiscal measures were introduced during the war, with the purpose of taxing the wartime profits of the merchants and farmers, and thus helping to relieve the strain on the public treasury. The first was the capital levy of November 1942,[64] which fell primarily on the commercial classes in the towns. For the agricultural population another form of taxation was introduced whereby the state compulsorily acquired a proportion of the crop at fixed prices. At first limited to wheat,

---

[61] Hershlag, in *Kyklos*, p. 332.   [62] Ibid. p. 339.

[63] Karpat, pp. 92–93; cf. Nasuhi Bursal, *Die Einkommensteuerreform in der Türkei* (1953).

[64] See above, pp. 297 ff.

rice, butter, and some other foodstuffs, the levy was later extended to almost all agricultural products.

The incidence of the two levies was very uneven. From the farmers, the state bought between a quarter and a half of their grain, paying from two to three times the pre-war price. It left them free to sell the remainder at free market prices, which at times rose to twenty times the pre-war level. The capital levy, which soon turned out to have other purposes beside the purely fiscal, was eventually abandoned. In the event it proved to have done little damage to the position of the non-Muslim capitalist class as a whole; it had of course done none to the new Turkish Muslim capitalist class that had been coming into being.

The Democratic Opposition, 1945–50

The end of the war found Turkey with a new class of rich men confident and ambitious; on the one hand they faced a mass of wage-earners and peasants who were distressed and discontented; on the other, a government of bureaucrats and soldiers who, by their wartime policies, had shown a dangerous incomprehension of business needs, a disrespect for the rights of property, and an economic paternalism that was both irksome and ineffective.[65]

There had, of course, been middle-class elements in Turkey before, but they were not Turkish and not Muslim. Separated from the dominant majority by both religion and language, the Greek, Armenian, and Jewish merchants and entrepreneurs of the Ottoman Empire had never been able to rise to the social and political role played by the new middle classes elsewhere. However great their economic power, it was to a large extent neutralized by the Ottoman system of communal organization, which effectively prevented them from exercising much influence on Turkish society or the Turkish state. If anything, they acted as a kind of buffer or shock-absorber, receiving the impulses that came from the West through commercial and financial contact, but not transmitting them to the Turkish, Muslim heart of the Ottoman state and society.

The appearance of a genuinely Turkish middle class, which was

---

[65] Note, for example, the sharp criticism of etatism at the economic congress held 22–27 Nov. 1948 (Jäschke, *Kalender*). cf. Karpat, pp. 92–93.

an essential part of the Turkish nation, was, therefore a development of the first importance. These new Turkish business men and managers were self-confident, self-reliant, and ambitious; they were becoming very resentful of the controls and restrictions imposed upon them by what they had begun to regard as the dead hand of officialdom. The civil servant was falling from the dizzy eminence that he once occupied in the Turkish social hierarchy. No longer was a civil service appointment the ultimate dream of every Turk with a secondary school education, nor a young bureaucrat the most sought-after bridegroom for a Turkish father with marriageable daughters. The appearance of a new and flourishing commercial class was radically changing the political balance of forces in the country, and affecting even her traditional social ethos.

The rise of this class was still hardly represented in the structure of government. Among the 453 deputies elected to the Assembly in 1943, 127 were public servants of various kinds, 67 members of the armed forces, 89 lawyers, and 59 teachers. Only 49 were merchants, 45 farmers, 15 bankers, and 3 industrialists.[66]

Land Reform

The new middle classes were already sharply critical of the government. They were soon joined by the landowners and country magnates. During the summer of 1945 the People's Party, returning to its populist origins, introduced a Land Reform Bill. On 14 May, after considerable preliminary argument, the Bill was submitted to the Assembly; on 11 June, after long parliamentary debates, it was passed and became law.

There had been earlier land reform laws under the Republic, but their scope had been limited and their effect, in application, still more so. The law of 1945 looked different. The objects of the law, as stated in the first paragraph, were to provide land and means for peasants with none or too little, and to ensure the full and effective use of the arable lands of the country. The method was to grant land to such peasants, together with twenty-year, interest-free loans for development, and other material help. The land was to come from unused state lands and pious endowments, municipal and other publicly owned land, reclaimed land, land of unknown ownership, and land expropriated from private

[66] *Vatan*, 11 Mar. 1943.

individuals. For the last-named category, all landed property in excess of 500 *dönüm* (123·5 acres) would be nationalized. Compensation would be paid on a sliding scale; the greater the area held, the lower the rate. It would be paid in instalments, over twenty years, in 4 per cent. treasury bonds. The law also laid down that the new holdings acquired under its provisions must not be split among heirs. It was estimated that about a third of the rural population, some 5 million persons, would benefit under the law, which, if fully applied, would effect a major revolution, transforming Turkey into a country of independent peasant smallholders.

The law was bitterly criticized; discussion in both the press and the Assembly was conducted with a vigour and acrimony unknown for many years. It was attacked from both left and right—by the left as Nazi, by the right as Communistic. Its defenders denied that it had anything to do with ideologies of left or right. It was a purely practical measure, carefully prepared, designed to bring a long overdue reform to Turkey's medieval countryside, and to free the peasants from thraldom to feudal landowners.[67]

The application of the law, delayed by political considerations, was excruciatingly slow, and in 1950, after further prolonged discussions, the nationalization limit was raised from 500 to 5,000 *dönüms*. The distribution began in 1947 with state lands and pious foundations, and by 1950 only a few score thousand *dönüms* had been distributed.

Workers and Peasants

The working class is a relatively new phenomenon in Turkey. In the nineteenth century there were barely a few thousand who could be properly so described, employed on the railways, the water works, and other public utilities, the state arsenal and ordnance factories, the coal mines at Ereğli, and a few factories for matches, carpets, cloth, and the like. A large proportion of the workers were women, girls, and children. Thus in 1897, 121 out of 201 workers employed at the Istanbul match factory were women; about half of the 1,000 workers at the cloth-mill at Bakırköy were children.[68]

[67] *Akşam*, 18 May 1945. On the Turkish land reform, which has been rather neglected by Western writers on Turkey, see Inalcık, in *Muslim Wld.*, xlv. 227–8; Barkan, in *R. Fac. Sci. Éc. Univ. Ist.* (1944–5), pp. 44–132 and his *Çiftçiyi Topraklandırma Kanunu* (1946); Karpat, pp. 99 ff.
[68] Sülker, pp. 7–9.

The first organized group seems to have been a 'society in favour of workmen' (*Ameleperver Cemiyeti*), founded in 1871, which may possibly have had some part in the strike at the naval arsenal at Kasımpaşa in 1872. This strike, the first in Turkey, was a joint effort of some 600 Muslim and Christian workmen, whose wages were several months in arrears. The workers struck after petitions and requests to the Sultan, the Grand Vezir, and the Ministry of the Navy had failed to produce results. On the principle of no pay, no work, they downed tools; they were paid a few days later.[69]

The illegal opposition movement of the 1890's also produced its labour wing, with the founding, in 1895, of the secret 'Ottoman Labour Society' (*Osmanlı Amele Cemiyeti*) among the workers at the ordnance factories at Tophane. The society lasted about a year, ending when its leaders were arrested and deported.[70]

The Young Turk Revolution of July 1908 unleashed a wave of strikes, of which nearly thirty occurred during the months of August and September. They were halted by a 'Provisional Law of Stoppage of Work' of 25 September, which showed clearly that the Committee of Union and Progress did not look with favour on the labour movement. The mutiny of April 1909, and the proclamation of martial law that followed it, provided the opportunity for further repressive measures, which severely limited the activities of the new labour unions and associations that were springing up.[71]

In the summer of 1909 the 'stoppage of work' law, despite charges that it served foreign economic interests, was passed by the parliament. A new 'Law of Associations', of the same year, also regulated labour organizations. Trade unions were permitted, except in 'enterprises that carry out public services' (Art. 8), a loose expression which covered the great majority of the working class.

This law, though permitting trade unions in private enterprises not providing public services, deprived the labour and union movement of the participation of those sections which had been most active and advanced, and in fact inhibited the growth of real trade unionism for nearly forty years. During the period of the armistice and the war of independence there was some revival of activity in Istanbul, within a patriotic rather than a

[69] Ibid. pp. 11–12; Erişçi, p. 8.   [70] Sülker, pp. 11–12; Erişçi, p. 8.
[71] Sülker, pp. 13 ff.; Erişçi, pp. 8 ff. According to Sülker (p. 16), the anti-strike law was demanded by German capitalists, and drafted by Count Ostrorog, Counsellor to the Ministry of Justice.

class framework, and the workers succeeded in obtaining separate representation at the Izmir economic congress in 1923.[72]

In the following years, however, economic pressure and authoritarian example led to an increasingly severe attitude towards labour, culminating in the draft labour law of 1932. This law, prepared under the aegis of the newly established Ministry of Economics, was passed by the Assembly in July 1936. The new law, which had been prepared with the help of German (not Nazi) advisers, dealt with conditions of employment and work, and provided for compulsory labour inspection and compulsory arbitration committees for disputes.[73] As far back as 1931 the People's Party, in its programme, had denounced the attempt to arouse class consciousness. The revised Law of Associations of July 1938 formally prohibited organizations on a class basis.[74]

During the war years the Turkish government, like many others, imposed extensive controls and assumed power of direction of labour. From 1945, however, as part of the general movement of political and economic liberalization, a new status was accorded to labour. On 7 January 1945 a Ministry of Labour was established; in 1946 a new Law of Associations repealed the ban on class organizations and a number of trade unions promptly appeared. Soon some of them were accused of Communist tendencies and disruptive activities, and were prosecuted under the martial law that was still in force. The position of the unions was finally regularized by the 'Workers' and Employers' Unions and Regional Federations Law' of 20 February 1947, drafted with the help of two British expert advisers. It still remains in force. This law still withheld the right to strike, but in other respects allowed the free formation of both unions and confederations. The number of unions rose to 73 in 1940, 77 in 1949, 88 in 1950, 137 in 1951, and 239 in 1952. An all-Turkish federation of unions was formed in Izmir in 1952, with an estimated membership of 150,000 workers.[75]

[72] See above, pp. 465–6.

[73] On the labour laws see Ferit H. Saymen, *Türk İş Hukuku* (1954); Cahit Talas, *La Législation du Travail en Turquie* (1948); and, more generally the International Labour Office report on *Labour Problems in Turkey* (1950).

[74] Art. 9: 'Associations on the basis or in the name of family, community, race, sex, or class may not be founded'; cf. Sülker, p. 33.

[75] Erişçi and Sülker, *passim*; also Tuna, 'The Organization of the Turkish Confederation of Trade Unions', *R. Fac. Sci. Écon. Univ. Ist.* (1953), pp. 109–19.

The peasants still had no distinctive organization of their own, and the various attempts to found a peasants' party, after both the First and Second World Wars, evoked little response.[76] The peasants were, however, increasing rapidly—and consciously—in status and political importance. The Republic had always paid lip-service to the Anatolian peasant, praising him as the backbone of the country—but deciding what was best for him, and sending government and party officials to enforce it. The peasant, accustomed for centuries, perhaps for millennia, to submit to the authority of the landlord and the state, had passively accepted this role.

The first major development in the Turkish countryside was the establishment of the Village Institutes. These, set up by a law of 1940, were to provide a five-year course of practical education for village boys and girls at public expense, and then send them back to their villages as schoolteachers and, more generally, as guides to more modern husbandry and hygiene. By their eighth anniversary, on 17 April 1948, there were twenty institutes with 15,000 pupils. A twenty-first was opened in Van in November of the same year.[77]

The Institutes were much criticized; they were at different times accused of inefficiency, of leftism, and of People's Party politics, and were eventually subjected to changes which modified their character very considerably. The awakening of the village, however, was no longer left to a few enthusiasts. In the 35,000 villages of Anatolia, the peasants of Turkey were at last stirring. Two fortunate harvests put the peasant on his feet economically; the return to party politics and free elections brought politicians to court his favour—and thus to enable him to demand something in return.

The really massive change in the Turkish countryside came after the war, with the new wave of economic development. Within a few years many thousands of tractors entered Turkey, transforming Turkish agriculture, revolutionizing the village society that lives by it, and even battering their way into the new Turkish literature that mirrors these changes. The tractor is not only a source of wealth; it also confers prestige and status on its owner, gives a sense of power and nobility to its driver, and serves the village community in a thousand unsuspected ways.

[76] On these parties see Tunaya, *Partiler, passim.*

[77] Jäschke, *Kalender,* 17 Apr. and 18 Nov. 1948. On the village institutes see further Karpat, pp. 377–80; Mahmut Makal, *A Village in Anatolia* (1954). This latter work is a most remarkable human document from a graduate of one of these institutes.

There were many other material improvements, bringing greater comfort to the villagers, and a closer degree of participation in the life of the national community. In the neighbourhood of the towns, bus services, piped water, electricity, daily newspapers, and access to urban amenities heralded the dawn of a new age; even in remoter places, a local road, a daily bus, and a few battery-operated wireless sets brought new contacts with the outside world, a new awareness of membership of the larger community, and the beginning of a new process of far-reaching social change.

The peasant, at first mistrustful, then with growing confidence, has responded to this situation. With means, comforts, and amenities undreamt of in an earlier age, he has become more confident and more independent. In recent years, he has begun to show an awareness of his political power and of his human dignity that is probably without precedent in the past history of the country and that has few parallels among her neighbours. The problems of the Turkish peasant are far from solved—social and religious, economic and technological questions of profound importance remain to be faced and overcome. But the Turkish peasantry, numbering over 70 per cent. of the population of the country, have emerged from their ancient submission, to participate in public affairs of their country, to speak their word on the formation and exercise of government. Kemalism had brought the revolution to the towns and townspeople of Turkey, but had barely touched the villages. A second, silent revolution was now reaching the deeper layers of the nation, and starting a new transformation.[78]

[78] On the change in the peasantry see the illuminating essay of H. A. Reed, 'A New Force at Work in Democratic Turkey', *MEJ*, vii (1953), 33–44; also Paul Stirling, 'Social Ranking in a Turkish Village', *Brit. J. Sociol.* iv (1953), 31–44; and Lerner, pp. 19 ff. and 111 ff. Social change in Turkey has also been discussed in a series of important studies by Dr. Karpat, listed in the bibliography.

CHAPTER XIV

Conclusions:
The Turkish Revolution

The success that we have won until today has done no more than open a road for us, towards progress and civilization. It has not yet brought us to progress and civilization. The duty that falls on us and on our grandsons is to advance, unhesitatingly, on this road.

KEMAL ATATÜRK.

A ruined land on the edge of a precipice . . . bloody battles with various enemies . . . years of struggle and then, respected at home and abroad, a new country, a new society, a new state, and, to achieve these, ceaseless revolutions—this, in a word, is the Turkish general revolution.

KEMAL ATATÜRK.

Those who have grasped the purpose of the Revolution will always be able to safeguard it.

KEMAL ATATÜRK.

THE Turkish Revolution began, in the formal sense, with the forcible overthrow of an old political order and the establishment of a new one in 1908. In another sense, however, it has been going on for nearly two centuries. It began when a series of defeats at the hands of once-despised enemies forced the Turks, for the sake of survival, to adopt European weapons, to invite European advisers, and thus, however reluctantly, to admit all the new ideas and institutions that underlie the modern state and army. The first reforms were the work of autocratic rulers, who sought only to train and equip better armies. The high cost of military modernization led to severer taxation and harsher rule. Reformers and rebels were not always the same people in the Turkish transformation, and often they were in conflict with one another. Some of the most active reformers were men of autocratic disposition and habit, wielding an accepted authority, and indeed giving it a new strength and pervasiveness. The overcoming of conservative resistance involved the abrogation or enfeeblement of the traditional checks on the sovereign power, which was further reinforced by modern instruments of control.

These changes, and the resulting growth of despotism, did not pass unchallenged, the more so in an age when Europe, the model and example of enlightenment, offered a wide choice of secular ideologies of revolt. Liberal, patriotic, and even revolutionary ideas infected the Turkish students and cadets, diplomats and military attachés, who came to explore the secrets of the mysterious Occident; in time these ideas found their way to Turkey, where they gave a new impetus and a new direction to the young officers and officials, and led to the successive constitutional and popular movements of 1876, 1908, and 1920.

The basic change in Turkey—from an Islamic Empire to a national Turkish state, from a medieval theocracy to a constitutional republic, from a bureaucratic feudalism to a modern capitalist economy—was accomplished over a long period, by successive waves of reformers and radicals.

Some have seen in the Turkish Revolution no more than a series of reluctant and tardy responses to external stimuli and influences—to military defeat and diplomatic pressure, to the loss of provinces to foreign rule and the penetration of the homeland by foreign culture and commerce. Certainly the sources of inspiration of both reformers and radicals came from foreign ideologies and the successive phases of both the Turkish reform and Revolution were opened by military and diplomatic events —though here, it may be noted, the most powerful stimuli were not those of the remote great powers of Europe, but of the former subject peoples, whose swift rise and progress inflicted a sharper lesson and a deeper humiliation. It was the Greek rising and the successes of Muhammad Ali that finally provoked Mahmud to rid himself of the useless Janissaries and experiment with something new; it was the Greeks again, landing at Izmir in 1919, who goaded the defeated and dispirited Turks to make a fresh and final effort to save and renew themselves. It would, however, be a gross over-simplification to attribute the whole Turkish movement, as some have done, to these European pressures and influences. Europe may have provided both the starting gun and the winning-post in the Turkish race against history; she did not provide the motive force.

It is natural to seek for parallels between the Young Turk and Kemalist Revolutions and the great European revolutions, in England, France, and Russia, and indeed points of resemblances are not lacking. In the Turkish *ancien régime* as in the others we can see such familiar pre-revolutionary features as financial stringency coupled with commercial expansion, administrative reform with governmental inefficiency, a questioning of fundamental allegiances among the rulers and intellectuals and a progressive withdrawal of consent on the part of important sections of the governed. In the Turkish Revolution we can see the characteristic succession of hope, terror, and dictatorship, in the transition from the constitutional millennium of 1908 to the repressions of the Young Turk triumvirate, and finally an authoritarian Republic in which Atatürk seems to take his place beside Bonaparte and Cromwell—even to the point of encountering and overcoming a Turkish La Vendée in the mountains of Kurdistan, and an Oxford among the ulema.

Yet, on closer examination, these resemblances seem to be superficial rather than fundamental. Although, as early as 1693, William Penn had proposed to include Turkish delegates in his proposed Diet of Europe, Ottoman Turkey was not a European country but an Islamic empire, drawing its inspiration from another faith, and shaped by another set of historical events and circumstances. True, Islam and Christendom had many elements in common, derived from the Hellenistic, Hebraic, and Middle Eastern heritage which both had shared—and perhaps these elements of unity made easier the ultimate transition of the Turks to a European civilization. But the great events and movements of European history had broken against the religious and military barriers that separated Islam from Christendom, leaving Turkey unaffected, even unaware. The struggle of Church and State, the Renaissance, the Reformation and Counter-Reformation, the scientific awakening, humanism, liberalism, rationalism, the Enlightenment—all the great European adventures and conflicts of ideas passed unnoticed and unreflected in a society to which they were profoundly alien and irrelevant. The same is true of the great social, economic, and political changes. The rise and fall of the baronage, the emergence of the communes, the rebirth of trade, the rise of the new middle class, the struggles of money and land, of city-state, nation-state, and Empire—all the swift yet complex evolution of European life and society, have no parallel in the Islamic and Middle Eastern civilization of the Ottomans. The growth and change and clash that preceded and shaped the

Turkish Revolution were thus radically different from those of the English, French, and even, though perhaps to a lesser extent, the Russian Revolutions.

The realization of these differences has led some observers to see in the Turkish transformation the prototype of the nationalist revolutions—of the struggle of the countries of the Middle East and Asia to throw off Western domination. Here too resemblances are not lacking. Though Turkey, unlike the Arab lands, Central Asia, India, and Indonesia, never fell under direct European rule, she nevertheless experienced many of the same processes as they did. The economic and diplomatic ascendancy of the Western powers in Turkey provided the setting—the well-intentioned reforming efforts of the Turkish régimes did the rest. The results were strikingly similar to those in the colonial empires: the old industries were destroyed by the competition of cheap manufactured imports; the old communal agrarian order was dislocated by the misguided introduction and rigid application of European legal concepts, which transformed tax-farmers into freeholders and added to the immemorial sufferings of the Oriental peasantry such new European afflictions as distraint and eviction; above all, an old and accepted system of social, economic, and political functions and responsibilities was disrupted and destroyed, leaving a void that was hard to fill. In Turkey, which remained an independent state, hasty and energetic reformers carried through their reforms with a ruthlessness and a precipitancy in striking contrast with the cautious conservatism of most Imperial authorities. In the event, they seem to have destroyed better than they built. While their Westernizing innovations often proved superficial and impermanent, their destruction of the old system of social bonds and obligations was final. Even the compensating advantages of the Imperial peace brought by the colonial régimes—security, unity, material advancement, efficient and conscientious government, the formation of a trained modern civil service—were lacking in Turkey, which encountered only the commercial and diplomatic pressures of Western power. This was an imperialism of interference without responsibility, which would neither create nor permit stable and orderly government.

It is perhaps by this point—the retention by the Turks of the final responsibility for their affairs—that we can explain some of the significant differences between the Turkish and other eastern revolutions. During the nineteenth and early twentieth centuries, the experience of Turkey in Westernization was in general shared with a number of other countries. Since 1918 there have been striking divergences. In Turkey the stream has been broadened and deepened—elsewhere it has been stopped, deflected, or reversed. In the Turkish, as in other modern revolutions, nationalism has been a tremendous force. It has, however, operated in a notably different way. Turkey is not a new state, where political thinking is still dominated by the problem of foreign rule and the fight to end it. Turkish leaders have accepted as well as asserted their responsibility for the affairs of their country, and have shown a cool realism and practical sense derived from long experience of government. They have been able to assess situations and define objectives, to make decisions related to facts and to abide by them —and the responsibility of leaders has been matched by the discipline of those whom they led.

Another significant difference between the Turkish and some other nationalist leaders was the different vision of history that determined their attitudes to the conflicting power blocks and ideologies of the modern world. For the Turks, as for the others, imperialism was the great enemy. But for the Turks the really important part of the imperialist phenomenon was not the maritime expansion, since the sixteenth century, of Western Europe, which had affected them only indirectly; it was the overland expansion, during the same period, of Eastern Europe, which had brought the old Turkish lands north and east of the Black Sea and the Caspian under Russian rule, and forced the Ottoman Empire to fight a long series of bitter wars, in a rearguard defence against the Russian advance to the Mediterranean. Thus, while other nationalists looked to Russia for sympathy and support against the West, Turkey looked to the West for help against Russia, and continued, even after many of the others had turned away, to see in the West and in the Western way of life the best hope for the future. The Turkish nationalist struggle in its final phase—that of 1919–23—was directed against Western and not Russian encroachments, but it was followed by a more radical and determined effort of Westernization than ever before. This was certainly made easier by the gain in confidence resulting from a victory over the West.

The attempt has been made, using methods derived from

European history, to explain the successive phases of the Turkish Revolution as a struggle between economically defined classes for control of the state, or as an upsurge of a popular movement, seeking freedom from tyranny. Though a love of freedom and a conflict of classes can both at times be discerned, neither provides a fully adequate approach to the facts of modern Turkish history. Though important class changes followed the actions of the revolutionary régimes, they do not seem to have caused them, or to have determined the functioning of the state, which lived and acted as a vital, dominating power in itself. Far more important than the ruling class—if indeed such a thing can be identified—was the ruling *élite*; the small, associated groups of men who, in conjunction with the sovereign authority itself, effectively controlled the day-to-day working of the apparatus of power. There were several of these administrative, religious, and military *élite* groups, defined not primarily by economic class, but by training, function, and method of recruitment. Their formation, rivalries, and vicissitudes are vital to the understanding of the Turkish Revolution, for in a sense the Kemalist Republic was the culmination of a long process, whereby the Turkish governing *élite* transformed itself, the state, and finally the country. Not the least important aspect of this change was the broadening and diversification of the *élite* itself, which came to draw, for its recruitment, on ever wider circles of the population, and thus involved more and more of the Turkish nation in an active interest and even participation in the conduct of public affairs. This process was accelerated by economic development, the spread of education, the development of mass media of communication, and the emergence of new social classes disinclined to acquiesce in the paternalistic government of the old ruling groups. In this way the *élite*, no doubt unconsciously, helped to prepare its own eventual supersession by a more democratic form of government resting on a new social and economic order.

Among the Turks, the two terms most frequently used to denote their revolution are nationalism and Westernization—and the two are not, as in other parts of the world, in contradiction with one another. Besides its international aspect, already noted, the Turkish nationalist Revolution has an important internal aspect. At one time, in Turkey, it was fashionable to speak of the Revolution as a rising of the Turks against the Ottomans, as the liberation of the last of the subject peoples of the Ottoman Empire. This interpretation, though at first sight it may seem a little fanciful, contains an important element of truth. The loss of most of the Rumelian provinces, the transfer of the capital to Ankara, the successful struggle of Turkish Anatolia, all make the change from the Ottoman Empire to the Turkish Republic more than one of nomenclature. Anatolia, the Turkish heartland, had always taken second place to Rumelia, the home of most of the cosmopolitan ruling class of the Empire—even the Young Turk Revolution, in its successive phases, had rested on Macedonia and Thrace, and Kemal himself was born in Salonika. But the shift in the centre of gravity and the cult of Anatolianism made Anatolia the real as well as the sentimental centre of the nation, and gave to the Anatolians an opportunity that they had not had before. The great Rumelian bureaucratic, religious, and military families are dwindling and losing their importance. The Anatolian country boys—*Memleket çocukları*—and still more the Anatolian country lords and gentry are inheriting their places, and making Turkey a Turkish state in fact as well as in name.

For many Turks, the great transformation which has taken place in their country is to be defined, not merely in terms of economy or society or government, but of civilization. The essential change attempted by the Turks in their Revolution was one of Westernization—another step in the westward march of the Turkish people that began 1,000 years ago, when they renounced China and turned to Islam. Now, renouncing a large part though not the whole of their Islamic heritage, they have turned to Europe, and made a sustained and determined effort to adopt and apply the European way of life in government, society, and culture. Opinions differ as to the measure of success achieved in this attempt; there can, however, be no doubt that in large and important areas of the public life of Turkey the Westernizing revolution is accomplished and irreversible.

In this transformation, the replacement of old, Islamic conceptions of identity, authority, and loyalty by new conceptions of European origin was of fundamental importance. In the theocratically conceived polity of Islam, God was to be twice replaced: as the source of sovereignty, by the people; as the object of worship, by the nation. It is no doubt due to our common human frailty that, in the first flush of enthusiasm, the second was easier to accomplish than the first.

There was a time when the causes of both faith and freedom seemed in grave danger in the Turkish Republic. Since then, there has been a marked improvement in the prospects of both. The rigid secularism of the past, which, in the words of one observer, was turning Turkey into a 'positivistic mausoleum', has been relaxed, some would say to the point of danger of a clerical counter-revolution.

The cause of freedom, too, has made important if hard-won advances. Since the apocalyptic days which followed the first free election in May 1950, there have been many disappointments, and few can doubt that the Turkish experiment in democracy has been going through grave difficulties. Just as in the times of trial which followed the Young Turk Revolution of 1908, so now also there are some who are ready to write off Turkish democracy as a failure and its exponents as fools or frauds. But for one who was present in Turkey in those days, it is difficult to believe that the great hopes of that time were wholly in vain, or that they have been wholly abandoned. Amid all the difficulties and setbacks, there is still much that gives encouragement for the future. The social changes that preceded and accompanied the rise of democracy have continued, and given greater strength and numbers to the new groups and elements whose interests and aspirations are with freedom; it is these groups which have made free institutions work, and are best able to preserve them. Finally—and perhaps most important of all—there is the personal quality that has been shown by so many Turks of different allegiances and from different walks of life—a quality of calm self-reliance, of responsibility, above all of civic courage. Without these, no attempt at democracy, however well-intentioned, can succeed. Against them, the ancient habits of autocracy and acquiescence cannot indefinitely survive.

SELECT BIBLIOGRAPHY

I. WORKS IN TURKISH

Abdullah, Fevziye. Mizancı Mehmed Murad Bey. *Tar. Derg.*, no. 3–4 (1950–1), 67–88. [*See also* Tansel.]

Adıvar, Halide Edib. *Türkiye'de Şark, Garp ve Amerikan Tesirleri*. Ist., 1956.

Adnan-Adıvar, Abdülhak. *Osmanlı Türklerinde Ilim*. Ist., 1943.

Ağaoğlu, Ahmet. *Serbest Fırka Hatıraları*. Ist., nd..

—— *Babamın Arkadaşları*. Ist., n.d.

Aksüt, Ali Kemali. *Sultan Aziz'in Mısır ve Avrupa Seyahati*. Ist., 1944.

Akyüz, Kenan. *Tevfik Fikret*. Ank., 1947.

—— ed. *Batı Tesirinde Türk Şiiri Antolojisi*. Ank., 1953.

Ali, Kılıç. *Istiklâl Mahkemesi Hatıraları*. Ist., 1955.

—— *Kılıç Ali Hatıralarını Anlatıyor*. Ist., 1955.

Aliye, Fatma. *Ahmed Cevdet Paşa ve zamanı*. Ist., 1332 A.H.

Amca, Hasan. *Doğmayan Hürriyet*. Ist., 1958.

Arıburnu, Kemal. *Millî Mücadele ve Inkılâplarla Ilgili Kanunlar . . .* I. Ank., 1957.

Arif, Mehmed. *Anadolu Inkılâbı*. Ist., 1923.

Arif, Mehmed. Humbaracı-başı Ahmed Paşa Bonneval. *TOEM*, pts. 18–20. (1328 A.H.).

Asım, Ahmed. *Asım Tarihi*. 2 vols. Ist., n.d.

Ata, Tayyarzade. *Tarih-i Ata*. 5 vols. Ist., 1291–3 A.H.

Atatürk, Kemal. *Atatürk'ün Söylev ve Demeçleri* (Collected Speeches). 3 vols. Ist., 1945–52.

—— *Nutuk*. 2 vols. Ank., 1950–2.

—— *Atatürk'ün Askerliğe dair Eserleri*. Ank., 1959.

Atay, Falih Rıfkı. *Başveren Inkılâpçı*. Ist., n.d.

—— *Niçin Kurtulmamak*. Ist., 1953.

Aydemir, Şevket Süreyya. *Suyu arayan Adam*. Ank., 1959.

—— *Tek Adam: Mustafa Kemal*, i (*1881–1919*); ii (*1919–1922*); iii (*1922–1938*). Ist., 1963–1965.

Barkan, Ömer Lûtfi. *Çiftçiyi Topraklandırma Kanunu*. Ist., 1946.

—— Türk Toprak Hukuku Tarihinde Tanzimat ve 1274 (1858) Tarihi Arazi Kanunnamesi, *in Tanzimat*, 321–421.

Baydar, Mustafa. *Atatürk Diyor ki*. Ist., 1957.

Baykal, Bekir Sıtkı. 93 Meşrutiyeti. *Bell.*, no. 21–22 (1942), 45–83.

—— Birinci Meşrutiyete dair belgeler. *Bell.*, no. 96 (1960), 601–36.

Baysun, Cavid. Mustafa Reşit Paşa, *in Tanzimat*, pp. 723–46.

Bayur, Hilmi Kâmil. *Sadrazam Kâmil Paşa Siyasî Hayatı*. Ank., 1954.

Bayur, Hikmet. *Türk Inkılâbı Tarihi*, i, ii, pts. 1–4, iii, pt. 1. Ist–Ank., 1940–53.

—— Ikinci Meşrutiyet Devri üzerinde bazı Düşünceler. *Bell.*, no. 90 (1959), 267–85.

—— *Türk Inkılâbı Tarihi.* I/1 & 2, 2nd revised ed. Ank., 1963–4.

—— *Atatürk Hayatı ve Eseri*, i. Ank., 1963.

Berkes, N. *Batıcılık, Ulusçuluk ve Toplumsal Devrimler.* Ist., 1965.

—— *Ikiyüz Yıldır neden Bocalıyoruz.* Ist., 1965.

Birand, Kâmiran. *Aydınlanma Devri Devlet Felsefesinin Tanzimatta Tesirleri.* Ank., 1955.

Bıyıklıoğlu, Tevfik. *Trakya'da Millî Mücadele.* 2 vols. Ank., 1955–6.

—— *Atatürk Anadolu'da, 1919–21*, i. Ank., 1959.

—— 'Birinci Türkiye Büyük Millet Meclisi'nin Hukukî Statüsü ve Ihtilâlcı Karakteri. *Bell.*, no. 96 (1960), 637–663.

—— Birinci Dünya Harbinde (1914–1918) ve Mondros Mütarekesi sıralarında (30 Ekim 1918–11 Ekim 1922), Boğazlar Problemi. *Bell.*, no. 97 (1961), 81–93.

Cebesoy, Gen. Ali Fuat. *Millî Mücadele Hatıraları.* Ist., 1953.

—— *Moskova Hatıraları.* Ist., 1955.

—— . . . *Siyasî Hatıraları.* Ist., 1957.

—— *Siyasi Hâtıralar.* Pt. ii. Ist., 1960.

Celaleddin, Mahmud. *Mirât-i hakikat. Tarih-i Mahmud Celaleddin Paşa.* 3 vols. Ist., 1326–7 A.H.

Cemal Paşa. *Hatırat, 1913–22.* Ist., 1922.

—— *Hatıralar.* Ist., 1959.

Cemalüddin Efendi. *Hâtırât-i Siyasiye.* Ist., 1336/1917.

Cevad, Mahmud. *Maarif-i Umumiye Nezareti Tarihçe-i Teşkilât ve Icraatı.* Ist., 1339 A.H.

Cevat, Ali. *Ikinci Meşrutiyetin Ilânı ve Otuzbir Mart Hâdisesi*, edited by Faik Reşit Unat. Ank., 1960.

Cevdet Paşa, Ahmed. *Tarih-i Cevdet.* 12 vols. Ist., 1301–9 A.H.

—— Maruzat. *TTEM*, 14th year (1340 A.H.), 15th year (1341 A.H.), 16th year (1926).

—— *Tezâkir*, ed. Cavid Baysun, i (1–12), ii (13–20), iii (21–39). Ank., 1953, 1960, 1963.

Danişmend, Ismail Hami. *Izahlı Osmanlı Tarihi Kronolojisi*, iv. Ist., 1955.

Daver, Bülent. *Türkiye Cümhuriyetinde Lâyiklik.* Ank., 1955.

Dursunoğlu, Cevat. *Millî Mücadelede Erzurum.* Ank., 1946.

Duru, Kâzım Nami. *Ittihat ve Terakki Hatıralarım.* Ist., 1957.

Durusoy, M. O. and Gökman, M. M., *Atatürk ve Devrimleri Biblio-yoğrafyası.* Ank., 1957.

Emre, Ahmet Cevat. *Atatürk'ün Inkılab Hedefi ve Tarih Tezi.* Ist., 1956.

Select Bibliography 491

Ergin, Osman [see also Nuri, Osman]. Türkiyede Şehirciliğin Tarihî Inkişafı. Ist., 1936.

—— Muallim Cevdet'in Hayatı, Eserleri ve Kütüphanesi. Ist., 1937.

—— Türkiye Maarif Tarihi. 5 vols. Ist., 1939–43.

Erişçi, Lütfü. Türkiyede Işçi Sınıfının Tarihi. Ist., 1951.

Ersoy, Osman. Türkiye'ye Matbaanın Girişi ve ilk basılan eserler. Ank., 1959.

Esad, Mehmed. Üss-i Zafer. Ist., 1243/1827.

Esad, Mehmed. Mirât-i Mühendishane. Ist., 1312 A.H.

Esmer, Ahmet Şükrü. Siyasî Tarih, 1919–39. Ank., 1953.

Feridun, Server. Anayasalar ve siyasal belgeler. Ist., 1962.

Fuad, Ali. Rical-i mühimme-i siyasiye. Ist., 1928.

Fuat, Ali. Ricali Tanzimattan Rifat Paşa. TTEM, n.s. (1930), 1–11. [See also Türkgeldi.]

Gerçek, Selim Nüzhet. Türk Gazeteciliği, 1831–1931. Ist., 1931.

—— Türk Matbaacılığı, i: Müteferrika Matbaası. Ist., 1939.

Gökalp, Ziya. Türkleşmek, Islâmlaşmak, Muasırlaşmak. Ist., 1918.

Gökbilgin, M. Tayyib. Millî Mücadele Başlarken. Ank., 1959.

—— Millî Mücadele Başlarken, Ank., 1959–65, 2 vols.

Gökman, Muzaffer. Atatürk ve Devrimleri Tarihi Bibliyografyası. Ist., 1963.

Gölpınarlı, Abdülbâki. Mevlânâ'dan sonra Mevlevîlik. Ist., 1953.

Göreli, Ismail Hakkı. Il Idaresi. Ank., 1952.

Gövsa, Ibrahim Alâettin. Türk Meşhurları Ansiklopedisi. Ist., n.d.

Gözübüyük, A. Ş. and S. Kili. Türk Anayasa Metinleri. Ank., 1957.

Gözübüyük, A. Ş. and Sezgin, Zekai. 1924 Anayasası Hakkındaki Meclis Görüşmeleri. Ank., 1957.

Halim Paşa, Prince Mehmed Said. Buhranlarımız. Ist., 1330–8 A.H.

Iğdemir, Uluğ. Kuleli Vakası hakkında bir Araştırma. Ank., 1937.

Ilmen, Süreyya. Zavallı Serbest Fırka. Ist., 1951.

Imece, Mustafa S. Atatürk'ün Şapka Devriminde Kastamonu ve Inebolu Seyahatları. Ank., 1959.

Inal, Mahmud Kemal. Osmanlı Devrinde Son Sadriazamlar. 14 pts. Ist., 1940–53.

—— Son Asır Türk Şairleri. Ist., 1930–42.

Inalcık, Halil. Tanzimat Nedir, in Tarih Araştırmaları. Ank., 1941, pp. 237–63.

Iskit, Server R. Türkiyede Neşriyat Hareketleri Tarihine bir Bakış. Ist., 1939.

—— Türkiyede Matbuat Rejimleri. Ist., 1939.

Islâm Ansiklopedisi. Istanbul, 1941–

[Inönü], Ismet Paşa. Inönü'nün Söylev ve Demeçleri. Ist., 1946.

Kâmil Paşa. Tarih-i Siyasî-i Devlet-i Aliye-i Osmaniye. 3 vols. Ist., 1327 A.H.

—— *Kâmil Paşanın Ayan reisi Said Paşaya Cevabları.* Ist., 1327 A.H.

—— *Hatırat-i Sadr-i Esbak Kâmil Paşa.* Ist., 1329 A.H.

Kaplan, Mehmed. *Namık Kemal; Hayatı ve Eserleri.* Ist., 1948.

Karabekir, Kâzım. *Istiklâl Harbimizin Esasları.* Ist., 1951.

—— *Istiklâl Harbimiz.* Ist., 1960.

Karal, Enver Ziya. Yunan Adalarının Fransızlar tarafından İşgali ve Osmanlı-Rus Münasebâtı, 1797–8. *Tar. Semineri Derg.*, i (1937), 100–25.

—— *Fransa-Mısır ve Osmanlı İmparatorluğu, 1797–1802.* Ist., 1940.

—— *Halet Efendinin Paris Büyük Elçiliği, 1802–6.* Ist., 1940.

—— Osmanlı Tarihine dair Vesikalar. *Bell.* no. 14–15 (1940), 175–89.

—— Nizam-i Cedide dair Layihalar. *Tar. Ves.*, i (1942), 414–25; ii (1942–3), 104–11, 342–51, 424–32.

—— *Osmanlı İmparatorluğunda ilk nüfus Sayımı.* Ank., 1943.

—— *Selim III'ün Hat-ti Hümayunları; Nizam-i Cedit.* Ank., 1946.

—— *Osmanlı Tarihi,* v–vii. Ank., 1947–56.

Karaosmanoğlu, Yakup Kadri. *Vatan Yolunda; Millî Mücadele Hâtıraları.* Ist., 1958.

—— *Zoraki Diplomat.* Ist., 1955.

Kaynar, Reşat. *Mustafa Reşit Paşa ve Tanzimat.* Ank., 1954.

Kemal, Mahmut. See Inal.

Kemal, Namık. *Vatan yahut Silistre,* ed. M. N. Özön. Ist., 1943.

—— *Külliyat-i Kemal,* iii, *Makalat-i siyasiye ve edebiye.* 6 parts. Ist., 1327 A.H.

Köprülü, M. Fuad. Vakıf Muessesesinin Hukukî mâhiyeti ve Tarihî Tekâmülü. *Vak. Derg.*, ii (1942), 1–35.

—— *Demokrasi yolunda; On the way to democracy.* Edited by T. Halasi-Kun. The Hague, 1964.

Koray, Enver. *Türkiye Tarih Yayınları Bibliyografyası 1729–1955.* Ist., 1959.

Kubalı, Hüseyin Nail. *Anayasa Hukuku.* Ist., 1964.

Kuntay, Mithat Cemal. *Namık Kemal.* 3 vols. Ist., 1944–56.

—— *Sarıklı İhtilâlcı Ali Suavi.* Ist., 1946.

Kuran, Ahmed Bedevi. *İnkılâp Tarihimiz ve Jön Türkler.* Ist., 1945.

—— *İnkılâp Tarihimiz ve İttihad ve Terakki.* Ist., 1948.

—— *Osmanlı İmparatorluğunda İnkılâp Hareketleri ve Millî Mücadele.* Ist., 1956.

—— *Osmanlı İmparatorluğunda ve Türkiye Cumhuriyetinde İnkılâp harekleri.* Ist., 1959.

Levend, A. S. *Türk Dilinde Gelişme ve Sadeleşme Safhaları.* Ank., 1949.

Lûtfi, Ahmed. *Tarih-i Lûtfi.* 8 vols. Ist., 1290–1328 A.H.

Mardin, Ebul'ulâ. *Medenî Hukuk Cephesinden Ahmet Cevdet Paşa.* Ist., 1946.

Mardin, Şerif. *Jön Türklerin Siyasi Fikirleri 1895–1908*. Ank., 1964.

Memduh Paşa, Mehmed. *Esvāt-i Sudur*. Izmir, 1328 A.H.

—— *Mirât-i şuûnat*. Izmir, 1328 A.H.

Midhat, Ahmed. *Üss-i Inkılâb*. Ist., 1294/1877.

Midhat, Ali Haydar. *Hâtıralarım, 1872–1946*. Ist., 1946.

Nadi, Yunus. *Ihtilâl ve Inkılâb-i Osmanî*. Ist., 1325 A.H.

Niyazi, Ahmed. *Hâtırât-i Niyazi*. Ist., 1326 A.H.

Nuri, Osman. *Abdülhamid-i Sani ve Devr-i Saltanatı*. 3 vols. Ist., 1327/1909.

Nuri, Osman. *Mecelle-i Umur-i Belediye*, i. Ist., 1922.

Nuri Paşa, Mustafa. *Netaic ül-Vukuat*. 4 vols. Ist., 1294–1327 A.H.

Okandan, Recai G. *Umumî âmme hukukumuzun ana hatlari*. i: *Osmanlı devletinin kuruluşundan inkırazına kadar*. Ist., 1948.

Ökte, Faik. *Varlık Vergisi Faciası*. Ist., 1951.

Öz, Tahsin. Fransa Kıralı Louis XVI ci'nin Selim III'e Namesi. *Tar. Ves.*, i/3 (1941), 198–202.

—— ed. Selim III ün Sırkatibi tarafından tutulan Ruzname. *Tar. Ves.*, iii (May 1949), 183–99.

Özçelik, A. Selçuk. Sened-i Ittifak. *Istanbul Universitesi Hukuk Fakültesi Mecmuası*, xxiv (1959), 1–12.

Özek, Çetin. *Türkiyede Lâiklik. Gelişim ve Koruyucu Ceza Hükümleri*. Ist., 1962.

Özön, Mustafa N. *Namık Kemal ve Ibret Gazetesi*. Ist., 1938.

—— *Son Asır Türk Edebiyatı Tarihi*. Ist., 1941.

Pâkalın, Mehmed Zeki. *Tanzimat maliye nazirları*. 2 vols. Ist., 1939–40.

—— *Son Sadrâzamlar ve Başvekiller*. 5 vols. Ist., 1940–8.

Rasim, Ahmed. *Osmanlı Tarihi*. 4 vols. Ist., 1326–30 A.H.

—— *Istibdaddan Hakimiyet-i Milliyeye*. 2 vols. Ist., 1923–5.

Rauf, Leskovikli Mehmed. *Ittihad ve Terakki Cemiyeti ne idi?* Ist., 1327 A.H.

Reşit Paşa. *Reşit Paşanın Hatıraları*, ed. Cevdet R. Yularkıran. Ist., 1939–40.

Rifat Paşa, Sadık. *Müntehabât-i Asar*. Ist., n.d.

Safa, Peyami. *Türk Inkılabına Bakışlar*. Ist., n.d.

Said Paşa. *Said Paşanın Hâtırâtı*. 3 vols. Ist., 1328 A.H.

Şanizade, Mehmed Ataullah. *Tarih*. 4 vols. Ist., 1290–1 A.H.

Sarç, Ömer Celâl. Tanzimat ve Sanayiimiz, in *Tanzimat*, pp. 423–40.

Saymen, Ferit H. *Türk Iş Hukuku*. Ist., 1954.

Şehsuvaroğlu, Haluk Y. *Sultan Aziz. Hayatı Hal'ı Ölümü*. Ist., 1949.

Selek, Sabahettin. *Millî Mücadele: Anadolu Ihtilâli*. 2 vols. Ist., 1965.

Şeref, Abdurrahman. *Tarih-i Devlet-i Osmaniye*. 2 vols. Ist., 1309 A.H.

—— *Tarih Musahabeleri*. Ist., 1340 A.H.

Simavi, Lûtfi. *Sultan Mehmed Reşad Hanın ve halefinin sarayında gördüklerim*. Ist., 1340 A.H.

Siyasal Bilgiler Fakültesi. *Kaza ve Vilâyet İdaresi üzerinde bir Araştırma.* Ank., 1957.

Sülker, Kemal. *Türkiyede Sendikacılık.* İst., 1955.

Sungu, İhsan. Galatasaray Lisesi'nin Kuruluşu. *Bell.*, no. 28 (1943), 315–47.

—— Tanzimat ve Yeni Osmanlılar, in *Tanzimat*, pp. 777–857.

—— Mekteb-i Maarif-i Adliyenin Tesisi. *Tar. Ves.*, i (1941), 212–25.

Süreyya, Mehmed. *Sicill-i Osmani.* 4 vols. İst., 1308–15 A.H.

Suvla, Refii Şükrü. Tanzimat Devrinde İstikrazlar, in *Tanzimat*, pp. 263–88.

Tahsin Paşa. *Abdülhamit ve Yıldız Hatıraları.* İst., 1931.

Talât Paşa. *Talât Paşa'nın Hatıraları*, ed. H. C. Yalçın. İst., 1946.

Tanör, Bülent, and Taner Beygo. *Türk anayasaları.* İst., 1964.

Tanpınar, Ahmet Hamdi. *XIX Asır Türk Edebiyatı Tarihi.* 2nd ed İst., 1956.

Tansel, Fevziye Abdullah. Arap Harflerinin Islâhı ve Değiştirilmesi hakkında ilk Teşebbüsler ve Neticeleri, 1862–84. *Bell.*, no. 66 (1953), 224–49.

Tansu, Samih Nafiz. *İki Devrin Perde Arkası.* İst., 1957.

Tarihi Muhakeme, i. İst., 1919.

Tevfik, Ebüzziya. *Nümûne-i Edebiyat-i Osmaniye.* 3rd ed. İst. 1306 A.H. (İst ed. 1296/1878).

—— Yeni Osmanlılar. *Yeni Tasvir-i Efkâr.* 1909.

Toğan, A. Zeki Velidi. *Bugünkü Türkili (Türkistan) ve yakın Tarihi.* 2 vols. İst., 1942–7.

Tuna, Orhan. Küçük San'atlar ve Kooperatifçilik Meseleleri. *İst. Üniv. Çanakkale Haftası 1952.* İst., 1953.

Tunaya, Tarık. Amme Hukukumuz bakımından ikinci Meşrutiyetin Siyasî Tefekküründe 'Garpçılık' Cereyanı. *İst. Üniv. Huk. Fak. Mec.*, xiv (1948), 586–630.

—— *Türkiyede Siyasî Partiler, 1859–1952.* İst., 1952.

—— Türkiye Büyük Meclisi Hükumeti'nin Kuruluşu ve Siyasî Karakteri. İst., n.d.

—— Amme Hukukumuz Bakımından, ikinci Meşrutiyetin Siyasî Tefekküründe 'Islamcılık' Cereyanı. *İst. Üniv. Huk. Fak. Mec.*, xix (1954).

—— Osmanlı İmparatorluğundan Türkiye Büyük Millet Meclisi Hükumeti Rejimine Geçiş', in *Prof. Muammer Raşit Seviğ'e Armağan.* İst., 1956.

—— Türkiyenin Siyasî Gelişme Seyri içinde İkinci 'Jön Türk' Hareketinin Fikrî Esasları, in *Prof. Tahir Taner'e Armağan.* İst., 1956.

—— and Reşit Ülker. *Mufassal Fihristli Özetli Milletvekilleri Seçimi Kanunu ve İlgili Mevzuat.* İst., 1954.

—— *Hürriyetin ilânı: ikinci Meşrutiyetin siyasî hayatına bakışlar.* Ist., 1959.
—— *Türkiyenin siyasî hayatında batılılaşma hareketleri.* Ist., 1960.
—— *Islâmcılık Cereyanı* Ist., 1962.
—— *Devrim Hareketleri içinde Atatürk ve Atatürkçülük.* Ist., 1964.
Tunçay, Mete. *Türkiye'de Sol Akımlar 1908–1925.* Ank. 1967.
Turan, Osman. Türkler ve Islamiyet, *Ank. Univ. Dil ve Tar.-Coğ. Fak. Derg.,* v (1945–6), 457–85.
Turhan, Mümtaz. *Kültür Değişmeleri.* Ist., 1951.
—— *Garblılaşmanın Neresindeyiz.* 2nd ed. Ist., 1959.
Türk Devrim Tarihi Enstitüsü Yayımları. *Cümhurbaşkanları, Başbakanlar ve Millî Eğitim Bakanlarının Millî Eğitimle ilgili Söylev ve Demeçleri,* i. Ank., 1946.
Turkey, Min. of Evkaf. *Evkâf-i Humayun Nezaretinin Tarihçe-i Teşkilâtı.* Ist., 1335 A.H.
—— Min. of Ed. *Tanzimat,* i. Ist., 1940.
Türkgeldi, Âli. *Mondros ve Mudanya Mütarekelerinin Tarihi.* Ank., 1948.
Türkgeldi, Ali Fuad. *Görüp Işittiklerim.* 2nd ed. Ank., 1951.
Ülgener, F. *Iktisadî Inhitat Tarihimizin Ahlâk ve Zihniyet Meseleleri.* Ist., 1951.
Ülken, Hilmi Ziya. *Türkiyede Çağdaş Düşünce Tarihi.* 2 vols. Konya, 1966.
Uluçay, M. Çağatay. *Saruhan'da Eşkıyalık ve Halk Hareketleri.* 2 vols. Manisa-Istanbul, 1944–5.
Unat, Faik Reşit. Ahmet III Devrine ait bir Islâhat Takriri. *Tar. Ves.,* i (1941), 107–21.
—— Atatürk'ün Askerlikten Istifası. *Tar. Ves.,* n.s., i (1955), 3–8.
—— Atatürk'ün II. Meşrutiyet Inkılâbının Hazırlanmasındaki Rolüne ait bir Belge. *Bell.,* no. 102 (1962), 339–348.
—— Başhoca Ishak Efendi. *Bell.,* no. 109 (1964), 89–115.
Us, Hakkı Tarık. *Meclis-i Meb'usân, 1293–1877.* 2 vols. Ist., 1940–54.
Uşaklıgil, Halid Ziya. *Saray ve Ötesi.* 3 vols. Ist., 1940–1.
Uzunçarşılı, Ismail Hakkı. Sadrazam Halil Hamit Paşa. *Türkiyat Mecmuası,* v (1936), 213–67.
—— Selim III'ün Veliaht iken Fransa Kralı Lüi XVI ile Muhabereleri. *Bell.,* no. 5–6 (1938), 191–246.
—— *Alemdar Mustafa Paşa.* Ist., 1942.
—— Ali Suâvi ve Çırağan Vak'ası. *Bell.,* no. 29 (1944), 71–118.
—— V Murad'i Tekrar Padişah Yapmak Isteyen K. Skaliyeri-Aziz Bey Komitesi. *Bell.,* no. 30 (1944), 245–328.
—— Çerkes Hasan Vak'ası. *Bell.,* no. 33 (1945), 89–133.
—— Beşinci Sultan Murad'ın Tedâvîsine ve Ölümüne ait Rapor ve Mektuplar 1876–1905. *Bell.,* no. 38 (1946), 317–67.

—— *Midhat ve Rüştü Paşaların Tevkiflerine dair Vesikalar.* Ank., 1946.
—— *Osmanlı Devletinin Merkez ve Bahriye Teşkilâtı.* Ank., 1948.
—— Ondokuzuncu Asır Başlarına kadar Türk-Ingiliz Münasebatına dair Vesikalar. *Bell.*, no. 51 (1949), 573–650.
—— *Midhat Paşa ve Taif Mahkûmları.* Ank., 1950.
—— Asâkir-i Mansure'ye Fes Giydirilmesi hakkında Sadr-i Âzam Takriri ve II Mahmud'un Hatt-i Humayunu. *Bell.*, no. 70 (1954), 223–30.
—— 1908 Yılında Ikinci Meşrutiyetin ne Surette Ilân Edildiğine dair Vesikalar. *Bell.*, no. 67 (1956), 103–74.
Yusuf, Akçuraoğlu. *Üç Tarz-i Siyaset.* Ist., 1327 A.H.
—— Türkcülük. *Türk Yılı*, i (1928), 289–455.

2. WORKS IN OTHER LANGUAGES

Abadan, Nermin. *Social change and Turkish women.* Ankara, 1963.

Adnan, A. *La Science chez les Turcs ottomans.* Paris, 1939.

Adnan-Adivar, Abdulhak. Interaction of Islamic and Western Thought in Turkey, *in* T. Cuyler Young, ed., *Near Eastern Culture and Society.* Princeton, 1951, 119–29.

Ahmad, F. Great Britain's Relations with the Young Turks, 1908–1914. *MES*, ii/4 (1966), 302–29.

—— *The Committee of Union and Progress in Turkish Politics, 1908–1913.* Unpublished Ph.D. thesis, London, 1966.

Akademiya Nauk SSSR Institut Vostokovedeniya. *Bibliografiya Turtsii (1917–1958).* Moscow, 1959.

Albrecht, W. *Grundriss des osmanischen Staatsrechts.* Berlin, 1905.

Allen, Henry E. *The Turkish Transformation: a study in social and religious development.* Chicago, 1935.

Alp, Tekin [Moise Cohen]. *Le Kemalisme.* Paris, 1937.

Aristarchi, G. *Législation ottomane.* 7 vols. Istanbul, 1873–88.

Armstrong, H. C. *Grey Wolf.* London, 1932.

[Atatürk, K.] *A Speech Delivered by Ghazi Mustapha Kemal, President of the Turkish Republic, October 1927.* Leipzig, 1929.

Babinger, F. *Stambuler Buchwesen im 18 Jahrhundert.* Leipzig, 1919.

—— *Die Geschichtsschreiber der Osmanen und ihre Werke.* Leipzig, 1927.

Bahrampour, Firouz. *Turkey: political and social transformation.* Brooklyn, N.Y., 1967.

Bailey, Frank Edgar. *British Policy and the Turkish Reform Movement.* Cambridge, Mass., 1942.

Bamberg, F. *Geschichte der orientalischen Angelegenheiten im Zeitraume des Pariser und des Berliner Friedens.* Berlin, 1892.

Barkan, Ömer Lutfi. La Loi sur la Distribution des Terres aux agriculteurs et les problèmes essentiels d'une réforme agraire en Turquie. *R. Fac. Sci. Éc. Univ. Ist.* (1944–5), 44–132.

Başgil, Ali Fuad and others. *La Turquie.* Paris, 1939. (No. VII in H. Levy-Ullmann and B. Mirkine-Guetzevitch, eds., *La Vie juridique des peuples.*)

Bastelberger, J. M. *Die militärischen Reformen unter Mahmud II, dem Retter des osmanischen Reiches.* Gotha, 1874.

Becker, C. H. *Islamstudien.* 2 vols. Leipzig, 1932.

Belin, [F.A.]. Étude sur la propriété foncière en pays musulman et specialement en Turquie. (*J. As.*, 1862). Reprint Paris, 1862.

Belin, [F.A.]. Essai sur l'histoire économique de la Turquie. (*J. As.*, 1885.) Reprint Paris, 1885.

Berkes, Niyazi. Historical Background of Turkish Secularism, *in* R. N. Frye, ed. *Islam and the West.* The Hague, 1957, pp. 41–68.

—— *The development of secularism in Turkey.* Montreal, 1964.

Birge, John K. *A Guide to Turkish Area Study.* Washington, 1949.

Blaisdell, D. C. *European Financial Control in the Ottoman Empire.* New York, 1929.

Bombaci, Alessio. *Storia della letteratura turca.* Milan, 1956.

Boppe, A. La France et le 'militaire turc' au XVIIIᵉ siècle. *Feuilles d'Histoire* (1912), 386–402 and 490–501.

Bremer, Marie Luise. *Die Memoiren des türkischen Derwischs Aşçi Dede Ibrahim.* Walldorf-Hessen, 1959.

Brice, W. C. The Population of Turkey in 1950. *The Geographical Journal*, cxx/3 (1954), 347–52.

Bursal, Nasuhi. *Die Einkommenssteurreform in der Türkei.* Wintherthur, 1953.

Butler, R., and Bury, J. P. T., editors. *Documents on British Foreign Policy, 1919–1939*, 1st series, xiii, *The Near and Middle East, January 1920–March 1921.* London, 1963.

Canard, M. Coiffure européenne et Islam. *Annales de l'Institut d'Études Orientales* (Algiers), viii (1949–50), 200–29.

Cahun, Léon. *Introduction à l'Histoire de l'Asie, Turcs et Mongols des Origines à 1405.* Paris, 1896.

—— Le monde islamique de 1840 à 1870, in E. Lavisse and A. Rambaud, *Histoire générale*, xi, Paris 1899, 527–60.

—— Le monde islamique de 1870 à nos jours, in E. Lavisse and A. Rambaud, *Histoire générale*, xii, Paris 1901, 479–503.

Castagné, J. La Latinisation de l'alphabet turk dans les républiques turko-tartares de l'U.R.S.S. *R. Ét. islam.*, i (1927), 321–53.

Caussin de Perceval, A. P. *Précis historique de la Destruction du Corps des Janissaires par le Sultan Mahmoud en 1826.* Paris, 1833.

Charmes, G. *L'Avenir de la Turquie. Le Panislamisme.* Paris, 1883.

Cillov, Halluk. Les Recensements industriels en Turquie. *R. Fac. Sci. Écon. Univ. Ist.*, xiii (1951–2), 162–77.

Colombe, M. Le Nouveau texte de la constitution turque. *C. Or. contemp.* iv (1946), 771–808.

—— Une Lettre d'un prince égyptien du XIXᵉ siècle au Sultan ottoman Abd al-Aziz. *Orient*, v (1958), 23–38.

—— La réforme des institutions dans l'empire ottoman au XIXᵉ siècle d'après le poète et ecrivain turc Namik Kemal. *Orient*, no. 13 (1960), 123–33.

Conker, O. and E. Witmeur. *Redressement économique et industrialisation de la nouvelle Turquie.* Paris, 1937.

Cunningham, Allan. The Wrong Horse?—A Study of Anglo-Turkish Relations before the first World War. *St. Antony's Papers. No. 17. Middle Eastern Affairs. No. four.* Oxford, 1965, 56–76.

Davison, R. H. Turkish Attitudes concerning Christian-Muslim Equality in the Nineteenth Century. *American Historical Review*, lix (1953–4), 844–64.

—— 'European Archives as a source for later Ottoman history', *in Report on Current Research on the Middle East 1958.* Washington, 1959, pp. 33–45.

—— 'The Question of Fuad Paşa's "Political Testament" '. *Belletin*, no. 89 (1959), 119–36.

—— Westernized Education in Ottoman Turkey. *MEJ* (Summer 1961), 289–301.

—— *Reform in the Ottoman Empire, 1856–1876.* Princeton, N.J., 1963.

Deny, Jean. L'adoption du Calendrier Grégorien en Turquie. *RMM*, xliii (1921), 46–53.

—— Les 'Souvenirs' du Gâzi Moustafa Kemal Pacha. *R. Ét. islam.*, i (1927), 117–222.

—— and R. Marchand. *Petit Manuel de la Turquie nouvelle.* Paris, 1933.

—— La Réforme actuelle de la langue turque. *En Terre d'Islam*, n.s., x (1935), 223–47.

Depont, O. and K. Coppolani. *Les Confréries religieuses musulmanes.* Algiers, 1897.

Devereux, R. *The First Ottoman Constitutional Period: A Study of the Midhat Constitution and Parliament.* Baltimore, 1963.

Djemal Pasha, Ahmed. *Memories of a Turkish Statesman, 1913–1919.* London–New York, 1922.

Doctrines et programmes des partis politiques ottomans. *RMM*, xxii (1913), 151–64.

Duda, H. W. Die Gesundung der türkischen Sprachreform. *Der Islam*, xxvi (1942), 77–100.

—— *Vom Kalifat zur Republik.* Vienna, 1948.

Duhamel, Georges. *La Turquie nouvelle.* Paris, 1954.

Dustūr. A Survey of the Constitutions of the Arab and Muslim States. Leiden, 1966.

Dwight, H. G. *Constantinople; Settings and Traits.* New York–London, 1926.

Eberhard, W. Nomads and Farmers in South-Eastern Turkey: Problems of Settlement. *Oriens,* vi (1953), 32–49.

Edib, Halide [Adıvar]. *Memoirs.* London, 1926.

—— *The Turkish Ordeal; being the Further Memoirs of Halide Edib.* London, 1928.

—— *Turkey Faces West.* New Haven, 1930.

—— *Conflict of East and West in Turkey.* 2nd ed. Lahore, 1935.

Eichmann, F. *Die Reformen des osmanischen Reiches, mit besonderer Berücksichtigung des Verhältnisses der Christen des Orients zur türkischen Herrschaft.* Berlin, 1858.

Eliot, Sir Charles [see Odysseus].

Elliot, Sir Henry. *Some Revolutions and Other Diplomatic Experiences.* London, 1922.

Emin, Ahmed. *The Development of Modern Turkey as measured by its Press.* New York, 1914.

—— *Turkey in the World War.* New Haven, 1930. [*See also* Yalman.]

Encyclopaedia of Islam. 1st ed. 4 vols and Suppl. Leiden, 1913–38. 2nd ed. 1954–

Engelhardt, Ed. *La Turquie et le Tanzimat.* 2 vols. Paris, 1882–4.

Erdentuğ, Nermin. *A study on the social structure of a Turkish village.* Ankara, 1959.

Fehmi, Youssouf. *Histoire de la Turquie.* Paris, 1909.

—— *La Révolution Ottomane (1908–1910).* Paris, 1911.

Fesch, Paul. *Constantinople aux derniers jours d'Abdul-Hamid.* Paris, 1907.

Fischer, A. *Aus der religiösen Reformbewegung in der Türkei.* Leipzig, 1922.

Franco, G. *Développements constitutionnels en Turquie.* Paris, 1925.

Franco, M. *Essai sur l'histoire des Israélites de l'Empire Ottoman.* Paris, 1897.

Frey, F. W. *The Turkish Political Elite.* Cambridge, Mass., 1965.

Frye, R. N., ed. *Islam and the West.* The Hague, 1957.

Gasanova, E. Yu. *Ideologiya buržuaznogo natsionalizma v Turtsii v period Mladoturok (1908–1914 gg).* Baku, 1966.

Gibb, E. J. W. *A History of Ottoman Poetry.* 6 vols. London, 1900–9,

Gibb, H. A. R. and Harold Bowen. *Islamic Society and the West,* i: *Islamic Society in the Eighteenth Century,* pt. 1. London, 1950. Pt. 2. London, 1957.

Gökalp, Ziya, trans. and ed. Niyazi Berkes. *Turkish Nationalism and Western Civilization.* London, 1959.

Gooch, G. P. and Temperley, Harold. *British Documents on the Origins of the War 1898–1914*, v. London, 1928; ix/i, London, 1933.

Gorvine, A. and L. L. Barber. *Organization and Functions of Turkish Ministries.* Ank., 1957.

Gorvine, A. *An Outline of Turkish Provincial and Local Government.* Ank., 1956.

Graves, P. *Briton and Turk.* London, 1941.

Grenville, Henry. *Observations sur l'état actuel de l'Empire ottoman*, ed. A. S. Ehrenkreutz. Ann Arbor, Mich., 1965.

Grunebaum, G. E. von, ed. *Unity and Variety in Muslim Civilization.* Chicago, 1955.

Hammer-Purgstall, J. von. *Geschichte des Osmanischen Reiches.* 10 vols. Pest, 1827–35. 2nd ed. 4 vols. Pest, 1835–40.

—— *Des osmanischen Reichs Staatsverfassung und Staatsverwaltung.* 2 vols. Vienna, 1815.

Harris, G. S. The Role of the Military in Turkish politics. *MEJ*, xix (1965), 54–66, 169–76.

Hartmann, M. *Der islamische Orient*, iii: *Unpolitische Briefe aus der Türkei.* Leipzig, 1910.

Haupt, G. Le début du mouvement socialiste en Turquie. *Le Mouvement Social*, no. 45 (1963), 121–37.

Heidborn, A. *Manuel de droit public et administratif de l'Empire Ottoman.* 2 vols. Vienna, 1908–12.

Hershlag, Z. Y. Turkey: Achievements and Failures in the Policy of Economic Development during the Inter-War Period 1919–39. *Kyklos* (1954), 323–50.

—— *Turkey; an Economy in Transition.* The Hague [1960].

—— *Introduction to the modern economic history of the Middle East.* Leiden, 1964.

Heyd, U. Islam in Modern Turkey. *R. C. As. J.*, xxxiv (1947), 299–308.

—— *Foundations of Turkish Nationalism.* London, 1950.

—— *Language Reform in Modern Turkey.* Jerusalem, 1954.

—— The Ottoman 'Ulemā and westernization in the time of Selim III and Mahmud II. *Scripta Hierosolymitana*, ix (1961), 63–96.

Horn, P. *Geschichte der türkischen Moderne.* Leipzig, 1902.

Hostler, C. W. Trends in Pan-Turanism. *MEA*, iii (1952), 3–13.

—— *Turkism and the Soviets.* New York, 1957.

Hüber, R. *Die Bagdadbahn.* Berlin, 1943.

Hurewitz, J. C. *Diplomacy in the Near and Middle East: a Documentary Record.* 2 vols. Princeton, N.J., 1956.

—— Ottoman Diplomacy and the European State System. *MEJ* (1961), 141–52.

Imhoff, Gen. Die Entstehung und der Zweck des Comités für Einheit und Fortschritt. *WI*, i (1913), 167–77.

Inalcık, Halil. Land Problems in Turkish History. *Muslim World*, xlv (1955), 221–28.

International Bank for Reconstruction and Development. *The Economy of Turkey*. Baltimore, 1951.

International Labour Office. *Labour Problems in Turkey*. Geneva, 1950.

Issawi, Charles, ed. *The economic history of the Middle East, 1800–1914: a book of readings*. Chicago, 1966.

Jäschke, G. Die Entwicklung des osmanischen Verfassungsstaates von den Anfängen bis zur Gegenwart. *WI*, v (1918), 5–56.

—— and Pritsch, E. Die Türkei seit dem Weltkriege. Geschichtskalender 1918–1928. *WI*, x (1927–9), 1–154.

—— Die Türkei seit dem Weltkriege. ii: Türkischer Geschichtskalender für 1929 mit neuem Nachtrag zu 1918–1928. iii: Für 1930. iv: Für 1931–1932. *WI*, xii (1930–1), 1–50, 137–66; xv (1933), 1–33.

—— Der Freiheitskampf des türkischen Volkes. *WI*, xiv (1932), 6–21.

—— Zur Geschichte des türkischen Nationalpakts. *MSOS*, xxxvi/2 (1933), 101–16.

—— Der Weg zur russisch-türkischen Freundschaft. *WI*, xvi (1934), 23–28.

—— Die grösseren Verwaltungsbezirke der Türkei seit 1918. *MSOS*, xxxviii (1935), 81–104.

—— Die Türkei in den Jahren 1933 und 1934. Geschichtskalender. *MSOS*, xxxviii (1935), 105–42.

—— Nationalismus und Religion im türkischen Befreiungskriege. *WI*, xviii (1936), 54–69.

—— Kommunismus und Islam im türkischen Befreiungskriege. *WI*, xx (1938), 110–17.

—— Die ersten Verfassungsentwürfe der Ankara-Türkei. *Mitt. Aus. Hoch. der Univ. Berlin*, xlii/2 (1939), 57–80.

—— Vom Osmanischen Reich zur Türkischen Republik. Zur Geschichte eines Namenswechsels. *WI*, xxi (1939), 85–93.

—— Der Turanismus der Jungtürken. Zur osmanischen Aussenpolitik im Weltkriege. *WI*, xxiii (1941), 1–54.

—— *Die Türkei in den Jahren 1935–1941*. Leipzig, 1943.

—— Der Turanismus und die kemalistische Türkei, *in* R. Hartmann and H. Scheel, eds. *Beiträge zur Arabistik, Semitistik und Islamwissenschaft*. Leipzig, 1944, pp. 468–73.

—— Zur Krisis des Islams in der Türkei. *Beitr. z. Arabistik, Semitistik und Islamwis.*, 1944, pp. 514–30.

—— Das osmanische Scheinkalifat von 1922. *WI*, n.s., i (1951), 195–217, 218–28.

—— Der Islam in der neuen Türkei. *WI*, n.s., i (1951).
—— Ankara wird Hauptstadt der neuen Türkei. *WI*, n.s., iii (1954), 262–7.
—— *Die Türkei in den Jahren 1942–1951.* Wiesbaden, 1955.
—— Beiträge zur Geschichte des Kampfes der Türkei um ihre Unabhängigkeit, *WI*, n.s., v (1957), 1–64.
—— Auf dem Wege zur türkischen Republik. *WI*, n.s., v (1958), 206–18.
—— Das Ende des osmanischen Sultanats. *Studien zur Auslandskunde, Vorderasien*, I/i, 113–36.
—— Le rôle du communisme dans les relations russo-turques de 1919 à 1922. *Orient*, no. 26 (1963), 31–44.
—— Mustafa Kemal et la proclamation de la Republique en Turquie. *Orient*, no. 27 (1963), 29–44.
Jonquière, A. de la. *Histoire de l'Empire Ottoman.* 2 vols. 3rd ed. Paris, 1914.
Jorga, N. *Geschichte des osmanischen Reiches.* 5 vols. Gotha, 1908–13.
Juchereau de Saint-Denys, A. de. *Révolutions de Constantinople en 1807 et 1808.* 2 vols. Paris, 1819.
—— *Histoire de l'Empire ottoman.* 4 vols. Paris, 1844.
Karal, E. Z. Turkey: from Oriental Empire to modern national state, in Métraux G. S. and F. Crouzet, eds. *The New Asia: readings in the history of Mankind.* New York–London, 1965, 59–81.
Karpat, K. H. *Turkey's Politics; the Transition to a Multi-Party System.* Princeton, 1959.
—— Social Themes in Contemporary Turkish Literature. *MEJ* (1960), 29–44, 153–68.
—— Social Effects of Farm Mechanization in Turkish Villages. *Social Research*, xxvii/1 (1960), 83–103.
—— The Turkish Elections of 1957. *The Western Political Quarterly*, xiv/2 (1961), 436–59.
—— Recent Political Developments in Turkey and their Social Background. *International Affairs*, xxxviii/3 (1962), 304–23.
—— The People's Houses in Turkey. Establishment and Growth. *MEJ* (1963), 55–67.
—— Society, Economics, and Politics in Contemporary Turkey. *World Politics*, xvii/1 (1964), 50–74.
—— Réflexions sur l'arrière-plan social de la révolution turque de 1960. *Orient*, no. 37 (1966), 27–55.
—— The Turkish Left. *Journal of Contemporary History*, i/2 (1966), 169–86.
[Kay, J. E. de]. *Sketches of Turkey in 1831 and 1832.* New York, 1833.

Keddie, Nikki R. The Pan-Islamic Appeal: Afghani and Abdülhamid II. *MES*, iii (1966), 46–67.

Kemal, Ismail. *The Memoirs of Ismail Kemal Bey*, ed. by Sommerville Story. London, 1920.

Kératry, E. de. *Mourad V: prince-sultan-prisonnier d'état (1840–1878), d'après des témoins de sa vie.* Paris, 1878.

Key, Kerim K. *An Outline of Modern Turkish Historiography.* Ist., 1954.

—— The Origins of Turkish Political Parties. *World Affairs Interpreter*, xxvi (1955), 49–60.

—— *Namık Kemal: Patriotic Poet of Turkey. An Inquiry into the Sources for a Study of Namik Kemal.* Washington, 1955.

—— *Origins of the Young Turk Movement, 1839–1908.* Washington, 1955.

—— Trends in Turkish Historiography, *in Report on Current Research on the Middle East 1957.* Washington, 1958, pp. 39–46.

—— Trends in Modern Turkish Literature. *Muslim World*, xlvii (1957), 318–28.

Khadduri, M. and Liebesny, H. J., eds. *Law in the Middle East.* Washington, 1955.

Kinross, Lord. *Atatürk: the Rebirth of a Nation.* London, 1964.

Köprülü, Fuad. L'institution du Vakouf: Sa nature juridique et son évolution historique. *Vakıflar dergisi*, ii (1942), partie française, 3–48.

Kortepeter, C. M. Another Look at the Tanzimat. *The Muslim World*, liv/1 (1964), 49–55.

Knight, E. F. *The Awakening of Turkey: a History of the Turkish Revolution.* London, 1909.

Kraelitz-Greifenhorst, F. von. *Die Verfassungsgesetze des osmanischen Reiches.* Vienna, 1919.

Kuran, Ercüment. Ottoman historiography of the Tanzimat period, in Lewis B., and Holt, P. M., editors, *Historians of the Middle East.* London, 1962, pp. 422–9.

—— *The Impact of Nationalism on the Turkish Elite in the nineteenth century.* Ank., 1966.

Lagarde, L. Note sur les journaux français de Constantinople à l'époque révolutionnaire. *J. As.*, ccxxxvi (1948), 271–6.

—— Note sur les journaux français de Smyrne à l'époque de Mahmoud II. *J. As.* (1950), 103–44.

Lane-Poole, S. *The Life of the Right Hon. Stratford Canning, Viscount Stratford de Redcliffe.* 2 vols. London, 1888.

Laqueur, W. Z. *Communism and Nationalism in the Middle East.* London–New York, 1956.

—— *The Soviet Union and the Middle East.* London–New York, 1959.

Lerner, D. *The Passing of Traditional Society.* Glencoe, 1958.

Levonian, Lutfy. *The Turkish Press; Selections from the Turkish Press showing Events and Opinions, 1925–32.* Athens, 1932.
—— *The Turkish Press, 1932–1936.* Beirut, 1937.
Lewis, Bernard. History-writing and National Revival in Turkey. *MEA,* iv (1953), 218–27.
—— The Impact of the French Revolution on Turkey. *Journal of World History,* i (1953), 105–25; revised version in Métraux, G. S. and Crouzet, F., eds., *The New Asia: readings in the history of mankind.* New York–London, 1965, 31–59.
—— Democracy in Turkey. *MEA,* x (1959), 55–72.
—— Ottoman Observers of Ottoman Decline. *Islamic Studies,* Karachi, i (1962), 71–87.
—— *Istanbul and the Civilization of the Ottoman Empire.* Norman, Okla., 1963.
—— *The Middle East and the West.* London–Bloomington Ind., 1964.
—— The Ottoman Empire in the Mid-Nineteenth Century: A Review. *MES,* i/3 (April 1965), 283–95.
Lewis, Geoffrey L. *Turkey,* revised ed. London, 1965.
Macfarlane, Charles. *Constantinople in 1828.* 2nd edition. 2 vols. London, 1829.
Makal, Mahmut. *A Village in Anatolia.* London, 1954.
Mantran, R. *Histoire de la Turquie.* Paris, 1961.
Marcère, E. de. *Une Ambassade à Constantinople; La Politique orientale de la Révolution française.* 2 vols. Paris, 1927.
Mardin, Ebul'ulâ. Development of the Shari'a under the Ottoman Empire, *in* M. Khadduri and H. J. Liebesny. *Law in the Middle East.* Washington, 1955, i, 287–91.
Mardin, Şerif. The mind of the Turkish reformer 1700–1900. *The Western Humanities Review,* xiv (1960), 413–36.
—— *The Genesis of Young Ottoman Thought: A Study in the Modernization of Turkish Political Ideas.* Princeton, 1962.
—— Libertarian movements in the Ottoman Empire 1878–1895. *MEJ,* xvi (1962), 169–82.
Marmorstein, E. Religious Opposition to Nationalism in the Middle East. *Int. Aff.,* xxviii (1952), 344–59.
Mary-Rousselière, A. *La Turquie constitutionnelle.* Rennes, 1935.
Matthews, A. T. J. *Emergent Turkish Administrators.* Ank., 1955.
McCullagh, F. *The Fall of Abd-ul-Hamid.* London, 1910.
Mears, E. G. and others. *Modern Turkey.* New York, 1924.
Midhat, Ali Haydar. *The Life of Midhat Pasha.* London, 1903.
Mikusch, D. von. *Mustapha Kemal.* London–New York, 1931.
Miller, A. F. *Mustafa Pasha Bayraktar.* Moscow, 1947.

Miller, W. *The Ottoman Empire and its Successors.* Cambridge, 1923.

Moltke, Helmut von. *Briefe über Zustände und Begebenheiten in der Türkei aus den Jahren 1835 bis 1839.* 5th ed. Berlin, 1891.

Morawitz, Charles. *Les Finances de Turquie.* Paris, 1902.

[Mordtmann, A. D.]. *Stambul und das moderne Türkenthum.* 2 vols. Leipzig, 1877.

—— *Anatolien, Skizzen und Reisebriefe (1850–1859).* Ed. Franz Babinger. Hannover, 1925.

Mosse, W. E. The Return of Reschid Pasha: An Incident in the Career of Lord Stratford de Redcliffe. *English Historical Review* 68:269 (1953), 546–73.

Muhiddin, Ahmed. *Die Kulturbewegung im modernen Türkentum.* Leipzig, 1921.

Mustafa, Seid. *Diatribe de l'ingénieur sur l'état actuel de l'art militaire, du génie et des sciences à Constantinople.* 1st ed. Scutari, 1803. 2nd ed. Paris, 1910.

Naff, T. Reform and the Conduct of Ottoman Diplomacy in the Reign of Selim III, 1789–1807. *Journal of the American Oriental Society,* lxxxiii/3 (1963), 295–315.

Nallino, C. A. La Fine del così detto califfato ottomano. *OM,* iv (1924), 137–53 (reprinted in *Raccolta di Scritti,* iii. Rome, 1941, pp. 260–83).

Nord, E. *Die Reform des türkischen Liegenschaftsrechts.* Leipzig, 1914.

Odysseus [Sir Charles Eliot]. *Turkey in Europe.* London, 1900. 2nd edition 1908.

d'Ohsson, Mouradgea. *Tableau général de l'Empire ottoman.* 7 vols. Paris, 1788–1824.

Orga, Irfan. *Phoenix Ascendant.* London, 1958.

Ostroróg, Count Léon. *The Angora Reform.* London, 1927.

Østrup, J. *Det Nye Tyrki.* Copenhagen, 1931.

Padel, W. and Steeg, L. *La Législation foncière ottomane.* Paris, 1904.

Parker, J. and C. Smith. *Modern Turkey.* London, 1940.

Pears, Sir E. *Forty Years in Constantinople.* London, 1916.

—— *Life of Abdul Hamid.* London, 1917.

Petrosian, Yu. A. *'Novye Osmani' i Borba za Konstitutsiyu 1876 g. v Turtsii.* Moscow, 1958.

Pritsch, E. Die türkische Verfassung vom 20 April 1924. *MSOS,* xxvi–xxvii/2 (1924), 164–251.

Ramsaur, E. E. The Bektashi Dervishes and the Young Turks. *Moslem World* (1942), 7–14.

—— *The Young Turks; Prelude to the Revolution of 1908.* Princeton, 1957.

Ramsay, Sir W. M. *Impressions of Turkey.* London [1897].

—— *The Revolution in Constantinople and Turkey.* London, 1909.

Reed, H. A. The Religious Life of Modern Turkish Muslims, *in* R. N. Frye, ed. *Islam and the West*. The Hague, 1957, pp. 108-48.

—— A New Force at Work in Democratic Turkey. *MEJ*, vii (1953), 33-44.

—— Revival of Islam in Secular Turkey. *MEJ*, viii (1954), 267-82.

—— The Faculty of Divinity in Ankara. *Muslim World*, xlvi (1956), 295-312 and xlvii (1957), 22-35.

—— Turkey's new Imam-Hatib Schools. *WI*, n.s., iv (1955), 150-63.

Robinson, R. D. *The First Turkish Republic: A Case Study in National Development*. Cambridge, Mass., 1963.

Rodinson, M. Araba. *J. As.*, ccxlv (1957), 273-80.

Rosen, G. *Geschichte der Türkei vom Siege der Reform im Jahre 1826 bis zum Pariser Traktat vom Jahre 1856*. 2 vols. Berlin–Leipzig, 1866-7.

Rossi, E. La Questione dell'alfabeto per le lingue turche. *OM*, vii (1927), 295-310.

—— Il decennale della Repubblica di Turchia (29 ottobre 1923-29 ottobre 1933). *OM*, xiii (1933), 541-57.

—— La Riforma linguistica in Turchia. *OM*, xv (1935), 45-57.

—— Un Decennio di Riforma linguistica in Turchia, 1932-42. *OM*, xxii (1942), 466-77.

—— Dall' Impero ottomano alla Repubblica di Turchia; Origine e sviluppi del nazionalismo turco sotto l'aspetto politico-culturale. *OM*, xxiii (1943), 359-88.

—— Venticinque anni di rivoluzione dell'alfabeto e venti di riforma linguistica in Turchia. *OM*, xxxiii (1953), 378-84.

Rummel, F. von. *Die Türkei auf dem Weg nach Europa*. Munich, 1952.

Rustow, D. A. The Army and the Founding of the Turkish Republic. *World Politics*, xi (1949), 513-52.

—— *Politics and Westernization in the Near East*. Princeton, 1956.

—— Politics and Islam in Turkey 1920–1935, *in* R. N. Frye, ed., *Islam and the West*. The Hague, 1957, pp. 69-107.

—— Foreign Policy of the Turkish Republic, *in* Macridis, R. C., ed., *Foreign Policy in World Politics*. Englewood Cliffs, N.J., 1958, pp. 295-322.

—— Turkey's Second Try at Democracy. *The Yale Review* (1963), 518-538.

—— Turkey: the Modernity of Tradition, in Pye, L. W. and Verba, S. (eds.), *Political Culture and Political Development*, Princeton, 1965, 171-98.

—— The development of parties in Turkey, in *Political Parties and Political Development*, eds. LaPalombara, J. and Weiner, M. Princeton, 1966, 107-33.

Ryan, Sir Andrew. *The Last of the Dragomans.* London, 1951.

Sarç, Ömer Celâl. Economic Policy of the New Turkey. *MEJ*, ii (1948), 430–46.

Sarrou, A. *La Jeune Turquie et la Révolution.* Paris–Nancy, 1912.

Sax, C. von. *Geschichte des Machtverfalls der Türkei.* 2nd ed. Vienna, 1913.

Schacht, J. *An Introduction to Islamic Law.* Oxford, 1964.

Schlechta-Wssehrd, O. M. von. Die osmanischen Geschichtsschreiber der neuren Zeit. *Denkschriften der phil. hist. Classe der Kaiserl. Ak. der Wissenschaften*, viii (1856), 1–47.

—— Die Revolutionen in Constantinopel in den Jahren 1807 und 1808. *SBAk. Wien* (1882), 184–8.

Senior, N. W. *Journal Kept in Turkey and Greece in the Autumn of 1857 and the Beginning of 1858.* London, 1859.

Shaw, S. J. The origins of Ottoman military reform: the Nizam-i Cedid Army of Sultan Selim III. *The Journal of Modern History*, xxxvii/3 (1965), 219–306.

—— The Established Ottoman Army Corps under Sultan Selim III (1789–1807). *Der Islam*, xl (1965), 142–84.

Slade, A. *Record of Travels in Turkey, Greece &c. . . . in the Years 1829, 1830, and 1831.* 2 vols. London, 1832 (2nd ed. 1854).

Smith, E. C. Debates on the Turkish Constitution of 1924. *Ankara Univ. Siyasal Bilgiler Fakültesi Dergisi*, xiii (1958), 82–105.

Smith, E. D. *Origins of the Kemalist Movement.* Washington, 1959.

Smith, W. C. *Islam in Modern History.* Princeton, 1957.

Snouck-Hurgronje, C. *Verspreide Geschriften*, iii. Bonn-Leipzig-Hague, 1923.

Societé pour l'Étude de l'histoire turque. *Histoire de la République turque.* Ist., 1935.

Stamatiadis, Epaminondas I. Βιογραφίαι τῶν Ἑλλήνων Μεγάλων Διερμηνέων τοῦ Ὀθωμανικοῦ Κράτους. Athens, 1865.

Stavrianos, L. S. *The Balkans since 1453.* New York, 1958.

Steegman, J. Turkish Painting. *The Studio*, May 1946, pp. 129–35.

Stirling, Paul. Social Ranking in a Turkish Village. *British Journal of Sociology*, iv (1953), 31–44.

—— Religious Change in Republican Turkey. *MEJ*, xii (1958). 395–408.

—— *Turkish Village.* London, 1965.

Sturm, A. L. and Mıhcıoğlu, Cemal. *Bibliography on Public Administration in Turkey 1928–1957, Selective and Annotated.* Ank., 1959.

Szyliowicz, J. S. *Political change in rural Turkey. Erdemli.* The Hague, 1966.

Tachau, F. The Search for National Identity among the Turks. *WI*, n.s. viii/3 (1963), 165–176.

Taeschner, Fr. Die geographische Literatur der Osmanen. *ZDMG*, n.s. 2, lxxvii (1923), 31–80.

—— and G. Jäschke. *Aus der Geschichte des islamischen Orients.* Tübingen, 1949.

[Taghizade, S. H.] Les Courants politiques dans la Turquie. *RMM*, xxi (1912). 158–221.

—— Le Panislamisme et le Panturquisme. *RMM*, xxii (1913), 179–220.

—— Les Rapports du mouvement politique et du mouvement social dans l'Empire ottoman. *RMM*, xxii (1913), 165–78.

Talas, Cahit. *La Législation du travail en Turquie.* Geneva, 1948.

Temperley, H. W. V. British Policy towards Parliamentary Rule and Constitutionalism in Turkey (1830–1914). *Cambridge Historical Journal*, iv (1932–34), 156–91.

—— *England and the Near East.* London, 1936.

Thomas, L. V. Recent Developments in Turkish Islam. *MEJ*, vi (1952), 22–40.

—— and R. N. Frye. *The United States and Turkey and Iran.* Cambridge, Mass., 1951.

Thornburg, M. W. and others. *Turkey, an Economic Appraisal.* New York, 1949.

Tibawi, A. L. Islam and Secularism in Turkey Today. *Quarterly Review* (1956), 325–7.

Tischendorf, P. A. von. *Das Lehnswesen in den moslemischen Staaten insbesondere im osmanischen Reiche.* Leipzig, 1872.

Toderini, G. *Letteratura turchesca.* 3 vols. Venice, 1787.

Tott, Baron F. de. *Mémoires.* 4 vols. Maestricht, 1785.

Toynbee, A. J. The Islamic World since the Peace Settlement. *Survey of International Affairs, 1925*, i.

—— and Kirkwood, K. P. *Turkey.* London, 1926.

Tschudi, R. *Das Chalifat.* Tübingen, 1926.

Tuna, Orhan. The Organization of the Turkish Confederation of Trade Unions. *R. Fac. Sci. Éc. Univ. Ist.*, (1953), 109–19.

Tunaya, T. Z. Elections in Turkish History. *MEA*, v (1954),116–20.

—— Ideological Character of the 1924 Constitution. *Annales de la Faculté de Droit d'Istanbul*, no. 15 (1960), 99–135.

Turhan, Mümtaz. *Where are we in westernization?* Translated from the Turkish by D. Garwood. Ist., 1965.

Turkish National Commission for UNESCO. *Atatürk.* Ank., 1963.

Türkkan, R. Oğuz. The Turkish Press. *MEA*, i (1950), 142–9.

Ubicini, A. *Lettres sur la Turquie.* 2 vols. Paris, 1853—4.

—— *La Turquie actuelle.* Paris, 1855.

—— *La constitution ottomane du 7 zilhidjé 1293.* Constantinople, 1877.

Ubicini, A. and P de Courteille. *Etat présent de l'Empire ottoman, statistique, gouvernement, administration, finances, armée, communautés non-musulmanes, etc.* Paris, 1876.

Ulman, A. Haluk and Tachau, Frank. Turkish politics: the attempt to reconcile rapid modernization with democracy. *MEJ,* xix (1965), 153–68.

UNESCO. The Reception of Foreign Law in Turkey. *International Social Science Bulletin,* ix/1 (1957), 7–81.

Unsal, Behcet. *Turkish Islamic Architecture.* London, 1959.

U.S. Dept. of Commerce. *Investment in Turkey.* Washington, 1956.

Vambéry, Arminius. *The Story of my Struggles.* London, n.d.

Van Lennep, H. J. *Travels in Little-Known Parts of Asia Minor.* 2 vols. London, 1870.

Velay, A. du. *Essai sur l'histoire financière de la Turquie.* Paris, 1903.

Vucinich, W. S. *The Ottoman Empire: its Record and Legacy.* Princeton, N.J., 1965.

Ward, R. E. and Rustow, D. A. (eds.) *Political Modernization in Japan and Turkey.* Princeton, N.J., 1964.

Washburn, G. *Fifty Years in Constantinople.* Boston-New York, 1909.

Webster, D. E. *The Turkey of Ataturk. Social Process in the Turkish Reformation.* Philadelphia, 1939.

Weiker, W. F. *The Turkish Revolution 1960–1961.* Washington, D.C., 1963.

Weinberger, S. J. Political Upset in Turkey. *MEA,* i (1950), 135–42.

White, Charles. *Three Years in Constantinople.* 3 vols. London, 1846.

Wittek, P. Türkentum und Islam, I. *Archiv für Sozialwissenschaft und Sozialpolitik,* lix (1928), 489–525.

—— Le Rôle des tribus turques dans l'empire ottoman. *Mélanges Georges Smets.* Brussels, 1952, pp. 554–76.

Wortham, H. E. *Mustapha Kemal of Turkey.* London, 1930.

Yalman, Ahmed Emin. *Turkey in my Time.* Norman, 1956. (*See also* Emin.)

Young, G. *Corps de droit ottoman.* 7 vols. Oxford, 1905–6.

Young, T. C. ed. *Near Eastern Culture and Society.* Princeton, 1951.

Ziemke, K. *Die neue Türkei, Politische Entwicklung 1914–1929.* Berlin–Leipzig, 1930.

Zinkeisen, J. W. *Geschichte des osmanischen Reiches in Europa.* 8 vols. Hamburg-Gotha, 1840–63.

Index

(*Note*: Until the general adoption of surnames in 1934, Turkish usage with regard to personal names differed considerably from that of the West.[1] For ease of reference, Turkish persons listed in this index have been placed under their last names where these are given—i.e. the surname for those who lived to adopt one—but under the last component of the personal name for those who did not. Titles which, in Turkish usage, follow the name—Ağa, Bey, Çelebi, Efendi, Hanım, Paşa—are not taken into account.) `

[1] See above, p. 289.

Maps

THE OTTOMAN EMPIRE
IN 1792

AUSTRIAN

BOSNI

MONTE
NEGRO

Mediterra

MOROCCO

ALGIERS

Algiers

Tunis

TUNIS

TRIPOLI

Tripoli

AUSTRIA - HUNGARY

BESSARABIA
To Russia, 1812

Belgrade

BOSNIA
Aust. Occup.
1878

SERBIA
Trib. 1815-17
Ind. 1878

RUMANIA

Independ. 1878

H

N
To Serbia
1878

Plevna

BULGARIA
Trib. 1878: Indep. 1908

M
To
M 1878

Sofia

E. RUMELIA
To Bulg. 1885

Edirne

Istanbul

MACEDONIA

To Greece
1881

THE BALKAN
PENINSULA IN 1878

Ottoman Boundary 179

Ottoman Empire 1878

Vassal States 1878

GREECE
Ind.
1829

Samos
Trib. 1832

H   Herzegovina
M   Montenegro
N   Novibazar

0   100   200

Scale of Miles

RUSSIA

75 →

MOLDAVIA
Jassy

1792
1774
1774

WALLACHIA

CRIMEA

Silistre

Black Sea

Caspian Sea

Ruschuk

LI
dirne

Istanbul

Trabzon

GEORGIA

Bursa

Ankara

Erzurum

Izmir

DEREBEYS

Kayseri

KURDISTAN

PERSIA

NOMAD TRIBES

Konya

Mosul

DEREBEYS

Adana

BAGHDAD

Aleppo

CYPRUS

Baghdad

Sea

Beyrut

Damascus

S Y R I A

Akka

Jerusalem

Alexandria

Cairo

WAHHABIS

E G Y P T

Red

H I J A Z

Medina

Aswan

Mecca

Jidda

Sea

Suakin

Approximate limits
of the Empire

North African States
under Ottoman suzerainty

Areas under autonomous
and tribal rulers

Lands lost, 1774-1792

Massawa

0   200   400

Scale of Miles

E. G. MORTON

THE OTTOMAN EMPIRE IN 1908

- - - Nominal Boundary
Dependent States
Territory occupied or protected by foreign powers
Lands lost since 1792

0   100   500
Scale of Miles

MOROCCO

ALGERIA
(French)

Tunis

TUNIS
(Fr. 1881)

Mediterran

Tripoli

Ghadames

TRIPOLI
(Ottoman direct rule from 1835)

FEZZAN
(Ottoman 1842)

Ghat

AUSTRIA - HUNGARY

RUMANIA

BOSNIA
(Austrian annexation 1908)

SERBIA

BULGARIA

To Rum.1913

MONTENEGRO

To Bulgaria 1885

To Bulgaria 1913

ALBANIA
Indep.1913

To Serbia 1913

To Bulgaria 1913

Edirne

Istanbul

To Greece 1913

GREECE

To Greece 1913

THE BALKAN
PENINSULA in 1913

Turkish Losses since 187

0   200
Scale of Miles

To Italy 1912

AUSTRI
BOSNI

MONTENEGRO

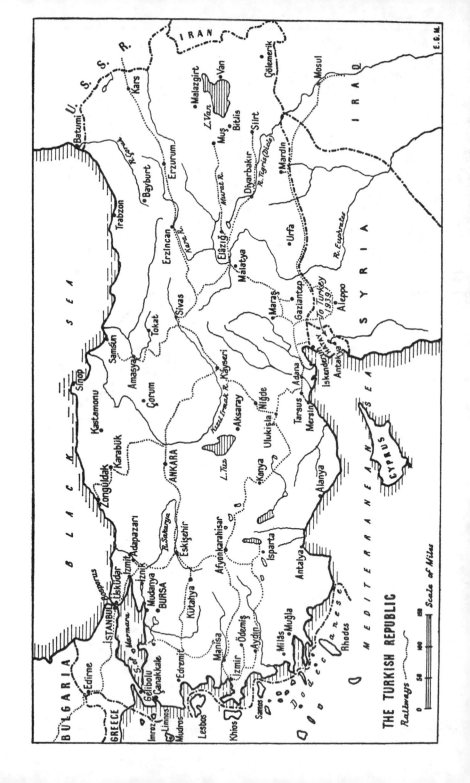

THE TURKISH REPUBLIC

Railways

Scale of Miles

0   50   100   150

E.B.M.

Please remember that this is a library book, and that it belongs only temporarily to each person who uses it. Be considerate. Do not write in this, or any, library book.